Microsoft® Office 365™
PUBLISHER 2016

COMPREHENSIVE

Microsoft Office 365™

PUBLISHER 2016

COMPREHENSIVE

JOY STARKS
Indiana University
Purdue University
Indianapolis

CENGAGE
Learning®

SHELLY CASHMAN SERIES®

Australia • Brazil • Japan • Korea • Mexico • Singapore • Spain • United Kingdom • United States

Shelly Cashman Microsoft Office 365 & Publisher 2016: Comprehensive
Joy L. Starks

SVP, GM Skills & Global Product Management: Dawn Gerrain

Product Director: Kathleen McMahon

Senior Product Team Manager: Lauren Murphy

Product Team Manager: Andrea Topping

Associate Product Manager: Melissa Stehler

Content Development Manager: Leigh Hefferon

Senior Content Developer: Alyssa Pratt

Developmental Editor: Lyn Markowicz

Product Assistant: Erica Chapman

Manuscript Quality Assurance Project Leader: Jeffrey Schwartz

Senior Production Director: Wendy Troeger

Production Director: Patty Stephan

Content Project Manager: Arul Joseph Raj, Lumina Datamatics

Manufacturing Planner: Julio Esperas

Designer: Diana Graham

Text Design: Joel Sadagursky

Cover Template Designer: Diana Graham

Cover Images: karawan/Shutterstock.com; Click Bestsellers/Shutterstock.com

Compositor: Lumina Datamatics

Vice President, Marketing: Brian Joyner

Marketing Director: Michele McTighe

For product information and technology assistance, contact us at
Cengage Learning Customer & Sales Support, 1-800-354-9706.

For permission to use material from this text or product,
submit all requests online at **www.cengage.com/permissions**.
Further permissions questions can be emailed to
permissionrequest@cengage.com.

Library of Congress Control Number: 2016939404

ISBN: 978-1-337-39197-9

Loose-leaf Edition:
ISBN: 978-1-305-87120-5

Cengage Learning
20 Channel Center Street
Boston, MA 02210
USA

Cengage Learning is a leading provider of customized learning solutions with employees residing in nearly 40 different countries and sales in more than 125 countries around the world. Find your local representative at **www.cengage.com.**

Cengage Learning products are represented in Canada by Nelson Education, Ltd.

To learn more about Cengage Learning, visit **www.cengage.com.**
Purchase any of our products at your local college store or at our preferred online store **www.cengagebrain.com.**

Printed in the United States of America
Print Number: 02   Print Year: 2017

Microsoft® Office 365™ PUBLISHER 2016

COMPREHENSIVE

Contents

Productivity Apps for School and Work
Introduction to OneNote 2016   **PA 2**
Introduction to Sway   **PA 6**
Introduction to Office Mix   **PA 10**
Introduction to Microsoft Edge   **PA 14**

Microsoft Office 2016 & Windows 10

Office 2016 & Windows 10: Essential Concepts and Skills
Objectives   **OFF 1**
  Roadmap   OFF 1
Introduction to the Windows 10 Operating System   **OFF 2**
  Using a Touch Screen and a Mouse   OFF 3
  Scrolling   OFF 4
  Keyboard Shortcuts   OFF 5
  Starting Windows   OFF 5
  To Sign In to an Account   OFF 6
  The Windows Desktop   OFF 8
Introduction to Microsoft Office 2016   **OFF 8**
  Microsoft Office 2016 Apps   OFF 8
  Microsoft Office 2016 Suites   OFF 9
Running and Using An App   **OFF 10**
  Publisher   OFF 10
  To Run an App Using the Start Menu and
    Create a Blank Publication   OFF 10
  To Maximize a Window   OFF 12
  Publisher Window, Ribbon, and Elements
    Common to Office Apps   OFF 13
  To Display a Different Tab on the Ribbon   OFF 17
  To Collapse and Expand the Ribbon and Use
    Full Screen Mode   OFF 18
  To Use a Shortcut Menu to Relocate the
    Quick Access Toolbar   OFF 19
  To Customize the Quick Access Toolbar   OFF 20
  To Zoom Using a Function Key   OFF 21
  To Enter Text in a Publication   OFF 22
Publication Properties   **OFF 23**
  To Change Publication Properties   OFF 23
Printing, Saving, and Organizing Files   **OFF 24**
  Printing a Publication   OFF 24
  To Print a Publication   OFF 25

Organizing Files and Folders   OFF 26
To Create a Folder   OFF 27
Folder Windows   OFF 29
To Create a Folder within a Folder   OFF 30
To Expand a Folder, Scroll through
  Folder Contents, and Collapse a Folder   OFF 30
To Switch from One App to Another   OFF 31
To Save a File in a Folder   OFF 32
Navigating in Dialog Boxes   OFF 35
To Minimize and Restore a Window   OFF 36
To Save a File on OneDrive   OFF 37
To Sign Out of a Microsoft Account   OFF 38
Screen Resolution   **OFF 39**
  To Change the Screen Resolution   OFF 40
  To Exit an App with One Publication Open   OFF 42
  To Copy a Folder to OneDrive   OFF 42
  To Unlink a OneDrive Account   OFF 44
Additional Common Features of Office Apps   **OFF 46**
  To Run an App Using the Search Box   OFF 46
  To Open an Existing File   OFF 47
  To Create a New Publication from the
    Backstage View   OFF 48
  To Close a File Using the Backstage View   OFF 49
  To Open a Recent File Using
    the Backstage View   OFF 50
  To Create a New Blank Publication from
    File Explorer   OFF 51
  To Run an App from File Explorer and Open
    a File   OFF 52
  To Save an Existing Office File with
    the Same File Name   OFF 52
  To Save a File with a New File Name   OFF 53
  To Exit an Office App   OFF 53
Renaming, Moving, and Deleting Files   **OFF 53**
  To Rename a File   OFF 54
  To Move a File   OFF 54
  To Delete a File   OFF 55
Microsoft Office and Windows Help   **OFF 56**
  To Open the Help Window in an Office App   OFF 56
  Moving and Resizing Windows   OFF 56
  To Move a Window by Dragging   OFF 56
  To Resize a Window by Dragging   OFF 57
  Using Office Help   OFF 57

To Obtain Help Using the Search Text Box | OFF 58
Obtaining Help while Working in an Office App | OFF 59
Using the Windows Search Box | OFF 59
To Use the Windows Search Box | OFF 59
Summary | **OFF 60**
Apply Your Knowledge | **OFF 61**
Extend Your Knowledge | **OFF 62**
Expand Your World | **OFF 62**
In the Labs | **OFF 63**

Microsoft **Office 365 & Publisher 2016**

MODULE ONE
Creating a Flyer

Objectives | **PUB 1**
Introduction | **PUB 1**
Project — 5K Flyer | **PUB 2**
Creating a Flyer | **PUB 2**
Templates | PUB 2
To Run Publisher and View Built-In Templates | PUB 4
To Select a Built-In Template | PUB 5
Customizing Templates | PUB 6
To Choose Publication Options | PUB 7
The Publisher Window | **PUB 10**
The Workspace | PUB 10
To Hide the Page Navigation Pane | PUB 12
Selecting Objects and Zooming | **PUB 12**
To Select | PUB 13
Zooming | PUB 13
To Zoom | PUB 14
Selecting and Entering Text | **PUB 15**
Text Boxes | PUB 15
To Replace Placeholder Text | PUB 15
To Replace Default Text | PUB 17
To Deselect an Object | PUB 18
Tear-Offs | PUB 18
To Enter Tear-Off Text | PUB 18
Deleting Objects | **PUB 19**
To Delete Objects | PUB 19
Checking the Spelling | **PUB 20**
To Check Spelling as You Type | PUB 20
Formatting Text | **PUB 22**
Fonts | PUB 23
Formatting Single versus Multiple Characters
    and Words | PUB 23
To Bold Text | PUB 23
To Underline Text | PUB 24
To Italicize Text | PUB 24
Autofitting Text | PUB 25
To Autofit Text | PUB 25
To Increase the Font Size | PUB 26
Using Graphics | **PUB 27**
To Use the Picture Placeholder | PUB 27
To Insert a Picture | PUB 29
Resizing, Moving, and Aligning Objects | **PUB 30**
To Resize an Object | PUB 30
To Move a Graphic | PUB 31
To Move a Text Box | PUB 31
To Align Text | PUB 32
To View Whole Page | PUB 32

To Print a Publication | PUB 33
Changing a Publication | **PUB 33**
To Open a Recent Publication | PUB 34
To Insert a Hyperlink | PUB 35
To Delete Using a Shortcut Menu | PUB 36
Creating a Webpage from a Publication | **PUB 37**
To Save a Print Publication as a
    Web Publication | PUB 37
To Preview the Web Publication in a Browser | PUB 38
Summary | **PUB 39**
Apply Your Knowledge | **PUB 40**
Extend Your Knowledge | **PUB 41**
Expand Your World | **PUB 43**
In the Labs | **PUB 44**

MODULE TWO
Publishing a Trifold Brochure

Objectives | **PUB 49**
Introduction | **PUB 49**
Project — Park Brochure | **PUB 49**
The Brochure Medium | **PUB 51**
Creating a Trifold Brochure | **PUB 52**
Making Choices about Brochure Options | PUB 52
To Select a Brochure Template | PUB 52
To Open and Maximize the Page Navigation Pane | PUB 53
To Edit Objects in the Right Panel | PUB 53
To Use the AutoCorrect Options Button | PUB 54
To Edit Objects in the Middle Panel | PUB 55
Copying, Cutting, and Pasting | **PUB 56**
To Copy and Paste | PUB 56
Paste Options Button | PUB 58
To Select a Paste Option | PUB 58
Typing Paragraphs of Text | **PUB 59**
To Edit Heading Text in the Left Panel | PUB 59
To Display Formatting Marks | PUB 60
To Wordwrap Text as You Type | PUB 60
Swapping Pictures | **PUB 61**
To Insert Multiple Pictures from a
    Storage Device | PUB 61
To Swap Pictures | PUB 62
To Use a Picture as a Background | PUB 63
Resetting Pictures and Picture Styles | **PUB 64**
To Reset Pictures | PUB 64
To Resize a Picture | PUB 65
To Apply a Picture Style | PUB 65
To Change the Border Color and Weight | PUB 66
To Change the Font Color | PUB 67
To AutoFit Headings | PUB 69
To Increase the Font Size of the Story | PUB 69
Shapes | **PUB 70**
To Insert a Shape | PUB 70
To Recolor a Shape | PUB 71
To Send a Shape Backward | PUB 72
Editing the Inside Panels of a Brochure | **PUB 73**
To Switch to Page 2 | PUB 73
To Insert and Format a Shape | PUB 73
To Edit the Left Panel on Page 2 | PUB 74
To Edit the Middle Panel on Page 2 | PUB 75
To Edit the Form | PUB 76
Stylistic Sets | **PUB 77**
To Format with a Stylistic Set | PUB 78

Online Pictures	**PUB 79**
To Search for Online Pictures	PUB 79
To Select Multiple Objects by Dragging	PUB 81
To Arrange Thumbnails	PUB 82
To Swap, Place, and Reset Pictures	PUB 83
Captions	**PUB 83**
To Edit Captions	PUB 84
To Ungroup	PUB 85
To Adjust Font Sizes on Page 2	PUB 86
To Use the Caption Gallery	PUB 86
Checking the Publication	**PUB 88**
To Check the Spelling of the Entire Publication	PUB 89
To Run the Design Checker	PUB 90
Previewing and Printing	**PUB 91**
To Preview Multiple Pages and Print	PUB 91
Printing Considerations	**PUB 92**
Paper Considerations	PUB 93
Color Considerations	PUB 94
Special Paper	PUB 95
Packing the Publication for the Printing Service	**PUB 95**
To Use the Pack and Go Wizard	PUB 95
Summary	**PUB 97**
Apply Your Knowledge	**PUB 98**
Extend Your Knowledge	**PUB 98**
Expand Your World	**PUB 101**
In the Labs	**PUB 101**

MODULE THREE
Designing a Newsletter

Objectives	**PUB 105**
Introduction	**PUB 105**
Project — Shelter Newsletter	**PUB 105**
Benefits and Advantages of Newsletters	PUB 107
Newsletter Design Choices	PUB 108
To Choose a Newsletter Template and Options	PUB 108
To Set Publisher Display Settings	PUB 109
To Set Page Options	PUB 110
Changing the Number of Pages in a Newsletter	PUB 113
Editing the Masthead	**PUB 113**
To Edit the Masthead	PUB 113
Newsletter Text	**PUB 114**
Replacing Placeholder Text Using an Imported File	PUB 115
To Edit the Lead Story Headline	PUB 116
To Import a Text File	PUB 116
To Edit the Secondary Story Headline	PUB 118
To Continue a Story across Pages	PUB 118
To Follow a Story across Pages	PUB 119
To Break a Text Box Link	PUB 120
To Manually Continue the Story across Pages	PUB 121
To Format with Continued Notices	PUB 122
To Edit the Headlines for the Continued Story	PUB 124
To Edit Page 2	PUB 125
To Delete Objects on Page 2 and Page 4	PUB 125
Customizing the Ribbon	**PUB 126**
To Customize the Publisher Ribbon	PUB 127
Editing Stories in Microsoft Word	**PUB 128**
To Edit a Story Using Microsoft Word	PUB 128
To Format while Editing in Microsoft Word	PUB 130

To Exit Word and Return to Publisher	PUB 130
To Edit Other Objects on Page 4	PUB 131
Marginal Elements	**PUB 132**
To Edit Sidebars	PUB 132
To Use a Soft Return	PUB 133
To Edit a Pull Quote	PUB 134
To Edit the Calendar	PUB 135
Using Graphics in a Newsletter	PUB 136
To Replace a Graphic Using the Shortcut Menu	PUB 136
To Replace the Graphic and Caption on Page 2	PUB 137
To Replace the Graphic and Caption on Page 3	PUB 138
To Insert a Graphic on Page 2	PUB 139
To Insert Graphics on Page 4	PUB 139
Revising a Newsletter	**PUB 140**
To Create a Drop Cap	PUB 140
To Customize a Drop Cap	PUB 141
To Reuse a Customized Drop Cap	PUB 142
Moving Text	PUB 142
To Drag and Drop Text	PUB 143
To Check the Spelling and Design	PUB 144
Hyphenation	PUB 145
To Check Hyphenation	PUB 145
To Print the Newsletter	PUB 147
Creating a Template	**PUB 148**
Saving the Template and Setting File Properties	PUB 149
To Create a Template with Property Changes	PUB 149
To Remove All Ribbon Customization and Exit Publisher	PUB 150
Summary	**PUB 151**
Apply Your Knowledge	**PUB 152**
Extend Your Knowledge	**PUB 154**
Expand Your World	**PUB 156**
In the Labs	**PUB 157**

MODULE FOUR
Creating a Custom Publication from Scratch

Objectives	**PUB 161**
Introduction	**PUB 161**
Project — Mailer	**PUB 161**
Custom-Sized Publication	**PUB 163**
To Select a Blank Publication	PUB 163
To Create a Custom Page Size	PUB 164
Custom Color Schemes	**PUB 166**
To Create a New Color Scheme	PUB 167
To Choose a Color Not in the Gallery	PUB 169
Custom Font Schemes	**PUB 170**
To Create a New Font Scheme	PUB 170
Editing Graphics	**PUB 172**
To Insert Pictures	PUB 172
To Resize the Castle Graphic	PUB 173
To Rotate	PUB 173
To Change the Proportion	PUB 174
To Set a Transparent Color	PUB 175
To Flip an Object	PUB 176
To Bring Forward and Resize	PUB 178
Grouping and Ungrouping Objects	PUB 178
To Group Objects	PUB 178
The WMF Format	PUB 179

Building Blocks **PUB 180**
To Save a Building Block PUB 180
To Snap an Object to the Margin Guide PUB 181
Picture Corrections **PUB 182**
To Select a Correction PUB 183
To Draw a Rectangle PUB 184
To Move the Logo onto the Page PUB 184
Text Effects **PUB 185**
To Draw a Text Box PUB 186
To Align Text and Format PUB 186
To Apply a Gradient to Text PUB 187
WordArt **PUB 189**
To Insert a WordArt Object PUB 190
To Change the WordArt Shape PUB 191
Paragraph Formatting **PUB 192**
Line Spacing PUB 193
To Change the Line Spacing PUB 193
Bulleted Lists PUB 194
To Create a Custom Bullet PUB 194
To Enter Text PUB 196
Advertisements **PUB 196**
To Insert a Coupon PUB 197
To Edit and Format the Coupon PUB 198
To Resize, Move, and Duplicate the Coupon PUB 198
To Enter Other Text PUB 199
To Check the Publication for Errors PUB 199
To Close a Publication without Exiting
Publisher PUB 200
Using Customized Sizes, Schemes,
and Building Blocks **PUB 200**
To Open a Customized Blank Page PUB 200
To Apply Customized Color and
Font Schemes PUB 201
Deleting Customizations **PUB 202**
To Delete Content from the Building
Block Library PUB 203
To Delete the Custom Color Scheme PUB 204
To Delete the Custom Font Scheme PUB 205
To Delete the Custom Page Size PUB 205
Summary **PUB 206**
Apply Your Knowledge **PUB 207**
Extend Your Knowledge **PUB 209**
Expand Your World **PUB 211**
In the Labs **PUB 212**

MODULE FIVE
Using Business Information Sets
Objectives PUB 217
Introduction PUB 217
Project — Letterhead and Business Cards PUB 218
Creating Letterhead PUB 218
To Open a Letterhead Template PUB 220
To Set Publisher Display Settings PUB 221
Creating a Logo **PUB 221**
To Crop a Picture PUB 221
Shape Fills PUB 223
To Fill a Shape with a Picture PUB 223
To Group Objects PUB 225
To Save as a Picture PUB 226
Business Information Sets **PUB 227**
To Create a Business Information Set PUB 227
To Insert a Business Information Field PUB 230

Using the Measurement Task Pane **PUB 231**
To Display the Measurement Task Pane PUB 232
To Position Objects Using the
Measurement Task Pane PUB 233
Creating a New Style **PUB 234**
To Sample a Font Color PUB 234
To Create a New Style PUB 235
To Apply the New Style PUB 237
To Edit the Masthead PUB 238
Customizing the Letterhead for Interactivity **PUB 238**
To Create a Text Box for Users PUB 239
To Use the Paragraph Dialog Box PUB 239
Text Wrapping PUB 240
To Set the Text Wrapping PUB 241
To Insert an Automatic Date PUB 242
To Set the Read-Only Attribute PUB 243
Using the Custom Letterhead Template **PUB 245**
To Open a Publication from the Recent List PUB 245
To Type the Beginning of the Letter PUB 245
To Create a Numbered List PUB 246
To Increase the Indent PUB 248
The Format Painter PUB 249
To Use the Format Painter PUB 249
To Save the Letter PUB 250
Envelopes **PUB 252**
To Create an Envelope PUB 252
To Address the Envelope PUB 254
To Set Options and Print the Envelope PUB 254
Award Certificates **PUB 255**
To Create and Edit an Award Certificate PUB 255
Business Cards **PUB 256**
To Create a Business Card PUB 256
To Print the Business Card PUB 258
To Set Publication Properties PUB 260
Creating Portable Files **PUB 260**
To Publish in a Portable Format PUB 261
Embedding Fonts **PUB 262**
To Embed Fonts PUB 263
To Delete the Business Information Set PUB 264
Summary **PUB 265**
Apply Your Knowledge **PUB 266**
Extend Your Knowledge **PUB 268**
Expand Your World **PUB 269**
In the Labs **PUB 270**

MODULE SIX
Working with Publisher Tables
Objectives PUB 273
Introduction PUB 273
Project — Table, Calendar, and Excel Functionality PUB 274
Reusable Parts **PUB 274**
To Select a Blank Publication and Adjust
Settings PUB 276
To Change the Page Orientation PUB 276
Creating a Business Information Set PUB 277
To Create a Business Information Set PUB 277
To Insert and Format a WordArt Object PUB 278
To Edit WordArt Alignment PUB 279
Shape Effects **PUB 280**
To Apply a Shape Effect PUB 280
To Fine-Tune a Shape Effect PUB 282
To Add an Object to the Building Block Library PUB 283

Using Tables   **PUB 284**
To Insert an Empty Table   PUB 284
To Apply a Table Format   PUB 285
Selecting Table Contents   PUB 287
To Delete a Column   PUB 287
To Insert Rows   PUB 289
To Resize the Table   PUB 290
To Merge Cells   PUB 290
To Create a Cell Diagonal   PUB 292
Table Borders   PUB 293
To Select a Table   PUB 293
To Change the Line Weight   PUB 294
To Change the Border Color   PUB 295
To Add Borders   PUB 295
Changing Row and Column Widths   PUB 297
To Select a Row   PUB 297
To Format Inside Borders   PUB 297
To Change the Fill and Font Color   PUB 298
To Format the Diagonal Border   PUB 299
To Edit Cell Alignment   PUB 299
To Align Other Cells   PUB 300
Entering Data in Tables   PUB 300
To Enter Data in a Table   PUB 301
Deleting Table Data   PUB 303
To Insert a Graphic in a Table Cell   PUB 303
To Finish the Table   PUB 304
Calendars   **PUB 304**
To Create a Calendar   PUB 305
Master Pages   **PUB 307**
To View the Master Page   PUB 307
BorderArt   PUB 309
To Add BorderArt   PUB 309
To Insert a Building Block   PUB 311
To Close the Master Page   PUB 312
To Insert Clip Art   PUB 313
To Edit Other Pages in the Calendar   PUB 313
Using Excel Tables   **PUB 314**
To Create the Letterhead   PUB 315
To Insert the Building Block   PUB 315
To Type the Letter   PUB 316
To Create an Embedded Table   PUB 317
To Format an Embedded Table   PUB 319
To Sum in an Embedded Table   PUB 320
To Move and Position the Table   PUB 322
Summary   **PUB 322**
Apply Your Knowledge   **PUB 323**
Extend Your Knowledge   **PUB 324**
Expand Your World   **PUB 325**
In the Labs   **PUB 326**

MODULE SEVEN
Advanced Formatting and Merging
Publications with Data
Objectives   PUB 329
Introduction   PUB 329
Project — Merging Form Letters and Tickets   **PUB 330**
To Run Publisher and Open a File   PUB 331
Watermarks   **PUB 332**
To Insert and Place the Watermark Graphic   PUB 332
To Change the Transparency of a Graphic   PUB 333
Spacing between Characters   **PUB 335**
To Kern Character Pairs   PUB 336

To Track Characters   PUB 337
The Character Spacing Dialog Box   PUB 338
To Create a Text Box   PUB 338
Working with Tabs and the Ruler   **PUB 339**
Setting Tabs   PUB 340
To Set a Tab Stop   PUB 341
To Enter Tabbed Text   PUB 342
Merging Data into Publications   **PUB 343**
Creating a Data Source   PUB 344
To Use the Mail Merge Wizard   PUB 345
To Customize Data Source Fields   PUB 347
Entering Data in the Data Source   PUB 348
To Enter Data in the Data Source File   PUB 349
To Save the Data Source   PUB 350
Inserting Field Codes   PUB 351
To Insert Grouped Field Codes   PUB 351
To Insert Individual Field Codes   PUB 354
Managing Merged Publications   PUB 356
To Preview the Form Letters   PUB 356
To Close the Mail Merge Task Pane   PUB 357
Editing a Merged Publication   **PUB 358**
To Connect with a Data Source   PUB 358
To Edit the Data Source   PUB 360
Creating Tickets   **PUB 362**
To Copy the Data Source File   PUB 362
Graphic Adjustments   **PUB 362**
To Open a File and Insert Graphics   PUB 364
To Recolor a Picture   PUB 364
To Edit the Brightness and Contrast   PUB 365
To Place Other Graphics   PUB 367
To Compress Pictures   PUB 368
To Insert Text   PUB 369
To Draw a Line   PUB 370
To Change the Text Direction   PUB 370
To Edit the Ticket Stub Further   PUB 371
Merging with Excel   **PUB 372**
To Select Recipients   PUB 372
To Filter Data   PUB 374
To Add Text to a Shape   PUB 375
To Insert Merge Field Codes   PUB 376
To Copy the Shape to the Ticket Stub and
    Check the Publication   PUB 378
To Print a Page of Tickets   PUB 378
To Save and Exit   PUB 381
Summary   **PUB 381**
Apply Your Knowledge   **PUB 382**
Extend Your Knowledge   **PUB 383**
Expand Your World   **PUB 384**
In the Labs   **PUB 385**

MODULE EIGHT
Generating Data-Driven Catalogs
Objectives   **PUB 389**
Introduction   **PUB 389**
Project — Intern Directory   **PUB 389**
Catalogs and Directories   **PUB 391**
To Create a Two-Page Spread   PUB 392
Alternating Master Pages   **PUB 394**
To Create the Background on Master Page A   PUB 394
Headers and Footers   PUB 395
To Create a Header   PUB 395
To Create a Mirrored Header   PUB 396

To Duplicate a Master Page PUB 396
To Remove Colored Background
    Shapes from Master Page B PUB 397
To Insert a Texture PUB 398
To Insert Alternating Footers PUB 400
To Apply a Number Style PUB 402
To Apply Master Pages PUB 402
Creating the Front Cover **PUB 404**
To Insert a Picture PUB 405
To Crop to Shape PUB 405
To Format the Border PUB 406
To Create a Reflection PUB 407
To Create a Title Graphic PUB 409
Generating the Catalog Merge **PUB 409**
To Copy the Data Source Files PUB 410
Catalog Pages **PUB 410**
To Insert Catalog Pages PUB 411
To Format the Catalog Pages PUB 411
To Delete a Two-Page Spread PUB 412
To Select the Data Source PUB 413
The Catalog Tools Format Tab PUB 414
To Insert a Picture Field PUB 415
To View Boundaries PUB 416
To Move and Resize the Picture Field PUB 417
To Insert Text Fields PUB 417
To Insert Other Text Fields PUB 418
To Align Objects PUB 419
To Find Entries PUB 421
To Turn Off Boundaries PUB 422
To Preview the Merge PUB 422
The Graphics Manager **PUB 423**
To Work with the Graphics Manager PUB 423
To Redisplay the Pictures and Close
    the Graphics Manager Task Pane PUB 426
Translating Text **PUB 426**
To Enter Text PUB 427
To Translate and Insert Text PUB 428
To Ignore Flagged Words and Check the
    Publication PUB 430
Merging Catalogs **PUB 430**
To Merge to a Printer PUB 430
To Exit Publisher PUB 433
Reopening Catalogs PUB 433
Summary **PUB 433**
Apply Your Knowledge **PUB 434**
Extend Your Knowledge **PUB 437**
Expand Your World **PUB 438**
In the Labs **PUB 439**

MODULE NINE
Sharing and Distributing Publications
Objectives **PUB 445**
Introduction **PUB 445**
Project — Distributed Publications **PUB 446**
Email Templates **PUB 448**
To Select an Email Template PUB 449
To Create the Publication and Customize
    the Workspace PUB 450
To Change the Email Newsletter Page Size PUB 450
To Set the Email Background Using a Pattern PUB 452
Reading Online PUB 454

To Edit the Heading PUB 455
To Edit Other Text Boxes at the Top of the Page PUB 455
To Complete the Lead Story PUB 456
To Complete the Second Story PUB 457
To Complete the Third Story PUB 458
To Edit the Comment Text Box PUB 459
To Complete the Sidebar PUB 460
Pictures PUB 460
To Insert Pictures PUB 461
To Fit a Picture PUB 462
To Insert and Fit Another Picture PUB 463
Symbols and Special Characters **PUB 464**
To Insert a Symbol from the Symbol Dialog Box PUB 464
To Insert a Special Character Using
    the Symbol Dialog Box PUB 466
Research Task Pane **PUB 467**
To Use the Research Task Pane PUB 468
To Create a Cited Reference PUB 469
Research Task Pane Options PUB 470
Creating Hyperlinks and Hot Spots **PUB 471**
To Insert a Hyperlink PUB 471
To Insert a Mailto Hyperlink PUB 472
To Create a Hot Spot PUB 474
Design Issues in Email PUB 475
To Edit the Color Scheme PUB 476
To Choose Design Checker Options PUB 477
To Check a Publication for Email Design Errors PUB 478
Troubleshooting Design Errors PUB 479
To Check for Spelling Errors PUB 479
Sending an Email Newsletter Using Publisher **PUB 480**
To Preview an Email Newsletter PUB 480
To Send an Email Newsletter Using Publisher PUB 481
Sending Print Publications as Email Newsletters PUB 482
To Save and Close the Publication PUB 483
Postcards **PUB 483**
To Open a Postcard Template PUB 484
To Edit a Postcard PUB 485
To Send a Postcard as an Attachment PUB 486
Greeting Cards **PUB 487**
To Customize a Greeting Card Template PUB 487
To Insert a Design Accent PUB 489
To Edit Text on Page 3 PUB 490
To Edit Text on Page 4 PUB 490
To Print a Folded Publication PUB 491
To Delete the Custom Color Scheme and
    Exit Publisher PUB 492
Summary **PUB 492**
Apply Your Knowledge **PUB 493**
Extend Your Knowledge **PUB 494**
Expand Your World **PUB 496**
In the Labs **PUB 497**

MODULE TEN
Editing Large-Scale Publications
Objectives **PUB 501**
Introduction **PUB 501**
Project — Creating a Short Story Booklet **PUB 501**
To Select a Blank Publication and Adjust Settings PUB 502
Designing the Layout **PUB 503**
To Insert Pages PUB 504
To Create Sections PUB 505

Pagination   **PUB 507**
   To Insert Page Numbers   PUB 507
   To Specify a Starting Page Number
      Using the Ribbon   PUB 508
   To Specify a Starting Page Number
      Using the Page Navigation Pane   PUB 510
   To Remove Page Numbering from Specific Pages   PUB 511
   To Apply a Background   PUB 512
   To Create the Title   PUB 512
   To Insert a Graphic   PUB 513
   To Enter the Subtitle   PUB 514
   To Collapse Sections   PUB 514
   To Create a Page Border   PUB 516
   To Insert Author Information   PUB 516
Cell and Text Box Margins   **PUB 517**
   To Create a Table of Contents   PUB 517
   To Change Cell Margins   PUB 518
   To Collapse the Front Matter Section   PUB 520
Ruler Guides   **PUB 520**
   To Select Ruler Guides   PUB 521
   Preparing Pages for Content   PUB 522
   To Duplicate a Page   PUB 523
   To Rearrange Pages   PUB 523
   To View a Two-Page Spread   PUB 524
   To Duplicate the Two-Page Spread   PUB 524
   To Link Text Boxes Using the Menu   PUB 527
Adding Content   **PUB 529**
   To Import Text   PUB 529
   To Use the Clipboard Task Pane   PUB 530
   To Paste from the Clipboard Task Pane   PUB 531
   To Edit the WordArt   PUB 532
   To Copy and Paste the Sidebar   PUB 532
   To Insert a Picture   PUB 533
   To Insert More Pictures   PUB 534
   To Change Text Wrapping Options   PUB 534
   To Copy the Wrapping Style   PUB 536
Find and Replace   **PUB 536**
   To Use the Find Command   PUB 537
   To Find Whole Words Only   PUB 539
   To Use the Replace Command   PUB 539
Thesaurus   **PUB 541**
   To Use the Thesaurus   PUB 541
Navigating through a Large-Scale Publication   **PUB 543**
   To Use the 'Go to Page' Command   PUB 543
   Page Breaks   PUB 544
   To Create a Text Break   PUB 544
   To Insert Other Breaks   PUB 546
   To Create a Section Heading   PUB 546
   To Copy and Paste the Section Heading   PUB 547
   Updating the Table of Contents   PUB 548
   To Update the Table of Contents   PUB 548
Bookmarks   **PUB 549**
   To Create a Bookmark   PUB 549
   To Create More Bookmarks   PUB 550
   To Use Bookmarks to Create Hyperlinks   PUB 550
   To Test a Hyperlink   PUB 552
   To Hyphenate the Publication   PUB 552
   To Check the Publication for Spelling
      and Design Errors   PUB 552
   To Save in the PDF Format   PUB 553
   To Navigate with Bookmarks in a PDF File   PUB 553

Summary   **PUB 555**
Apply Your Knowledge   **PUB 555**
Extend Your Knowledge   **PUB 558**
Expand Your World   **PUB 559**
In the Labs   **PUB 560**

MODULE ELEVEN
Advanced Features in Publisher
Objectives   **PUB 565**
Introduction   **PUB 565**
Project — Creating an Interactive Website   **PUB 566**
Using Online Templates   **PUB 567**
   To Search for an Online Template   PUB 568
   To Choose a Color Scheme and Save   PUB 569
   Picture Formats   PUB 570
   To Convert a Picture and Ungroup   PUB 570
   To Fill with a Custom RGB Color   PUB 572
   To Copy the Formatting   PUB 573
   To Fill Other Shapes   PUB 574
   To Regroup and Save as a Picture   PUB 575
Installing Fonts   **PUB 575**
   To Install a New Font   PUB 575
Webpages and Websites   **PUB 576**
   To Open a Web Publication   PUB 577
   To Change the Size of the Webpage   PUB 577
   To Apply a Background   PUB 578
   To Create Custom Ruler Guides   PUB 579
   To Save the Publication in a New Folder   PUB 580
Web Mastheads and Navigation Bars   **PUB 581**
   To Create a Web Masthead   PUB 582
   To Reformat the Masthead   PUB 583
   To Use the Installed Font   PUB 584
   To Insert a Navigation Bar   PUB 584
   To Add a Secondary Page to a Website   PUB 585
Web Graphics   **PUB 586**
   To Insert an Animated Graphic   PUB 586
   To Preview an Animated Graphic   PUB 587
   Alternative Text   PUB 587
   To Add Alternative Text   PUB 587
   To Insert Another Graphic   PUB 588
   To Complete Page 1   PUB 589
Publishing the Website   **PUB 589**
   To Publish a Website   PUB 590
Form Controls   **PUB 591**
   To Create Text Boxes   PUB 592
   To Change a Navigation Button   PUB 592
   To Insert Option Button Form Controls   PUB 593
   To Edit Option Button Form Control
      Properties   PUB 594
   To Insert Textbox Form Controls   PUB 596
   To Edit Textbox Form Control Properties   PUB 596
   To Insert Submit Form Controls   PUB 597
   To Edit Form Properties   PUB 599
Web Page Options   **PUB 600**
   To Edit Webpage Options   PUB 600
   Audio   PUB 601
   To Insert an Audio File   PUB 601
   To Edit Webpage Options on Page 2   PUB 602
   To Republish to the Web   PUB 603
Testing a Website   **PUB 603**
   To Test a Website   PUB 603

Visual Basic for Applications   **PUB 605**
    To Display the Developer Tab   PUB 606
    Using the Visual Basic Editor   PUB 607
    To Open the VBA Code Window   PUB 607
    Entering Code Statements and Comments   PUB 608
    To Program a BeforeClose Event   PUB 608
Security Levels   **PUB 610**
    To Set a Security Level in Publisher   PUB 610
Completing the Website   **PUB 611**
    To Check the Publication   PUB 611
    To Save and Republish   PUB 612

    Testing the Website   PUB 612
    To Hide the Developer Tab   PUB 612
    To Test the Macro   PUB 613
Summary   **PUB 613**
Apply Your Knowledge   **PUB 614**
Extend Your Knowledge   **PUB 616**
Expand Your World   **PUB 618**
In the Labs   **PUB 619**

Index   **IND 1**

Microsoft® Office 365™
PUBLISHER 2016

COMPREHENSIVE

Productivity Apps for School and Work

OneNote
Sway
Office Mix
Edge

Corinne Hoisington

Lochlan keeps track of his class notes, football plays, and internship meetings with OneNote.

Zoe is using the annotation features of Microsoft Edge to take and save web notes for her research paper.

Nori is creating a Sway site to highlight this year's activities for the Student Government Association.

Hunter is adding interactive videos and screen recordings to his PowerPoint resume.

© Rawpixel/Shutterstock.com

Being computer literate no longer means mastery of only Word, Excel, PowerPoint, Outlook, and Access. To become technology power users, Hunter, Nori, Zoe, and Lochlan are exploring Microsoft OneNote, Sway, Mix, and Edge in Office 2016 and Windows 10.

In this Module

Introduction to OneNote 2016 2
Introduction to Sway 6
Introduction to Office Mix 10
Introduction to Microsoft Edge............. 14

Learn to use productivity apps!
Links to companion **Sways**, featuring **videos** with hands-on instructions, are located on www.cengagebrain.com.

Introduction to OneNote 2016

notebook | section tab | To Do tag | screen clipping | note | template | Microsoft OneNote Mobile app | sync | drawing canvas | inked handwriting | Ink to Text

Bottom Line

- OneNote is a note-taking app for your academic and professional life.
- Use OneNote to get organized by gathering your ideas, sketches, webpages, photos, videos, and notes in one place.

As you glance around any classroom, you invariably see paper notebooks and notepads on each desk. Because deciphering and sharing handwritten notes can be a challenge, Microsoft OneNote 2016 replaces physical notebooks, binders, and paper notes with a searchable, digital notebook. OneNote captures your ideas and schoolwork on any device so you can stay organized, share notes, and work with others on projects. Whether you are a student taking class notes as shown in Figure 1 or an employee taking notes in company meetings, OneNote is the one place to keep notes for all of your projects.

Figure 1: OneNote 2016 notebook

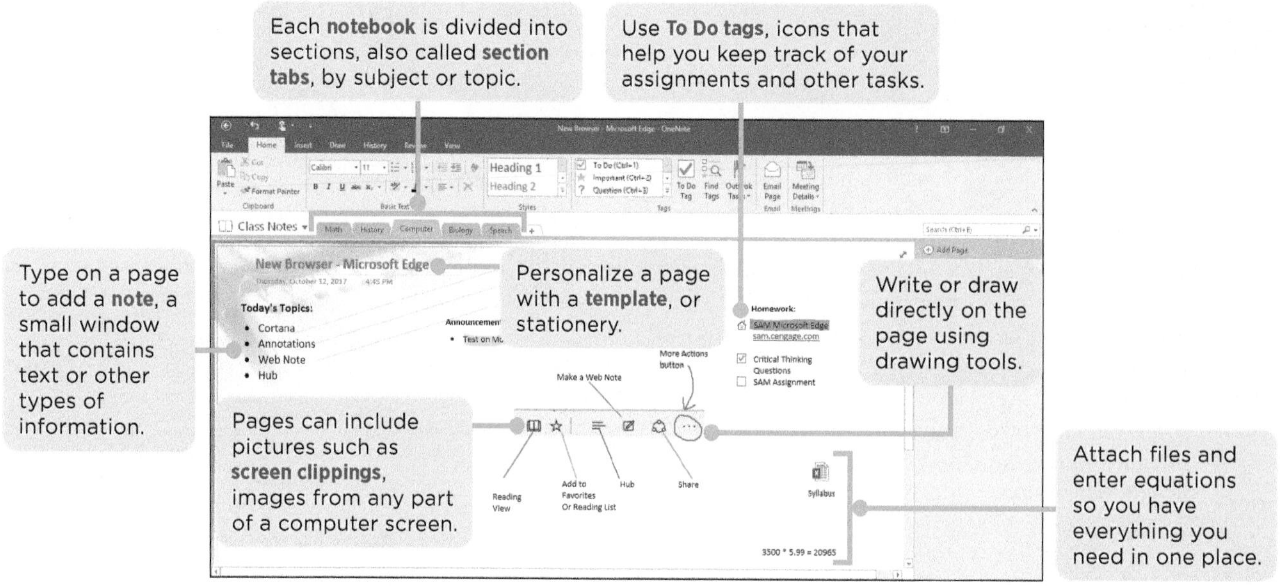

Each **notebook** is divided into sections, also called **section tabs**, by subject or topic.

Use **To Do tags**, icons that help you keep track of your assignments and other tasks.

Type on a page to add a **note**, a small window that contains text or other types of information.

Personalize a page with a **template**, or stationery.

Write or draw directly on the page using drawing tools.

Pages can include pictures such as **screen clippings**, images from any part of a computer screen.

Attach files and enter equations so you have everything you need in one place.

Creating a OneNote Notebook

OneNote is divided into sections similar to those in a spiral-bound notebook. Each OneNote notebook contains sections, pages, and other notebooks. You can use One-Note for school, business, and personal projects. Store information for each type of project in different notebooks to keep your tasks separate, or use any other organization that suits you. OneNote is flexible enough to adapt to the way you want to work.

When you create a notebook, it contains a blank page with a plain white background by default, though you can use templates, or stationery, to apply designs in categories such as Academic, Business, Decorative, and Planners. Start typing or use the buttons on the Insert tab to insert notes, which are small resizable windows that can contain text, equations, tables, on-screen writing, images, audio and video recordings, to-do lists, file attachments, and file printouts. Add as many notes as you need to each page.

Learn to use OneNote!

Links to companion **Sways**, featuring **videos** with hands-on instructions, are located on www.cengagebrain.com.

Syncing a Notebook to the Cloud

OneNote saves your notes every time you make a change in a notebook. To make sure you can access your notebooks with a laptop, tablet, or smartphone wherever you are, OneNote uses cloud-based storage, such as OneDrive or SharePoint. **Microsoft OneNote Mobile app**, a lightweight version of OneNote 2016 shown in Figure 2, is available for free in the Windows Store, Google Play for Android devices, and the AppStore for iOS devices.

If you have a Microsoft account, OneNote saves your notes on OneDrive automatically for all your mobile devices and computers, which is called **syncing**. For example, you can use OneNote to take notes on your laptop during class, and then open OneNote on your phone to study later. To use a notebook stored on your computer with your OneNote Mobile app, move the notebook to OneDrive. You can quickly share notebook content with other people using OneDrive.

Figure 2: Microsoft OneNote Mobile app

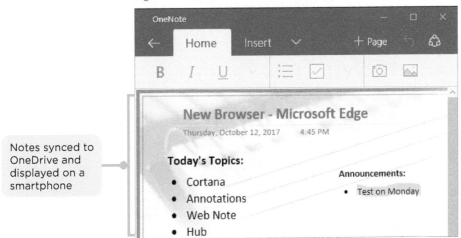

Notes synced to OneDrive and displayed on a smartphone

Taking Notes

Use OneNote pages to organize your notes by class and topic or lecture. Beyond simple typed notes, OneNote stores drawings, converts handwriting to searchable text and mathematical sketches to equations, and records audio and video.

OneNote includes drawing tools that let you sketch freehand drawings such as biological cell diagrams and financial supply-and-demand charts. As shown in Figure 3, the Draw tab on the ribbon provides these drawing tools along with shapes so you can insert diagrams and other illustrations to represent your ideas. When you draw on a page, OneNote creates a **drawing canvas**, which is a container for shapes and lines.

On the Job Now

OneNote is ideal for taking notes during meetings, whether you are recording minutes, documenting a discussion, sketching product diagrams, or listing follow-up items. Use a meeting template to add pages with content appropriate for meetings.

Figure 3: Tools on the Draw tab

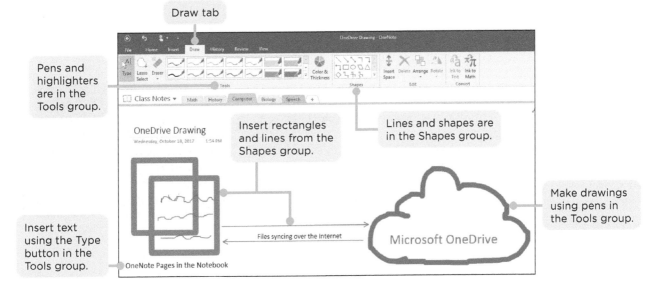

Draw tab

Pens and highlighters are in the Tools group.

Insert rectangles and lines from the Shapes group.

Lines and shapes are in the Shapes group.

Make drawings using pens in the Tools group.

Insert text using the Type button in the Tools group.

Converting Handwriting to Text

When you use a pen tool to write on a notebook page, the text you enter is called **inked handwriting**. OneNote can convert inked handwriting to typed text when you use the **Ink to Text** button in the Convert group on the Draw tab, as shown in Figure 4. After OneNote converts the handwriting to text, you can use the Search box to find terms in the converted text or any other note in your notebooks.

Figure 4: Converting handwriting to text

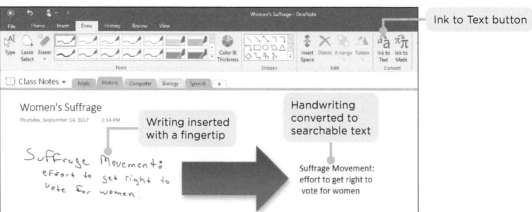

Ink to Text button

Women's Suffrage

Writing inserted with a fingertip

Handwriting converted to searchable text

Suffrage Movement: effort to get right to vote for women

On the Job Now

Use OneNote as a place to brainstorm ongoing work projects. If a notebook contains sensitive material, you can password-protect some or all of the notebook so that only certain people can open it.

Recording a Lecture

If your computer or mobile device has a microphone or camera, OneNote can record the audio or video from a lecture or business meeting as shown in **Figure 5**. When you record a lecture (with your instructor's permission), you can follow along, take regular notes at your own pace, and review the video recording later. You can control the start, pause, and stop motions of the recording when you play back the recording of your notes.

Figure 5: Video inserted in a notebook

Record Video button

Audio & Video Recording tab

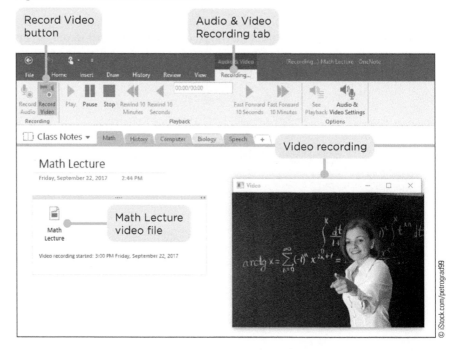

Video recording

Math Lecture

Math Lecture video file

© iStock.com/petrograd99

Try This Now

1: Taking Notes for a Week

As a student, you can get organized by using OneNote to take detailed notes in your classes. Perform the following tasks:

    a. Create a new OneNote notebook on your Microsoft OneDrive account (the default location for new notebooks). Name the notebook with your first name followed by "Notes," as in **Caleb Notes**.

    b. Create four section tabs, each with a different class name.

    c. Take detailed notes in those classes for one week. Be sure to include notes, drawings, and other types of content.

    d. Sync your notes with your OneDrive. Submit your assignment in the format specified by your instructor.

2: Using OneNote to Organize a Research Paper

You have a research paper due on the topic of three habits of successful students. Use OneNote to organize your research. Perform the following tasks:

    a. Create a new OneNote notebook on your Microsoft OneDrive account. Name the notebook **Success Research**.

    b. Create three section tabs with the following names:

- **Take Detailed Notes**
- **Be Respectful in Class**
- **Come to Class Prepared**

    c. On the web, research the topics and find three sources for each section. Copy a sentence from each source and paste the sentence into the appropriate section. When you paste the sentence, OneNote inserts it in a note with a link to the source.

    d. Sync your notes with your OneDrive. Submit your assignment in the format specified by your instructor.

3: Planning Your Career

Note: This activity requires a webcam or built-in video camera on any type of device.

Consider an occupation that interests you. Using OneNote, examine the responsibilities, education requirements, potential salary, and employment outlook of a specific career. Perform the following tasks:

    a. Create a new OneNote notebook on your Microsoft OneDrive account. Name the notebook with your first name followed by a career title, such as **Kara - App Developer**.

    b. Create four section tabs with the names **Responsibilities, Education Requirements, Median Salary**, and **Employment Outlook.**

    c. Research the responsibilities of your career path. Using OneNote, record a short video (approximately 30 seconds) of yourself explaining the responsibilities of your career path. Place the video in the Responsibilities section.

    d. On the web, research the educational requirements for your career path and find two appropriate sources. Copy a paragraph from each source and paste them into the appropriate section. When you paste a paragraph, OneNote inserts it in a note with a link to the source.

    e. Research the median salary for a single year for this career. Create a mathematical equation in the Median Salary section that multiplies the amount of the median salary times 20 years to calculate how much you will possibly earn.

    f. For the Employment Outlook section, research the outlook for your career path. Take at least four notes about what you find when researching the topic.

    g. Sync your notes with your OneDrive. Submit your assignment in the format specified by your instructor.

Introduction to Sway

Sway site | responsive design | Storyline | card | Creative Commons license | animation emphasis effects | Docs.com

Expressing your ideas in a presentation typically means creating PowerPoint slides or a Word document. Microsoft Sway gives you another way to engage an audience. Sway is a free Microsoft tool available at Sway.com or as an app in Office 365. Using Sway, you can combine text, images, videos, and social media in a website called a **Sway site** that you can share and display on any device. To get started, you create a digital story on a web-based canvas without borders, slides, cells, or page breaks. A Sway site organizes the text, images, and video into a **responsive design**, which means your content adapts perfectly to any screen size as shown in Figure 6. You store a Sway site in the cloud on OneDrive using a free Microsoft account.

Figure 6: Sway site with responsive design

You can display a Sway presentation in a web browser.

Sway uses responsive design to make sure pages fit perfectly on any device.

© iStock.com/marinello, © iStock.com/marekuliasz

Creating a Sway Presentation

You can use Sway to build a digital flyer, a club newsletter, a vacation blog, an informational site, a digital art portfolio, or a new product rollout. After you select your topic and sign into Sway with your Microsoft account, a **Storyline** opens, providing tools and a work area for composing your digital story. See Figure 7. Each story can include text, images, and videos. You create a Sway by adding text and media content into a Storyline section, or **card**. To add pictures, videos, or documents, select a card in the left pane and then select the Insert Content button. The first card in a Sway presentation contains a title and background image.

Figure 7: Creating a Sway site

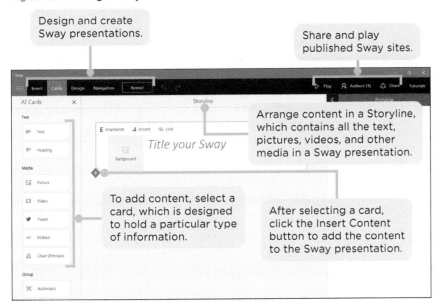

Design and create Sway presentations.

Share and play published Sway sites.

Arrange content in a Storyline, which contains all the text, pictures, videos, and other media in a Sway presentation.

To add content, select a card, which is designed to hold a particular type of information.

After selecting a card, click the Insert Content button to add the content to the Sway presentation.

Adding Content to Build a Story

As you work, Sway searches the Internet to help you find relevant images, videos, tweets, and other content from online sources such as Bing, YouTube, Twitter, and Facebook. You can drag content from the search results right into the Storyline. In addition, you can upload your own images and videos directly in the presentation. For example, if you are creating a Sway presentation about the market for commercial drones, Sway suggests content to incorporate into the presentation by displaying it in the left pane as search results. The search results include drone images tagged with a **Creative Commons license** at online sources as shown in **Figure 8**. A Creative Commons license is a public copyright license that allows the free distribution of an otherwise copyrighted work. In addition, you can specify the source of the media. For example, you can add your own Facebook or OneNote pictures and videos in Sway without leaving the app.

On the Job Now

If you have a Microsoft Word document containing an outline of your business content, drag the outline into Sway to create a card for each topic.

Figure 8: Images in Sway search results

Select the source of media objects

Information about Creative Commons licenses

Storyline title

The Market for Commercial Drones

Drag an image to the picture placeholder box

Suggested images in the search results

Designing a Sway

Sway professionally designs your Storyline content by resizing background images and fonts to fit your display, and by floating text, animating media, embedding video, and removing images as a page scrolls out of view. Sway also evaluates the images in your Storyline and suggests a color palette based on colors that appear in your photos. Use the Design button to display tools including color palettes, font choices, **animation emphasis effects**, and style templates to provide a personality for a Sway presentation. Instead of creating your own design, you can click the Remix button, which randomly selects unique designs for your Sway site.

Publishing a Sway

Use the Play button to display your finished Sway presentation as a website. The Address bar includes a unique web address where others can view your Sway site. As the author, you can edit a published Sway site by clicking the Edit button (pencil icon) on the Sway toolbar.

Sharing a Sway

When you are ready to share your Sway website, you have several options as shown in **Figure 9**. Use the Share slider button to share the Sway site publically or keep it private. If you add the Sway site to the Microsoft **Docs.com** public gallery, anyone worldwide can use Bing, Google, or other search engines to find, view, and share your Sway site. You can also share your Sway site using Facebook, Twitter, Google+, Yammer, and other social media sites. Link your presentation to any webpage or email the link to your audience. Sway can also generate a code for embedding the link within another webpage.

Figure 9: Sharing a Sway site

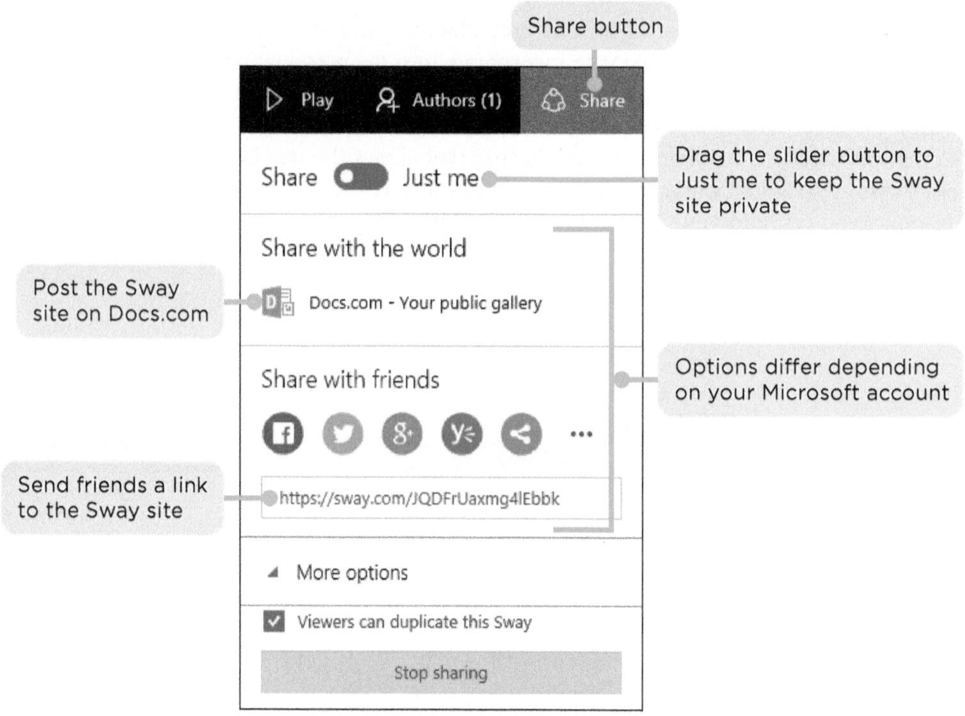

Share button

| ▷ Play | ♀₊ Authors (1) | ⟳ Share |

Share ⬤ Just me — Drag the slider button to Just me to keep the Sway site private

Share with the world

Post the Sway site on Docs.com — 🄳 Docs.com - Your public gallery

Share with friends

🅕 🐦 8⁺ ℽ₌ ⦿ ⋯ — Options differ depending on your Microsoft account

Send friends a link to the Sway site — https://sway.com/JQDFrUaxmg4lEbbk

◢ More options

☑ Viewers can duplicate this Sway

Stop sharing

Try This Now

Learn to use Sway!
Links to companion **Sways**, featuring **videos** with hands-on instructions, are located on www.cengagebrain.com.

1: Creating a Sway Resume

Sway is a digital storytelling app. Create a Sway resume to share the skills, job experiences, and achievements you have that match the requirements of a future job interest. Perform the following tasks:

a. Create a new presentation in Sway to use as a digital resume. Title the Sway Storyline with your full name and then select a background image.

b. Create three separate sections titled **Academic Background, Work Experience**, and **Skills**, and insert text, a picture, and a paragraph or bulleted points in each section. Be sure to include your own picture.

c. Add a fourth section that includes a video about your school that you find online.

d. Customize the design of your presentation.

e. Submit your assignment link in the format specified by your instructor.

2: Creating an Online Sway Newsletter

Newsletters are designed to capture the attention of their target audience. Using Sway, create a newsletter for a club, organization, or your favorite music group. Perform the following tasks:

a. Create a new presentation in Sway to use as a digital newsletter for a club, organization, or your favorite music group. Provide a title for the Sway Storyline and select an appropriate background image.

b. Select three separate sections with appropriate titles, such as Upcoming Events. In each section, insert text, a picture, and a paragraph or bulleted points.

c. Add a fourth section that includes a video about your selected topic.

d. Customize the design of your presentation.

e. Submit your assignment link in the format specified by your instructor.

3: Creating and Sharing a Technology Presentation

To place a Sway presentation in the hands of your entire audience, you can share a link to the Sway presentation. Create a Sway presentation on a new technology and share it with your class. Perform the following tasks:

a. Create a new presentation in Sway about a cutting-edge technology topic. Provide a title for the Sway Storyline and select a background image.

b. Create four separate sections about your topic, and include text, a picture, and a paragraph in each section.

c. Add a fifth section that includes a video about your topic.

d. Customize the design of your presentation.

e. Share the link to your Sway with your classmates and submit your assignment link in the format specified by your instructor.

Introduction to Office Mix

add-in | clip | slide recording | Slide Notes | screen recording | free-response quiz

Bottom Line
- Office Mix is a free PowerPoint add-in from Microsoft that adds features to PowerPoint.
- The Mix tab on the PowerPoint ribbon provides tools for creating screen recordings, videos, interactive quizzes, and live webpages.

To enliven business meetings and lectures, Microsoft adds a new dimension to presentations with a powerful toolset called Office Mix, a free add-in for PowerPoint. (An **add-in** is software that works with an installed app to extend its features.) Using Office Mix, you can record yourself on video, capture still and moving images on your desktop, and insert interactive elements such as quizzes and live webpages directly into PowerPoint slides. When you post the finished presentation to OneDrive, Office Mix provides a link you can share with friends and colleagues. Anyone with an Internet connection and a web browser can watch a published Office Mix presentation, such as the one in Figure 10, on a computer or mobile device.

Figure 10: Office Mix presentation

Learn to use Office Mix!
Links to companion **Sways**, featuring **videos** with hands-on instructions, are located on www.cengagebrain.com.

Adding Office Mix to PowerPoint

To get started, you create an Office Mix account at the website mix.office.com using an email address or a Facebook or Google account. Next, you download and install the Office Mix add-in (see Figure 11). Office Mix appears as a new tab named Mix on the PowerPoint ribbon in versions of Office 2013 and Office 2016 running on personal computers (PCs).

Figure 11: Getting started with Office Mix

Capturing Video Clips

A **clip** is a short segment of audio, such as music, or video. After finishing the content on a PowerPoint slide, you can use Office Mix to add a video clip to animate or illustrate the content. Office Mix creates video clips in two ways: by recording live action on a webcam and by capturing screen images and movements. If your computer has a webcam, you can record yourself and annotate the slide to create a **slide recording** as shown in Figure 12.

On the Job Now

Companies are using Office Mix to train employees about new products, to explain benefit packages to new workers, and to educate interns about office procedures.

Figure 12: Making a slide recording

When you are making a slide recording, you can record your spoken narration at the same time. The **Slide Notes** feature works like a teleprompter to help you focus on your presentation content instead of memorizing your narration. Use the Inking tools to make annotations or add highlighting using different pen types and colors. After finishing a recording, edit the video in PowerPoint to trim the length or set playback options.

The second way to create a video is to capture on-screen images and actions with or without a voiceover. This method is ideal if you want to show how to use your favorite website or demonstrate an app such as OneNote. To share your screen with an audience, select the part of the screen you want to show in the video. Office Mix captures everything that happens in that area to create a **screen recording**, as shown in Figure 13. Office Mix inserts the screen recording as a video in the slide.

On the Job Now

To make your video recordings accessible to people with hearing impairments, use the Office Mix closed-captioning tools. You can also use closed captions to supplement audio that is difficult to understand and to provide an aid for those learning to read.

Figure 13: Making a screen recording

Inserting Quizzes, Live Webpages, and Apps

To enhance and assess audience understanding, make your slides interactive by adding quizzes, live webpages, and apps. Quizzes give immediate feedback to the user as shown in Figure 14. Office Mix supports several quiz formats, including a **free-response quiz** similar to a short answer quiz, and true/false, multiple-choice, and multiple-response formats.

Figure 14: Creating an interactive quiz

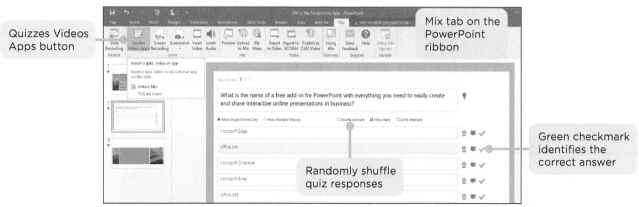

Sharing an Office Mix Presentation

When you complete your work with Office Mix, upload the presentation to your personal Office Mix dashboard as shown in Figure 15. Users of PCs, Macs, iOS devices, and Android devices can access and play Office Mix presentations. The Office Mix dashboard displays built-in analytics that include the quiz results and how much time viewers spent on each slide. You can play completed Office Mix presentations online or download them as movies.

Figure 15: Sharing an Office Mix presentation

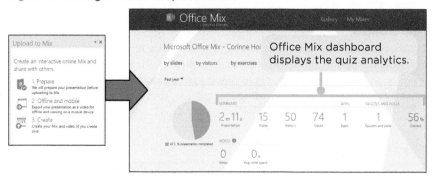

Try This Now

1: Creating an Office Mix Tutorial for OneNote

Note: This activity requires a microphone on your computer.

Office Mix makes it easy to record screens and their contents. Create PowerPoint slides with an Office Mix screen recording to show OneNote 2016 features. Perform the following tasks:

    a. Create a PowerPoint presentation with the Ion Boardroom template. Create an opening slide with the title **My Favorite OneNote Features** and enter your name in the subtitle.

    b. Create three additional slides, each titled with a new feature of OneNote. Open OneNote and use the Mix tab in PowerPoint to capture three separate screen recordings that teach your favorite features.

    c. Add a fifth slide that quizzes the user with a multiple-choice question about OneNote and includes four responses. Be sure to insert a checkmark indicating the correct response.

    d. Upload the completed presentation to your Office Mix dashboard and share the link with your instructor.

    e. Submit your assignment link in the format specified by your instructor.

2: Teaching Augmented Reality with Office Mix

Note: This activity requires a webcam or built-in video camera on your computer.

A local elementary school has asked you to teach augmented reality to its students using Office Mix. Perform the following tasks:

    a. Research augmented reality using your favorite online search tools.

    b. Create a PowerPoint presentation with the Frame template. Create an opening slide with the title **Augmented Reality** and enter your name in the subtitle.

    c. Create a slide with four bullets summarizing your research of augmented reality. Create a 20-second slide recording of yourself providing a quick overview of augmented reality.

    d. Create another slide with a 30-second screen recording of a video about augmented reality from a site such as YouTube or another video-sharing site.

    e. Add a final slide that quizzes the user with a true/false question about augmented reality. Be sure to insert a checkmark indicating the correct response.

    f. Upload the completed presentation to your Office Mix dashboard and share the link with your instructor.

    g. Submit your assignment link in the format specified by your instructor.

3: Marketing a Travel Destination with Office Mix

Note: This activity requires a webcam or built-in video camera on your computer.

To convince your audience to travel to a particular city, create a slide presentation marketing any city in the world using a slide recording, screen recording, and a quiz. Perform the following tasks:

    a. Create a PowerPoint presentation with any template. Create an opening slide with the title of the city you are marketing as a travel destination and your name in the subtitle.

    b. Create a slide with four bullets about the featured city. Create a 30-second slide recording of yourself explaining why this city is the perfect vacation destination.

    c. Create another slide with a 20-second screen recording of a travel video about the city from a site such as YouTube or another video-sharing site.

    d. Add a final slide that quizzes the user with a multiple-choice question about the featured city with five responses. Be sure to include a checkmark indicating the correct response.

    e. Upload the completed presentation to your Office Mix dashboard and share your link with your instructor.

    f. Submit your assignment link in the format specified by your instructor.

Learn to use Office Mix! Links to companion **Sways**, featuring **videos** with hands-on instructions, are located on www.cengagebrain.com.

Introduction to Microsoft Edge

Reading view | Hub | Cortana | Web Note | Inking | sandbox

Bottom Line

- Microsoft Edge is the name of the new web browser built into Windows 10.
- Microsoft Edge allows you to search the web faster, take web notes, read webpages without distractions, and get instant assistance from Cortana.

Microsoft Edge is the default web browser developed for the Windows 10 operating system as a replacement for Internet Explorer. Unlike its predecessor, Edge lets you write on webpages, read webpages without advertisements and other distractions, and search for information using a virtual personal assistant. The Edge interface is clean and basic, as shown in Figure 16, meaning you can pay more attention to the webpage content.

Figure 16: Microsoft Edge tools

Forward button • New tab button • Web address in the Address bar • Add to favorites or reading list button • Back button • Reading view button • More button • Refresh (F5) button • Hub (Favorites, reading list, history, and downloads) button • Share Web Note button • Make a Web Note button

Learn to use Edge!

Links to companion **Sways**, featuring **videos** with hands-on instructions, are located on www.cengagebrain.com.

On the Job Now

Businesses started adopting Internet Explorer more than 20 years ago simply to view webpages. Today, Microsoft Edge has a different purpose: to promote interaction with the web and share its contents with colleagues.

Browsing the Web with Microsoft Edge

One of the fastest browsers available, Edge allows you to type search text directly in the Address bar. As you view the resulting webpage, you can switch to **Reading view**, which is available for most news and research sites, to eliminate distracting advertisements. For example, if you are catching up on technology news online, the webpage might be difficult to read due to a busy layout cluttered with ads. Switch to Reading view to refresh the page and remove the original page formatting, ads, and menu sidebars to read the article distraction-free.

Consider the **Hub** in Microsoft Edge as providing one-stop access to all the things you collect on the web, such as your favorite websites, reading list, surfing history, and downloaded files.

Locating Information with Cortana

Cortana, the Windows 10 virtual assistant, plays an important role in Microsoft Edge. After you turn on Cortana, it appears as an animated circle in the Address bar when you might need assistance, as shown in the restaurant website in Figure 17. When you click the Cortana icon, a pane slides in from the right of the browser window to display detailed information about the restaurant, including maps and reviews. Cortana can also assist you in defining words, finding the weather, suggesting coupons for shopping, updating stock market information, and calculating math.

Figure 17: Cortana providing restaurant information

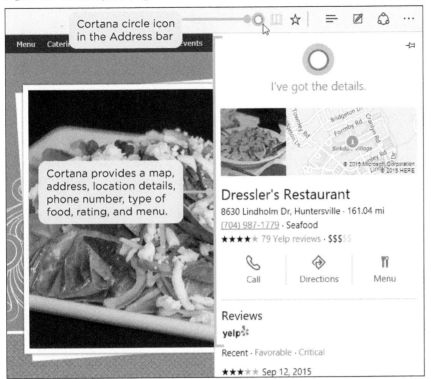

Cortana circle icon in the Address bar

Cortana provides a map, address, location details, phone number, type of food, rating, and menu.

I've got the details.

Dressler's Restaurant
8630 Lindholm Dr, Huntersville · 161.04 mi
(704) 987-1779 · Seafood
★★★★☆ 79 Yelp reviews · $$$$$

| Call | Directions | Menu |

Reviews
yelp

Recent · Favorable · Critical
★★★☆☆ Sep 12, 2015

Annotating Webpages

One of the most impressive Microsoft Edge features are the **Web Note** tools, which you use to write on a webpage or to highlight text. When you click the Make a Web Note button, an **Inking** toolbar appears, as shown in **Figure 18**, that provides writing and drawing tools. These tools include an eraser, a pen, and a highlighter with different colors. You can also insert a typed note and copy a screen image (called a screen clipping). You can draw with a pointing device, fingertip, or stylus using different pen colors. Whether you add notes to a recipe, annotate sources for a research paper, or select a product while shopping online, the Web Note tools can enhance your productivity. After you complete your notes, click the Save button to save the annotations to OneNote, your Favorites list, or your Reading list. You can share the inked page with others using the Share Web Note button.

On the Job Now

To enhance security, Microsoft Edge runs in a partial sandbox, an arrangement that prevents attackers from gaining control of your computer. Browsing within the **sandbox** protects computer resources and information from hackers.

Figure 18: Web Note tools in Microsoft Edge

Inking toolbar with Web Note tools for making annotations

Writing and drawing created with the Pen tool

Highlighted text

Work anywhere

The integrated Kickstand features multiple positions so you can work comfortably whether you're on a plane, at your desk, or in front of the television.

I am considering purchasing the new Surface Pro for school

Save a copy of the webpage with annotations

Typed note

Try This Now

Learn to use Edge!
Links to companion **Sways**, featuring **videos** with hands-on instructions, are located on www.cengagebrain.com.

1: Using Cortana in Microsoft Edge

Note: This activity requires using Microsoft Edge on a Windows 10 computer.

Cortana can assist you in finding information on a webpage in Microsoft Edge. Perform the following tasks:

a. Create a Word document using the Word Screen Clipping tool to capture the following screenshots.

- Screenshot A—Using Microsoft Edge, open a webpage with a technology news article. Right-click a term in the article and ask Cortana to define it.
- Screenshot B—Using Microsoft Edge, open the website of a fancy restaurant in a city near you. Make sure the Cortana circle icon is displayed in the Address bar. (If it's not displayed, find a different restaurant website.) Click the Cortana circle icon to display a pane with information about the restaurant.
- Screenshot C—Using Microsoft Edge, type **10 USD to Euros** in the Address bar without pressing the Enter key. Cortana converts the U.S. dollars to Euros.
- Screenshot D—Using Microsoft Edge, type **Apple stock** in the Address bar without pressing the Enter key. Cortana displays the current stock quote.

b. Submit your assignment in the format specified by your instructor.

2: Viewing Online News with Reading View

Note: This activity requires using Microsoft Edge on a Windows 10 computer.

Reading view in Microsoft Edge can make a webpage less cluttered with ads and other distractions. Perform the following tasks:

a. Create a Word document using the Word Screen Clipping tool to capture the following screenshots.

- Screenshot A—Using Microsoft Edge, open the website **mashable.com**. Open a technology article. Click the Reading view button to display an ad-free page that uses only basic text formatting.
- Screenshot B—Using Microsoft Edge, open the website **bbc.com**. Open any news article. Click the Reading view button to display an ad-free page that uses only basic text formatting.
- Screenshot C—Make three types of annotations (Pen, Highlighter, and Add a typed note) on the BBC article page displayed in Reading view.

b. Submit your assignment in the format specified by your instructor.

3: Inking with Microsoft Edge

Note: This activity requires using Microsoft Edge on a Windows 10 computer.

Microsoft Edge provides many annotation options to record your ideas. Perform the following tasks:

a. Open the website **wolframalpha.com** in the Microsoft Edge browser. Wolfram Alpha is a well-respected academic search engine. Type **US$100 1965 dollars in 2015** in the Wolfram Alpha search text box and press the Enter key.

b. Click the Make a Web Note button to display the Web Note tools. Using the Pen tool, draw a circle around the result on the webpage. Save the page to OneNote.

c. In the Wolfram Alpha search text box, type the name of the city closest to where you live and press the Enter key. Using the Highlighter tool, highlight at least three interesting results. Add a note and then type a sentence about what you learned about this city. Save the page to OneNote. Share your OneNote notebook with your instructor.

d. Submit your assignment link in the format specified by your instructor.

Office 2016 and Windows 10: Essential Concepts and Skills

Objectives

You will have mastered the material in this module when you can:

- Use a touch screen
- Perform basic mouse operations
- Start Windows and sign in to an account
- Identify the objects on the Windows 10 desktop
- Identify the versions and apps of Microsoft Office 2016
- Run an app
- Identify the components of the Microsoft Office ribbon

- Create folders
- Save files
- Change screen resolution
- Perform basic tasks in Microsoft Office apps
- Manage files
- Use Microsoft Office Help and Windows Help

This introductory module uses Publisher 2016 to cover features and functions common to Office 2016 apps, as well as the basics of Windows 10.

Roadmap

In this module, you will learn how to perform basic tasks in Windows and Publisher. The following roadmap identifies general activities you will perform as you progress through this module:

1. SIGN IN to an account.
2. USE WINDOWS.
3. USE features in Publisher that are common across Office APPS.
4. FILE and folder MANAGEMENT.
5. SWITCH between APPS.
6. SAVE and manage FILES.
7. CHANGE SCREEN RESOLUTION.

8. EXIT APPS.

9. USE ADDITIONAL Office APP FEATURES.

10. USE Office and Windows HELP.

At the beginning of the step instructions throughout each module, you will see an abbreviated form of this roadmap. The abbreviated roadmap uses colors to indicate module progress: gray means the module is beyond that activity, blue means the task being shown is covered in that activity, and black means that activity is yet to be covered. For example, the following abbreviated roadmap indicates the module would be showing a task in the USE APPS activity.

1 SIGN IN | 2 USE WINDOWS | 3 USE APPS | 4 FILE MANAGEMENT | 5 SWITCH APPS | 6 SAVE FILES
7 CHANGE SCREEN RESOLUTION | 8 EXIT APPS | 9 USE ADDITIONAL APP FEATURES | 10 USE HELP

Use the abbreviated roadmap as a progress guide while you read or step through the instructions in this module.

Introduction to the Windows 10 Operating System

Windows 10 is the newest version of Microsoft Windows, which is a popular and widely used operating system (Figure 1). An **operating system (OS)** is a set of programs that coordinate all the activities among computer or mobile device hardware.

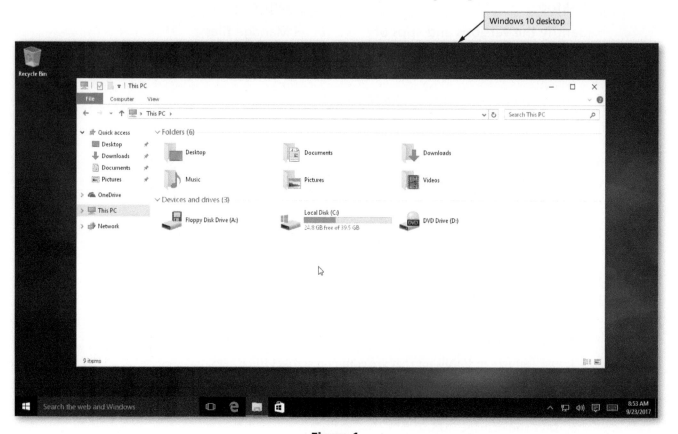

Windows 10 desktop

Figure 1

The Windows operating system simplifies the process of working with publications and apps by organizing the manner in which you interact with the computer. Windows is used to run apps. An application, or **app**, consists of programs designed to make users more productive and/or assist them with personal tasks, such as desktop publishing or browsing the web.

Using a Touch Screen and a Mouse

Windows users who have computers or devices with touch screen capability can interact with the screen using gestures. A **gesture** is a motion you make on a touch screen with the tip of one or more fingers or your hand. Touch screens are convenient because they do not require a separate device for input. Table 1 presents common ways to interact with a touch screen.

If you are using your finger on a touch screen and are having difficulty completing the steps in this module, consider using a stylus. Many people find it easier to be precise with a stylus than with a finger. In addition, with a stylus you see the pointer. If you still are having trouble completing the steps with a stylus, try using a mouse.

Table 1 Touch Screen Gestures

Motion	Description	Common Uses	Equivalent Mouse Operation
Tap	Quickly touch and release one finger one time.	Activate a link (built-in connection). Press a button. Run a program or an app.	Click
Double-tap	Quickly touch and release one finger two times.	Run a program or an app. Zoom in (show a smaller area on the screen, so that contents appear larger) at the location of the double-tap.	Double-click
Press and hold	Press and hold one finger to cause an action to occur, or until an action occurs.	Display a shortcut menu (immediate access to allowable actions). Activate a mode enabling you to move an item with one finger to a new location.	Right-click
Drag, or slide	Press and hold one finger on an object and then move the finger to the new location.	Move an item around the screen. Scroll.	Drag
Swipe	Press and hold one finger and then move the finger horizontally or vertically on the screen.	Select an object. Swipe from edge to display a bar such as the Action Center, Apps bar, and Navigation bar (all discussed later).	Drag
Stretch	Move two fingers apart.	Zoom in (show a smaller area on the screen, so that contents appear larger).	None
Pinch	Move two fingers together.	Zoom out (show a larger area on the screen, so that contents appear smaller).	None

Will the screen look different if you are using a touch screen?
The Windows and Microsoft Office interface varies slightly if you are using a touch screen. For this reason, you might notice that your Windows or Publisher screens looks slightly different from the screens in this book.

CONSIDER THIS

BTW
Pointer
If you are using a touch screen, the pointer may not appear on the screen as you perform touch gestures. The pointer will reappear when you begin using the mouse.

Windows users who do not have touch screen capabilities typically work with a mouse that has at least two buttons. For a right-handed user, the left button usually is the primary mouse button, and the right mouse button is the secondary mouse button. Left-handed people, however, can reverse the function of these buttons.

Table 2 explains how to perform a variety of mouse operations. Some apps also use keys in combination with the mouse to perform certain actions. For example, when you hold down the CTRL key while rolling the mouse wheel, text on the screen may become larger or smaller based on the direction you roll the wheel. The function of the mouse buttons and the wheel varies depending on the app.

Table 2 Mouse Operations

Operation	Mouse Action	Example*	Equivalent Touch Gesture
Point	Move the mouse until the pointer on the desktop is positioned on the item of choice.	Position the pointer on the screen.	None
Click	Press and release the primary mouse button, which usually is the left mouse button.	Select or deselect items on the screen or run an app or app feature.	Tap
Right-click	Press and release the secondary mouse button, which usually is the right mouse button.	Display a shortcut menu.	Press and hold
Double-click	Quickly press and release the primary mouse button twice without moving the mouse.	Run an app or app feature.	Double-tap
Triple-click	Quickly press and release the primary mouse button three times without moving the mouse.	Select a paragraph.	Triple-tap
Drag	Point to an item, hold down the primary mouse button, move the item to the desired location on the screen, and then release the mouse button.	Move an object from one location to another or draw pictures.	Drag or slide
Right-drag	Point to an item, hold down the right mouse button, move the item to the desired location on the screen, and then release the right mouse button.	Display a shortcut menu after moving an object from one location to another.	Press and hold, then drag
Rotate wheel	Roll the wheel forward or backward.	Scroll vertically (up and down).	Swipe
Free-spin wheel	Whirl the wheel forward or backward so that it spins freely on its own.	Scroll through many pages in seconds.	Swipe
Press wheel	Press the wheel button while moving the mouse.	Scroll continuously.	None
Tilt wheel	Press the wheel toward the right or left.	Scroll horizontally (left and right).	None
Press thumb button	Press the button on the side of the mouse with your thumb.	Move forward or backward through webpages and/or control media, games, etc.	None

*Note: The examples presented in this column are discussed as they are demonstrated in this module.

Scrolling

A **scroll bar** is a horizontal or vertical bar that appears when the contents of an area may not be visible completely on the screen (Figure 2). A scroll bar contains **scroll arrows** and a **scroll box** that enable you to view areas that currently cannot be seen on the screen. Clicking the up and down scroll arrows moves the screen content up or down one line. You also can click above or below the scroll box to move up or down a section, or drag the scroll box up or down to move to a specific location.

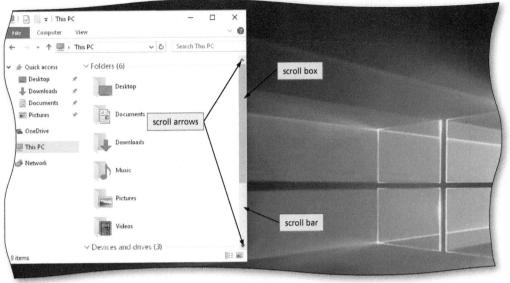

Figure 2

Keyboard Shortcuts

In many cases, you can use the keyboard instead of the mouse to accomplish a task. To perform tasks using the keyboard, you press one or more keyboard keys, sometimes identified as a **keyboard shortcut**. Some keyboard shortcuts consist of a single key, such as the F1 key. For example, to obtain help in many apps, you can press the F1 key. Other keyboard shortcuts consist of multiple keys, in which case a plus sign separates the key names, such as CTRL+ESC. This notation means to press and hold down the first key listed, press one or more additional keys, and then release all keys. For example, to display the Start menu, press CTRL+ESC, that is, hold down the CTRL key, press the ESC key, and then release both keys.

Starting Windows

It is not unusual for multiple people to use the same computer in a work, educational, recreational, or home setting. Windows enables each user to establish a **user account**, which identifies to Windows the resources, such as apps and storage locations, a user can access when working with the computer.

Each user account has a user name and may have a password and an icon, as well. A **user name** is a unique combination of letters or numbers that identifies a specific user to Windows. A **password** is a private combination of letters, numbers, and special characters associated with the user name that allows access to a user's account resources. An icon is a small image that represents an object; thus, a **user icon** is a picture associated with a user name.

When you turn on a computer, Windows starts and displays a **lock screen** consisting of the time and date (Figure 3). To unlock the screen, click the lock screen. Depending on your computer's settings, Windows may or may not display a sign-in screen that shows the user names and user icons for users who have accounts on the computer. This **sign-in screen** enables you to sign in to your user account and makes the computer available for use (shown in Figure 4). Clicking the user icon begins the process of signing in, also called logging on, to your user account.

BTW
Minimize Wrist Injury
Computer users frequently switch between the keyboard and the mouse while using Publisher; such switching strains the wrist. To help prevent wrist injury, minimize switching. For instance, if your fingers already are on the keyboard, use keyboard keys to scroll. If your hand already is on the mouse, use the mouse to scroll. If your hand is on the touch screen, use touch gestures to scroll.

Figure 3

At the bottom of the sign-in screen (shown in Figure 4) is the 'Connect to Internet' button, 'Ease of access' button, and a Shut down button. Clicking the 'Connect to Internet' button displays a list of each network connection and its status. You also can connect to or disconnect from a network. Clicking the 'Ease of access' button displays the Ease of access menu, which provides tools to optimize a computer to accommodate the needs of the mobility, hearing, and vision impaired users. Clicking the Shut down button displays a menu containing commands related to putting the computer or mobile device in a low-power state, shutting it down, and restarting the computer or mobile device. The commands available on your computer or mobile device may differ.

- The Sleep command saves your work, turns off the computer fans and hard drive, and places the computer in a lower-power state. To wake the computer from sleep mode, press the power button or lift a laptop's cover, and sign in to your account.

- The Shut down command exits running apps, shuts down Windows, and then turns off the computer.

- The Restart command exits running apps, shuts down Windows, and then restarts Windows.

To Sign In to an Account

1 SIGN IN | 2 USE WINDOWS | 3 USE APPS | 4 FILE MANAGEMENT | 5 SWITCH APPS | 6 SAVE FILES
7 CHANGE SCREEN RESOLUTION | 8 EXIT APPS | 9 USE ADDITIONAL APP FEATURES | 10 USE HELP

The following steps, which use SCSeries as the user name, sign in to an account based on a typical Windows installation. *Why? After starting Windows, you might be required to sign in to an account to access the computer or mobile device's resources.* You may need to ask your instructor how to sign in to your account.

1

- Click the lock screen (shown in Figure 3) to display a sign-in screen.

- Click the user icon (for SCSeries, in this case) on the sign-in screen, which depending on settings, either will display a second sign-in screen that contains a Password text box (Figure 4) or will display the Windows desktop (shown in Figure 5).

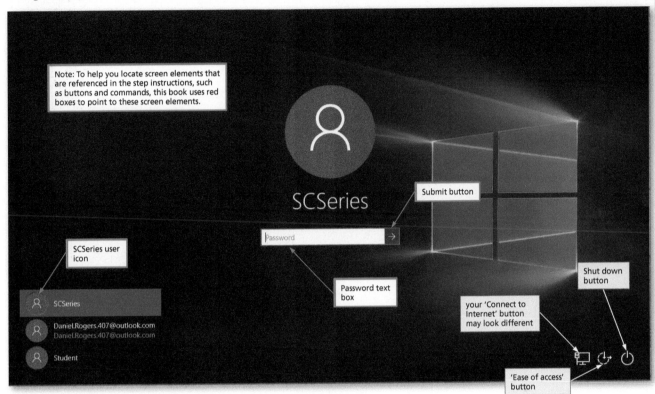

Figure 4

Office 2016 and Windows 10 Module

Q&A Why do I not see a user icon?
Your computer may require you to type a user name instead of clicking an icon.

What is a text box?
A text box is a rectangular box in which you type text.

Why does my screen not show a Password text box?
Your account does not require a password.

- If Windows displays a sign-in screen with a Password text box, type your password in the text box.

2

- Click the Submit button (shown in Figure 4) to sign in to your account and display the Windows desktop (Figure 5).

Q&A Why does my desktop look different from the one in Figure 5?
The Windows desktop is customizable, and your school or employer may have modified the desktop to meet its needs. Also, your screen resolution, which affects the size of the elements on the screen, may differ from the screen resolution used in this book. Later in this module, you learn how to change screen resolution.

How do I type if my tablet has no keyboard?
You can use your fingers to press keys on a keyboard that appears on the screen, called an on-screen keyboard, or you can purchase a separate physical keyboard that attaches to or wirelessly communicates with the tablet.

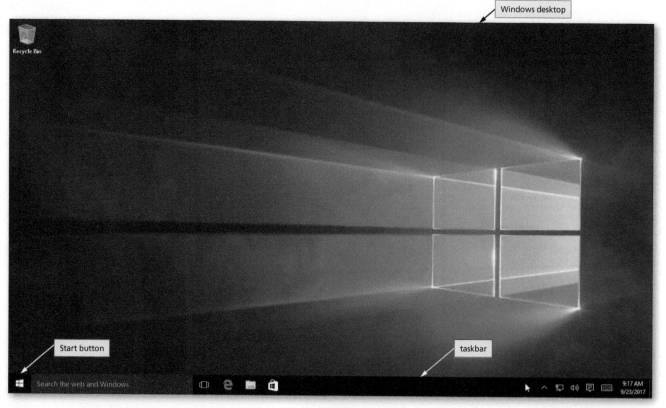

Figure 5

The Windows Desktop

The Windows 10 desktop (Figure 5) and the objects on the desktop emulate a work area in an office. Think of the Windows desktop as an electronic version of the top of your desk. You can perform tasks such as placing objects on the desktop, moving the objects around the desktop, and removing items from the desktop.

When you run an app in Windows 10, it appears on the desktop. Some icons also may be displayed on the desktop. For instance, the icon for the **Recycle Bin**, the location of files that have been deleted, appears on the desktop by default. A **file** is a named unit of storage. Files can contain text, images, audio, and/or video. You can customize your desktop so that icons representing programs and files you use often appear on your desktop.

Introduction to Microsoft Office 2016

Microsoft Office 2016 is the newest version of Microsoft Office, offering features that provide users with better functionality and easier ways to work with the various files they create. This version of Office also is designed to work more optimally on mobile devices and online.

Microsoft Office 2016 Apps

Microsoft Office 2016 includes a wide variety of apps, such as Word, PowerPoint, Excel, Access, Outlook, Publisher, and OneNote:

- **Microsoft Word 2016**, or Word, is a full-featured word processing app that allows you to create professional-looking documents and revise them easily.

- **Microsoft PowerPoint 2016**, or PowerPoint, is a complete presentation app that enables you to produce professional-looking presentations and then deliver them to an audience.

- **Microsoft Excel 2016**, or Excel, is a powerful spreadsheet app that allows you to organize data, complete calculations, make decisions, graph data, develop professional-looking reports, publish organized data to the web, and access real-time data from websites.

- **Microsoft Access 2016**, or Access, is a database management system that enables you to create a database; add, change, and delete data in the database; ask questions concerning the data in the database; and create forms and reports using the data in the database.

- **Microsoft Outlook 2016**, or Outlook, is a communications and scheduling app that allows you to manage email accounts, calendars, contacts, and access to other Internet content.

- **Microsoft Publisher 2016**, or Publisher, is a desktop publishing app that helps you create professional-quality publications and marketing materials that can be shared easily.

- **Microsoft OneNote 2016**, or OneNote, is a note-taking app that allows you to store and share information in notebooks with other people.

Microsoft Office 2016 Suites

A **suite** is a collection of individual apps available together as a unit. Microsoft offers a variety of Office suites, including a stand-alone desktop app, Microsoft Office 365, and Microsoft Office Online. **Microsoft Office 365**, or Office 365, provides plans that allow organizations to use Office in a mobile setting while also being able to communicate and share files, depending upon the type of plan selected by the organization. **Microsoft Office Online** includes apps that allow you to edit and share files on the web using the familiar Office interface.

During the Office 365 installation, you select a plan, and depending on your plan, you receive different apps and services. Office Online apps do not require a local installation and can be accessed through OneDrive and your browser. **OneDrive** is a cloud storage service that provides storage and other services, such as Office Online, to computer and mobile device users.

How do you sign up for a OneDrive account?

- Use your browser to navigate to onedrive.live.com.

- Create a Microsoft account by clicking the Sign up button and then entering your information to create the account.

- Sign in to OneDrive using your new account or use it in Publisher to save your files on OneDrive.

CONSIDER THIS

Apps in a suite, such as Microsoft Office, typically use a similar interface and share features. Once you are comfortable working with the elements and the interface, and performing tasks in one app, the similarity can help you apply the knowledge and skills you have learned to another app(s) in the suite. For example, the process for saving a file in Publisher is the same in Word, PowerPoint, Excel, and some of the other Office apps. While briefly showing how to use Publisher, this module illustrates some of the common functions across the Office apps and identifies the characteristics unique to Publisher.

Running and Using An App

To use an app, you must instruct the operating system to run the app. Windows provides many different ways to run an app, one of which is presented in this section (other ways to run an app are presented throughout this module). After an app is running, you can use it to perform a variety of tasks. The following pages use Publisher to discuss some elements of the Office interface and to perform tasks that are common to other Office apps.

Publisher

Publisher is a full-featured desktop publishing app that allows you to create many types of personal and business publications, including flyers, brochures, advertisements, catalogs, mailing labels, and newsletters. Publisher also provides tools that enable you to create webpages and save these webpages directly on a web server. Publisher has many features designed to simplify the production of publications and add visual appeal. Using Publisher, you easily can change the shape, size, and color of text. You also can include borders, shading, tables, images, pictures, charts, and web addresses in publications.

To Run an App Using the Start Menu and Create a Blank Publication

1 SIGN IN | 2 USE WINDOWS | 3 USE APPS | 4 FILE MANAGEMENT | 5 SWITCH APPS | 6 SAVE FILES
7 CHANGE SCREEN RESOLUTION | 8 EXIT APPS | 9 USE ADDITIONAL APP FEATURES | 10 USE HELP

Across the bottom of the Windows 10 desktop is the taskbar. The taskbar contains the **Start button**, which you use to access apps, files, folders, and settings. A **folder** is a named location on a storage medium that usually contains related publications.

Clicking the Start button displays the Start menu. The **Start menu** allows you to access programs, folders, and files on the computer or mobile device and contains commands that allow you to run programs, store and search for publications, customize the computer or mobile device, and sign out of a user account or shut down the computer or mobile device. A **menu** is a list of related items, including folders, programs, and commands. Each **command** on a menu performs a specific action, such as saving a file or obtaining help. *Why? When you install an app, for example, the app's name will be added to the All apps list on the Start menu.*

The following steps, which assume Windows is running, use the Start menu to run Publisher and create a blank publication based on a typical installation. You may need to ask your instructor how to run Publisher on your computer. Although the steps illustrate running the Publisher app, the steps to run any Office app are similar.

- Click the Start button on the Windows 10 taskbar to display the Start menu (Figure 6).

Figure 6

2

- Click All apps at the bottom of the left pane of the Start menu to display a list of apps installed on the computer or mobile device. If necessary, scroll to display the app you wish to run, Publisher 2016, in this case (Figure 7).

Figure 7

3

- If the app you wish to run is located in a folder, click or scroll to and then click the folder in the All apps list to display a list of the folder's contents.

- Click, or scroll to and then click the app name (Publisher 2016, in this case) in the list to run the selected app (Figure 8).

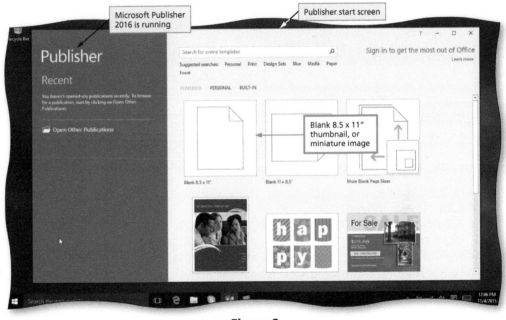

Figure 8

4

- Click the Blank 8.5 X 11" thumbnail on the Publisher start screen to create a blank publication in the Publisher window (Figure 9).

Q&A

Publisher opened with a blank publication. Did I do something wrong?

No. Someone may have turned off the New template gallery. To turn it back on, click File on the ribbon, click the Options tab (Backstage view), and then click the 'Show the New template gallery when starting Publisher' check box (Publisher Options dialog box).

What happens when you run an app?

Some apps provide a means for you to create a blank publication, as shown in Figure 8; others immediately display a blank publication in an app window, such as the Publisher window shown in Figure 9. A **window** is a rectangular area that displays data and information. The top of a window has a **title bar**, which is a horizontal space that contains the window's name.

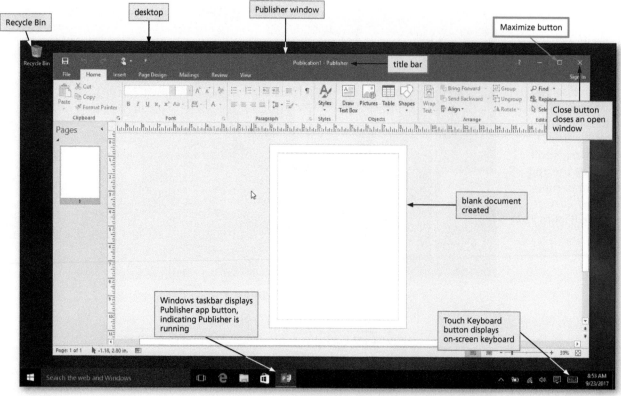

Figure 9

Other Ways

1. Type app name in search box, click app name in results list

2. Double-click file created in app you want to run

To Maximize a Window

Sometimes content is not visible completely in a window. One method of displaying the entire contents of a window is to **maximize** it, or enlarge the window so that it fills the entire screen. The following step maximizes the Publisher window; however, any Office app's window can be maximized using this step. *Why? A maximized window provides the most space available for using the app.*

- If the Publisher window is not maximized already, click the Maximize button (shown in Figure 9) next to the Close button on the Publisher window's title bar to maximize the window (Figure 10).

Q&A What happened to the Maximize button?
It changed to a Restore Down button, which you can use to return a window to its size and location before you maximized it.

How do I know whether a window is maximized?
A window is maximized if it fills the entire display area and the Restore Down button is displayed on the title bar.

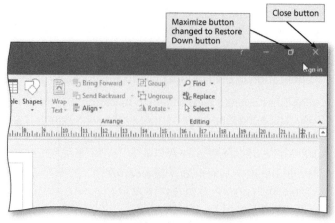

Figure 10

Other Ways

1. Double-click title bar

2. Drag title bar to top of screen

Publisher Window, Ribbon, and Elements Common to Office Apps

The Publisher window consists of a variety of components to make your work more efficient and publications more professional. These include the ribbon, mini toolbar, shortcut menus, workspace, Quick Access Toolbar, and Microsoft Account area. Most of these components are common to other Microsoft Office apps; others are unique to Publisher.

When you run Publisher, the default (preset) view is Single Page view, which shows the publication on a mock sheet of paper in the workspace (Figure 11).

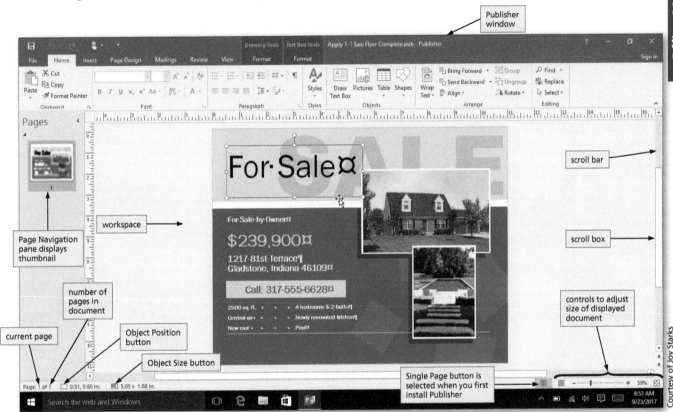

Figure 11

Courtesy of Joy Starks

Scroll Bars You use a scroll bar to display different portions of a publication in the workspace. At the right edge of the workspace is a vertical scroll bar. If a publication is too wide to fit in the workspace, a horizontal scroll bar also appears at the bottom of the workspace. On a scroll bar, the position of the scroll box reflects the location of the portion of the publication that is displayed in the workspace.

Status Bar The status bar, located at the bottom of the Publisher window above the Windows taskbar, presents information about the publication, the dimensions and location of selected objects, and the status of certain commands and keys; it also provides controls for viewing the publication. As you type text or perform certain tasks, various indicators and buttons may appear on the status bar.

The left side of the status bar in Figure 11 shows the current page followed by the total number of pages in the publication, the Object Position button, and the Object Size button. The right side of the status bar includes buttons and controls you can use to change the view of a publication and adjust the size of the displayed publication.

BTW
Touch Keyboard
To display the on-screen touch keyboard, click the Touch Keyboard button on the Windows taskbar (shown in Figure 9). When finished using the touch keyboard, click the X button on the touch keyboard to close the keyboard.

Ribbon The ribbon, located near the top of the window below the title bar, is the control center in Publisher and other Office apps (Figure 12). The ribbon provides easy, central access to the tasks you perform while creating a publication. The ribbon consists of tabs, groups, and commands. Each **tab** contains a collection of groups, and each **group** contains related commands. When you run an Office app, such as Publisher, it initially displays several main tabs, also called default or top-level tabs. All Office apps have a Home tab, which contains the more frequently used commands.

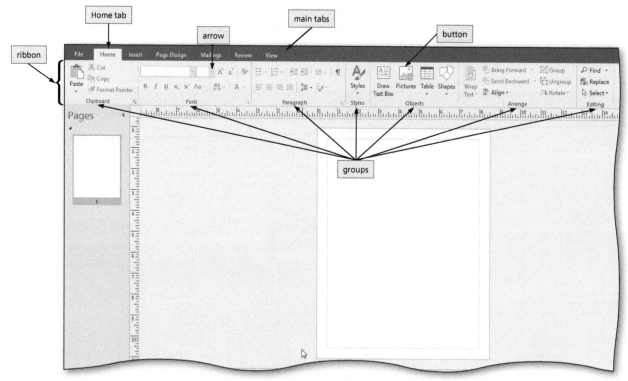

Figure 12

BTW
Customizing the Ribbon
In addition to customizing the Quick Access Toolbar, you can add items to and remove items from the ribbon. To customize the ribbon, click File on the ribbon to open the Backstage view, click the Options tab in the Backstage view, and then click Customize Ribbon in the left pane of the Options dialog box. More information about customizing the ribbon is presented in a later module.

In addition to the main tabs, the Office apps display **tool tabs**, also called contextual tabs (Figure 13), when you perform certain tasks or work with objects such as pictures or tables. If you insert a picture in a Publisher publication, for example, the Picture Tools tab and its related subordinate Format tab appear, collectively referred to as the Picture Tools Format tab. When you are finished working with the picture, the Picture Tools Format tab disappears from the ribbon. Publisher and other Office apps determine when tool tabs should appear and disappear based on tasks you perform. Some tool tabs, such as the Table Tools tab, have more than one related subordinate tab.

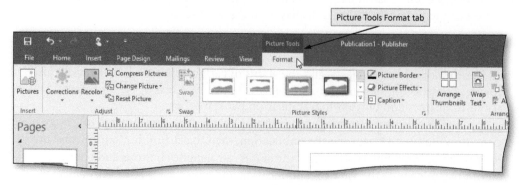

Figure 13

Items on the ribbon include buttons, boxes, and galleries (shown in Figure 13). A **gallery** is a set of choices, often graphical, arranged in a grid or in a list. You can scroll through choices in an in-ribbon gallery by clicking the gallery's scroll arrows. Or, you can click a gallery's More button to view more gallery options on the screen at a time.

Some buttons and boxes have arrows that, when clicked, also display a gallery; others always cause a gallery to be displayed when clicked. Most galleries support **live preview**, which is a feature that allows you to point to a gallery choice and see its effect in the publication — without actually selecting the choice (Figure 14). Live preview works only if you are using a mouse; if you are using a touch screen, you will not be able to view live previews.

BTW
Tell Me Box
Some apps display a **Tell Me box** that appears to the right of the tabs on the ribbon, which functions as a type of search box that helps you to perform specific tasks in an Office app. As you type in the Tell Me box, the word-wheeling feature displays search results that are refined as you type. The Tell Me box also lists the last five commands accessed from the box.

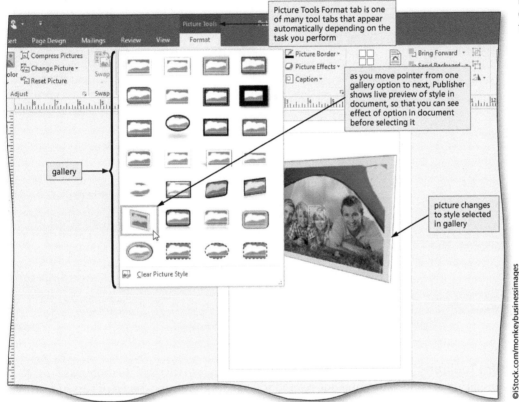

Figure 14

Some commands on the ribbon display an image to help you remember their function. When you point to a command on the ribbon, all or part of the command becomes highlighted in a shade of gray, and a ScreenTip appears on the screen. A **ScreenTip** is an on-screen note that provides the name of the command, available keyboard shortcut(s), a description of the command, and sometimes instructions for how to obtain help about the command (Figure 15).

BTW
ScreenTips
You can turn ScreenTips on and off in the Publisher Options dialog box (Backstage View | Options tab).

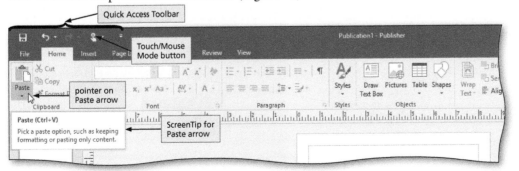

Figure 15

BTW
Touch Mode
The Office and Windows interfaces may vary if you are using Touch mode. For this reason, you might notice that the function or appearance of your touch screen in Publisher differs slightly from this module's presentation.

Some groups on the ribbon have a small arrow in the lower-right corner, called a **Dialog Box Launcher**, that when clicked, displays a dialog box or a task pane with additional options for the group (Figure 16). When presented with a dialog box, you make selections and must close the dialog box before returning to the publication. A **task pane**, in contrast to a dialog box, is a window that can remain open and visible while you work in the publication.

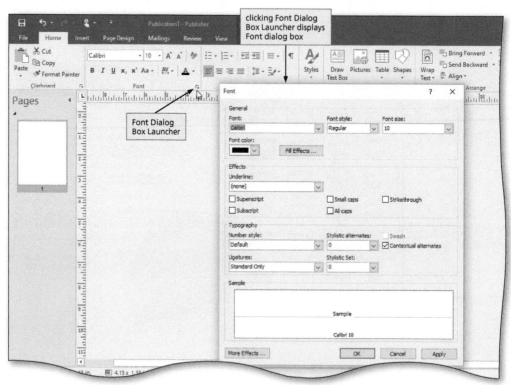

Figure 16

BTW
Turning Off the Mini Toolbar
If you do not want the mini toolbar to appear, click File on the ribbon to open the Backstage view, click the Options tab in the Backstage view, if necessary, click General (Options dialog box), remove the check mark from the `Show Mini Toolbar on selection' check box, and then click the OK button.

Mini Toolbar   The **mini toolbar**, which appears automatically based on tasks you perform, contains commands related to changing the appearance of text in a publication (Figure 17). If you do not use the mini toolbar, it disappears from the screen. The buttons, arrows, and boxes on the mini toolbar vary, depending on whether you are using Touch mode versus Mouse mode. If you right-click an object in the publication, Publisher displays both the mini toolbar and a shortcut menu, which is discussed in a later section in this module.

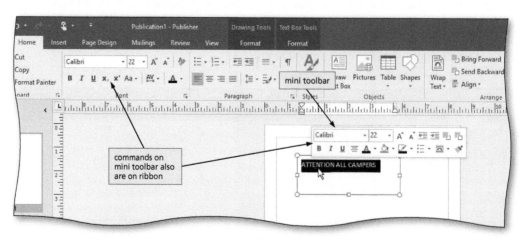

Figure 17

All commands on the mini toolbar also exist on the ribbon. The purpose of the mini toolbar is to minimize hand or mouse movement.

Quick Access Toolbar   The **Quick Access Toolbar**, located initially (by default) above the ribbon at the left edge of the title bar, provides convenient, one-click access to frequently used commands (shown in Figure 15). The commands on the Quick Access Toolbar always are available, regardless of the task you are performing. The Touch/Mouse Mode button on the Quick Access Toolbar allows you to switch between Touch mode and Mouse mode. If you primarily are using touch gestures, Touch mode will add more space between commands on menus and on the ribbon so that they are easier to tap. While touch gestures are convenient ways to interact with Office apps, not all features are supported when you are using Touch mode. If you are using a mouse, Mouse mode will not add the extra space between buttons and commands. The Quick Access Toolbar is discussed in more depth later in the module.

KeyTips   If you prefer using the keyboard instead of the mouse, you can press the ALT key on the keyboard to display **KeyTips**, or keyboard code icons, for certain commands (Figure 18). To select a command using the keyboard, press the letter or number displayed in the KeyTip, which may cause additional KeyTips related to the selected command to appear. To remove KeyTips from the screen, press the ALT key or the ESC key until all KeyTips disappear, or click anywhere in the app window.

BTW
Full Screen Mode
Some apps have a **Full Screen mode**, which hides all the commands and just displays the current file or document.

BTW
More Ribbon Options
Some apps display a 'Ribbon Display Options' button on the title bar with additional ribbon commands, such as Auto-hide.

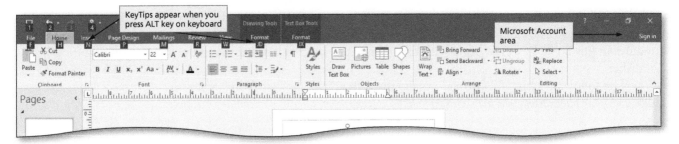

Figure 18

Microsoft Account Area   In this area, you can use the Sign in link to sign in to your Microsoft account. Once signed in, you will see your account information. Some apps also display a picture if you have included one in your Microsoft account.

To Display a Different Tab on the Ribbon

1 SIGN IN | 2 USE WINDOWS | 3 USE APPS | 4 FILE MANAGEMENT | 5 SWITCH APPS | 6 SAVE FILES
7 CHANGE SCREEN RESOLUTION | 8 EXIT APPS | 9 USE ADDITIONAL APP FEATURES | 10 USE HELP

When you run Publisher, the ribbon displays seven main tabs: File, Home, Insert, Page Design, Mailings, Review, and View. The tab currently displayed is called the **active tab**.

The following step displays the Insert tab, that is, makes it the active tab. *Why? When working with an Office app, you may need to switch tabs to access other options for working with a publication.*

1

- Click Insert on the ribbon to display the Insert tab (Figure 19).

(P) **Experiment**

- Click the other tabs on the ribbon to view their contents. When you are finished, click Insert on the ribbon to redisplay the Insert tab.

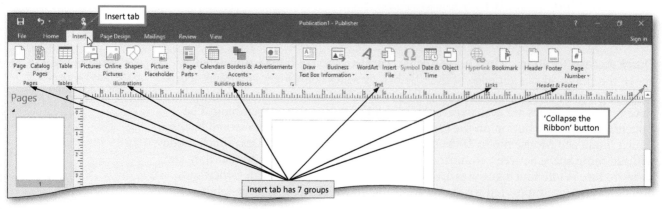

Figure 19

Other Ways

1. Press ALT, press letter corresponding to tab to display

2. Press ALT, press LEFT ARROW or RIGHT ARROW until desired tab is displayed

To Collapse and Expand the Ribbon

1 SIGN IN | 2 USE WINDOWS | 3 USE APPS | **4 FILE MANAGEMENT** | **5 SWITCH APPS** | **6 SAVE FILES**
7 CHANGE SCREEN RESOLUTION | **8 EXIT APPS** | **9 USE ADDITIONAL APP FEATURES** | **10 USE HELP**

To display more of a publication or other item in the window of an Office app, some users prefer to collapse the ribbon, which hides the groups on the ribbon and displays only the main tabs. Each time you run an Office app, such as Publisher, the ribbon appears the same way it did the last time you used that Office app. The modules in this book, however, begin with the ribbon appearing as it did at the initial installation of Office or Publisher.

The following steps collapse and expand the ribbon in Publisher. ***Why?*** *If you need more space on the screen to work with your publication, you may consider collapsing the ribbon to gain additional workspace.*

- Click the 'Collapse the Ribbon' button on the ribbon (shown in Figure 19) to collapse the ribbon (Figure 20).

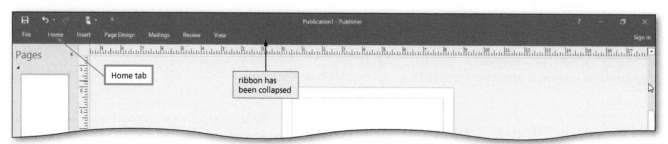

Figure 20

Q&A
What happened to the 'Collapse the Ribbon' button?
The 'Pin the ribbon' button replaces the 'Collapse the Ribbon' button when the ribbon is collapsed. You will see the 'Pin the ribbon' button only when you expand a ribbon by clicking a tab.

- Click Home on the ribbon to expand the Home tab (Figure 21).

Figure 21

Q&A | Why would I click the Home tab?

If you want to use a command on a collapsed ribbon, click the main tab to display the groups for that tab. After you select a command on the ribbon and resume working in the publication, the groups will be collapsed once again. If you decide not to use a command on the ribbon, you can collapse the groups by clicking the same main tab or clicking in the app window.

(P) Experiment

- Click Home on the ribbon to collapse the groups again. Click Home on the ribbon to expand the Home tab.

- Click the 'Pin the ribbon' button on the expanded Home tab to restore the ribbon.

Other Ways

1. Double-click a main tab on the ribbon
2. Press CTRL+F1

To Use a Shortcut Menu to Relocate the Quick Access Toolbar

1 SIGN IN | 2 USE WINDOWS | 3 USE APPS | 4 FILE MANAGEMENT | 5 SWITCH APPS | 6 SAVE FILES
7 CHANGE SCREEN RESOLUTION | 8 EXIT APPS | 9 USE ADDITIONAL APP FEATURES | 10 USE HELP

When you right-click certain areas of the Publisher and other Office app windows, a shortcut menu will appear. A **shortcut menu** is a list of frequently used commands that relate to an object. *Why? You can use shortcut menus to access common commands quickly.* When you right-click the status bar, for example, a shortcut menu appears with commands related to the status bar. When you right-click the Quick Access Toolbar, a shortcut menu appears with commands related to the Quick Access Toolbar. The following steps use a shortcut menu to move the Quick Access Toolbar, which by default is located on the title bar.

1

- Right-click the Quick Access Toolbar to display a shortcut menu that presents a list of commands related to the Quick Access Toolbar (Figure 22).

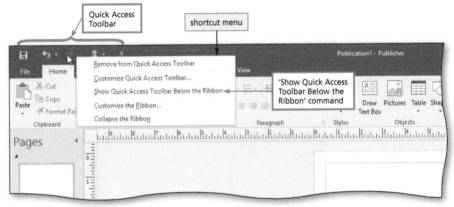

Figure 22

2

- Click 'Show Quick Access Toolbar Below the Ribbon' on the shortcut menu to display the Quick Access Toolbar below the ribbon (Figure 23).

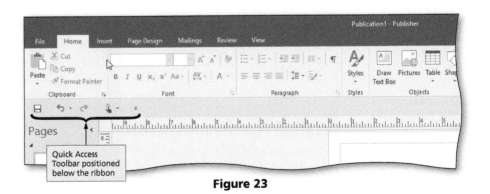

Figure 23

- Right-click the Quick Access Toolbar again to display the shortcut menu (Figure 24).

- Click 'Show Quick Access Toolbar Above the Ribbon' on the shortcut menu to return the Quick Access Toolbar to its original position.

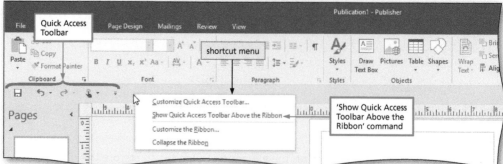

Figure 24

Other Ways

1. Click 'Customize Quick Access Toolbar' button on Quick Access Toolbar, click 'Show Below the Ribbon' or 'Show Above the Ribbon'

To Customize the Quick Access Toolbar

1 SIGN IN | 2 USE WINDOWS | 3 USE APPS | 4 FILE MANAGEMENT | 5 SWITCH APPS | 6 SAVE FILES
7 CHANGE SCREEN RESOLUTION | 8 EXIT APPS | 9 USE ADDITIONAL APP FEATURES | 10 USE HELP

The Quick Access Toolbar provides easy access to some of the more frequently used commands in the Office apps. By default, the Quick Access Toolbar contains buttons for the Save, Undo, and Redo commands. If your computer or mobile device has a touch screen, the Quick Access Toolbar also might display the Touch/Mouse Mode button. You can customize the Quick Access Toolbar by changing its location in the window, as shown in the previous steps, and by adding more buttons to reflect commands you would like to access easily. The following steps add the Quick Print button to the Quick Access Toolbar in the Publisher window. *Why? Adding the Quick Print button to the Quick Access Toolbar speeds up the process of printing.*

- Click the 'Customize Quick Access Toolbar' button to display the Customize Quick Access Toolbar menu (Figure 25).

Q&A Which commands are listed on the Customize Quick Access Toolbar menu?
It lists commands that commonly are added to the Quick Access Toolbar.

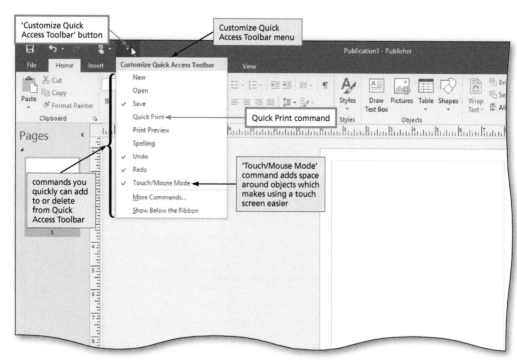

Figure 25

- Click Quick Print on the Customize Quick Access Toolbar menu to add the Quick Print button to the Quick Access Toolbar (Figure 26).

Q&A How would I remove a button from the Quick Access Toolbar?
You would right-click the button you wish to remove and then click 'Remove from Quick Access Toolbar' on the shortcut menu or click the 'Customize Quick Access Toolbar' button on the Quick Access Toolbar and then click the button name in the Customize Quick Access Toolbar menu to remove the check mark.

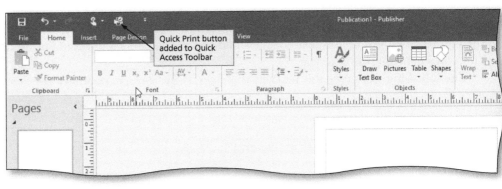

Figure 26

To Zoom Using a Function Key

1 SIGN IN | 2 USE WINDOWS | 3 USE APPS | 4 FILE MANAGEMENT | 5 SWITCH APPS | 6 SAVE FILES
7 CHANGE SCREEN RESOLUTION | 8 EXIT APPS | 9 USE ADDITIONAL APP FEATURES | 10 USE HELP

If text is too small to read easily, or if objects are too small to manipulate, you may want to zoom. When you zoom, Publisher changes the magnification of the text or other object on the page. Zooming does not change the font size of text; nor does it change the size of objects, such as pictures and shapes. The following step uses the F9 key to change the magnification to 100%. *Why? The function key is a quick way to zoom; you will learn many ways to zoom in future modules.*

- Press the F9 key on the keyboard. If your mobile device does not display function keys, click the Zoom In button on the task bar several times until your display is magnified to 100% (Figure 27).

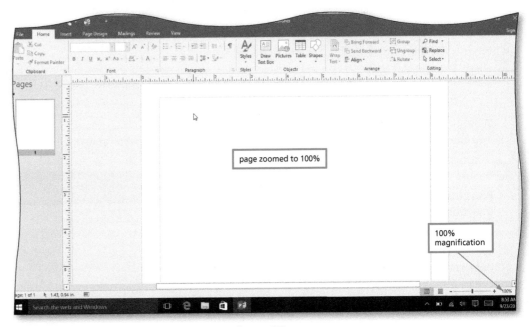

Figure 27

Other Ways

1. Click 100% button (View tab | Zoom group)
2. Type 100% in Zoom box (View tab | Zoom group)
3. Drag Zoom slider on taskbar

To Enter Text in a Publication

Many times, the first step in creating a publication is to enter text or replace text in a template by typing on the keyboard. Publisher uses text boxes to hold text. If the publication contains no text box, Publisher creates one for you when you begin to type.

The following steps type this first line of a flyer. *Why? To begin creating a flyer, for example, you type the headline in the publication.*

- Type **ATTENTION ALL CAMPERS** as the text (Figure 28).

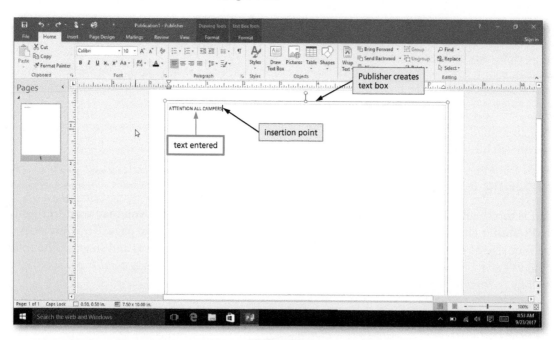

Figure 28

Q&A

What is the blinking vertical bar to the right of the text?
The blinking bar is the insertion point, which indicates where text, graphics, and other items will be inserted in the publication. As you type, the insertion point moves to the right, and when you reach the end of a line, it moves down to the beginning of the next line.

What if I make an error while typing?
You can press the BACKSPACE key until you have deleted the text in error and then retype the text correctly.

- Press the ENTER key to move the insertion point to the beginning of the next line (Figure 29).

Q&A

Why did blank space appear between the entered text and the insertion point?
Each time you press the ENTER key, Publisher creates a new paragraph and inserts blank space between the two paragraphs. Depending on your settings, Publisher may or may not insert a blank space between the two paragraphs.

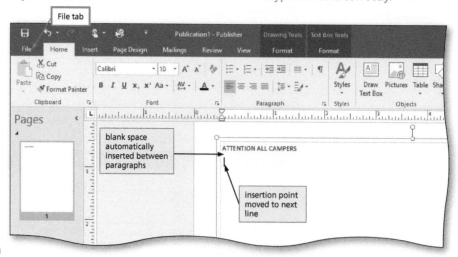

Figure 29

Publication Properties

You can organize and identify your files by using publication properties, which are the details about a file, such as the project author, title, and subject. For example, a class name or publication topic can describe the file's purpose or content.

Why would you want to assign publication properties to a publication?
Publication properties are valuable for a variety of reasons:

• Users can save time locating a particular file, because they can view a file's publication properties without opening the file.

• By creating consistent properties for files having similar content, users can better organize their files.

• Some organizations require users to add publication properties so that other employees can view details about these files.

To Change Publication Properties

1 SIGN IN | 2 USE WINDOWS | 3 USE APPS | 4 FILE MANAGEMENT | **5 SWITCH APPS** | **6 SAVE FILES**
7 CHANGE SCREEN RESOLUTION | **8 EXIT APPS** | **9 USE ADDITIONAL APP FEATURES** | **10 USE HELP**

You can change the publication properties while working with the file in an Office app. When you save the file, the Office app (Publisher, in this case) will save the publication properties with the file. The following steps change publication properties. *Why? Adding publication properties will help you identify characteristics of the file without opening it.*

• Click File on the ribbon (shown in Figure 29) to open the Backstage view and then, if necessary, click the Info tab in the Backstage view to display the Info gallery.

• Click the Publication Properties button (Backstage view | Info tab) to display the Publication Properties menu (Figure 30).

Q&A What is the purpose of the File tab on the ribbon and what is the Backstage view?
The File tab opens the Backstage view for each Office app, including Publisher. The **Backstage view** contains a set of commands that enable you to manage publications and provides data about the publications.

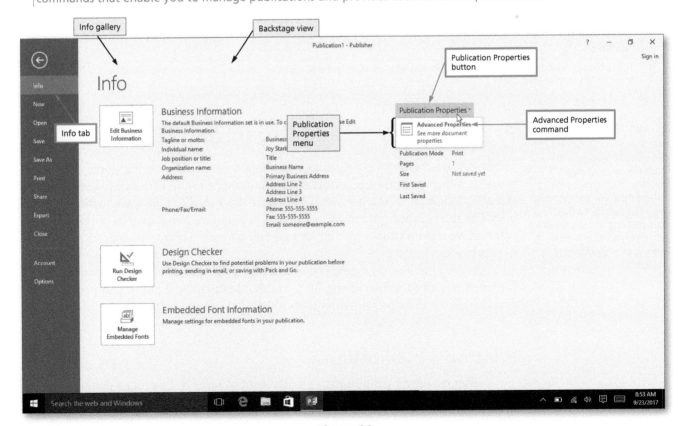

Figure 30

- Click Advanced Properties on the menu to display the Publication1 Properties dialog box.

- Click the Comments text box (Publication1 Properties dialog box) and then type CIS 101 Assignment in the text box (Figure 31).

Q&A

What is the purpose of the Info gallery in the Backstage view?
The Info tab, which is selected by default when you click File on the ribbon, displays the Info gallery, where you can protect a publication, inspect a publication, and manage versions of a publication, as well as view all the file properties, such as when the file was created.

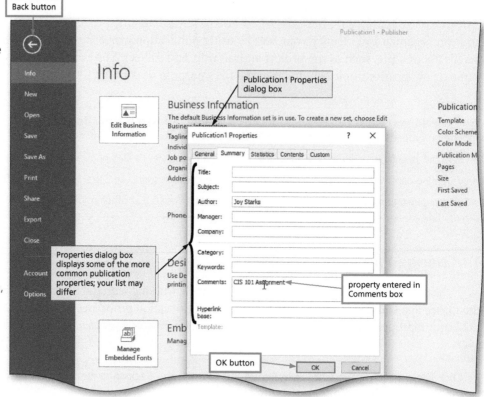

Figure 31

- Click the OK button (Publication1 Properties dialog box) to close the dialog box.

- Click the Back button in the upper-left corner of the Backstage view to return to the publication.

Other Ways

1. In File Explorer window, right-click file icon, click Properties on shortcut menu, click Comments text box (Properties dialog box), enter comment, click OK button

BTW
Document Properties
Some apps allow you to make property changes directly in Backstage view. In Microsoft Word, for example, you can click to the right of the property on the Info tab, to display a text box allowing you to enter or change that property.

Printing, Saving, and Organizing Files

While you are creating a publication, the computer or mobile device stores it in memory. When you save a publication, the computer or mobile device places it on a storage medium, such as a hard disk, solid state drive (SSD), USB flash drive, or optical disc. The storage medium can be permanent in your computer, may be portable where you remove it from your computer, or may be on a web server you access through a network or the Internet.

A saved publication is referred to as a file. A **file name** is the name assigned to a file when it is saved. When saving files, you should organize them so that you easily can find them later. Windows provides tools to help you organize files.

Printing a Publication

After creating a publication, you may want to print it. Printing a publication enables you to distribute it to others in a form that can be read or viewed but typically not edited.

What is the best method for distributing a publication?

The traditional method of distributing a publication uses a printer to produce a hard copy. A **hard copy** or **printout** is information that exists on a physical medium, such as paper. Hard copies can be useful for the following reasons:

- Some people prefer proofreading a hard copy of a publication rather than viewing it on the screen to check for errors and readability.

- Hard copies can serve as a backup reference if your storage medium is lost or becomes corrupted and you need to recreate the publication.

Instead of distributing a hard copy of a publication, users can distribute the publication as an electronic image that mirrors the original publication's appearance. The electronic image of the publication can be sent as an email attachment, posted on a website, or copied to a portable storage medium, such as a USB flash drive. Two popular electronic image formats, sometimes called fixed formats, are PDF by Adobe Systems and XPS by Microsoft. In Publisher, you can create electronic image files through the Save As dialog box and the Export, Share, and Print tabs in the Backstage view. Electronic images of publications, such as PDF and XPS, can be useful for the following reasons:

- Users can view electronic images of publications without the software that created the original publication (e.g., Publisher). For example, to view a PDF file you use a program called Adobe Reader, which can be downloaded free from Adobe's website.

- Sending electronic publications saves paper and printer supplies. Society encourages users to contribute to **green computing**, which involves reducing the electricity consumed and environmental waste generated when using computers, mobile devices, and related technologies.

To Print a Publication

1 SIGN IN | 2 USE WINDOWS | 3 USE APPS | 4 FILE MANAGEMENT | 5 SWITCH APPS | 6 SAVE FILES
7 CHANGE SCREEN RESOLUTION | 8 EXIT APPS | 9 USE ADDITIONAL APP FEATURES | 10 USE HELP

With the publication opened, you may want to print it. *Why? Because you want to see how the text will appear on paper; you want to print a hard copy on a printer.* The following steps print a hard copy of the contents of the publication.

1

- Click File on the ribbon to open the Backstage view.
- Click the Print tab in the Backstage view to display the Print gallery (Figure 32).

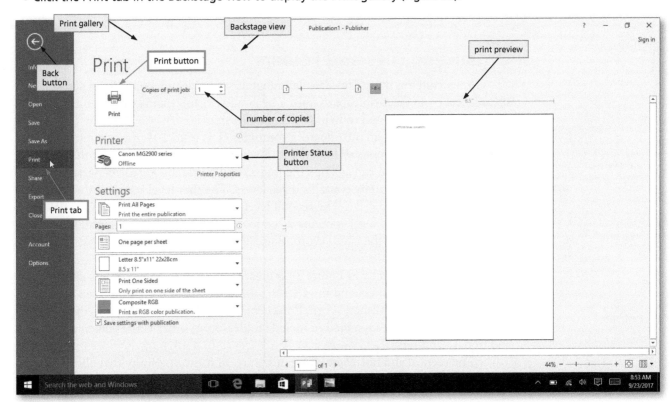

Figure 32

How can I print multiple copies of my publication?
Increase the number in the 'Copies of print job' box in the Print gallery.

What if I decide not to print the publication at this time?
Click the Back button in the upper-left corner of the Backstage view to return to the publication.

- Verify that the selected printer will print a hard copy of the publication. If necessary, click the Printer Status button to display a list of available printer options and then click the desired printer to change the currently selected printer.

- Click the Print button in the Print gallery to print the publication on the currently selected printer.

- When the printer stops, retrieve the hard copy (Figure 33).

What if I want to print an electronic image of a publication instead of a hard copy?
You would click the Printer Status button in the Print gallery and then select the desired electronic image option, such as Microsoft XPS Document Writer, which would create an XPS file.

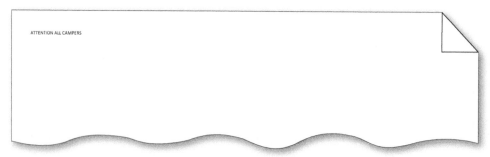

ATTENTION ALL CAMPERS

Figure 33

Other Ways

1. Press CTRL+P

Organizing Files and Folders

A file contains data. This data can range from a research paper to an accounting spreadsheet to an electronic math quiz. You should organize and store files in folders to avoid misplacing a file and to help you find a file quickly.

If you are taking an introductory computer class (CIS 101, for example), you may want to design a series of folders for the different subjects covered in the class. To accomplish this, you can arrange the folders in a hierarchy for the class, as shown in Figure 34. The hierarchy contains three levels. The first level contains the storage medium, such as a hard drive. The second level contains the class folder (CIS 101, in this case), and the third level contains seven folders, one each for a different Office app that will be covered in the class (Word, PowerPoint, Excel, Access, Outlook, Publisher, and OneNote).

When the hierarchy in Figure 34 is created, the storage medium is said to contain the CIS 101 folder, and the CIS 101 folder is said to contain the separate Office folders (i.e., Publisher, Word, PowerPoint, Excel, etc.). In addition, this hierarchy easily can be expanded to include folders from other classes taken during additional semesters.

The vertical and horizontal lines in Figure 34 form a pathway that allows you to navigate to a drive or folder on a computer or network. A **path** consists of a drive letter

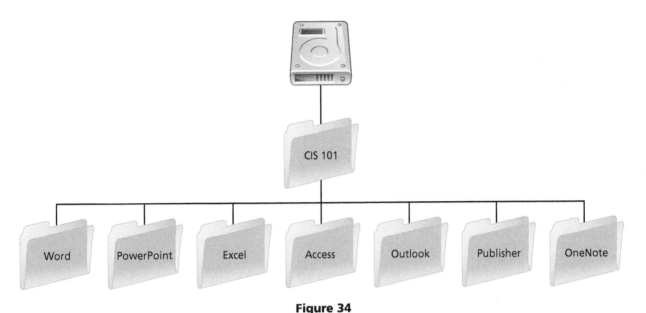

Figure 34

(preceded by a drive name when necessary) and colon, to identify the storage device, and one or more folder names. A hard drive typically has a drive letter of C. Each drive or folder in the hierarchy has a corresponding path.

By default, Windows saves publications in the Documents folder, music in the Music folder, photos in the Pictures folder, videos in the Videos folder, and downloads in the Downloads folder.

The following pages illustrate the steps to organize the folders for this class and save a file in a folder:

1. Create the folder identifying your class.
2. Create the Publisher folder in the folder identifying your class.
3. Save a file in the Publisher folder.
4. Verify the location of the saved file.

To Create a Folder

1 SIGN IN | 2 USE WINDOWS | 3 USE APPS | 4 FILE MANAGEMENT | **5 SWITCH APPS** | **6 SAVE FILES**
7 CHANGE SCREEN RESOLUTION | 8 EXIT APPS | 9 USE ADDITIONAL APP FEATURES | 10 USE HELP

When you create a folder, such as the CIS 101 folder shown in Figure 34, you must name the folder. A folder name should describe the folder and its contents. A folder name can contain spaces and any uppercase or lowercase characters, except a backslash (\), slash (/), colon (:), asterisk (*), question mark (?), quotation marks ("), less than symbol (<), greater than symbol (>), or vertical bar (|). Folder names cannot be CON, AUX, COM1, COM2, COM3, COM4, LPT1, LPT2, LPT3, PRN, or NUL. The same rules for naming folders also apply to naming files.

The following steps create a class folder (CIS 101, in this case) in the Documents folder. *Why? When storing files, you should organize the files so that it will be easier to find them later.*

● Click the File Explorer button on the taskbar to run File Explorer.

● If necessary, double-click This PC in the navigation pane to expand the contents of your computer.

● If necessary, click the 'Expand the Ribbon' button to expand the ribbon.

● Click the Documents folder in the navigation pane to display the contents of the Documents folder in the file list (Figure 35).

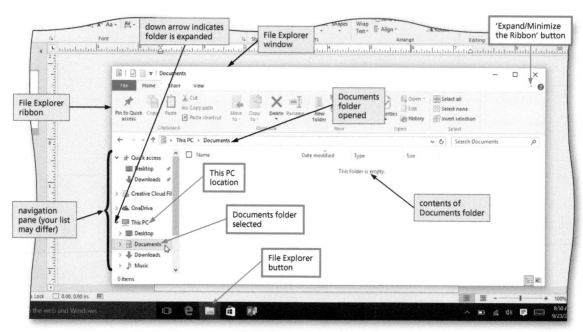

Figure 35

2

- Click the New folder button on the Quick Access Toolbar to create a new folder with the name, New folder, selected in a text box (Figure 36).

Q&A Why is the folder icon displayed differently on my computer or mobile device?
Windows might be configured to display contents differently on your computer or mobile device.

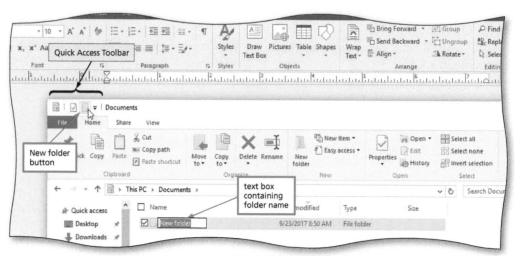

Figure 36

3

- Type CIS 101 (or your class code) in the text box as the new folder name.

  If requested by your instructor, add your last name to the end of the folder name.

- Press the ENTER key to change the folder name from New folder to a folder name identifying your class (Figure 37).

Q&A What happens when I press the ENTER key?
The class folder (CIS 101, in this case) is displayed in the file list, which contains the folder name, date modified, type, and size.

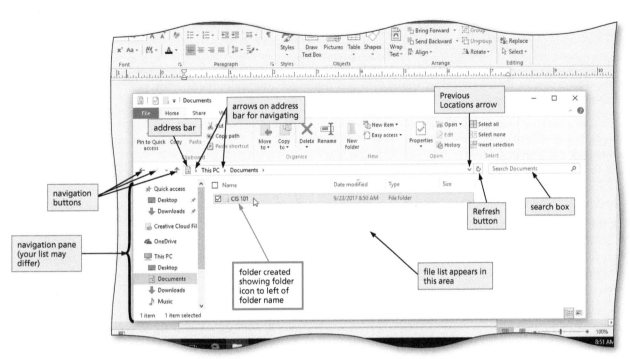

Figure 37

Folder Windows

The File Explorer window is called a folder window. Recall that a folder is a specific named location on a storage medium that contains related files. Most users rely on **folder windows** for finding, viewing, and managing information on their computers. Folder windows have common design elements, including the following (shown in Figure 37).

- The **address bar** provides quick navigation options. The arrows on the address bar allow you to visit different locations on the computer or mobile device.
- The buttons to the left of the address bar allow you to navigate the contents of the navigation pane and view recent pages.
- The **Previous Locations arrow** displays the locations you have visited.
- The **Refresh button** on the right side of the address bar refreshes the contents of the folder list.
- The **Search box** contains the dimmed words, Search Documents. You can type a term in the search box for a list of files, folders, shortcuts, and elements containing that term within the location you are searching.
- The **ribbon** contains four tabs used to accomplish various tasks on the computer or mobile device related to organizing and managing the contents of the open window. This ribbon works similarly to the ribbon in the Office apps.
- The **navigation pane** on the left contains the Quick access area, the OneDrive area, the This PC area, and the Network area.
- The **Quick access area** shows locations you access frequently. By default, this list contains links only to your Desktop, Downloads, Documents, and Pictures.

To Create a Folder within a Folder

With the class folder created, you can create folders that will store the files you create using Publisher. The following step creates a Publisher folder in the CIS 101 folder (or the folder identifying your class). *Why? To be able to organize your files, you should create a folder structure.*

- Double-click the icon or folder name for the CIS 101 folder (or the folder identifying your class) in the file list to open the folder.

- Click the New folder button on the Quick Access Toolbar to create a new folder with the name, New folder, selected in a text box folder.

- Type **Publisher** in the text box as the new folder name.

- Press the ENTER key to rename the folder (Figure 38).

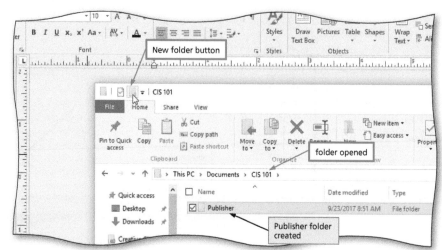

Figure 38

Other Ways
1. Press CTRL+SHIFT+N
2. Click New folder button (Home tab | New group)

To Expand a Folder, Scroll through Folder Contents, and Collapse a Folder

Folder windows display the hierarchy of items and the contents of drives and folders in the file list. You might want to expand a folder in the navigation pane to view its contents, scroll through its contents, and collapse it when you are finished viewing its contents. *Why? When a folder is expanded, you can see all the folders it contains. By contrast, a collapsed folder hides the folders it contains.* The following steps expand, scroll through, and then collapse the folder identifying your class (CIS 101, in this case).

- Double-click the Documents folder in the This PC area of the navigation pane, which expands the folder to display its contents and displays a down arrow to the left of the Documents folder icon (Figure 39).

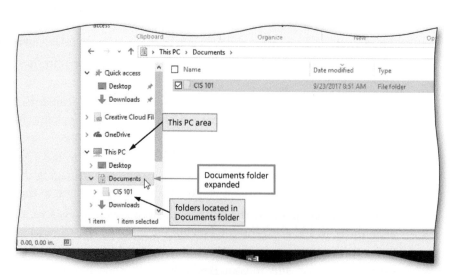

Figure 39

②

• Double-click the CIS 101 folder, which expands the folder to display its contents and displays a down arrow to the left of the folder icon (Figure 40).

 Experiment

• Drag the scroll box down or click the down scroll arrow on the vertical scroll bar to display additional folders at the bottom of the navigation pane. Drag the scroll box up or click the scroll bar above the scroll box to move the scroll box to the top of the navigation pane. Drag the scroll box down the scroll bar until the scroll box is halfway down the scroll bar.

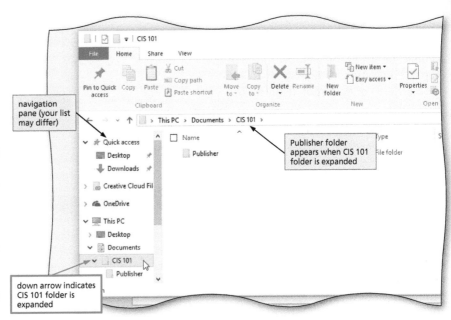

Figure 40

③

• Double-click the folder identifying your class (CIS 101, in this case) to collapse the folder (Figure 41).

Q&A
Why are some folders indented below others?
A folder contains the indented folders below it.

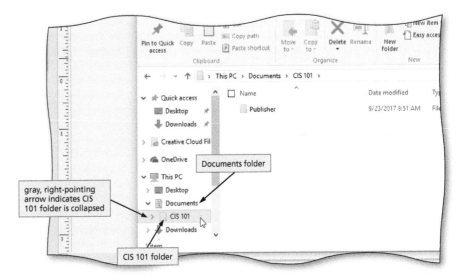

Figure 41

Other Ways
1. Point to display arrows in navigation pane, click arrow to expand or collapse	2. Select folder to expand or collapse using arrow keys, press RIGHT ARROW to expand; press LEFT ARROW to collapse

---

To Switch from One App to Another

1 SIGN IN | 2 USE WINDOWS | 3 USE APPS | 4 FILE MANAGEMENT | 5 SWITCH APPS | **6 SAVE FILES**
7 CHANGE SCREEN RESOLUTION | 8 EXIT APPS | 9 USE ADDITIONAL APP FEATURES | 10 USE HELP

The next step is to save the Publisher file containing the headline you typed earlier. Publisher, however, currently is not the active window. You can use the button on the taskbar and live preview to switch to Publisher and then save the publication in the Publisher window.

Why? *By clicking the appropriate app button on the taskbar, you can switch to the running app you want to use.* The following steps switch to the Publisher window; however, the steps are the same for any active Office app currently displayed as a button on the taskbar.

1

- Point to the Publisher app button on the taskbar to see a live preview of the open publication(s) or the window title(s) of the open publication(s), depending on your computer's configuration (Figure 42).

Q&A
What if I am using a touch screen?
Live preview will not work if you are using a touch screen. If you are using a touch screen and do not have a mouse, proceed to Step 2.

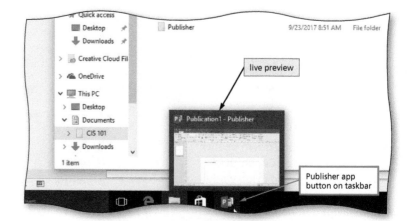

Figure 42

2

- Click the Publisher app button or the live preview to make the app associated with the app button the active window (Figure 43).

Q&A
What if multiple publications are open in an app?
Click the desired live preview to switch to the window you want to use.

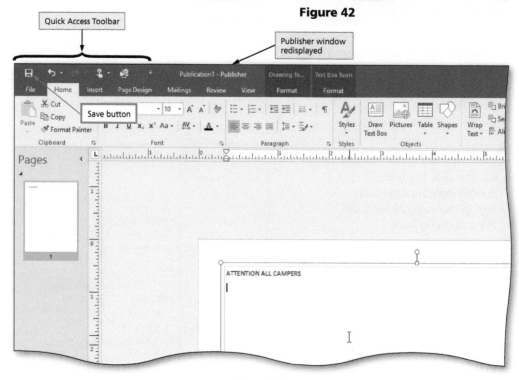

Figure 43

Other Ways

1. Press ALT+TAB until app you wish to display is selected

To Save a File in a Folder

1 SIGN IN | 2 USE WINDOWS | 3 USE APPS | 4 FILE MANAGEMENT | 5 SWITCH APPS | 6 SAVE FILES
7 CHANGE SCREEN RESOLUTION | 8 EXIT APPS | 9 USE ADDITIONAL APP FEATURES | 10 USE HELP

With the Publisher folder created, you can save the publication shown in the Publisher window in the Publisher folder. *Why? Without saving a file, you may lose all the work you have completed and will be unable to reuse or share it with others later.* The following steps save a file in the Publisher folder contained in your class folder (CIS 101, in this case) using the file name, Campers.

1

- Click the Save button (shown in Figure 43) on the Quick Access Toolbar, which depending on settings, will display either the Save As gallery in the Backstage view (Figure 44) or the Save As dialog box (Figure 45).

Q&A What if the Save As gallery is not displayed in the Backstage view?
Click the Save As tab to display the Save As gallery.

How do I close the Backstage view?
Click the Back button in the upper-left corner of the Backstage view to return to the Publisher window.

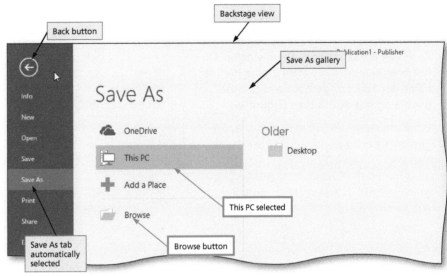

Figure 44

2

- If your screen displays the Backstage view, click This PC, if necessary, to display options related to saving on your computer or mobile device; if your screen already displays the Save As dialog box, proceed to Step 3.

Q&A What if I wanted to save on OneDrive instead?
You would click OneDrive. Saving on OneDrive is discussed in a later section in this module.

- Click the Browse button to display the Save As dialog box (Figure 45).

Q&A Why does a file name already appear in the File name box?
Publisher automatically suggests a file name the first time you save a publication. The file name normally consists of the first few words contained in the publication. Because the suggested file name is selected, you do not need to delete it; as soon as you begin typing, the new file name replaces the selected text.

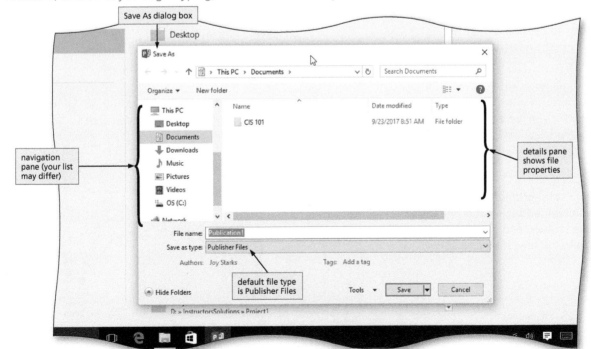

Figure 45

• Type **Campers** in the File name box (Save As dialog box) to change the file name. Do not press the ENTER key after typing the file name because you do not want to close the dialog box at this time (Figure 46).

Q&A

What characters can I use in a file name? The only invalid characters are the backslash (\), slash (/), colon (:), asterisk (*), question mark (?), quotation mark ("), less than symbol (<), greater than symbol (>), and vertical bar (|).

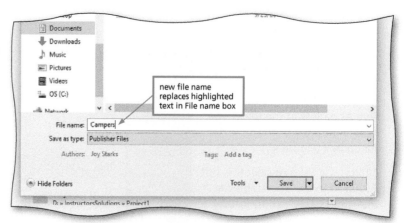

Figure 46

• Navigate to the desired save location (in this case, the Publisher folder in the CIS 101 folder [or your class folder] in the Documents folder) by performing the tasks in Steps 4a and 4b.

• If the Documents folder is not displayed in the navigation pane, drag the scroll bar in the navigation pane until Documents appears.

• If the Documents folder is not expanded in the navigation pane, double-click Documents to display its folders in the navigation pane.

• If your class folder (CIS 101, in this case) is not expanded, double-click the CIS 101 folder to select the folder and display its contents in the navigation pane (Figure 47).

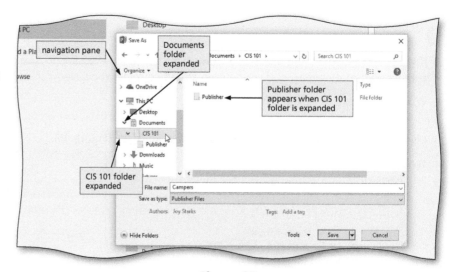

Figure 47

Q&A

What if I do not want to save in a folder? Although storing files in folders is an effective technique for organizing files, some users prefer not to store files in folders. If you prefer not to save this file in a folder, select the storage device on which you wish to save the file and then proceed to Step 5.

• Click the Publisher folder in the navigation pane to select it as the new save location and display its contents in the file list (Figure 48).

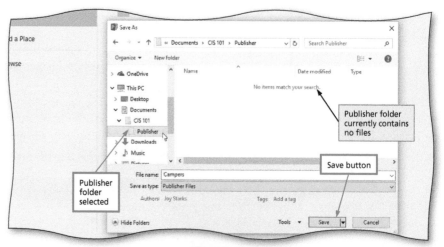

Figure 48

⑤

- Click the Save button (Save As dialog box) to save the publication in the selected folder in the selected location with the entered file name (Figure 49).

Q&A How do I know that the file is saved?

While an Office app, such as Publisher, is saving a file, it briefly displays a message on the status bar indicating the amount of the file saved. In addition, the file name appears on the title bar.

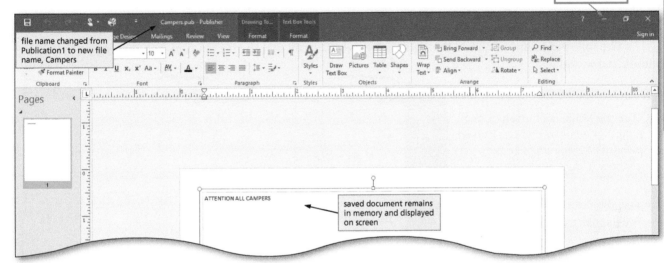

file name changed from Publication1 to new file name, Campers

Minimize button

ATTENTION ALL CAMPERS

saved document remains in memory and displayed on screen

Figure 49

Other Ways

1. Click File on ribbon, click Save As tab in Backstage view, click This PC, click Browse button, type file name (Save As dialog box), navigate to desired save location, click Save button

2. Press F12, type file name (Save As dialog box), navigate to desired save location, click Save button

CONSIDER THIS

How often should you save a publication?

It is important to save a publication frequently for the following reasons:

- The publication in memory might be lost if the computer is turned off or you lose electrical power while an app is running.
- If you run out of time before completing a project, you may finish it at a future time without starting over.

Navigating in Dialog Boxes

Navigating is the process of finding a location on a storage device. While saving the Campers file, for example, Steps 4a and 4b navigated to the Publisher folder located in the CIS 101 folder in the Documents folder. When performing certain functions in Windows apps, such as saving a file, opening a file, or inserting a picture in an existing publication, you most likely will have to navigate to the location where you want to save the file or to the folder containing the file you want to open or insert. Most dialog boxes in Windows apps requiring navigation follow a similar procedure; that is, the way you navigate to a folder in one dialog box, such as the Save As dialog box, is similar to how you might navigate in another dialog box, such as the Open dialog box. If you chose to navigate to a specific location in a dialog box, you would follow the instructions in Steps 4a and 4b.

BTW

File Type
Depending on your Windows settings, the file type .pub may be displayed immediately to the right of the file name after you save the file. The file type .pub is a Publisher file.

To Minimize and Restore a Window

Before continuing, you can verify that the Publisher file was saved properly. To do this, you will minimize the Publisher window and then open the CIS 101 window so that you can verify the file is stored in the CIS 101 folder on the hard drive. A **minimized window** is an open window that is hidden from view but can be displayed quickly by clicking the window's button on the taskbar.

In the following example, Publisher is used to illustrate minimizing and restoring windows; however, you would follow the same steps regardless of the Office app you are using. *Why? Before closing an app, you should make sure your file saved correctly so that you can find it later.*

The following steps minimize the Publisher window, verify that the file is saved, and then restore the minimized window.

1

- Click the Minimize button on the Publisher window title bar (shown in Figure 49) to minimize the window (Figure 50).

Q&A Is the minimized window still available?
The minimized window, Publisher in this case, remains available but no longer is the active window. It is minimized as a button on the taskbar.

- If the File Explorer window is not open on the screen, click the File Explorer button on the taskbar to make the File Explorer window the active window.

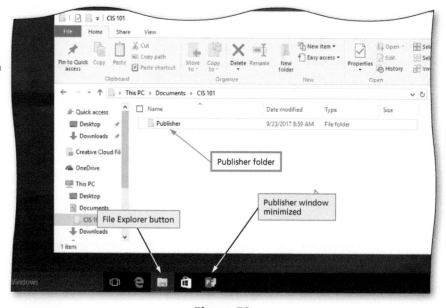

Figure 50

2

- Double-click the Publisher folder in the file list to select the folder and display its contents (Figure 51).

Q&A Why does the File Explorer button on the taskbar change?
A selected app button indicates that the app is active on the screen. When the button is not selected, the app is running but not active.

3

- After viewing the contents of the selected folder, click the Publisher button on the taskbar to restore the minimized window (as shown in Figure 49).

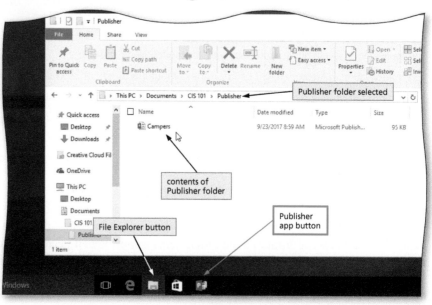

Figure 51

Other Ways

1. Right-click title bar, click Minimize on shortcut menu, click taskbar button in taskbar button area
2. Press WINDOWS+M, press WINDOWS+SHIFT+M
3. Click Publisher app button on taskbar to minimize window; click Publisher app button again to restore window

To Save a File on OneDrive

One of the features of Office is the capability to save files on OneDrive so that you can use the files on multiple computers or mobile devices without having to use an external storage device, such as a USB flash drive. Storing files on OneDrive also enables you to share files more efficiently with others, such as when using Office Online and Office 365.

In the following example, Publisher is used to save a file on OneDrive. *Why? Storing files on OneDrive provides more portability options than are available from storing files in the Documents folder.*

You can save files directly on OneDrive from within an Office app. The following steps save the current Publisher file on OneDrive. These steps require you have a Microsoft account and an Internet connection.

1

- Click File on the ribbon to open the Backstage view.

- Click the Save As tab in the Backstage view to display the Save As gallery.

- Click OneDrive in the left pane to display OneDrive saving options or a Sign In button, if you are not signed in to your Microsoft account already (Figure 52).

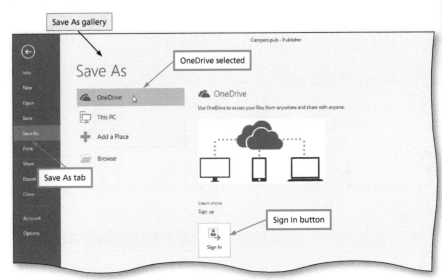

Figure 52

2

- If your screen displays a Sign In button (shown in Figure 52), click it to display the Sign in dialog box (Figure 53).

Q&A
What if the Sign In button does not appear?

If you already are signed into your Microsoft account, the Sign In button will not be displayed. In this case, proceed to Step 3.

- Follow the instructions on the screen to sign in to your Microsoft account.

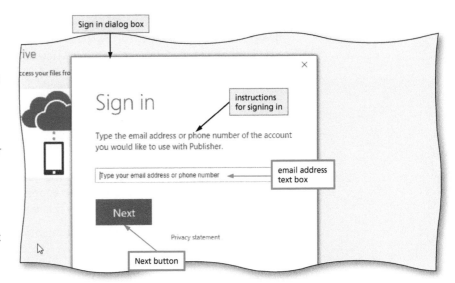

Figure 53

3

- Click the Documents folder in the right pane to display the Save As dialog box (Figure 54).

Q&A Why does the path in the OneDrive address bar in the Save As dialog box contain various letters and numbers? The letters and numbers in the address bar uniquely identify the location of your OneDrive files and folders.

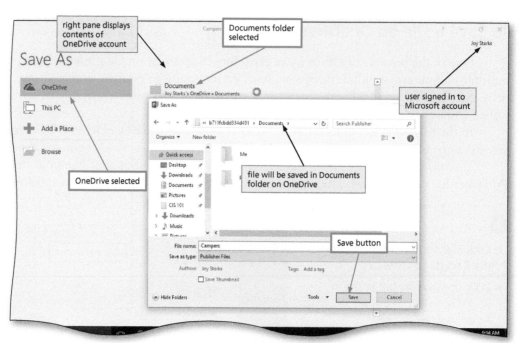

Figure 54

4

- Click the Save button (Save As dialog box) to save the file on OneDrive.

To Sign Out of a Microsoft Account

If you are using a public computer or otherwise wish to sign out of your Microsoft account, you should sign out of the account from the Accounts gallery in the Backstage view. Signing out of the account is the safest way to make sure that nobody else can access online files or settings stored in your Microsoft account. *Why? For security reasons, you should sign out of your Microsoft account when you are finished using a public or shared computer. Staying signed in to your Microsoft account might enable others to access your files.*

The following steps sign out of a Microsoft account from Publisher. You would use the same steps in any Office app. If you do not wish to sign out of your Microsoft account, read these steps without performing them.

1 Click File on the ribbon to open the Backstage view.

2 Click the Account tab to display the Account gallery (Figure 55).

3 Click the Sign out link, which displays the Remove Account dialog box. If a Can't remove Windows accounts dialog box appears instead of the Remove Account dialog box, click the OK button and skip the remaining steps.

Q&A Why does a Can't remove Windows accounts dialog box appear?
If you signed in to Windows using your Microsoft account, then you also must sign out from Windows, rather than signing out from within Publisher. When you are finished using Windows, be sure to sign out at that time.

4 Click the Yes button (Remove Account dialog box) to sign out of your Microsoft account on this computer or mobile device.

Q&A Should I sign out of Windows after removing my Microsoft account?
When you are finished using the computer, you should sign out of Windows for maximum security.

5 Click the Back button in the upper-left corner of the Backstage view to return to the publication.

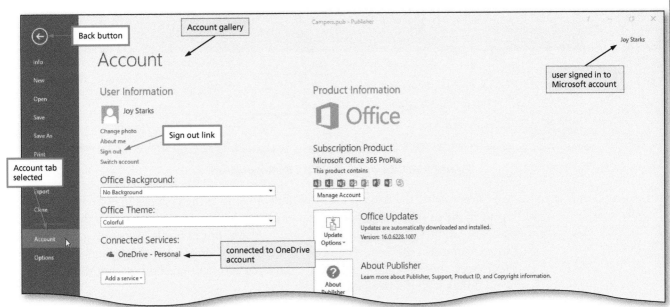

Figure 55

Screen Resolution

Screen resolution indicates the number of pixels (dots) that the computer uses to display the letters, numbers, graphics, and background you see on the screen. When you increase the screen resolution, Windows displays more information on the screen, but the information decreases in size. The reverse also is true: as you decrease the screen resolution, Windows displays less information on the screen, but the information increases in size.

Screen resolution usually is stated as the product of two numbers, such as 1366 × 768 (pronounced "thirteen sixty-six by seven sixty-eight"). A 1366 × 768 screen resolution results in a display of 1366 distinct pixels on each of 768 lines, or about 1,050,624 pixels. Changing the screen resolution affects how the ribbon appears in Office apps and some Windows dialog boxes. Figure 56, for example, shows the Publisher ribbon at screen resolutions of 1366 × 768 and 1024 × 768. All of the same commands are available regardless of screen resolution. The app (Publisher, in this case), however, makes changes to the groups and the buttons within the groups to accommodate the various screen resolutions. The result is that certain commands may need to be accessed differently depending on the resolution chosen. A command that is visible on the ribbon and available by clicking a button at one resolution may not be visible and may need to be accessed using its Dialog Box Launcher at a different resolution.

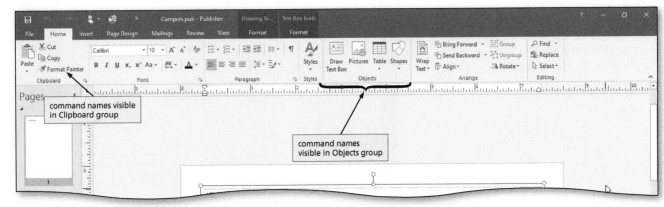

Figure 56a Ribbon at 1366 x 768 Resolution

Figure 56b Ribbon at 1024 x 768 Resolution

Comparing the two ribbons in Figure 56, notice the changes in content and layout of the groups and galleries. In some cases, the content of a group is the same in each resolution, but the layout of the group differs. For example, the same gallery and buttons appear in the Objects groups in the two resolutions, but the layouts differ. In other cases, the content and layout are the same across the resolution, but the level of detail differs with the resolution.

To Change the Screen Resolution

1 SIGN IN | 2 USE WINDOWS | 3 USE APPS | 4 FILE MANAGEMENT | 5 SWITCH APPS | 6 SAVE FILES
7 CHANGE SCREEN RESOLUTION | 8 EXIT APPS | 9 USE ADDITIONAL APP FEATURES | 10 USE HELP

If you are using a computer to step through the modules in this book and you want your screen to match the figures, you may need to change your screen's resolution. *Why? The figures in this book use a screen resolution of 1366 × 768.* The following steps change the screen resolution to 1366 × 768. Your computer already may be set to 1366 × 768. Keep in mind that many computer labs prevent users from changing the screen resolution; in that case, read the following steps for illustration purposes.

- Click the Show desktop button, which is located at the far-right edge of the taskbar, to display the Windows desktop.

- Right-click an empty area on the Windows desktop to display a shortcut menu that contains a list of commands related to the desktop (Figure 57).

Q&A Why does my shortcut menu display different commands?
Depending on your computer's hardware and configuration, different commands might appear on the shortcut menu.

- Click Display settings on the shortcut menu to open the Settings app window. If necessary, scroll to display the 'Advanced display settings' link (Figure 58).

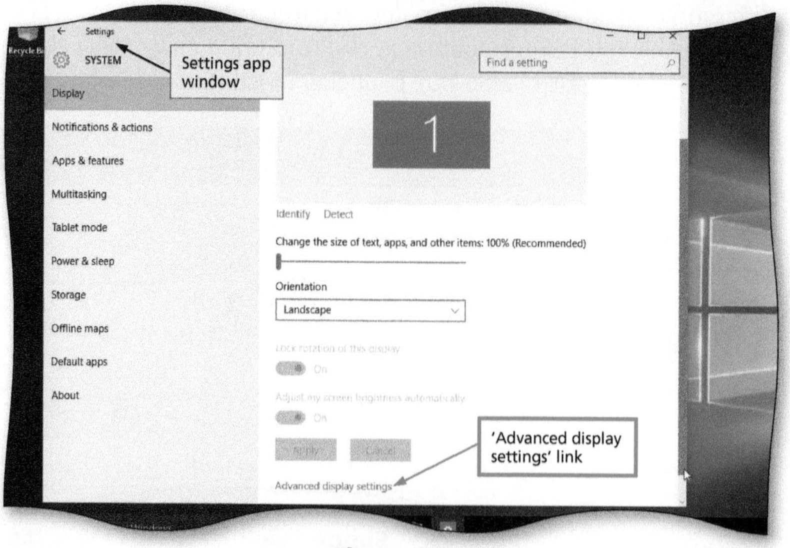

Figure 57

Figure 58

- Click the 'Advanced display settings' link in the Settings app window to display the advanced display settings.
- If necessary, scroll to display the Resolution box (Figure 59).

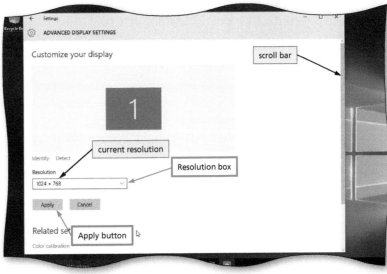

Figure 59

- Click the Resolution box to display a list of available screen resolutions (Figure 60).
- If necessary, scroll to and then click 1366 × 768 to select the screen resolution.

Q&A What if my computer does not support the 1366 × 768 resolution?
Some computers do not support the 1366 × 768 resolution. In this case, select a resolution that is close to the 1366 × 768 resolution.

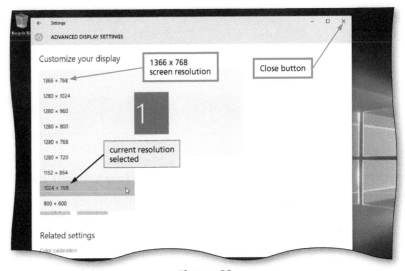

Figure 60

- Click the Apply button (Advanced Display Settings window), shown in Figure 59, to change the screen resolution and a confirmation message (Figure 61).
- Click the Keep changes button to accept the new screen resolution.
- Click the Close button (shown in Figure 60) to close the Settings app window.

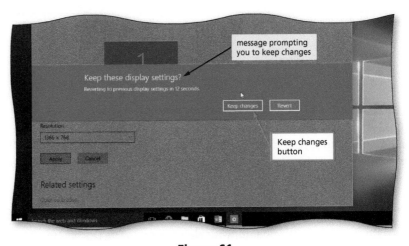

Figure 61

Other Ways

1. Click Start button, click Settings, click System, click Display, click 'Advanced display settings,' select desired resolution in Resolution box, click Apply button, click Keep changes button

2. Type `screen resolution` in search box, click 'Change the screen resolution,' select desired resolution in Resolution box, click Apply button, click Keep changes button

To Exit an App with One Publication Open

When you exit an Office app, such as Publisher, if you have made changes to a file since the last time the file was saved, the app displays a dialog box asking if you want to save the changes you made to the file before it closes the app window. *Why? The dialog box contains three buttons with these resulting actions: the Save button saves the changes and then exits the app, the Don't Save button exits the app without saving changes, and the Cancel button closes the dialog box and redisplays the file without saving the changes.*

If no changes have been made to an open publication since the last time the file was saved, the app will close the window without displaying a dialog box.

The following steps exit Publisher. You would follow similar steps in other Office apps.

- If necessary, click the Publisher app button on the taskbar to display the Publisher window on the desktop (Figure 62).

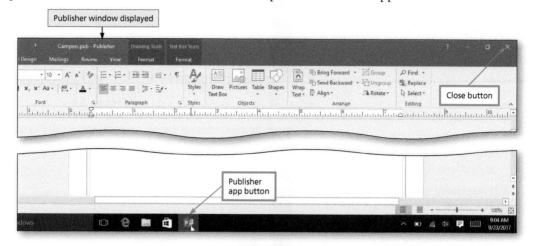

Publisher window displayed

Close button

Publisher app button

Figure 62

- Click the Close button on the right side of the Publisher window title bar to close the publication and exit Publisher. If a Microsoft Publisher dialog box appears, click the Save button to save any changes made to the publication since the last save.

Q&A

What if I have more than one publication open in Publisher?

You could click the Close button for each open publication. When you click the last open publication's Close button, you also exit Publisher. As an alternative that is more efficient, you could right-click the Publisher app button on the taskbar and then click 'Close all windows' on the shortcut menu to close all open publications and exit Publisher.

Other Ways

1. Right-click Publisher app button on Windows taskbar, click 'Close all windows' on shortcut menu   2. Press ALT+F4

To Copy a Folder to OneDrive

To back up your files or easily make them available on another computer or mobile device, you can copy them to OneDrive. The following steps copy your CIS 101 folder to OneDrive. If you do not have access to a OneDrive account, read the following steps without performing them. *Why? It often is good practice to have a backup of your files so that they are available in case something happens to your original copies.*

- Click the File Explorer button on the taskbar to make the folder window the active window.

- Navigate to the CIS 101 folder (or your class folder) in the Documents folder.

- Click Documents in the This PC area of the navigation pane to display the CIS 101 folder in the file list.

Q&A What if my CIS 101 folder is stored in a different location? Use the navigation pane to navigate to the location of your CIS 101 folder. The CIS 101 folder should be displayed in the file list once you have located it.

- Click the CIS 101 folder in the file list to select it (Figure 63).

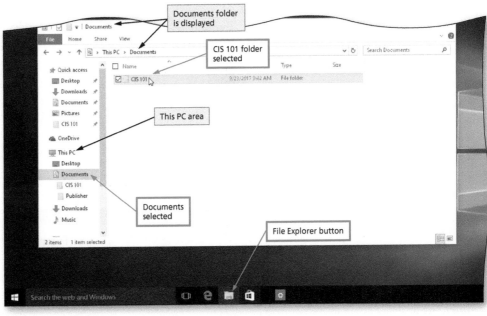

Figure 63

2

- Click Home on the ribbon to display the Home tab.
- Click the Copy to button (Home tab | Organize group) to display the Copy to menu (Figure 64).

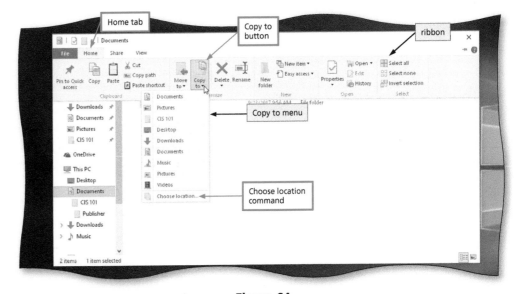

Figure 64

3

- Click Choose location on the Copy to menu to display the Copy Items dialog box.
- Click OneDrive (Copy Items dialog box) to select it (Figure 65).

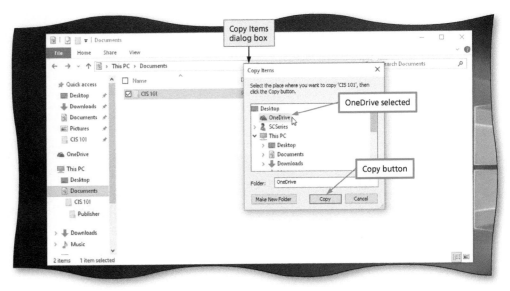

Figure 65

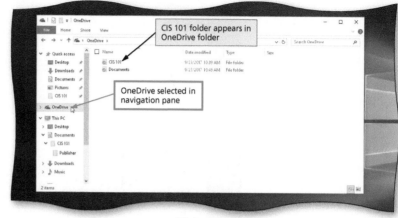

- Click the Copy button (Copy Items dialog box) to copy the selected folder to OneDrive.

- Click OneDrive in the navigation pane to verify the CIS 101 folder displays in the file list (Figure 66).

Q&A

Why does a Microsoft OneDrive dialog box appear when I click OneDrive in the navigation pane?

If you are not currently signed in to Windows using a Microsoft account, you will manually need to sign in to a Microsoft account to save files to OneDrive.

Follow the instructions on the screen to sign in to your Microsoft account.

Figure 66

Other Ways

1. In File Explorer, select folder to copy, click Copy button (Home tab | Clipboard group), display contents of OneDrive in file list, click Paste button (Home tab | Clipboard group)

2. In File Explorer, select folder to copy, press CTRL+C, display contents of OneDrive in file list, press CTRL+V

3. Drag folder to copy to OneDrive in navigation pane

To Unlink a OneDrive Account

1 SIGN IN | 2 USE WINDOWS | 3 USE APPS | **4 FILE MANAGEMENT** | 5 SWITCH APPS | 6 SAVE FILES
7 CHANGE SCREEN RESOLUTION | 8 EXIT APPS | **9 USE ADDITIONAL APP FEATURES** | **10 USE HELP**

If you are using a public computer and are not signed in to Windows with a Microsoft account, you should unlink your OneDrive account so that other users cannot access it. *Why? If you do not unlink your OneDrive account, other people accessing the same user account on the computer will be able to view, remove, and add to files stored in your OneDrive account.*

The following steps unlink your OneDrive account. If you do not wish to sign out of your Microsoft account, read these steps without performing them.

- Click the 'Show hidden icons' button on the Windows taskbar to show a menu of hidden icons (Figure 67).

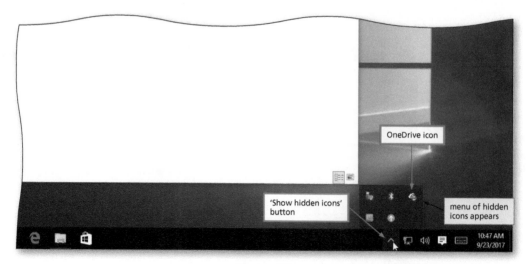

Figure 67

2

- Right-click the OneDrive icon (shown in Figure 67) to display a shortcut menu (Figure 68).

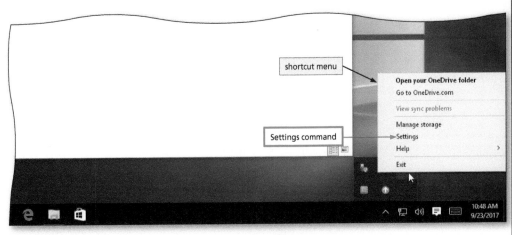

Figure 68

3

- Click Settings on the shortcut menu to display the Microsoft OneDrive dialog box (Figure 69).

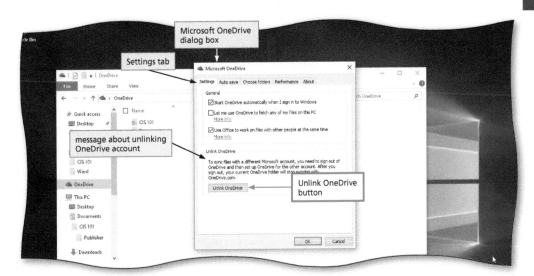

Figure 69

4

- If necessary, click the Settings tab.

- Click the Unlink OneDrive button (Microsoft OneDrive dialog box) to unlink the OneDrive account (Figure 70).

- When the Microsoft OneDrive dialog box appears with a Welcome to OneDrive message, click the Close button.

- Minimize the File Explorer window.

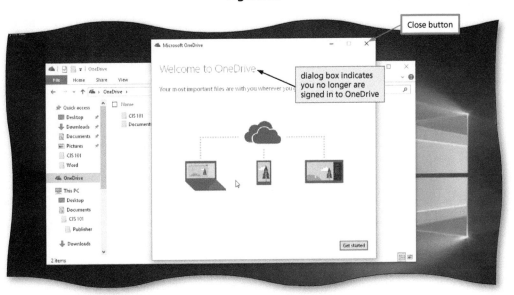

Figure 70

Break Point: If you wish to take a break, this is a good place to do so. To resume at a later time, continue to follow the steps from this location forward.

Additional Common Features of Office Apps

The previous section used Publisher to illustrate common features of Office and some basic elements unique to Publisher. The following sections continue to use Publisher to present additional common features of Office.

In the following pages, you will learn how to do the following:

1. Run Publisher using the search box.
2. Open a publication in Publisher.
3. Close the publication.
4. Reopen the publication just closed.
5. Create a blank Publisher publication from Windows Explorer and then open the file.
6. Save a publication with a new file name.

To Run an App Using the Search Box

1 SIGN IN | **2 USE WINDOWS** | 3 USE APPS | 4 FILE MANAGEMENT | 5 SWITCH APPS | 6 SAVE FILES
7 CHANGE SCREEN RESOLUTION | 8 EXIT APPS | **9 USE ADDITIONAL APP FEATURES** | 10 USE HELP

The following steps, which assume Windows is running, use the search box to run Publisher based on a typical installation; however, you would follow similar steps to run any app. *Why? Some people prefer to use the search box to locate and run an app, as opposed to searching through a list of all apps on the Start menu.* You may need to ask your instructor how to run Publisher on your computer.

- Type **Publisher 2016** as the search text in the search box and watch the search results appear in the search results (Figure 71).

Q&A Do I need to type the complete app name or use correct capitalization?
No, you need to type just enough characters of the app name for it to appear in the search results. For example, you may be able to type Publisher or publisher, instead of Publisher 2016.

What if the search does not locate the Publisher app on my computer?
You may need to adjust the Windows search settings. Search for the word, index; click 'Indexing Options Control Panel'; click the Modify button (Indexing Options dialog box); expand the Local Disk, if necessary; place a check mark beside all Program Files entries; and then click the OK button. It may take a few minutes for the index to rebuild. If it still does not work, you may need to click the Advanced button (Indexing Options dialog box) and then click the Rebuild button (Advanced Options dialog box).

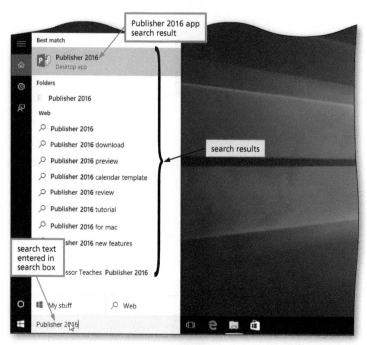

Figure 71

- Click the app name, Publisher 2016 in this case, in the search results to run Publisher and display the Publisher start screen.
- Click the Blank 8.5 × 11" publication thumbnail on the Publisher start screen (shown earlier in this module in Figure 8) to create a blank publication and display it in the Publisher window.

- If the Publisher window is not maximized, click the Maximize button on its title bar to maximize the window (Figure 72).

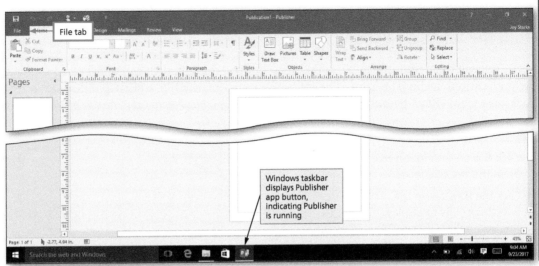

Figure 72

To Open an Existing File

1 SIGN IN | 2 USE WINDOWS | 3 USE APPS | 4 FILE MANAGEMENT | 5 SWITCH APPS | 6 SAVE FILES
7 CHANGE SCREEN RESOLUTION | 8 EXIT APPS | 9 USE ADDITIONAL APP FEATURES | **10 USE HELP**

As discussed earlier, the Backstage view contains a set of commands that enable you to manage publications and data about the publications. *Why? From the Backstage view in Publisher, for example, you can create, open, print, and save publications. You also can share publications, manage versions, set permissions, and modify publication properties. In other Office apps, the Backstage view may contain features specific to those apps.* The following steps open a saved file, specifically the Campers file, which recently was saved.

1

- Click File on the ribbon (shown in Figure 72) to open the Backstage view and then click the Open tab in the Backstage view to display the Open gallery in the Backstage view.

- Click the Browse button to display the Open dialog box.

- If necessary, navigate to the location of the file to open (Publisher folder in the CIS 101 folder).

- Click the file to open, Campers in this case, to select the file (Figure 73).

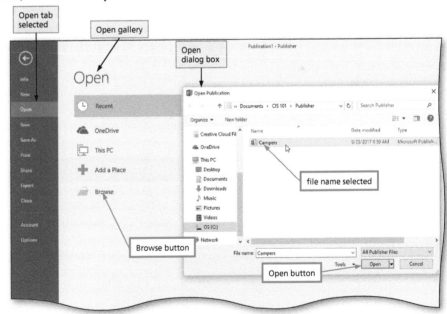

Figure 73

2

- Click the Open button (Open dialog box) to open the file. If necessary, click the Enable Content button.

Q&A | Why did a Security Warning appear?
The Security Warning appears when you open an Office file that might contain harmful content. The files you create in this module are not harmful, but you should be cautious when opening files from other people.

Other Ways

1. Press CTRL+O

2. Navigate to file in File Explorer window, double-click file name

To Create a New Publication from the Backstage View

You can open multiple publications in an Office program, such as Publisher, so that you can work on the publications at the same time. The following steps create a file, a blank publication in this case, from the Backstage view. *Why? You want to create a new publication while keeping the current publication open.*

1

- Click File on the ribbon to open the Backstage view.
- Click the New tab in the Backstage view to display the New gallery (Figure 74).

Q&A Can I create publications through the Backstage view in other Office apps?
Yes. If the Office app has a New tab in the Backstage view, the New gallery displays various options for creating a new file.

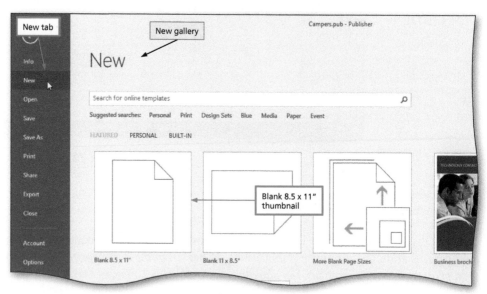

Figure 74

2

- Click the Blank 8.5 × 11" thumbnail in the New gallery to create a new publication (Figure 75).

Q&A Why does the title bar now say Publication2?
While Publisher is running, it assigns new files a numbered and temporary file name on the title bar so that you can differentiate among publications. Because the Campers file is open already, this new file becomes the second publication, or Publication2.

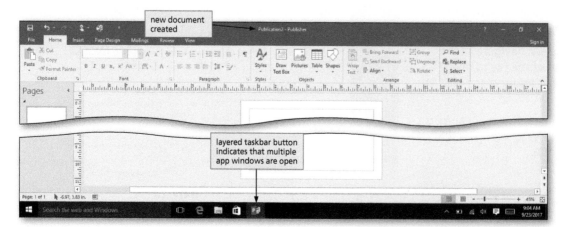

Figure 75

Other Ways

1. Press CTRL+N

To Enter Text in a Publication

The next publication identifies camping rates. The following step enters the first line of text in the new publication.

1 Press the F9 key to zoom to 100%.

2 Type `List of Camping Rates` and then press the ENTER key (Figure 76).

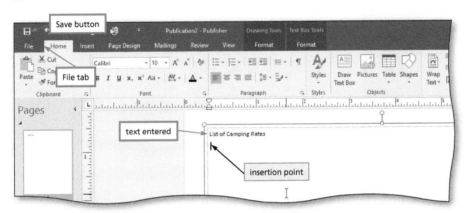

Figure 76

To Save a File in a Folder

The following steps save the second publication in the Publisher folder in the class folder (CIS 101, in this case) in the Documents folder using the file name, Camping Rates.

1 Click the Save button on the Quick Access Toolbar, which depending on settings, will display either the Save As gallery in the Backstage view or the Save As dialog box.

2 If your screen displays the Backstage view, click This PC, if necessary, to display options in the right pane related to saving on your computer; if your screen already displays the Save As dialog box, proceed to Step 4.

3 Click the Browse button in the left pane to display the Save As dialog box.

4 If necessary, type `Camping Rates` in the File name box (Save As dialog box) to change the file name. Do not press the ENTER key after typing the file name because you do not want to close the dialog box at this time.

5 If necessary, navigate to the desired save location (in this case, the Publisher folder in the CIS 101 folder [or your class folder] in the Documents folder). For specific instructions, perform the tasks in Steps 4a and 4b in the previous section in this module titled To Save a File in a Folder.

6 Click the Save button (Save As dialog box) to save the publication in the selected folder on the selected drive with the entered file name.

To Close a File Using the Backstage View

1 SIGN IN | 2 USE WINDOWS | 3 USE APPS | 4 FILE MANAGEMENT | 5 SWITCH APPS | 6 SAVE FILES
7 CHANGE SCREEN RESOLUTION | 8 EXIT APPS | 9 USE ADDITIONAL APP FEATURES | 10 USE HELP

Sometimes, you may want to close an Office file, such as a Publisher publication, entirely and start over with a new file. You also may want to close a file when you are done working with it. **Why?** *You should close a file when you are done working with it so that you do not make inadvertent changes to it.* The following steps close the current active Publisher file, that is, the Camping Rates publication, without exiting Publisher.

- Click File on the ribbon to open the Backstage view (Figure 77).

- Click Close in the Backstage view to close the open file (Camping Rates, in this case) without exiting the active app (Publisher).

Q&A What if Publisher displays a dialog box about saving?
Click the Save button if you want to save the changes, click the Don't Save button if you want to ignore the changes since the last time you saved, and click the Cancel button if you do not want to close the publication.

Can I use the Backstage view to close an open file in other Office apps, such as PowerPoint and Excel?
Yes.

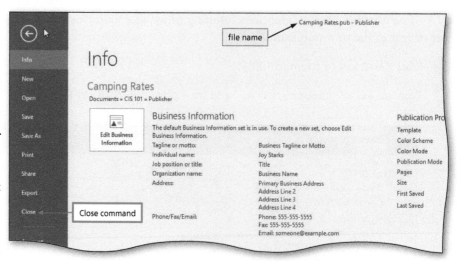

Figure 77

Other Ways

1. Press CTRL+F4

To Open a Recent File Using the Backstage View

1 SIGN IN | 2 USE WINDOWS | 3 USE APPS | 4 FILE MANAGEMENT | 5 SWITCH APPS | 6 SAVE FILES
7 CHANGE SCREEN RESOLUTION | 8 EXIT APPS | 9 USE ADDITIONAL APP FEATURES | 10 USE HELP

You sometimes need to open a file that you recently modified. **Why?** *You may have more changes to make, such as adding more content or correcting errors.* The Backstage view allows you to access recent files easily. The following steps reopen the Camping Rates file just closed.

1

- Click File on the ribbon to open the Backstage view.
- Click the Open tab in the Backstage view to display the Open gallery (Figure 78).

2

- Click the desired file name in the Recent list, Camping Rates in this case, to open the file.

Q&A Can I use the Backstage view to open a recent file in other Office apps, such as PowerPoint and Excel?
Yes, as long as the file name appears in the list of recent files.

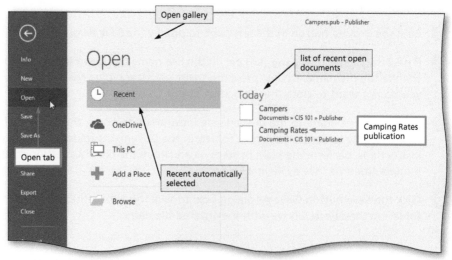

Figure 78

Other Ways

1. Click File on ribbon, click Open in Backstage view, click Browse button, navigate to file (Open dialog box), click Open button

To Create a New Blank Publication from File Explorer

File Explorer provides a means to create a blank Office publication without running an Office app. The following steps use File Explorer to create a blank Publisher publication. *Why? Sometimes you might need to create a blank publication and then return to it later for editing.*

- Click the File Explorer button on the taskbar to make the folder window the active window.
- If necessary, double-click the Documents folder in the navigation pane to expand the Documents folder.
- If necessary, double-click your class folder (CIS 101, in this case) in the navigation pane to expand the folder.
- Click the Publisher folder in the navigation pane to display its contents in the file list.
- With the Publisher folder selected, right-click an open area in the file list to display a shortcut menu.
- Point to New on the shortcut menu to display the New submenu (Figure 79).

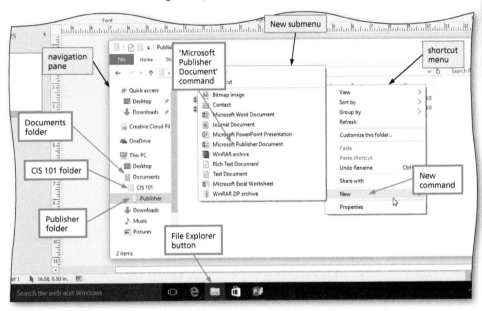

Figure 79

- Click 'Microsoft Publisher Document' on the New submenu to display an icon and text box for a new file in the current folder window with the file name, New Microsoft Publisher Document, selected (Figure 80).

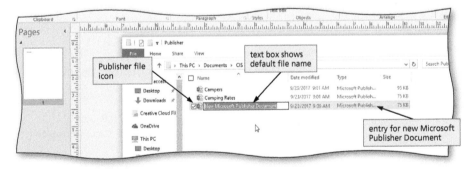

Figure 80

- Type **Recommended Campgrounds** in the text box and then press the ENTER key to assign a new file name to the new file in the current folder (Figure 81).

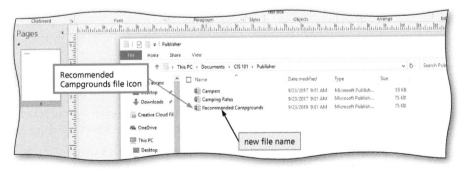

Figure 81

To Run an App from File Explorer and Open a File

Previously in this module, you learned how to run Publisher using the Start menu and the search box. The following steps, which assume Windows is running, use File Explorer to run Publisher based on a typical installation. *Why? Another way to run an Office app is to open an existing file from File Explorer, which causes the app in which the file was created to run and then open the selected file.* You may need to ask your instructor how to run Publisher for your computer.

- If necessary, display the file to open in the folder window in File Explorer (shown in Figure 81).

- Right-click the file icon or file name you want to open (Recommended Campgrounds, in this case) to display a shortcut menu (Figure 82).

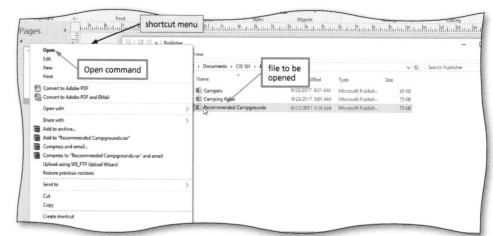

Figure 82

- Click Open on the shortcut menu to open the selected file in the app used to create the file, Publisher in this case (shown in Figure 83).

- If the window is not maximized, click the Maximize button on the title bar to maximize the window.

Other Ways
1. Double-click file name in file list

To Enter Text in a Publication

The next step is to enter text in the blank Publisher publication. The following step enters a line of text.

1 Zoom to 100%.

2 Type `List of Recommended Campgrounds` and then press the ENTER key (shown in Figure 83).

To Save an Existing Office File with the Same File Name

Saving frequently cannot be overemphasized. *Why? You have made modifications to the file (publication) since you created it. Thus, you should save again. Similarly, you should continue saving files frequently so that you do not lose the changes you have made since the time you last saved the file.* You can use the same file name, such as Recommended Campgrounds, to save the changes made to the publication. The following step saves a file again with the same file name.

1

- Click the Save button on the Quick Access Toolbar to overwrite the previously saved file (Recommended Campgrounds, in this case) in the Publisher folder (Figure 83).

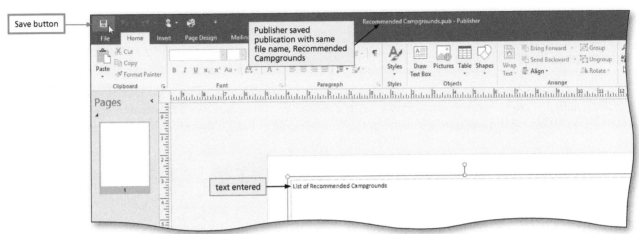

Figure 83

Other Ways

1. Press CTRL+S

2. Press SHIFT+F12

To Save a File with a New File Name

You might want to save a file with a different file name or to a different location. For example, you might start a homework assignment with a data file and then save it with a final file name for submission to your instructor, saving it to a location designated by your instructor. The following steps save a file with a different file name.

1 Click the File tab to open the Backstage view.

2 Click the Save As tab to display the Save As gallery.

3 If necessary, click This PC to display options in the right pane related to saving on your computer.

4 Click the Browse button in the left pane to display the Save As dialog box.

5 Type `Campgrounds` in the File name box (Save As dialog box) to change the file name. Do not press the ENTER key after typing the file name because you do not want to close the dialog box at this time.

6 If necessary, navigate to the desired save location (in this case, the Publisher folder in the CIS 101 folder [or your class folder] in the Documents folder). For specific instructions, perform the tasks in Steps 4a and 4b in the previous section titled To Save a File in a Folder.

7 Click the Save button (Save As dialog box) to save the publication in the selected folder on the selected drive with the entered file name.

To Exit an Office App

You are finished using Publisher. The following steps exit Publisher.

1 Because you have multiple Publisher publications open, right-click the Publisher app button on the taskbar and then click 'Close all windows' on the shortcut menu to close all open publications and exit Publisher.

2 If a dialog box appears, click the Save button to save any changes made to the file since the last save.

Renaming, Moving, and Deleting Files

Earlier in this module, you learned how to organize files in folders, which is part of a process known as **file management**. The following sections cover additional file management topics including renaming, moving, and deleting files.

To Rename a File

In some circumstances, you may want to change the name of, or rename, a file or a folder. *Why? You may want to distinguish a file in one folder or drive from a copy of a similar file, or you may decide to rename a file to better identify its contents.* The following steps change the name of the Campers file in the Publisher folder to Campers Flyer.

- If necessary, click the File Explorer button on the taskbar to make the folder window the active window.

- Navigate to the location of the file to be renamed (in this case, the Publisher folder in the CIS 101 [or your class folder] folder in the Documents folder) to display the file(s) it contains in the file list.

- Click the file to be renamed, the Campers icon or file name in the file list in this case, to select it.

- Right-click the selected file to display a shortcut menu that presents a list of commands related to files (Figure 84).

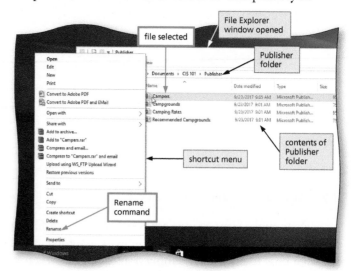

Figure 84

2

- Click Rename on the shortcut menu to place the current file name in a text box.

- Type `Campers Flyer` in the text box and then press the ENTER key (Figure 85).

Q&A

Are any risks involved in renaming files that are located on a hard drive?

If you inadvertently rename a file that is associated with certain apps, the apps may not be able to find the file and, therefore, may not run properly. Always use caution when renaming files.

Can I rename a file when it is open?

No, a file must be closed to change the file name.

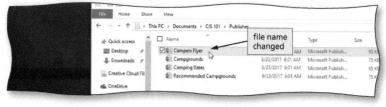

Figure 85

Other Ways

1. Select file, press F2, type new file name, press ENTER

2. Select file, click Rename button (Home tab | Organize group), type new file name, press ENTER

To Move a File

Why? At some time, you may want to move a file from one folder, called the source folder, to another, called the destination folder. When you move a file, it no longer appears in the original folder. If the destination and the source folders are on the same media, you can move a file by dragging it. If the folders are on different media, you will need to right-drag the file and then click Move here on the shortcut menu. The following step moves the Recommended Campgrounds file from the Publisher folder to the CIS 101 folder.

1

- If necessary, in File Explorer, navigate to the location of the file to be moved (in this case, the Publisher folder in the CIS 101 folder [or your class folder] in the Documents folder).

- If necessary, click the Publisher folder in the navigation pane to display the files it contains in the right pane.

- Drag the file to be moved, the Recommended Campgrounds file in the right pane in this case, to the CIS 101 folder in the navigation pane (Figure 86).

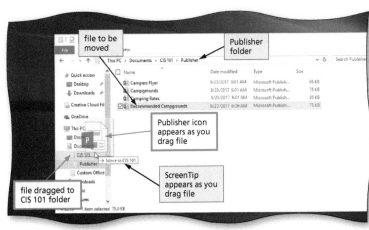

Figure 86

 Experiment

- Click the CIS 101 folder in the navigation pane to verify that the file was moved.

Other Ways

1. Right-click file to move, click Cut on shortcut menu, right-click destination folder, click Paste on shortcut menu	2. Select file to move, press CTRL+X, select destination folder, press CTRL+V

To Delete a File

1 SIGN IN | 2 USE WINDOWS | 3 USE APPS | **4 FILE MANAGEMENT** | 5 SWITCH APPS | 6 SAVE FILES
7 CHANGE SCREEN RESOLUTION | 8 EXIT APPS | 9 USE ADDITIONAL APP FEATURES | **10 USE HELP**

A final task you may want to perform is to delete a file. Exercise extreme caution when deleting a file or files. When you delete a file from a hard drive, the deleted file is stored in the Recycle Bin where you can recover it until you empty the Recycle Bin. If you delete a file from removable media, such as a USB flash drive, the file is deleted permanently. The next steps delete the Recommended Campgrounds file from the CIS 101 folder. *Why? When a file no longer is needed, you can delete it to conserve space on your storage location.*

1

- If necessary, in File Explorer, navigate to the location of the file to be deleted (in this case, the CIS 101 folder [or your class folder] in the Documents folder).

- Click the file to be deleted, the Recommended Campgrounds icon or file name in the right pane in this case, to select the file.

- Right-click the selected file to display a shortcut menu (Figure 87).

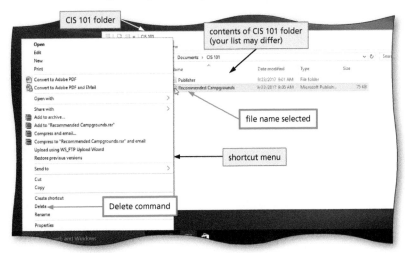

2

- Click Delete on the shortcut menu to delete the file.

Figure 87

- If a dialog box appears, click the Yes button to delete the file.

Q&A Can I use this same technique to delete a folder?

Yes. Right-click the folder and then click Delete on the shortcut menu. When you delete a folder, all of the files and folders contained in the folder you are deleting, together with any files and folders on lower hierarchical levels, are deleted as well. For example, if you delete the CIS 101 folder, you will delete all folders and files inside the CIS 101 folder.

Other Ways

1. Select file, press DELETE

Microsoft Office and Windows Help

At any time while you are using one of the Office apps, such as Publisher, you can use Office Help to display information about all topics associated with the app. Help in other Office apps operates in a similar fashion.

In Office, Help is presented in a window that has browser-style navigation buttons. Each Office app has its own Help home page, which is the starting Help page that is displayed in the Help window. If your computer is connected to the Internet, the contents of the Help page reflect both the local help files installed on the computer and material from Microsoft's website.

To Open the Help Window in an Office App

1 SIGN IN | 2 USE WINDOWS | 3 USE APPS | 4 FILE MANAGEMENT | 5 SWITCH APPS | 6 SAVE FILES
7 CHANGE SCREEN RESOLUTION | 8 EXIT APPS | 9 USE ADDITIONAL APP FEATURES | **10 USE HELP**

The following step opens the Publisher 2016 Help window. ***Why?*** *You might not understand how certain commands or operations work in Publisher, so you can obtain the necessary information using help.*

- Run Publisher.
- Click the Blank 8.5 x 11" thumbnail to display a blank publication.
- Press F1 to open the Publisher 2016 Help window (Figure 88).

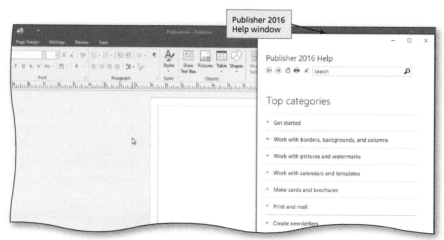

Figure 88

Moving and Resizing Windows

At times, it is useful, or even necessary, to have more than one window open and visible on the screen at the same time. You can resize and move these open windows so that you can view different areas of and elements in the window. In the case of the Publisher 2016 Help window, for example, it could be covering publication text in the Publisher window that you need to see.

To Move a Window by Dragging

1 SIGN IN | **2 USE WINDOWS** | 3 USE APPS | 4 FILE MANAGEMENT | 5 SWITCH APPS | 6 SAVE FILES
7 CHANGE SCREEN RESOLUTION | 8 EXIT APPS | 9 USE ADDITIONAL APP FEATURES | 10 USE HELP

You can move any open window that is not maximized to another location on the desktop by dragging the title bar of the window. ***Why?*** *You might want to have a better view of what is behind the window or just want to move the window so that you can see it better.* The following step drags the Publisher 2016 Help window to the upper-left corner of the desktop.

1

- Drag the window title bar (the Publisher 2016 Help window title bar, in this case) so that the window moves to the upper-left corner of the desktop, as shown in Figure 89.

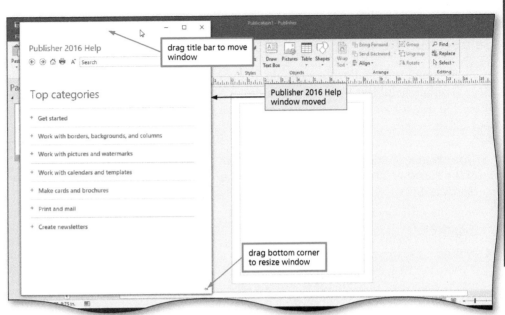

Figure 89

To Resize a Window by Dragging

1 SIGN IN | **2 USE WINDOWS** | 3 USE APPS | 4 FILE MANAGEMENT | 5 SWITCH APPS | 6 SAVE FILES
7 CHANGE SCREEN RESOLUTION | 8 EXIT APPS | 9 USE ADDITIONAL APP FEATURES | 10 USE HELP

A method used to change the size of the window is to drag the window borders. The following step changes the size of the Publisher 2016 Help window by dragging its borders. *Why? Sometimes, information is not visible completely in a window, and you want to increase the size of the window.*

1

- Point to the lower-right corner of the window (the Publisher 2016 Help window, in this case) until the pointer changes to a two-headed arrow.

- Drag the bottom border as necessary to display more of the active window (Figure 90).

Q&A Can I drag other borders on the window to enlarge or shrink the window?
Yes, you can drag the left, right, and top borders and any window corner to resize a window.

Will Windows remember the new size of the window after I close it?
Yes. When you reopen the window, Windows will display it at the same size it was when you closed it.

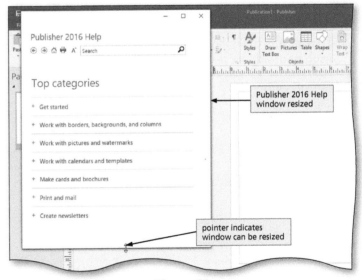

Figure 90

Using Office Help

Once an Office app's Help window is open, several methods exist for navigating Help. You can search for help by using any of the three following methods from the Help window:

1. Enter search text in the Search text box.
2. Click the links in the Help window.
3. Use the Table of Contents.

To Obtain Help Using the Search Text Box

Assume for the following example that you want to know more about fonts. The following steps use the 'Search online help' text box to obtain useful information about fonts by entering the word, fonts, as search text. *Why? You may not know the exact help topic you are looking to find, so using keywords can help narrow your search.*

- Type **fonts** in the Search text box at the top of the Publisher 2016 Help window to enter the search text.

- Press the ENTER key to display the search results (Figure 91).

 | Why do my search results differ?
If you do not have an Internet connection, your results will reflect only the content of the Help files on your computer. When searching for help online, results also can change as content is added, deleted, and updated on the online Help webpages maintained by Microsoft.

Why were my search results not very helpful? When initiating a search, be sure to check the spelling of the search text; also, keep your search specific to return the most accurate results.

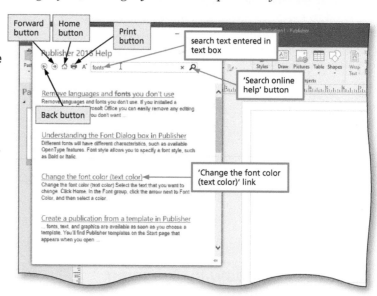

Figure 91

- Click the 'Change the font color (text color)', or a similar, link to display the Help information associated with the selected topic (Figure 92).

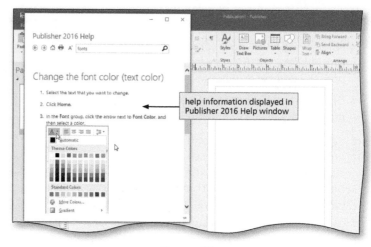

Figure 92

- Click the Home button in the Publisher 2016 Help window to clear the search results and redisplay the Help home page (Figure 93).

- Click the Close button in the Publisher 2016 Help window to close the window.

- Exit Microsoft Publisher.

Figure 93

Obtaining Help while Working in an Office App

Help in the Office apps, such as Publisher, provides you with the ability to obtain help directly, without opening the Help window and initiating a search. For example, you may be unsure about how a particular command works, or you may be presented with a dialog box that you are not sure how to use.

Figure 94 shows one option for obtaining help while working in an Office app. If you want to learn more about a command, point to its button and wait for the ScreenTip to appear. If the Help icon and 'Tell me more' link appear in the ScreenTip, click the 'Tell me more' link or press the F1 key while pointing to the button to open the Help window associated with that command.

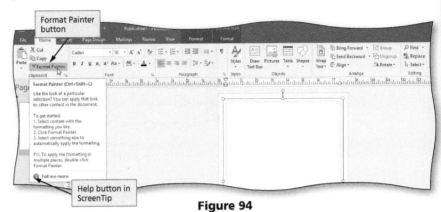

Figure 94

Figure 95 shows a dialog box that contains a Help button. Clicking the Help button or pressing the F1 key while the dialog box is displayed opens a Help window. The Help window contains help about that dialog box, if available. If no help file is available for that particular dialog box, then the main Help window opens.

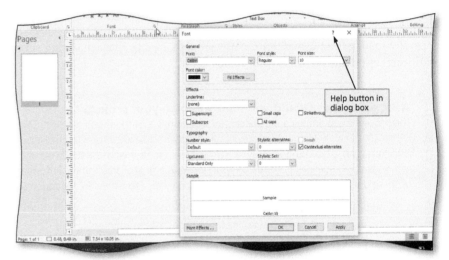

Figure 95

Using the Windows Search Box

One of the more powerful Windows features is the Windows search box. The search box is a central location from where you can type search text and quickly access related Windows commands or web search results. In addition, **Cortana** is a new search tool in Windows that you can access using the search box. It can act as a personal assistant by performing functions such as providing ideas; searching for apps, files, and folders; and setting reminders. In addition to typing search text in the search box, you also can use your computer or mobile device's microphone to give verbal commands.

To Use the Windows Search Box

1 SIGN IN | 2 USE WINDOWS | 3 USE APPS | 4 FILE MANAGEMENT | 5 SWITCH APPS | 6 SAVE FILES
7 CHANGE SCREEN RESOLUTION | 8 EXIT APPS | 9 USE ADDITIONAL APP FEATURES | 10 USE HELP

The following step uses the Windows search box to search for a Windows command. *Why? Using the search box to locate apps, settings, folders, and files can be faster than navigating windows and dialog boxes to search for the desired content.*

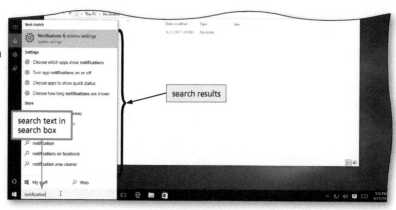

1

- Type **notification** in the search box to display the search results. The search results include related Windows settings, Windows Store apps, and web search results (Figure 96).

- Click an empty area of the desktop to close the search results.

Figure 96

Summary

In this module, you learned how to use the Windows interface, several touch screen and mouse operations, and file and folder management. You also learned some basic features of Publisher and discovered the common elements that exist among Microsoft Office apps. Topics covered included signing in, using Windows, using apps, file management, switching between apps, saving files, changing screen resolution, exiting apps, using additional app features, and using Help.

CONSIDER THIS: PLAN AHEAD

What guidelines should you follow to plan your projects?

The process of communicating specific information is a learned, rational skill. Computers and software, especially Microsoft Office 2016, can help you develop ideas and present detailed information to a particular audience and minimize much of the laborious work of drafting and revising projects. No matter what method you use to plan a project, it is beneficial to follow some specific guidelines from the onset to arrive at a final product that is informative, relevant, and effective. Use some aspects of these guidelines every time you undertake a project, and others as needed in specific instances.

1. Determine the project's purpose.

  a) Clearly define why you are undertaking this assignment.

  b) Begin to draft ideas of how best to communicate information by handwriting ideas on paper; composing directly on a laptop, tablet, or mobile device; or developing a strategy that fits your particular thinking and writing style.

2. Analyze your audience.

  a) Learn about the people who will read, analyze, or view your work.

  b) Determine their interests and needs so that you can present the information they need to know and omit the information they already possess.

  c) Form a mental picture of these people or find photos of people who fit this profile so that you can develop a project with the audience in mind.

3. Gather possible content.

  a) Locate existing information that may reside in spreadsheets, databases, or other files.

  b) Conduct a web search to find relevant websites.

  c) Read pamphlets, magazine and newspaper articles, and books to gain insights of how others have approached your topic.

  d) Conduct personal interviews to obtain perspectives not available by any other means.

  e) Consider video and audio clips as potential sources for material that might complement or support the factual data you uncover.

4. Determine what content to present to your audience.

  a) Write three or four major ideas you want an audience member to remember after reading or viewing your project.

  b) Envision your project's endpoint, the key fact you wish to emphasize, so that all project elements lead to this final element.

  c) Determine relevant time factors, such as the length of time to develop the project, how long readers will spend reviewing your project, or the amount of time allocated for your speaking engagement.

  d) Decide whether a graph, photo, or artistic element can express or enhance a particular concept.

  e) Be mindful of the order in which you plan to present the content, and place the most important material at the top or bottom of the page, because readers and audience members generally remember the first and last pieces of information they see and hear.

CONSIDER THIS

How should you submit solutions to questions in the assignments identified with a ✺ symbol?

Every assignment in this book contains one or more questions with a ✺ symbol. These questions require you to think beyond the assigned file. Present your solutions to the question in the format required by your instructor. Possible formats may include one or more of these options: write the answer; create a publication that contains the answer; present your answer to the class; discuss your answer in a group; record the answer as audio or video using a webcam, smartphone, or portable media player; or post answers on a blog, wiki, or website.

Apply Your Knowledge

Reinforce the skills and apply the concepts you learned in this module.

Creating a Folder and a Publication

Instructions: You will create a Publisher Assignments folder and then create a publication and save it in the folder.

Perform the following tasks:

1. Open the File Explorer window and then double-click to open the Documents folder.
2. Click the New folder button on the Quick Access Toolbar to display a new folder icon and text box for the folder name.
3. Type **Publisher Assignments** in the text box to name the folder. Press the ENTER key to create the folder in the Documents folder.
4. Run Publisher and create a new blank publication.
5. Press the F9 key to zoom to 100%.
6. Type **Contact Information** and then press then ENTER key to enter a line of text (Figure 97).
7. If requested by your instructor, enter your name, phone number, and email address in the Publisher publication.
8. Click the Save button on the Quick Access Toolbar. Navigate to the Publisher Assignments folder in the Documents folder and then save the publication using the file name, Apply 1 Publication.
9. If your Quick Access Toolbar does not show the Quick Print button, add the Quick Print button to the Quick Access Toolbar. Print the publication using the Quick Print button on the Quick Access Toolbar. When you are finished printing, remove the Quick Print button from the Quick Access Toolbar.

Figure 97

10. Submit the printout to your instructor.
11. Exit Publisher.
12. ✺ What other commands might you find useful to include on the Quick Access Toolbar?

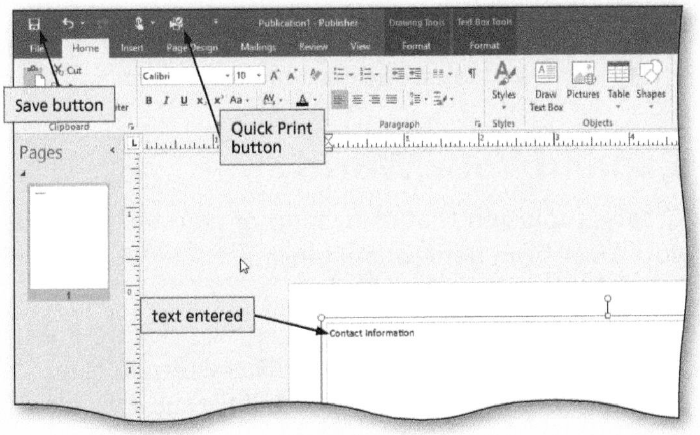

Extend Your Knowledge

Extend the skills you learned in this module and experiment with new skills. You will use Help to complete the assignment.

Using Help

Instructions: Use Publisher 2016 Help to perform the following tasks.

Perform the following tasks:

1. Run Publisher.
2. Press the F1 key to open the Publisher 2016 Help window (shown in Figure 88).
3. Search Publisher 2016 Help to answer the following questions.
   a. What are three new features of Publisher 2016?
   b. What type of training is available through Publisher 2016 Help?
   c. What are the steps to customize the ribbon?
   d. What is the purpose of the Office Clipboard?
   e. How do you cascade Publisher windows?
   f. Why would you use mail merge?
   g. How do you insert pictures?
   h. How do you change the size of text?
   i. What are the steps to zoom in and out of a publication?
   j. What is the purpose of the Design Checker pane? How do you display it?
4. Type the answers from your searches in a new blank Publisher publication. Save the publication with a new file name and then submit it in the format specified by your instructor.
5. If requested by your instructor, enter your name in the Publisher publication.
6. Exit Publisher.
7. ✸ What search text did you use to perform the searches above? Did it take multiple attempts to search and locate the exact information for which you were searching?

Expand Your World

Create a solution that uses cloud or web technologies by learning and investigating on your own from general guidance.

Creating Folders on OneDrive and Using the Publisher Online App

Instructions: You will create the folders shown in Figure 98 on OneDrive. Then, you will use the Publisher Online app to create a small file and save it in a folder on OneDrive.

Perform the following tasks:

1. Sign in to OneDrive in your browser.
2. Use the New button to create the folder structure shown in Figure 98.
3. In the Upcoming Events folder, use the New button to create a Publisher publication with the file name, Extend 1 Task List, that contains the text, Prepare agenda for Tuesday's meeting.

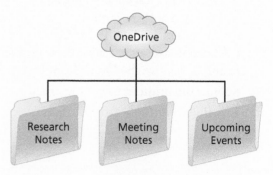

Figure 98

4. If requested by your instructor, add your name to the publication.

5. Save the publication in the Upcoming Events folder.

6. Submit the assignment in the format specified by your instructor.

7. ✸ Based on your current knowledge of OneDrive, do you think you will use it? What about the Publisher Online app?

In the Labs

Design, create, modify, and/or use files following the guidelines, concepts, and skills presented in this module. Labs 1 and 2, which increase in difficulty, require you to create solutions based on what you learned in the module; Lab 3 requires you to apply your creative thinking and problem-solving skills to design and implement a solution.

Lab 1: **Creating Folders for a Bookstore**

Problem: Your friend works for a local bookstore. He would like to organize his files in relation to the types of books available in the store. He has seven main categories: fiction, biography, children, humor, social science, nonfiction, and medical. You are to create a folder structure similar to Figure 99.

Perform the following tasks:

1. Click the File Explorer button on the taskbar and display the contents of the Documents folder.

2. In the Documents folder, create the main folder and name it Book Categories.

3. Navigate to the Book Categories folder.

4. Within the Book Categories folder, create a folder for each of the following: Fiction, Biography, Children, Humor, Social Science, Nonfiction, and Medical.

5. Within the Fiction folder, create two additional folders: Science Fiction and Western.

6. If requested by your instructor, add another folder using your last name as the folder name.

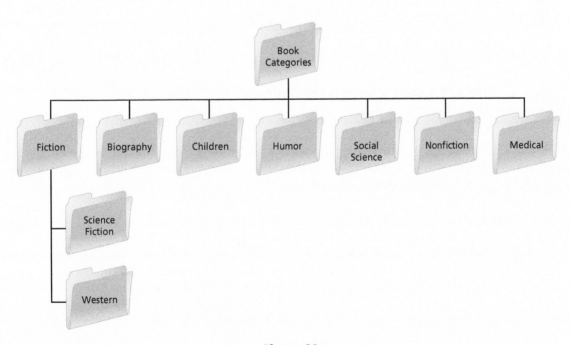

Figure 99

Continued >

In the Labs *continued*

7. Submit the assignment in the format specified by your instructor.

8. ✹ Think about how you use your computer for various tasks (personal, professional, and academic). What folders might be required on your computer to store the files you save?

Lab 2: Creating Publisher Publications and Saving Them in Appropriate Folders

Problem: You are taking a class that requires you to complete three Publisher modules. You will save the work completed in each module in a different folder (Figure 100).

Perform the following tasks:

1. Create the folders shown in Figure 100.

2. Create a Publisher publication containing the text, Module 1 Notes.

3. In the Backstage view, click Save As and then click This PC.

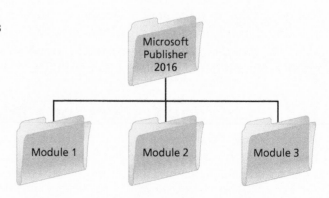

Figure 100

4. Click the Browse button to display the Save As dialog box. Click Documents to open the Documents folder. Navigate to the Module 1 folder and then save the file in the Publisher folder using the file name, Lab 2 Module 1 Notes.

5. Create another publication containing the text, Module 2 Notes, and then save it in the Module 2 folder using the file name, Lab 2 Module 2 Notes.

6. Create a third publication containing the text, Module 3 Notes, and then save it in the Module 3 folder using the file name, Lab 2 Module 3 Notes.

7. If requested by your instructor, add your name to each of the three Publisher publications.

8. Submit the assignment in the format specified by your instructor.

9. ✹ Based on your current knowledge of Windows and Publisher, how will you organize folders for assignments in this class? Why?

Lab 3: Consider This: Your Turn

Performing Research about Malware

Problem: You have just installed a new computer with the Windows 10 operating system. Because you want to be sure that it is protected from the threat of malware, you decide to research malware, malware protection, and removing malware.

Perform the following tasks:

Part 1:   Research the following three topics: malware, malware protection, and removing malware. Use the concepts and techniques presented in this module to use the search box to find information regarding these topics. Create a publication that contains steps to safeguard a computer properly from malware, ways to prevent malware, as well as different ways to remove malware or a virus should your computer become infected. Submit your assignment in the format specified by your instructor.

Part 2:   ✹ You made several decisions while searching for this assignment. What decisions did you make? What was the rationale behind these decisions? How did you locate the required information about malware?

1 Creating a Flyer

Objectives

You will have mastered the material in this module when you can:

- Choose Publisher template options
- Describe the Publisher window
- Select objects and zoom
- Replace Publisher placeholder and default text
- Delete objects
- Check spelling as you type
- Format text and autofit

- Use graphics
- Insert a photo
- Move, align, and resize objects
- Print a publication
- Open and modify a publication
- Create a hyperlink
- Save a print publication as a web publication

Introduction

To publicize an event, advertise a sale or service, promote a business, or convey a message to the community, you may want to create a flyer and post it in a public location. A **flyer** is a single-page publication, which may be printed on various sizes of paper, announcing personal items for sale or rent (car, boat, apartment); garage or block sales; services being offered (housecleaning, lessons, carpooling); membership, sponsorship, or charity events (religious organization, club); and other messages. Flyers are an inexpensive means of reaching the community, yet many go unnoticed because they are designed poorly. A good flyer, or any publication, must deliver a message in the clearest, most attractive and effective way possible. You must clarify your purpose and know your target audience. You need to gather ideas and plan for the printing. Finally, you must edit, proofread, and then publish your flyer. Flyers must stand out to be noticed.

Flyers also can be posted on the web. Electronic bulletin boards, social networking sites, and online auction websites are good places to reach people with flyers, advertising everything from a bake sale to a part-time job.

To illustrate the features of Publisher, this book presents a series of projects that create publications similar to those you will encounter in academic and business environments.

Project — 5K Flyer

The project in this module uses Publisher and a template to create the flyer shown in Figure 1–1. This attractive flyer advertises a local 5K walk/run for charity. The date of the event appears in the upper-right corner. The title runs across the center and clearly identifies the purpose of the flyer, using large, bold letters. Below the title, to maintain consistency, the same font is used for the description of the event. The shoe graphic is placed to be eye-catching; it entices people to stop and look at the flyer. The QR code graphic allows mobile devices to access the event's webpage quickly. The tear-offs, aligned at the bottom of the flyer, include the phone number for more information. Finally, the font and color schemes support the topic and make the text stand out.

The following roadmap identifies general activities you will perform as you progress through this module:

1. CUSTOMIZE the TEMPLATE options such as choice, color scheme, and font scheme.
2. NAVIGATE the interface and SELECT objects.
3. REPLACE placeholder TEXT.
4. DELETE OBJECTS you do not plan to use in the publication, if any.
5. FORMAT the TEXT in the flyer.
6. INSERT GRAPHICS in placeholders and in other locations, as necessary.
7. ENHANCE the PAGE by repositioning and aligning objects.
8. After saving, OPEN and REVISE the publication.

Creating a Flyer

Publisher provides many ways to begin the process of creating and editing a publication. You can:

- Create a new publication from a template.
- Create a new publication from scratch.
- Create a new publication based on an existing one.
- Open an existing publication.

Choosing the appropriate method depends on your experience with desktop publishing and on how you have used Publisher in the past.

Templates

Because many people find that composing and designing from scratch is a difficult process, Publisher provides templates to assist in publication preparation. Publisher has hundreds of templates to create professionally designed and unique publications. A **template** is a tool that helps you through the design process by offering you publication options — changing your publication accordingly — and preset objects placed in an attractive layout. A template is similar to a blueprint you can use over and over, filling in the blanks, replacing prewritten text as necessary, and changing the art to fit your needs.

For an introduction to Windows and instruction about how to perform basic Windows tasks, read the Office and Windows module at the beginning of this book, where you can learn how to resize windows, change screen resolution, create folders, move and rename files, use Windows Help, and much more.

BTW
Featured Template Gallery
You may have to wait a few minutes for Publisher to populate the FEATURED template gallery, because Microsoft updates the gallery every day.

BTW
Templates
Choose a template that suits the purpose of the publication, with headline and graphic placement that attracts your audience. Choose a style that complements the topic.

April 8, 2017

5K Family Walk/Run for Children's Hospital

Friends of Children's Hospital

Support **Children's Hospital** by bringing your family out for the 5K Family Walk/Run on April 8. Check-in begins at 7:00 a.m. Race begins at 8:30 a.m. Register by phone or on the web at 5Kwalkrun.org. The first 50 people to register online receive a <u>free T-shirt</u>.

Call: (214) 555-1306

For more information, call:
(214) 555-1306

For more information, call:
(214) 555-1306

For more information, call:
(214) 555-1306

For more information, call:
(214) 555-1306

For more information, call:
(214) 555-1306

For more information, call:
(214) 555-1306

For more information, call:
(214) 555-1306

For more information, call:
(214) 555-1306

For more information, call:
(214) 555-1306

For more information, call:
(214) 555-1306

For more information, call:
(214) 555-1306

Figure 1–1

Publisher provides two kinds of templates. **Featured templates** (shown in Figure 1–2) are downloaded from Office.com and customized for specific situations. **Built-in templates** are more generic and require no downloading. In this first project, as you begin to learn about the features of Publisher, a series of steps is presented to create a publication using a built-in template.

To Run Publisher and View Built-In Templates

1 CUSTOMIZE TEMPLATES | 2 NAVIGATE & SELECT | 3 REPLACE TEXT | 4 DELETE OBJECTS
5 FORMAT TEXT | 6 INSERT GRAPHICS | 7 ENHANCE PAGE | 8 OPEN & REVISE

The following steps run Publisher and view the built-in templates.

1

- Run Publisher. If the Publisher window is not maximized, click the Maximize button on its title bar to maximize the window (Figure 1–2).

Q&A Why does my list of templates look different?
It may be that someone has downloaded additional templates on your system. Or, the resolution on your screen may be different. Thus, the size and number of displayed templates may vary.

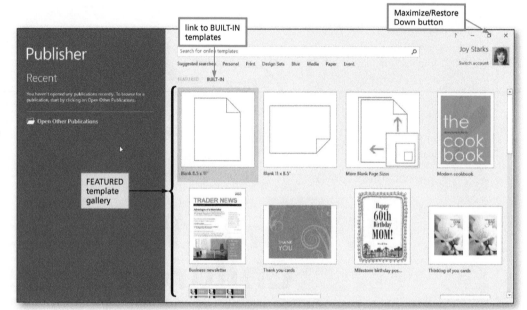

Figure 1–2

2

- In the Publisher start screen, click BUILT-IN to display the built-in templates (Figure 1–3).

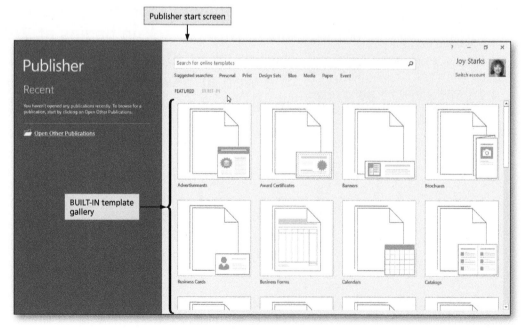

Figure 1–3

Creating a Flyer **Publisher Module 1** **PUB** 5

1 CUSTOMIZE TEMPLATES | **2 NAVIGATE & SELECT** | **3 REPLACE TEXT** | **4 DELETE OBJECTS**
5 FORMAT TEXT | **6 INSERT GRAPHICS** | **7 ENHANCE PAGE** | **8 OPEN & REVISE**

Publisher Module 1

To Select a Built-In Template

Built-in templates are organized by publication type (for example, Flyers); within publication type, they are organized by purpose or category (for example, Marketing) and then alphabetically by design type. Publisher groups additional templates into folders. Once you select a built-in template, Publisher displays the **template information pane** on the right with a larger preview of the selected template, along with some customization options.

The following steps select an event flyer template. *Why?* *An event flyer template contains many of the objects needed to create the desired flyer.*

①

• If necessary, scroll down to display the desired publication type (in this case, Flyers) (Figure 1–4).

🔍 **Experiment**

• Scroll through the available template types.

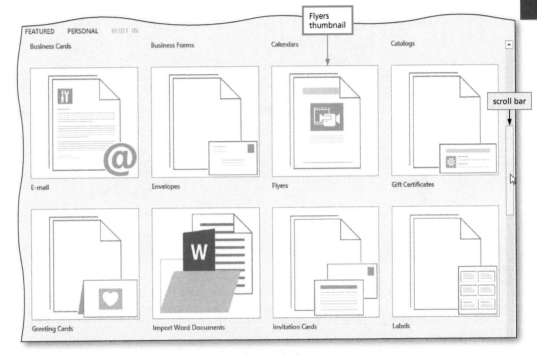

Figure 1–4

②

• Click the Flyers thumbnail to display the Flyer templates and folders of additional templates (Figure 1–5).

Q&A Can I go back and choose a different category of templates?
Yes, you can click the Back button in the upper-left corner of the template gallery, or you can click Home or Flyers in the navigation trail to move back to those previous locations.

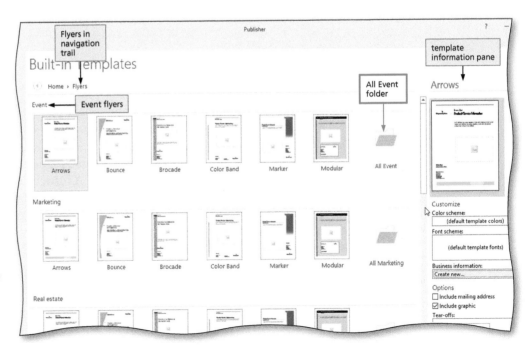

Figure 1–5

3

- Click the All Event folder to open it.

- Scroll down to display the Informational templates in the More Installed Templates area.

- Click the Capsules thumbnail to select it (Figure 1–6).

Q&A
Could I use a different template?
You could, but it does not have the same features as the template used in this module.

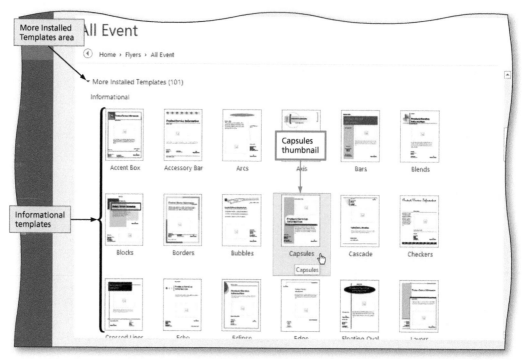

Figure 1–6

CONSIDER THIS

Does it make any difference which color scheme and font scheme you use?
Yes. The choice of an appropriate template, font, and color scheme is determined by the flyer's purpose and intended audience. For example, in this 5K Flyer about a walk/run, the Sagebrush color scheme helps connect the audience with the outdoor nature of the event. The Online font scheme uses a Verdana Bold font for the heading. Verdana Bold is a sans serif font, meaning it has no flourishes on individual letters and is suitable for print publications.

BTW
Font Schemes
Choose a font scheme that gives your flyer a consistent, professional appearance and that characterizes your subject. Make intentional decisions about the font style and type. Avoid common reading fonts such as Arial, Times New Roman, and Helvetica that are used in other kinds of print publications. Flyers are more effective with stronger or unusual font schemes.

Customizing Templates

Once you choose a template, you should make choices about the color scheme, font scheme, and other components of the publication. A **color scheme** is a defined set of colors that complement each other when used in the same publication. Each Publisher color scheme provides four complementary colors. A **font scheme** is a defined set of fonts associated with a publication. A **font**, or typeface, defines the appearance and shape of the letters, numbers, and special characters. A font scheme contains one font for headings and another font for body text and captions. Font schemes make it easy to change all the fonts in a publication to give it a new look. Other customization options allow you to choose to include business information, a mailing address, a graphic, or tear-offs.

Creating a Flyer **Publisher Module 1** **PUB** 7

Publisher Module 1

1 CUSTOMIZE TEMPLATES | 2 NAVIGATE & SELECT | 3 REPLACE TEXT | 4 DELETE OBJECTS
5 FORMAT TEXT | 6 INSERT GRAPHICS | 7 ENHANCE PAGE | 8 OPEN & REVISE

To Choose Publication Options

The following steps choose customization options for the template. *Why? You typically will want to customize a template with an appropriate font and color scheme, determined by the flyer's purpose and intended audience.*

1

• Click the Color scheme button in the Customize area to display the Color scheme gallery (Figure 1–7).

Q&A What are the individual colors used for in each scheme?

By default, the text will be black and the background will be white in each color scheme. Publisher uses the first and second scheme colors for major color accents within a publication. The third and fourth colors are used for shading and secondary accents.

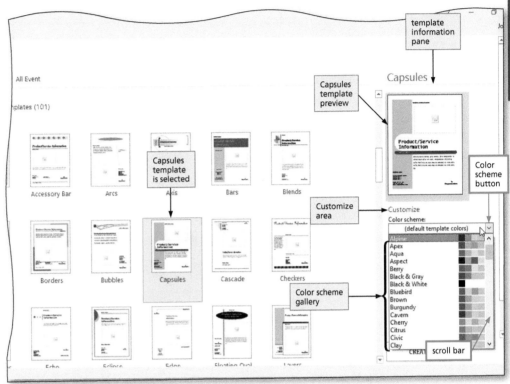

Figure 1–7

2

• Scroll as necessary and then click Sagebrush in the Color scheme gallery to select it (Figure 1–8).

Experiment

• Click various color schemes and watch the changes in all of the thumbnails. When you finish experimenting, click Sagebrush in the Color scheme gallery.

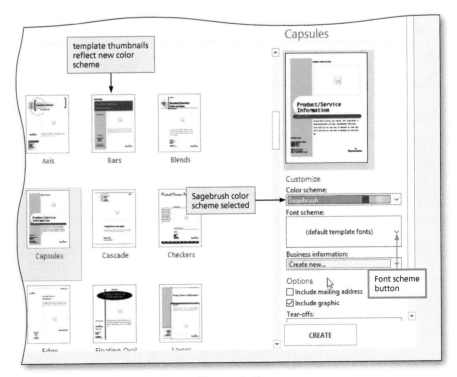

Figure 1–8

3

- Click the Font scheme button in the Customize area to display the Font scheme gallery (Figure 1–9).

Q&A How are the font schemes organized?
The font schemes are organized alphabetically by the generic name of the scheme that appears above the major font in the list.

Experiment

- Click various font schemes and watch the changes in all of the thumbnails.

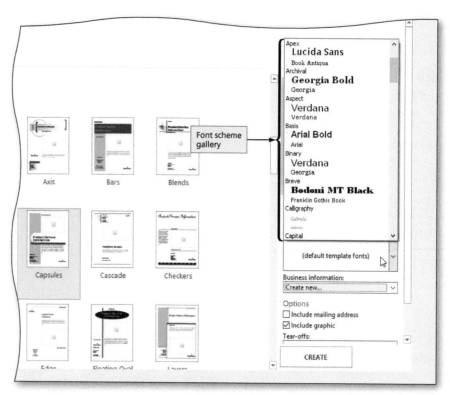

Figure 1–9

4

- Scroll as necessary and then click the Online font scheme in the Font scheme gallery to select it.

- If necessary, scroll to display the Options area of the template information pane (Figure 1–10).

Q&A What are the three items listed in each scheme?
The first line is the generic name of the scheme. Below that, both a major font and a minor font are specified. Generally, a major font is used for titles and headings, and a minor font is used for body text. In the Online font scheme, for example, Online is the generic name of the scheme, Verdana Bold is the major font, and Verdana is the minor font.

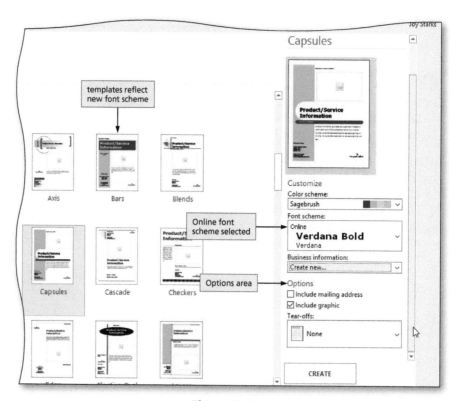

Figure 1–10

5

- Click the Tear-offs button in the Options area to display the Tear-offs gallery (Figure 1–11).

 What are the other kinds of tear-offs?

You can choose to display tear-offs for coupons, order forms, response forms, and sign-up forms.

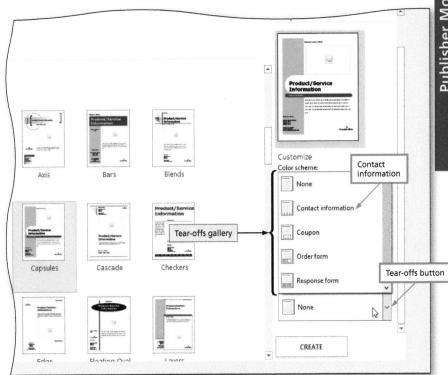

Figure 1–11

6

- Click Contact information in the Tear-offs gallery to select tear-offs that will display contact information (Figure 1–12).

Q&A Should I change the check boxes?

No, the flyer you create in this module uses the default value of no mailing address, but includes a graphic.

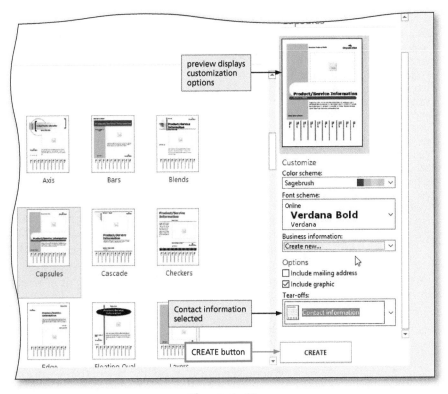

Figure 1–12

• Click the CREATE button to create the publication using the selected template and options (Figure 1–13).

Q&A

How can I go back if I change my mind?
You can click File on the ribbon and start a new publication, or you can make changes to the template, font scheme, color scheme, and other options using the ribbon, as you will see in this and subsequent modules.

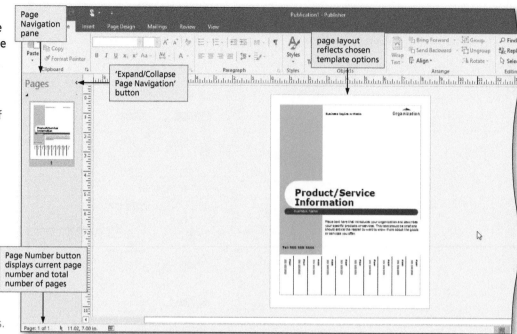

Figure 1–13

BTW

Publisher Help
At any time while using Publisher, you can find answers to questions and display information about various topics through Publisher Help. Used properly, this form of assistance can increase your productivity and reduce your frustrations by minimizing the time you spend learning how to use Publisher. For instruction about Publisher Help and exercises that will help you gain confidence in using it, read the Office and Windows module at the beginning of this book.

The Publisher Window

The Publisher window consists of a variety of components to make your work more efficient and your publications more professional. The following sections discuss these components.

The Workspace

The **workspace** contains several elements similar to the document windows of other applications, as well as some elements unique to Publisher. In Publisher, as you create a publication, the page layout, rulers, scroll bars, guides, the Page Navigation pane, and the status bar are displayed in the workspace (Figure 1–14). Objects can be placed on the page layout or in the gray scratch area.

Page Layout   The **page layout** contains a view of the publication page, all the objects contained therein, plus the guides and boundaries for the page and its objects. The page layout can be changed to accommodate multipage spreads. You also can use the Special Paper command to view your page layout as it will appear when printed on special paper or see the final copy after preparing your publication for a printing service.

Rulers   Two rulers outline the workspace at the top and left. A **ruler** is used to measure and place objects on the page. Although the vertical and horizontal rulers are displayed at the left and top of the workspace, they can be moved and placed anywhere you need them. You use the rulers to measure and align objects on the page, set tab stops, adjust text frames, and change margins. Additionally, the rulers can be hidden to show more of the workspace. You will learn more about rulers in a later module.

BTW

Boundaries
If you want to see all object boundaries, click the Boundaries check box (View tab | Show group).

Objects   The elements you want to place in your publication are called **objects**, which include text, WordArt, tear-offs, graphics, pictures, bookmarks, bullets, lines, and web tools.

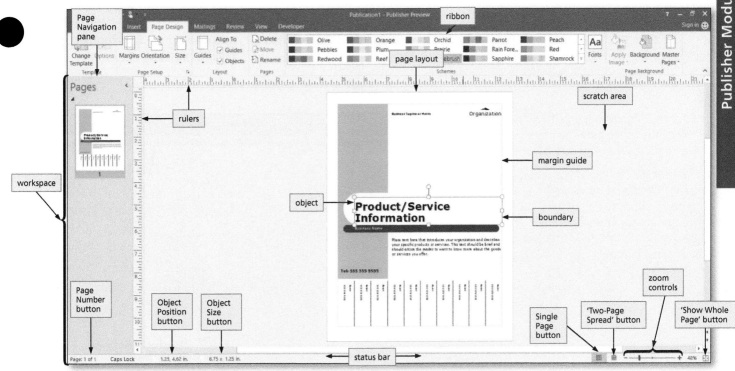

Figure 1–14

Guides and Boundaries Publisher's page layout displays guides and boundaries of the page and selected objects. A **boundary** is the gray, dotted line surrounding an object. Boundaries are useful when you want to move or resize objects on the page. Boundaries and guides can be turned on and off using the View tab. They do not display on printed copies. **Margin guides** automatically are displayed in blue at all four margins. Other guides include grid guides, which you can turn on to help organize objects in rows and columns, pink visual layout guides that display as you move objects, and baseline guides that help you align text horizontally across text boxes.

Status Bar As you learned in the Office and Windows module, the Publisher status bar contains buttons and controls you can use to view the position and size of objects, change the view of a publication, and adjust the size of the displayed publication.

The **Page Number button** allows you to show or hide the Page Navigation button, and also displays the current page and number of pages in the publication. A Caps Lock notification will appear next to the Page Number button in the status bar when the Caps Lock button is engaged on the keyboard. The **Object Position button** and **Object Size button** serve as guidelines for lining up objects from the left and top margins. The exact position and size of a selected object is displayed in inches as you create or move it. You may choose to have the measurement displayed in pixels, picas, points, or centimeters. If no object is selected, the Object Position button displays the location of the pointer. Clicking either button will display the Measurements toolbar. You will learn more about the Measurements toolbar in a later module.

The right side of the status bar includes the Single Page, 'Two-Page Spread', and 'Show Whole Page' buttons, as well as the zoom controls. If you right-click the status bar, you can choose which controls to display.

Page Navigation Pane The Page Navigation pane displays all of the current pages in the publication as thumbnails in a panel on the left side of the workspace. Clicking a thumbnail displays that page in the workspace.

BTW

Screen Resolution
If you are using a computer or mobile device to step through the project in this module and you want your screens to match the figures in this book, you should change your screen's resolution to 1366 × 768. For information about how to change a computer's resolution, refer to the Office and Windows module at the beginning of this book.

BTW

The Ribbon and Screen Resolution
Publisher may change how the groups and buttons within the groups appear on the ribbon, depending on the computer or mobile device's screen resolution. Thus, your ribbon may look different from the ones in this book if you are using a screen resolution other than 1366 × 768.

To Hide the Page Navigation Pane

Because the flyer contains only one page, you will hide the Page Navigation pane using the Page Number button on the status bar. *Why? Hiding the pane gives you more room on the screen for viewing and editing the flyer.* The following step hides the Page Navigation pane.

1

• Click the Page Number button on the status bar to hide the Page Navigation pane (Figure 1–15).

Q&A I do not see the Page Navigation pane. What did I do wrong?
It may be that someone has hidden the Page Navigation pane already. The Page Number button opens and closes the Page Navigation pane. Click it again.

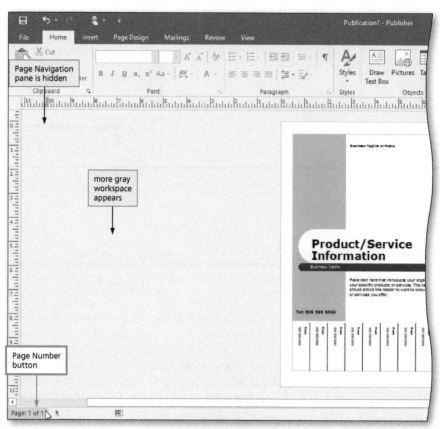

Figure 1–15

Other Ways

1. Click Page Navigation check box (View tab | Show group)

TO COLLAPSE AND EXPAND THE PAGE NAVIGATION PANE

An alternative to hiding the Page Navigation pane is to collapse or minimize it. If you wanted to collapse the Page Navigation pane, you would perform the following steps.

1. If the Page Navigation pane is not open, click the Page Number button on the status bar to display the Page Navigation pane.

2. Click the 'Collapse Page Navigation Pane' button in the upper-right corner of the pane.

3. If you want to expand a collapsed Page Navigation pane, click the 'Expand Page Navigation Pane' button in the upper-right corner of the pane.

BTW
Selecting
If your screen normally displays dark letters on a light background, which is the default setting in Publisher, then selected text displays as light letters on a dark background.

Selecting Objects and Zooming

Pointing to an object in Publisher causes the object to display its boundary, helping you to determine the edges and general shape of the object. When you **select** an object by clicking it, the object appears surrounded by a solid **selection rectangle**, which has small squares and circles, called **handles**, at each corner and middle location. Many objects also display a **rotation handle** connected to the top of the object or a yellow **adjustment handle** diamond used to change the shape of some objects. A selected object can be resized, rotated, moved, deleted, or grouped with other objects.

Objects such as photos, clip art, and shapes are easy to select. You simply click them. With other objects such as text boxes, logos, and placeholders, you first must point to them — to display their boundaries — and then click the boundary. Selecting text does not necessarily select the text box object that holds the text; rather, it may select the text itself. Clicking the boundary is the best way to select a text box object.

To Select

1 CUSTOMIZE TEMPLATES | 2 NAVIGATE & SELECT | 3 REPLACE TEXT | 4 DELETE OBJECTS
5 FORMAT TEXT | 6 INSERT GRAPHICS | 7 ENHANCE PAGE | 8 OPEN & REVISE

The following step selects the box that surrounds the title in the flyer. *Why? Before you can edit an object, you first must select it.*

1

• Point near the desired object or click the boundary of the desired object (in this case, the title text box) to select the object rather than the text (Figure 1–16).

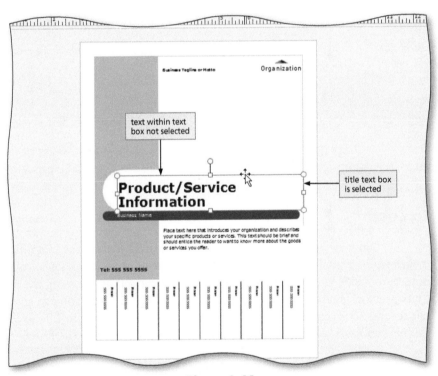

Figure 1–16

Other Ways

1. With no object selected, press TAB key until desired object is selected

Zooming

Once selected, the size of the object might be small and, therefore, difficult to edit. Publisher provides several ways to **zoom**, or change the magnification of an object, to facilitate viewing and editing.

Table 1–1 shows several zoom methods.

Table 1–1 Zoom Methods

Tool	Method	Result
Function key	To zoom in on an object, press the F9 key on the keyboard, press the F9 key again to return to the previous magnification.	Selected object appears centered in the workspace at 100% magnification.
Keyboard shortcut	To zoom to page width, press CTRL+SHIFT+L.	Page layout is magnified as large as possible in the workspace.
Mouse wheel	To change the magnification, press and hold the CTRL key and then move the mouse wheel down or up.	Page layout appears 20% smaller or larger.
Page Width button	To zoom to page width, click the Page Width button (View tab | Zoom group).	Page layout expands to fill the workspace horizontally.
Ribbon	To use the ribbon, click the View tab. In the Zoom group, click the desired button.	Page layout appears at selected magnification.
Selected Objects button	To zoom to objects, click the Selected Objects button (View tab | Zoom group).	Selected object is magnified as large as possible to fit on the screen.
Shortcut menu	To zoom in on an object, right-click the object, point to Zoom on the shortcut menu, click the desired magnification.	Object appears at selected magnification.
'Show Whole Page' button	To zoom to whole page, click the 'Show Whole Page' button on the status bar.	Page layout is magnified as large as possible in the workspace.
Whole Page button	To zoom to whole page, click the Whole Page button (View tab | Zoom group).	Page layout is magnified as large as possible in the workspace.
Zoom box	To change the magnification, enter a magnification percentage in the Zoom box (View tab | Zoom group).	Page layout appears at entered magnification.
Zoom arrow	To change the magnification, click Zoom arrow (View tab | Zoom group) and then click desired magnification.	Page layout appears at selected magnification.
Zoom Out button Zoom In button	To increment or decrement magnification, click the Zoom Out or Zoom In button on the status bar.	Page layout appears 10% smaller or larger with each click.
Zoom slider	To change the magnification of the entire page, drag the Zoom slider on the status bar.	Objects appear at selected magnification.
100% button	To zoom to page width, click the 100% button (View tab | Zoom group).	Page layout is magnified to 100%.

To Zoom

1 CUSTOMIZE TEMPLATES | 2 NAVIGATE & SELECT | 3 REPLACE TEXT | 4 DELETE OBJECTS
5 FORMAT TEXT | 6 INSERT GRAPHICS | 7 ENHANCE PAGE | 8 OPEN & REVISE

When viewing an entire printed page, 8½ × 11 inches, the magnification is approximately 48%, which makes reading small text difficult. If your keyboard has function keys, you can press the F9 key to enlarge selected objects to 100% and center them in the Publisher window. Pressing the F9 key a second time returns the layout to its previous magnification. If you are using touch gestures, you can stretch to zoom in. Alternately, Publisher has several zoom controls on the status bar and on the View tab. The following step zooms in on the title. *Why?* *Editing small areas of text is easier if you use zooming techniques to enlarge the view of the publication.*

1

- Press the F9 key to zoom the selected object to approximately 100% (Figure 1–17).

 What is the best way to zoom? It really is your personal preference. The Zoom controls on the status bar allow you to change the magnification percentage in 10% increments. The Zoom group on the View tab contains some preset sizes as well as custom size text boxes.

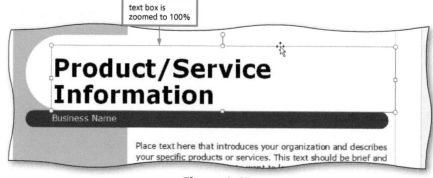

Figure 1–17

Other Ways

1. Click Zoom arrow (View tab | Zoom group), click desired magnification
2. Click Selected Objects button (View tab | Zoom group)
3. Right-click object, point to Zoom on shortcut menu, click desired magnification on Zoom menu
4. Drag Zoom slider on status bar
5. Click Zoom In button or Zoom Out button on status bar

Selecting and Entering Text

The first step in editing a publication template is to replace its text by typing on the keyboard. You may have to scroll and zoom in the page layout to make careful edits. In a later section of this module, you will learn how to format, or change the appearance of, the entered text.

Text Boxes

Most of Publisher's templates come with text already inserted into text boxes. A **text box** is an object in a publication designed to hold text in a specific shape, size, and style. Text boxes also can be drawn on the page using the 'Draw a Text Box' button (Home tab | Objects group). Text boxes can be formatted using the ribbon, the mini toolbar, or the shortcut menu. A text box has changeable properties. A **property** is an attribute or characteristic of an object. Within text boxes, you can **edit**, or make changes to, many properties such as font, spacing, alignment, line/border style, fill color, and margins, among others.

As you type, if you make a mistake you can backspace or use the DELETE key as you do in word processing. You also can **undo** typing by clicking the Undo button on the Quick Access Toolbar or by pressing CTRL+Z.

When you create a new text box, it is empty, ready for you to type. In the templates, however, Publisher insert two types of text in template text boxes. As you will see in the next steps, placeholder text and default text are selected differently, and used for different purposes.

BTW
Selected Objects Button
When you click the Selected Objects button (View tab | Zoom group), the selected object is magnified to fill the window, even if that is more than 100 percent.

BTW
Organizing Files and Folders
You should organize and store files in folders so that you easily can find the files later. For example, if you are taking an introductory technology class called CIS 101, a good practice would be to save all Publisher files in a Publisher folder in a CIS 101 folder. For a discussion of folders and detailed examples of creating folders, refer to the Office and Windows module at the beginning of this book.

To Replace Placeholder Text

1 CUSTOMIZE TEMPLATES | 2 NAVIGATE & SELECT | 3 REPLACE TEXT | **4 DELETE OBJECTS**

5 FORMAT TEXT | 6 INSERT GRAPHICS | 7 ENHANCE PAGE | 8 OPEN & REVISE

You select **placeholder text**, such as that in the flyer title, with a single click. *Why? Clicking once to select text allows you to begin typing immediately without having to select the text or press the DELETE key.*

The following steps select and replace placeholder text.

1
- Click the title text to select it (Figure 1–18).

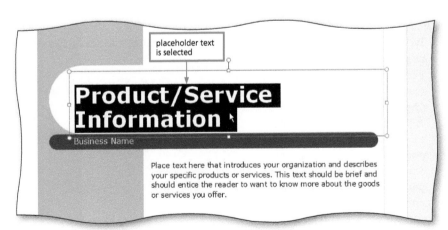

placeholder text is selected

Product/Service Information

Business Name

Place text here that introduces your organization and describes your specific products or services. This text should be brief and should entice the reader to want to know more about the goods or services you offer.

Figure 1–18

2

- Type 5K Family Walk/Run
for Children's Hospital
(Figure 1–19).

Q&A | What if I make an error while
typing?
Common word processing
techniques work in Publisher text
boxes. For example, you can press
the BACKSPACE key until you have
deleted the text in error and then
retype the text correctly.

Figure 1–19

3

- Below the Business Name box,
click the text in the description
text box to select the placeholder
text (Figure 1–20).

Q&A | Am I skipping the Business Name
text box?
The text in the Business Name text
box is not selected with a single
click. You will edit that text later
in the module.

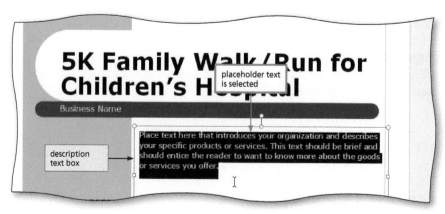

Figure 1–20

4

- Type Support Children's
Hospital by bringing your
family out for the 5K
Family Walk/Run on April 8.
Check-in begins at
7:00 a.m. Race begins
at 8:30 a.m. Register by
phone or on the web at
5kwalkrun.org. The first 50
people to register online
receive a free T-shirt. to
complete the text (Figure 1–21).

Figure 1–21

5

- On the left side of the flyer, click the text in the phone number text box to select the placeholder text.

- Type `Call: (214) 555-1306` to replace the text (Figure 1–22).

Figure 1–22

1 CUSTOMIZE TEMPLATES | 2 NAVIGATE & SELECT | 3 REPLACE TEXT | **4 DELETE OBJECTS**
5 FORMAT TEXT | 6 INSERT GRAPHICS | 7 ENHANCE PAGE | 8 OPEN & REVISE

To Replace Default Text

In the following steps, you replace the **default text**, or preset text, in other template text boxes. Text, such as the business name, address, or tag line, is selected by dragging through the text, double-clicking specific words, or by pressing CTRL+A to select all of the text in the text box. Then, you simply type to replace the text. *Why?* *Default text is different from placeholder text that is selected with a single click.* In a future module, you will learn that default text also may be edited by changing the business information set.

1

- Click the text in the Business Name text box to position the insertion point inside the text box (Figure 1–23).

Q&A What is the button that displays the letter, i?
It is the smart tag button. If you click it, Publisher offers to fill in the text for you with various options. **Smart tag buttons** appear when you point to certain text boxes that are part of the business information set or when you click a logo.

My business name is different. Did I do something wrong?
No. Someone may have changed the business name during installation. You will replace it in the next steps.

Figure 1–23

2

- Drag through the text in the Business Name text box to select all of the text in the text box (Figure 1–24).

Q&A Could I press CTRL+A?
Yes, as long as the insertion point is positioned inside the text box, CTRL+A will select all of the text in the text box.

Figure 1–24

- Type `Friends of Children's Hospital` to complete the text (Figure 1–25).

Should I press the DELETE key before typing?
It is not necessary to press the DELETE key; the text you type deletes the selected text automatically.

Figure 1–25

Other Ways

1. Select text box, click Select button (Home tab | Editing group), click 'Select All Text in Text Box', type new text

2. Position insertion point in text box, press CTRL+A, type new text

---

1 CUSTOMIZE TEMPLATES | 2 NAVIGATE & SELECT | 3 REPLACE TEXT | **4 DELETE OBJECTS**
5 FORMAT TEXT | 6 INSERT GRAPHICS | 7 ENHANCE PAGE | 8 OPEN & REVISE

To Deselect an Object

For various reasons, you may want to deselect or remove the selection from an object. For example, when a Publisher object is selected, scrolling is limited. **Why?** *Publisher assumes you would not want to scroll past the end of the object.* The following step deselects the object by clicking outside of its boundaries.

- Click outside of the selected object (in this case, the text box) to deselect it (Figure 1–26).

Exactly where should I click?
As long as you do not select another object, anywhere in the workspace is fine. You may want to click just to the left of the selection rectangle or in the scratch area.

Figure 1–26

Other Ways

1. Press ESC

Tear-Offs

Across the lower portion of the flyer are contact information tear-offs. **Tear-offs** are small, ready-to-be scored text boxes with some combination of name, phone number, fax, email, or address information. Designed for customer use, tear-offs typically are perforated so that a person walking by can tear off a tab to keep, rather than having to stop, find a pen and paper, and write down the name and phone number. Traditionally, small businesses or individuals wanting to advertise something locally used tear-offs, but more recently, large companies are mass-producing advertising flyers with tear-offs to post at shopping centers, display in offices, and advertise on college campuses.

Publisher tear-offs contain placeholder text and are **synchronized**, which means when you finish editing one of the tear-off text boxes, the others change to match it automatically.

1 CUSTOMIZE TEMPLATES | 2 NAVIGATE & SELECT | 3 REPLACE TEXT | **4 DELETE OBJECTS**
5 FORMAT TEXT | 6 INSERT GRAPHICS | 7 ENHANCE PAGE | 8 OPEN & REVISE

To Enter Tear-Off Text

The following steps edit the tear-off text boxes. **Why?** *The tear-offs must contain information to contact the flyer's creator or to request more information.*

- Scroll to display the lower portion of the flyer.
- Click the text in one of the tear-off text boxes to select it (Figure 1–27).

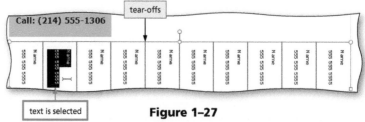

Figure 1–27

2

- Type `For more information, call:` and then press the ENTER key.

- Type `(214) 555-1306` to complete the tear-off text (Figure 1–28).

- If requested by your instructor, enter your phone number instead of (214) 555-1306 in the tear-off.

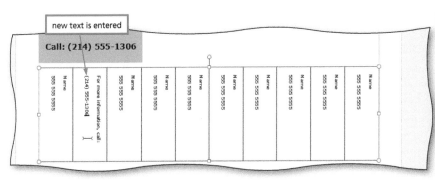

Figure 1–28

3

- Click outside of the text box to synchronize the other tear-offs (Figure 1–29).

Q&A What if I want to make each tear-off different?

Typically, all of the tear-offs are the same, but you can undo synchronization by clicking the Undo button on the Quick Access Toolbar and then entering the text for other tear-offs.

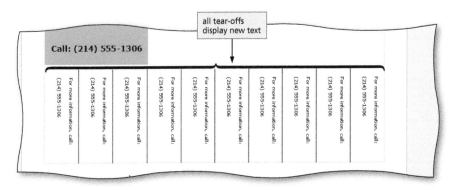

Figure 1–29

Deleting Objects

Templates may display objects in the page layout that you do not wish to use. In those cases, or when you change your mind about including an inserted object, you must delete objects.

To Delete Objects

1 CUSTOMIZE TEMPLATES | 2 NAVIGATE & SELECT | 3 REPLACE TEXT | 4 DELETE OBJECTS
5 FORMAT TEXT | 6 INSERT GRAPHICS | 7 ENHANCE PAGE | 8 OPEN & REVISE

In order to delete an object, it must be selected. In the following steps, you delete the organization logo. **Why?** *The logo is not used in this flyer.*

1

- Scroll to the top of the flyer to display the organization logo. Click the Zoom In button on the status bar several times to increase the magnification.

- Point to the logo to display the boundary and then click the boundary to select the object. Avoid clicking the text in the logo (Figure 1–30).

Q&A What if I want to delete just part of the logo?

The template logo is a small picture and the word, Organization, grouped together. To delete one or the other, select the logo first, and then click only the part of the object you wish to delete. Press the DELETE key to delete that part of the grouped object.

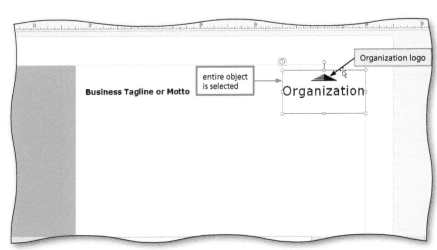

Figure 1–30

2

- Press the DELETE key to delete the selected object (Figure 1–31).

Q&A

Why did only the text disappear?
You may have selected the text or the boundary of the text box instead of the boundary of the entire logo. Select the remaining object and then press the DELETE key.

What if I delete an object accidentally?
Press CTRL+Z to undo the most recent step, or click the Undo button on the Quick Access Toolbar. The object will reappear in the original location.

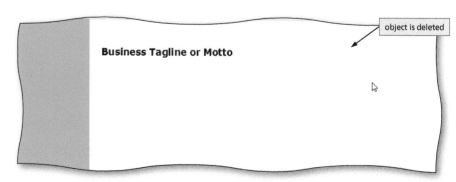

Business Tagline or Motto

object is deleted

Figure 1–31

Other Ways

1. Right-click object, click Delete Object on shortcut menu   2. Select object, press BACKSPACE

TO DELETE A TEXT BOX

If you wanted to delete a text box, you would follow these steps.

1. Point to the text box until the dotted border is displayed and the pointer changes to a double two-headed arrow.
2. Click the border to select the text box rather than the text.
3. Press the DELETE key to delete the text box.

Checking the Spelling

As you type text in a publication, Publisher checks your typing for possible spelling errors. Publisher **flags** any potential error in the publication window with a red wavy underline. A red wavy underline means the flagged text is not in Publisher's dictionary (because it is a proper name, a slang term, or misspelled). Although you can check the entire publication for spelling errors at once, you also can check these flagged errors as they appear on the screen.

To display a list of corrections for flagged text, right-click the flagged text. Publisher displays a list of suggested spelling corrections on the shortcut menu. A flagged word, however, is not necessarily misspelled. For example, many names, abbreviations, and specialized terms are not in Publisher's main dictionary. In these cases, you instruct Publisher to ignore the flagged word. As you type, Publisher also detects duplicate words while checking for spelling errors. For example, if your publication contains the phrase, to the the store, Publisher places a red wavy underline below the second occurrence of the word, the.

BTW
Automatic Spelling Correction
As you type, Publisher automatically corrects some misspelled words. For example, if you type, recieve, Publisher automatically corrects the misspelling and displays the word, receive, when you press the SPACEBAR or type a punctuation mark.

BTW
Automatically Corrected Words
To see a complete list of automatically corrected words, click File on the ribbon to open the Backstage view, click the Options tab in the Backstage view, click Proofing in the left pane (Publisher Options dialog box), click the AutoCorrect Options button, and then scroll through the list near the bottom of the dialog box.

To Check Spelling as You Type

1 CUSTOMIZE TEMPLATES | 2 NAVIGATE & SELECT | 3 REPLACE TEXT | 4 DELETE OBJECTS
5 FORMAT TEXT | 6 INSERT GRAPHICS | 7 ENHANCE PAGE | 8 OPEN & REVISE

In the following steps, the word, April, is misspelled intentionally as Aprl to illustrate Publisher's check spelling as you type feature. If you are doing this project on a computer, your flyer may contain different misspelled words. **Why?** *You may have made spelling or typographical errors, if your typing was not accurate.*

1

- Click the text in the 'Business Tagline or Motto' text box to position the insertion point inside the text box.

- Drag through the text or press CTRL+A to select all of the text in the text box (Figure 1–32).

Q&A Why does my template list a different business name?

The person who installed Microsoft Office on your computer or network may have set or customized the field.

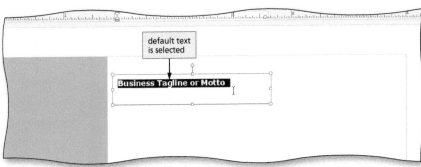

Figure 1–32

2

- Type Aprl 8, 2017, misspelling the word, April, so that a red wavy underline appears (Figure 1–33).

Q&A What if Publisher does not flag my spelling errors with wavy underlines?

To verify that the check spelling as you type features are enabled, click File on the ribbon to open the Backstage view and then click the Options tab. Click Proofing in the left pane and then ensure that the 'Check spelling as you type' check box contains a check mark. Also, ensure the 'Hide spelling and grammar errors' check box does not have a check mark.

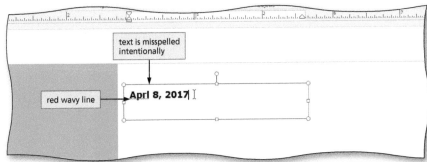

Figure 1–33

3

- Right-click the flagged word (Aprl, in this case) to display a shortcut menu that presents a list of suggested spelling corrections for the flagged word (Figure 1–34).

Q&A What if, when I right-click the misspelled word, my desired correction is not in the list on the shortcut menu?

You can click outside the shortcut menu to close the shortcut menu and then retype the correct word.

What toolbar was displayed when I selected the text?

Recall from the Office and Windows module that the mini toolbar appears automatically and contains commands related to changing the appearance of text in a publication. If you do not use the mini toolbar, it disappears from the screen.

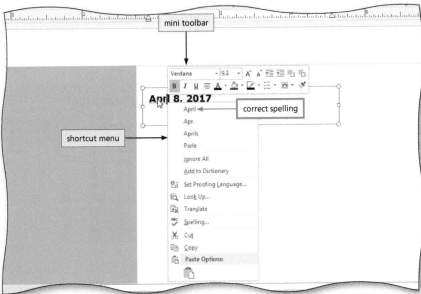

Figure 1–34

● Click the correct spelling (in this case, April) on the shortcut menu to replace the misspelled word with a correctly spelled word (Figure 1–35).

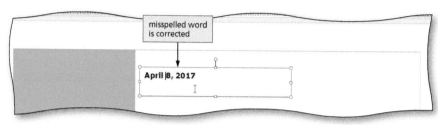

Q&A What if a flagged word actually is a proper name and spelled correctly?

Right-click the word, and then click Ignore All on the shortcut menu to instruct Publisher not to flag future occurrences of the same word in this publication.

Figure 1–35

● Save the publication on your hard drive, OneDrive, or other storage location using the file name, 5K Flyer.

Q&A Why should I save the publication at this time?

You have performed many tasks while creating this publication and do not want to risk losing work completed thus far.

Break Point: If you wish to take a break, this is a good place to do so. Exit Publisher. To resume at a later time, run Publisher, open the file named 5K Flyer, and continue following the steps from this location forward.

Formatting Text

Although you can format text before you type, many Publisher users enter text first and then format the existing text. Publisher provides many ways to modify the appearance, or **format**, of selected text. Some formatting options include editing the font, paragraph, alignment, typography, copy fitting, and text effects. The more common formatting commands are shown in the Font group on the Home tab on the ribbon (Figure 1–36) or on the Text Box Tools Format tab. Many of these formatting tools also appear on a mini toolbar when you point to text. These include the capability to change the font size, color, style, and effects. You will learn more about each of the formatting options in the Font group as you use them.

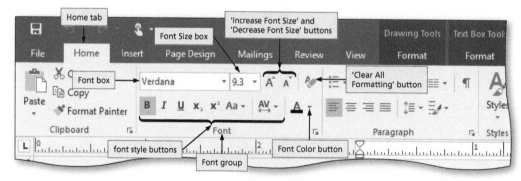

Figure 1–36

A third way to format text involves using the shortcut menu, which appears when you right-click an object, or when you press SHIFT+F10. The shortcut menu is a list of frequently used commands that relate to the selected object. If you right-click some items, Publisher displays both the mini toolbar and a shortcut menu.

Fonts

Characters that appear on the screen are a specific shape and size, determined by the template you choose or the settings you apply. Recall that the font, or typeface, defines the appearance and shape of the letters, numbers, and special characters. The name of the font appears in the Font box (Home tab | Font group). You can leave characters in the default font or change them to a different font. **Font size** specifies the size of the characters and is determined by a measurement system called points. A single **point** is about 1/72 of one inch in height. Thus, a character with a font size of 12 is about 12/72 or 1/6 of one inch in height. You can increase or decrease the font size of characters in a publication, as well as change the capitalization.

In addition to the common bold, italic, and underline formatting options, Publisher also allows you to apply special text effects and highlights.

Formatting Single versus Multiple Characters and Words

To format a single character, the character must be selected. To format a word, however, you simply can position the insertion point in the word, to make it the current word, and then format the word. You will learn in a later module that paragraph formatting, such as alignment and bullets, also can be applied without first selecting it; however, if you want to format multiple characters or words, you first must select the words you want to format and then format the selection.

To Bold Text

1 CUSTOMIZE TEMPLATES | 2 NAVIGATE & SELECT | 3 REPLACE TEXT | 4 DELETE OBJECTS
5 FORMAT TEXT | 6 INSERT GRAPHICS | 7 ENHANCE PAGE | 8 OPEN & REVISE

Bold characters appear somewhat thicker and darker than those that are not bold. To format the name of the hospital, you first will select the text. **Why?** *Multiple words must be selected in order to apply formatting.* The following step adds bold formatting to the name of the hospital.

1

- Click Home on the ribbon to display the Home tab.
- In the publication, scroll to the description text box and then drag through the text you wish to format (in this case, Children's Hospital) to select it.
- With the text selected, click the Bold button (Home tab | Font group) to bold the selected text (Figure 1–37).

Q&A How would I remove a bold format?
You would click the Bold button a second time, or you immediately could click the Undo button on the Quick Access Toolbar, or press CTRL+Z.

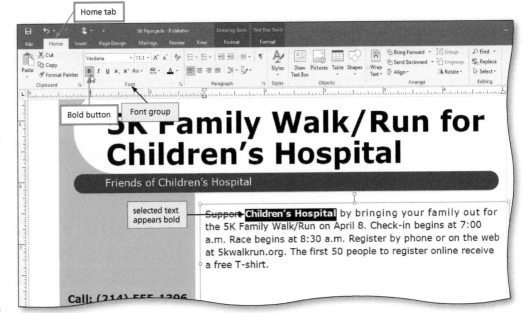

Figure 1–37

Other Ways

1. Click Font Dialog Box Launcher (Home tab | Font group), click Bold in Font style list (Font dialog box), click OK button
2. Click Bold button on mini toolbar
3. Right-click text, point to Change Text on shortcut menu, click Font, click Bold in Font style list (Font dialog box), click OK button
4. Press CTRL+B

To Underline Text

Underlines are used to emphasize or draw attention to specific text. **Underlined** text prints with an underscore (_) below each character including spaces. *Why? Underlining the spaces between words provides continuity.* The following step selects the text, free T-shirt, and formats it with an underline.

- Drag through the text, free T-shirt, to select it.

- With the text selected, click the Underline button (Home tab | Font group) to underline the selected text (Figure 1–38).

Q&A How can I tell what formatting has been applied to text?
The selected buttons and boxes on the Home tab show formatting characteristics of the location of the insertion point.

Figure 1–38

Other Ways

1. Click Font Dialog Box Launcher (Home tab | Font group), click Underline in Font style list (Font dialog box), click OK button
2. Click Underline button on mini toolbar
3. Right-click text, point to Change Text on shortcut menu, click Font, click Underline in Font Style list (Font dialog box), click OK button
4. Press CTRL+U

To Italicize Text

Italic text has a slanted appearance. The following step formats the phone number in italics. *Why? The italicized text draws attention and makes the text stand out.*

- Select the text in the phone number text box.
- With the text selected, click the Italic button (Home tab | Font group) to italicize the selected text (Figure 1–39).

Q&A Why is the Bold button enabled?
The Capsules template displayed the phone number in bold. You are adding italics to the formatting.

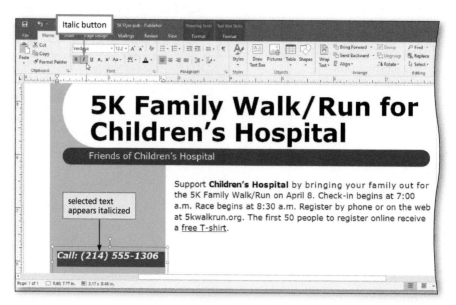

Figure 1–39

Other Ways

1. Click Font Dialog Box Launcher (Home tab | Font group), click Italic in Font style list (Font dialog box), click OK button
2. Click Italic button on mini toolbar
3. Right-click text, point to Change Text on shortcut menu, click Font on Change Text submenu, click Italic in Font Style list (Font dialog box), click OK button
4. Press CTRL+I

Autofitting Text

Other advanced text formatting commands are located on the Text Box Tools Format tab that is displayed when a text box is selected. You can autofit text, change the text direction, and hyphenate, as well as make changes to the alignment, styles, and typography.

Sometimes, the replacement text that you enter into a template does not fit the same way as the original template text — you might have too much text to fit, or too little text to fill the box. In those cases, you may want **autofit**, or **copy fit**, the text to adjust the way the text fits into the text box. Publisher autofitting choices are listed in Table 1–2.

BTW
Print Publications
When creating a print publication, you must consider paper type, color options, number of copies, and the plan for publishing. Does the publication have to be in print to reach the target audience? How will readers find the printed publication? Keep the limitations of printed material in mind when deciding what to include in the layout.

Table 1–2   Types of Autofitting

Type of Autofitting	Result
Best Fit	Shrinks or expands text to fit in the text box, even when the text box is resized
Shrink Text On Overflow	Reduces the point size of text until no text is in overflow
Grow Text Box to Fit	Enlarges text box to fit all of the text at its current size
Do Not Autofit	Text appears at its original size

To Autofit Text

1 CUSTOMIZE TEMPLATES | 2 NAVIGATE & SELECT | 3 REPLACE TEXT | 4 DELETE OBJECTS
5 FORMAT TEXT | **6 INSERT GRAPHICS** | **7 ENHANCE PAGE** | **8 OPEN & REVISE**

The following steps autofit the text in the description text box. **Why?** *You want the text to appear as large as possible.*

1
- Click the description text and then click Text Box Tools Format on the ribbon to display the Text Box Tools Format tab.

- Click the Text Fit button (Text Box Tools Format tab | Text group) to display the Text Fit menu (Figure 1–40).

Q&A Do I have to select all of the text in a text box in order to autofit it?
No. Because all of the text in the text box is included automatically in autofitting, you do not need to select the text in order to autofit it.

Figure 1–40

2

- Click Best Fit on the Text Fit menu to autofit the text in the text box (Figure 1–41).

Q&A
Could I use the 'Increase Font Size' button to make the title larger? Yes, but you would have to estimate how big to make the text, and future editing might be displayed incorrectly. Autofitting is different from using the 'Increase Font Size' button. With autofitting, the text and any future text is increased or decreased to fit the given size of the text box automatically.

Figure 1–41

Other Ways

1. Right-click text, click Best Fit on shortcut menu

To Increase the Font Size

1 CUSTOMIZE TEMPLATES | 2 NAVIGATE & SELECT | 3 REPLACE TEXT | 4 DELETE OBJECTS
5 FORMAT TEXT | 6 INSERT GRAPHICS | 7 ENHANCE PAGE | 8 OPEN & REVISE

The following step uses the 'Increase Font Size' button to enlarge the date text to make it easier to read. *Why? The organization wants to be sure viewers know about the event.* If no text is selected, the current word will be increased.

1

- Scroll as necessary to display the text in the date text box.

- Click the text and then press CTRL+A to select all of the text in the text box.

- Click the 'Increase Font Size' button (Home tab | Font group) several times until the text fills the text box without wrapping to a second line, to approximately a font size of 24. If the line wraps, click the 'Decrease Font Size' button (Home tab | Font group) one time (Figure 1–42).

Q&A
Do I have to select the text first? If no text is selected, only the current word will be increased when you click the 'Increase Font Size' button.

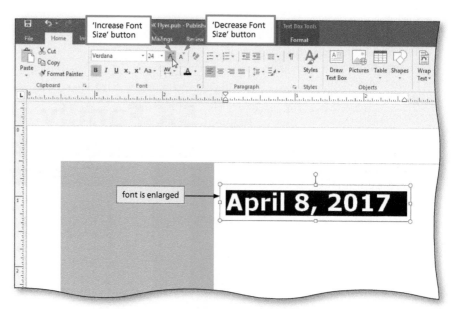

Figure 1–42

Other Ways

1. Select text, click Font Size arrow (Home tab | Font group), click larger font size   2. Press CTRL+>

Using Graphics

Files containing graphical images, also called **graphics**, are available from a variety of sources. For example, a **clip** is a single media file, such as art, sound, or animation that you can insert and use in print publications, web publications, and other Microsoft Office documents. You also can insert pictures stored on your computer or storage location or search for pictures on the web. You will learn about other kinds of graphics in future modules.

Many templates have picture placeholders that provide a size and shape to hold selected pictures. A **picture placeholder** has boundaries called the picture frame and a picture icon that is displayed only when you point to it. You can click the picture icon in a template to access the Insert Pictures dialog box; Publisher offers you three choices to locate a picture or graphic: from a file, from an online search, or from your OneDrive account, if you are signed in. In this module, you will insert a picture from a file. In a future module, you will use the online search. You also can insert an empty picture placeholder to reserve space for pictures you want to add later.

BTW
Using Graphics
When you insert a graphic, Publisher automatically displays the Picture Tools Format tab that contains buttons and tools to help you format the picture.

How do you choose appropriate graphics?

If your client or business has not provided you with a graphic, you should look for a graphic that enhances your topic with strong bright colors. Try to coordinate graphic colors and the Publisher color scheme. Perhaps the most important consideration, however, is ownership. Photos and clip art are not always free. Some web clip art galleries might specify royalty-free images for one-time use, but not for commercial use intended to generate profit. For other uses, you must purchase clip art. It is important to read all licensing agreements carefully. The usage of some artwork requires written permission. Copyright laws apply to all images equally — the right of legal use depends on the intended use and conditions of the copyright owner. All images are copyrighted, regardless of whether they are marked as copyrighted.

CONSIDER THIS

To Use the Picture Placeholder

1 CUSTOMIZE TEMPLATES | 2 NAVIGATE & SELECT | 3 REPLACE TEXT | 4 DELETE OBJECTS
5 FORMAT TEXT | 6 INSERT GRAPHICS | **7 ENHANCE PAGE** | 8 OPEN & REVISE

Many templates contain picture placeholders whose size and shape fit in with the template style. *Why? Publications with pictures attract attention and add a sense of realism; most users want pictures in their publications.* The following steps use the picture placeholder to place a photo that is located in the Data Files. Please contact your instructor for information about accessing the Data Files.

1

- Click the area above the title to display the boundary of the picture placeholder and the picture icon (Figure 1–43).

Q&A

I am not using a mouse. Can I make the boundary visible so that I can see it without pointing to it?
Yes. Tap the Boundaries check box (View tab | Show group), which will display the boundaries on all objects.

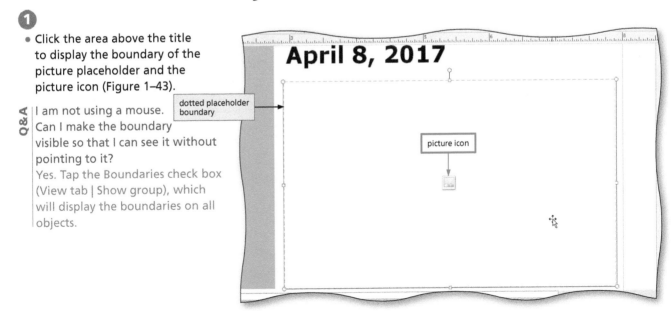

Figure 1–43

2
- Click the picture icon to display the Insert Pictures dialog box (Figure 1–44).

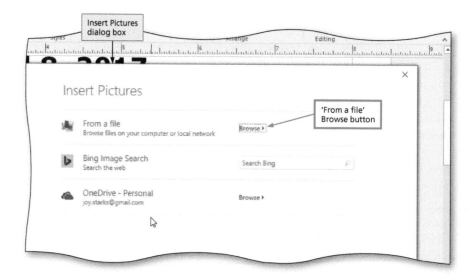

Figure 1–44

3
- Click the 'From a file' Browse button to display the Insert Picture dialog box.
- Navigate to the Data Files and the Module 01 folder. Scroll down in the list, as necessary, to display the file named, Shoes (Figure 1–45).

Q&A If I decide not to add a picture, will the placeholder print?
No. Graphic placeholders do not print. Placeholder text will print, however.

Why is my view different?
The default view for graphic files is to display a medium icon. To change the view, click the More options arrow.

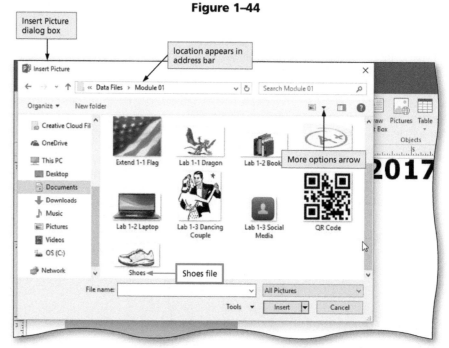

Figure 1–45

4
- Double-click the file named Shoes to insert the chosen picture into the publication (Figure 1–46).

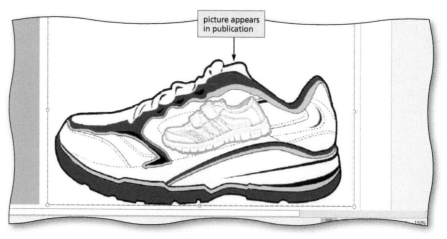

Figure 1–46

To Insert a Picture

You do not have to have a picture placeholder to insert pictures into a publication. *Why? You may want to use a picture as is and not have it conform to the size of the placeholder.* You can insert both online pictures and those from storage, using the Publisher ribbon.

The following steps insert a picture without the use of a picture placeholder. To complete this assignment, you will be required to use the Data Files. Please contact your instructor for information about accessing the Data Files.

1
- Click outside the page layout so that no object is selected.
- Click Insert on the ribbon to display the Insert tab (Figure 1–47).

Figure 1–47

2
- Click the Pictures button (Insert tab | Illustrations group) to display the Insert Picture dialog box.
- Navigate to the location of the Data Files and the Module 01 folder.
- Double-click the desired picture (in this case, the QR Code file) to insert the graphic into the publication (Figure 1–48).

Q&A How did Publisher decide where to place the picture?
Publisher inserts the picture in the middle of the screen, regardless of the magnification or scrolled area. You will resize and move it in the next series of steps.

Figure 1–48

Resizing, Moving, and Aligning Objects

Many times, even when using a template, you will want to enhance the page by resizing objects, moving objects around on the page layout, and aligning them with other objects.

Sometimes pictures and graphics are not the right size. In that case, you need to resize them. To **resize** any object in Publisher, select the object and then drag a handle. Recall that a handle is one of several small shapes displayed around an object when the object is selected. Pressing the CTRL key while dragging (CTRL+drag) keeps the center of the graphic in the same place while resizing. Pressing the SHIFT key while dragging (SHIFT+drag) maintains the graphic's proportions while resizing. Finally, pressing the SHIFT and CTRL keys while dragging (SHIFT+CTRL+drag) maintains the proportions and keeps the center in the same place.

To **move** an object, it must be selected. The pointer changes to a double two-headed arrow, and you then drag the object to the new location or to the scratch area. If you press and hold the SHIFT key while dragging, the object moves in a straight line. Pressing the CTRL key while dragging creates a copy of the object. As you move an object, Publisher displays visual **layout guides** to help you place and align the object to other objects on the page layout. When you **align** an object to another object, its edge or center lines up, either vertically or horizontally. The visual layout guides display as pink lines that move from object to object as you drag. Visual layout guides appear when aligning to the left, right, top, bottom, or middle of objects.

If you want to align the text within a text box rather than aligning the text box itself, Publisher provides four alignment options: Align Right, Center, Align Left, and Justify. Justify aligns text on both the left and right, padding it with extra spaces if necessary. The align tools are on the Home tab, in the Paragraph group. You will learn more about paragraph options in a later module.

To Resize an Object

1 CUSTOMIZE TEMPLATES | 2 NAVIGATE & SELECT | 3 REPLACE TEXT | 4 DELETE OBJECTS
5 FORMAT TEXT | 6 INSERT GRAPHICS | 7 ENHANCE PAGE | **8 OPEN & REVISE**

The next step resizes the QR code to make it smaller. *Why? The QR code eventually will need to fit in a smaller space.*

- Scroll as necessary and then select the object to be resized (in this case, the QR code).
- SHIFT+drag the lower-right sizing handle up and left, until the status bar displays a size of approximately 1.33 by 1.33 inches (Figure 1–49).

Q&A Why do I have to use the SHIFT key?
Using the SHIFT key keeps the QR code proportional in size.

Figure 1–49

Other Ways

1. Enter new width and height on Measurement toolbar	2. Enter new width and height (Drawing Tools Format tab | Size group)	3. Enter new width and height (Picture Tools Format tab | Size group)

To Move a Graphic

The following steps move the QR code from its current centered location to a location to the left of and aligned with the date. *Why? Moving the graphic up gives it a more prominent place in the flyer and aligns it for consistency.*

1

- If necessary, select the graphic (in this case, the QR code).

- Drag the graphic up and to the left side of the flyer, until the pink layout guide appears and is aligned horizontally with the date (Figure 1–50).

Q&A When do the layout guides appear?

As you drag an object, when one of its borders or its center aligns with another object on the page, Publisher displays a pink guide showing you the possible alignment.

Figure 1–50

2

- Release the mouse button, if necessary, to finish moving the object.

Other Ways

1. Select object, press ARROW key

2. Select object, click Object Position button on status bar, enter new *x* and *y* coordinates on Measurement toolbar

To Move a Text Box

The following step moves the date text box and aligns it with the right margin by dragging its border. *Why? If you drag the text inside a text box, you may move the text, rather than the entire text box object.* In the overall design of the flyer, aligning the date on the right provides a tiered effect among central objects to infer movement from right to left in the flyer.

1

- Select the text box you wish to move (in this case, the date text box) by clicking its border.

- SHIFT+drag the text box to move it in a straight line until it aligns with the right margin as noted by the pink vertical layout guide (Figure 1–51).

Q&A Why did Publisher change to the Home tab?

The Publisher ribbon is context-sensitive, which means it senses whether you are working with text, graphics, tables, etc., and displays the appropriate ribbon with the tools you might need.

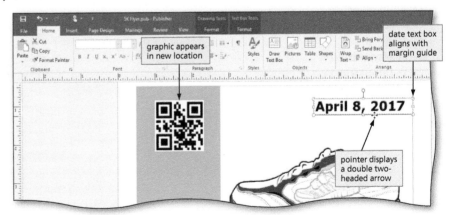

Figure 1–51

Other Ways

1. Select text box border, press ARROW key

2. Select text box, click Object Position button on status bar, enter new *x* and *y* coordinates on Measurement toolbar

To Align Text

The following step right-aligns the text in the title. *Why? Aligning the title text on the right will match the general alignment of the top half of the flyer.*

1

• Click the text in the title.

• Click the Align Right button (Home tab | Paragraph group) to align the text on the right (Figure 1–52).

Q&A Will it align both lines?
Yes, the align buttons are paragraph-based.

Figure 1–52

Other Ways

1. Click Paragraph Spacing button (Home tab | Paragraph group), click 'Paragraph Spacing Options' on Paragraph Spacing menu, click Alignment button (Paragraph dialog box), click Right, click OK button

2. Press CTRL+R

To View Whole Page

The following steps view the entire page layout. *Why? Before you save the publication again, you may want to see how it looks so far.*

1

• Click outside of any selected object to deselect it.

• Click the 'Show Whole Page' button on the status bar to view the entire page (Figure 1–53).

2

• Click the Save button on the Quick Access Toolbar to save the file with the same file name and to overwrite the previously saved file.

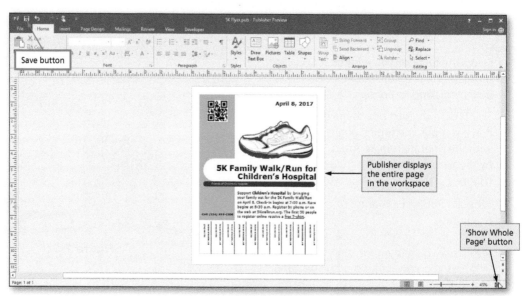

Figure 1–53

Other Ways

1. Click Whole Page button (View tab | Zoom group)

2. Press SHIFT+CTRL+L

CONSIDER THIS

What is the best method for distributing a publication?
The traditional method of distributing a publication uses a printer to produce a hard copy. A **hard copy** or **printout** is information that exists on a physical medium such as paper. Hard copies can be useful for the following reasons:

• Some people prefer proofreading a hard copy of a publication rather than viewing it on the screen to check for errors and readability.

• Hard copies can serve as a backup reference if your storage medium is lost or becomes corrupted and you need to recreate the publication.

Instead of distributing a hard copy of a publication, users can distribute the publication as an electronic image that mirrors the original publication's appearance. The electronic image of the publication can be sent as an email attachment, posted on a website, or copied to a portable storage medium such as a USB flash drive. Two popular electronic image formats, sometimes called fixed formats, are PDF by Adobe Systems and XPS by Microsoft. In Publisher, you can create electronic image files through the Save As dialog box and the Export, Share, and Print tabs in the Backstage view. Electronic images of publications, such as PDF and XPS, can be useful, as users can view electronic images of publications without the software that created the original publication (e.g., Publisher). Specifically, to view a PDF file, you use a program called Adobe Reader, which can be downloaded free from Adobe's website. Similarly, to view an XPS file, you use a program called XPS Viewer, which is included in the latest versions of Windows and Internet Explorer.

Sending electronic publications saves paper and printer supplies. Society encourages users to contribute to **green computing**, which involves reducing the electricity consumed and environmental waste generated when using computers, mobile devices, and related technologies, as well as saving paper.

To Print a Publication

After creating a publication, you may want to print it. Printing a publication enables you to distribute it to others in a form that can be read or viewed, but typically not edited. It is a good practice to save a publication before printing it, in case you experience difficulties printing.

The following steps print a hard copy of the contents of the saved 5K Flyer publication.

1 Click File on the ribbon to open the Backstage view.

2 Click the Print tab in the Backstage view to display the Print gallery.

3 Verify the printer name listed on the Printer Status button will print a hard copy of the publication. If necessary, click the Printer Status button to display a list of available printer options and then click the desired printer to change the currently selected printer.

4 Click the Print button in the Print gallery to print the publication on the currently selected printer.

5 When the printer stops, retrieve the hard copy.

6 Exit Publisher. If a Microsoft Publisher dialog box appears, click the Save button to save any changes made to the publication since the last save.

Break Point: If you wish to take a break, this is a good place to do so. To resume at a later time, continue following the steps from this location forward.

Changing a Publication

After creating a publication, you often will find that you must make changes to it. Changes can be required because the publication contains an error or because of new circumstances. The types of changes made to publications normally fall into one of the three following categories: deletions, additions, or modifications.

BTW

Conserving Ink and Toner
If you want to conserve ink or toner, you can instruct Publisher to print draft quality documents by clicking Print in the Backstage view to display the Print gallery, clicking the Printer Properties link, and then, depending on your printer, click the Print Quality button and choose Draft in the list.

Deletions Sometimes deletions are necessary in a publication because objects are incorrect or no longer are needed. For example, to place this advertising flyer on a website, the tear-offs no longer are needed. In that case, you would delete them from the page layout.

Additions Additional text, objects, or formatting may be required in the publication. For example, in the 5K Flyer you may want to insert a text box that could be displayed when the flyer is published on the web.

Modifications If you make modifications to text or graphics, normal techniques of inserting, deleting, editing, and formatting apply. Publisher provides several methods for detecting problems in a publication and making modifications, including spell checking and design checking.

In the following sections, you will make changes to the flyer to prepare it for publishing to the web.

To Open a Recent Publication

1 CUSTOMIZE TEMPLATES | 2 NAVIGATE & SELECT | 3 REPLACE TEXT | 4 DELETE OBJECTS
5 FORMAT TEXT | 6 INSERT GRAPHICS | 7 ENHANCE PAGE | **8 OPEN & REVISE**

Earlier in this module, you saved your publication using the file name, 5K Flyer. Publisher maintains a list of the last few publications that have been opened or saved on your computer. The **Recent list** allows you to click the name of the publication to open it, without browsing to the location. The following steps run Publisher and open the 5K Flyer file from the Recent Publication list.

1
• Run Publisher (Figure 1–54).

Q&A
My list of recent publications is different. Did I do something wrong?
No, your list will differ depending on what publications you have opened in the past.

The file does not appear in the Recent list. What should I do?
If the file you wish to open does not appear in the Recent list, click 'Open Other Publications' and then navigate to the location of the file to be opened. Double-click the file name to open it.

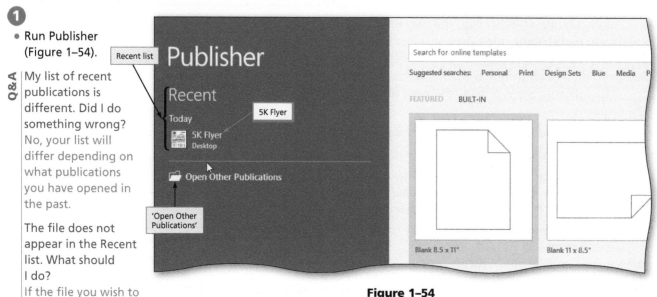

Figure 1–54

2
• In the Recent list, click 5K Flyer to open the publication.

Q&A
Can I change the total number of publications listed in the Recent list?
Yes. In the Backstage view, click the Options tab, click Advanced (Publisher Options dialog box), and then in the Display area, change the number in the 'Show this number of Recent Publications' text box.

To Insert a Hyperlink

A **hyperlink**, or link, is a clickable link or reference to another location. A hyperlink can link to a page on the web, to an email address, to a location on a storage device, or another location within a publication. The following steps create a link to the event website. *Why? This version of the flyer will be seen on the web, where users may want to click to register.*

1

- Select the text you wish to make a hyperlink (in this case, the web address in the description text box) and then zoom to 100% (Figure 1–55).

Figure 1–55

2

- Click Insert on the ribbon to display the Insert tab.

- Click the 'Add a Hyperlink' button (Insert tab | Links group) to display the Insert Hyperlink dialog box.

- If necessary, click the Address text box to position the insertion point and then type **www.5Kwalkrun.org** to enter the web address. Publisher will add the http:// protocol to your web address (Figure 1–56).

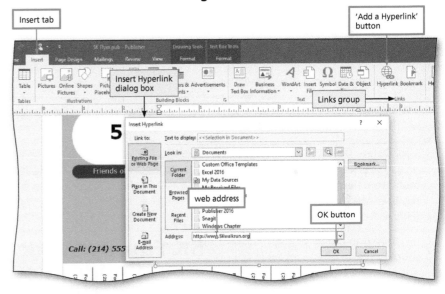

Figure 1–56

3

- Click the OK button (Insert Hyperlink dialog box) to assign the hyperlink (Figure 1–57).

Q&A How can I tell if it is a hyperlink?
Publisher will underline a hyperlink and use a purple or blue font. When a user hovers over a hyperlink, the pointer will appear as a hand.

Figure 1–57

Other Ways

1. Right-click text, click Hyperlink on shortcut menu, enter web address in Address text box (Insert Hyperlink dialog box), click OK button

2. Press CTRL+K, enter web address in Address text box (Insert Hyperlink dialog box), click OK button

To Delete Using a Shortcut Menu

If this flyer is displayed on a website, the tear-offs are unnecessary and should be deleted. The following steps delete the tear-offs using the shortcut menu. *Why? In many cases, executing a command from the shortcut menu is faster because you do not have to move the pointer.*

1

- Scroll to the lower portion of the flyer.

- Right-click any one of the tear-offs to display the shortcut menu (Figure 1–58).

Q&A My shortcut menu is different. Did I do something wrong?
No. Shortcut menus are context-sensitive, so they are displayed slightly different if you click the text versus the border of the text box.

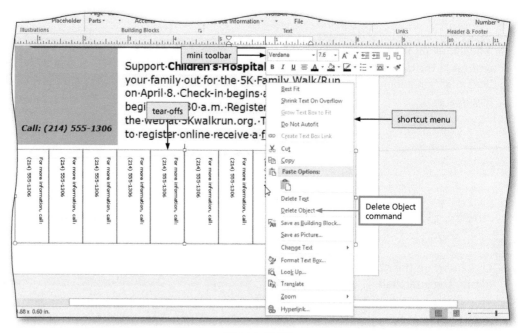

Figure 1–58

2

- Click Delete Object on the shortcut menu to delete the tear-offs (Figure 1–59).

Q&A What do I do if my shortcut menu does not display a Delete Object command?
Click in a slightly different location within the tear-offs.

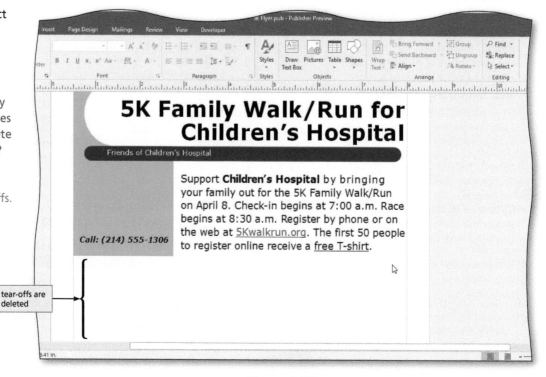

Figure 1–59

Creating a Webpage from a Publication

You can create several types of publications with Microsoft Publisher, other than standard print publications. A **web publication** is one suitable for publishing to the web, containing certain objects, formatting options, hyperlinks, and other features specific to webpages. You can create a web publication from scratch, or you can save the print publication as a web publication. The following sections create a web version of the flyer that might be posted on a campus website or social networking site.

BTW
Web Publications
When converting to a web publication, determine which objects will work effectively on the web and which ones will not, modifying the publication as necessary. Will the publication be accessible on the web? Is the target audience common web users? If so, determine whether an email or website would be the most efficient means of communication.

To Save a Print Publication as a Web Publication

1 CUSTOMIZE TEMPLATES | 2 NAVIGATE & SELECT | 3 REPLACE TEXT | 4 DELETE OBJECTS
5 FORMAT TEXT | 6 INSERT GRAPHICS | 7 ENHANCE PAGE | **8 OPEN & REVISE**

The Export tab in the Backstage view includes a group of commands that allow you to save publications as different file types or to package publications for sending to other users. In the following steps, you will export the publication by publishing it to the web. **Publishing HTML** or **publishing to the web** is the process of making webpages available to others, for example, on the World Wide Web or on a company's intranet.

A **Hypertext Markup Language** (**HTML**) file is a file capable of being stored and transferred electronically on a file server in order to display on the web.

The **Mime Hypertext Markup Language** (**MHTML**) is a small, single-file format that does not create a supporting folder of resources. The following steps save the publication as a web flyer in the MHTML format. *Why? The MHTML file can be published to and downloaded from the web quickly.*

1

- Click File on the ribbon to open the Backstage view.
- Click the Export tab in the Backstage view to display the Export gallery.
- Click the Publish HTML tab to display its options.
- Click the 'Web Page (HTML)' button to display options for publishing HTML (Figure 1–60).

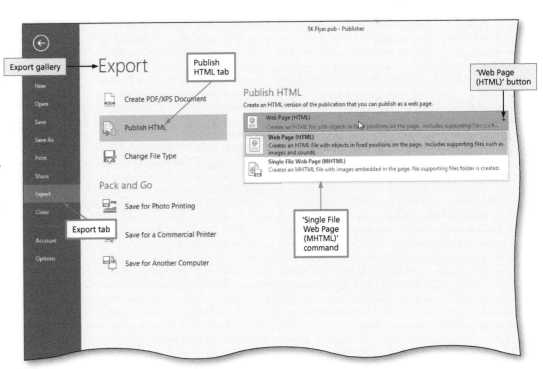

Figure 1–60

2

- Click 'Single File Web Page (MHTML)' to select it.

- Click the Publish HTML button in the Backstage view to display the Save As dialog box.

- Type **5K Web Flyer** in the File name text box (Save As dialog box). Do not press the ENTER key after typing the file name.

- Navigate to your storage location (Figure 1–61).

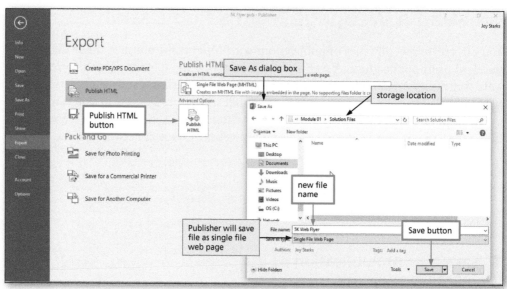

Figure 1–61

How do I move the the dialog box out of the way?

In general, you can move dialog boxes by dragging the title bar. You also can resize them to view different parts of your screen.

3

- Click the Save button (Save As dialog box) to save the publication as a single file web page.

Other Ways

1. Click Save As in Backstage view, click storage location, enter file name, click 'Save as type' button, click 'Single File Web Page (*.mht;*.mhtml)', click Save button (Save As dialog box)

To Preview the Web Publication in a Browser

1 CUSTOMIZE TEMPLATES | 2 NAVIGATE & SELECT | 3 REPLACE TEXT | 4 DELETE OBJECTS
5 FORMAT TEXT | 6 INSERT GRAPHICS | 7 ENHANCE PAGE | **8 OPEN & REVISE**

The following steps preview the web publication. *Why? Previewing is the best way to test the look and feel of the webpage and to test the hyperlink.* You will open the MHTML file from its storage location.

- Click the folder icon on your taskbar to run the File Explorer. When the File Explorer window opens, navigate to your storage location (Figure 1–62).

Figure 1–62

- Double-click the 5K Web Flyer file.

- When the browser window opens, if necessary, maximize the window and scroll to display the hyperlink (Figure 1–63).

Q&A Why does my display look different?
Each brand and version of browser software displays information in a slightly different manner.

Figure 1–63

3

- Click the Close button on the browser window's title bar and then click the Close button on the File Explorer window's title bar.

- Exit Publisher. If a Microsoft Publisher dialog box appears, click the Don't Save button to exit Publisher.

- Sign out of your Microsoft Account if necessary.

Summary

In this module, you learned some basic Publisher techniques as you created a flyer from a template. You learned how to choose a publication template and set font and color schemes. You learned how to enter and edit both placeholder and default text. After creating synchronized tear-offs, you formatted text with bold, underline, and italics. You added a graphic using a picture placeholder and then inserted a picture without a placeholder. You learned how to delete, resize, move, and align objects. After checking the spelling, you saved the file and reopened it for revisions, such as creating a hyperlink and removing tear-offs in the publication. Finally, you saved a print publication as a web publication.

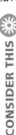

CONSIDER THIS

What decisions will you need to make when creating your next publication?
Use these guidelines as you complete the assignments in this module and create your own publications outside of this class.

1. Select template options.
    a) Select a template that matches your need.
    b) Choose font and color schemes determined by the flyer's purpose and audience.
2. Choose words for the text.
    a) Replace all placeholder and default text.
    b) Add other objects as necessary; delete unused items.
3. Identify how to format various objects in the flyer.
    a) Use bold, underline, and italics for emphasis.
    b) Autofit the text to make the flyer easy to read.
4. Find and insert the appropriate graphic(s).
    a) Resize, move, and align as necessary.
5. Determine whether the flyer will be more effective as a print publication, web publication, or both.
    a) Insert any necessary hyperlinks.
    b) Consider creating a background for a web publication.

Apply Your Knowledge

Reinforce the skills and apply the concepts you learned in this module.

Editing a Flyer with Text and Graphics

Note: To complete this assignment, you will be required to use the Data Files. Please contact your instructor for information about accessing the Data Files.

Instructions: Run Publisher and open the file named Apply 1-1 Sale Flyer from the Data Files. The document contains a flyer to advertise a home for sale that you are to modify. The modified flyer is shown in Figure 1–64.

Perform the following tasks:

1. Select the default text in the Price text box. Type `$239,900` to replace the text.
2. Select the default text in the address text box. Type `1217 81st Terrace` and then press the ENTER key. Type `Gladstone, Indiana 46109` to replace the text.
3. With the insertion point still positioned in the address text box, click the Text Box Tools Format tab. Click the Text Fit button (Text Box Tools Format tab | Text group) and then click Best Fit on the Text Fit menu.
4. Select the default text in the phone number text box. Type `Call: 317-555-6628` to replace the text.

Figure 1–64

5. If instructed to do so, change the phone number in Step 4 to your phone number.

6. Select the default text in the description text box. Type `2500 sq. ft.` and then press the TAB key 3 times. Type `4 bedrooms & 2 baths` and then press the ENTER key.

7. Type `Central air` and then press the TAB key four times. Type `Newly renovated kitchen` and then press the ENTER key.

8. Type `New roof` and then press the TAB key four times. Type `Pool` to complete the description text.

9. Delete the More Information text box.

10. On the right side of the flyer, select the picture placeholder. In the picture placeholder, click the picture icon to display the Insert Pictures dialog box. Browse to the Data Files and the Module 1 folder. Insert the picture called Apply 1-1 Home. Deselect the picture.

11. Click the Pictures button (Insert tab | Illustrations group). Browse to the Data Files and the Module 1 folder. Insert the picture Apply 1-1 Pool. Move the picture to a location below and slightly overlapping the picture of the house, as shown in Figure 1–64.

12. Save the flyer on your storage location with the file name, Apply 1-1 Sale Flyer Complete.

13. Submit the completed publication in the format specified by your instructor, which may involve printing a hard copy.

14. ✺ What would you add or delete if you were to publish this flyer in the MHTML format on the web? Why?

Extend Your Knowledge

Extend the skills you learned in this module and experiment with new skills. You may need to use Help to complete the assignment.

Creating a Flyer from Scratch

Note: To complete this assignment, you will be required to use the Data Files. Please contact your instructor for information about accessing the Data Files.

Instructions: Run Publisher and open a blank 8.5 × 11" template. Use Publisher to create the flyer shown in Figure 1–65 by inserting graphics, drawing text boxes, applying picture styles, and formatting the text.

Perform the following tasks:

1. Click the Pictures button (Insert tab | Illustrations group). Insert the graphic named, Extend 1-1 Decorative Rectangle, which is located in the Data Files. Move it as necessary to approximately the center of the page.

2. Insert a second picture named, Extend 1-1 Blue Rectangle, which is located in the Data Files. Move it to the upper-center as shown in Figure 1–65.

3. Insert a third picture named, Extend 1-1 Flag, which is located in the Data Files. Move it above the blue rectangle as shown in Figure 1–65.

4. Use Help to read about applying picture styles. Use the More button (Picture Tools Format | Picture styles group) to apply a picture style, such as Relaxed Perspective, White, to the flag graphic.

5. Use Help to read about drawing text boxes and then perform the following tasks, zooming as necessary:

   a. Use the 'Draw a Text Box' button (Home tab | Objects group) to create a text box on top of the blue rectangle, filling the area below the flag graphic.

   b. Before typing the text, return to the Home tab. Click the Font Color arrow (Home tab | Font group) and then choose a white color. Type the text, `Register to Vote!` and then autofit it.

Continued >

Extend Your Knowledge *continued*

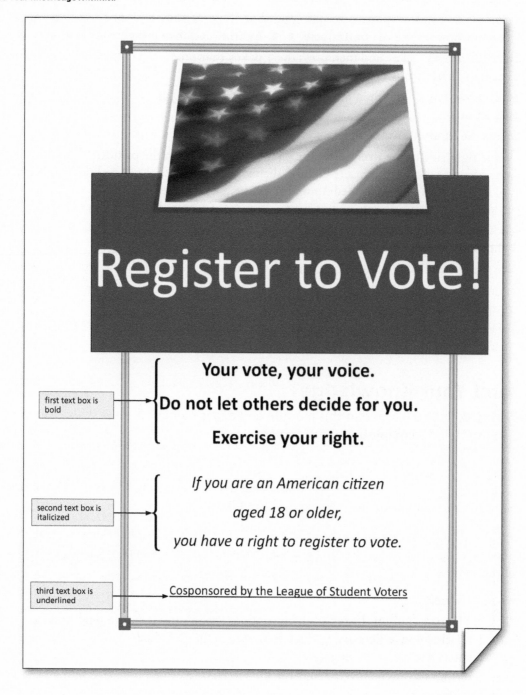

first text box is bold

second text box is italicized

third text box is underlined

Figure 1–65

c. Draw another text box below the first one. Return to the Home tab. Click the Font Color arrow (Home tab | Font group) and then choose a black color. Click the Center button (Home tab | Paragraph group).

d. Click the Bold button (Home tab | Font group) and then type the text shown in Figure 1–65. Use the 'Increase Font Size' button (Home tab | Font group) to change the font size to approximately 24 pt.

e. Repeat Step 5c for the next text box and format the text italic. Increase the font size to approximately 20 pt. Type the text as shown in Figure 1-65. If Publisher automatically capitalizes some letters, fix them as necessary.

f. Repeat Step 5c for the last text box and format the text underlined. Increase the font size to approximately 16 pt. Type the text as shown in Figure 1-65.

g. If requested to do so by your instructor, add the name of your voting location to the flyer.

6. Save the file with the file name, Extend 1-1 Vote Flyer Complete.

7. Submit the file in the format specified by your instructor.

8. ☀ When would you use a template instead of creating a flyer from scratch that contains only the objects you need? Was formatting the font before you typed easier than selecting text and formatting it afterward? Why?

Expand Your World

Create a solution that uses cloud and web technologies by learning and investigating on your own from general guidance.

Modifying and Exporting a Publication

Note: To complete this assignment, you will be required to use the Data Files. Please contact your instructor for information about accessing the Data Files.

Instructions: Run Publisher and open the file Expand 1-1 Spring Break Ad from the Data Files. The file contains a flyer to advertise a spring break trip that you are to modify and post on OneDrive. The modified flyer is shown in Figure 1–66.

Figure 1–66

Continued >

Expand Your World *continued*

Perform the following tasks:

1. Replace the placeholder text, Attention Grabber, with the name of your school. Replace the Date placeholder text with the date of your school's spring break.

2. If requested to do so by your instructor, change the phone number to your phone number.

3. Save the presentation on OneDrive using the file name, Expand 1-1 Spring Break Ad Complete.

4. Submit the assignment in the format specified by your instructor.

5. ✳ On what occasions might you save one of your files for school or your job on OneDrive? Do you think using OneDrive enhances collaboration efforts? Why?

In the Labs

Design, create, modify, and/or use a publication following the guidelines, concepts, and skills presented in this module. Labs 1 and 2, which increase in difficulty, require you to create solutions based on what you learned in the module; Lab 3 requires you to apply your creative thinking and problem-solving skills to design and implement a solution.

Lab 1: **Creating a Multipurpose Flyer**

Note: To complete this assignment, you will be required to use the Data Files. Please contact your instructor for information about accessing the Data Files.

Problem: The Computer Club on campus is sponsoring a video game tournament and would like you to create a flyer for print and web posting. You decide to look through Publisher's templates for an appropriate flyer to use as a starting point. You create the flyer shown in Figure 1–67.

Perform the following tasks:

1. Run Publisher.

2. Click BUILT-IN templates.

3. Click the Flyers thumbnail to display the Flyer templates and folders of additional templates. Click the All Event folder to open it. Scroll down to display the 'More Installed Templates' area and the Special Offer flyers. Click the Blocks thumbnail to select it.

4. Customize the template with the Mountain color scheme and the Etched font scheme. If necessary, in the Options area, click the Tear-offs button and then click None.

5. Click the OK button to create the publication.

6. At the top of the flyer, zoom in to make the following changes:

   a. Select the Business Name text. Type `Computer Club`. Right-click the text box to display the shortcut menu, and then click Best Fit to autofit the text.

   b. If instructed to do so, change the name of the club in Step 6a to the name of a club or group of which you are a member.

   c. Click the border of the 'Business Tagline or Motto' text box to select it. Press the DELETE key to delete the text box.

   d. Select all of the text in the Date text box. Type `October 7, 2017` to replace the text. Autofit the text.

   e. Change the Time text to `Start: 10:00 a.m.` Autofit the text.

   f. Delete the logo.

Figure 1–67

7. Scroll to the center of the flyer and make the following changes.

  a. Click the Promotion Title placeholder text to select it. Type **Dragon Tournament** to replace the text.

  b. Click the description placeholder text to select it. Press the F9 key to zoom to 100%. Type the following text, pressing the ENTER key at the end of each line.

  Dragons: 12-player maximum

  Event Format: League rules

  Cost: Free! You may preregister your spot online for $3.00.

  c. In the same box, type the following text that purposefully has a misspelled word (in this case, acheivements).

  Event Details: Players will be assigned a character. Play in each pod lasts 4 hours. Prizes will be awarded for outstanding acheivements and good play!

  d. Right-click the misspelled word and choose the correct spelling from the list.

Continued >

In the Labs *continued*

    e. Autofit the description text box.

    f. Click the border of the bulleted list text box to select it. Press the DELETE key to delete the text box.

    g. Resize the description text box by selecting it and dragging the center-right handle to the right to fill in the space left by the bulleted list.

8. Scroll to the lower portion of the flyer and make the following changes:

    a. Delete the organization logo.

    b. Click the lower-right area in the flyer to display the boundary of the picture placeholder and the picture icon. Click the picture icon to display the Insert Pictures dialog box. Click the 'From a file' Browse button to display the Insert Picture dialog box. Navigate to the Data Files and the Module 01 folder. Double-click the file named, Lab 1-1 Dragon, to insert the chosen picture into the publication. Deselect the graphic.

    c. Click the Pictures button (Insert tab | Illustrations group) to display the Insert Picture dialog box. Navigate to the location of the Data Files and the Module 01 folder. Double-click the desired picture (in this case, the QR Code file) to insert the file into the publication. Resize the picture to approximately 1.33 × 1.33 inches. Move the QR code to the lower-left corner of the flyer.

9. Save the flyer on your storage location with the file name, Lab 1-1 Tournament Flyer.

10. Print a hardcopy of the flyer.

11. To convert the flyer to a web flyer, perform the following steps.

    a. At the top of the flyer, select the text, Computer Club.

    b. Click the 'Add a Hyperlink' button (Insert tab | Links group) to display the Insert Hyperlink dialog box. If necessary, click the Address text box to position the insertion point, and then type **www.cengagecomputerclub.org** to enter the web address.

    c. Click the OK button (Insert Hyperlink dialog box) to assign the hyperlink.

    d. Delete the QR code.

    e. Click File on the ribbon to open the Backstage view and then click the Export tab to display the Export gallery.

    f. Click Publish HTML to display its options.

    g. Click the 'Web Page (HTML)' button to display options for publishing HTML. Click 'Single File Web Page (MHTML)' to select it.

    h. Click the Publish HTML button to display the Save As dialog box.

    i. Type **Lab 1-1 Web Flyer** in the File name text box. Do not press the ENTER key after typing the file name. Navigate to your storage location. Click the Save button (Save As dialog box) to save the publication as a single file web page.

    j. Preview the web flyer in a browser.

12. Submit the file as directed by your instructor.

13. ✳ As you see QR codes in public places, where are they normally placed on the object? How are they placed differently on products versus advertisements? Why do you think that is true?

Lab 2: **Customizing a Flyer**

Note: To complete this assignment, you will be required to use the Data Files. Please contact your instructor for information about accessing the Data Files.

Problem: Your friend wants to earn some extra money by tutoring. He wants you to create a flyer that he can post on dormitory bulletin boards. You create the flyer shown in Figure 1–68.

Publisher Module 1**PUB**

STUDENT ASSIGNMENTS   Publisher Module 1

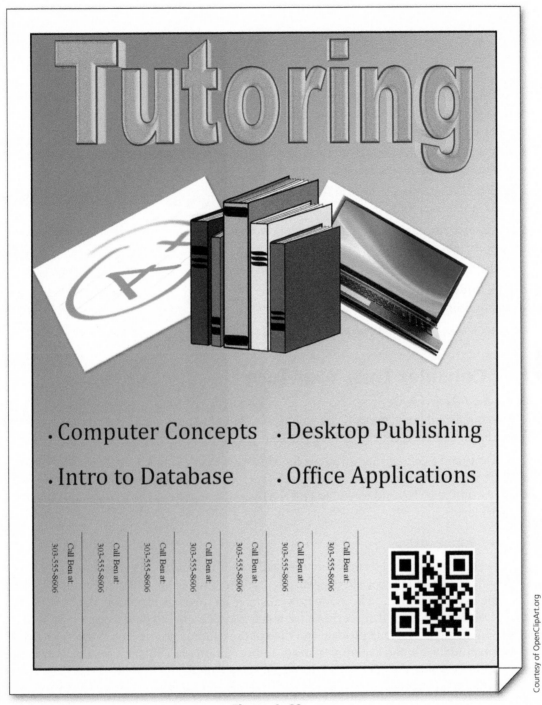

Figure 1–68

Courtesy of OpenClipArt.org

Perform the following tasks:

1. Run Publisher. Open the flyer named Lab 1-2 Tutoring Flyer, which is located in the Data Files.

2. Select the description placeholder text in the bulleted list. Press the F9 key to zoom to 100%. Type the following lines, pressing the ENTER key after each one.

```
Computer Concepts
Intro to Database
Desktop Publishing
Office Applications
```

In the Labs *continued*

3. If instructed to do so, change the four tutoring topics in Step 2 to the name of four classes you have taken.

4. Click a single tear-off. Press CTRL+A to select all of the text in the tear-off. Type `Call Ben at:` and then press the ENTER key. Type `303-555-8606` to complete the tear-off. If requested by your instructor, use your name and phone number in the tear-offs. Click outside the tear-offs to synchronize them.

5. Locate the picture placeholder on the upper-right. Insert the picture named Lab 1-2 Laptop, which is located in the Data Files.

6. Locate the picture placeholder on the left. Insert the picture named Lab 1-2 Grade, which is located in the Data Files.

7. Insert the picture named QR Code, which is located in the Data Files. Resize it and place it in the lower-right corner of the flyer.

8. Save the flyer on your storage location with the file name, Lab 1-2 Tutoring Flyer Complete.

9. Print a hardcopy of the flyer.

10. Submit the file as directed by your instructor.

11. ✳ Which elements would you change if this were a flyer on the web? Why?

Lab 3: **Consider This: Your Turn**

Creating an Advertisement

Note: To complete this assignment, you will be required to use the Data Files. Please contact your instructor for information about accessing the Data Files.

Problem: You attend a college that is famous for its Department of Dance. Students who major in dance are required to complete internships as dance instructors. Because you are a computer technology major, they have asked you to create a flyer that advertises the lessons and includes a social media logo.

Perform the following tasks:

Part 1: Use the concepts and techniques presented in this module to design and create an advertising flyer. Use an appropriate template, font scheme, and color scheme. Replace placeholder text. Include wording such as, "The graduate students from the Department of Dance will teach Ballroom Dancing. No prior dance experience is necessary. Come and have a great time — it is a great date night, guys!!" Include the date and time of the dance lessons. Choose text for a hyperlink and your email address as the hyperlink address. In the picture placeholder, click the picture icon for the template graphic, and insert the Lab 1-3 Dancing Couple file from the Data Files. Insert the Lab 1-3 Social Media logo from the Data Files and use an appropriate text reference. Submit your assignment in the format specified by your instructor.

Part 2: ✳ You made several decisions while determining the appropriate template, schemes, text, and graphics. How did you choose the template? What did you consider when choosing the color and font schemes? How did you decide on graphic placement?

2 Publishing a Trifold Brochure

Objectives

You will have mastered the material in this module when you can:

- Discuss advantages of the brochure medium
- Choose brochure options
- Copy and paste with paste options
- Wordwrap text
- Swap pictures using the scratch area
- Use a picture as a background
- Insert and format a shape
- Use stylistic sets

- Search for online pictures
- Arrange thumbnails
- Edit captions and caption styles
- Check the spelling of the entire publication
- Run the Design Checker
- Choose appropriate printing services, paper, and color libraries
- Package a publication for a printing service

Introduction

Whether you want to advertise a service, an event, or a product, or merely want to inform the public about a current topic of interest, brochures are a popular type of promotional publication. A **brochure**, or pamphlet, usually is a high-quality publication with lots of color and graphics, created for advertising purposes. Businesses that may not be able to reach potential clientele effectively through traditional advertising, such as web, newspapers, and radio, can create a long-lasting advertisement with a well-designed brochure.

Brochures come in all shapes and sizes. Colleges and universities produce brochures about their programs. The travel industry uses brochures to entice tourists. Service industries and manufacturers display their products using this visual, hands-on medium.

Project — Park Brochure

The project in this module shows you how to build the two-page, trifold brochure shown in Figure 2–1. The brochure informs potential visitors about activities at a state park. Each side of the brochure has three panels. Page 1 (Figure 2–1a) contains the front and back panels, as well as the inside fold. Page 2 (Figure 2–1b) contains a three-panel display that, when opened completely, provides the reader with more details about the park and a response form.

On page 1, the front panel contains shapes, text boxes, graphics, and a background designed to draw the reader's attention and inform the reader of the intent of the brochure. The back panel, which displays in the middle of page 1, contains the name of the park, the address, phone and fax numbers, and an email address. The inside fold, on the left, contains a map and information about camping and hiking.

The three inside panels on page 2 contain more information about the park and a form the reader may use to request more information.

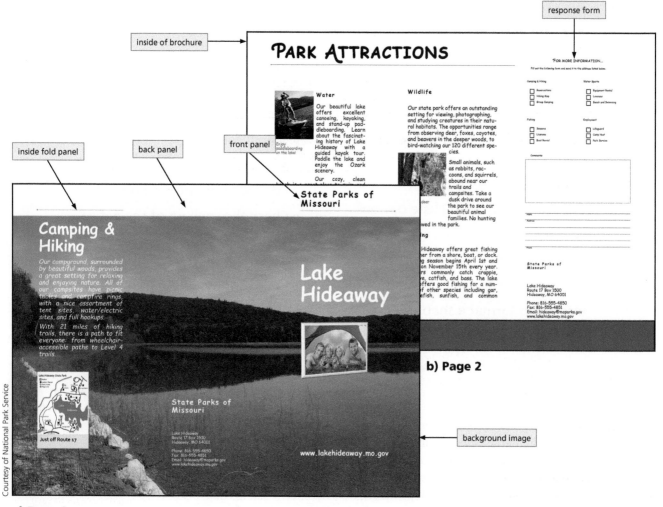

Figure 2–1

The following roadmap identifies general activities you will perform as you progress through this module:

1. CUSTOMIZE the BROCHURE template options such as page size, color scheme, and font scheme.
2. EDIT template TEXT and OBJECTS.
3. SWAP PICTURES and use picture backgrounds.
4. CREATE PICTURE STYLES and SHAPES.
5. USE STYLISTIC SETS to enhance brochure text.
6. SEARCH for ONLINE PICTURES.

7. INSERT CAPTIONS for each photo.

8. CHECK the PUBLICATION for errors.

9. PACK the publication for a printing service.

The Brochure Medium

Professionals commonly print brochures on special paper to provide long-lasting documents and to enhance the graphics. The brochure medium intentionally is tactile; brochures are meant to be touched, carried home, passed along, and looked at, again and again. Newspapers and flyers usually have short-term readership and are printed on paper that readers throw away or recycle. Brochures, on the other hand, frequently use a heavier stock of paper so that they can stand better in a display rack.

How do you decide on the purpose, shelf life, and layout of a brochure?
Spend time brainstorming ideas for the brochure. Think about why you want to create one. Decide on the purpose of the brochure. Is it to inform, sell, attract, or advertise an event? Adjust your template, fonts, colors, and graphics to match that purpose. Brochures commonly have a wider audience than flyers. They need to last longer, so carefully consider whether to add dated material or prices. Create a timeline of effectiveness and plan to have the brochure ready far in advance. Decide how many panels your brochure should be and how often you are going to produce it. If you are working for someone, draw a storyboard and get it approved before you begin. Think about alignment of objects, proximity of similar data, contrast, and repetition.

The content of a brochure needs to last longer, too. On occasion, the intent of a brochure is to educate, such as a brochure on health issues in a doctor's office. More commonly, though, the intent is to market a product or sell a service. Prices and dated materials that are subject to frequent change affect the usable life of a brochure.

Typically, brochures use a great deal of color, and they include actual photos instead of drawings or clip art. Photos give a sense of realism to a publication and show people, places, or objects that are real, whereas images or drawings more appropriately are used to convey concepts or ideas.

Brochures, designed to be in circulation for longer periods as a type of advertising, ordinarily are published in greater quantities and on more expensive paper than other single-page publications, so they can be more costly. The cost, however, is less prohibitive when produced **in-house** using desktop publishing software rather than hiring an outside service. The cost per copy is lower when producing brochures in mass quantities.

Table 2–1 lists some benefits and advantages of using the brochure medium.

BTW
How Brochures Differ
Each brochure template produces two pages of graphics, business information text boxes, and story boxes. Brochures are differentiated by the look and feel of the front panel, the location and style of the shapes and graphics, the design of any panel dividers, and the specific kind of decorations unique to each publication set.

Table 2–1 Benefits and Advantages of Using the Brochure Medium	
Exposure	An attention-getter in displays
	A take-along document encouraging second looks
	A long-lasting publication due to paper and content
	An easily distributed publication — mass mailings, advertising sites
Information	An in-depth look at a product or service
	An opportunity to inform in a nonrestrictive environment
	An opportunity for focused feedback using forms
Audience	Interested clientele and potential customers
Communication	An effective medium to highlight products and services
	A source of free information to build credibility
	An easier method to disseminate information than a magazine

BTW
Gatefolds
A gatefold is a four-panel brochure where both ends fold toward the center. Gatefolds, also called foldouts, commonly are used in advertising, for menus, or as inserts in magazines.

Creating a Trifold Brochure

Publisher-supplied templates use proven design strategies and combinations of objects, which are placed to attract attention and disseminate information effectively. The options for brochures differ from other publications in that they allow you to choose from page sizes, special kinds of forms, and panel/page layout options.

Making Choices about Brochure Options

For the park brochure publication, you will use an informational brochure template, making changes to its color scheme, font scheme, page size, and forms. When choosing a template, **page size** refers to the number of panels in the brochure. **Form options**, which appear on page 2 of the brochure, include an order form, response form, and sign-up form, or no form at all. The **order form** displays fields for the description of items ordered, as well as types of payment information, including blank fields for entering items, quantities, and prices. The **response form** displays check box choices for up to four multiple-choice questions and a comment section. The **sign-up form** displays check box choices, fields for time and price, and payment information. Each form contains blanks for the name and address of prospective customers or clients. A company not only verifies the marketing power of its brochure, it also is able to create a customer database with the information. All three forms are meant to be detached as turnaround documents.

To Select a Brochure Template

1 CUSTOMIZE BROCHURE | 2 EDIT TEXT & OBJECTS | 3 SWAP PICTURES | 4 CREATE PICTURE STYLES & SHAPES
5 USE STYLISTIC SETS | 6 SEARCH ONLINE PICTURES | 7 INSERT CAPTIONS | 8 CHECK PUBLICATION | 9 PACK

The following steps select a brochure template. *Why? You should use a template until you are more experienced in designing brochures.*

- Run Publisher and then click BUILT-IN to display the built-in templates.
- Click Brochures and then click Simple Divider in the Informational area to select the template.
- Click the Color scheme button and then select the Pebbles color scheme.
- Click the Font scheme button and then select the Casual font scheme.
- Click the Page size button in the Options area and then, if necessary, click 3-panel to choose the number of panels. If necessary, click to remove the check mark in the 'Include customer address' check box.
- Scroll down and then click the Form button in the Options area. Click Response form to choose the type of form (Figure 2–2).

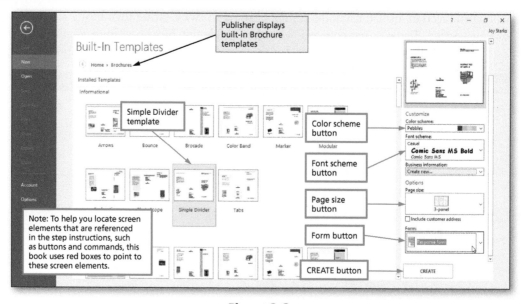

Figure 2–2

2

• Click the CREATE button to create the publication using the selected template and options.

Q&A What if I change my mind about the brochure options? You can choose a different template by using the Change Template button (Page Design tab | Template group) or change the color and fonts schemes using buttons in the Schemes group on the Page Design tab.

3

• Save the publication on your hard drive, OneDrive, or other storage location using the file name, Lake Hideaway Brochure (Figure 2–3).

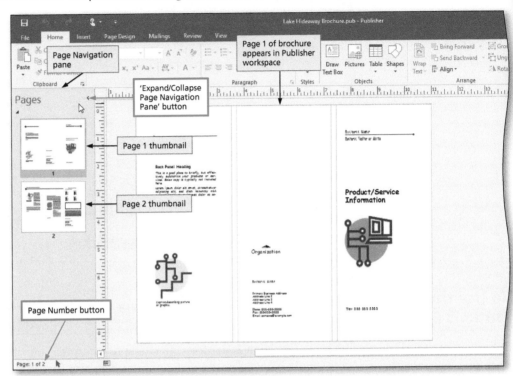

Figure 2–3

To Open and Maximize the Page Navigation Pane

The following step opens the Page Navigation pane to display both pages of the brochure.

1 If the Page Navigation pane is not displayed, click the Page Number button on the status bar to open the Page Navigation pane. If the Page Navigation pane is minimized, click the 'Expand Page Navigation Pane' button to maximize it.

To Edit Objects in the Right Panel

The front of the brochure displays in the right panel of page 1 and contains default text, placeholder text, and some synchronized text boxes. Recall that default text must be selected by dragging or pressing CTRL+A. Placeholder text is selected with a single click. You may want to zoom and scroll to make careful edits. The Business Name text box is a synchronized object that appears in both the right and middle panels. Recall that changing synchronized text in one location will change the text in other locations. The following steps edit objects in the publication's right panel.

1 In the right panel, select the default text, Business Name, by dragging through the text. Use the Zoom In button on the status bar to zoom to approximately 130%.

2 Type `State Parks of` and then press the ENTER key. Type `Missouri` to finish the text.

3 Select the border of the 'Business Tagline or Motto' text box. Delete the text box.

4 Click the Product/Service Information placeholder text to select it. Type `Lake Hideaway` to replace the text (Figure 2–4).

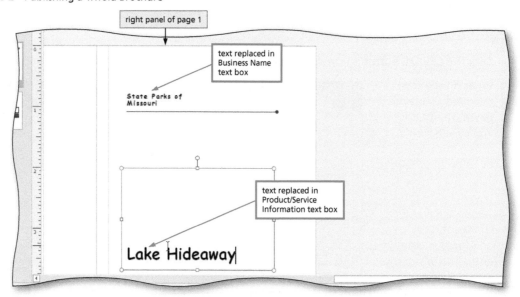

Figure 2–4

To Use the AutoCorrect Options Button

1 CUSTOMIZE BROCHURE | **2 EDIT TEXT & OBJECTS** | **3 SWAP PICTURES** | **4 CREATE PICTURE STYLES & SHAPES**
5 USE STYLISTIC SETS | **6 SEARCH ONLINE PICTURES** | **7 INSERT CAPTIONS** | **8 CHECK PUBLICATION** | **9 PACK**

Sometimes, Publisher changes a word or letter for you, trying to interpret your meaning or to help you with sentence structure and spelling. When you position the pointer near text that Publisher has corrected automatically, a small blue box appears below the text. It is a minimized AutoCorrect Options button. If you point to the button, Publisher displays the maximized AutoCorrect Options button. When you click the AutoCorrect Options button, Publisher displays a menu. *Why? The menu allows you to undo a correction or change how Publisher handles future automatic corrections of this type.* The following steps use the AutoCorrect Options button and menu.

 1

- Scroll to the lower portion of the right panel. Select the phone number default text by dragging through the text.

- Type **www.lakehideaway.mo.gov** to replace the text, and watch Publisher capitalize the first letter automatically.

- Move the mouse pointer close to the capital W to display the minimized AutoCorrect Options button (Figure 2–5).

Q&A Why did Publisher change this to a capital W?
Publisher interprets the web address as the beginning of a sentence and capitalizes the first letter.

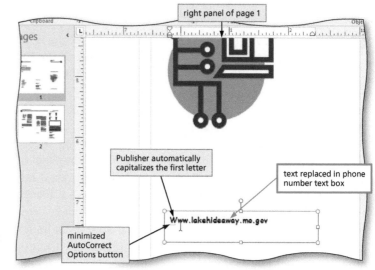

Figure 2–5

2

- Point to the minimized AutoCorrect Options button. When it appears maximized, click it to display the AutoCorrect Options menu (Figure 2–6).

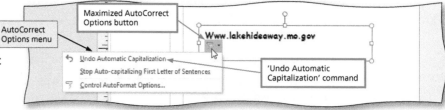

Figure 2–6

3
- Click 'Undo Automatic Capitalization' to cause the text to revert to lowercase (Figure 2–7).

Q&A How do I remove the AutoCorrect Options button from the screen?
When you move the mouse pointer, the AutoCorrect Options button will disappear from the screen. Alternatively, you can press the ESCAPE key twice. It does not print.

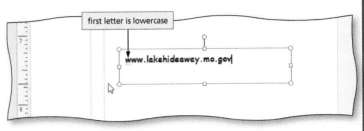

Figure 2–7

To Edit Objects in the Middle Panel

When folded, the middle panel will display on the back of the trifold brochure. It contains text boxes for the business address, phone numbers, and email address. The following steps edit the text in the middle panel.

1 Scroll as necessary to display the middle panel. Zoom to approximately 150%.

2 Delete the organization logo. Note that the business name text has been replaced already.

3 Drag to select all of the text in the Primary Business Address text box. Type **Lake Hideaway** and then press the ENTER key to finish the first line of the address and advance to the next address line.

4 Type **Route 17 Box 1500** and then press the ENTER key to finish the second line. Type **Hideaway, MO 64001** to finish entering the address text. Do not press the ENTER key after the last line.

If requested by your instructor, enter your name, address, city, and state instead of those in Steps 3 and 4. Do not press the ENTER key after the last line.

5 Drag to select the phone and fax numbers and the email address text. Type **Phone: 816-555-4850** and then press the ENTER key to finish entering the first line. Type **Fax: 816-555-4851** and then press the ENTER key to finish entering the second line. Type **Email: hideaway@moparks.gov** and then press the ENTER key to create a new line for future text (Figure 2–8).

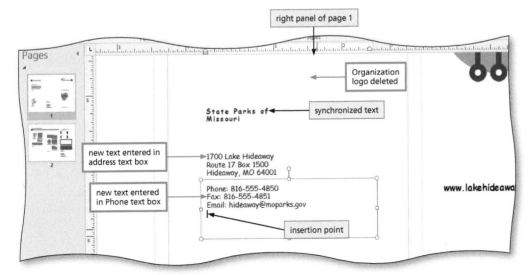

Figure 2–8

BTW
Smart Tags
The AutoCorrect Options button and the Paste Options button are smart tags. Recall from Module 1 that a smart tag appears when Publisher has options to show you, such as the Information button that appears as an uppercase I.

Copying, Cutting, and Pasting

In each of the Office 2016 applications, you can store or copy text and objects for later use. The **Office Clipboard** is a temporary storage area that holds up to 24 items (text or graphics) copied from any Office program. The Office Clipboard is different from the **Windows Clipboard** associated with the operating system, which can contain only one item at a time.

Copying is the process of placing items on the Office Clipboard; the item also remains in the publication. **Cutting**, by contrast, removes the item from the publication before placing it on the clipboard. The copy and cut functions transfer text or objects to the Windows Clipboard as well as to the Office Clipboard. Cutting is different from deleting. Deleted items are not placed on either clipboard. **Pasting** is the process of copying an item from either clipboard into the publication at the location of the insertion point or selection.

Table 2–2 describes various methods to copy, cut, paste, and delete selected text.

BTW
Stylus
If you are using your finger on a touch screen and are having difficulty completing the steps in this module, consider using a stylus. Many people find it easier to be precise with a stylus rather than with a finger. In addition, with a stylus you see the pointer. If you still are having trouble completing the steps with a stylus, try using a mouse.

Table 2–2 Copy, Cut, Paste, and Delete

Method	Copy	Cut	Paste	Delete
shortcut menu	Right-click to display the shortcut menu and then click Copy	Right-click to display the shortcut menu and then click Cut	Right-click to display the shortcut menu and then click Paste	Right-click to display the shortcut menu and then click Delete Text
ribbon	Click the Copy button (Home tab | Clipboard group)	Click the Cut button (Home tab | Clipboard group)	Click the Paste button (Home tab | Clipboard group)	Not available
keyboard	Press CTRL+C	Press CTRL+X	Press CTRL+V	Press the DELETE key or BACKSPACE key

BTW
Touch Galleries
If you are using a mouse or stylus, galleries, such as the Font Color gallery, display their choices in small, colored squares. If you are displaying the gallery via touch gestures, Windows 10 senses the touch gesture and displays the gallery with much larger, colored squares, making it easier to tap the one you want.

In Publisher, you can copy, cut, paste, and delete objects as well as text. If you are copying text, it is advisable to select from the beginning letter of the text and include any ending spaces, tabs, punctuation, or paragraph marks. That way, when you cut or paste, the text will be spaced properly. If you are copying, cutting, pasting, and deleting objects, the object must be selected. Publisher normally pastes objects from either clipboard into the center of the displayed page layout if no object is selected.

The next step in editing the brochure is to include the website address at the bottom of the center panel. One way to enter this information in the brochure is to type it. Recall, however, that you already typed this information on the right panel. Thus, a timesaving alternative would be to copy and paste the text.

To Copy and Paste

1 CUSTOMIZE BROCHURE | 2 EDIT TEXT & OBJECTS | 3 SWAP PICTURES | 4 CREATE PICTURE STYLES & SHAPES
5 USE STYLISTIC SETS | 6 SEARCH ONLINE PICTURES | 7 INSERT CAPTIONS | 8 CHECK PUBLICATION | 9 PACK

In the brochure, you want to copy the website address from one panel to the other. *Why? Copying and pasting reduces errors that might result from retyping information.* The following steps copy and paste the website address.

1

- Scroll until the lower portion of both the right and middle panels are visible.
- Click the website address text box to select it.
- Drag through the text to be copied (the website address in this case).
- Click the Copy button (Home tab | Clipboard group) to copy the selected item in the publication to the Office Clipboard (Figure 2–9).

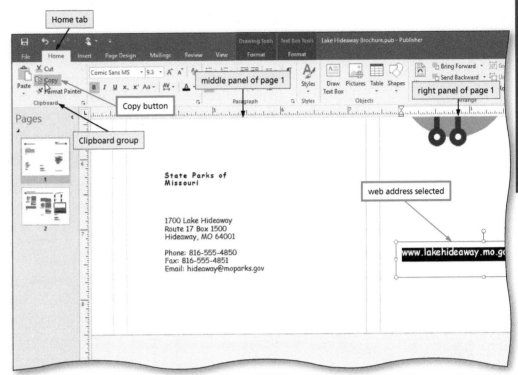

Figure 2–9

2

- Click the phone number text box at the bottom of the center panel and position the insertion point on the blank line underneath the email address.
- Click the Paste button (Home tab | Clipboard group) to paste the copied item into the text box. Do not press any other keys (Figure 2–10).

Q&A Should I select the text before pasting? No. If you are not replacing text, you position the insertion point at the desired location and then paste.

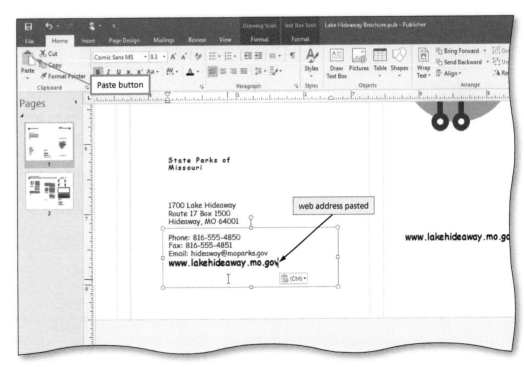

Figure 2–10

Other Ways

1. Right-click selected item, click Copy on shortcut menu, right-click where item is to be pasted, click desired Paste button on shortcut menu

2. Select item, press CTRL+C, position insertion point at paste location, press CTRL+V

BTW
Touch Screen
Differences
The Office and Windows interfaces may vary if you are using a touch screen. For this reason, you might notice that the function or appearance of your touch screen differs slightly from this module's presentation.

Paste Options Button

After you paste, Publisher may display the Paste Options button. Clicking the **Paste Options** button displays the Paste Options menu, which contains buttons representing formatting choices. They also appear when you click the Paste arrow (Home tab | Clipboard group). Table 2–3 describes some of the Paste options. Depending on the contents of the clipboard, you may see different buttons with advanced options for pasting, especially when cutting and pasting graphics.

Table 2–3 Paste Options		
Button	**Option**	**Result**
	Paste	Pastes the copied content *as is* without any formatting changes
	Keep Source Formatting	Keeps the formatting of the text you copied
	Merge Formatting	Changes the formatting so that it matches the text around it
	Keep Text Only	Pastes the copied text as plain unformatted text and removes any styles or hyperlinks

To Select a Paste Option

1 CUSTOMIZE BROCHURE | 2 EDIT TEXT & OBJECTS | 3 SWAP PICTURES | 4 CREATE PICTURE STYLES & SHAPES
5 USE STYLISTIC SETS | 6 SEARCH ONLINE PICTURES | 7 INSERT CAPTIONS | 8 CHECK PUBLICATION | 9 PACK

The following steps select the 'Keep Text Only' paste option. *Why? The website address should match the font style in the center panel.*

1

- Click the Paste Options button that appears below the pasted information to display the Paste Options menu (Figure 2–11).

 Experiment

- Point to each of the Paste Options buttons to see their ScreenTips.

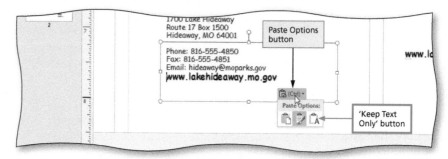

Figure 2–11

2

- Click the 'Keep Text Only' button to paste without the original bold formatting (Figure 2–12).

Q&A Can I change my mind and choose a different paste option?
Yes, if you change it before typing anything else. Otherwise, you would have to delete and paste again.

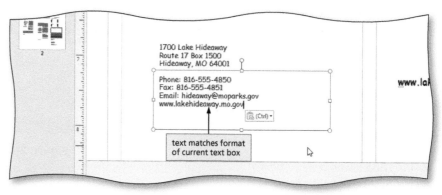

Figure 2–12

Other Ways

1. Press CTRL key, click Paste Options button
2. Click Paste arrow (Home tab | Clipboard group), click Paste Options button
3. Click Paste Options button on shortcut menu

Typing Paragraphs of Text

When you type paragraphs of text, you will use Publisher's wordwrap feature. **Wordwrap** allows you to type words in a text box continually without pressing the ENTER key at the end of each line. When the insertion point reaches the right margin of a text box, Publisher automatically positions the insertion point at the beginning of the next line. As you type, if a word extends beyond the right margin, Publisher automatically positions that word on the next line or hyphenates the word and moves the insertion point.

How do you decide on a brochure's content?

Gather all the information, such as stories, graphics, logos, colors, shapes, style information, and watermarks. Save copies or versions along the way. If you have to create objects from scratch, have someone else evaluate your work and give you constructive feedback. If you are using forms in your brochure, verify the manner in which the viewer will return the form. Check and double-check all prices, addresses, and phone numbers.

CONSIDER THIS

Publisher creates a new paragraph, or **hard return,** each time you press the ENTER key. Thus, as you type text in a text box, do not press the ENTER key when the insertion point reaches the right margin. Instead, press the ENTER key only in these circumstances:

- To insert blank lines in a text box
- To begin a new paragraph
- To terminate a short line of text and advance to the next line
- To respond to questions or prompts in Publisher dialog boxes, panes, and other on-screen objects

To view where in a publication you pressed the ENTER key or SPACEBAR key, you may find it helpful to display formatting marks. A **formatting mark**, sometimes called a **nonprinting character**, is a special character that Publisher displays on the screen, but one that is not visible on a printed publication. For example, the paragraph mark (¶) is a formatting mark that indicates where you pressed the ENTER key. A raised dot (·) appears where you pressed the spacebar. An end of field marker (¤) is displayed to indicate the end of text in a text box. Other formatting marks are discussed as they appear on the screen.

BTW

Moving Text

If you want to use your mouse to move text from one location to another, you can select the text and then drag it to the new location. Publisher will display a small rectangle attached to the pointer as you position the pointer in the new location. Moving text or objects also can be accomplished by cutting and then pasting.

To Edit Heading Text in the Left Panel

The left panel will appear as the inside fold when the brochure is first opened. It contains text boxes for a heading and summary text. The following steps edit the heading text.

1️⃣ Scroll to the top of the left panel.

2️⃣ In the left panel, click to select the Back Panel Heading placeholder text. Type `Camping & Hiking` to replace the text (Figure 2–13).

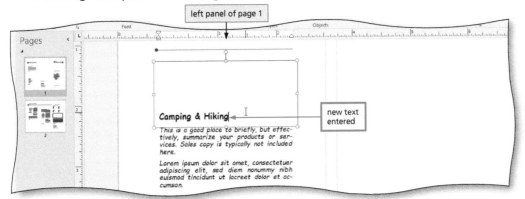

Figure 2–13

To Display Formatting Marks

The following step displays formatting marks, if they do not show already on the screen. *Why? The formatting marks help you see where you pressed the* ENTER *key and the* SPACEBAR *key, among other actions.*

- If it is not selected already, click the Special Characters button (Home tab | Paragraph group) to display formatting marks (Figure 2–14).

Q&A

What if I do not want formatting marks to show on the screen?
If you feel the formatting marks clutter the screen, you can hide them by clicking the Special Characters button again. The figures presented in the rest of this module show the formatting marks.

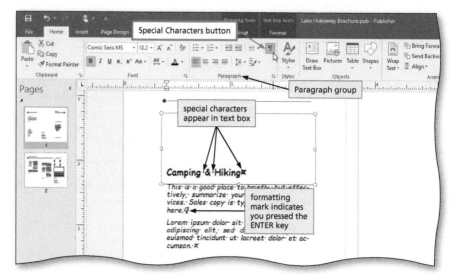

Figure 2–14

Other Ways

1. Press CTRL+SHIFT+Y

To Wordwrap Text as You Type

The next step in creating the brochure is to type the text in the left panel. The following steps wordwrap the text in the text box. *Why? Using wordwrap ensures consistent margins.*

- Click to select the placeholder text in the text box below the heading.
- Type Our campground, surrounded by beautiful woods, provides a great setting for relaxing and enjoying nature. All of our campsites have picnic tables and campfire rings, with a nice assortment of tent sites, water/electric sites, and full hookups. and notice that Publisher wraps the text when you get close to the right edge of the text box.
- Press the ENTER key to finish the first paragraph.
- Type With 21 miles of hiking trails, there is a path to fit everyone: from wheelchair-accessible paths to Level 4 trails. to finish the text (Figure 2–15).

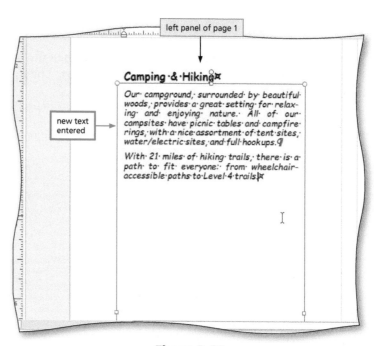

Figure 2–15

Swapping Pictures

In Publisher 2016, you can use the scratch area to manipulate and swap pictures. Recall that the **scratch area** is the gray area that appears outside the publication page. It is used as a temporary holding area; if you are not sure where you want to move an item, you can drag it to the scratch area. When inserting a single picture, you can drag it to the scratch area. When you insert multiple pictures at one time, Publisher arranges the thumbnails or puts them in a column in the scratch area, instead of on top of one another on your page. Unlike the clipboard, the scratch area is saved with the publication. The pictures in the scratch area will still be there the next time you open the publication. The scratch area does not print and contains the same items, regardless of which page of the publication is displayed.

Recall that many templates include picture placeholders, each with a picture icon. After the placeholder is replaced with a picture, the icon changes to a **swap icon**. Pictures in the scratch area also have swap icons. You can drag the swap icon to swap pictures with one another, or you can right-click the swap icon to display a shortcut menu with more options.

BTW

Organizing Files and Folders
You should organize and store files in folders so that you easily can find the files later. For example, if you are taking an introductory computer class called CIS 101, a good practice would be to save all Publisher files in a Publisher folder in a CIS 101 folder. For a discussion of folders and detailed examples of creating folders, refer to the Office and Windows module at the beginning of this book.

To Insert Multiple Pictures from a Storage Device

1 CUSTOMIZE BROCHURE | 2 EDIT TEXT & OBJECTS | 3 SWAP PICTURES | **4 CREATE PICTURE STYLES & SHAPES**

5 USE STYLISTIC SETS | 6 SEARCH ONLINE PICTURES | 7 INSERT CAPTIONS | 8 CHECK PUBLICATION | 9 PACK

The following steps insert multiple pictures from a storage device. *Why? Selecting and placing multiple pictures in the scratch area allows you to see what different pictures might look like in the publication.* To complete these steps, you will need to use the photos located in the Data Files. Please contact your instructor for information about accessing the Data Files.

- On the status bar, click the 'Show Whole Page' button to display the entire page.

- Click Insert on the ribbon to display the Insert tab.

- Click the Pictures button (Insert tab | Illustrations group) to display the Insert Picture dialog box.

- Navigate to the Data Files and the Module 02 folder.

- One at a time, CTRL+click the files, Campers, Lake, and Map to select the three pictures (Figure 2–16).

Q&A Why do I have to use the CTRL key?
CTRL+clicking allows you to select multiple items, rather than selecting them one at a time.

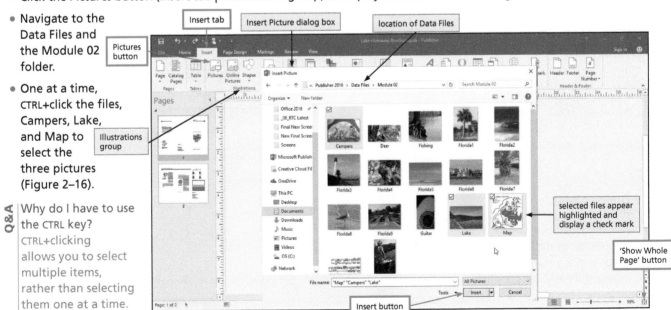

Figure 2–16

My file list looks different. Did I do something wrong?
No. Your window probably is set for a different view. Right-click the window, click View, and then select a different view.

2

- Click the Insert button (Insert Picture dialog box) to place the pictures in the scratch area (Figure 2–17).

Q&A My picture displays in the middle of the publication rather than in the scratch area. What did I do wrong?

If you choose just one picture, it is displayed in the middle of the publication. Multiple selections appear in the scratch area. You can drag your picture to the scratch area, if necessary.

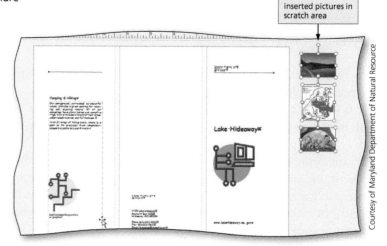

inserted pictures in scratch area

Courtesy of Maryland Department of Natural Resource

Figure 2–17

To Swap Pictures

1 CUSTOMIZE BROCHURE | 2 EDIT TEXT & OBJECTS | 3 SWAP PICTURES | 4 CREATE PICTURE STYLES & SHAPES
5 USE STYLISTIC SETS | 6 SEARCH ONLINE PICTURES | 7 INSERT CAPTIONS | 8 CHECK PUBLICATION | 9 PACK

When you decide to swap one picture for another, you drag the new picture toward the old picture. When Publisher displays a pink boundary, release the mouse button (or lift your finger away from the screen if you are using touch gestures). It is a good idea to swap pictures that have the same orientation. *Why? Pictures with the same orientation as the template fit the area better and are not scaled disproportionately.* **Portrait** pictures are taller than they are wide; **landscape** pictures are wider than they are tall. The following steps swap the pictures from the scratch area with the template graphics in the brochure.

1

- Click the scratch area away from the pictures to deselect them.

- In the scratch area, click the photo you wish to use in the brochure (in this case the picture of the campers) to display the swap icon (Figure 2–18).

Q&A The swap icon disappeared. Did I do something wrong?

You may have moved the pointer away from the picture. Move the pointer back over the top of the selected picture to display the swap icon.

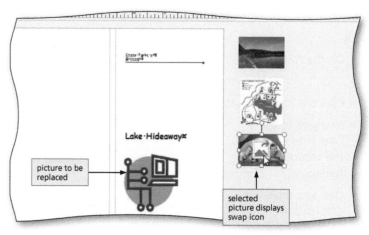

picture to be replaced

selected picture displays swap icon

Figure 2–18

2

- From the scratch area, drag the swap icon of the photo you wish to swap to a location over a current graphic on the page. (In this case, drag the picture of the campers to a location over the graphic in the right panel.) Do not release the mouse button (Figure 2–19).

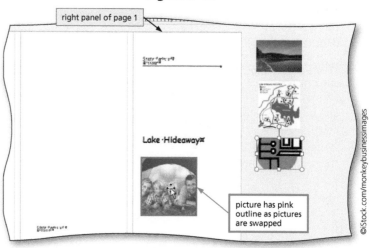

right panel of page 1

picture has pink outline as pictures are swapped

©iStock.com/monkeybusinessimages

Figure 2–19

③
- When the pink boundary is displayed, release the mouse button to swap the pictures (Figure 2–20).

Q&A My picture is no longer in full color. Did I do something wrong? No. Publisher applies the color scheme to swapped pictures. You will change that later in the module.

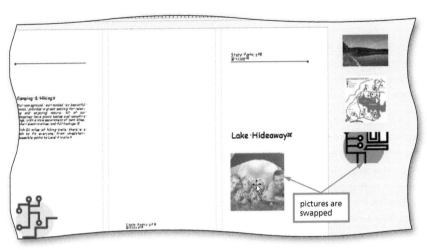

Figure 2–20

④
- Repeat Steps 1 through 3 to swap the map with the picture on the left panel (Figure 2–21).

Q&A Should I edit the caption? No, you will edit the caption later in the module.

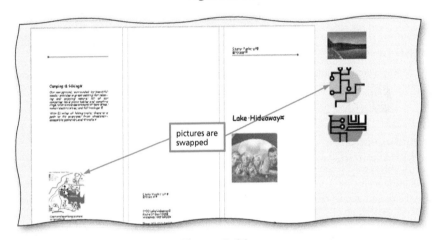

Figure 2–21

Other Ways

1. Select two pictures, click Swap button (Picture Tools Format tab | Swap group)

To Use a Picture as a Background

1 CUSTOMIZE BROCHURE | 2 EDIT TEXT & OBJECTS | 3 SWAP PICTURES | 4 CREATE PICTURE STYLES & SHAPES
5 USE STYLISTIC SETS | 6 SEARCH ONLINE PICTURES | 7 INSERT CAPTIONS | 8 CHECK PUBLICATION | 9 PACK

Many brochures use pictures in the background. *Why? A picture adds interest and removes the stark white color around objects in the brochure.* In this brochure, you will apply a picture to the background, using a picture from the scratch area and the shortcut menu. The following steps apply a picture to the background of page 1 of the brochure.

①
- Right-click the picture you wish to use as a background (in this case, the lake picture) to display the shortcut menu.
- Point to 'Apply to Background' on the shortcut menu to display the Apply to Background submenu (Figure 2–22).

Q&A Will the picture also be placed on page 2? No, not unless you go to page 2 and apply it there. Each page of a publication has a unique background area.

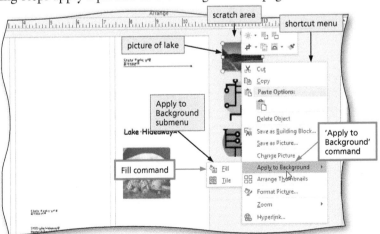

Figure 2–22

2

- Click Fill on the Apply to Background submenu to place the picture in the background of the page (Figure 2–23).

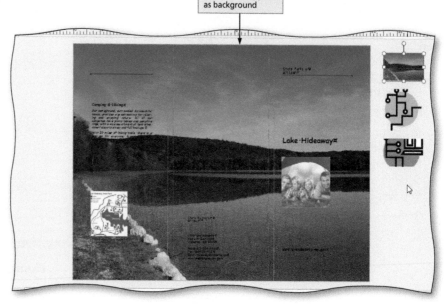

lake picture appears as background

 Experiment

- Press CTRL+Z to remove the picture from the background. Right-click the lake picture again, click 'Apply to Background', and then click Tile to view the difference between Fill and Tile. When you are finished, perform Steps 1 and 2 again.

Figure 2–23

Other Ways

1. Click Background button (Page Design tab | Page Background group), click More Backgrounds in Background gallery, click 'Picture or texture fill', click File, navigate to picture, double-click picture, click OK button (Format Background dialog box)

Resetting Pictures and Picture Styles

If Publisher applies a color scheme to your graphic, or if the picture does not fit correctly in the picture placeholder, you can use the **Reset command** to revert the picture to its original coloring and better fit it in the placeholder. Publisher also provides **picture styles** that allow you easily to change the basic rectangle format to a more visually appealing style and designer look. The Picture Style gallery has more than 20 picture styles that include a variety of shapes, borders, and scallops. The Picture Tools Format tab on the ribbon contains other adjustments, such as adding a border and picture formatting options that you will learn about in a later module.

1 CUSTOMIZE BROCHURE | 2 EDIT TEXT & OBJECTS | 3 SWAP PICTURES | 4 CREATE PICTURE STYLES & SHAPES
5 USE STYLISTIC SETS | 6 SEARCH ONLINE PICTURES | 7 INSERT CAPTIONS | 8 CHECK PUBLICATION | 9 PACK

To Reset Pictures

The following steps reset both pictures on page 1 of the brochure to remove the color scheme changes.

1

- Select the picture you wish to reset (in this case the picture of the campers on the right panel).

- Click the Reset Picture button (Picture Tools Format tab | Adjust group) to reset the picture (Figure 2–24).

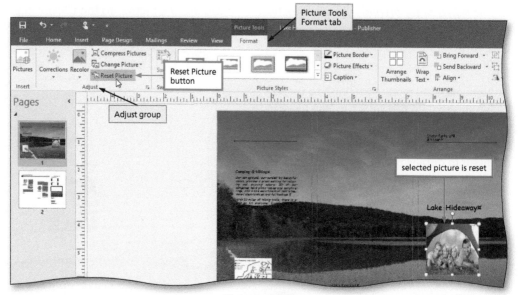

Picture Tools Format tab

Reset Picture button

Adjust group

selected picture is reset

Figure 2–24

2
- Select the map graphic in the left panel. Click the Reset Picture button (Picture Tools Format tab | Adjust group) to reset the picture (Figure 2–25).

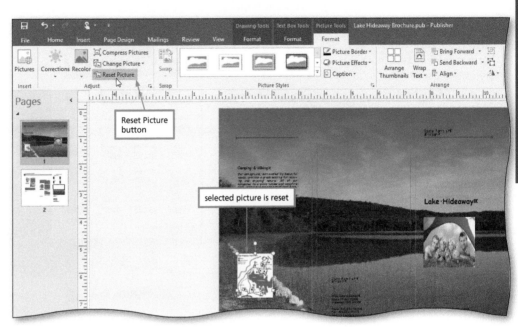

Figure 2–25

To Resize a Picture

The following step resizes the graphic in the right panel of page 1.

1 Select the picture of the campers in the right panel. Drag the lower-right handle until the picture is approximately 2 inches by 1.33 inches (shown in Figure 2–26).

To Apply a Picture Style

1 CUSTOMIZE BROCHURE | 2 EDIT TEXT & OBJECTS | 3 SWAP PICTURES | 4 CREATE PICTURE STYLES & SHAPES
5 USE STYLISTIC SETS | 6 SEARCH ONLINE PICTURES | 7 INSERT CAPTIONS | 8 CHECK PUBLICATION | 9 PACK

The picture on the front of the brochure will use a picture style slanting up and right. *Why? Researchers say that an upward slant adds energy to a publication and directs the reader's eye toward the inside of the brochure, with a 3-D look.* The following steps apply a picture style to the picture on the front of the brochure.

1
- If necessary, select the desired picture (in this case the picture of the campers in the right panel).
- On the ribbon, click Picture Tools Format to display the Picture Tools Format tab (Figure 2–26).

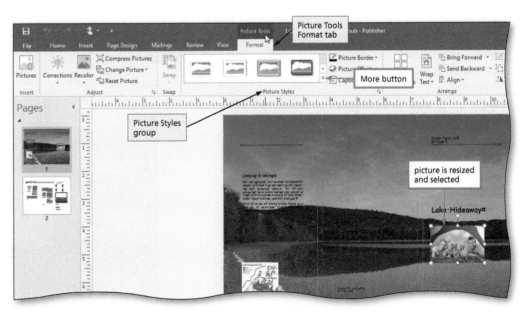

Figure 2–26

- Click the More button (Picture Tools Format tab | Picture Styles group) to display the Picture Styles gallery (Figure 2–27).

🔎 **Experiment**

- Point to various picture styles in the Picture Styles gallery and watch the format of the picture change in the publication window.

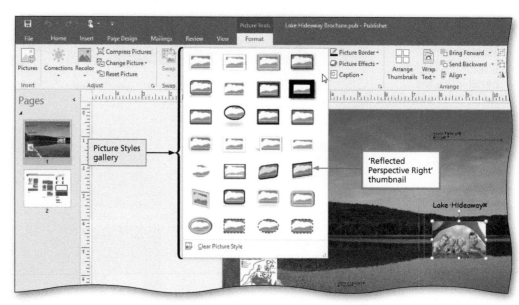

Figure 2–27

- Click the 'Reflected Perspective Right' thumbnail in the Picture Styles gallery to apply the selected style to the picture (Figure 2–28).

Figure 2–28

To Change the Border Color and Weight

1 CUSTOMIZE BROCHURE | 2 EDIT TEXT & OBJECTS | 3 SWAP PICTURES | 4 CREATE PICTURE STYLES & SHAPES

5 USE STYLISTIC SETS | 6 SEARCH ONLINE PICTURES | 7 INSERT CAPTIONS | 8 CHECK PUBLICATION | 9 PACK

The following steps change the border color of the picture and the weight, or size, of the border. *Why? A lighter, stronger border will make the picture stand out from the background.*

1

- Select the picture of the campers, if necessary.

- Click the Picture Border button (Picture Tools Format tab | Picture Styles group) to display the Picture Border gallery (Figure 2–29).

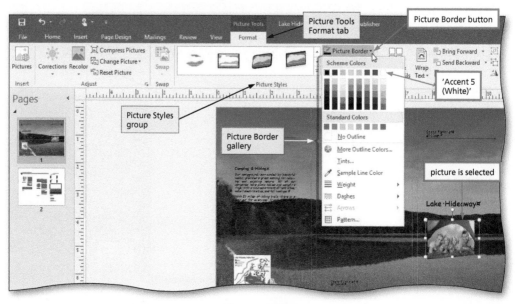

Figure 2–29

● Click 'Accent 5 (White)' in the Scheme Colors area to change the border.

● Click the Picture Border button (Picture Tools Format tab | Picture Styles group) again, to display the Picture Border gallery.

● Point to the Weight command to display the Weight submenu (Figure 2–30).

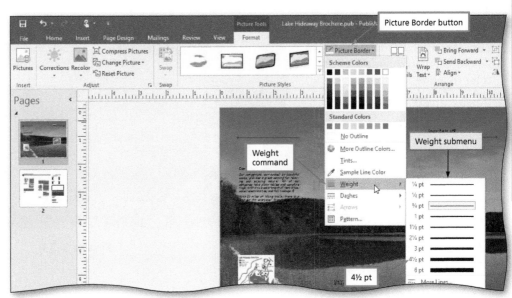

Figure 2–30

● Click 4½ pt on the Weight menu to change the weight of the border (Figure 2–31).

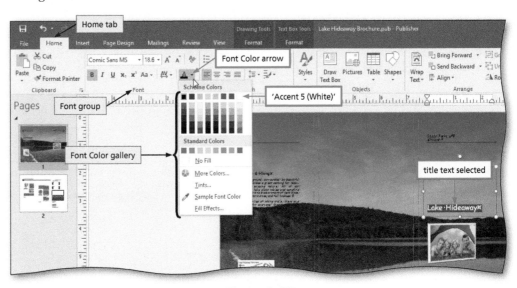

Figure 2–31

Other Ways

1. To change border color, right-click shape, click Format Picture on shortcut menu, click Colors and Lines tab (Format Picture dialog box), in Line area click Color button, click desired color

2. To change border weight, right-click shape, click Format Picture on shortcut menu, click Colors and Lines tab (Format Picture dialog box), in Line area click width up or down button

1 CUSTOMIZE BROCHURE | 2 EDIT TEXT & OBJECTS | 3 SWAP PICTURES | 4 CREATE PICTURE STYLES & SHAPES

To Change the Font Color

5 USE STYLISTIC SETS | 6 SEARCH ONLINE PICTURES | 7 INSERT CAPTIONS | 8 CHECK PUBLICATION | 9 PACK

The following steps change the font color to white in several text boxes. *Why? White lettering will be easier to read with the dark picture background.*

● Select the text in the title, Lake Hideaway.

● Click the Font Color arrow (Home tab | Font Group) to display the Font Color gallery (Figure 2–32).

Figure 2–32

2

- Click 'Accent 5 (White)' in the Font Color gallery to change the font color to white.

- Deselect the text to view the white text (Figure 2–33).

Figure 2–33

3

- Repeat Steps 1 and 2 to change the font color for all of the other text boxes on page 1, with the exception of the text box in the upper portion of the right panel (Figure 2–34).

Q&A Is there a way to change all of the font color faster?

It would be difficult to change text color globally; however, you can use CTRL+A to select all of the text in a text box, which may be faster than dragging through it. And, once you have the font color chosen, the Font Color button retains the color so you can just click it for subsequent color changes without having to display the gallery.

Could I use the format painter to copy the formatting?

No, not for white only. The format painter would also copy the font and font size to the other locations.

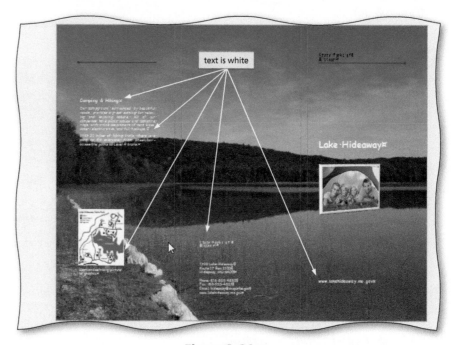

Figure 2–34

Other Ways

1. Click Font Color arrow on mini toolbar, click desired color

2. Click Font Color arrow (Text Box Tools Format tab | Font Group), click desired color

3. Right-click selected text, point to Change Text on shortcut menu, click Font on Change Text submenu, click Font color arrow (Font dialog box), click desired color, click OK button

To AutoFit Headings

The following step uses the Best Fit option to autofit the headings on page 1.

1 One a time, right-click the text in each heading text box and the text in the URL text box, and then click Best Fit on the shortcut menu (Figure 2–35).

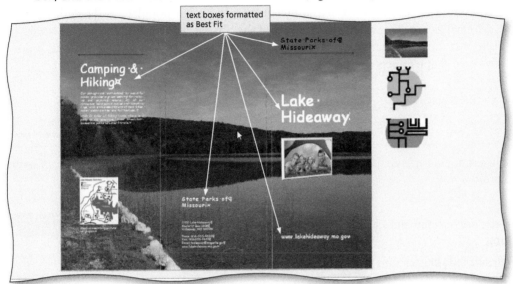

Figure 2–35

To Increase the Font Size of the Story

The following steps use the 'Increase Font Size' button to make the text bigger on page 1.

1 Select the story text in the left panel.

2 Click the 'Increase Font Size' button (Home tab | Font group) several times until the text is enlarged to 12 pt (Figure 2–36).

3 Deselect the text.

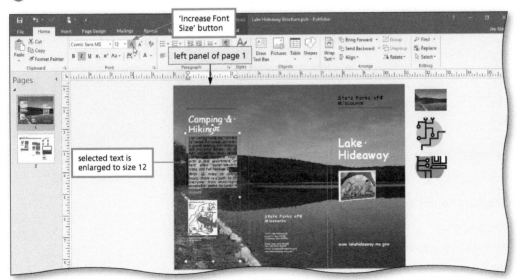

Figure 2–36

BTW
Superscripts and Subscripts
Two special font effects are superscript and subscript. A superscript is a character that appears slightly higher than other text on a line, such as that used in footnotes (reference[1]). A subscript is text that is slightly lower than other text on a line, such as that used in scientific formulas (H_2O).

Shapes

Publisher has more than 150 shapes that you can use to create logos, graphics, banners, illustrations, and other ornamental objects. You can apply fill effects, shadows, reflections, glows, pictures, and other special effects to shapes. When you click the Shapes button (Insert tab | Illustrations group), Publisher populates a Recently Used Shapes area that appears at the top of the Shapes gallery. You can choose your desired shape from that area or from the regular categories. You will learn about more advanced shape effects in a later module.

1 CUSTOMIZE BROCHURE | 2 EDIT TEXT & OBJECTS | 3 SWAP PICTURES | 4 CREATE PICTURE STYLES & SHAPES
5 USE STYLISTIC SETS | 6 SEARCH ONLINE PICTURES | 7 INSERT CAPTIONS | 8 CHECK PUBLICATION | 9 PACK

To Insert a Shape

The following steps insert a rectangle shape across the top of the publication. ***Why?*** *The rectangle will serve as a kind of banner for the brochure.*

1

- Make sure no text or objects are selected and then display the Insert tab.

- Click the Shapes button (Insert tab | Illustrations group) to display the Shapes gallery (Figure 2–37).

Q&A Why is my gallery different?
Publisher displays the most recently used shapes at the top of the gallery. The recently used shapes on your computer may differ.

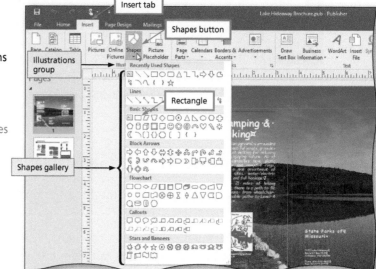

Figure 2–37

2

- Click the desired shape button (in this case, Rectangle) in the Basic Shapes category to select it.

- Move the pointer into the workspace. Beginning in the upper left corner of the page layout, drag a shape across

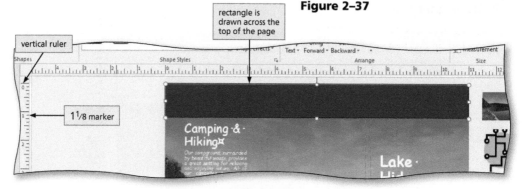

Figure 2–38

the top of page 1, approximately 1⅛ inches high (Figure 2–38).

Q&A How can I tell how high the shape is?
Use the vertical ruler to estimate 1⅛ inches.

Why did the rectangle fill with blue?
Blue is the default shape color assigned by the color scheme. You will change it in the next steps.

Other Ways

1. Click More button (Drawing Tools Format tab | Insert Shapes group), click desired shape button in gallery, draw shape

To Recolor a Shape

In the following steps, you will change the fill color of the shape and its outline to white. *Why? Publisher uses the color scheme when creating shapes. This color scheme uses a dark blue fill and a black outline.*

1

- With the shape still selected, click the Shape Fill arrow (Drawing Tools Format tab | Shape Styles group) to display the Shape Fill gallery (Figure 2–39).

Q&A Why did the Drawing Tools Format tab appear? When a shape is selected, Publisher automatically displays the Drawing Tools Format tab.

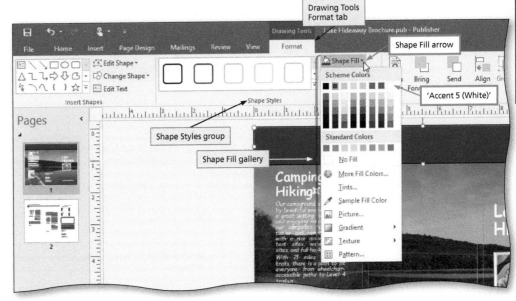

Figure 2–39

2

- Click 'Accent 5 (White)' in the Scheme Colors area in the gallery to change the shape color.

- With the shape still selected, click the Shape Outline arrow (Drawing Tools Format tab | Shape Styles group) to display the Shape Outline gallery (Figure 2–40).

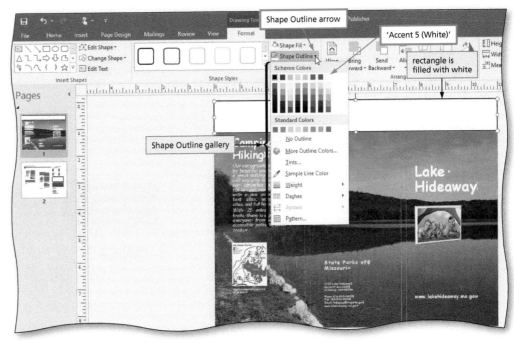

Figure 2–40

3

- Click White in the color gallery to change the outline color (Figure 2–41).

Q&A

Did the outline border change?

Yes. The only outline you may see is the selection border.

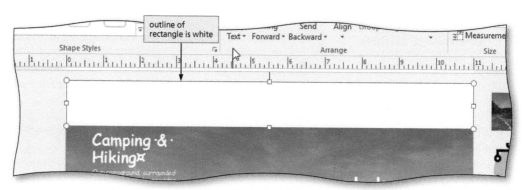

Figure 2–41

Other Ways

1. To change fill color, click Shape Fill arrow on mini toolbar, click desired color
2. To change fill color, right-click shape, click Format AutoShape on shortcut menu, click Color button in Fill area, click desired color
3. To change border color, click Shape outline arrow on mini toolbar, click desired color
4. To change border color, right-click shape, click Format AutoShape on shortcut menu, click Color arrow in Line area, click desired color

To Send a Shape Backward

1 CUSTOMIZE BROCHURE | 2 EDIT TEXT & OBJECTS | 3 SWAP PICTURES | 4 CREATE PICTURE STYLES & SHAPES
5 USE STYLISTIC SETS | 6 SEARCH ONLINE PICTURES | 7 INSERT CAPTIONS | 8 CHECK PUBLICATION | 9 PACK

In Publisher, **layering**, or **ordering**, means to make purposeful decisions on how objects appear in front of one another. For example, when you are using a template, any new object you insert appears in front of template objects automatically. When objects are layered, the most forward object will eclipse the objects below it. Building a publication in layers from the back to the front ensures that you will be aware of any objects that might obstruct one another and that your choices provide interesting backgrounds. You can reorder most objects, including shapes, tables, text boxes, pictures, and clip art.

The following steps move the rectangle behind the text and decorative lines. *Why? The recently inserted shape is obstructing the view of the objects below it.* You also will save the file again in the last step.

1

- With the shape still selected, click the Send Backward button (Drawing Tools Format tab | Arrange group) three times (Figure 2–42).

Q&A

Should I click the upper part of the button or the arrow below it?

Click the upper part, which is the button itself.

Why should I click it three times?

Publisher reorders objects one at a time. In this case, there are two lines and a text box that need to come forward.

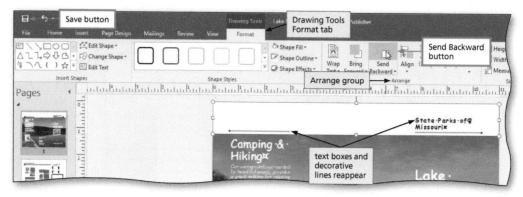

Figure 2–42

2

- Click the Save button on the Quick Access Toolbar to overwrite the previously saved file.

Break Point: If you wish to take a break, this is a good place to do so. Exit Publisher. To resume at a later time, run Publisher, open the file called Lake Hideaway Brochure, and continue following the steps from this location forward.

Editing the Inside Panels of a Brochure

As you edit the inside panels of the brochure, you will change text, edit the form text boxes, and change the pictures and captions. Headings introduce information about the topic and describe specific products or services. Secondary headings and the stories below them organize topics to make it easier for readers to understand the information.

1 CUSTOMIZE BROCHURE | 2 EDIT TEXT & OBJECTS | 3 SWAP PICTURES | 4 CREATE PICTURE STYLES & SHAPES

5 USE STYLISTIC SETS | 6 SEARCH ONLINE PICTURES | 7 INSERT CAPTIONS | 8 CHECK PUBLICATION | 9 PACK

To Switch to Page 2

The following step uses the Page Navigation pane to move to page 2. *Why? The Page Navigation pane is the only way to move among pages by clicking; however, you can press the F5 key and enter the new page number.*

1
- Click the Page 2 icon in the Page Navigation pane to display page 2.
- If necessary, zoom to Whole Page view (Figure 2–43).

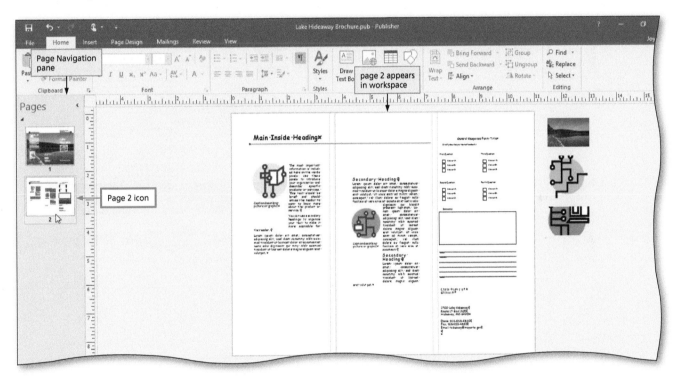

Figure 2–43

Other Ways

1. Press F5, enter page number, click OK button

To Insert and Format a Shape

The following steps insert a blue rectangle at the bottom of page 2 to provide continuity between the pages.

1 Display the Insert tab.

2 Click the Shapes button (Insert tab | Illustrations group) to display the Shapes gallery.

③ Click the desired shape button (in this case, the Rectangle) in the Basic Shapes category to select it.

④ Move the pointer into the workspace and then drag a shape across the bottom of page 2, approximately ¾ inches high.

⑤ If the Phone text box does not display the website, right-click the text box and then click Best Fit on the shortcut menu (Figure 2–44).

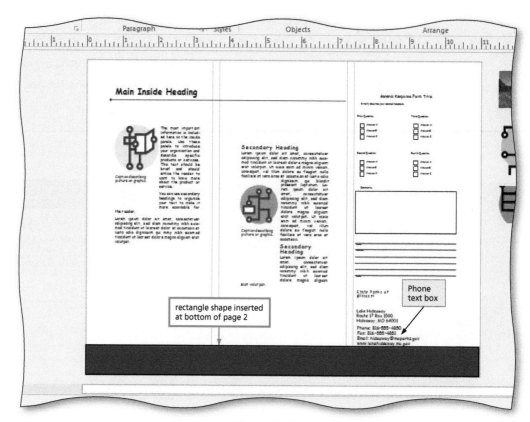

Figure 2–44

To Edit the Left Panel on Page 2

The following steps edit the text on the left panel of page 2. As you edit the text, zoom and scroll as necessary to view the text.

① In the left panel of page 2, click the placeholder text in the 'Main Inside Heading' text box to select it.

② Type **Park Attractions** to complete the page heading.

③ Click the placeholder text for the story in the left panel.

④ To create the story heading, press CTRL+B to bold the text. Type **Water** and then press the ENTER key. Press CTRL+B to turn off bold and press the ENTER key again.

⑤ Type **Our beautiful lake offers excellent canoeing, kayaking, and stand-up paddleboarding. Learn about the fascinating history of Lake Hideaway with a guided kayak tour. Paddle the lake and enjoy the Ozark scenery.** and then press the ENTER key to create the first paragraph.

6 Type `Our cozy, clean beach is a great place to swim and play. Bring your sunscreen, beach chair, picnic, and board! Or, you can rent canoes, kayaks, and paddleboards at the park office.` to complete the story (Figure 2–45).

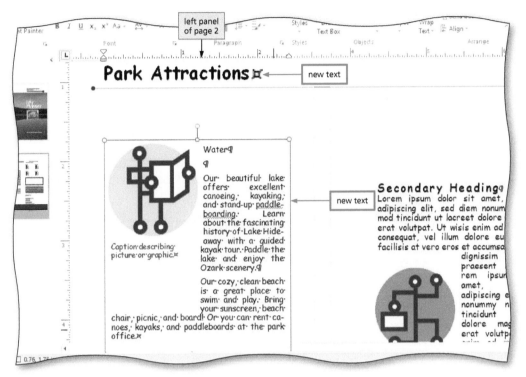

Figure 2–45

To Edit the Middle Panel on Page 2

The following steps edit the text in the middle panel of page 2. As you edit the text, zoom and scroll as necessary to view the text. Later in the module, you will format the text.

1 In the middle panel of page 2, click the first Secondary Heading placeholder text in the middle panel to select it.

2 Type `Wildlife` to complete the text.

3 Click the story below the heading to select the placeholder text.

4 Type `Our state park offers an outstanding setting for viewing, photographing, and studying creatures in their natural habitats. The opportunities range from observing deer, foxes, coyotes, and beavers in the deeper woods, to bird-watching our 120 different species.` and then press the ENTER key to create the first paragraph.

5 Type `Small animals, such as rabbits, raccoons, and squirrels, abound near our trails and campsites. Take a dusk drive around the park to see our beautiful animal families. No hunting is allowed in the park.` to complete the story.

6 Click the second Secondary Heading placeholder text on the middle panel to select it.

7 Type `Fishing` to complete the text.

8 Click the story below the heading to select the placeholder text.

⑨ Type `Lake Hideaway offers great fishing whether from a shore, boat, or dock. Fishing season begins on the last Saturday in April and ends on November 15th every year. Anglers commonly catch crappie, walleye, catfish, and bass. The lake also offers good fishing for a number of other species including gar, paddlefish, sunfish, and common carp.` to complete the story (Figure 2–46).

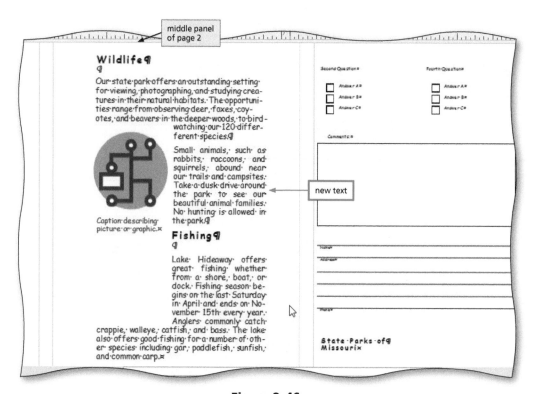

Figure 2–46

To Edit the Form

Publisher forms consist of text boxes, graphic boxes, and lines position in an attractive and usable format. The check boxes consist of a graphic and a text box grouped together. A **grouped object** consists of more than one object linked together for logical reasons, such as the parts of a masthead or a picture with its caption. Grouped objects are moved, edited, and formatted together as one. When necessary, grouped objects can be formatted individually by clicking a specific object after selecting the group. They can be ungrouped if you want to move or resize them independently. Alternately, individual objects can be grouped if you want to keep them together.

The following steps edit form text boxes and the grouped check boxes in the right panel of page 2.

① On the right panel of page 2, click the text in the General Response Form Title text box to select the placeholder text.

② Click the Zoom In button on the status bar to zoom to approximately 230%.

③ Type `For more information...` to complete the text.

④ Click the instruction text box below the heading to select the placeholder text.

⑤ Type `Fill out the following form and send it to the address listed below.` to finish entering the text.

⑥ If necessary, scroll down to display the check box area.

⑦ Click the First Question heading to select the placeholder text.

⑧ Type `Camping & Hiking` to change the heading and then click outside the text box to deselect it.

⑨ Repeat the process to replace each of the other three headings shown in Figure 2–47.

⑩ Click the text, Answer A, below the Camping & Hiking heading, in order to select only the placeholder text, not the check box. Do not double-click.

⑪ Type `Reservations` to change the placeholder text.

⑫ Repeat the process to edit all of the other check boxes in the form as shown in Figure 2–47.

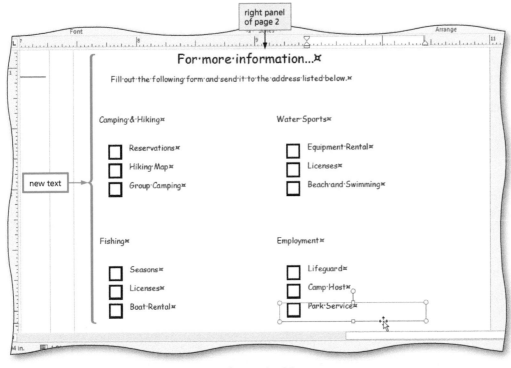

Figure 2–47

Stylistic Sets

Publisher includes a special kind of font feature called a stylistic set. A **stylistic set** is an organized set of alternate letters and glyphs, allowing you to change what a font looks like. A **glyph** is a special stroke that appears in text that is not part of the normal font set. Diacritical marks, such as the umlaut (ä) or cedilla (ç), use glyphs.

Besides its regular display, almost every font has three common stylistic sets: bold, italic, and the combination of bold and italic. The letters are displayed in the same font but use a heavier or slanted glyph. Another example with which you may be familiar is a font family that has both serif and sans serif stylistic sets. A **serif** is

BTW
Stylistic Alternate Sets
If you use a script font that looks like cursive writing, a stylistic alternate can simulate handwriting by using a set of randomly chosen glyphs with slight differences in appearance.

BTW
Character Typography
Typography also includes scaling, tracking, and kerning of characters. You will learn about these spacing options in a future module.

BTW
Serif Fonts
Serif fonts are considered Oldstyle when they display a slanted serif. Fonts are considered Modern when they use horizontal serifs.

BTW
Swashes
A swash is an exaggerated serif or glyph that typically runs into the space above or below the next letter. Some swashes can cause an unattractive appearance when used with adjacent descending letters such as g, j, or y; however, when used correctly, a swash produces a flowing, linear appearance that adds interest to the font.

small line, flourish, or embellishment that crosses the strokes of letters in some fonts. A **sans serif**, meaning without flourish, set has no extra embellishment at the end of characters. Other stylistic sets include alternates for characters such as e, j, g, or y. The extra characters with accompanying glyphs have to be a part of the font set when it is installed. On a typical Publisher installation, only a few font families contain complete stylistic sets. Some fonts, such as Gabriola, allow you to choose a **stylistic alternate** set, which creates a random pattern from among the various stylistic sets available for the current font.

Typography refers to specialized effects and fonts, including stylistic sets, drop caps, number styles, and glyphs. Ligatures, stylistic sets, swashes, and stylistic alternates, as well as some alphabetic characters that are not part of the English language, also are created with glyphs. You will learn more about typography in future modules.

To Format with a Stylistic Set

1 CUSTOMIZE BROCHURE | 2 EDIT TEXT & OBJECTS | 3 SWAP PICTURES | 4 CREATE PICTURE STYLES & SHAPES
5 USE STYLISTIC SETS | 6 SEARCH ONLINE PICTURES | 7 INSERT CAPTIONS | 8 CHECK PUBLICATION | 9 PACK

The following steps choose a stylistic set for the heading. *Why? Stylistic sets add interest and flair to headings.*

1
- Select the text, For more information…, at the top of the right panel of page 2.
- Click Text Box Tools Format on the ribbon to display the Text Box Tools Format tab.
- With the text selected, click the Stylistic Sets button (Text Box Tools Format tab | Typography group) to display the Stylistic Sets gallery (Figure 2–48).

Experiment
- Point to each stylistic set and watch the live preview in the text box.

Q&A Do all fonts have fancy stylistic sets?
No, usually only **OpenType** or scalable fonts contain stylistic sets other than bold and italic.

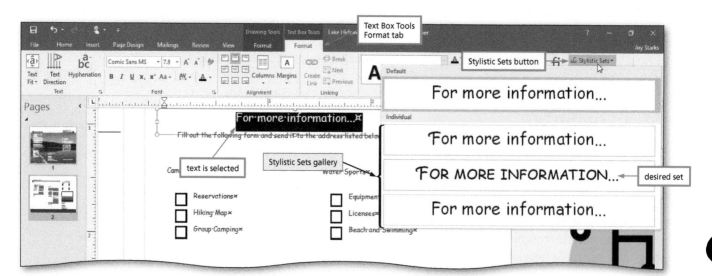

Figure 2–48

2

- Click the desired set (in this case, the second one from the bottom) to apply the stylistic set to the selected text (Figure 2–49).

Q&A Are any fancier stylistic sets available?

Yes. The Gabriola font has some fancier stylistic sets with large glyphs, but those will not fit in with the style of the brochure.

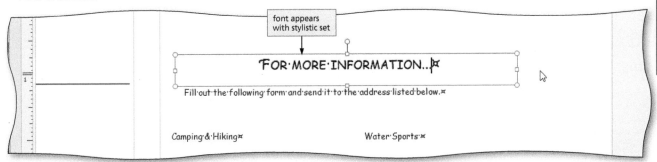

Figure 2–49

3

- Scroll to the left panel on page 2 and Select the text, **Park Attractions** at the top of the right panel.

- With the text selected, click the Stylistic Sets button (Text Box Tools Format tab | Typography group) to display the Stylistic Sets gallery.

- Click the desired set (in this case, the second one from the bottom) to apply the stylistic set to the selected text (Figure 2–50).

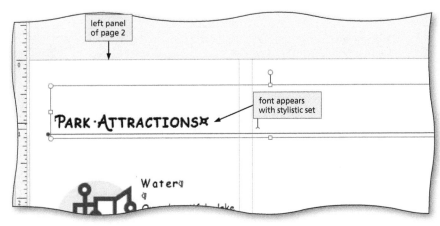

Figure 2–50

Online Pictures

Sometimes you may want to locate images or clip art from the web, also called **online pictures**. Publisher 2016 uses a Bing Image Search to help you locate images licensed under Creative Commons. The resulting images may or may not be royalty and copyright free. You must read the specific license for any image you plan to use, even for educational purposes.

To Search for Online Pictures

1 CUSTOMIZE BROCHURE | 2 EDIT TEXT & OBJECTS | 3 SWAP PICTURES | 4 CREATE PICTURE STYLES & SHAPES
5 USE STYLISTIC SETS | 6 SEARCH ONLINE PICTURES | **7 INSERT CAPTIONS** | **8 CHECK PUBLICATION** | **9 PACK**

The following steps use the Bing Image Search to locate pictures of a paddleboard and a deer. If you cannot find the specific image, you may use another appropriate image. Make sure you review the license to ensure you can comply. The size of your pictures may vary. If you want to use the exact image shown in the figures, you may retrieve the image from the Data Files.

1

- Zoom to display the entire page. Deselect any objects or pictures.

- Display the Insert tab and then click the Online Pictures button (Insert tab | Illustrations group) to display the Insert Pictures dialog box.

- Type **paddleboard** in the Bing Image Search text box to enter the search term. Press the ENTER key to display pictures related to paddleboards.

- Click a picture of a paddleboard similar to the one shown in Figure 2–51.

Q&A My pictures are different. Did I do something wrong?
No. The results of your search will be different from that shown in the figure.

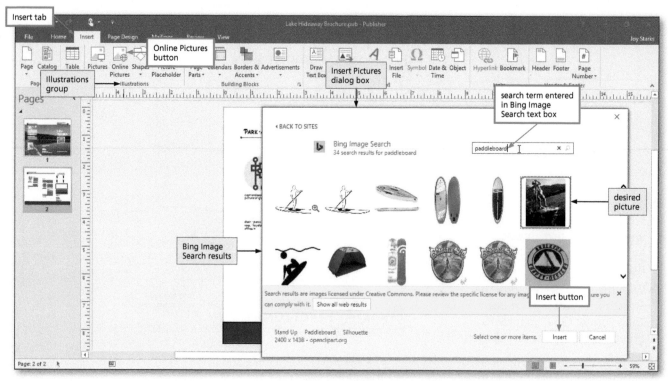

Figure 2–51

2

- Click the Insert button (Insert Pictures dialog box) to place the selected picture in the publication.

- Drag the picture to the scratch area (Figure 2–52).

Q&A I would like to use the exact picture. What should I do?
If you cannot find the exact picture with your Bing search and want to use it, you may insert the picture from the Data Files using the Pictures button (Insert tab | Illustrations group). Please contact your instructor for information about accessing the Data Files.

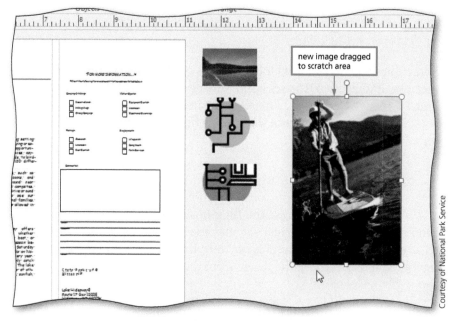

Figure 2–52

3

- Repeat Steps 1 and 2 to insert a picture of a deer and a picture of someone fishing. Scroll and zoom as necessary to view all of the pictures in the scratch area (Figure 2–53).

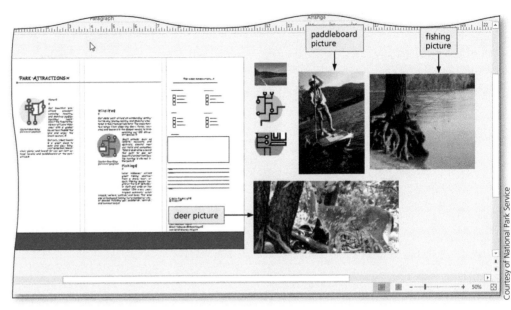

Courtesy of National Park Service

Figure 2–53

Other Ways

1. Click Insert Pictures button (Picture Tools Format tab | Insert group), enter search term (Insert Pictures dialog box), press ENTER key

2. Right-click picture, point Change Picture on shortcut menu, click Change Picture on Change Picture submenu, enter search term (Insert Pictures dialog box), press ENTER key

To Select Multiple Objects by Dragging

1 CUSTOMIZE BROCHURE | 2 EDIT TEXT & OBJECTS | 3 SWAP PICTURES | 4 CREATE PICTURE STYLES & SHAPES
5 USE STYLISTIC SETS | 6 SEARCH ONLINE PICTURES | **7 INSERT CAPTIONS** | 8 CHECK PUBLICATION | 9 PACK

The following steps select all of the pictures in the scratch area. *Why? They must be selected in order to arrange them in the next series of steps.*

1

- In the scratch area, drag, starting above and to the left of the first thumbnail, moving down and to the right, to include all of the pictures. Do not release the mouse button (or, if you are using touch, do not lift your finger) (Figure 2–54).

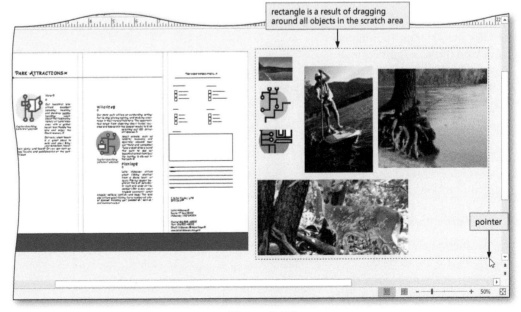

Figure 2–54

2

- Release the mouse button to select all of the pictures (Figure 2–55).

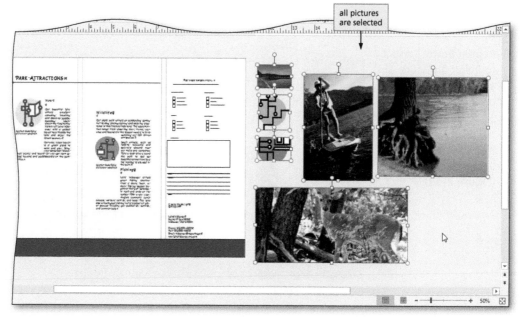

all pictures are selected

Figure 2–55

Other Ways

1. CTRL+click each object in the scratch area

To Arrange Thumbnails

1 CUSTOMIZE BROCHURE | 2 EDIT TEXT & OBJECTS | 3 SWAP PICTURES | 4 CREATE PICTURE STYLES & SHAPES
5 USE STYLISTIC SETS | 6 SEARCH ONLINE PICTURES | 7 INSERT CAPTIONS | 8 CHECK PUBLICATION | 9 PACK

When you **arrange thumbnails** in the scratch area, all of the pictures are reduced to thumbnail size and are aligned in rows and columns. *Why? A **thumbnail** is a reduced-size version of a larger graphic image used to help recognize and organize pictures, and to save space.* The following step arranges thumbnails.

1

- With the pictures selected, display the Picture Tools Format tab.

- Click the Arrange Thumbnails button (Picture Tools Format tab | Arrange group) to arrange the thumbnails (Figure 2–56).

Q&A

My tab disappeared. Did I do something wrong?
No. The Picture Tools Format tab displays only when a picture is selected. Arranging the thumbnails may have deselected the pictures.

My thumbnails are in a different order. Did I do something wrong?
No. Your thumbnails will differ.

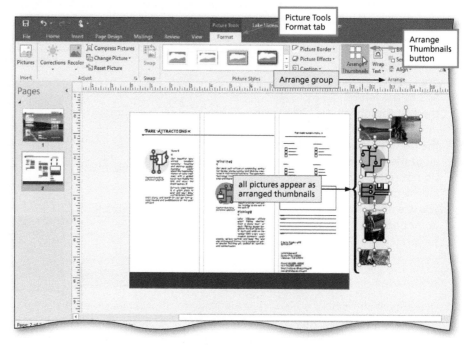

Picture Tools Format tab

Arrange Thumbnails button

Arrange group

all pictures appear as arranged thumbnails

Figure 2–56

Other Ways

1. Select pictures in scratch area, right-click any picture, click Arrange Thumbnails on shortcut menu

To Swap, Place, and Reset Pictures

The following steps change the pictures on page 2. Later in the module, you will resize them and edit the captions.

① Zoom to Whole Page view, if necessary.

② In the scratch area, click the photo you wish to use in the left panel of the brochure (in this case, the picture of the paddleboard) to display the swap icon.

③ From the scratch area, drag the swap icon of the photo to a location over the graphic in the left panel. When you see a pink boundary, drop the picture.

④ Click the paddleboard picture again to select only the picture, not the caption. Click the Reset Picture button (Picture Tools Format tab | Adjust group) to remove the color scheme.

⑤ Repeat Steps 2 through 4 to swap and reset the deer picture in the middle panel.

⑥ Drag the fishing picture from the scratch area to the bottom of the left panel, right-aligned with the text above it (Figure 2–57).

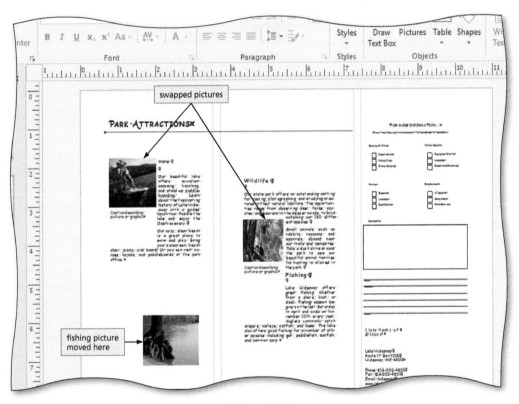

Figure 2–57

Captions

A **caption** is explanatory or identification text or a title that accompanies a graphic, figure, or photo. A caption can be as simple as a figure number, as you see in the figures of this book, or a caption can identify people, places, objects, or actions occurring in the graphic. When using Publisher templates, some captions already exist near a graphic. In those cases, the caption is a text box grouped with a graphic. If a graphic or photo does not have a caption, you can add one using the Caption gallery.

To Edit Captions

The following steps edit the text in the captions on page 2. *Why? A caption explains the graphic to the reader.*

1

- Scroll to the desired caption (in this case, the left panel of page 2).

- Click the caption text below the photo to select it, and then type `Enjoy` and then press the ENTER key. Type **paddleboarding** and then press the ENTER key. Type **on the lake!** to replace the text. If Publisher capitalizes the first letter on lines 2 and 3, use the AutoCorrect Options button as you did earlier in the module.

- If necessary, drag the right handle of the picture and caption grouping to the left until the picture is better proportioned (Figure 2–58).

Q&A | Can you delete a caption?
Yes, but be sure to delete the text box as well as the text. If the caption is part of a group, click once to select the group, then point to the border of the text box and click to select it. Finally, press the DELETE key to delete the caption text box.

Should I fix the red wavy line below the word, paddleboarding?
No. You check spelling later in the module.

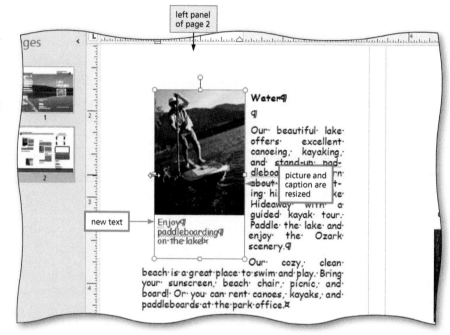

Figure 2–58

2

- Scroll to the caption on the middle panel of page 2 and then click the caption text below the photo to select it.

- Type **We guarantee deer** and then press the ENTER key. Type **sightings!** to complete the caption (Figure 2–59).

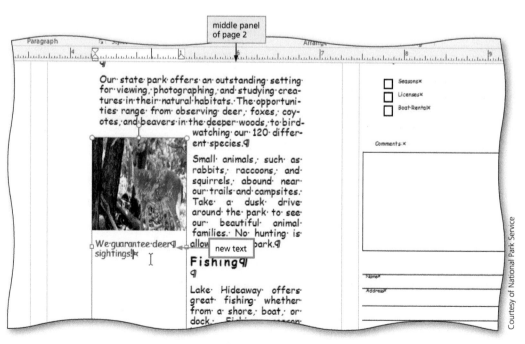

Figure 2–59

1 CUSTOMIZE BROCHURE | 2 EDIT TEXT & OBJECTS | 3 SWAP PICTURES | 4 CREATE PICTURE STYLES & SHAPES

5 USE STYLISTIC SETS | 6 SEARCH ONLINE PICTURES | 7 INSERT CAPTIONS | **8 CHECK PUBLICATION** | **9 PACK**

To Ungroup

The picture and caption are grouped or linked together in order to make moving them easier. The following steps ungroup the caption. **Why?** *Ungrouped, the caption text box can be resized.*

1

- With the picture/ caption group selected, display the Home tab, if necessary.

- Click the Ungroup button (Home tab | Arrange group) to ungroup (Figure 2–60).

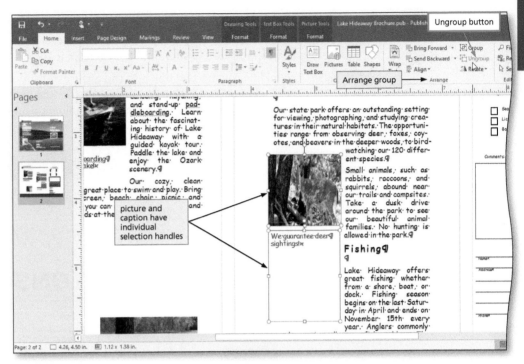

Figure 2–60

2

- Deselect and then select only the caption text box. Resize the text box by dragging the lower-center handle upward as shown in Figure 2–61.

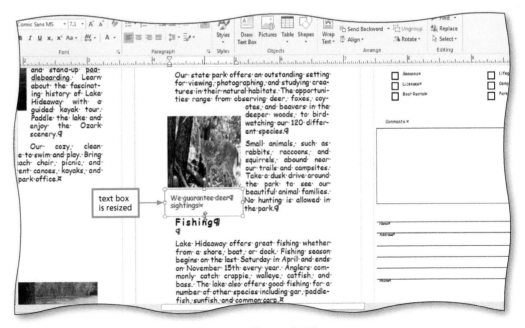

Figure 2–61

Other Ways

1. Select grouped object, press CTRL+SHIFT+G

To Adjust Font Sizes on Page 2

The following steps adjust font sizes in several text boxes on page 2 to make the text larger and more legible.

1 Right-click the heading text, Park Attractions, and then click Best Fit on the shortcut menu.

2 Select the text in the left column (not the caption). Click the Increase Font size button (Home tab | Font group) until the text size is 10.

3 Select the text in the middle column (not the caption). Click the Increase Font size button (Home tab | Font group) until the text size is 10.

4 Select the middle column text box (not the picture or caption). Drag the upper-center sizing handle upward until the title aligns with the title in the left column, and so that all of the text is displayed at the bottom of the middle panel (Figure 2–62).

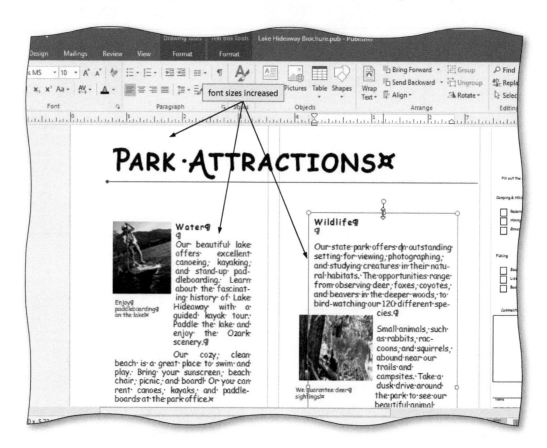

Figure 2–62

To Use the Caption Gallery

1 CUSTOMIZE BROCHURE | 2 EDIT TEXT & OBJECTS | 3 SWAP PICTURES | 4 CREATE PICTURE STYLES & SHAPES
5 USE STYLISTIC SETS | 6 SEARCH ONLINE PICTURES | 7 INSERT CAPTIONS | **8 CHECK PUBLICATION** | 9 PACK

The following steps add a decorative caption to an existing photo using the Caption gallery. *Why? A decorative caption adds interest and color.*

1

- Click the fishing picture to select it and zoom to 150%.
- Click Picture Tools Format on the ribbon to display the Picture Tools Format tab.

- Click the Caption button (Picture Tools Format tab | Picture Styles group) to display its gallery and then scroll to the bottom of the gallery (Figure 2–63).

Experiment

- Point to each caption style in the gallery to see its effect on the publication.

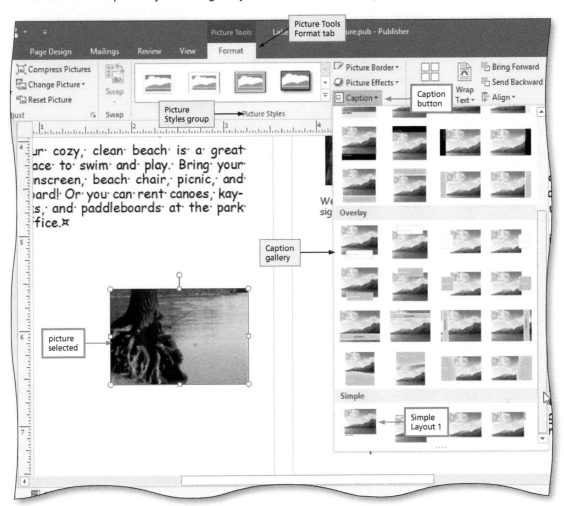

Figure 2–63

2

- Click the Simple Layout 1 thumbnail to apply the caption style to the picture.

- Select the caption text and then type **Relax while fishing!** to enter the caption.

- Select the caption text again, click the Font Color arrow (Home tab | Font group), and then click 'Accent 1 (Dark Blue)' in the Font Color gallery to match the color of the other captions. If necessary, change the font to Comic Sans MS.

- Click outside the text to remove the selection (Figure 2–64).

Figure 2–64

3

- Click the Page 1 icon in the Page Navigation pane to return to page 1.

- Click the map and then click the Caption button (Picture Tools Format tab | Picture Styles group) to display its gallery.

Q&A My Caption button is dimmed. What should I do?
Click the Ungroup button (Home tab |Arrange group). Select the textbox and delete it. Select the picture. The Caption button should be enabled at that point.

- Click the 'Tint Layout 1' thumbnail in the Formatted section in the Picture Styles gallery to apply the caption style to the picture.

- Select the caption and then type
Just off Route 17 to replace the caption text below the map (Figure 2–65).

Figure 2–65

BTW

Brochure Features
Many brochures incorporate newspaper features, such as columns and a masthead, and add eye appeal with logos, sidebars, shapes, and graphics. Small brochures typically have folded panels. Larger brochures resemble small magazines, with multiple pages and stapled bindings.

Checking the Publication

Recall that you checked a publication for spelling errors as you typed in Module 1. A wavy, red line indicated a word that was not in Publisher's dictionary. You then used the shortcut menu to choose the correct word. Additionally, Publisher can check the entire publication once you have finished editing it. The process of checking your entire publication for spelling errors moves from text box to text box and offers suggestions for words it does not find in its dictionary. Publisher does not look for grammatical errors.

CONSIDER THIS

What is the best way to eliminate errors in the brochure?

If possible, proofread the brochure with a fresh set of eyes, that is, at least one to two days after completing the first draft. Insert repeated elements and special objects, such as watermarks and logos, which need to be placed around, or behind, other objects. Look at text wrapping on every graphic. Ask someone else to proofread the brochure and give you suggestions for improvements. Revise it as necessary and then use the spelling and design checking features of the software.

BTW

Design Problems
If you want to learn more about specific design problems, click the problem in the 'Select an item to fix' box (Design Checker task pane). Click the gray arrow that appears and then click Explain to obtain more information.

A second kind of publication check is called the Design Checker. The **Design Checker** finds potential design problems in the publication, such as objects hidden behind other objects, text that does not fit in its text box, or a picture that is scaled disproportionately. As with the spelling check, you can choose to correct or ignore each design problem.

To Check the Spelling of the Entire Publication

The following steps check the entire brochure for spelling errors. *Why? You should check the spelling on every publication after you finish editing it.*

1

- Click Review on the ribbon to display the Review tab.

- Click the Spelling button (Review tab | Proofing group) to begin the spelling check in the current location, which in this case is inside the caption text box (Figure 2–66).

Q&A Can I check spelling of just a section of a publication?
Yes, select the text before starting the spelling check.

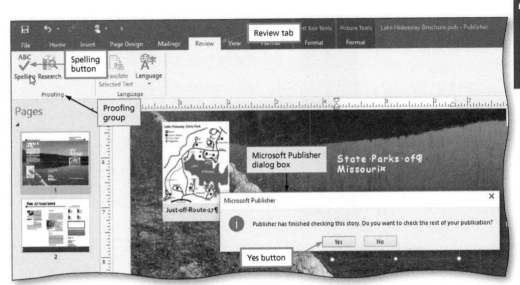

Figure 2–66

2

- When Publisher finishes checking the caption text box, click the Yes button (Microsoft Publisher dialog box) to tell Publisher to check the rest of the publication. If your publication displays a different error, accept or ignore it as necessary (Figure 2–67).

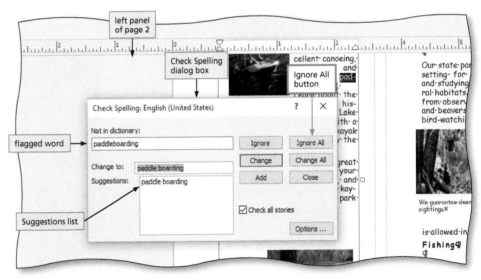

Figure 2–67

3

- Click the Ignore All button (Check Spelling dialog box) to ignore the flagged word each time it occurs (in this case, paddleboarding).

- If Publisher flags any other words, choose the correct spelling in the Suggestions list, click the Change button, and then continue the spelling check until the next error is identified or the end of the publication is reached.

- When the Microsoft Publisher dialog box is displayed indicating the spelling check is complete, click the OK button to close the dialog box.

Other Ways

1. Right-click flagged word, click Spelling on shortcut menu   2. Press F7

To Run the Design Checker

The following steps run the Design Checker. *Why? The Design Checker troubleshoots and identifies potential design problems in the publication.*

1

• Click File on the ribbon to open the Backstage view and, by default, select the Info tab (Figure 2–68).

Q&A Will the Design Checker fix the problems automatically?
In some cases, you will have the option of choosing an automatic fix for the issue; in other cases, you will have to fix the problem manually.

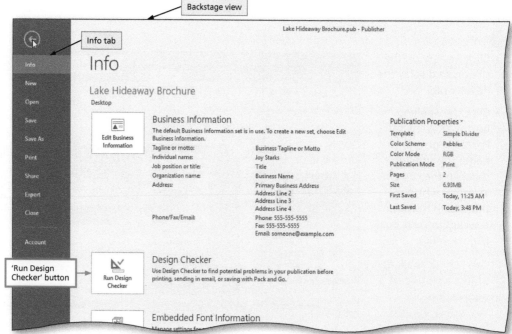

Figure 2–68

2

• Click the 'Run Design Checker' button in the Info gallery to display the Design Checker task pane (Figure 2–69).

Q&A What are the links at the bottom of the Design Checker task pane?
You can click the link, Design Checker Options, to specify the order in which the Design Checker checks the pages of your publication or to specify which kinds of design issues to include. The second link offers tips from the Publisher Help system about running the Design Checker.

What are the listed design problems?
A small amount of space appears between the margin of the page and the closest object to the margin. This is intentional and was part of the template, but the Design Checker notes the problem for your information only. Publication objects may be close to the printable area margin. This also is just a warning. The brochure will print correctly.

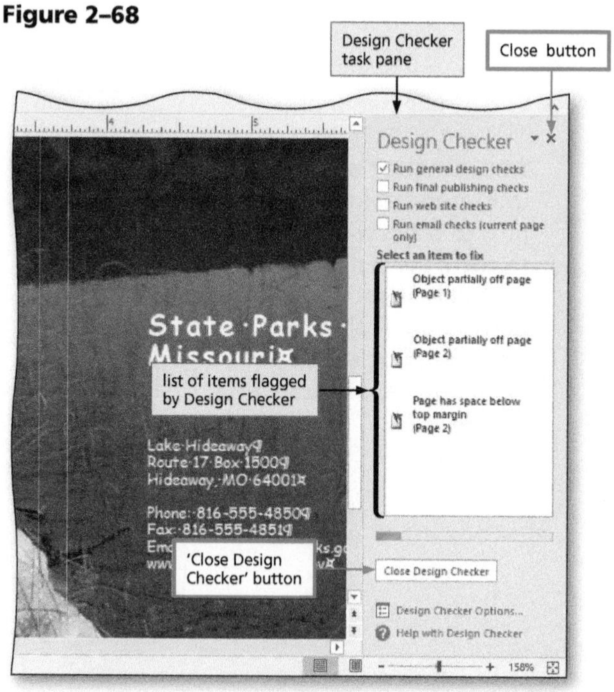

3

• Fix any issues not related to space or low resolution images. Click the 'Close Design Checker' button in the Design Checker task pane to close the Design Checker and return to the publication.

• Click the Save button on the Quick Access Toolbar to overwrite the previously saved file.

Q&A How do I fix a picture that is not scaled proportionally?
In the Design Checker task pane, point to the error, and then click the button that appears to the right of the error. On the resulting menu, click 'Fix Rescale Picture'.

Figure 2–69

Break Point: If you wish to take a break, this is a good place to do so. Exit Publisher. To resume at a later time, run Publisher, open the file called Lake Hideaway Brochure, and continue following the steps from this location forward.

Previewing and Printing

When you work with multi-page publications, it is a good idea to preview each page before printing. Additionally, if you decide to print on special paper, or print on both sides of the paper, you must adjust certain settings on the Print tab in the Backstage view.

To Preview Multiple Pages and Print

1 CUSTOMIZE BROCHURE | 2 EDIT TEXT & OBJECTS | 3 SWAP PICTURES | 4 CREATE PICTURE STYLES & SHAPES
5 USE STYLISTIC SETS | 6 SEARCH ONLINE PICTURES | 7 INSERT CAPTIONS | **8 CHECK PUBLICATION** | **9 PACK**

Previewing both pages in the publications is the first step in getting it ready for outside printing as you examine what the printed copy will look like from your desktop. The following steps preview and then print the brochure on both sides. *Why? Printing on both sides gives you the opportunity to check your panels and folds and to view the brochure as your readers will view it.* If your printer does not have the capability to print double-sided, follow your printer's specifications to print one side of the brochure, turn it over, and then print the reverse side.

- If necessary, display page 1.
- Click File on the ribbon to open the Backstage view.
- Click the Print tab in the Backstage view to display the Print gallery.
- Click the 'View Multiple Sheets' button to display the Multiple Sheets gallery (Figure 2–70).

Q&A | What are the rulers in the Print gallery?
Publisher displays rulers at the top and left of the print preview to help you verify the size of the printed page. You can turn off the ruler display by clicking the Ruler button.

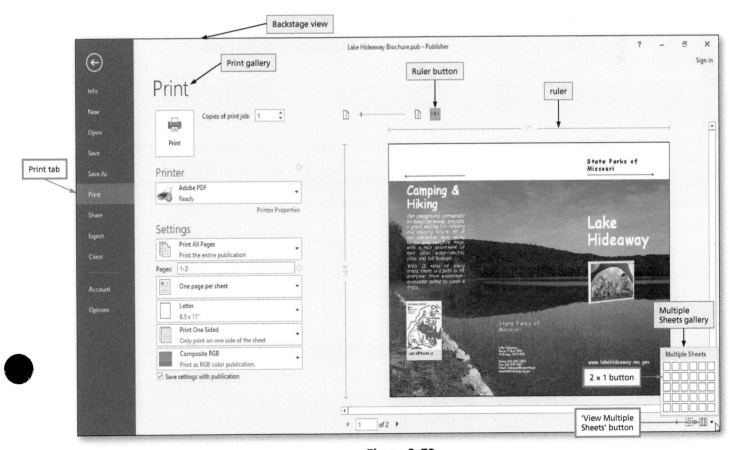

Figure 2–70

2

- Click the '2 × 1' button to display the pages above one another.
- Click the 'Print One Sided' button to display the list of options (Figure 2–71).

Q&A

If the brochure has only two pages, why do all of those preview grids exist?
Publisher allows for more pages in every kind of publication, should you decide to add them. If you click a button in the grid for more than two pages — either horizontally or vertically — the size of the preview is reduced.

Is that the best way to preview the brochure?
Viewing two full pages with intensive graphics and text may give you a good overview of the publication; however, do not substitute the preview for checking the publication for errors by reading the content carefully and running the spelling and design checking tools.

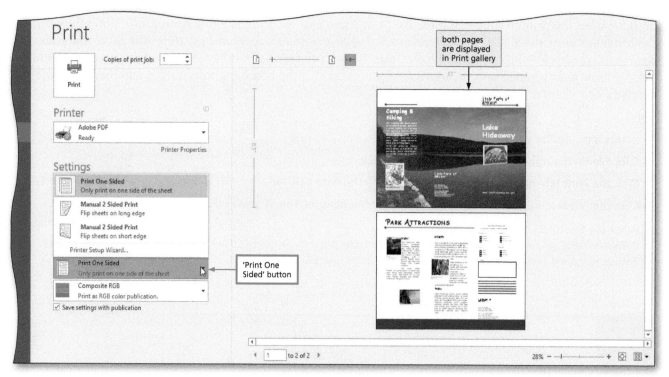

Figure 2–71

3

- If your list displays a 'Print On Both Sides (Flip sheets on long edge)' command, click it to select automatic printing of both sides.
- If your list displays a 'Manual 2 Sided Print (Flip sheets on long edge)' command, click it to select manual printing.
- Click the Print button to print the brochure. When the printer stops, retrieve the printed publication.

Other Ways

1. Press CTRL+P, choose settings, click Print button (Print gallery)

BTW
View Multiple
Sheets Grid
In multipage publications, you can use the View Multiple Sheets grid to choose how the pages display in the print preview. For example, choosing 5 × 2 in the grid will cause Publisher to display five pages vertically (high) and two pages across (wide) for a total display of 10 pages.

Printing Considerations

When they need mass quantities of publications, businesses generally **outsource**, or submit their publications to an outside printer, for duplicating. You must make special considerations when preparing a publication for outside printing.

How do you make wise, professional printing choices?
Make a firm decision that quality matters, and consult with several commercial printers ahead of time. Get prices, color modes, copies, paper, and folding options in writing before you finish your brochure. Brochures are more effective on heavier paper, with strong colors and a glossy feel. Together with the commercial printer, select a paper that is going to last. Check to make sure the commercial printer can accept Microsoft Publisher 2016 files.

If you start a publication from scratch, it is best to **set up** the publication for the type of printing you want before you place objects on the page. Otherwise, you may be forced to make design changes at the last minute. You also may set up an existing publication for a printing service. In order to provide you with experience in setting up a publication for outside printing, this project guides you through the preparation steps — even if you are submitting this publication only to your instructor.

Printing options, such as whether to use a copy shop or commercial printer, have advantages and limitations. You may have to make some trade-offs before deciding on the best printing option. Table 2–4 shows some of the questions you can ask yourself about printing.

BTW

Printer Memory
Some printers do not have enough memory to print a wide variety of images and colors. In these cases, the printer prints up to a certain point on a page and then stops — resulting in only the top portion of the publication printing. Check with your instructor to see if your printer has enough memory to work with colors.

Table 2–4 Choosing a Printing Option

Consideration	Questions to Ask	Desktop Option	Professional Options
Color	Is the quality of photos and color a high priority?	Low to medium quality	High quality
Convenience	Do I want the easy way?	Very convenient and familiar	Time needed to explore different methods, unfamiliarity
Cost	How much do I want to pay?	Printer supplies and personal time	High-resolution color/high quality is expensive; the more you print, the less expensive the per-copy price
Quality	How formal is the purpose of my publication?	Local event; narrow, personal audience	Business, marketing, professional services
Quantity	How many copies do I need?	1 to 10 copies	10 to 500 copies: use a copy shop; 500+ copies: use a commercial printer
Turnaround	How soon do I need it?	Immediate	Rush outside printing is probably an extra cost

Paper Considerations

Professional brochures are printed on a high grade of paper to enhance the graphics and provide a longer lasting document. Grades of paper are based on weight. Desktop printers commonly use **20-lb. bond paper**, which means they use a lightweight paper intended for writing and printing. A commercial printer might use 60-lb. glossy or linen paper.

The finishing options and their costs are important considerations that may take additional time to explore. **Glossy paper** is a coated paper, produced using a heat process with clay and titanium. **Linen paper**, with its mild texture or grain, can support high-quality graphics without the shine and slick feel of glossy paper. Users sometimes choose a special stock of paper, such as cover stock, card stock, or text stock. This textbook is printed on 45-lb. blade-coated paper. **Blade-coated paper** is coated and then skimmed and smoothed to create the pages you see here.

BTW

Distributing a Document
Instead of printing and distributing a hard copy of a document, you can distribute the document electronically. Options include sending the document via email; posting it on cloud storage (such as OneDrive) and sharing the file with others; posting it on a social networking site, blog, or other website; and sharing a link associated with an online location of the document. You also can create and share a PDF or XPS image of the document.

These paper and finishing options may seem burdensome, but they are becoming conveniently available to desktop publishers. Local office supply stores have shelf after shelf of various types of computer paper specifically designed for laser and ink-jet printers. Some of the paper you can purchase has been prescored for specific folding.

Color Considerations

When printing colors, Publisher uses a color scheme called RGB. **RGB** stands for the three colors — red, green, and blue — used to print the combined colors of your publication. RGB provides the best color matching for graphics and photos. Desktop printers may convert the RGB specifications to CMYK, which stands for cyan, magenta, yellow, and key (black). Professional printers, on the other hand, can print your publication using color scheme processes, or **libraries**. These processes include black and white, spot color, and process color.

In **black-and-white printing**, the printer uses only one color of ink (usually black, but you can choose a different color if you want). You can add accent colors to your publication by using different shades of gray or by printing on colored paper. Your publication can have the same range of subtleties as a black-and-white photo.

A **spot color** is used to accent a black-and-white publication. Newspapers, for example, may print their masthead in a bright, eye-catching color on page 1 but print the rest of the publication in black and white. **Spot-color printing** uses semitransparent, premixed inks typically chosen from standard color-matching guides, such as Pantone. Choosing colors from a **color-matching library** helps ensure high-quality results, because printing professionals who license the libraries agree to maintain the specifications, control, and quality.

In a spot-color publication, each spot color is **separated** on its own plate and printed on an offset printing press. The use of spot colors has become more creative in the last few years. Printing services use spot colors of metallic or florescent inks, as well as screen tints, to provide color variations without increasing the number of color separations and cost. If your publication includes a logo with one or two colors, or if you want to use color to emphasize line art or text, then consider using spot-color printing.

Process-color printing, or four-color printing, means your publication can include color photos and any color or combination of colors, using a print shop's CMYK process-color library.

Process-color printing is the most expensive proposition; black-and-white printing is the cheapest. Using color increases the cost and time it takes to process the publication. When using either the spot-color or the process-color method, the printer first must output the publication to film on an **image setter**, which recreates the publication on film or photographic paper. The film then is used to create color **printing plates**. Each printing plate transfers one of the colors in the publication onto paper in an offset process. Publisher can print a preview of these individual sheets showing how the colors will separate before you take your publication to the printer.

A newer printing technology called **digital printing** uses toner instead of ink to reproduce a full range of colors. Digital printing does not require separate printing plates. Digital printing usually is cheaper than offset printing without sacrificing any quality.

Special Paper

Printing the brochure on a high grade of paper results in a professional look. A heavier stock paper helps the brochure to stand up better in display racks, although any paper will suffice. **Brochure paper** is a special paper with creases that create a professional-looking fold and with a paper finish that works well with color and graphics.

TO PRINT ON SPECIAL PAPER

If you have special paper, you would perform the following steps to choose that special paper before printing. See your instructor for assistance in choosing the correct option associated with your printer.

1. Open the Backstage view and then click the Print tab.
2. Click the Printer Properties link below the Printer Status box to display your printer's Properties dialog box.
3. Find the paper or quality setting and then choose the paper.
4. Click the OK button in the Printer Properties dialog box to return to the Backstage view.

Packing the Publication for the Printing Service

The publication file can be packed for the printing service in two ways. The first way is to give the printing service the Publisher file in Publisher format using the Pack and Go Wizard. The second way is to save the file in a format called Encapsulated PostScript. Both of these methods are discussed in the following sections. Alternately, some printing services will take a Publisher document in its native format (.pub) without any packing; although, in that case, the printing service may not have the exact fonts and will substitute.

BTW
PostScript Files
If you decide to submit a PostScript dump, or file, to an outside printer or service bureau, include a copy of the original document as well — for backup purposes. Many shops slowly are changing over from Macintosh-based to cross-platform based operations. If an error occurs, the printer technician can correct the error from the original document without requiring you to make another trip to the print shop.

To Use the Pack and Go Wizard

1 CUSTOMIZE BROCHURE | 2 EDIT TEXT & OBJECTS | 3 SWAP PICTURES | 4 CREATE PICTURE STYLES & SHAPES
5 USE STYLISTIC SETS | 6 SEARCH ONLINE PICTURES | 7 INSERT CAPTIONS | 8 CHECK PUBLICATION | **9 PACK**

The **Pack and Go Wizard** guides you through the steps to collect and pack all the files the printing service needs and then compresses the files. *Why? Publisher checks for and embeds the TrueType fonts used in the publication, in case the printing service does not have those fonts available.* The following steps use the Pack and Go Wizard to ready the publication for submission to a commercial printing service. These steps create a compressed, or zipped, folder on your storage device.

- Click File on the ribbon to open the Backstage view.
- Click the Export tab in the Backstage view to display the Export gallery.
- In the Pack and Go area, click the 'Save for a Commercial Printer' tab.
- Click the 'Pack and Go Wizard' button to begin the Pack and Go Wizard.
- If necessary, use the Browse button in the Pack and Go Wizard dialog box to navigate to and select your storage location (Figure 2–72).

Q&A Should I save my file first?
You do not have to save it again; however, if you plan to store the publication on a storage device other than the one on which you previously saved the brochure, save it again on the new medium before beginning the process.

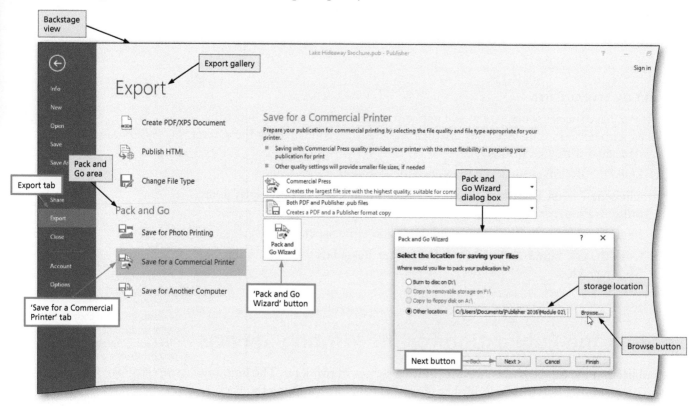

Figure 2–72

2

- When Publisher displays the next Pack and Go Wizard dialog box, if necessary, click the Next button to save the compressed file.

- When the final Pack and Go Wizard dialog box is displayed, remove the check mark in the 'Print a composite proof' check box (Figure 2–73).

Q&A What if I make a change to the publication after running the Pack and Go Wizard?
The file is saved in a compressed format on your storage location, with the same file name as your Publisher file. If you make changes to the publication after packing the files, be sure to run the Pack and Go Wizard again so that the changes are part of the packed publication.

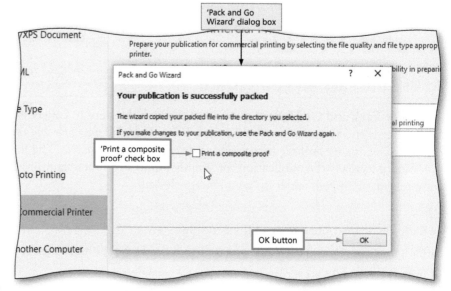

Figure 2–73

3
- Click the OK button to close the Pack and Go Wizard dialog box.
- Exit Publisher. If a Microsoft Publisher dialog box appears, click the Don't Save button to exit Publisher.
- Sign out of your Microsoft Account if necessary.

Summary

In this module, you have learned how to choose make choices about brochures and brochure templates as you edited headings and other text boxes. You copied and pasted using special paste options, and you displayed formatting marks as the text wrapped in paragraphs. Then, you swapped pictures and reset them. After applying a picture style, you changed the border and fill color of the picture and an added shape. On the inside page of the brochure, you used a stylistic set for the headings. Then, you inserted pictures using an online search. You edited all captions and used the caption gallery. Finally, you checked the spelling and the design of the publication before packing it for a printing service.

BTW
Automatic Saving
Publisher can save your publication at regular intervals for you. In the Backstage view, click the Options tab and then click Save (Publisher Options dialog box). Select the 'Save AutoRecover information every 10 minutes' check box. In the minutes box, specify how often you want Publisher to save files. Do not use AutoRecover as a substitute for regularly saving your work.

CONSIDER THIS

What decisions will you need to make when creating your next publication?
Use these guidelines as you complete the assignments in this module and create your own publications outside of this class.

1. Decide on the purpose, shelf life, and layout.
    a) Select a template that matches your need.
    b) Choose font and color schemes determined by the brochure's purpose and audience.
2. Create the brochure.
    a) Replace all placeholder and default text.
    b) Copy and paste text when possible to prevent the introduction of new errors.
    c) Edit forms.
    d) Use appropriate pictures with captions.
    e) Swap pictures when possible so that they will fit in the space.
3. Identify how to format various objects in the brochure.
    a) Copy formats for consistency.
    b) Use stylistic sets to enhance the brochure.
4. Proofread and check the publication.
    a) Read the brochure.
    b) Ask another person to read it.
    c) Use the spelling check feature.
    d) Use the Design Checker.
5. Plan for printing and packing.
    a) Choose correct printing options.
    b) Consult with a commercial printing service.
    c) Use the Pack and Go Wizard.

STUDENT ASSIGNMENTS

Apply Your Knowledge

Reinforce the skills and apply the concepts you learned in this module.

Swapping Graphics

Note: To complete this assignment, you will be required to use the Data Files. Please contact your instructor for information about accessing the Data Files.

Instructions: Run Publisher and open the file called Apply 2–1 Picture Collage from the Data Files. The document contains pictures from your recent Florida vacation. You produce the collage shown in Figure 2–74.

Figure 2–74

Courtesy of Joy Starks

Perform the following tasks:

1. Click the Pictures button (Insert tab | Illustrations group). Navigate to the Data Files and the Module 02 folder. CTRL+click each of the Florida pictures to select them. Click the Insert button to insert the multiple pictures into the publication, and if necessary, move them to the scratch area.

2. With the pictures still selected, click the Arrange Thumbnails button (Picture Tools Format tab | Arrange Group).

3. One at a time, swap the pictures for the empty picture placeholders. Arrange the pictures on the page layout as desired.

4. If requested by your instructor, replace one of the pictures with a picture of you.

5. Choose one picture for the background. To apply it, right-click its swap icon, point to 'Apply to Background' on the shortcut menu, and then click Fill on the Apply to Background submenu.

6. Save the collage on your storage device with the file name, Apply 2–1 Picture Collage Complete.

7. Submit the revised document in the format specified by your instructor.

8. ✺ Do you think a caption on each picture would make the publication look cluttered? Why or why not?

Extend Your Knowledge

Extend the skills you learned in this module and experiment with new skills. You may need to use Help to complete the assignment.

Creating a Brochure from Scratch

Note: To complete this assignment, you will be required to use the Data Files. Please contact your instructor for information about accessing the Data Files.

Instructions: Run Publisher. You are to start from scratch and create the brochure shown in Figure 2–75. You will insert images you obtain online, change the color and font scheme, create panel guides, and add other formatting to the brochure.

Perform the following tasks:

1. Click BUILT-IN, and then click Brochures. Scroll to the Blank Sizes area, and then click the Letter (Landscape) thumbnail.

2. Choose the Maroon color scheme and the Office 1 font scheme. Click the CREATE button to create the publication.

3. When the publication is displayed, maximize the window, if necessary. If necessary, click the Special Characters button (Home tab | Paragraph group) to display special characters.

4. Use Help to read about creating guides and then perform the following tasks:

   a. To create panel guides, drag from the vertical ruler into the publication to create a nonprinting guide, stopping at 3⅝" as measured on the horizontal ruler. Drag another guide from the vertical ruler into the publication, stopping at 7⅜".

   b. In the Page Navigation pane, right-click the page 1 icon, and then click 'Insert Duplicate Page' on the shortcut menu. You will leave page 2 blank for future content.

   c. If necessary, click the Page 1 icon in the Page Navigation pane to return to page 1 in the brochure.

   d. Save the publication on your storage device with the file name, Extend 2–1 Team Training Brochure.

5. Click the Online Pictures button (Insert tab | Illustrations group). Use Bing Image Search to insert a picture of the earth or a globe similar to the one shown in Figure 2–75. Be sure you review the specific copyright license of any pictures you use from the web. Drag the picture to the scratch area and then click the Arrange Thumbnails button (Picture Tools Format tab | Arrange group) to reduce the size of the thumbnail.

6. Repeat Step 5 to insert three photos of state map outlines — you may have to enter the search term of a specific state, such as Kentucky state outline. Review the specific copyright license of any pictures you use from the web.

7. To create the right panel, which serves as the front of the brochure, do the following:

   a. Drag the earth to the right panel. Position it approximately in the center, vertically; and resize it so that it almost fills the panel horizontally. Click the More button (Picture Tools Format | Pictures Styles), and choose an appropriate picture style, such as the Drop Shadow Rectangle. Deselect the picture.

   b. Click the 'Draw Text Box' button (Home tab | Objects group). Drag to create a text box at the top of the right panel, approximately 1½" tall. Stay within the margin and guides. Type **Early Response Team Training** to enter the text. Right-click the text, and then click Best Fit on the shortcut menu.

   c. Click the 'Draw Text Box' button (Home tab | Objects group). Drag to create another text box in the lower portion of the right panel. Type **A collaborative effort to provide a caring presence in the aftermath of disaster** to enter the text in the text box. Right-click the text, and then click Best Fit on the shortcut menu.

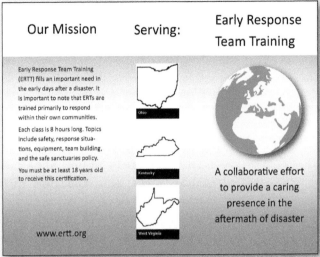

Figure 2–75

Continued >

STUDENT ASSIGNMENTS

8. To create the left panel:

   a. Create another text box in upper part of the left panel. Type **Our Mission** in the text box Use the 'Increase Font Size' button to make the font size approximately 36.

   b. Create a larger text box below the Our Mission text box, approximately 4½" high. Click inside the text box, and change the font size to 16. Type the following paragraphs letting Publisher wrap the text:

   Early Response Team Training (ERTT) fills an important need in the early days after a disaster. It is important to note that ERTs are trained primarily to respond within their own communities.
   Each class is 8 hours long. Topics include safety, response situations, equipment, team building, and the safe sanctuaries policy.
   You must be at least 18 years old to receive this certification.

   c. Create a text box at the bottom of the panel, still within the margins and guides of the left panel. Type **www.ertt.org** to enter the web address. When Publisher capitalizes the first letter, use the AutoCorrect Options button to remove the capitalization. Autofit the text.

   d. If requested by your instructor, change the web address to your webpage or Facebook page.

9. Use Help to read about the Align and Distribute commands related to objects.

10. To create the middle panel of page 1:

    a. Create another text box in upper part of the center panel. Type **Serving:**. Use the 'Increase Font Size' button (Home tab | Font group) to make the font size approximately 36.

    b. One at a time, drag the state outline graphics from the scratch area to the middle panel. Place them in the approximate locations shown in Figure 2–75.

    c. Select one of the state outline graphics. Click the Caption button (Picture Tools Format tab | Picture Styles group) and choose a caption style, such as Reversed Layout 1. Type the name of the state in the resulting caption text box. Repeat the process for the other two state outline graphics.

    d. Drag around all three graphics and captions in the middle panel. Click the Align Objects button (Drawing Tools Format tab | Arrange group) and then click Distribute Vertically on the Align Objects menu.

11. Click the Background button (Page Design tab | Page Background group) and then click 'Accent 2 Horizontal Gradient' in the Background gallery.

12. Click the Shapes button (Insert tab | Illustrations group) and then click the Rectangle shape in the Shapes gallery. Drag a rectangle across the top of page 1. With the rectangle selected, click the Shape Outline arrow and then click 'Accent 5 (White)' in the Shape Outline gallery. Click the Shape Fill arrow (Drawing Tools Format tab | Shapes Styles group) and then click 'Accent 5 (White)' in the Shape Fill gallery. Click the Send Backward button (Drawing Tools Format tab | Arrange group) three times to move the rectangle behind the text boxes.

13. Check the brochure for spelling errors and design errors and fix them as necessary. Save the file again.

14. Use the Pack and Go Wizard as described in the module, to pack the publication.

15. Preview the publication using the Print gallery. If possible, print the publication on special brochure paper

16. ✹ When would you use a template instead of creating a brochure from scratch? Would formatting the font before you type be easier than selecting text and formatting it afterward?

Expand Your World

Create a solution that uses cloud and web technologies by learning and investigating on your own from general guidance.

Creating a Webpage with a Brochure Link

Instructions: If you do not have a OneDrive account, create one. For a detailed example of the procedure, refer to the Office and Windows module. Run Publisher and open one of your brochures. Save the brochure on OneDrive. You would like to create a webpage with a link to download one of your brochures stored on the cloud, because many company websites include a link to download a print copy of various brochures.

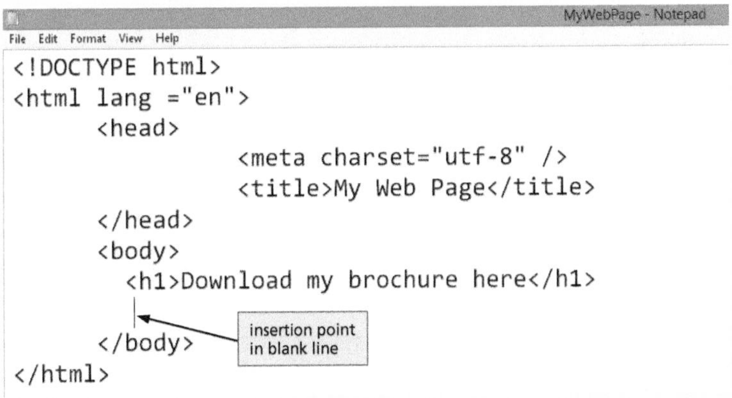

Perform the following tasks:

1. Run the Notepad app or other text editor app on your computer. Enter the code from Figure 2–76, leaving the ninth line blank, as shown.

2. If requested to do so by your instructor, change the words, My Web Page, to your name in line five.

3. Save the file on your storage device, using MyWebPage.html as the file name. Do not close the text editor window.

```
                                                    MyWebPage - Notepad
File  Edit  Format  View  Help
<!DOCTYPE html>
<html lang ="en">
      <head>
                      <meta charset="utf-8" />
                      <title>My Web Page</title>
      </head>
      <body>
        <h1>Download my brochure here</h1>

      </body>              insertion point
</html>                     in blank line
```

Figure 2–76

4. Run a browser and navigate to your OneDrive account.

5. Right-click the stored brochure file to display the shortcut menu, and then click Embed. When prompted, click the Generate button (Embed dialog box). When OneDrive displays the HTML code, press CTRL+C to copy the highlighted code.

6. Go back to the text editor window and position the insertion point on line nine. Press CTRL+V to paste the code into the file. If necessary, click Format on the menu bar and then click Word Wrap to enable the feature. Save the HTML file again and then close the window.

7. To view your webpage, open a File Explorer window and then navigate to the location of your saved HTML file. Double-click the MyWebPage.html file. If the browser asks permission to run the ActiveX content, click the 'Allow blocked content' button.

8. Submit the assignment in the format specified by your instructor.

9. ✸ Does your school provide a brochure about its program? Can you download the brochure from the school's website? Do you think it still is good to have a hard copy? Why?

In the Labs

Design, create, modify, and/or use a publication following the guidelines, concepts, and skills presented in this module. Labs 1 and 2, which increase in difficulty, require you to create solutions based on what you learned in the module; Lab 3 requires you to apply your creative thinking and problem-solving skills to design and implement a solution.

Lab 1: Creating a Bi-Fold DVD Insert

Note: To complete this assignment, you will be required to use the Data Files. Please contact your instructor for information about accessing the Data Files.

Continued >

In the Labs *continued*

Problem: A friend of yours has produced a DVD of original music. She would like you to design the insert that will be packaged with the DVD. You decide to look through Publisher's templates for an appropriate file to use as a starting point. You create the CD/DVD label shown in Figure 2–77.

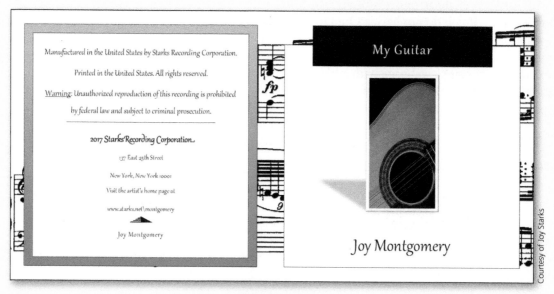

Figure 2–77

Perform the following tasks:

1. Run Publisher. Click BUILT-IN and then scroll as necessary to click the Labels thumbnail. Click the All Media folder.

2. In the CD/DVD Labels area, click CD/DVD Booklet thumbnail.

3. In the Customization area, choose the Parrot color scheme and the Calligraphy font scheme.

4. Click the CREATE button.

5. Use the Pictures button (Insert tab | Illustrations group) to insert the picture of the music from the Data Files. Move the picture to the scratch area. Right-click the picture, point to 'Apply to Background' on the shortcut menu, and then click Fill on the Apply to Background menu to place the picture in the background of the page.

6. Perform the following steps to edit objects in the right panel:

   a. Click the CD Title and then type **My Guitar** to complete the name of the DVD. Right-click the text and then click Best Fit on the shortcut menu. Click the Performer's Name text and then type **Joy Montgomery** to enter the performer. Right-click the text and then click Best Fit on the shortcut menu. Select the text and then press CTRL+C to copy it to the Clipboard.

   b. If requested by your instructor, replace Joy Montgomery with your name.

   c. Right-click the graphic, point to Change Picture on the shortcut menu, and then click Change Picture on the Change Picture menu to display the Insert Pictures dialog box. Navigate to the Data Files and then double-click the file named Guitar. Click the Reset Picture button (Picture Tools Format tab | Adjust group) to reset the picture.

   d. With the picture selected, click the More button (Picture Tools Format tab | Picture Styles group) and then click 'Perspective Shadow, White' in the Picture Style gallery.

   e. With the picture still selected, click the Picture Border button (Picture Tools Format tab | Picture Styles group), point to the Weight command, and then click 3 to change the weight of the border.

7. Perform the following steps to edit objects in the left panel:

   a. Click the text in the first text box and then type the following text, pressing the ENTER key and the end of each sentence.

   `Manufactured in the United States by Starks`
   `Recording Corporation.`
   `Printed in the United States. All rights reserved.`
   `Warning: Unauthorized reproduction of this`
   `recording is prohibited by federal law and subject`
   `to criminal prosecution.`

   b. Select the text in the Business Name text box. Type `2017 Starks Recording Corporation` to complete the text. Right-click the text and then click Best Fit on the shortcut menu. Select the text. Click the Stylistic Sets button (Text Box Tools Format tab | Typography group) and then choose the last stylistic set in the gallery.

   c. Select the text in the Address text box. Type `137 East 25th Street` and then press the ENTER key. Type `New York, New York 10001` to complete the text. Right-click the text and then click Best Fit on the shortcut menu.

   d. Select the text in the Phone text box. Type `Visit the artist's home page at` and then press the ENTER key. Type `www.starks.net\montgomery` to complete the text. Right-click the text and then click Best Fit on the shortcut menu.

   e. Click the text, Organization. Press CTRL+V to paste the text from the clipboard. Click the Paste Options button and then click the 'Keep Text Only' button.

8. Check the publication for spelling and design errors, and fix them as necessary. Save the file with the name, Lab 2–1 DVD Label.

9. Use the Pack and Go Wizard as described in the module to pack the publication.

10. Submit the file in the format specified by your instructor.

11. ✹ For extra credit, right-click Page 1 in the Page Navigation pane, and insert a new page. Insert pictures of your favorite artist. Create a text box with a list of songs. How did you decide on picture and text box placement?

Lab 2: **Editing an Order Form with Stylistic Sets**

Note: To complete this assignment, you will be required to use the Data Files. Please contact your instructor for information about accessing the Data Files.

Problem: The Biology Club is selling poinsettias and wreaths for the Christmas season. The members started creating a form, but they would like you to make it more appealing. You create the form shown in Figure 2–78.

Perform the following tasks:

1. Run Publisher and open the file called Lab 2–2 Order Form from the Data Files.

2. Click the heading. Type `Biology Club Order Form` to replace the text. Change the font to Gabriola. Change the font size to 22. Change the font color to red. Resize the text box as necessary to display all of the text.

3. If requested by your instructor, change the name of the club to an organization with which you have an affiliation.

Continued >

In the Labs *continued*

4. With the heading text still selected, click the Stylistic Sets button (Text Box Tools Format tab | Typography group). Select a fancy stylistic set. Resize the text box as necessary to display all of the glyphs.

5. Select the text in the Item # text box. Change the font to Gabriola and the font size to 11. double-click the Format Painter button (Home tab | Clipboard group) to copy the formatting.

6. One at a time, select each of the other text boxes on the form to apply the formatting. It is okay if the alignment changes. If necessary, resize any text boxes that are too small to accommodate the font change. When formatting is complete, click the Format Painter button again to turn off the format painter.

7. Select the picture. Click the Caption button (Picture Tools Format tab | Picture Styles group) to display the Caption gallery. Choose the Offset – Layout 3 caption style. Edit the caption to say: We deliver on campus!

8. Check the brochure for spelling errors and design errors, and fix them as necessary. Save the order form on your storage device with the file name, Lab 2–2 Order Form Complete.

9. Submit the file as directed by your instructor.

10. ✳ How might you have created this order form from scratch? Does Publisher have the individual components that you could add? Would that have been easier than trying to customize a built-in form?

Figure 2–78

Lab 3: Consider This: Your Turn

Creating a Youth Baseball League Brochure

Problem: Your brother has asked you to help him create a brochure announcing the sign-up dates for the youth baseball league that he coaches.

Perform the following tasks:

Part 1:   Pick an appropriate color and font scheme for the brochure, and include a sign-up form. Type **Preseason Sign-Up** as the brochure title. Type **Youth Baseball League** to replace the Business Name text. Type your address and phone number in the appropriate text boxes. Delete the logo. Replace all graphics with sports-related clip art. Edit the captions to match. Edit the sign-up form with appropriate events, such as T-Ball, Coach Pitched, and Little League. Include times and prices. The league commissioner will send you content for the stories at a later date.

Part 2:   ✳ On a separate piece of paper, make a table similar to Table 2–1 in this module, listing the type of exposure, information, audience, and purpose of the communication. Turn in the table with your printout.

3 Designing a Newsletter

Objectives

You will have mastered the material in this module when you can:

- Describe the advantages of using the newsletter medium and identify the steps in its design process
- Edit a newsletter template
- Set page options
- Edit a masthead
- Import text files
- Navigate pages
- Continue a story across pages and insert continued notices

- Customize the ribbon
- Use Publisher's Edit Story in Microsoft Word feature
- Insert and edit marginal elements
- Revise a newsletter
- Apply decorative drop caps
- Drag and drop text
- Check hyphenation in stories
- Create a template with property changes

Introduction

Desktop publishing is becoming an increasingly popular way for businesses of all sizes to produce their printed publications. The desktop aspects of design and production make it easy and inexpensive to produce high-quality publications in a short time. **Desktop publishing** (DTP) encompasses performing all publishing tasks from a desk, including the planning, designing, writing, and layout, as well as printing, collating, and distributing. With a personal computer and a software program, such as Publisher, you can create a professional publication from your computer without the cost and time of using a professional printing service.

Project — Shelter Newsletter

Newsletters are a popular way for offices, businesses, schools, and other organizations to distribute information to their clientele. A **newsletter** usually is a double-sided multipage publication with newspaper features, such as columns and a masthead, and the added eye appeal of sidebars, pictures, and other graphics.

Newsletters have several advantages over other publication media. Typically, they are cheaper to produce than brochures. Brochures, designed to be in circulation longer as a type of advertising, are published in greater quantities and on more expensive paper than newsletters, making brochures more costly. Newsletters also differ from brochures in that newsletters commonly have a shorter shelf life, making newsletters a perfect forum for information with dates. Newsletters are narrower and more focused in scope than newspapers; their eye appeal is more distinctive. Many companies distribute newsletters to interested audiences; however, newsletters also are becoming an integral part of many marketing plans to widen audiences, because they offer a legitimate medium by which to communicate services, successes, and issues.

The project in this module uses a Publisher newsletter template to produce the Shelter Days newsletter shown in Figure 3–1. This monthly publication informs readers about the Brisbane County Animal Shelter. The shelter's four-page newsletter contains a masthead, headings, stories, sidebars, pullquotes, a calendar, and graphics.

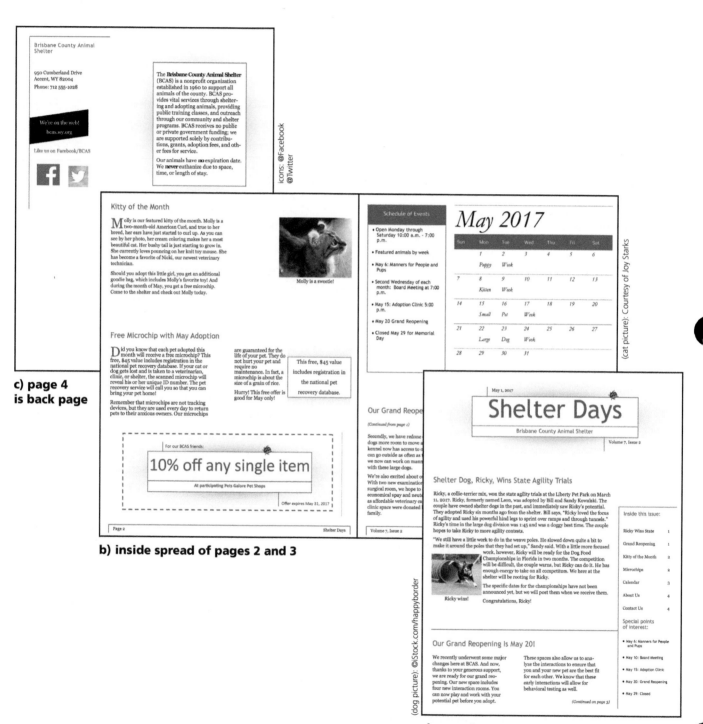

c) page 4 is back page

b) inside spread of pages 2 and 3

a) page 1

Figure 3–1

The following roadmap identifies general activities you will perform as you progress through this module:

1. Select a newsletter template and EDIT PUBLICATION OPTIONS.
2. IMPORT text from files and CONNECT STORIES across pages.
3. USE CONTINUED NOTICES.
4. CUSTOMIZE the RIBBON.
5. EDIT USING Microsoft WORD when necessary.
6. INSERT MARGINAL ELEMENTS.
7. APPLY DROP CAPS and HYPHENATE.
8. CREATE a TEMPLATE and change properties.

BTW
Organizing Files and Folders
You should organize and store files in folders so that you easily can find the files later. For example, if you are taking an introductory computer class called CIS 101, a good practice would be to save all Publisher files in a Publisher folder in a CIS 101 folder. For a discussion of folders and detailed examples of creating folders, refer to the Office and Windows module at the beginning of this book.

CONSIDER THIS

How do you decide on the purpose and audience of a newsletter?

Designing an effective newsletter involves a great deal of planning in order to deliver a message in the clearest, most attractive, and most effective way possible. Spend time brainstorming ideas for the newsletter with other members of the organization. Ask yourself why you want to create a newsletter in the first place and what message you want to convey. Remember that newsletters both communicate and educate. Identify the scope of the newsletter and whether you want the topic to be general in nature or more specific — perhaps about only one aspect of the organization. Use the phrase, "I want to tell <audience> about <topic> because <purpose>." Decide on one purpose, and adjust your plans to match that purpose.

As you decide on your audience, ask yourself these questions:

• Who will be reading the stories?

• What are the demographics of this population? That is, what are their characteristics, such as gender, age, educational background, and heritage?

• Why do you want those people to read your newsletter?

Decide if the audience is composed of local, interested clientele, patrons, employees, prospective customers, or family members. Keep in mind the age of your readers and their backgrounds, including both present and future readers.

Benefits and Advantages of Newsletters

Table 3–1 lists some benefits and advantages of using the newsletter medium.

Table 3–1	Benefits and Advantages of Using a Newsletter
Purpose	**Benefits and Advantages**
Exposure	An easily distributed publication via office mail, by bulk mail, or electronically
	A pass-along publication for other interested parties
	A coffee-table reading item in reception areas
Education	An opportunity to inform in a nonrestrictive environment
	A directed education forum for clientele
	Increased, focused feedback that is unavailable in most advertising
Contacts	A form of legitimized contact
	A source of free information to build credibility
	An easier way to expand a contact database than other marketing tools
Communication	An effective medium to highlight the inner workings of a company
	A way to create a discussion forum
	A method to disseminate more information than a brochure
Cost	An easily designed medium using desktop publishing software
	An inexpensive method of mass production
	A reusable design using a newsletter template

For an introduction to Windows and instructions about how to perform basic Windows tasks, read the Office and Windows module at the beginning of this book, where you can learn how to resize windows, change screen resolution, create folders, move and rename files, use Windows Help, and much more.

Publisher's newsletter templates include stories, graphics, sidebars, and other elements typical of newsletters using a rich collection of intuitive design, layout, typography, and graphic tools. Because Publisher takes care of many of the design issues, using a template to begin a newsletter gives you the advantage of proven layouts with fewer chances of publication errors.

Newsletter Design Choices

Publisher's many design-planning features include more than 100 different newsletter templates from which you may choose, each with its own set of design, color, font, and layout schemes. Each newsletter template produces four pages of stories, graphics, page numbers, and other objects in the same way. The difference is the location and style of the shapes and graphics, as well as the specific kind of decorations unique to each publication set. A **publication set** is a predefined group of shapes, designed in patterns to create a template style. A publication set is consistant across publication types; for example, the Bars newsletter template has the same shapes and style of objects as does the Bars brochure template. A publication set helps in branding a company across publication types.

Another choice you have when making decisions about newsletter design is how the pages will be organized and ultimately printed. A **one-page spread** displays and prints the pages individually in portrait mode — the printed pages would need to be stapled or bound in some way. A **two-page spread** displays the first and last pages individually, but displays the middle pages as two facing pages similar to a book format. If you have special newsletter paper, such as 11 × 17, the pages print landscape, so you can fold the newsletter. Other print sizes are available as built-in templates, listed within the Blank Pages section. In the workspace, a two-page spread makes it easier to see how the pages will look when open. Stories and figures spanning a two-page spread rarely need notices about continuation. In a two-page spread, the page on the left is called a **verso page**. The page on the right is called a **recto page**.

To Choose a Newsletter Template and Options

The following steps choose a newsletter template and change its options.

1. Run Publisher and then click BUILT-IN to display the built-in templates.
2. Scroll as necessary and then click the Newsletters thumbnail to display the Newsletter templates.
3. Scroll to the section labeled, More Installed Templates, and then click the Nature thumbnail to choose the template.
4. Click the Color scheme button in the template information pane. Scroll as necessary and then click Orange to choose the color scheme.
5. Click the Font scheme button, scroll as necessary, and then click Urban to choose the font scheme.
6. Do not click the Business information button because it is not used in this publication.
7. Click the Page size button in the Options area and then, if necessary, click 'Two-page spread' to choose how the template will display.
8. If necessary, click to remove the check mark in the 'Include customer address' check box (Figure 3–2).
9. Click the CREATE button to create the publication based on the template settings.

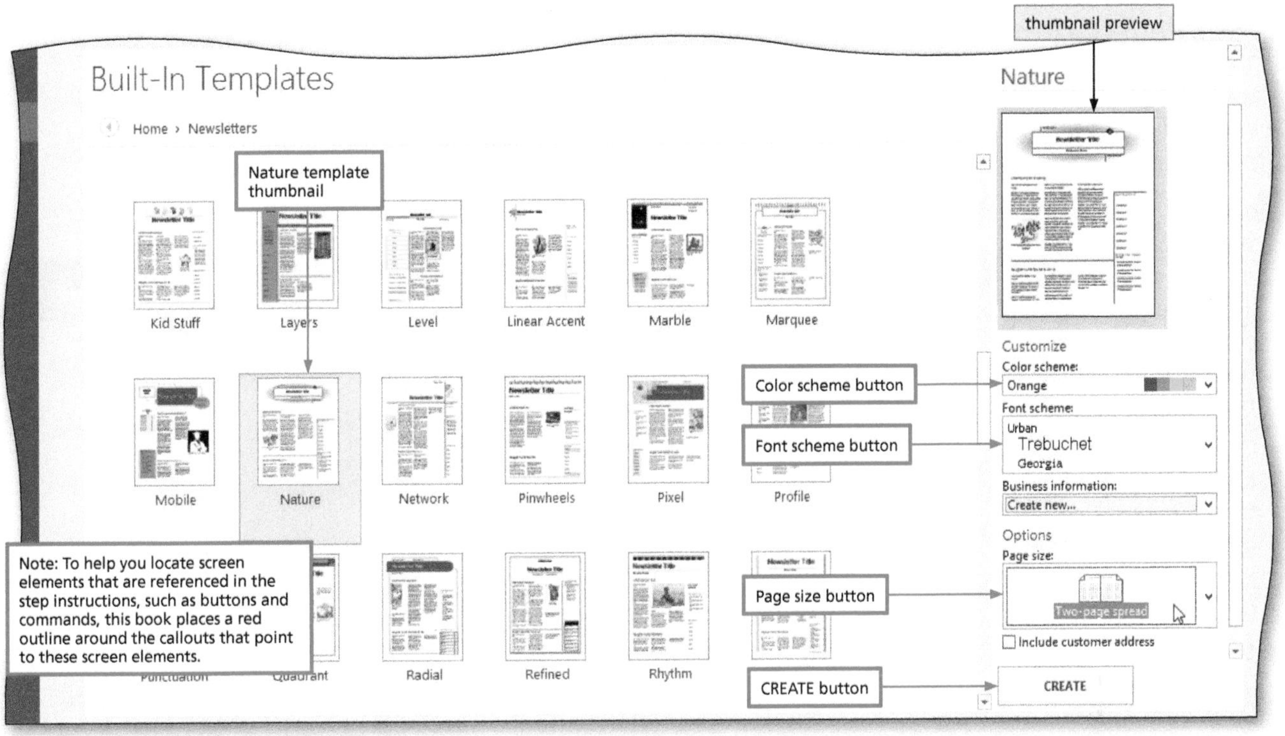

Built-In Templates

Home › Newsletters

thumbnail preview

Nature

Nature template thumbnail

Kid Stuff Layers Level Linear Accent Marble Marquee

Mobile Nature Network Pinwheels Pixel Profile

Note: To help you locate screen elements that are referenced in the step instructions, such as buttons and commands, this book places a red outline around the callouts that point to these screen elements.

Punctuation Quadrant Radial Refined Rhythm

Color scheme button
Font scheme button

Page size button

CREATE button

Customize
Color scheme:
Orange
Font scheme:
Urban
   Trebuchet
   Georgia
Business information:
Create new...

Options
Page size:
Two-page spread
☐ Include customer address

CREATE

Figure 3–2

To Set Publisher Display Settings

As discussed in Module 2, it is helpful to display formatting marks, which indicate where in the publication you pressed the ENTER key, the SPACEBAR key, and other keys. The following steps display formatting marks and open the Page Navigation pane to display all of the pages of the newsletter.

1 If the Special Characters button (Home tab | Paragraph group) is not selected already, click it to display formatting marks on the screen.

2 If the Page Navigation pane is not displayed, click the Page Number button on the status bar to open the Page Navigation pane. If the Page Navigation pane is minimized, click the 'Expand Page Navigation Pane' button to maximize it.

How do you decide about options for the layout and printing?
Choosing a layout and printing option before you even write the stories is a daunting, yet extremely important, task. The kind of printing process and paper you will be using will affect the cost and, therefore, the length of the newsletter. Depending on what you can afford to produce and distribute, the layout may need more or fewer stories, graphics, columns, and sidebars. Base your decisions on content that will be repeated in future newsletters.

Make informed decisions about the kind of alignment you plan to use. Choose the paper size and determine how columns, a masthead, and graphics will affect your layout. Decide what kinds of features in the newsletter should be close to each other. A consistent look and feel with simple, eye-catching graphics normally is the best choice for the publication set. Plan to include one graphic with each story. Because newsletters usually are mass-produced, collated, and stapled, you should make a plan for printing and decide if you are going to publish it in-house or externally. Choose a paper that is going to last until the next newsletter.

CONSIDER THIS

To Set Page Options

Publisher newsletters can display one, two, or three columns of story text, or mix the format. *Why?* *Changing the number of columns in a story or mixing the format adds visual interest.* Inside pages also can display calendars and forms. The following steps select page options for the various pages in the newsletter.

1
- With page 1 of the newsletter displayed in the workspace, click Page Design on the ribbon to display the Page Design tab.
- Click the Options button (Page Design tab | Template group) to display the Page Content dialog box.
- Click the Columns button to display its list (Figure 3–3).

Q&A Does the column choice affect the objects down the right side of the newsletter page?
No, the number of columns that you choose will be displayed in the stories only, and the choice affects only the current page.

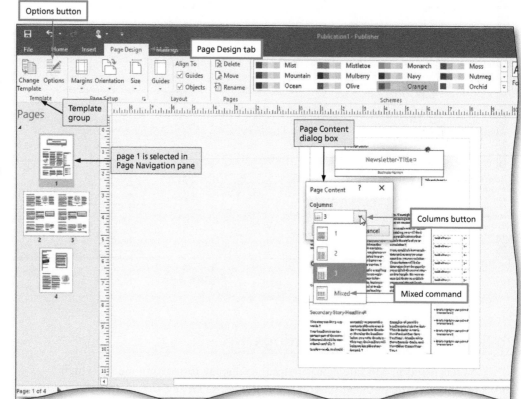

Figure 3–3

2
- Click Mixed in the Columns list to choose a mixed number of columns for the stories on page 1.
- Click the OK button (Page Content dialog box) to change the options for the page (Figure 3–4).

 Q&A Is one choice better than another one?
No, it is a personal or customer preference. Longer stories may need to be continued at different places, depending upon how many columns of text you have. The more columns you have, the more white space is created on the page.

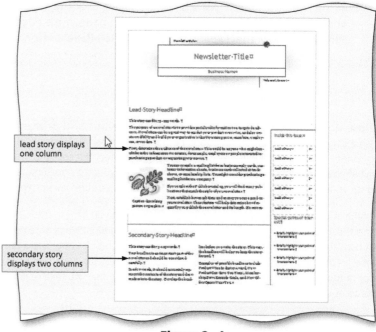

Figure 3–4

3

- In the Page Navigation pane, click the 'Page 2 and Page 3' icon to display the pages in the workspace.
- Click the Options button (Page Design tab | Template group) to display the Page Content dialog box.
- Click the 'Select a page to modify' button to display its list (Figure 3–5).

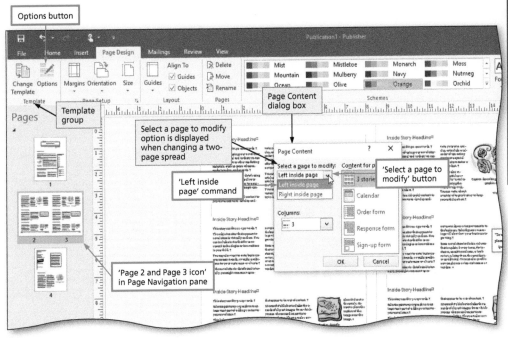

Figure 3–5

4

- Click 'Left inside page' to choose the verso page, if necessary.
- Click the Columns button to display its list (Figure 3–6).

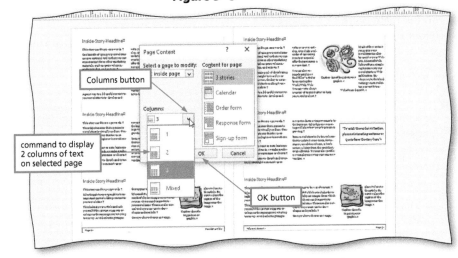

Figure 3–6

5

- Click 2 in the Columns list to choose a two-column format for the stories on page 2.
- Click the OK button (Page Content dialog box) to close the dialog box (Figure 3–7).

Q&A Can I move pages around in my newsletter?
Yes, you can right-click in the Page Navigation pane and then choose Move on the shortcut menu. Publisher will display a dialog box, allowing you to specify which page to move and the new location.

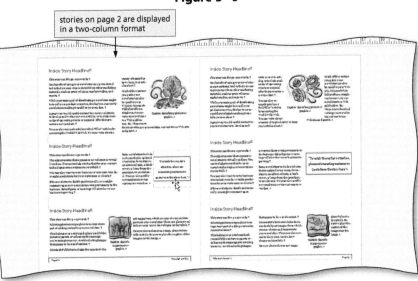

Figure 3–7

6
- Click the Options button (Page Design tab | Template group) to display the Page Content dialog box again.
- Click the 'Select a page to modify' button and then click 'Right inside page' to choose the recto page.
- Click the Columns button and then click 2 in the Columns list to choose 2 columns.
- In the Content for page area, click Calendar to insert a calendar on the recto page (Figure 3–8).

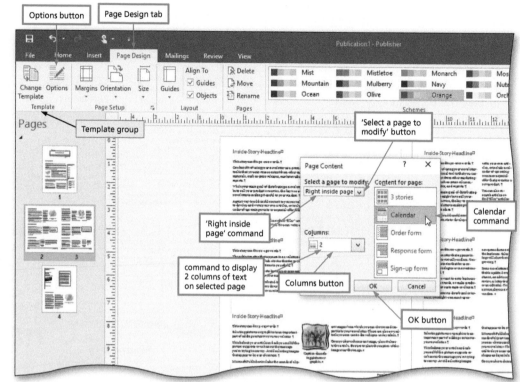

Figure 3–8

7
- Click the OK button (Page Content dialog box) to close the dialog box.
- Click the Save button on the Quick Access Toolbar. Browse to the storage location. Save the file with the file name, Shelter Newsletter (Figure 3–9).

Q&A
My calendar is different. Did I do something wrong?
No. The calendar option uses the current month on your system. Any month is acceptable for this project. You will learn how to change calendar dates in a later module.

Should I change the options for the back page?
No. You will edit those objects individually later in the module.

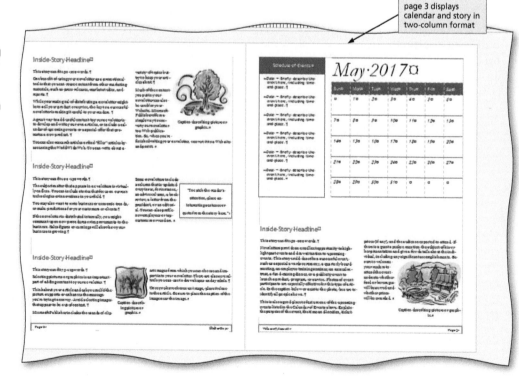

Figure 3–9

Changing the Number of Pages in a Newsletter

Not all newsletters are four pages long. Some will have more or fewer pages. The following sections describe how to delete pages from or add pages to a newsletter template.

TO DELETE PAGES FROM A NEWSLETTER

If you were designing a newsletter with only two pages, it would be best to delete pages 2 and 3 because page 4 already is formatted to be a back page in most templates. Pages 2 and 3 have inside page numbers and graphics. If you wanted to delete pages 2 and 3, you would perform the following steps.

1. Right-click the 'Page 2 and Page 3' icon in the Page Navigation pane to display the shortcut menu.
2. Click Delete on the shortcut menu to delete pages 2 and 3. When Publisher displays the Delete Page dialog box for confirmation, click Both pages and then click the OK button (Delete Page dialog box).

TO ADD PAGES TO A NEWSLETTER

If you wanted to add extra pages to a newsletter, you would perform the following steps.

1. Right-click the 'Page 2 and Page 3' icon in the Page Navigation pane to display the shortcut menu.
2. Click Insert Page on the shortcut menu to insert a new page. Follow the directions in the Insert Newsletter Pages dialog box to insert either a left-hand page, a right-hand page, or both, and then click the OK button (Insert Newsletter Pages dialog box).

Editing the Masthead

Most newsletters contain a masthead similar to those used in newspapers. A **masthead** is a box or section printed in each issue that lists information, such as the name, publisher, location, volume, and date. The Publisher-designed masthead, included in the Nature newsletter publication set, contains several text boxes and colors that create an attractive, eye-catching graphic to complement the set.

BTW

Zooming
Recall that the F9 key toggles between the current page view and 100% magnification or actual size. **Toggle** means the same key will alternate views, or turn a feature on and off. Editing text is easier if you view the text at 100% magnification or higher.

To Edit the Masthead

1 EDIT PUBLICATION OPTIONS | 2 IMPORT & CONNECT STORIES | 3 USE CONTINUED NOTICES | 4 CUSTOMIZE RIBBON
5 EDIT USING WORD | 6 INSERT MARGINAL ELEMENTS | 7 APPLY DROP CAPS & HYPHENATE | 8 CREATE TEMPLATE

The following steps edit text in the masthead, including the volume and issue number. *Why? Publications typically use volume numbers to indicate the number of years the publication has been in existence. The issue number indicates its sequence. Volume numbers and issue numbers do not necessarily correlate to the calendar year and months. Schools, for example, sometimes start in the fall with Volume 1, Issue 1.*

- Click the Page 1 icon in the Page Navigation pane to change the display to page 1.
- Click the text, Newsletter Title, to select it and then zoom to 150%.
- Type **Shelter Days** to replace the text. Right-click the text and then click Best Fit on the shortcut menu (Figure 3–10).

Q&A Why does my font look different?
Publisher replaces the selected text with the font from the publication set. Your font may differ from the one shown.

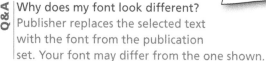
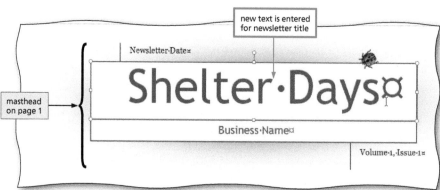

Figure 3–10

- Click the default text in the Business Name text box and then press CTRL+A to select all of the text.
- Type **Brisbane County Animal Shelter** to replace the text (Figure 3–11).

Figure 3–11

3

- Click the placeholder text in the Newsletter Date text box to select it.
- Type **May 1, 2017** to replace the text.
- Click the placeholder text in the Volume 1, Issue 1 text box to select it.
- Type **Volume 7, Issue 2** to replace the text (Figure 3–12).

Figure 3–12

BTW

Text in Overflow
The overflow area is an invisible storage location within a publication that holds extra text. You can move text out of overflow and back into a publication by one of several means: flowing text into a new text box, autofitting text, enlarging the text box, changing the text size, changing the margins within the text box, or deleting some of the text in the text box.

Newsletter Text

Newsletter content may come to you, as the desktop publisher, in various ways. Authors may submit their stories in email or as attachments. Others may post a Microsoft Word document or a graphic on the company's common storage location. Still other authors may handwrite their stories or record them on a recording device. In those cases, you will have to type the story yourself.

How do you gather topics and research stories?

Gather credible, relevant information in the form of stories, pictures, dates, figures, tables, and discussion threads. Plan far enough ahead so that you have time to take pictures or gather graphics for each story — even if you end up not using them. Stay organized; keep folders of information and store pictures and stories together. If you have to write a story from scratch, gather your data, do your research, and have an informed reader go over your content.

The same principles of audience, purpose, and topic apply to individual stories, just as they do for the newsletter as a whole. Evaluate your sources for authority, timeliness, and accuracy. Be especially wary of information obtained from the web. Any person, company, or organization can publish a webpage on the Internet. Ask yourself these questions about the source:

- Authority: Does a reputable institution or group support the source? Is the information presented without bias? Are the author's credentials listed and verifiable?

- Timeliness: Is the information up to date? Are the dates of sources listed? What is the last date that the information was revised or updated?

- Accuracy: Is the information free of errors? Is it verifiable? Are the sources clearly identified?

Identify the sources for your text and graphics. Notify all writers of important dates, and allow time for gathering the data. Make a list for each story: include the author's name, the approximate length of the story, the electronic format, and associated graphics. Ask the author for suggestions for headlines. Consult with colleagues about other graphics, features, sidebars, and the masthead.

Acknowledge all sources of information; do not plagiarize. Not only is plagiarism unethical, it also is considered an academic crime that can have severe consequences, such as failing a course or being expelled from school.

When you summarize, paraphrase (rewrite information in your own words), present facts, give statistics, quote exact words, or show a map, chart, or other graphical image, you must acknowledge the source. Information that commonly is known or accessible to the audience constitutes **common knowledge** and does not need to be acknowledged. If, however, you question whether certain information is common knowledge, you should document it — just to be safe.

Publisher allows users to import text and graphics from many sources, from a variety of different programs, and in many different file formats. Publisher uses the term, **importing**, to describe inserting text or objects from any other source into the Publisher workspace. Publisher uses the term, **story**, when referring to text that is contained within a single text box or a chain of linked text boxes. Each newsletter template provides **linked text boxes,** or text boxes whose text flows from one to another. In the templates, two or three text boxes may be linked automatically; however, if a story is too long to fit in the linked text boxes, Publisher will offer to link even more text boxes for easy reading.

Replacing Placeholder Text Using an Imported File

Publisher suggests that 175 to 225 words will fit in the space allocated for the lead story. The story is displayed in a two-column text box format that connects, or links, the running text from one text box to the next. Publisher links text boxes according to your settings, and it displays arrow buttons to navigate to the next and previous text boxes.

This edition of Shelter Days contains several stories, some of which have been typed previously and stored using Microsoft Word, as they might be in a business setting. The stories, located in the Data Files, are ready to be used in the newsletter. Please contact your instructor for information about accessing the Data Files. The final story you will type yourself. Each story will include a **headline**, which is a short phrase printed at the top of a story, usually in a bigger font than the story. A headline summarizes the story that follows it.

BTW

The Ribbon and Screen Resolution
Publisher may change how the groups and buttons within the groups appear on the ribbon, depending on the computer's screen resolution. Thus, your ribbon may look different from the ones in this book if you are using a screen resolution other than 1366 × 768.

BTW

Publisher Help
At any time while using Publisher, you can find answers to questions and display information about various topics through Publisher Help. Used properly, this form of assistance can increase your productivity and reduce your frustrations by minimizing the time you spend learning how to use Publisher. For instruction about Publisher Help and exercises that will help you gain confidence in using it, read the Office and Windows module at the beginning of this book.

To Edit the Lead Story Headline

The following steps edit the Lead Story Headline placeholder text.

1 Click the placeholder text, Lead Story Headline, on page 1 to select it.

2 Type `Shelter Dog, Ricky, Wins State Agility Trials` to replace the text (Figure 3–13).

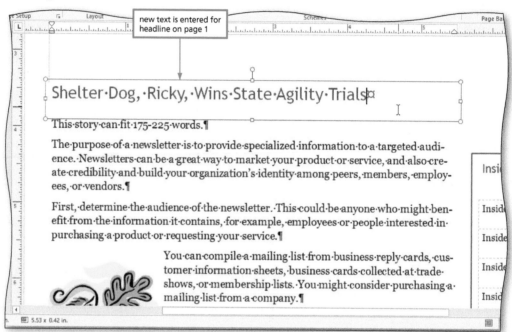

Figure 3–13

To Import a Text File

1 EDIT PUBLICATION OPTIONS | 2 IMPORT & CONNECT STORIES | 3 USE CONTINUED NOTICES | 4 CUSTOMIZE RIBBON
5 EDIT USING WORD | 6 INSERT MARGINAL ELEMENTS | 7 APPLY DROP CAPS & HYPHENATE | 8 CREATE TEMPLATE

The following steps import a text file to replace the Publisher-supplied placeholder text for the lead story. **Why?** *Importing the story prevents typographical errors created by retyping the text.* To complete these steps, you will be required to use the Data Files. Please contact your instructor for information about accessing the Data Files.

1

- Scroll down to display the story below the headline. Zoom to approximately 120%.

- Click the placeholder text in the story to select it (Figure 3–14).

🔍 **Experiment**

- Read the placeholder text in order to learn about design suggestions related to newsletter publications.

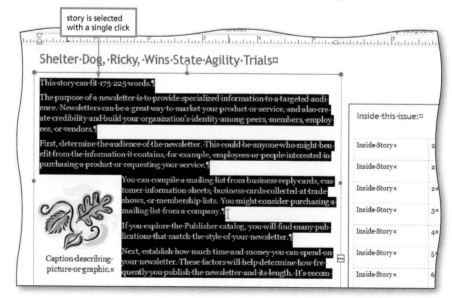

Figure 3–14

2

- Display the Insert tab.

- Click the Insert File button (Insert tab | Text group) to display the Insert Text dialog box.

- Navigate to the location of the file to be opened (in this case, the Module 03 folder in the Publisher Data Files) (Figure 3–15).

Q&A What kinds of text files can Publisher import?

Publisher can import files from most popular applications. If you click the 'All Text Formats' button (Insert Text dialog box), you can see a list of specific file types.

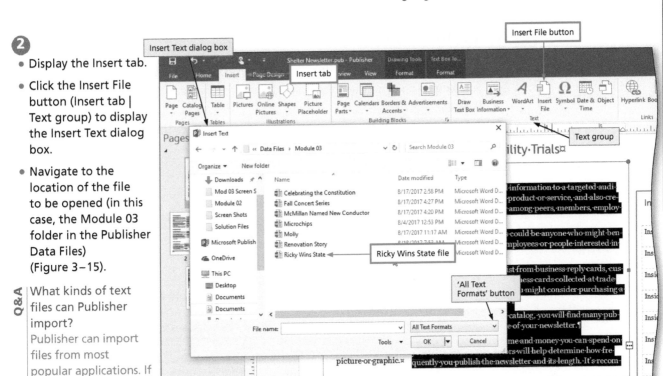

Figure 3–15

3

- Double-click the Ricky Wins State file to insert the text into the newsletter (Figure 3–16).

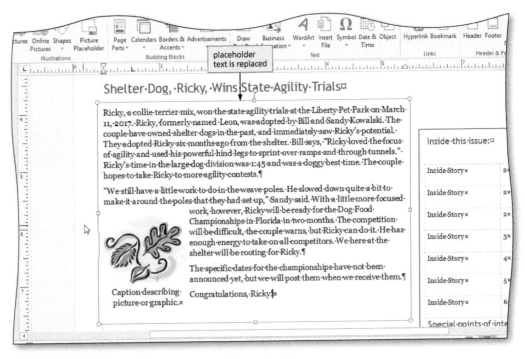

Shelter·Dog,·Ricky,·Wins·State·Agility·Trials¤

Ricky,·a·collie-terrier·mix,·won·the·state·agility·trials·at·the·Liberty·Pet·Park·on·March·11,·2017.·Ricky,·formerly·named·Leon,·was·adopted·by·Bill·and·Sandy·Kowalski.·The·couple·have·owned·shelter·dogs·in·the·past,·and·immediately·saw·Ricky's·potential.·They·adopted·Ricky·six·months·ago·from·the·shelter.·Bill·says,·"Ricky·loved·the·focus·of·agility·and·used·his·powerful·hind·legs·to·sprint·over·ramps·and·through·tunnels."·Ricky's·time·in·the·large·dog·division·was·1:45·and·was·a·doggy·best·time.·The·couple·hopes·to·take·Ricky·to·more·agility·contests.¶

"We·still·have·a·little·work·to·do·in·the·weave·poles.·He·slowed·down·quite·a·bit·to·make·it·around·the·poles·that·they·had·set·up,"·Sandy·said.·With·a·little·more·focused·work,·however,·Ricky·will·be·ready·for·the·Dog·Food·Championships·in·Florida·in·two·months.·The·competition·will·be·difficult,·the·couple·warns,·but·Ricky·can·do·it.·He·has·enough·energy·to·take·on·all·competitors.·We·here·at·the·shelter·will·be·rooting·for·Ricky.¶

The·specific·dates·for·the·championships·have·not·been·announced·yet,·but·we·will·post·them·when·we·receive·them.¶

Caption·describing· picture·or·graphic.¤   Congratulations,·Ricky!¤

Figure 3–16

Other Ways

1. Right-click story, point to Change Text on shortcut menu, click Text File on Change Text submenu, click file name, click OK button (Insert Text dialog box)

To Edit the Secondary Story Headline

The following steps edit the Secondary Story Headline placeholder text.

1 Scroll down on page 1 and then click the placeholder text, 'Secondary Story Headline', to select it.

2 Type `Our Grand Reopening Is May 20!` to replace the text (Figure 3–17).

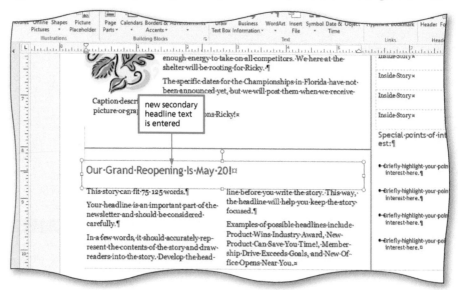

Figure 3–17

To Continue a Story across Pages

1 EDIT PUBLICATION OPTIONS | 2 IMPORT & CONNECT STORIES | 3 USE CONTINUED NOTICES | 4 CUSTOMIZE RIBBON
5 EDIT USING WORD | 6 INSERT MARGINAL ELEMENTS | 7 APPLY DROP CAPS & HYPHENATE | 8 CREATE TEMPLATE

As you import text, if a story contains more text than will fit in the default text box, Publisher displays a message to warn you. *Why? You then have the option to allow Publisher to connect, or* **autoflow***, the text to another available text box or to flow the text yourself, manually.* The following steps import a story and continue it from page 1 to page 2 using Publisher dialog boxes. To complete these steps, you will be required to use the Data Files. Please contact your instructor for information about accessing the Data Files.

1
- Click the secondary story placeholder text on page 1 to select it.
- Click the Insert File button (Insert tab | Text group) to display the Insert Text dialog box.
- If necessary, navigate to the location of the Data Files and then double-click the file named, Renovation Story, to insert the text file (Figure 3–18).

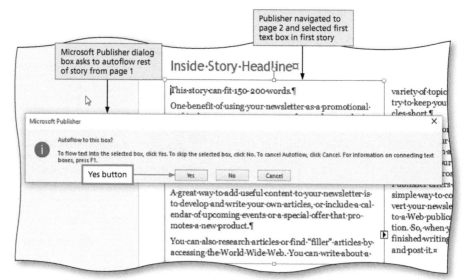

Figure 3–18

Q&A
Why did Publisher display a dialog box and move to page 2?
The story was too large to fit in the space provided on page 1. Publisher moved to the first available text box with default or placeholder story text.

2

- In the Microsoft Publisher dialog box, click the Yes button to autoflow the story to the selected text box (Figure 3–19).

Q&A What do the three Autoflow buttons do?

If you click the Yes button, as you did here, Publisher will insert the rest of the text in the currently selected text box. If you click the No button, Publisher will move to the next story text box and ask again. If you click the Cancel button, you will have to flow the text manually.

What if I have no more spare text boxes in which to flow the text?

Publisher will ask if you want new text boxes created. If you answer yes, Publisher automatically will create a new page with new text boxes.

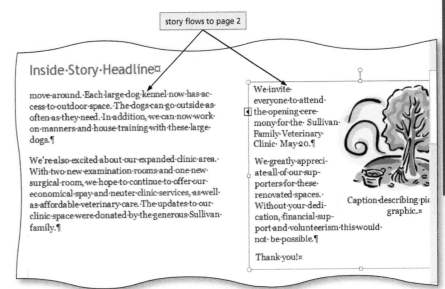

Figure 3–19

To Follow a Story across Pages

1 EDIT PUBLICATION OPTIONS | 2 IMPORT & CONNECT STORIES | 3 USE CONTINUED NOTICES | 4 CUSTOMIZE RIBBON
5 EDIT USING WORD | 6 INSERT MARGINAL ELEMENTS | 7 APPLY DROP CAPS & HYPHENATE | 8 CREATE TEMPLATE

Publisher provides a way to move quickly back and forth through a continued story. *Why? While reading and editing the story, you may forget where the rest of the story is located or want to jump to its location quickly.* The following steps use the Next and Previous buttons to follow the story from text box to text box, across pages.

1

- Click the Page 1 icon in the Page Navigation pane and navigate to the Our Grand Reopening Is May 20! story at the bottom of the page.

- Click the second text box in the story to display the Previous and Next buttons (Figure 3–20).

Q&A Do all text boxes have Previous and Next buttons?

No. Only text boxes that contain a linked story display the buttons.

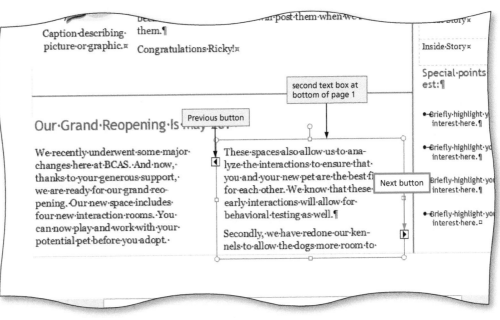

Figure 3–20

2

- Click the Next button to move to the rest of the story — the first text box at the top of page 2 (Figure 3–21).

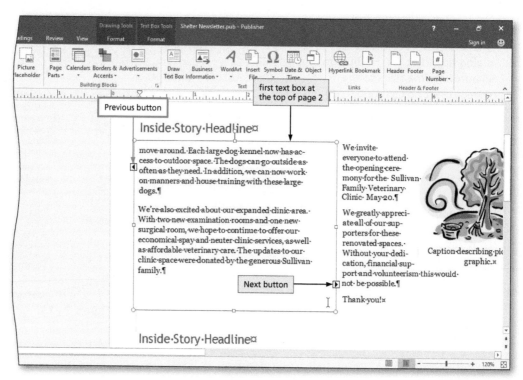

Figure 3–21

3

- Click the Previous button to move back to the first part of the story — the second text box at the bottom of page 1 (Figure 3–22).

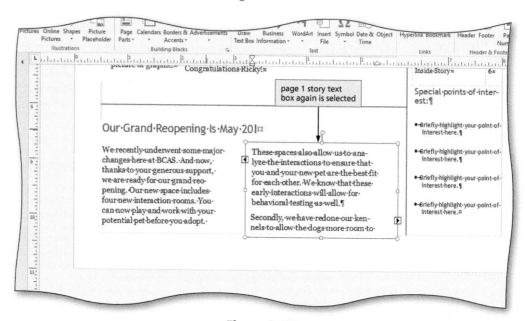

Figure 3–22

Other Ways

1. Select text box, click Previous or Next button (Text Box Tools Format tab | Linking group)

To Break a Text Box Link

1 EDIT PUBLICATION OPTIONS | 2 IMPORT & CONNECT STORIES | 3 USE CONTINUED NOTICES | 4 CUSTOMIZE RIBBON
5 EDIT USING WORD | 6 INSERT MARGINAL ELEMENTS | 7 APPLY DROP CAPS & HYPHENATE | 8 CREATE TEMPLATE

Sometimes, you might change your mind about where to continue a story. In that case, you have two choices. You can undo the previous insertion and autoflow again, or you can break the connection and create a manual one. When you break a connection, the extra text that cannot fit in the text box is placed in **overflow**. *Why? Unlike the Clipboard, the overflow area is maintained when you save the publication, allowing you to access it at any time.* The following step breaks the connection between the story at the bottom of page 1 and its continuation at the top of page 2.

1

- If necessary, navigate to page 1 and the story at the bottom of the page and then click the second column in the story to select the text box.
- Display the Text Box Tools Format tab.
- Click the Break button (Text Box Tools Format tab | Linking group) to break the connection to the rest of the story (Figure 3–23).

Q&A Where is the rest of the story now?
Publisher places it in a special overflow area as indicated by the 'Text in Overflow' button in Figure 3–23. The text box on page 2 becomes blank.

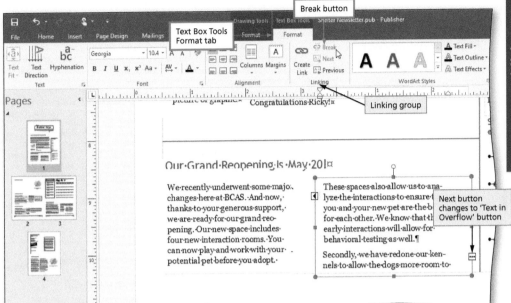

Figure 3–23

To Manually Continue the Story across Pages

1 EDIT PUBLICATION OPTIONS | 2 IMPORT & CONNECT STORIES | 3 USE CONTINUED NOTICES | 4 CUSTOMIZE RIBBON
5 EDIT USING WORD | 6 INSERT MARGINAL ELEMENTS | 7 APPLY DROP CAPS & HYPHENATE | 8 CREATE TEMPLATE

The following steps manually move the text from the overflow area to another text box. **Why?** *You cannot see the text while it is in overflow.*

1

- If necessary, select the text box that displays the 'Text in Overflow' button.
- Click the 'Text in Overflow' button to display the pitcher-shaped pointer (Figure 3–24).

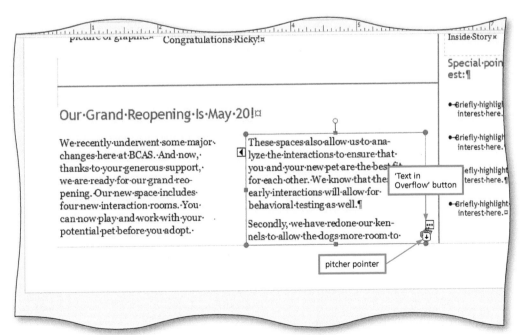

Figure 3–24

2

- Click the 'Page 2 and Page 3' icon in the Page Navigation pane to display the pages.

- Scroll as necessary to display the story at the bottom of page 3.

- With the pitcher-shaped pointer, click the placeholder text in the story to continue the Our Grand Reopening Is May 20! text (Figure 3–25).

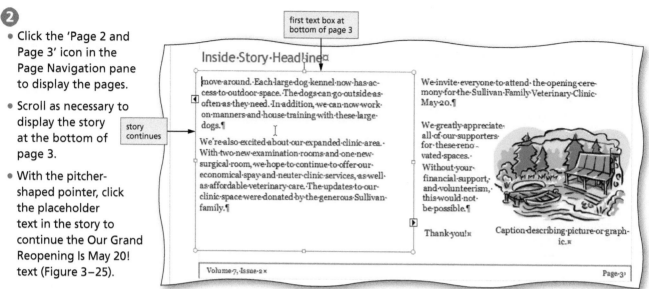

Figure 3–25

Q&A What if I change my mind and want to continue to a different text box?
You can click the Undo button on the Quick Access Toolbar, or you can click the last column of the story on page 1 and then click the Break button (Text Box Tools Format tab | Linking Group). You then can click the 'Text in Overflow' button again.

Other Ways

1. Select unlinked text box, click Create Link button (Text Box Tools Format tab | Linking group), click new text box

---

To Format with Continued Notices

1 EDIT PUBLICATION OPTIONS | 2 IMPORT & CONNECT STORIES | 3 USE CONTINUED NOTICES | **4 CUSTOMIZE RIBBON**
5 EDIT USING WORD | 6 INSERT MARGINAL ELEMENTS | 7 APPLY DROP CAPS & HYPHENATE | 8 CREATE TEMPLATE

In print publications for stories that flow from one page to another, it is good practice to add **continued notices**, or **jump lines**, to guide readers through the story. **Why?** *A continued notice helps readers find the rest of the story easily.* The following steps format the last text box on page 1 with a continued on notice. Then, on page 3, the first text box in the rest of the story is formatted with a continued from notice.

1

- Click the Page 1 icon in the Page Navigation pane and then navigate to the bottom of the page.

- Right-click the second column of text in the lead story to display the shortcut menu (Figure 3–26).

Q&A Will Publisher ask me what page number to use?
No. The placement of the notices and the page numbering are automatic.

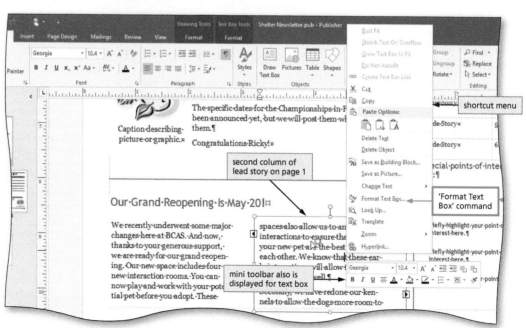

Figure 3–26

②

- Click 'Format Text Box' on the shortcut menu to display the Format Text Box dialog box.
- Click the Text Box tab to display its settings.
- Click to display a check mark in the 'Include "Continued on page…"' check box (Figure 3–27).

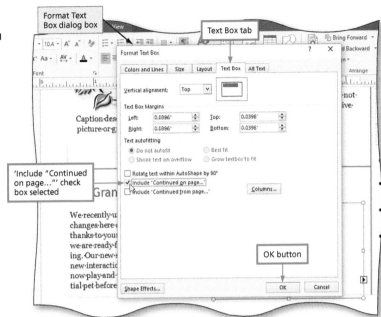

Figure 3–27

③

- Click the OK button (Format Text Box dialog box) to insert the continued on notice (Figure 3–28).

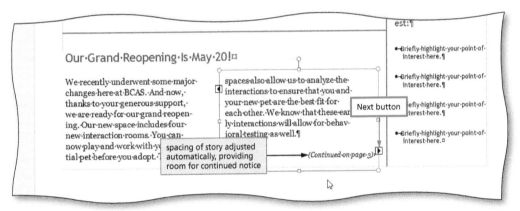

Our·Grand·Reopening·Is·May·20!¤

We·recently·underwent·some·major· changes·here·at·BCAS.··And·now,· thanks·to·your·generous·support,· we·are·ready·for·our·grand·reopen-ing.·Our·new·space·includes·four· new·interaction·rooms.·You·can· now·play·and·work·with·y… tial·pet·before·you·adopt.·

spaces·also·allow·us·to·analyze·the· interactions·to·ensure·that·you·and· your·new·pet·are·the·best·fit·for· each·other.·We·know·that·these·ear-ly·interactions·will·allow·for·behav-ioral·testing·as·well.¶

(Continued·on·page·3)

Figure 3–28

④

- Click the Next button to move to the rest of the story on page 3.
- Right-click the text in the first text box to display the shortcut menu and then click 'Format Text Box' on the shortcut menu to display the Format Text Box dialog box.
- If necessary, click the Text Box tab (Format Text Box dialog box) to display its settings.
- Click to display a check mark in the 'Include "Continued from page…"' check box (Figure 3–29).

Q&A What do I do if my dialog box is covering up the text box?
The setting changes will take place when you click the OK button. If you want to see both the dialog box and the text box, you can drag the title bar of the dialog box to a better location.

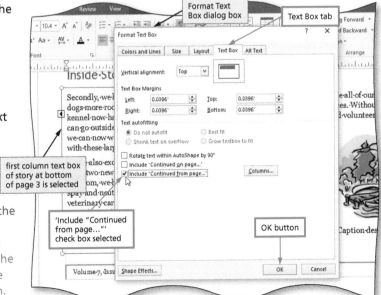

Figure 3–29

⑤

- Click the OK button (Format Text Box dialog box) to insert the continued from notice (Figure 3–30).

🔍 **Experiment**

- Use the Next and Previous buttons to move between the linked text boxes on pages 1 and 3. Examine the continued notices with the supplied page numbers.

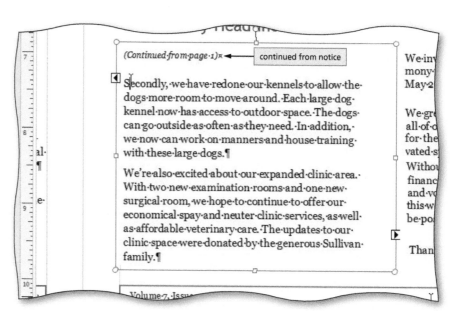

(Continued from page 1) ← continued from notice

Secondly, we have redone our kennels to allow the dogs more room to move around. Each large dog kennel now has access to outdoor space. The dogs can go outside as often as they need. In addition, we now can work on manners and house training with these large dogs.¶

We're also excited about our expanded clinic area. With two new examination rooms and one new surgical room, we hope to continue to offer our economical spay and neuter clinic services, as well as affordable veterinary care. The updates to our clinic space were donated by the generous Sullivan family.¶

Figure 3–30

Other Ways

1. Select text box, click Format Text Box Dialog Box Launcher (Text Box Tools Format tab | Text group), click Text Box tab (Format Text Box dialog box), click 'Include "Continued on page…"' or 'Include "Continued from page…"', click OK button

---

To Edit the Headlines for the Continued Story

The following step edits the inside headline for the continued story.

① Click the Inside Story Headline placeholder text to select it and then type `Our Grand Reopening Is May 20!` to replace the text (Figure 3–31).

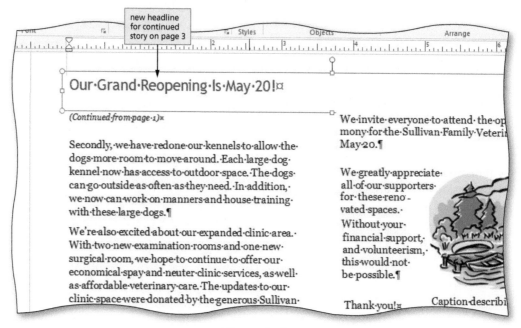

new headline for continued story on page 3

Our Grand Reopening Is May 20!¤

(Continued from page 1)

Secondly, we have redone our kennels to allow the dogs more room to move around. Each large dog kennel now has access to outdoor space. The dogs can go outside as often as they need. In addition, we now can work on manners and house training with these large dogs.¶

We're also excited about our expanded clinic area. With two new examination rooms and one new surgical room, we hope to continue to offer our economical spay and neuter clinic services, as well as affordable veterinary care. The updates to our clinic space were donated by the generous Sullivan

We invite everyone to attend the op mony for the Sullivan Family Veterin May 20.¶

We greatly appreciate all of our supporters for these reno vated spaces.

Without your financial support, and volunteerism, this would not be possible.¶

Thank you!¤   Caption describi

Figure 3–31

To Edit Page 2

The following steps edit the headline and import the text for two stories on page 2, and delete the third story to make room for later content. To complete these steps, you will be required to use the Data Files. Please contact your instructor for information about accessing the Data Files.

1 Scroll to display the top portion of page 2 and then click the Inside Story Headline placeholder text above the first story to select it. Recall that the first story text box is blank because of the autoflow change.

2 Type `Kitty of the Month` to replace the selected headline.

3 Click inside the empty story text box to position the insertion point.

4 Click the Insert File button (Insert tab | Text group) to display the Insert Text dialog box.

5 If necessary, navigate to the Data Files and then double-click the file named, Molly, to insert the text file.

6 Repeat steps 1 through 5 for the second story on page 2. Use the text, Free Microchip with May Adoption, as the headline. Insert the text file named Microchips for the story.

7 Zoom to approximately 80% to display both stories and headlines (Figure 3–32).

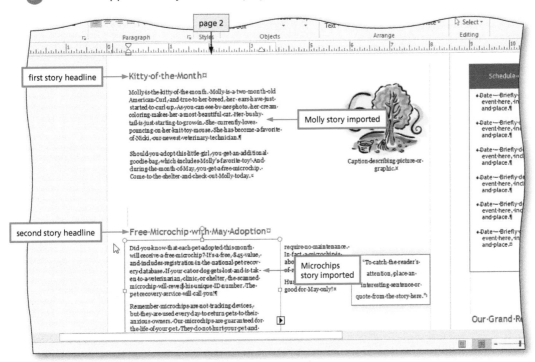

Figure 3–32

To Delete Objects on Page 2 and Page 4

The following steps remove the headline, story, and graphic on page 2. You will fill that area later in the module. The steps also remove the headline, story, and graphic at the bottom of page 4. The organization plans to fold the newsletter and mail it, so the bottom of page 4 will be reserved for mailing labels and postage.

1 Navigate to the bottom of page 2.

2 Drag to select the template headline, story, graphic, and caption.

③ Press the DELETE key to delete the selected objects.

④ Navigate to the top of page 2. Click between the graphic and story to select the second text box of the story, which is empty. Press the DELETE key.

⑤ Navigate to the bottom of page 4. Drag to select the template headline, story, graphic, and caption (Figure 3–33).

⑥ Press the DELETE key to delete the selected items.

⑦ Click the Save button on the Quick Access Toolbar to save the file again with the same file name, and in the same location.

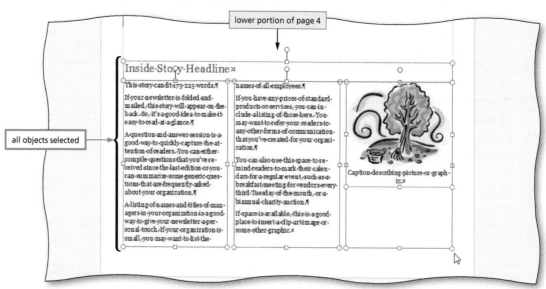

Figure 3–33

Break Point: If you wish to take a break, this is a good place to do so. Exit Publisher. To resume at a later time, run Publisher, open the file called Shelter Newsletter, and continue following the steps from this location forward.

Customizing the Ribbon

It is easy to **customize**, or personalize, the ribbon the way that you want it. You can

- Create custom groups and custom tabs to contain frequently used commands
- Rearrange or rename buttons, groups, and tabs to fit your work style
- Rename or remove buttons and boxes from an existing tab and group
- Add new buttons to a custom group

When you add new buttons to the ribbon, you may choose from a list that includes commands that you may use elsewhere in Publisher such as those on shortcut menus, commands from the Backstage view, or other commands that are not on the ribbon. Or, you can create a new button that executes a command or set of commands that you record. You will create such a button later in this book. In this module, you will create a custom group on the Review tab and add a command that is not currently on the ribbon. The command will appear as a button in the new custom group.

You can customize the ribbon in all of the Microsoft Office applications, but the customizations are application-specific. The changes you make to the Publisher ribbon will not change the ribbon in any other Microsoft Office application. When you no longer need the customization, it can be removed individually, or the entire ribbon can be reset to its default settings, removing all customizations.

To Customize the Publisher Ribbon

The following steps add the Edit Story in Microsoft Word button to a new group on the Review tab on the ribbon. *Why? The Review tab has empty space to hold custom groups. The other tabs are full. Adding a custom group to one of the other tabs would compress the existing groups, which might make it more difficult to locate buttons and boxes.*

1

- Click File on the ribbon to open the Backstage view and then click Options to display the Publisher Options dialog box.

- Click the Customize Ribbon tab in the left pane (Publisher Options dialog box) to display the options for customizing the ribbon.

- Click the 'Choose commands from' button to view the list of commands (Figure 3–34).

Q&A Why are some commands not in the ribbon?
Publisher is a powerful program with many commands. Including all of the available commands on the ribbon would be overwhelming to many users. Publisher includes the more frequently used or popular commands in its default set.

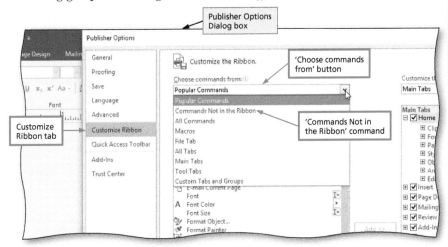

Figure 3–34

2

- Click 'Commands Not in the Ribbon' to display the list.

- Click the command you want to add (in this case, the 'Edit Story in Microsoft Word' command).

- Click Review in the list of Main Tabs to select the destination tab and then click the New Group button to create a custom group.

- Click the Add button to add the chosen command to the new group (Figure 3–35).

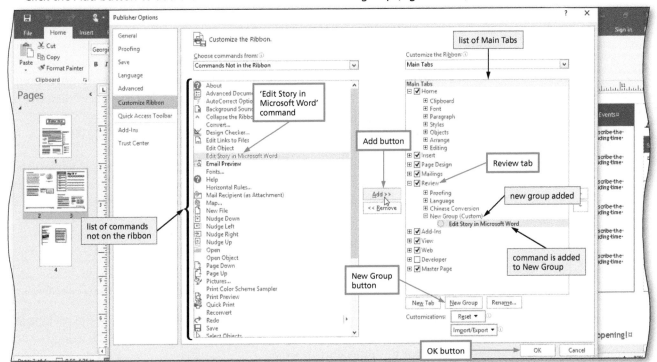

Figure 3–35

Can I add more than one command to the ribbon?
Yes, but you have to add them one at a time.

Do I have to add commands to a new group?
Yes. Commands can be added only to custom groups. The default tabs and groups cannot be changed.

3

- Click the OK button (Publisher Options dialog box) to close the dialog box and to create the custom group.

- Click Review on the ribbon to display the Review tab and its new group and button (Figure 3–36).

 Can I rename the custom group?
Yes, you can rename any group or command by clicking the Rename button in the Publisher Options dialog box. As you rename, you can choose a custom icon for the command.

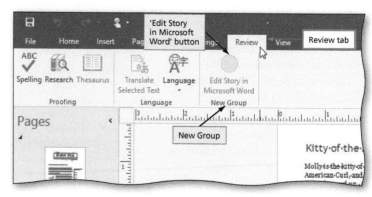

Figure 3–36

Other Ways

1. Right-click ribbon, click 'Customize the Ribbon' on shortcut menu, choose or create groups, add commands, click OK button (Publisher Options dialog box)

BTW
Whole Page View
The 'Show Whole Page' button on the right side of the Publisher status bar displays the entire page. Page editing techniques, such as moving graphics, inserting new objects, and aligning objects, are performed more easily in Show Whole Page view. You also may choose different magnifications and views by clicking the Zoom arrow (View tab | Zoom group).

Editing Stories in Microsoft Word

You have seen that you can edit text directly in Microsoft Publisher or import text from a previously stored file. A third way to edit text is to use Microsoft Word as your editor. Publisher provides an easy link between the two applications.

If you need to edit only a few words, it is faster to continue using Publisher. If you need to edit a longer story or one that is not available on your storage device, it sometimes is easier to edit the story in Word. Many users are accustomed to working in Word and want to take advantage of available Word features, such as grammar checking and revision tracking. It may be easier to drag and drop paragraphs in a Word window than to perform the same task in a Publisher window, especially when it involves moving across pages in a larger Publisher publication. Editing your stories in Word allows you to manipulate the text using the full capabilities of a word processing program.

While you are editing a story in Word, you cannot edit the corresponding text box in Publisher; Publisher displays a gray box instead of the text. When you close Word, control returns to Publisher and the text appears.

Occasionally, if you have many applications running, such as virus protection and other memory-taxing programs, Publisher may warn you that you are low on computer memory. In that case, exit the other applications and try editing the story in Word again.

To Edit a Story Using Microsoft Word

1 EDIT PUBLICATION OPTIONS | 2 IMPORT & CONNECT STORIES | 3 USE CONTINUED NOTICES | 4 CUSTOMIZE RIBBON
5 EDIT USING WORD | 6 INSERT MARGINAL ELEMENTS | 7 APPLY DROP CAPS & HYPHENATE | 8 CREATE TEMPLATE

The following steps use Microsoft Word in conjunction with Publisher to create the text on the back page of the newsletter. *Why? Some people find it easier to edit stories using Microsoft Word.* Microsoft Word version 6.0 or later must be installed on your computer for this procedure to work.

1

- If necessary, navigate to page 4 and then scroll to display the story text box in the upper portion of page 4.
- Click the placeholder text in the story to select it.
- If necessary, display the Review tab (Figure 3–37).

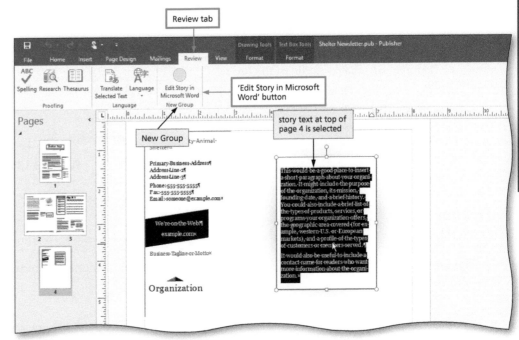

Figure 3–37

2

- Click the 'Edit Story in Microsoft Word' button (Review tab | New Group) to run the Word program.
- Press CTRL+A to select all of the text, and then type `The Brisbane County Animal Shelter (BCAS) is a nonprofit organization established in 1960 to support all animals of the county. BCAS provides vital services through sheltering and adopting animals, providing public training classes, and outreach through our community and shelter programs. BCAS receives no public or private government funding; we are supported solely by contributions, grants, adoption fees, and other fees for service.` to replace the placeholder text. Press the ENTER key to finish the first paragraph (Figure 3–38).

Q&A Why are my formatting marks not showing in Microsoft Word?
It is possible that someone has turned off formatting marks. Click the 'Show/Hide ¶' button (Word Home tab | Paragraph Group) to turn them on and off.

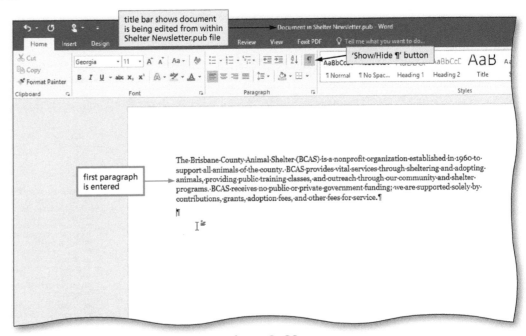

Figure 3–38

• Type `Our animals have no expiration date. We never euthanize due to space, time, or length of stay.` to finish the text (Figure 3–39).

Q&A | Why are my fonts different?
Usually, the Word text displays the same formatting as the previous text in Publisher. Your display may differ depending on available fonts.

The·Brisbane·County·Animal·Shelter·(BCAS)·is·a·nonprofit·organization·established·in·1960·to·support·all·animals·of·the·county.·BCAS·provides·vital·services·through·sheltering·and·adopting·animals,·providing·public·training·classes,·and·outreach·through·our·community·and·shelter·programs.·BCAS·receives·no·public·or·private·government·funding;·we·are·supported·solely·by·contributions,·grants,·adoption·fees,·and·other·fees·for·service.¶

Our·animals·have·no·expiration·date.·We·never·euthanize·due·to·space,·time,·or·length·of·stay.¶

¶

[second paragraph is entered]

Figure 3–39

To Format while Editing in Microsoft Word

1 EDIT PUBLICATION OPTIONS | 2 IMPORT & CONNECT STORIES | 3 USE CONTINUED NOTICES | 4 CUSTOMIZE RIBBON
5 EDIT USING WORD | **6 INSERT MARGINAL ELEMENTS** | 7 APPLY DROP CAPS & HYPHENATE | 8 CREATE TEMPLATE

The following step uses the CTRL key to select multiple sections of nonadjacent text and format them in Microsoft Word. **Why?** *You cannot select nonadjacent text in Publisher.*

• Drag to select the words, Brisbane County Animal Shelter, in the first paragraph.

• One at a time, CTRL+drag to select the words, no and never, in the second paragraph.

• Click the Bold button (Home tab | Font group) on the Word ribbon to bold the selected text (Figure 3–40).

[Bold button]

[Close button]

[nonadjacent text is selected and bolded]

The·**Brisbane·County·Animal·Shelter**·(BCAS)·is·a·nonprofit·organization·established·in·1960·to·support·all·animals·of·the·county.·BCAS·provides·vital·services·through·sheltering·and·adopting·animals,·providing·public·training·classes,·and·outreach·through·our·community·and·shelter·programs.·BCAS·receives·no·public·or·private·government·funding;·we·are·supported·solely·by·contributions,·grants,·adoption·fees,·and·other·fees·for·service.¶

Our·animals·have·**no**·expiration·date.·We·**never**·euthanize·due·to·space,·time,·or·length·of·stay.¶
¶

Figure 3–40

To Exit Word and Return to Publisher

1 EDIT PUBLICATION OPTIONS | 2 IMPORT & CONNECT STORIES | 3 USE CONTINUED NOTICES | 4 CUSTOMIZE RIBBON
5 EDIT USING WORD | **6 INSERT MARGINAL ELEMENTS** | 7 APPLY DROP CAPS & HYPHENATE | 8 CREATE TEMPLATE

The following step exits Word and returns to Publisher. **Why?** *You must exit Word in order to edit the text box in Publisher.*

• Click the Close button on the title bar of the Document in Shelter Newsletter.pub - Word window to exit Word (Figure 3–41).

Q&A | Why do I see only gray lines instead of the text?
Running Microsoft Word from within Microsoft Publisher is a drain on your system's memory and on the refresh rate of your screen. Try navigating to page 1 and then back to page 4 to refresh the screen.

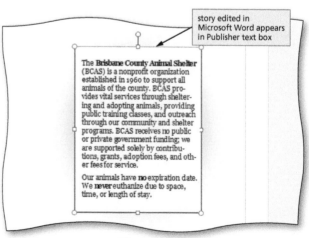

[story edited in Microsoft Word appears in Publisher text box]

The **Brisbane County Animal Shelter** (BCAS) is a nonprofit organization established in 1960 to support all animals of the county. BCAS provides vital services through sheltering and adopting animals, providing public training classes, and outreach through our community and shelter programs. BCAS receives no public or private government funding; we are supported solely by contributions, grants, adoption fees, and other fees for service.

Our animals have **no** expiration date. We **never** euthanize due to space, time, or length of stay.

Figure 3–41

To Edit Other Objects on Page 4

Table 3–2 lists text and deletions for the other objects on page 4.

Table 3–2 Text for Page 4	
Location	**Text**
Organization logo	<delete>
Business Name	Brisbane County Animal Shelter
Primary Business Address	950 Cumberland Drive Accent, WY 82004
Phone, Fax, Email text box	Phone: 712 555-1028
Business Tagline or Motto	Like us on Facebook/BCAS
Attention getter	We're on the web! bcas.wy.org

The following steps delete the logo and edit other text boxes on page 4. As you edit the text boxes, zoom and scroll as necessary.

1. In the left portion of page 4, select the Organization logo and delete it.

2. If necessary, select the default Business Name text and replace it with the text from Table 3–2.

3. Click the default text in the Primary Business Address text box. Press CTRL+A to select all of the text. Enter the text from Table 3–2.

4. Select the default text in the Phone, Fax, Email text box and then enter the text from Table 3–2.

5. Select the Business Tagline or Motto placeholder text and then enter the text from Table 3–2. If necessary, right-click the text and then click Best Fit on the shortcut menu.

6. Select the text in the attention getter. Right-click to display the shortcut menu and then, if Best Fit does not display a check mark, click Best Fit on the shortcut menu. Enter the text from Table 3–2. As you enter the web address, if Publisher changes the first letter to an uppercase B, point to the letter, click the AutoCorrect Options button, and then click 'Undo Automatic Capitalization' (Figure 3–42).

7. Click the Save button on the Quick Access Toolbar to save the file again with the same file name and in the same location.

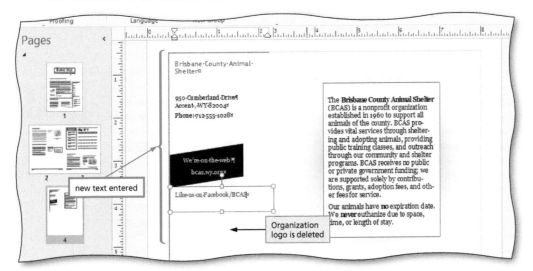

Figure 3–42

BTW
**Bullets and Soft
Returns**
If you are editing a bulleted list, a soft return will not repeat the bullet. This is ideal for short phrases and lists within a single bullet.

Marginal Elements

Publisher newsletter templates include marginal elements and layout features to make the newsletter more attractive and to add interest to the page. A **sidebar**, or breakout, is a small piece of text, set off with a box or graphic, and placed beside a story. It contains text that is not vital for understanding the main text but usually adds interest or additional information. Tables of contents, art boxes, and bulleted points of interest are examples of sidebars. A newsletter **table of contents**, or margin table, usually is a narrow, short list that is used to refer readers to specific pages or to present listed or numeric items in the margin area. A **pull quote**, or **pullout**, is an excerpt from the main story used to highlight the concepts within the story or to attract readers. Pull quotes, like sidebars, can be set off with a box or graphic. Graphics, shapes, and borders also are used sometimes as marginal elements.

To Edit Sidebars

1 EDIT PUBLICATION OPTIONS | 2 IMPORT & CONNECT STORIES | 3 USE CONTINUED NOTICES | 4 CUSTOMIZE RIBBON
5 EDIT USING WORD | 6 INSERT MARGINAL ELEMENTS | **7 APPLY DROP CAPS & HYPHENATE** | **8 CREATE TEMPLATE**

The newsletter template used in this module includes two sidebars on page 1. The first one is a table of contents. The second is a bulleted list about special points of interest. *Why? Some newsletters use a sidebar table as an index to locate stories in longer newsletters; sidebars also are used to break up a page with lots of text and attract readers to inside pages. Other newsletters use sidebar tables to display numerical data and lists.* Table 3–3 lists the text for the sidebars that you will edit in the following steps.

Table 3–3 Text for Sidebars		
Inside this issue:	Ricky Wins State	1
	Grand Reopening	1
	Kitty of the Month	2
	Microchips	2
	Calendar	3
	About Us	4
	Contact Us	4
Special points of interest:	May 6: Manners for People and Pups	
	May 10: Board Meeting	
	May 15: Adoption Clinic	
	May 20: Grand Reopening	
	May 20: Closed	

1
- Navigate to page 1.
- Locate the Inside this issue sidebar and then click Inside Story in the first row to select it. Zoom as necessary (Figure 3–43).

Q&A What are the dotted gray lines in the table?
Publisher displays dotted gray lines to indicate the size of each cell in the table. A **cell** is the text box located where a table column and table row intersect. The lines do not print.

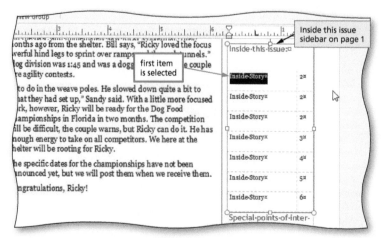

Figure 3–43

2

- Type `Ricky Wins State` to replace the text and then press the TAB key. Complete the table with the data from Table 3–3. Use the TAB key to move from cell to cell.

- Scroll down to the second sidebar, Special points of interest, and then click the bulleted list to select it.

- Type the list as shown in Table 3–3, pressing the ENTER key at the end of each line (Figure 3–44).

Q&A Could I click the next cell instead of using the TAB key?
You could click the cell, but you then would need to select the page number and type to replace it. Pressing the TAB key both advances to and selects the data in the next cell.

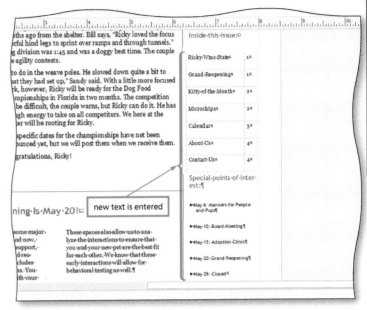

Figure 3–44

To Use a Soft Return

1 EDIT PUBLICATION OPTIONS | 2 IMPORT & CONNECT STORIES | 3 USE CONTINUED NOTICES | 4 CUSTOMIZE RIBBON
5 EDIT USING WORD | 6 INSERT MARGINAL ELEMENTS | **7 APPLY DROP CAPS & HYPHENATE** | **8 CREATE TEMPLATE**

The following steps edit the title of the Special points of interest sidebar, so that it appears on two lines, without the hyphen. *Why? A title or heading looks better without hyphens. A title also looks better when the line lengths are balanced or more equal in length.*

Recall that a hard return is created when you press the ENTER key. A hard return also creates a new paragraph with appropriate paragraph spacing. For example, a typical setting might be that lines are single-spaced as they wrap, but paragraphs are double-spaced — meaning Publisher creates a blank line between paragraphs. If you do not want paragraph spacing but you do want a new line, you can use a **soft return** or **manual line break**. To create a soft return you press the SHIFT+ENTER keys.

1

- Navigate to the Special points of interest title.

- Click the title to select it and then type `Special points` to create the first line.

- Press SHIFT+ENTER to create a soft return (Figure 3–45).

Q&A What is the symbol that appeared at the end of the line?
Publisher displays the curved arrow or manual line break symbol when you press SHIFT+ENTER, so that you can see the keystroke and differentiate it from a paragraph mark or hard return. The symbol does not print.

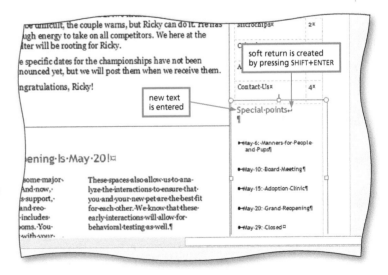

Figure 3–45

2

- Type of interest to complete the heading (Figure 3–46).

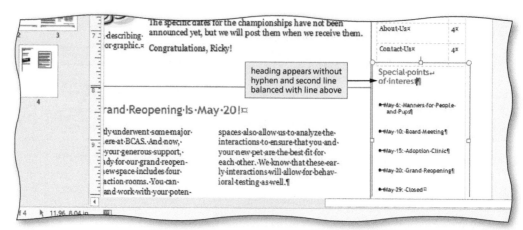

Figure 3–46

To Edit a Pull Quote

1 EDIT PUBLICATION OPTIONS | 2 IMPORT & CONNECT STORIES | 3 USE CONTINUED NOTICES | 4 CUSTOMIZE RIBBON
5 EDIT USING WORD | 6 INSERT MARGINAL ELEMENTS | **7 APPLY DROP CAPS & HYPHENATE** | 8 CREATE TEMPLATE

People often make reading decisions based on the size of the story. Using a pull quote brings a small portion of the text to their attention. ***Why?*** *Pull quotes invite the reader to read the story; they also are useful for breaking the monotony of long columns of text and for adding visual interest.* The following steps insert a pull quote using function keys to copy and paste the quote from the story.

1

- Navigate to the second story, Free Microchip with May Adoption, on page 2.

- Drag to select the text in the second sentence.

- Press CTRL+C to copy the sentence to the Clipboard (Figure 3–47).

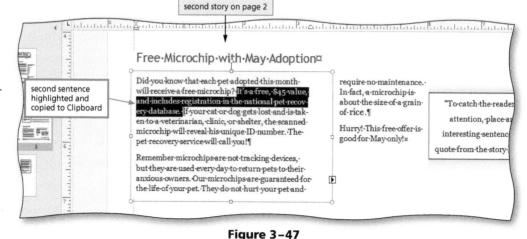

Figure 3–47

Q&A

How should I choose the text for the pull quote?

Layout specialists say pull quotes should summarize the intended message in one or two sentences.

2

- Click to select the pull quote placeholder text to the right of the story (Figure 3–48).

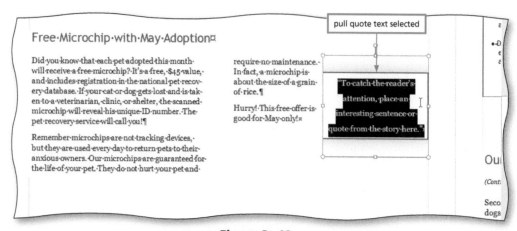

Figure 3–48

3

- Press CTRL+V to paste the sentence from the Clipboard.

- Click the Paste Options button and then click the 'Keep Text Only' button to accept the destination formatting (Figure 3–49).

Q&A

How would I insert a pull quote if one did not exist?

Click the Page Parts button (Insert tab | Building Blocks group) to display the Page Parts gallery. Choose a pull quote in the Pull Quotes area. When the pull quote appears in the publication, move it to the desired location and then edit the text.

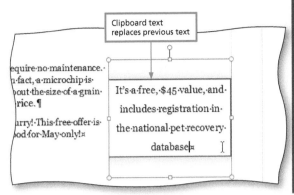

Figure 3–49

To Edit the Calendar

The following steps edit the calendar on page 3. On the left side of the calendar is a bulleted list similar to that on page 1. On the right side is a table of dates. Each date is a text box that you can edit. You will learn more about tables in a later module.

1 Navigate to the top of page 3 and zoom to approximately 110%.

2 Click the Schedule of Events bulleted list. Type the following list, pressing the ENTER key at the end of every line except the last:

```
Open Monday through Saturday 10:00 a.m. - 7:00 p.m.

Featured animals by week

May 6: Manners for People and Pups

Second Wednesday of each month: Board Meeting at 7:00 p.m.

May 15: Adoption Clinic 5:00 p.m.

May 20: Grand Reopening

Closed May 29 for Memorial Day
```

3 Click to the right of the number on the first Monday of the calendar. Press the ENTER key and then type `Puppy` as the notation. Do not press the ENTER key after typing the word.

4 Using Figure 3–50 as a guide, enter the other calendar date notations in a similar manner (Figure 3–50).

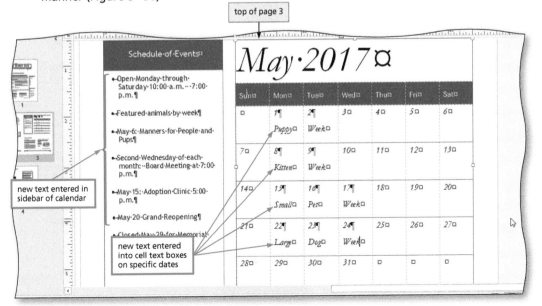

Figure 3–50

Using Graphics in a Newsletter

Marginal elements and stories in newsletters often contain graphics and pictures. Most graphic designers employ a simple technique for deciding how many graphics are too many: They hold the publication at arm's length and glance at it. Then, closing their eyes, they count the number of things they remember. Remembering more than five graphics indicates too many; fewer than two indicates too few. Without question, graphics can make or break a publication. The world has come to expect them. Used correctly, graphics enhance the text, attract the eye, and brighten the look of the publication. If you use graphics from the web, make sure you review the copyright licenses to ensure you can comply with copyright restrictions.

CONSIDER THIS

How do you decide on the best layout?

As you insert graphics and arrange stories, follow any guidelines from the authors or from the company for which you are creating the newsletter. Together, determine the best layout for visual appeal and reliable dissemination of content. Make any required changes. Print a copy and mark the places where sidebars and pull quotes would make sense. Verify that all photos have captions.

In newsletters, you should use photos as true-to-life representations for stories about employees, services, and products. Drawings, on the other hand, can explain, instruct, entertain, or represent images for which you have no picture. The careful use of graphics can add flair and distinction to your publication.

To Replace a Graphic Using the Shortcut Menu

1 EDIT PUBLICATION OPTIONS | 2 IMPORT & CONNECT STORIES | 3 USE CONTINUED NOTICES | 4 CUSTOMIZE RIBBON

5 EDIT USING WORD | 6 INSERT MARGINAL ELEMENTS | **7 APPLY DROP CAPS & HYPHENATE** | 8 CREATE TEMPLATE

The following steps replace a graphic using the shortcut menu. *Why? Using the shortcut menu is a quick way to change a picture without having to navigate the ribbon.* To complete these steps, you will be required to use the Data Files. Please contact your instructor for information about accessing the Data Files.

- Navigate to page 1.
- Click the graphic and caption in the lead story and then click the graphic again to select only the graphic.
- Press the F9 key to zoom the object to 100%.
- Right-click the graphic to display the shortcut menu and then point to Change Picture on the shortcut menu to display the Change Picture submenu (Figure 3–51).

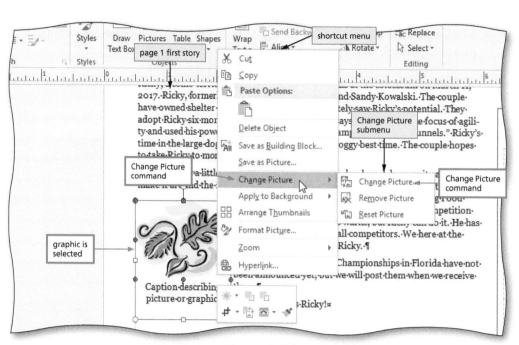

Figure 3–51

2

- Click Change Picture on the Change Picture submenu to display the Insert Pictures dialog box (Figure 3–52).

Q&A What do the other choices on the Change Picture submenu do?

The Remove Picture command deletes the picture but retains the picture placeholder. The Reset Picture command removes any previous cropping or resizing.

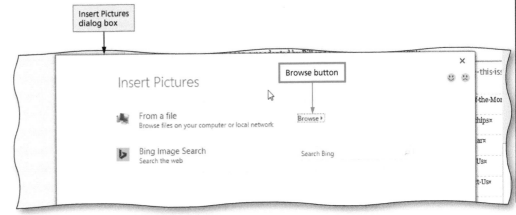

Figure 3–52

3

- Click the Browse button (Insert Pictures dialog box) in the From a file area to display the Insert Picture dialog box.

- Navigate to the location of the Data Files and double-click the file named Ricky to replace the picture.

- Select the placeholder text in the caption and then type `Ricky wins!` to replace the caption (Figure 3–53).

Q&A What if I choose a larger or smaller picture?

Because you are replacing the graphic, rather than inserting a picture, Publisher resizes the picture to fit the space. The picture automatically is scaled in proportion.

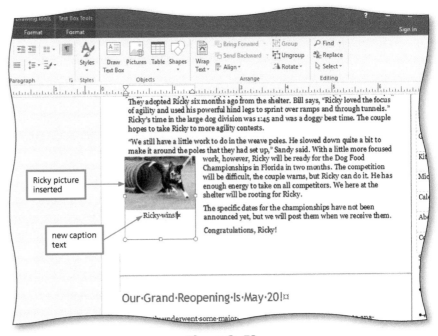

Figure 3–53

To Replace the Graphic and Caption on Page 2

The following steps use the Bing Image Search to locate a picture of a kitten. If you cannot find the specific image, you may use another appropriate image. Make sure you review the license to ensure you can comply with copyright laws. The size of your pictures may vary. If you want to use the exact image shown in the figures, you may retrieve the image from the Data Files. Please contact your instructor for information about accessing the Data Files.

1 Navigate to the top of page 2.

2 Select only the graphic beside the first story. Right-click the graphic, point to Change Picture on the shortcut menu, and then click Change Picture on the Change Picture submenu to display the Insert Pictures dialog box.

③ Type `kitten` in the Bing Image Search box and then press the ENTER key to begin the search.

④ Scroll as necessary in the Bing Image Search dialog box and then double-click a picture similar to the one in Figure 3–54 to replace the graphic.

⑤ Replace the caption by typing, `Molly is a sweetie!` as the caption text (Figure 3–54).

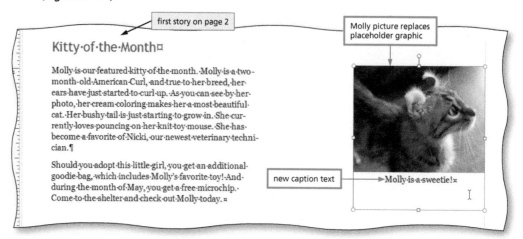

Figure 3–54

To Replace the Graphic and Caption on Page 3

The following steps use the Bing Image Search to locate a picture of an animal shelter. If you cannot find the specific image, you may use another appropriate image. Make sure you review the license to ensure you can comply with its restrictions. The size of your pictures may vary. If you want to use the exact image shown in the figures, you may retrieve the image from the Data Files. Please contact your instructor for information about accessing the Data Files.

① Navigate to the bottom of page 3.

② Right click the existing graphic and use the shortcut menu to replace the graphic. Use a Bing Image Search for the term, animal shelter. Use a graphic similar to the one in Figure 3–55.

③ Replace the caption by typing, `Brisbane County Animal Shelter` as the caption text.

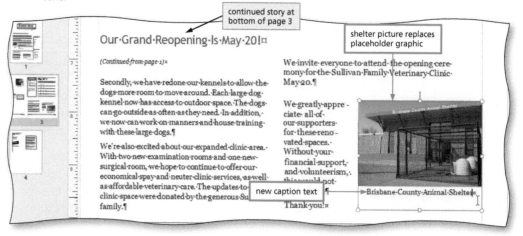

Figure 3–55

To Insert a Graphic on Page 2

The following steps insert a graphic on page 2 from the Data Files. Please contact your instructor for information about accessing the Data Files.

1 Navigate to the bottom of page 2.

2 Display the Insert tab.

3 Click the Pictures button (Insert tab | Illustrations group) to display the Insert Picture dialog box.

4 Navigate to the Data Files and then insert the Coupon graphic.

5 In the publication, drag the graphic to the empty space at the bottom of page 2.

6 Click outside the graphic to deselect it (Figure 3–56).

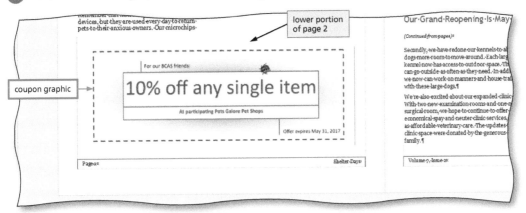

Figure 3–56

To Insert Graphics on Page 4

The following steps insert graphics on page 4 from the Data Files. Please contact your instructor for information about accessing the Data Files.

1 Navigate to page 4. One at a time, insert the Facebook graphic and the Twitter graphic. Resize if necessary and then move the graphics to a location below the Facebook notation in the middle of the page (Figure 3–57).

2 Click the Save button on the Quick Access Toolbar to save the file again, with the same file name and in the same location.

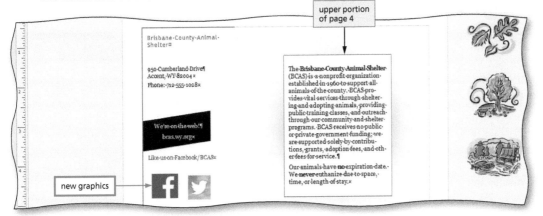

Figure 3–57

Break Point: If you wish to take a break, this is a good place to do so. Exit Publisher. To resume at a later time, run Publisher, open the file called Shelter Newsletter, and continue following the steps from this location forward.

BTW
Conserving Ink and Toner
If you want to conserve ink or toner, you can instruct Publisher to print draft quality documents by tapping or clicking File on the ribbon to open the Backstage view and then tapping or clicking the Print tab in the Backstage view to display the Print gallery. Click the Printer Properties link and then, depending on your printer, click the Print Quality button and choose Draft in the list. Close the Printer Properties dialog box and then click the Print button as usual.

Revising a Newsletter

As discussed in Module 1, once you complete a publication, you may find it necessary to make changes to it. Before submitting a newsletter to a customer or printing service, you should proofread it. While **proofreading**, you look for grammatical errors and spelling errors. You want to be sure the layout, graphics, and stories make sense. If you find errors, you must correct, make changes to, or edit the newsletter. Other readers, perhaps customers or editors, may want to proofread your publication and make changes, such as moving text or adding embellishments, such as a drop cap. You also should check how Publisher has hyphenated your stories.

How should you proofread and revise a newsletter?

As you proofread the newsletter, look for ways to improve it. Check all grammar, spelling, and punctuation. Be sure the text is logical and transitions are smooth. Where necessary, add text, delete text, reword text, and move text to different locations. Ask yourself these questions:

• Does the title suggest the topic?

• Does the first line of the story entice the reader to continue?

• Is the purpose of the newsletter clear?

• Are all sources acknowledged?

The final phase of the design process is a synthesis involving proofreading, editing, and publishing. Publisher offers several methods to check for errors in your newsletter. None of these methods is a replacement for careful reading and proofreading.

To Create a Drop Cap

1 EDIT PUBLICATION OPTIONS | 2 IMPORT & CONNECT STORIES | 3 USE CONTINUED NOTICES | 4 CUSTOMIZE RIBBON
5 EDIT USING WORD | 6 INSERT MARGINAL ELEMENTS | **7 APPLY DROP CAPS & HYPHENATE** | **8 CREATE TEMPLATE**

A dropped capital letter, or **drop cap**, is a decorative, large initial capital letter extending down below the other letters in the line. If the text wraps to more than one line, the paragraph typically wraps around the dropped capital letter. The following steps create a dropped capital letter M to begin the word, Molly, in the story on page 2. *Why? A drop cap will set off the paragraph and draw the reader's eye toward the beginning of the story.*

1

• Navigate to page 2 and then click to the left of the letter, M, at the beginning of the story about Molly to position the insertion point. Zoom to approximately 120%.

• Display the Text Box Tools Format tab.

• Click the Drop Cap button (Text Box Tools Format tab | Typography group) to display the Drop Cap gallery (Figure 3–58).

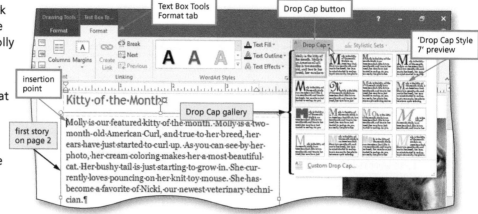

Figure 3–58

• Point to each of the available drop caps in the Drop Cap gallery to preview the different styles.

2

- Click the 'Drop Cap Style 7' preview to select it (Figure 3–59).

Q&A Will this drop cap look inconsistent with the other fonts on the page?
The font is still Georgia, which will match the rest of the paragraph's characters.

Figure 3–59

To Customize a Drop Cap

1 EDIT PUBLICATION OPTIONS | 2 IMPORT & CONNECT STORIES | 3 USE CONTINUED NOTICES | 4 CUSTOMIZE RIBBON
5 EDIT USING WORD | 6 INSERT MARGINAL ELEMENTS | 7 APPLY DROP CAPS & HYPHENATE | 8 CREATE TEMPLATE

The Drop Cap dialog box allows you to customize the drop cap. You can format the number of lines in the drop cap or even change it to an **up cap**, in which the larger letter extends up above the rest of the text. You also can change the font, font style, and color of the text.

Once created, the customized style is added to the Drop Cap gallery for the current publication. *Why? Publisher makes it available to use in other portions of the publication, if desired.* The following steps change the drop cap size to two lines.

1

- With the insertion point still positioned before the desired letter (in this case, the M of Molly), click the Drop Cap button (Text Box Tools Format tab | Typography group) again to display the Drop Cap gallery (Figure 3–60).

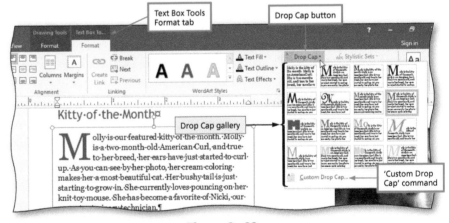

Figure 3–60

2

- Click 'Custom Drop Cap' at the bottom of the gallery to display the Drop Cap dialog box.

- Click the 'Size of letters' down arrow until the height of the drop cap is 2 lines high (Figure 3–61).

Experiment

- Change other settings in the Drop Cap dialog box and watch the contents of the Preview area change. When you are finished experimenting, return all options to the settings in Figure 3–61.

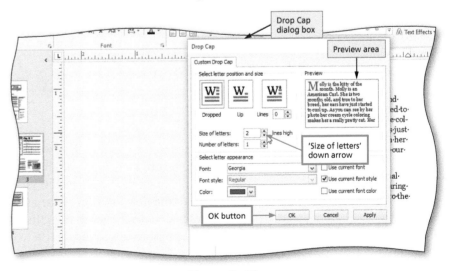

Figure 3–61

3

- Click the OK button (Drop Cap dialog box) to apply the formatting (Figure 3–62).

Q&A Is a drop cap limited to a single letter?

No, you can format up to 15 contiguous letters and spaces as drop caps at the beginning of each paragraph.

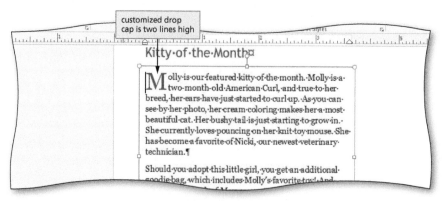

Figure 3–62

To Reuse a Customized Drop Cap

1 EDIT PUBLICATION OPTIONS | 2 IMPORT & CONNECT STORIES | 3 USE CONTINUED NOTICES | 4 CUSTOMIZE RIBBON
5 EDIT USING WORD | 6 INSERT MARGINAL ELEMENTS | 7 APPLY DROP CAPS & HYPHENATE | 8 CREATE TEMPLATE

Anytime you use a special feature in a multipage publication, it is a good idea to use it more than once when possible. **Why?** *That way, your feature does not look like an afterthought or a mistake, but like a conscious design decision.* The following steps use the customized drop cap again for a second story.

1

- Navigate to the second story on page 2.

- Position the insertion point before the letter, D, in the word, Did, at the beginning of the story.

- Click the Drop Cap button (Text Box Tools Format tab | Typography group) to display the Drop Cap gallery (Figure 3–63).

2

- Click 'Custom Drop Cap Number 1' in the gallery to apply the recently created drop cap.

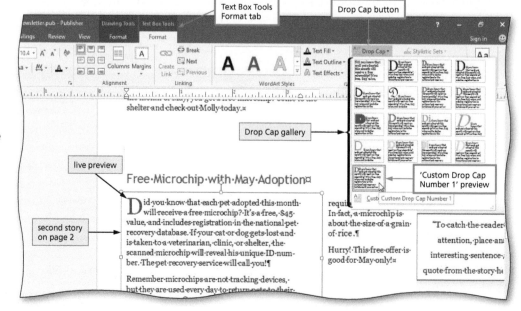

Figure 3–63

Moving Text

If you decide to move text, such as words, characters, sentences, or paragraphs, you first select the text to be moved and then use drag-and-drop editing or the cut-and-paste technique to move the selected text. With **drag-and-drop editing**, you drag the selected item to the new location and then insert, or drop, it there. Moving text in this manner does not transfer data to the Office Clipboard or the Windows Clipboard, nor does it cause Publisher to display the Paste Options button. Any format changes to the text must be made manually.

When moving text between pages, use the cut-and-paste method. When moving text a long distance or between apps, use the Office Clipboard task pane to cut and paste. When moving text a short distance, the drag-and-drop technique is more efficient; thus, the following steps demonstrate drag-and-drop editing.

To Drag and Drop Text

1 EDIT PUBLICATION OPTIONS | 2 IMPORT & CONNECT STORIES | 3 USE CONTINUED NOTICES | 4 CUSTOMIZE RIBBON
5 EDIT USING WORD | 6 INSERT MARGINAL ELEMENTS | **7 APPLY DROP CAPS & HYPHENATE** | **8 CREATE TEMPLATE**

The editor of the newsletter has decided that two paragraphs on page 3 should be inverted. *Why? The editor feels that the story will read better with the change.* The following steps move paragraphs by dragging and dropping.

1

- Navigate to the continued story at the bottom of page 3.

- Triple-click to select the next to the last paragraph (Figure 3–64).

Q&A Could I drag to select the paragraph?
Yes; however, it is more efficient to triple-click, which automatically selects the entire paragraph and the paragraph mark at the end.

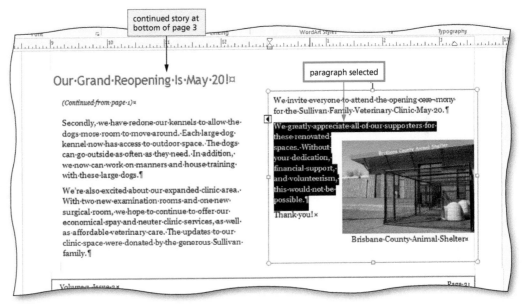

Figure 3–64

2

- Drag the selection to the beginning of the previous paragraph. Do not release the mouse button (Figure 3–65).

Q&A I am not able to drag the selection. What did I do wrong?
It may be that someone has turned off drag-and-drop editing. Click File on the ribbon to open the Backstage view. Click the Options tab and then click Advanced in the Publisher Options dialog box. Make sure a check mark appears in the 'Allow text to be dragged and dropped' check box.

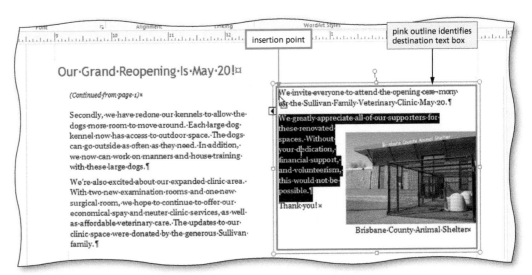

Figure 3–65

3

- Release the mouse button (or, if you are using a touch screen, lift your finger) to move the selected text to the location of the pointer.

- Click outside the selection to deselect (Figure 3–66).

Q&A What if I accidentally drag text to the wrong location?
Click the Undo button on the Quick Access Toolbar or press CTRL+Z and try again.

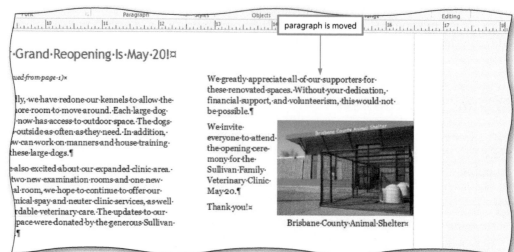

Figure 3–66

(image text, partially visible):

·Grand·Reopening·Is·May·20!¤

ued·from·page·1)×

lly,·we·have·redone·our·kennels·to·allow·the·
ore·room·to·move·around.·Each·large·dog·
·now·has·access·to·outdoor·space.·The·dogs·
·outside·as·often·as·they·need.·In·addition,·
w·can·work·on·manners·and·house·training·
these·large·dogs.¶

e·also·excited·about·our·expanded·clinic·area.·
two·new·examination·rooms·and·one·new·
al·room,·we·hope·to·continue·to·offer·our·
nical·spay·and·neuter·clinic·services,·as·well·
rdable·veterinary·care.·The·updates·to·our·
pace·were·donated·by·the·generous·Sullivan·
¶

paragraph is moved

We·greatly·appreciate·all·of·our·supporters·for·
these·renovated·spaces.·Without·your·dedication,·
financial·support,·and·volunteerism,·this·would·not·
be·possible.¶

We·invite·
everyone·to·attend·
the·opening·cere-
mony·for·the·
Sullivan·Family·
Veterinary·Clinic·
May·20.¶

Thank·you!×

Brisbane·County·Animal·Shelter×

Can I use drag-and-drop editing to move any selected item?
Yes, you can select words, sentences, phrases, and graphics and then use drag-and-drop editing to move them.

To Check the Spelling and Design

The following steps check the entire publication for spelling errors and then run the Design Checker.

1 Press the F7 key to begin the spelling check in the current location, which in this case is inside the caption text box.

2 If Publisher flags any words, choose the correct spelling in the Suggestions list, click the Change button (Check Spelling dialog box), and then continue the spelling check until the next error is identified or the end of the text box is reached.

3 Click the Yes button (Microsoft Publisher dialog box) to tell Publisher to check the rest of the publication. If the publication displays a different error, correct or ignore it as necessary.

4 Click the OK button (Microsoft Publisher dialog box) to close the dialog box.

5 Click File on the ribbon to open the Backstage view and, by default, select the Info tab.

6 Click the 'Run Design Checker' button in the Info gallery to display the Design Checker task pane.

7 If your publication has problems other than objects near the margin, point to the error in the Select an item to fix list (Design Checker task pane). When an arrow appears on the right side of the error, click the arrow and then click 'Go to this Item' on the menu. Fix or ignore the flagged item as necessary.

8 Click the Close button on the Design Checker task pane to close the Design Checker and return to the publication.

Hyphenation

Hyphenation refers to splitting a word that otherwise would extend beyond the right margin. Because Publisher bases hyphenation only on words in its dictionary, it is a good idea to review the hyphenation. Publisher's hyphenation feature allows you to hyphenate the text automatically or manually, insert optional or **nonbreaking hyphens,** and set the maximum amount of space allowed between a word and the right margin without hyphenating the word. When you use **automatic hyphenation,** Publisher automatically inserts hyphens where they are needed. When you use **manual hyphenation,** Publisher searches for the text to hyphenate and asks you whether you want to insert the hyphens in the text. Some rules for hyphenation include:

- Hyphenate only at standard syllable breaks.
- Do not change the hyphen location of words that already are hyphenated.
- Avoid hyphenating words in the first or last line of a paragraph.
- Avoid hyphenations that leave only two letters at the beginning or end of a line.
- Avoid hyphenating two lines in a row.
- Avoid hyphenating a line across text boxes or pages.
- Avoid hyphenating proper nouns.

BTW
Choosing a Different Hyphenation Location
When using the Hyphenation dialog box, Publisher shows all the possible hyphenation locations at appropriate syllable breaks (shown in Figure 3–68). The current choice is highlighted in blue. You can choose to hyphenate at one of the other places in the word by clicking the hyphen and then clicking the Yes button.

To Check Hyphenation

1 EDIT PUBLICATION OPTIONS | 2 IMPORT & CONNECT STORIES | 3 USE CONTINUED NOTICES | 4 CUSTOMIZE RIBBON
5 EDIT USING WORD | 6 INSERT MARGINAL ELEMENTS | **7 APPLY DROP CAPS & HYPHENATE** | **8 CREATE TEMPLATE**

The following steps hyphenate the stories. **Why?** *Hyphenating allows you to make decisions about where the hyphens will be placed.* You will choose to hyphenate manually, which means you can specify where the hyphen should occur, or if it should occur, rather than have Publisher hyphenate the story automatically.

1
- Navigate to page 1 and click the lead story.
- Display the Text Box Tools Format tab.
- Click the Hyphenation button (Text Box Tools Format tab | Text group) to display the Hyphenation dialog box (Figure 3–67).

Q&A What is the hyphenation zone? The **hyphenation zone** is the maximum amount of space Publisher allows between a word and the right margin without hyphenating the word. To reduce the number of hyphens, increase the hyphenation zone. To reduce the ragged edge of the right margin, decrease the hyphenation zone.

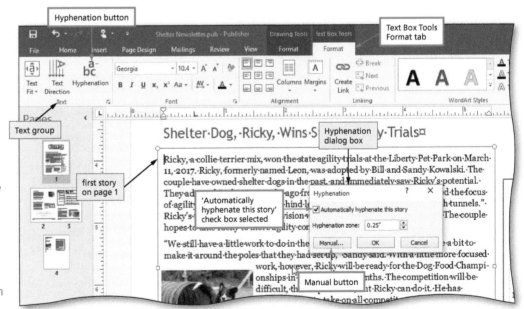

Figure 3–67

- Click to remove the check mark in the 'Automatically hyphenate this story' check box (Hyphenation dialog box shown in Figure 3-67).

- Click the Manual button (Hyphenation dialog box) to hyphenate the story manually and to display the Hyphenate dialog box, which displays the first hyphenation choice (Figure 3-68).

Figure 3-68

Why is the text already hyphenated?

The default value is automatic hyphenation. Publisher hyphenates after the standard syllables.

- Click the No button (Hyphenate dialog box) because this word, Championship, is a proper noun.

- If Publisher stops at the word, announced, click the No button because this word is on the first line of the third paragraph and it results in two-character hyphenation. When no other hyphenation choices exist in the current story, Publisher will display a dialog box as shown in Figure 3-69.

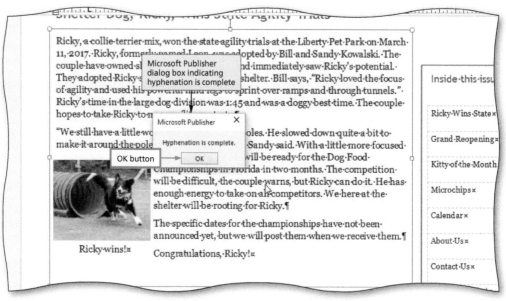

Figure 3-69

My hyphenation stopped on a different word. What should I do?

Because of fonts and resolution, your system may stop at a different word. Use the rules discussed in this module to evaluate your word and choose the correct hyphenation.

- Click the OK button when the hyphenation for the story is complete.

- One at a time, repeat Steps 1 through 3 for the other stories and sidebars in the publication, adjusting the hyphens as necessary.

- Continue to click the Yes or No button (Hyphenation dialog box) using the hyphenation rules listed previously.

Q&A
What sort of hyphenation issues might I find?
You may have to choose to hyphenate at a different location by clicking the hyphen in the Hyphenate dialog box. You may find the hyphenation correct, in which case you will click the Yes button. Or, you may decide not to hyphenate because it would create two hyphens in a row.

⑤

- When you are finished hyphenating all of the stories, click the Save button on the Quick Access Toolbar to overwrite the previously saved file.

Other Ways

1. Press CTRL+SHIFT+H, choose settings, click OK button (Hyphenation dialog box), make hyphenation choices, click OK button (Microsoft Publisher dialog box)

To Print the Newsletter

1 EDIT PUBLICATION OPTIONS | 2 IMPORT & CONNECT STORIES | 3 USE CONTINUED NOTICES | 4 CUSTOMIZE RIBBON
5 EDIT USING WORD | 6 INSERT MARGINAL ELEMENTS | **7 APPLY DROP CAPS & HYPHENATE** | **8 CREATE TEMPLATE**

While it often is cheaper in business situations to outsource newsletter printing, you may want to print a copy on a desktop printer. ***Why?*** *Printing will allow you to proofread more easily and also assess the look and feel of the newsletter.*

If you have access to a printer that can accept **tabloid** size, 17×11.5 inch paper, you can print double-sided and then fold the paper to create the newsletter. If you want to print double-sided on 8.5×11 inch paper, the newsletter will print on the back and front of two pages that you then can staple. The following steps make choices about printing the newsletter.

①

- Click File on the ribbon to open the Backstage view and then click the Print tab to display the Print gallery.

- In the Settings area, click the 'One page per sheet' button to display its list (Figure 3–70).

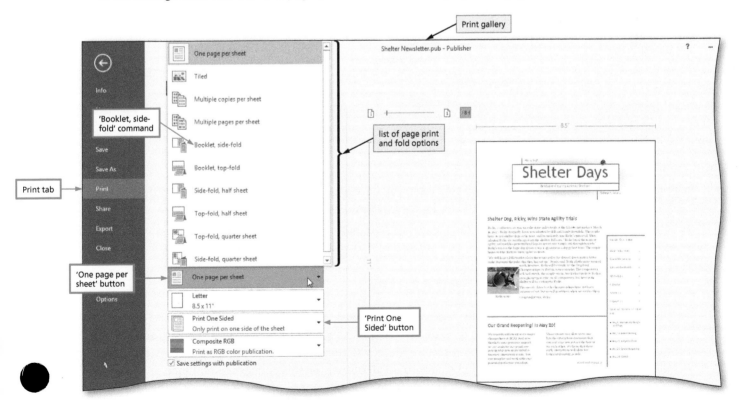

Figure 3–70

2

- Click 'Booklet, side-fold' to specify how the newsletter will print.
- Click the 'Print One Sided' button and then click the appropriate manual or duplex print setting (Figure 3–71).

⊘ Experiment

- Click the Back button on the status bar to see the inside two-page spread. If necessary, click the 'Fit to Sheet' button on the Print gallery task bar.

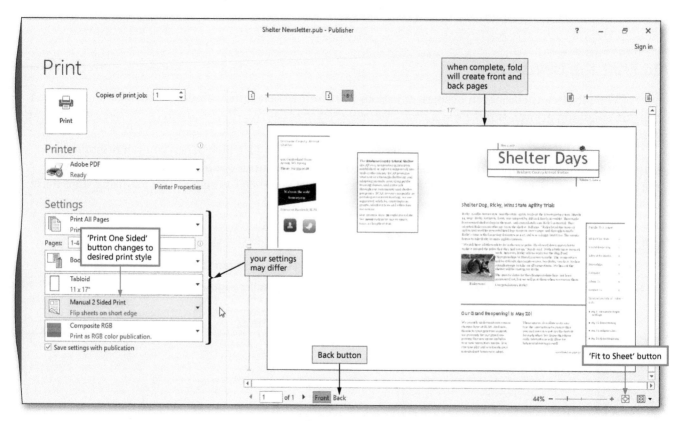

Figure 3–71

3

- If the printer is capable of handling oversized paper and you have access to 17 × 11.5 inch paper, load the paper into the printer and then click the Print button in the Print gallery.
- If you cannot do oversize printing, click the Backstage view Back button to return to the publication workspace.

Creating a Template

Newsletters typically retain their masthead, color scheme, font scheme, and other graphics from issue to issue. In a first issue, you must make design choices and implement them to make sure the newsletter is displayed correctly, and reviewing that takes time. You will not have to do all of that for subsequent issues. Once the decisions have been made and the publication has been distributed, you can reuse the same publication as a template. Additionally, Publisher allows you to add it to the templates on your computer.

Saving the Template and Setting File Properties

Recall that in the Office and Windows module at the beginning of this book, you set file properties using properties in the Backstage view (Info tab); however, two specific properties can be set at the time you save a publication or template. The author and tag properties can be entered in any of the Save As dialog boxes, which can save you several steps. A **tag** is a custom property that helps you find and organize files.

Where should a company store its templates?

On a business computer, for an organization that routinely uses templates, templates should be saved in the default location. Publisher stores templates within the program data in a folder named, Custom Office Templates. Templates stored in the default location are displayed in the catalog when you click the My Templates button. Templates, however, can be stored in several places: on a personal computer, on a web server, or on a common drive for use by multiple employees or students.

To Create a Template with Property Changes

1 EDIT PUBLICATION OPTIONS | 2 IMPORT & CONNECT STORIES | 3 USE CONTINUED NOTICES | 4 CUSTOMIZE RIBBON

5 EDIT USING WORD | 6 INSERT MARGINAL ELEMENTS | 7 APPLY DROP CAPS & HYPHENATE | **8 CREATE TEMPLATE**

The following steps create a template with property changes and save it on a personal storage device. *Why? It is not recommended to save templates on lab computers or computers belonging to other people, because you may not want others to use your templates due to privacy issues.*

- Click File on the ribbon to open the Backstage view.
- Click the Export tab, and then click the 'Change File Type' tab to display the Save Publication gallery.
- Click Template in the Publisher File Types area to save the file as a Publisher template (Figure 3–72).

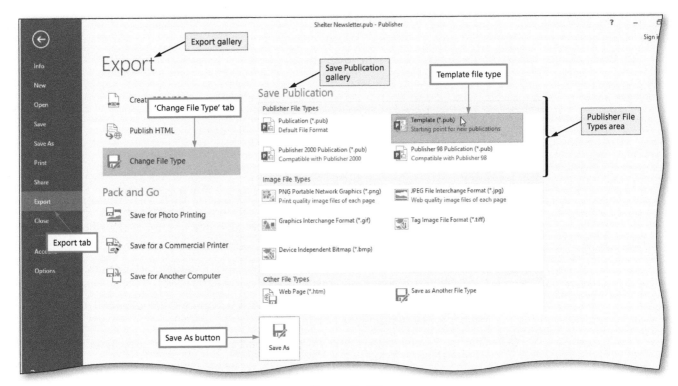

Figure 3–72

2

- Click the Save As button to display the Save as Template dialog box.

- Type **Newsletter Template** to change the name of the publication. Do not press the ENTER key.

- Navigate to your preferred storage location.

  If requested by your instructor, double-click the Authors text box in the lower portion of the dialog box and then type your name to replace the text.

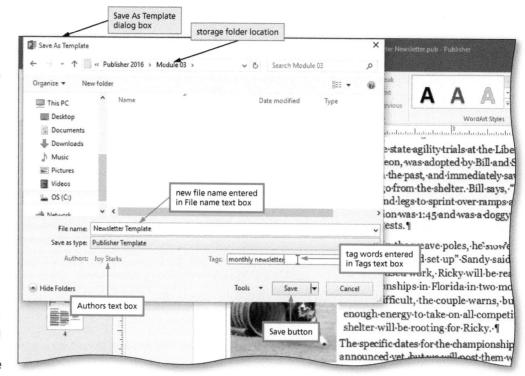

Figure 3–73

- Click the Tags text box and then type **monthly newsletter** to add the tag words (Figure 3–73). The current text in the Tags text box will disappear as you start to type.

Q&A | Can I make the newsletter template read-only so that users will have to save updates with a different file name?
Yes. After saving and exiting Publisher, open the File Explorer window. Right-click the file name, click Properties on the shortcut menu, and then place a check mark in the Read-only attribute (Publication Properties dialog box | General tab).

3

- Click the Save button (Save As dialog box) to save the template.

Other Ways

1. In Backstage view, click Save As, choose location (Save As dialog box), enter name of newsletter, click 'Save as type' button, click Publisher Template, click Save button

---

To Remove All Ribbon Customization and Exit Publisher

When working in a lab environment, it is advisable to remove the ribbon customization. The following steps remove all ribbon customization.

1 Click File on the ribbon to open the Backstage view and then click Options to display the Publisher Options dialog box.

2 Click Customize Ribbon in the left pane (Publisher Options dialog box) to display the options for customizing the ribbon.

3 Click the Reset button (Publisher Options dialog box) and then click 'Reset all customizations' in the list.

④ Click the Yes button (Microsoft Office dialog box).

⑤ Click the OK button (Publisher Options dialog box) to close the dialog box.

⑥ To exit Publisher, click the Close button on the right side of the title bar.

⑦ If a Microsoft Publisher dialog box is displayed, click the Don't Save button so that any changes you have made are not saved.

Summary

In this module, you learned how to select template options for a newsletter, such as the number of columns and special content. After editing the masthead components, you imported stories from external files and created original stories using the Edit Story in Microsoft Word command. As stories flowed across pages, you inserted continued notices. You edited sidebars, pull quotes, and the calendar. In revising the newsletter, you applied decorative drop caps, used drag-and-drop editing techniques, hyphenated the stories, checked the spelling, and ran the Design Checker. Finally, you saved the newsletter both as a Publisher file and as a Publisher template that the company can edit each month.

What decisions will you need to make when creating your next newsletter?
Use these guidelines as you complete the assignments in this module and create your own publications outside of this class.

1. Decide on the layout.

    a) Select a template and options that matches your need.

    b) Set columns and options for each page purpose and audience.

2. Edit the masthead.

3. Gather the text content.

    a) Import stories when possible.

    b) Edit stories in Microsoft Word when necessary.

    c) Flow long stories to other text boxes.

    d) Format continued stories with continued notices.

4. Create and edit marginal elements.

5. Insert other elements, such as advertisements.

6. Edit graphics and captions.

7. Revise as necessary.

    a) Proofread and check the publication.

    b) Run a hyphenation check.

8. Create a template for future use.

CONSIDER THIS

Apply Your Knowledge

Reinforce the skills and apply the concepts you learned in this module.

Creating a Newsletter

Note: To complete this assignment, you will be required to use the Data Files. Please contact your instructor for information about accessing the Data Files.

Instructions: A fifth-grade teacher would like you to create a newsletter for her class and parents. They have provided some stories and will give you others at a later time. You produce the first page of the newsletter shown in Figure 3–74.

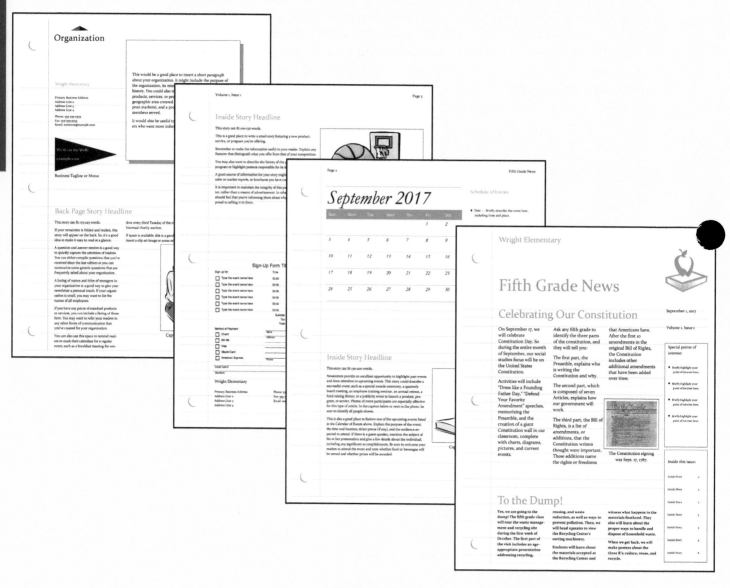

Figure 3–74

Perform the following tasks:

1. Run Publisher. Click BUILT-IN and then click Newsletters.

2. Choose the School newsletter template, the Office color scheme, and the Paper font scheme. Set the Page size to Two-page spread.

3. Create the publication. Navigate to page 2. Use the Options button (Page Design tab | Template group) to include a calendar and a 2-column format on the left inside page. The date of your calendar may differ. Click the Options button (Page Design tab | Template group) again for the right-inside page, and include a sign-up form and a 1-column format.

4. Edit the masthead as shown in Figure 3–74.

5. For the lead story, use the headline, Celebrating Our Constitution. Import the story, Celebrating the Constitution, from the Data Files.

6. Click the Hyphenation button (Text Box Tools format tab | Text group) to display the Hyphenation dialog box. Remove the check mark from the 'Automatically hyphenate this story' check box. Click the Manual button (Hyphenation dialog box) to hyphenate the story manually and to display the first hyphenation choice. Click Yes or No as appropriate, using the rules discussed earlier in this module in the section titled, Hyphenation. Remember that proper names, such as Constitution, should not be hyphenated.

7. If necessary, customize the ribbon to display the 'Edit Story in Microsoft Word' button (Review tab | New Group). Refer to the section in this module titled, To Edit a Story Using Microsoft Word.

8. For the secondary story on page 1, right-click the headline and then click Best Fit on the shortcut menu. Type the headline `To the Dump!` Click the placeholder text of the story. Click the 'Edit Story in Microsoft Word' button (Review tab | New Group). When Word is running, press CTRL+A to select all of the text. Change the font size to 8. Type the following text, pressing the ENTER key at the end of each paragraph except the last:

   `Yes, we are going to the dump! The fifth grade class will tour the waste management and recycling site during the first week of October. The first part of the visit includes an age-appropriate presentation addressing recycling, reusing, and waste reduction, as well as ways to prevent pollution. Then, we will head upstairs to view the Recycling Center's sorting machinery.`

   `Students will learn about the materials accepted at the Recycling Center and witness what happens to the materials firsthand. They also will learn about the proper ways to handle and dispose of household waste.`

   `When we get back, we will make posters about the three R's: reduce, reuse, and recycle.`

9. Exit Word to return to Publisher. Hyphenate the second story as you did the first (in Step 6).

10. On page 1, click the graphic twice to select it. Use the shortcut menu to change the picture. Use the Bing Image Search to locate photos related to the search term, preamble. (An appropriate image also is included in the Data Files.) Change the caption to read: The Constitution signing was Sept. 17, 1787.

11. If requested by your instructor, change other text and graphics such as the table of contents sidebar, sign-up form, and calendar. Use your name and address at the top of page 4.

12. Save the file with the file name, Apply 3–1 Fifth Grade Newsletter.

13. Remove the ribbon customization as described in the section titled, To Remove All Ribbon Customization and Exit Publisher, earlier in this module.

14. Submit the publication in the format specified by your instructor.

Continued >

Apply Your Knowledge *continued*

15. ✹ Do you think adding a calendar and sign-up form to pages 2 and 3 make them too busy? Why or why not? Would you rather type the story in Step 8 in Publisher or Word? Why?

Extend Your Knowledge

Extend the skills you learned in this module and experiment with new skills. You may need to use Help to complete the assignment.

Creating Page 1 of a Newsletter from Scratch

Instructions: Run Publisher. Your school is planning a first-time callout for a new fellowship club called the Coffee Cup. You have been asked to create a sample page 1, to promote meetings and events. You decide to start from scratch to create the newsletter page shown in Figure 3–75.

Figure 3–75

Perform the following tasks:

1. Click BUILT-IN and then click Newsletters. Scroll to the Blank Sizes area and then click the '1/2 A4 Booklet 5.827 × 8.268' thumbnail to choose a paper size.

2. Choose the Cavern color scheme and the Textbook font scheme. Click the CREATE button to create the publication. When Publisher asks to insert pages automatically, click the Yes button.

3. Use Help to read about Building Blocks. Click the Page Parts button (Insert tab | Building Blocks group) to display the Page Parts gallery and then, in the Headings area, choose the Convention heading to use as a masthead. *Hint:* Point to each heading to see its name. When Publisher inserts the heading, move it to the top of the page. Resize it to fit within the margins.

4. Right-click the Title text, and choose Best Fit on the shortcut menu. Type **THE COFFEE CUP** to change the title. Right-click the subtitle text and then choose Best Fit on the shortcut menu. Change the subtitle to LIBERAL ARTS STUDENT ORGANIZATION.

5. If requested to do so by your instructor, replace the subtitle with the name of your school.

6. Click the Background button (Page Design tab | Page Background group). In the Gradient Background area, click 'Accent 3 Vertical Gradient'.

7. Again using the Page Parts button (Insert tab | Building Blocks group), insert the Convention (Layout 3) sidebar. Resize the sidebar to fit the space below the masthead and at the right margin as shown in Figure 3–75. Your display may differ, depending on how you resize the sidebar.

8. Type **CALL-OUT** to replace the title text. Type **ORGANIZATIONAL MEETING** to replace the sidebar subtitle text. Right-click the text and then click Best Fit on the shortcut menu to autofit the text.

9. Select the text at the bottom of the sidebar. Type **Join us Saturday, Feb. 4, at 10:00 a.m. in the Student Union Coffee Shop for a free cup of coffee with your student ID.** to replace the text.

10. Use the 'Draw Text Box' button (Home tab | Objects group) to add a text box just below the masthead, approximately .5 inches high and 2.5 inches wide. Insert the text, **Volume 1, Issue 1** and then press CTRL+ENTER to create a soft return. Type **Jan. 23, 2017** to insert the date.

11. If instructed to do so, change the date to your birthday.

12. Draw a text box below the masthead, approximately .5 inches tall and 2.5 inches wide. Insert the text, Lead Story Headline, as the new text. Right-click the text and then click Best Fit on the shortcut menu.

13. Draw a text box below the lead story headline to fill the empty space, approximately 4.45 inches tall and 2.5 inches wide.

14. If necessary, customize the ribbon to display the 'Edit Story in Microsoft Word' button (Review tab | New group).

15. Click the first empty text box. Click the 'Edit Story in Microsoft Word' button (Review tab | New group). When Word is displayed, type **=rand(2,3)** and then press the ENTER key to generate random text. Delete any extra hard returns at the end of the text. Exit Word to return to Publisher.

16. Click one of the pictures in the side bar twice, to select only the picture. Replace the picture with a photo you find using the search term, coffee. Repeat the process for the other two pictures.

17. Save the file with the file name, Extend 3–1 Coffee Newsletter.

18. Remove the ribbon customization as described earlier in this module.

19. Submit the file in the format specified by your instructor.

Continued >

Extend Your Knowledge *continued*

20. ✳ When would you use a template instead of creating a newsletter from scratch? What other page parts might you add to subsequent pages? Why?

Expand Your World

Create a solution that uses cloud and web technologies by learning and investigating on your own from general guidance.

Converting Files

Instructions: Run a browser and navigate to zamzar.com (Figure 3–76). You would like to explore converting your newsletter to formats other than the .pub Publisher format. While Publisher has many formats in the Save as type list, a cloud tool may have even more choices.

Figure 3–76

Perform the following tasks:

1. In Step 1 on the Convert Files tab, click the Browse button or the Choose Files button (depending on your browser) and then navigate to one of your completed newsletters.

2. In Step 2, click the 'Convert files(s) to:' box and choose a conversion format, such as html or an e-book format.

3. In Step 3, enter your email address.

4. In Step 4, click the Convert button to send the converted file to your email. If you receive a message indicating the conversion is about to happen, click the OK button.

5. When you receive the email from Zamzar, click the link provided and then click the Download Now button. Your browser should direct you to save the download.

6. If your download is a compressed file, right-click the zipped file to display a shortcut menu. Click Extract or Extract All to extract the file.

7. Open the converted file.

8. Submit the assignment in the format specified by your instructor.

9. ✻ What format might you use to post your newsletter on the web? Would an HTML file be better than a download link? Why or why not? When might you convert to a PDF format?

In the Labs

Design, create, modify, and/or use a publication following the guidelines, concepts, and skills presented in this module. Labs 1 and 2, which increase in difficulty, require you to create solutions based on what you learned in the module; Lab 3 requires you to apply your creative thinking and problem-solving skills to design and implement a solution.

Lab 1: **Creating a Symphony Newsletter**

Note: To complete this assignment, you will be required to use the Data Files. Please contact your instructor for information about accessing the Data Files.

Problem: The symphonic orchestra has asked you to create a newsletter they can distribute to their patrons. Currently, they have given you some content for page 1 and page 4. You are to leave placeholder text and graphics on the inside pages. You create the newsletter shown in Figure 3–77.

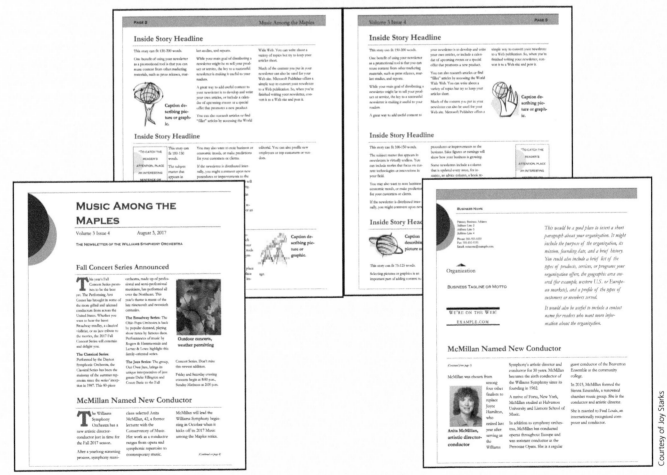

Figure 3–77

Continued >

In the Labs *continued*

Perform the following tasks:

1. Run Publisher. In the template gallery, click BUILT-IN and then click Newsletters.

2. In the More Installed Templates area, choose the Eclipse template.

3. Select the Aspect color scheme and the Etched font scheme. Choose to use a two-page spread. Create the publication.

4. As you make changes to the newsletter, scroll and zoom as necessary. Turn on the display of formatting characters if desired.

5. Use the following text to edit the masthead on page 1:

   Newsletter Title: Music Among the Maples

   Volume and Issue: Volume 3 Issue 4

   Newsletter Date: August 3, 2017

   Business Name: The Newsletter of the Williams Symphony Orchestra

6. For the lead story, use the headline, Fall Concert Series Announced. Import the lead story, Fall Concert Series, from the Data Files.

7. Position the insertion point at the beginning of the story. Click the Drop Cap button (Text Box Tools Format tab | Typography group) to display the Drop Cap gallery and then click the 'Drop Cap Style 13' preview.

8. Delete both the Special Points of Interest sidebar and the Inside this Issue sidebar on page 1.

9. Replace the graphic on page 1 using the shortcut menu. Search for the term, maples. Edit the caption to read Outdoor concerts, weather permitting.

10. For the second story on page 1, use McMillan Named New Conductor as the headline. Import the story, McMillan Named New Conductor, from the Data Files. When Publisher prompts you, flow the story to the last story on page 4. Use the same headline on page 4.

11. Navigate to the last text box of the story on page 1. Right-click the story to display the shortcut menu. Click 'Format Text Box' on the shortcut menu to display the Format Text Box dialog box. Click the Text Box tab and then place a check mark in the 'Include "Continued on page…"' check box (Format Text Box dialog box).

12. Navigate to the first text box of the story on page 4. Repeat Step 11 to include a Continued from notice. Use the Previous and Next buttons to follow the story from beginning to end, and double-check your continued notices.

13. Go back to the beginning of the story on page 1 and create a drop cap as you did in Step 7.

14. At the bottom of page 4, click the graphic twice to select it. Replace the graphic using the shortcut menu. Browse to the Data Files and insert the Conductor graphic. Click the Fit button (Picture Tools Format tab | Crop group) to make the graphic fit the area.

15. If requested to do so by your instructor, use your photo instead of the one supplied in the Data Files.

16. Edit the caption to read: Anita McMillan, artistic director-conductor. Check your publication for spelling and design errors, and fix or ignore the flagged items as necessary. Hyphenate the stories according to the hyphenation rules discussed in this module. Delete any graphics in the scratch area.

17. Save the newsletter on your storage device with the file name, Lab 3 – 1 Symphony Newsletter. Save the file again, this time as a Publisher template, named Lab 3 – 1 Symphony Newsletter Template.

18. Submit the file as directed by your instructor.

19. ✳ How do the font scheme and color scheme complement the topic of the newsletter? How do you think page 1 would have looked if you had changed it to a mixed column format? Why might you want to change the format?

Lab 2: **Publisher Newsletter Choices**

Note: To complete this assignment, you will be required to use the Data Files. Please contact your instructor for information about accessing the Data Files.

Problem: Use a copy of a newsletter that you regularly receive, or obtain one from a friend, organization, or school. Using the principles in this module, analyze the newsletter.

Perform the following tasks:

1. Run Publisher.

2. Open the publication, Lab 3 – 2 Newsletter Analysis Table, from the Data Files (Figure 3-78).

3. Use the skills you learned in editing sidebars to fill in each of the empty cells in the table as it applies to your selected newsletter. The topics to look for are listed below:
   - Purpose
   - Audience
   - Paper
   - Distribution
   - Font and color scheme
   - Consistency
   - Alignment
   - Repeated elements
   - Continued notices and ease of navigation
   - Sidebars, pull quotes, patterns, etc.

4. If requested by your instructor, insert your name in the text box at the top of the newsletter, along with the current date.

5. Print the publication and attach a copy of the newsletter. Submit both to your instructor.

Continued >

In the Labs *continued*

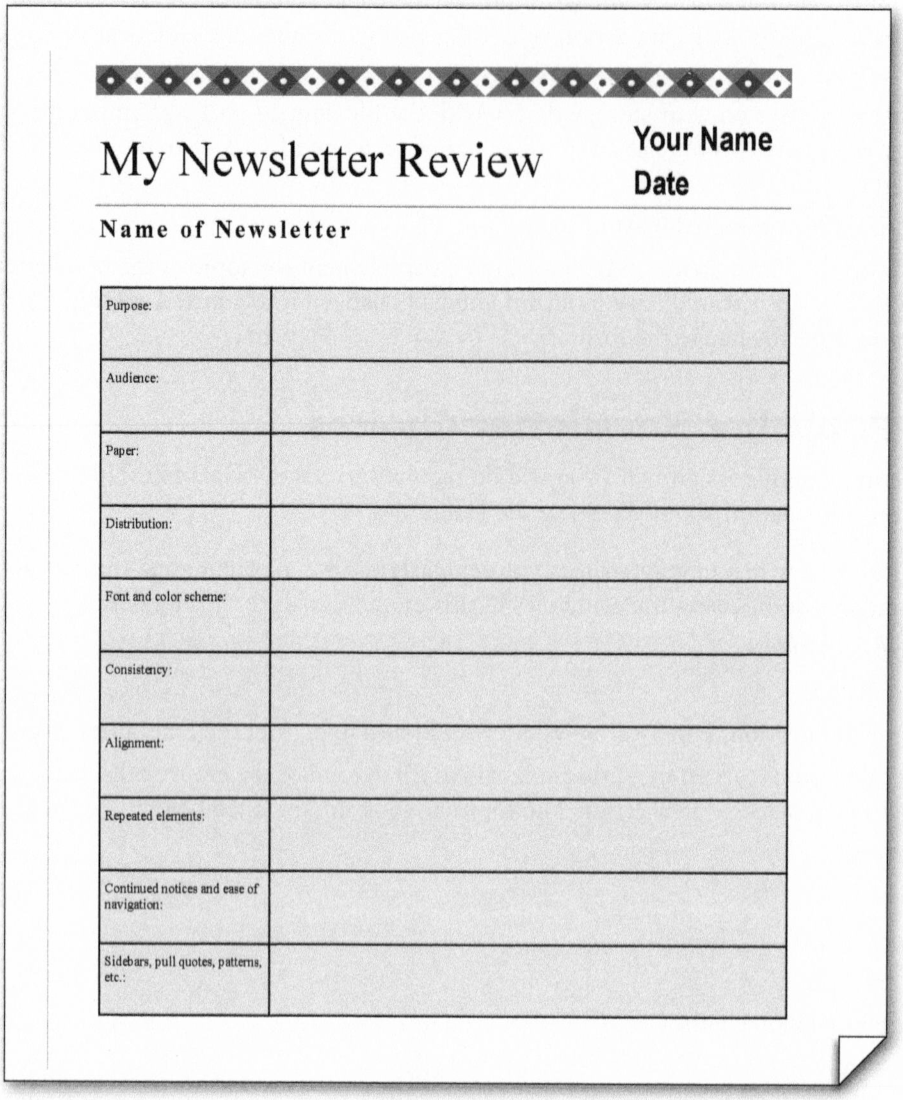

My Newsletter Review   **Your Name**
Date

Name of Newsletter

Purpose:	
Audience:	
Paper:	
Distribution:	
Font and color scheme:	
Consistency:	
Alignment:	
Repeated elements:	
Continued notices and ease of navigation:	
Sidebars, pull quotes, patterns, etc.:	

Figure 3–78

Lab 3: **Consider This: Your Turn**

Creating a Money Newsletter

Problem: A financial literacy group has asked you to create a newsletter about the wise use of money and spending. You decided to create a newsletter from scratch.

Part 1:   Run Publisher. Use the Cascade newsletter template. Use the Green Color Scheme and the Trek font scheme. Use the title, You and Your Money. On page 1, change the lead story headline to The Road to Financial Freedom (you may use the default text in the story itself). Change the secondary story headline to You Take over the Wheel (you may use the default text in the story itself). Link the story to one of the stories on page 2, and change the headline there as well. Create a pull quote from the story if your template does not have one already. Replace the graphics with suitable pictures and caption. Submit your assignment in the format specified by your instructor.

Part 2: 🕸 What other kinds of stories might you include in a financial newsletter such as this one? Where might those stories come from? Who might be the author/organization for this newsletter? Who might be the audience?

4 Creating a Custom Publication from Scratch

Objectives

You will have mastered the material in this module when you can:

- Create a custom publication size
- Create color and font schemes
- Rotate, flip, and change the proportion of graphics
- Set a transparent color
- Group and ungroup objects
- Create a building block

- Make picture corrections
- Apply text effects
- Use WordArt
- Change the line spacing of text
- Adjust paragraph formatting
- Create a custom bullet
- Apply and delete customizations

Introduction

Customizing publications, tailored to a specific organization, with font schemes, color schemes, page dimensions, and margins, allows desktop publishers to be more creative and provide made-to-order publications for their clients. The process of developing a publication that communicates a company brand and specific requirements entails careful analysis and planning. Coordinating design choices with the customer and gathering necessary information will determine the design and style that will be most successful in delivering the company's message. Whether you are creating a publication from scratch or using a template, many settings and preferences can be customized and saved. Once saved, the publication can be reused, resulting in increased productivity and continuity across publications.

Project — Mailer

Module 4 uses Publisher to create a mailer. **Mailers** commonly are smaller, single-page publications used for advertising and marketing. Mailers include information about the organization, pictures, contact information, and other pertinent information with many color and eye-catching graphics. Mailers also may include coupons. The mailer created in this module advertises specials and coupons for a pizza restaurant named Pizza Palace and includes graphics, bulleted items, and WordArt. The completed publication is shown in Figure 4–1.

To illustrate some of the customizable features of Microsoft Publisher, this project presents a series of steps to create the mailer with a customized color scheme that uses the company colors: red, gold, and light blue. A customized font scheme will include the Gabriola font for the heading and the secondary font, Arial, for the body text.

The graphics combine clip art with shapes and fills, repeating the color scheme. With a solid picture in the background, three graphics are edited and repurposed as a logo for the Pizza Palace. Finally, a WordArt object and a bulleted list provide the text content as shown in Figure 4–1. Coupons appear in the lower-right corner.

Figure 4–1

The following roadmap identifies general activities you will perform as you progress through this module:

1. CUSTOMIZE the PUBLICATION editing the page size, margins, font schemes, and color schemes.
2. EDIT GRAPHICS.
3. Create and USE BUILDING BLOCKS.
4. Edit and FORMAT TEXT with line spacing, text effects, and gradient fills.
5. USE WORDART.
6. Change paragraph formatting and CREATE BULLETED LISTS.
7. INSERT and edit a COUPON advertisement.
8. APPLY CUSTOMIZATIONS.
9. DELETE CUSTOMIZATIONS.

Custom-Sized Publication

Publications come in many different sizes and shapes. Customers and designers do not always want to use one of the preset sizes, such as 8½ × 11. In those cases, you may want to create a **custom-sized publication** with specific dimensions, orientation, and margins. Custom-sized publications are used for everything from newspaper advertisements to greeting cards to church bulletins.

What steps should I take when creating a custom publication?
Define the purpose of the publication. Choose a font scheme and color scheme to match the customer's logo or company colors. Define which pieces of business information you plan to use. Does the proposed publication fulfill the need? If you are working from scratch, look at similar publication templates. Choose margins and a paper size that will help standardize the publication with others used in the industry.

BTW
Blank Publications
If you want Publisher to start with a blank publication rather than the list of templates, each time you run the program, do the following. Click the File tab to open the Backstage view and then click the Options tab. Click the General tab (Publisher Options dialog box) and then remove the check mark in the 'Show the New template' gallery when starting Publisher' check box.

To Select a Blank Publication

When you first run Publisher, the template gallery displays a list of featured and built-in templates, as well as blank publications. Most users select a publication template and then begin editing. It is not always the case, however, that a template will fit every situation. Sometimes you want to think through a publication while manipulating objects on a blank page, trying different shapes, colors, graphics, and effects. Other times you may have specific goals for a publication, such as size or orientation, that do not match any of the templates. For these cases, Publisher provides **blank publications** with no preset objects or design, allowing you to start from scratch.

The following steps select a blank print publication.

1. Run Publisher.

2. Click the 'Blank 8.5 × 11"' thumbnail in the template gallery to create a blank publication in the Publisher window.

3. If the Publisher window is not maximized, click the Maximize button on the title bar.

4. If the Special Characters button (Home tab | Paragraph group) is not selected already, click it to display formatting marks on the screen.

5. If the Page Navigation pane is displayed, click the Page Number button on the status bar to hide the Page Navigation pane (Figure 4–2).

Figure 4–2

To Create a Custom Page Size

The following steps create a new, custom page size. *Why? The customer has requested a mailer that measures 7.75 × 5 inches.* Publisher and other Office applications use the term **page setup** to refer to the process of changing the document margins, orientation, and size, among other settings.

- Click Page Design on the ribbon to display the Page Design tab.

- Click the 'Choose Page Size' button (Page Design tab | Page Setup group) to display the Page Size menu, which lists standard page sizes and options for other sizes (Figure 4–3).

Q&A How does the 'Create New Page Size' command differ from the Page Setup command?
When you choose the 'Create New Page Size' command, you can name and save the settings. A new thumbnail will appear in the template gallery every time you run Publisher, which allows you to reuse the page size for other publications. The Page Setup command affects only the current publication.

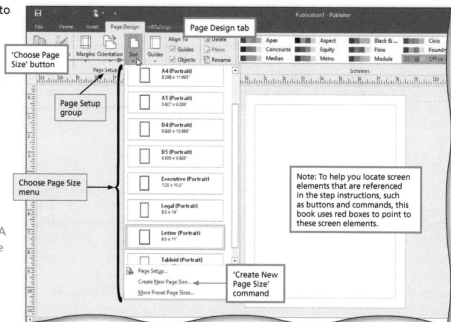

Figure 4–3

- Click 'Create New Page Size' at the bottom of the Choose Page Size menu to display the Create New Page Size dialog box.

- In the Name text box (Create New Page Size dialog box), type **Mailer** to name the custom size.

- Click the Layout type button to display the list of layouts (Figure 4–4).

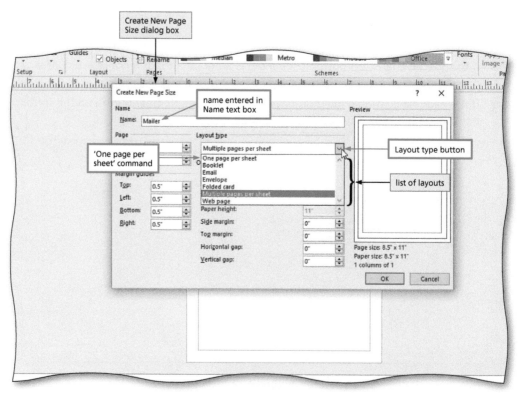

Figure 4–4

Experiment

- One at a time, click each of the layout types in the list to view additional settings that may appear. Note how the preview changes.

3

- Click 'One page per sheet' to display the settings associated with single publications on a sheet of paper.
- Select the text in the Width box and then type 7.75 to set the width for the publication.
- Select the text in the Height box and then type 5 to set the height for the publication.
- One at a time, select the text in each of the four Margin guides boxes and type 0.25 to change the margin on each side of the publication (Figure 4–5).

Q&A | Why are the margins set to .25?
Many desktop printers cannot print to the exact edge of the paper, and leaving a little space frames the content.

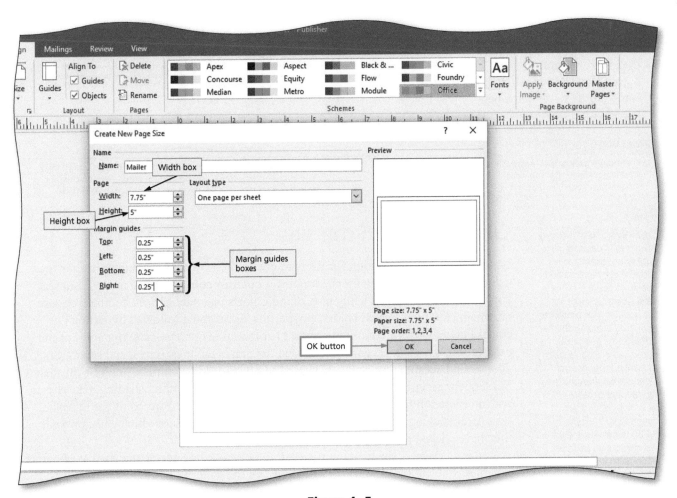

Figure 4–5

4

- Click the OK button (Create New Page Size dialog box) to save the page size and margins.

- Zoom to 100% if necessary (Figure 4–6).

Q&A

Where will the custom layout be saved?

The saved layout will appear in the template gallery when you first run Publisher, or when you click File on the ribbon and then click the New tab. To view custom sizes in the template gallery, click the 'More Blank Page Sizes' thumbnail.

Experiment

- Click the 'Choose Page Size' button (Page Design tab | Page Setup group) to verify the new page size has been saved.

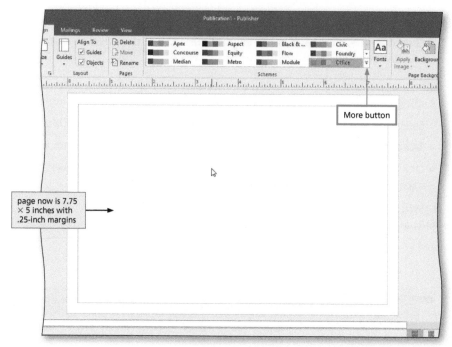

Figure 4–6

Other Ways

1. In template gallery, click 'More Blank Page Sizes' thumbnail, click 'Create new page size' thumbnail, enter values, click OK button (Create New Page Size dialog box)

2. To change margins, click Adjust Margins button (Page Design tab | Page Setup group), click Custom Margins, enter margin values on Margin Guides tab, click OK button (Layout Guides dialog box)

Custom Color Schemes

Publisher provides an option for users to create their own color schemes rather than using one of the predefined sets. Creating a **custom color scheme** means choosing your own colors that will apply to text and objects in a publication. You may choose one main color, five accent colors, a hyperlink color, and a followed hyperlink color. The main color commonly is used for text in major, eye-catching areas of the publication. The first accent color is used for graphical lines, boxes, and separators. The second accent color typically is used as fill color in prominent publication shapes. Subsequent accent colors may be used in several ways, including shading, text effects, and alternate font colors. The hyperlink color is used as the font color for hyperlink text. After clicking a hyperlink, its color changes to show users which path, or trail, they have clicked previously.

Once created, the name of the custom color scheme appears in the list of color schemes. The chosen colors also will appear in the galleries related to shapes, fills, and outlines. A **gallery** is a set of choices, often graphical, arranged in a grid or in a list. You can scroll through choices in a gallery by clicking the gallery's scroll arrows. Recall that some buttons and boxes have arrows that, when clicked, also display a gallery. Most galleries support **live preview**, a feature that allows you to point to a gallery choice and see its effect in the publication, without actually selecting the choice.

To Create a New Color Scheme

The publication will use accent colors of red, gold, and light blue, as well as a black main color for text. *Why? The customer wants to emulate the colors of his product, red for the pizza sauce and gold for the crust.* The following steps create a custom color scheme.

1

- Click the More button (Page Design tab | Schemes group) (shown in Figure 4–6) to display the Color Scheme gallery (Figure 4–7).

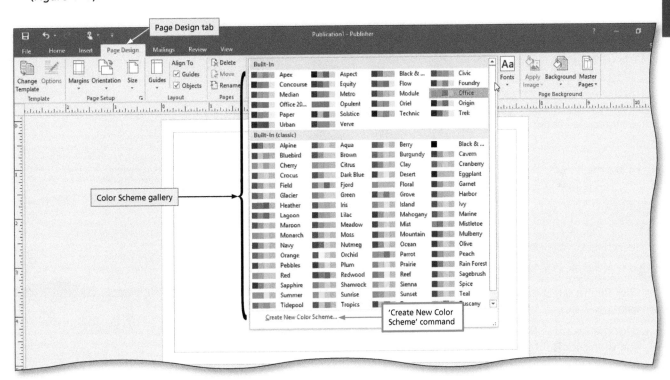

Figure 4–7

2

- Click 'Create New Color Scheme' to display the Create New Color Scheme dialog box.

- Type `Pizza Palace` in the 'Color scheme name' text box (Create New Color Scheme dialog box) to name the color scheme with the same name as the company (Figure 4–8).

Q&A What if I do not enter a name for the modified color scheme?
Publisher assigns a name that begins with the word, Custom, followed by a number (i.e., Custom 8).

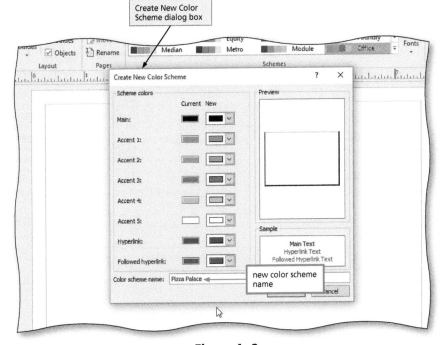

Figure 4–8

• In the Scheme colors area, click the New button next to the Accent 1 color to display a gallery of color choices (Figure 4–9).

Experiment

• Point to each color in the gallery to display its name.

Q&A
Why is this color gallery different from others?
This color gallery is a general palette of colors. It does not display the typical accent colors across the top, because you are choosing the accent colors in this dialog box.

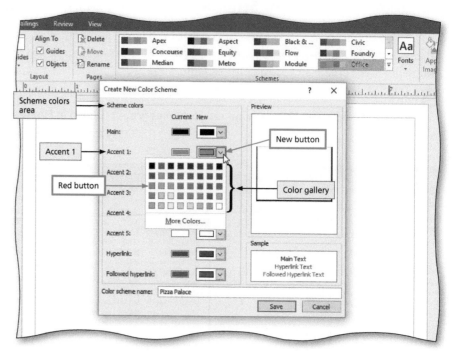

Figure 4–9

• Click Red to select the Accent 1 color.

• Click the Accent 2, New button, and then click Gold to select the Accent 2 color.

• Do not close the Create New Color Scheme dialog box (Figure 4–10).

Q&A
Can I delete a color scheme once I create it?
Yes. To delete a color scheme, first display the list of color schemes, right-click the custom color scheme, and then click Delete Scheme on the shortcut menu.

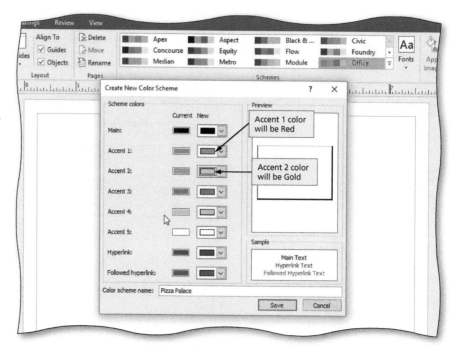

Figure 4–10

Other Ways

1. In template information pane, click Color scheme box, scroll to end of list, click Create new, enter values, click Save button (Create New Color Scheme dialog box)

To Choose a Color Not in the Gallery

Most Publisher color galleries display approximately 40 common colors. For example, in the Font Color gallery, the 40 colors are variations of the chosen color scheme. Some galleries also display recently used colors. All color galleries display a More Colors command. *Why? When clicked, the command allows the user to choose from other Standard colors, Custom colors, and Pantone colors.* The following steps choose a color from the Standard colors.

- In the Create New Color Scheme dialog box, click the New button associated with Accent 3 to display the color gallery (Figure 4–11).

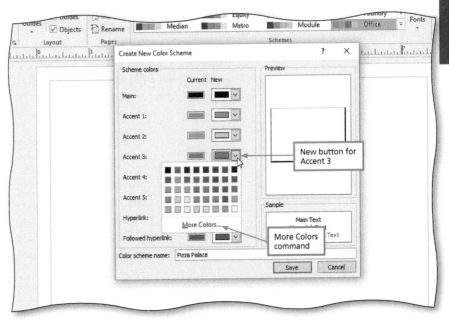

Figure 4–11

- Click More Colors in the color gallery to display the Colors dialog box.

- If necessary, click the Standard tab, and then click the desired color (in this case, the light blue color in the fifth row and sixth from the left) (Figure 4–12).

Experiment

- Click each of the tabs in the Colors dialog box to see the types of colors and color systems from which you can choose.

- Click the OK button (Colors dialog box) to select the chosen color.

- Click the Save button (Create New Color Scheme dialog box) to save the new color scheme.

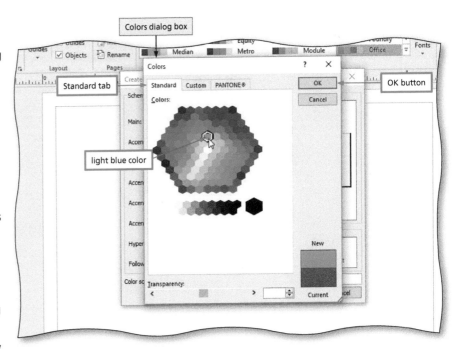

Figure 4–12

Other Ways

1. In any color gallery, click More Colors, click desired color, click OK button (Colors dialog box)

Custom Font Schemes

Publisher provides an option for users to create their own font schemes rather than using one of the predefined sets. Creating a **custom font scheme** means choosing your own fonts to use in a publication. You may choose one heading font and one body font. Choosing complementary fonts takes practice. In general, either the heading font and body font should match exactly but perhaps appear in different sizes or formats (such as italics), or the two fonts should contrast with each other dramatically in features such as size, type ornamentation, and direction. **Type ornamentation** refers to serif, structure, form, or style.

Custom font schemes contain a name that will appear in the font scheme list. The chosen fonts also will appear in the Styles list. The body font will be the default font for new text boxes.

To Create a New Font Scheme

1 CUSTOMIZE PUBLICATION | 2 EDIT GRAPHICS | 3 USE BUILDING BLOCKS | 4 FORMAT TEXT | 5 USE WORDART
6 CREATE BULLETED LISTS | 7 INSERT COUPON | 8 APPLY CUSTOMIZATIONS | 9 DELETE CUSTOMIZATIONS

Because the Pizza Palace company wants to portray royalty and clarity as well as good food, a customized font scheme will include the Gabriola font, which has fancy stylistic sets and glyphs. Gabriola is a Microsoft font that has been optimized to improve legibility on the screen. A body font of Arial provides a nice contrast with the Gabriola heading font. *Why? Arial is a sans-serif, TrueType font and is easily legible in print publications. TrueType refers to scalable fonts that produce high-quality characters on both computer screens and printers.* The following steps create a new font scheme.

• Click the Scheme Fonts button (Page Design tab | Schemes group) to display the Scheme Fonts gallery (Figure 4–13).

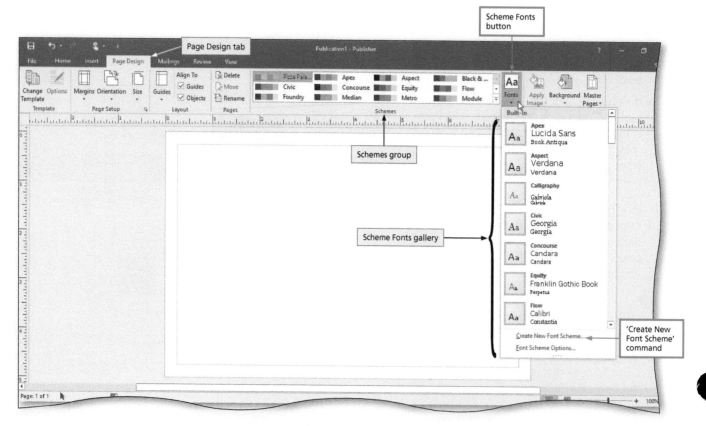

Figure 4–13

2

- Click 'Create New Font Scheme' in the Scheme Fonts gallery to display the Create New Font Scheme dialog box.

- Type `Pizza Palace` in the Font scheme name text box (Create New Font Scheme dialog box) to name the font scheme with the same name as the company (Figure 4–14).

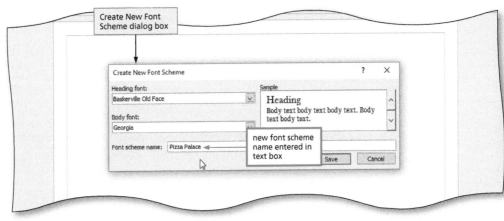

Figure 4–14

3

- Click the Heading font arrow to display the list of fonts (Figure 4–15).

🔍 **Experiment**

- Click different fonts and watch the Sample box change. When you are finished, click the Heading font arrow again.

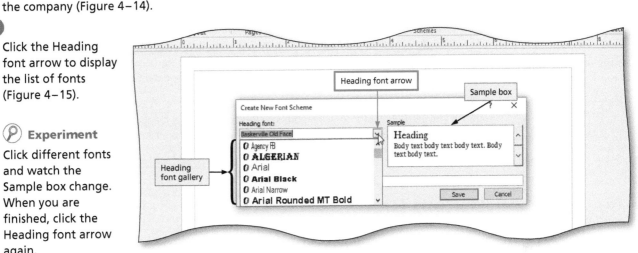

Figure 4–15

4

- Scroll as necessary and then click Gabriola to select the heading font.

- Click the Body font arrow, scroll as necessary, and then click Arial to select the body font (Figure 4–16).

Q&A

Can I delete a font scheme once I create it?

Yes. To delete a font scheme, display the list of font schemes, right-click the custom font scheme, and then click Delete Scheme on the shortcut menu. You also can rename or duplicate the scheme.

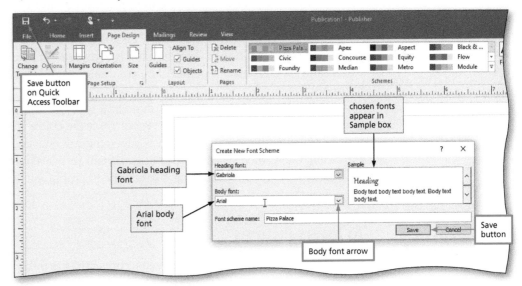

Figure 4–16

⑤

- Click the Save button (Create New Font Scheme dialog box) to save the new font scheme.

Q&A Where is the new font scheme stored?
Each font scheme that you create will appear at the top of the gallery, alphabetized by name.

⑥

- Click the Save button on the Quick Access Toolbar. Navigate to your storage location and then save the file with the file name, Pizza Palace Mailer.

Other Ways

1. In template information pane, click Font scheme box, scroll to end of list, click Create new, enter values, click Save button (Create New Font Scheme dialog box)

What is the best way to choose a layout and elements?
Carefully consider the necessary elements and their placement. Choose margins and a paper size that will help standardize the publication. Decide whether to add dated material or prices. Think about alignment of elements and proximity of similar data. Create appropriate contrast or repetition when using fonts and colors.

If you are working for someone, draw a storyboard and get it approved before you begin. If you need to create objects from scratch, have someone else evaluate your work and give you constructive feedback.

BTW
Cropping vs. Resizing
Cropping is different from resizing. Both techniques reduce the overall size of the graphic display; however, with cropping, you eliminate part of the graphic from the display while maintaining the size of the objects in the picture. With resizing, the entire graphic becomes smaller or larger. For additional editing possibilities, you can resize a cropped graphic or crop a resized graphic. If you want to undo a cropping effect, you can click the Reset Picture button (Picture Tools Format tab | Adjust group).

BTW
Using the CTRL Key
When you CTRL+drag a sizing handle, the graphic is resized, keeping the center of the graphic in the same place. This is true whether you use a corner handle to resize or a side handle to change the proportion.

Editing Graphics

Recall that you have inserted graphics or pictures into publications by choosing them online or by importing them from a file. Graphics add value and visual flair to publications; however, to create a unique publication for a business, it is good to enhance and customize the graphic through editing. Many times customers are bored by stock graphics and clip art because of their overuse. A well-edited graphic not only contributes to the uniqueness of the publication but also adds a personal touch. Publications with edited graphics do not look rigid or computer generated.

The main graphic for the Pizza Palace is a picture of a palace with a pizza delivery person on a moped. This graphic is composed of three separate graphics, edited, and then grouped together. The combined graphic is saved as a logo for future use.

With Publisher, you can perform several types of adjustments or edits on graphics. You can rotate and flip; correct or reset the color; set a transparent color; resize or change the proportion; add borders, picture effects, and captions; and, if it is a drawing, curve, or clip art, you can erase or edit just certain portions of the graphic. You will learn more about making corrections to graphics in a future module.

To Insert Pictures

The following steps insert three pictures into the publication. To complete these steps, you will be required to use the Data Files. Please contact your instructor for information about accessing the Data Files.

① Display the Insert tab.

② Click the Pictures button (Insert tab | Illustrations group) to display the Insert Picture dialog box. Browse to the location of the Data Files and the Module 04 folder.

③ CTRL+click the picture files named Delivery, Castle, and Road.

④ Click the Insert button (Insert Picture dialog box) to insert the pictures into the scratch area.

⑤ Click the scratch area away from the graphics to deselect them (Figure 4–17).

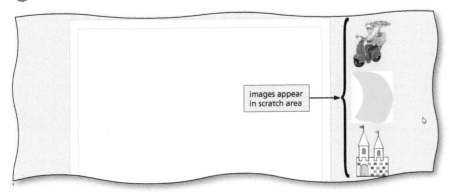

Figure 4–17

To Resize the Castle Graphic

The following steps resize the castle graphic.

① Drag the castle graphic to the right, away from the others in the scratch area for further editing. Scroll as necessary to display the entire graphic.

② SHIFT+drag the lower-right handle until the castle is approximately 2 inches by 3.13 inches as noted on the status bar (Figure 4–18).

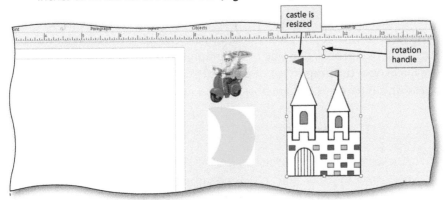

Figure 4–18

To Rotate

1 CUSTOMIZE PUBLICATION | 2 EDIT GRAPHICS | 3 USE BUILDING BLOCKS | 4 FORMAT TEXT | 5 USE WORDART
6 CREATE BULLETED LISTS | 7 INSERT COUPON | 8 APPLY CUSTOMIZATIONS | 9 DELETE CUSTOMIZATIONS

When you **rotate** an object in Publisher, you turn it so that the top of the object faces a different direction. For example, a picture of a person could be rotated to look like that person was standing on his or her head. Each selected object in Publisher displays one or more rotation handles used to rotate the object freely. To rotate in 15-degree increments, hold down the SHIFT key while dragging a rotation handle. To rotate an object on its base, hold down the CTRL key and drag the rotation handle — the object will rotate in a circle by pivoting around the handle. You can enter other rotation percentages using the Rotate Objects button (Picture Tools Format tab | Arrange group).

The following steps rotate the road graphic. *Why? The road graphic needs to be turned to look like a road leading to the castle.*

- Select the road graphic.

- Point to the rotation handle. When the pointer changes to a rotation pointer, SHIFT+drag the road graphic approximately 150° clockwise as shown in Figure 4–19.

Q&A Can I rotate objects other than drawing objects?
Yes, you can rotate all objects including shapes, text boxes, and tables. Rotate Objects buttons also appear on multiple tabs on the ribbon.

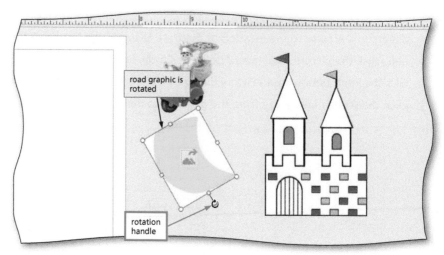

Figure 4–19

- Deselect the graphic.

Other Ways

1. Click Rotate Objects button (Picture Tools Format tab | Arrange group), click desired rotation

2. Right-click object, click Format Picture on shortcut menu, click Size tab (Format Picture dialog box), enter rotation percentage, click OK button

3. Click Object Size button (status bar), enter rotation percentage on Measurement task pane

To Change the Proportion

1 CUSTOMIZE PUBLICATION | 2 EDIT GRAPHICS | 3 USE BUILDING BLOCKS | 4 FORMAT TEXT | 5 USE WORDART
6 CREATE BULLETED LISTS | 7 INSERT COUPON | 8 APPLY CUSTOMIZATIONS | 9 DELETE CUSTOMIZATIONS

Recall that you have resized a graphic, which changes the width and height proportionally; the picture looks the same, just large or smaller. If you want to change the proportion, you are changing the ratio between the width and height. Changing the proportion exaggerates one side of the graphic and should be done only with a purpose in mind. The following step changes the proportion of the road graphic. *Why? The top of the road needs to be approximately the size of the castle door, but the curve and length of the road need to remain the same.*

- If necessary, select the road graphic.

- Drag the right sizing handle to the left to make the road narrower (Figure 4–20).

Figure 4–20

To Set a Transparent Color

Publisher allows you to set a transparent color in most graphics. *Why? Sometimes you will not want to use or see a certain portion of a graphic.* The background then will show through behind the chosen color. Setting a transparent color is part of the recoloring process that also includes changing the color of the entire graphic to match one of the theme colors, or to change the brightness/contrast of the graphic using the Format Picture dialog box. The picture's original color information remains stored with the image, so you can restore the picture's original colors at any time.

The following steps set a transparent color.

1
- If necessary, select the road graphic.
- Display the Picture Tools Format tab.
- Click the Recolor button (Picture Tools Format tab | Adjust group) to display the Recolor gallery (Figure 4–21).

🔍 **Experiment**
- Point to each of the thumbnails in the Recolor gallery to see each one's effect on the graphic.

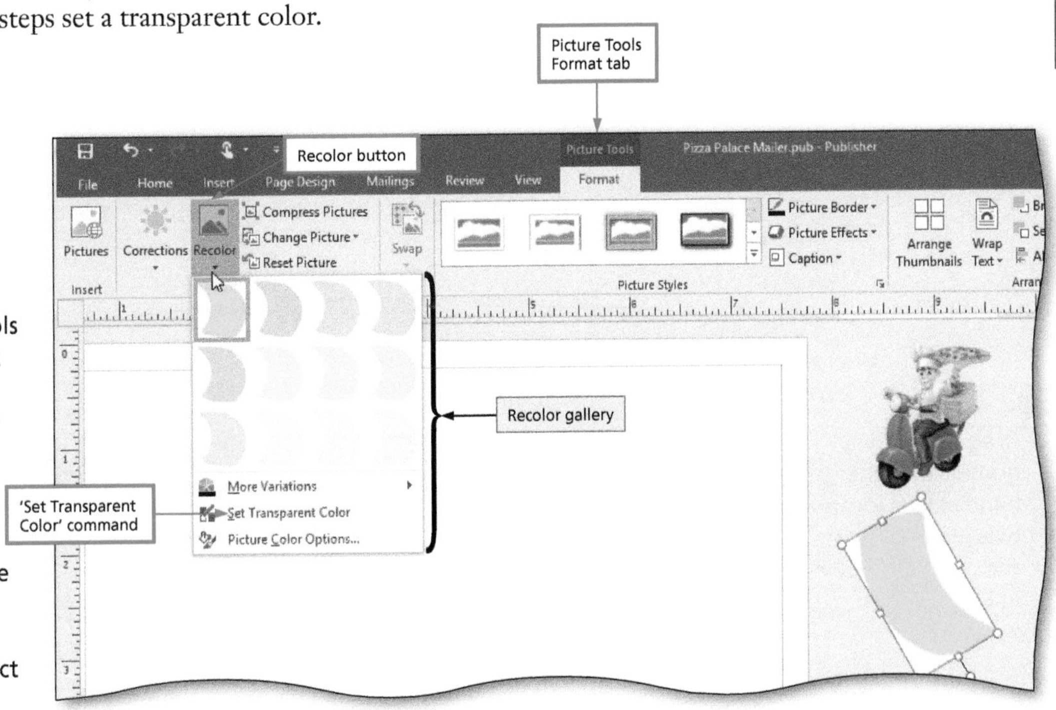

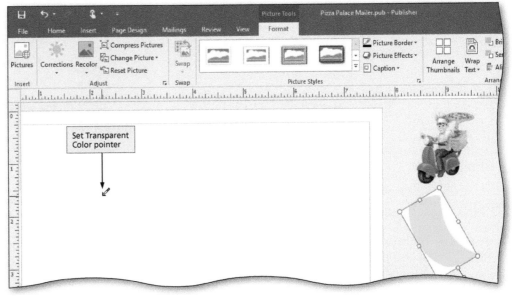

Figure 4–21

2
- Click 'Set Transparent Color' in the Recolor gallery to display the new pointer (Figure 4–22).

Figure 4–22

- Click the white portion of the road graphic (Figure 4–23).

Q&A Why am I making the white area transparent?
When the graphic is grouped to become a company logo, the white should not appear.

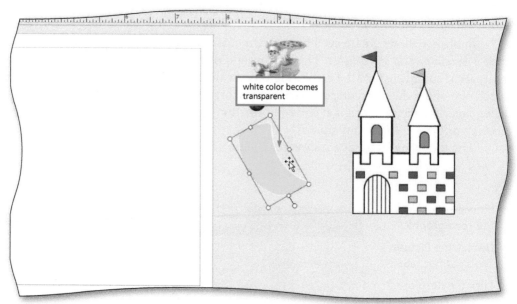

Figure 4–23

- Drag the road graphic (not the handle) to a location below the door of the castle as shown in Figure 4–24.

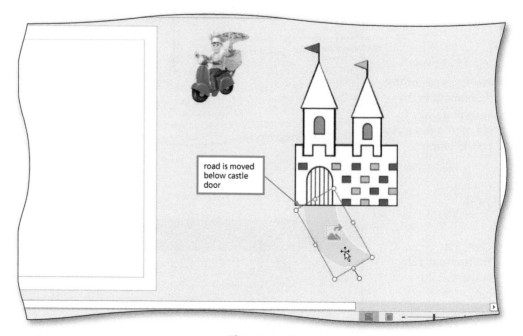

Figure 4–24

To Flip an Object

Publisher also allows you to **flip** objects, changing the left to right or the top to bottom orientation of a picture or graphic. The following steps flip the delivery graphic horizontally. *Why?* *The delivery person needs to face the other way, as if he were coming out of the castle.*

①

- Select the delivery graphic.
- Click the Rotate Objects button (Picture Tools Format tab | Arrange group) to display the Rotate Objects gallery (Figure 4–25).

Experiment

- Point to each rotation option in the gallery and watch how the graphic changes in the page layout.

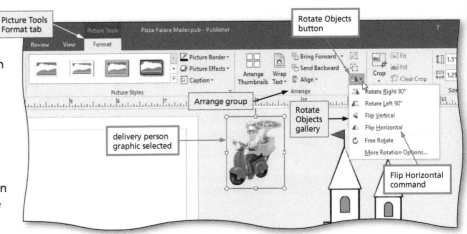

Figure 4–25

②

- Click Flip Horizontal in the gallery to flip the graphic (Figure 4–26).

Q&A Can I flip objects other than graphics?
Yes, as with rotating, you can flip most objects.

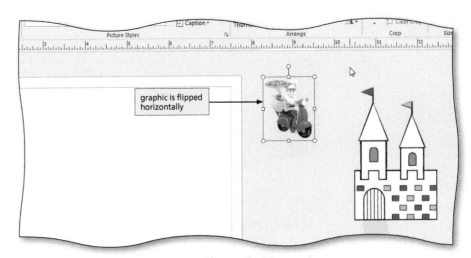

Figure 4–26

③

- Drag the graphic to a location on the road as shown in Figure 4–27.

Q&A Why did the delivery graphic display behind the road and castle?
Publisher inserts graphics from back to front. The delivery graphic was alphabetically first in the three pictures files inserted previously. Because it technically was placed first into the publication, Publisher loaded the other graphics in front of that one.

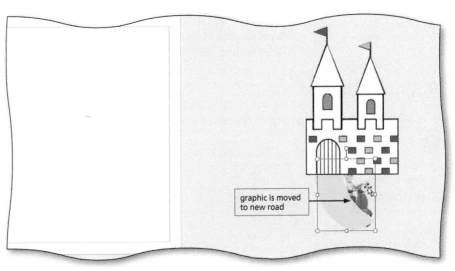

Figure 4–27

Other Ways

1. Click Rotate Objects button (Picture Tools Format tab | Arrange group) or (Home tab | Arrange group), click Free Rotate in Rotate Objects gallery, rotate object

2. Right-click object, click Format Picture on shortcut menu, click Size tab (Format Picture dialog box), enter rotation percentage, click OK button

3. Click Object Size button (status bar), enter rotation percentage on Measurement task pane

To Bring Forward and Resize

Recall that you can change the layering order of objects by using the Bring Forward or Send Backward buttons (Picture Tools Format tab | Arrange group). The following steps bring the delivery graphic forward and resize it.

1 With the delivery graphic still selected, click the Bring Forward button (Picture Tools Format tab | Arrange group) twice, so that the graphic appears in its entirety.

2 Resize the delivery graphic to approximately 1.50 × 1.80 inches as noted on the status bar (Figure 4–28).

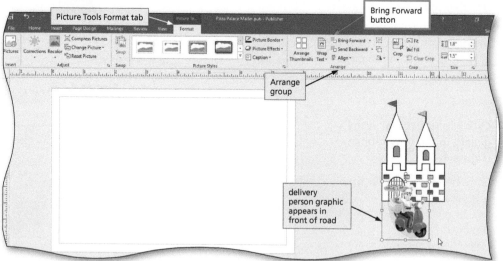

Figure 4–28

Grouping and Ungrouping Objects

Many clip art graphics are a combination of line drawings and shapes. When multiple objects are selected, you can **group** them, which means they stay together for purposes such as cutting, pasting, moving, and formatting. Alternately, when you **ungroup** objects, their parts can be selected and manipulated individually. Some clip art pictures first must be converted to a different format, the Microsoft Office drawing object format, before ungrouping.

To Group Objects

1 CUSTOMIZE PUBLICATION | 2 EDIT GRAPHICS | 3 USE BUILDING BLOCKS | 4 FORMAT TEXT | 5 USE WORDART
6 CREATE BULLETED LISTS | 7 INSERT COUPON | 8 APPLY CUSTOMIZATIONS | 9 DELETE CUSTOMIZATIONS

The following steps group the three graphics. **Why?** *It is easier to move and save the graphic if it is grouped.*

- Select the objects you wish to group (in this case, drag around the entire castle, road, and delivery graphics) to create a selection of the multiple parts (Figure 4–29).

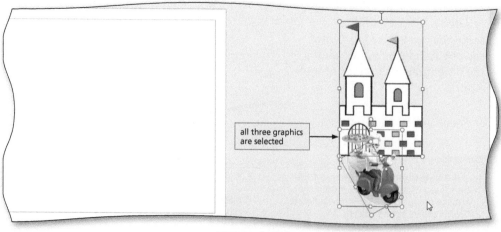

Figure 4–29

- Click the Group button (Picture Tools Format tab | Arrange group) to group the graphic (Figure 4–30).

Q&A Why did Publisher display the Drawing Tools Format tab?
When you group objects, they become a **drawing object**, which includes objects such as shapes, text boxes, and some clip art files.

❸

- Click the Save button on the Quick Access Toolbar to save the file again with the same file name and in the same location.

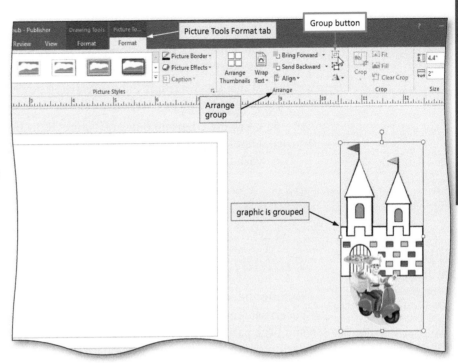

Figure 4–30

Other Ways

1. Right-click selected objects, click Group on shortcut menu   2. Select objects, press CTRL+SHIFT+G

To Ungroup a Graphic

If you wanted to ungroup a grouped graphic, you would perform the following steps.

1. Select the grouped graphic.
2. Display the Drawing Tools Format tab.
3. Click the Ungroup button (Drawing Tools Format tab | Arrange group) to ungroup the graphic or press CTRL+SHIFT+G.

The WMF Format

Many of the clip art images supplied in previous versions of Office were stored in the **Windows Metafile Format (.wmf)**. A wmf file is a format portable across Office applications, composed of drawn graphics and shapes. Ungrouping and editing wmf files required some specific manipulations, not common to other file formats. Specifically, you had to convert the picture into a Microsoft Office Drawing Object and then ungroup and edit the pieces.

To Convert a Picture to a Drawing Object

If you wanted to edit a picture that was stored in the wmf format, you would perform the following steps to convert the picture to a Microsoft Office Drawing Object and then ungroup it.

BTW

Fitting Graphics
The Fit button (Picture Tools Format tab | Crop group) places the entire, original graphic within the cropping handle dimensions, even if that means creating a disproportional image. The Fill command (Picture Tools Format tab | Crop group) places the original graphic within the cropping handles maintaining proportions, which sometimes means a slight cropping occurs if the cropping handle dimensions are not the same shape as the original. The Clear Crop (Picture Tools Format tab | Crop group) command resets the graphic to its original size and dimension with no cropping. The commands become enabled after an initial crop.

1. If necessary, select the picture and display the Picture Tools Format tab.
2. Click the Ungroup button (Picture Tools Format tab | Arrange group) to begin the ungroup process.
3. When the Microsoft Publisher dialog box is displayed, click the Yes button to convert the picture to a Microsoft Office drawing object.
4. Click the Ungroup button (Picture Tools Format tab | Arrange group) again. Deselect by clicking outside of the selected parts and then click the part you wish to edit.

Break Point: If you wish to take a break, this is a good place to do so. Exit Publisher. To resume at a later time, run Publisher, open the file called Pizza Palace Mailer, and continue following the steps from this location forward.

BTW
Building Block Categories
In the Create New Building Block dialog box, you cannot change the Gallery list, but you can enter a new category and save your graphic to that new category. Once you click the OK button, the new category will appear each time you access the Building Block Library.

Building Blocks

Building blocks are graphical elements that you can insert in a publication, including advertisement items, business information components, calendars, design accents, and page parts. To insert a building block into a publication, you click the appropriate button on the Insert tab, such as calendars or advertisements. You also can create your own building blocks and add them to the Building Block Library. The **Building Block Library** displays folders of building block components. When saving a building block, you can enter a title, description, and keywords to help you find the building block later. You also can choose the gallery and category in which you wish to save.

Alternately, you can save edited graphics on your storage device as pictures. Saving the graphic as a picture allows you to use that graphic in other applications, whereas building blocks are available only in Publisher.

To Save a Building Block

1 CUSTOMIZE PUBLICATION | 2 EDIT GRAPHICS | 3 USE BUILDING BLOCKS | 4 FORMAT TEXT | 5 USE WORDART
6 CREATE BULLETED LISTS | 7 INSERT COUPON | 8 APPLY CUSTOMIZATIONS | 9 DELETE CUSTOMIZATIONS

The following steps save the grouped graphic as a building block to use as a company logo. *Why? The graphic becomes reusable across multiple publications.*

- Right-click the desired graphic or object (in this case, the grouped castle, road, and delivery graphic) to display the shortcut menu (Figure 4–31).

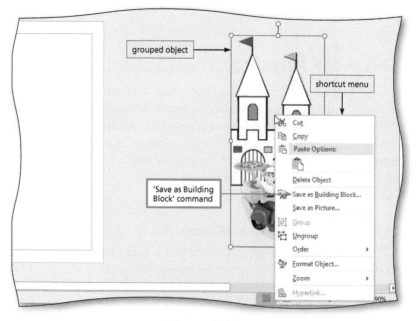

Figure 4–31

2

- Click 'Save as Building Block' on the shortcut menu to display the Create New Building Block dialog box.

- Type `Pizza Palace Logo` in the Title text box.

- Press the TAB key to move to the Description text box, and then type `This logo is a grouped graphic of a castle, road, and delivery person.`

- Click the Keywords text box. Type `pizza, castle, delivery` to enter keywords (Figure 4–32).

3

- Click the OK button (Create New Building Block dialog box) to save the building block.

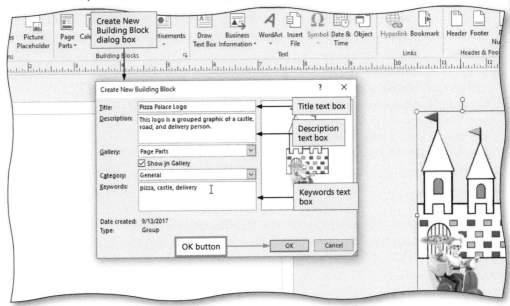

Figure 4–32

TO SAVE THE GRAPHIC AS A PICTURE

If you wanted to use the logo in another application, such as Microsoft Word or Microsoft PowerPoint, you would perform the following steps to save the graphic as a picture on your storage device.

1. Right-click the object and then click 'Save as Picture' to display the Save As dialog box.
2. Type the name of your graphic in the File name box.
3. Navigate to your storage location.
4. Edit property tags as desired and then click the Save button (Save As dialog box) to save the graphic as a picture.

To Snap an Object to the Margin Guide

1 CUSTOMIZE PUBLICATION | 2 EDIT GRAPHICS | 3 USE BUILDING BLOCKS | **4 FORMAT TEXT** | 5 USE WORDART

6 CREATE BULLETED LISTS | **7 INSERT COUPON** | **8 APPLY CUSTOMIZATIONS** | **9 DELETE CUSTOMIZATIONS**

The following steps insert a picture and snap it to the margin. *Why? Snapping is a magnet-like alignment that occurs between object borders and margin guides. Snapping is an easy way to align objects with the margin or with other objects, and snapping is better than dragging to an approximate location.* You also will resize the picture, changing its proportions. To complete these steps, you will be required to use the Data Files. Please contact your instructor for information about accessing the Data Files.

1

- Insert the picture named Pizza from the Data Files.

- Display the Page Design tab.

- Verify that both the Guides and Objects check boxes (Page Design tab | Layout group) contain check marks.

- Drag the border of the object (in this case, the pizza picture) toward the top margin guide and the left margin guide until the blue snapping lines appear. Do not release the mouse button (Figure 4–33).

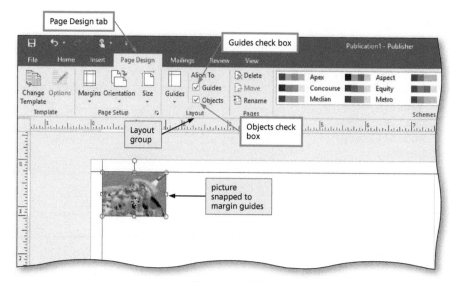

Figure 4–33

Q&A How do I place objects more precisely?

In a later module, you will learn about the Measurements task pane. Alternatively, you can right-click the object and then click Format Object on the shortcut menu. The Format Object dialog box contains a Layout tab in which you can enter the precise measurements in the 'Position on page' text boxes.

2

- Release the mouse button to snap the object to the margin guide.

- Drag the lower-center handle of the selected picture down to snap with the bottom margin.

- Drag the right-center handle of the picture to the right to snap with the right margin changing the proportion (Figure 4–34).

Q&A Could I have just filled the background with the picture?

When you use a background fill, Publisher stretches the picture to the edge of the paper. In this publication, the mailer needs a .25 margin on all four sides.

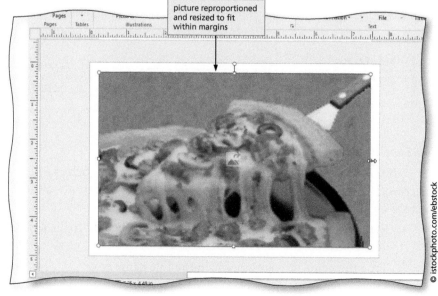

© istockphoto.com/ebstock

Figure 4–34

Picture Corrections

Sometimes you have to make corrections to pictures — either to enhance the colors and improve the picture or to purposefully change the picture for a special effect. The Corrections button (Picture Tools Format tab | Adjust group) displays a gallery to correct or adjust the brightness and contrast in a picture. **Brightness** is the percentage of black or white added to a main color. The higher the brightness percentage, the more white the image contains. **Contrast** is the saturation or intensity of the color. The higher the contrast percentage, the more intense the color.

Creating a Custom Publication from Scratch **Publisher Module 4** **PUB** 183

Publisher Module 4

1 CUSTOMIZE PUBLICATION | 2 EDIT GRAPHICS | 3 USE BUILDING BLOCKS | **4 FORMAT TEXT** | **5 USE WORDART**
6 CREATE BULLETED LISTS | **7 INSERT COUPON** | **8 APPLY CUSTOMIZATIONS** | **9 DELETE CUSTOMIZATIONS**

To Select a Correction

The following steps select a correction for the picture of the pizza. *Why? You need to reduce the contrast in the picture so that future added text will be more readable.*

1

- With the pizza picture selected, click the Corrections button (Picture Tools Format tab | Adjust group) to display the Corrections gallery (Figure 4–35).

Experiment

- Point to each correction in the gallery and watch the picture change. Note the ScreenTips.

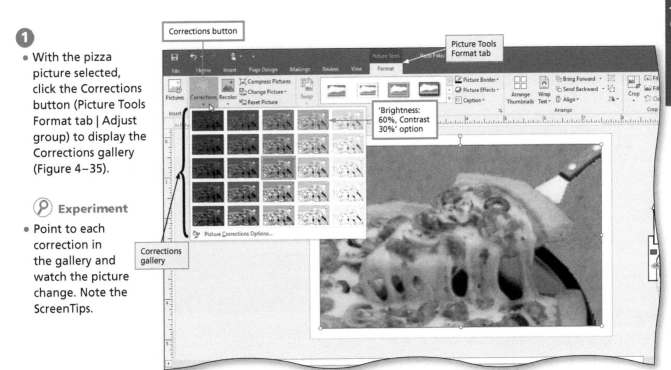

Figure 4–35

2

- Click 'Brightness: 60%, Contrast 30%' (row 1, column 4) to correct the picture (Figure 4–36).

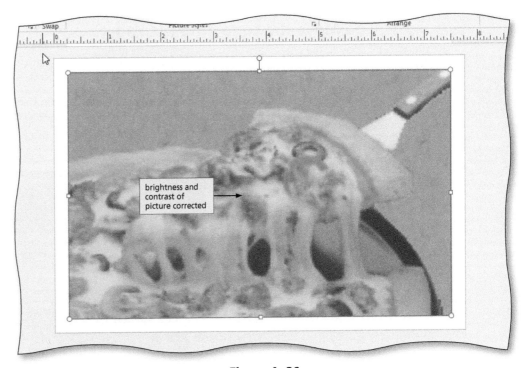

Figure 4–36

To Draw a Rectangle

The following steps draw a rectangle in the mailer that will become a background for the header text.

① Click the Shapes button (Insert tab | Illustrations group) to display the Shapes gallery.

② Click the Rectangle shape in the Basic Shapes area in the Shapes gallery.

③ Draw a rectangle, approximately 1.4 inches tall, across the top of the mailer, snapping it to the margins.

④ Click the Shape Fill arrow (Drawing Tools Format tab | Shape Styles group) and then click Main (Black) in the Shape Styles gallery (Figure 4–37).

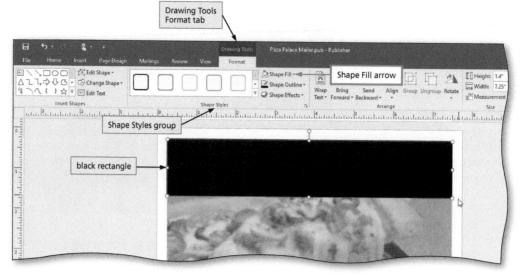

Figure 4–37

To Move the Logo onto the Page

The following step moves the logo into the publication and snaps it to the left margin.

① Drag the logo from the scratch area to the publication page until it snaps to the left and bottom margins (Figure 4–38). If the logo appears behind the pizza or rectangle, click the Bring Forward button (Picture Tools Format tab | Arrange group).

Figure 4–38

Text Effects

Recall that you have entered text in text boxes created by various templates. In a new, blank publication, if you start typing text, Publisher creates a large text box for you that fills the page. If any other object exists, Publisher will warn you about creating a text box first, before typing. By creating a text box, you can create a specific size and location, and format the text separately from the rest of the publication.

Like many word processing programs, Publisher allows you to format text with all kinds of font, color, and line spacing choices. In Publisher, you can **fill** or paint text with a color or with a special effect. You also can apply effects to the **outline** around the text, similar to adding a border or stroke around each letter. Table 4–1 displays the fill effects for text. Table 4–2 displays the outline effects for text.

Table 4–1 Text Fill Effects

Fill Effect	Settings	Result
No fill	None	Text is transparent (best used over a solid color)
Solid fill	Color button Transparency slider	Text appears with a solid color (default setting)
Gradient fill	Preset gradients button Type button Direction button Angle box Gradient stops Color button Position box Transparency slider Rotate with shape check box	Gradual progression of colors and shades

Table 4–2 Text Outline Effects

Fill Effect	Settings	Result
No line	None	Text displays fill effect or default settings with no outline
Solid line	Color button Transparency slider Width box Compound type button Dash type button Cap type button Join type button	Outline appears as a solid color at specified width and type settings
Gradient fill	Preset gradients button Type button Direction button Angle box Gradient stops Color button Position box Transparency slider Width box Compound type button Dash type button Cap type button Join type button	Outline appears with gradual progression of colors and shades at specified width and type settings

BTW
Shapes
Determining what shape to use with pictures is an important decision. Consider the choice of shape that will work with your picture. If your picture is square, you can insert it into a circle, but you may lose some of the edges or your picture may be distorted slightly. If your picture is rectangular, however, an oval shape may be interesting and aesthetically pleasing. If you want to focus on the center of your picture, a star shape may help direct the viewer's attention.

To Draw a Text Box

The main heading will appear at the top of the mailer, centered within the right two-thirds of the mailer. The following step draws a text box in the scratch area. ***Why?*** *You cannot type directly in the publication or in the scratch area without first creating a text box.* After formatting the text, you will move it in front of the black rectangle.

1

- Display the Home tab.
- Click the 'Draw a Text Box' button (Home tab | Objects group).
- In the scratch area, drag a text box approximately 5 inches wide and 1.25 inches tall (Figure 4–39).

 What are the default settings for text boxes?

The text is black, the alignment is left-justified, and the font is the body font of the font scheme. The margins within the text box are set to 0.04 inches. All of the settings can be changed.

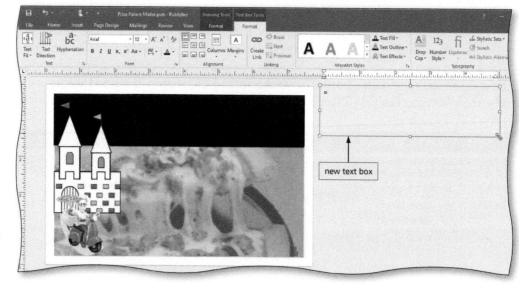

Figure 4–39

Other Ways

1. Click 'Draw a Text Box' button (Insert tab | Text group)

To Align Text and Format

Publisher allows you to align text in any one of nine different places using buttons on the Text Box Tools Format tab in the Alignment group. The following steps align the text along the bottom of the text box, centered. ***Why?*** *Placing the text along the bottom allows room for glyphs that rise above the text.*

1

- If necessary, display the Text Box Tools Format tab.
- Click the 'Align Bottom Center' button (Text Box Tools Format tab | Alignment group) to center the text along the bottom of the text box (Figure 4–40).

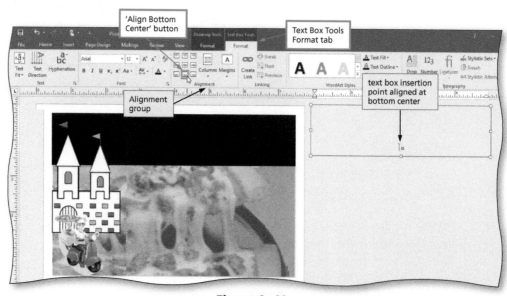

Figure 4–40

2
- Click the Font box and type `Gabriola` to select the heading font.
- Click the Font Size box and type `48` to set the font size.
- In the text box, type `Pizza Palace` to enter the text.
- Scroll the workspace to the right slightly and then select the text in the text box.
- Click the Stylistic Sets button (Text Box Tools Format tab | Typography group) to display the Stylistic Sets gallery (Figure 4–41).

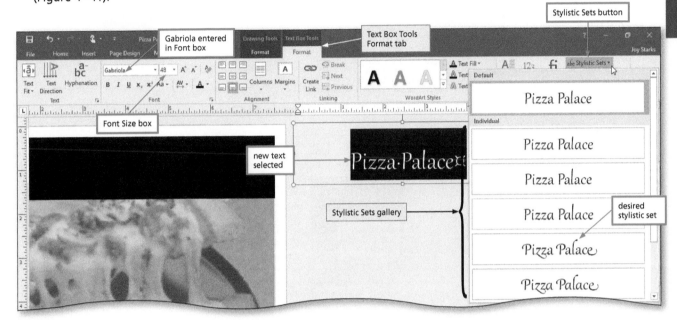

Figure 4–41

3
- Click the fourth stylistic set in the gallery to choose it (Figure 4–42).

Figure 4–42

To Apply a Gradient to Text

1 CUSTOMIZE PUBLICATION | 2 EDIT GRAPHICS | 3 USE BUILDING BLOCKS | 4 FORMAT TEXT | 5 USE WORDART
6 CREATE BULLETED LISTS | 7 INSERT COUPON | 8 APPLY CUSTOMIZATIONS | 9 DELETE CUSTOMIZATIONS

A **gradient** is a gradual progression of colors and shades, usually from one color to another color or from one shade to another shade of the same color. Recall that you used a gradient background from the Background gallery in a previous module. When editing a gradient, you either can choose a preset or you can make specific choices about the type of gradient, the direction, and the colors. A **color stop** is a button on a slider to set exactly where the color should start to change in the gradient.

The following steps apply a gradient fill to the text. *Why? Gradient fills create a sense of movement to draw attention and add dimension to a publication.*

1

- If necessary, select the desired text (in this case, Pizza Palace).

- Click the Font Color arrow (Home tab | Font group) to display the Font Color gallery (Figure 4–43).

Figure 4–43

2

- Click Fill Effects to display the Format Shape dialog box.

- Click the Gradient fill option button (Format Shape dialog box) to display the gradient settings.

- Click the Preset gradients button to display the Preset gradients gallery (Figure 4–44).

Q&A What is the purpose of the Type button?

Publisher offers three different types of gradients. A **linear gradient** applies the color change in a straight line. A **radial gradient** displays the color change in a circle radiating outward. A **rectangular gradient** displays the colors in a rectangular fashion.

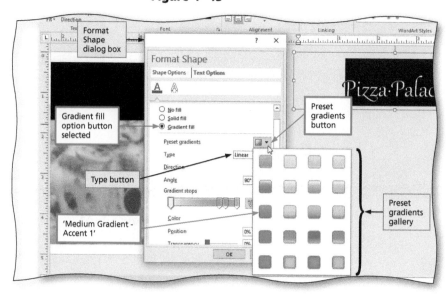

Figure 4–44

3

- Click the desired gradient (in this case, 'Medium Gradient - Accent 1') to select the preset.

- Scroll down in the dialog box as necessary to show the rest of the gradient commands.

- Click the Direction button to display the Direction gallery (Figure 4–45).

Q&A What is the purpose of the Transparency slider?

When you choose one color for your gradient, the Transparency slider allows you to specify what percentage of **transparency**, or opacity, for the beginning and end of the gradient. A 100% transparency appears white. A 0% transparency displays the chosen color as a solid.

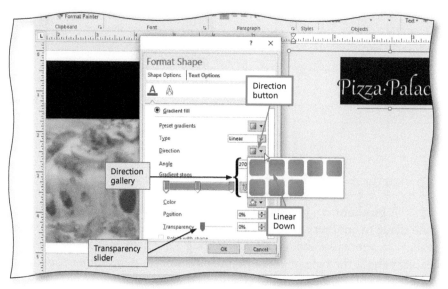

Figure 4–45

4

- Click the desired direction (in this case, Linear Down) to select the direction.
- Click the gradient stop you wish to change (in this case, 'Stop 2 of 3').
- Scroll, if necessary, and then click the Position up or down arrow until the Position box displays 75% to change the location of the stop (Figure 4–46).

Q&A | What is a color stop?
Color stops are points in the color bar to specify the location of a color change.

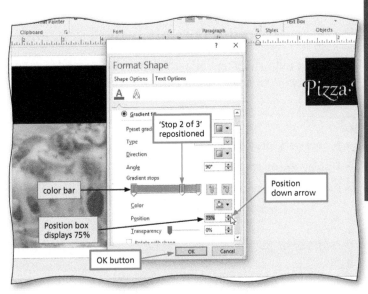

Figure 4–46

5

- Click the OK button to close the Format Shape dialog box.
- Drag the border of the text box to move it to a location in the upper-right portion of the black rectangle as shown in Figure 4–47.
- Deselect the text, if necessary, to view the fill effect.
- Center the publication in the workspace.

Q&A | Is it acceptable for some of the textbox to overlap into the workspace?
Yes, it will not cause any printing issues; the area is blank.

Figure 4–47

Other Ways

1. Click Format Shape Dialog Box Launcher (Drawing Tools Format tab | Shape Styles group), click Colors and Lines tab (Format Text Box dialog box), click Fill Effects button, choose settings, click OK button (Format Shape dialog box), click OK button (Format Text Box dialog box)

2. Right-click selection, click Format Text Box on shortcut menu, click Colors and Lines tab (Format Text Box dialog box), click Fill Effects button, choose settings, click OK button (Format Shape dialog box), click OK button (Format Text Box dialog box)

WordArt

WordArt is a gallery of text styles that works with Publisher to create fancy text effects. A WordArt object actually is a graphic, not text. Publication designers typically use WordArt to create eye-catching headlines, banners, or watermark images. Most designers agree that you should use WordArt sparingly and, at most, only once per page, unless you are trying to achieve some kind of special effect or illustration.

WordArt has its own tab on the ribbon that is displayed only when a WordArt object is selected. On the WordArt tab, you can change many settings, such as the fill, outline, warp, height, and alignment, as well as edit the color, shape, and shape effect.

BTW

WordArt Spelling
Keep in mind that WordArt objects are drawing objects; they are not Publisher text. Thus, if you misspell the contents of a WordArt object and then check the publication, Publisher will not flag the misspelled word(s) in the WordArt text.

To Insert a WordArt Object

The following steps add a WordArt object at the top of the mailer. *Why? While a formatted text box with font effects might create a similar effect, using WordArt increases the number of special effect possibilities and options.*

1

- If necessary, deselect any selected objects on the page or in the scratch area.
- Display the Insert tab.
- Click the Insert WordArt button (Insert tab | Text group) to display the WordArt gallery (Figure 4–48).

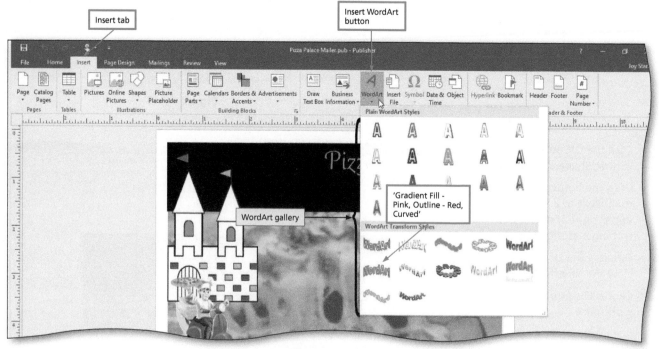

Figure 4–48

2

- Click the desired style (in this case, 'Gradient Fill - Pink, Outline - Red, Curved') in the WordArt gallery to select it.

- Type **Always Free Delivery** in the Text text box (Edit WordArt Text dialog box) to enter the text.

- Click the Font arrow, scroll as necessary, and then click Gabriola in the Font list.

- Click the Size arrow, scroll as necessary, and then click 24 in the Size list (Figure 4–49).

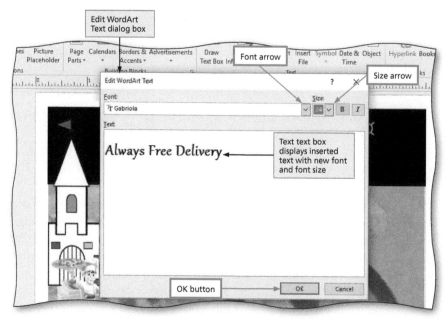

Figure 4–49

3

- Click the OK button to close the Edit WordArt Text dialog box and insert the WordArt graphic (Figure 4–50).

Q&A My WordArt graphic appeared in a different location. Should I move it?
No, you can work with it in any location on the worksheet. You will place it in the heading area later in the module.

Figure 4–50

To Change the WordArt Shape

1 CUSTOMIZE PUBLICATION | 2 EDIT GRAPHICS | 3 USE BUILDING BLOCKS | 4 FORMAT TEXT | **5 USE WORDART**
6 CREATE BULLETED LISTS | **7 INSERT COUPON** | **8 APPLY CUSTOMIZATIONS** | **9 DELETE CUSTOMIZATIONS**

The following steps change the WordArt's shape. *Why? The owner of Pizza Palace wants an upward pointing shape.*

1

- Click the 'Change WordArt Shape' button (WordArt Tools Format tab | WordArt Styles group) to display the Change WordArt Shape gallery (Figure 4–51).

Experiment

- Point to each effect in the gallery to display a preview of the effect in the publication.

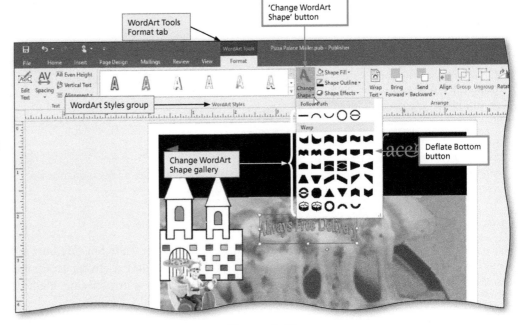

Figure 4–51

2

- Click the Deflate Bottom button (row 2, column 6) in the gallery to select it (Figure 4–52).

Figure 4–52

3

- Drag the WordArt object to a location directly below the words, Pizza Palace.

- Drag the right handle of the WordArt object to the right until it is approximately 3 inches wide and positioned as shown in Figure 4–53.

4

- Click the Save button on the Quick Access Toolbar to save the file again with the same file name and in the same location.

Figure 4–53

Break Point: If you wish to take a break, this is a good place to do so. Exit Publisher. To resume at a later time, run Publisher, open the file called Pizza Palace Mailer, and continue following the steps from this location forward.

BTW
Background Transparency
If the shape or text box has white in the background, you may want to remove it so that the objects behind show through. Select the shape or text box and then press CTRL+T to make the object transparent.

Paragraph Formatting

To change the line spacing, you click the Line Spacing button (Home tab | Paragraph group) on the ribbon (Figure 4–54). The Paragraph group includes buttons and boxes to help you format lines of text, including line spacing, alignment, columns, bullets, and numbering.

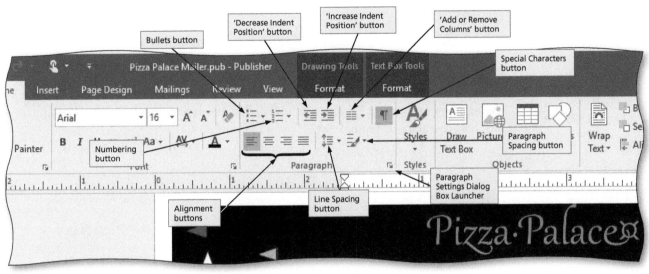

Figure 4–54

Line Spacing

Line spacing is the amount of space from the bottom of one line of text to the bottom of the next line, which determines the amount of vertical space between lines of text in a paragraph. By default, the Normal style is single spaced, but because Publisher accommodates the largest font in any given line, plus a small amount of extra space for glyphs and ornamentation, the default line spacing for new text boxes is 1.19.

To Change the Line Spacing

1 CUSTOMIZE PUBLICATION | 2 EDIT GRAPHICS | 3 USE BUILDING BLOCKS | 4 FORMAT TEXT | 5 USE WORDART
6 CREATE BULLETED LISTS | **7 INSERT COUPON** | 8 APPLY CUSTOMIZATIONS | 9 DELETE CUSTOMIZATIONS

The following steps create a text box and then reduce the line spacing. *Why? To include all of the specials and leave room for a coupon inserted later in the module, the line spacing needs to be single-spaced.*

1

- If necessary, display the Home tab.

- Click the 'Draw a Text Box' button (Home tab | Objects group) and then draw a text box approximately 5 inches wide and 1.9 inches tall. Watch the Object Size button on the status bar as you drag.

- With the insertion point inside the text box, click the Line Spacing button (Home tab | Paragraph group) to display the Line Spacing gallery (Figure 4–55).

2

- Click 1.0 in the Line Spacing gallery to change the line spacing to single spaced.

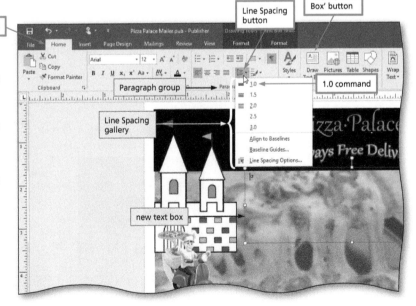

Figure 4–55

Other Ways

1. Click Paragraph Settings Dialog Box Launcher (Home tab | Paragraph group), enter settings, click OK button (Paragraph dialog box)

2. Right-click text, point to Change Text on shortcut menu, click Paragraph on Change Text submenu, enter settings, click OK button (Paragraph dialog box)

Bulleted Lists

A **bulleted list** is a series of lines, each beginning with a bullet character. When you click the Bullets button (Home tab | Paragraph group), Publisher displays the Bullet Styles gallery, which is a clickable list of thumbnails and commands that show different bullet styles. You can choose a standard bullet character (•) and adjust its size and how far the text is indented. You also can customize the bullet by choosing a different character or symbol.

To Create a Custom Bullet

1 CUSTOMIZE PUBLICATION | 2 EDIT GRAPHICS | 3 USE BUILDING BLOCKS | 4 FORMAT TEXT | 5 USE WORDART
6 CREATE BULLETED LISTS | **7 INSERT COUPON** | **8 APPLY CUSTOMIZATIONS** | **9 DELETE CUSTOMIZATIONS**

The following steps create a bulleted list using a custom character. *Why? The owner of Pizza Palace wants the bullet to look like a rook chess piece.*

- Click the Bullets button (Home tab | Paragraph group) to display the Bullets gallery (Figure 4–56).

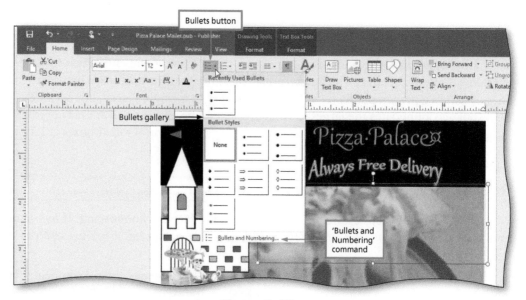

Figure 4–56

- Click 'Bullets and Numbering' in the Bullets gallery to display the Bullets and Numbering dialog box.

- Click any Bullet character, other than a blank one (Figure 4–57).

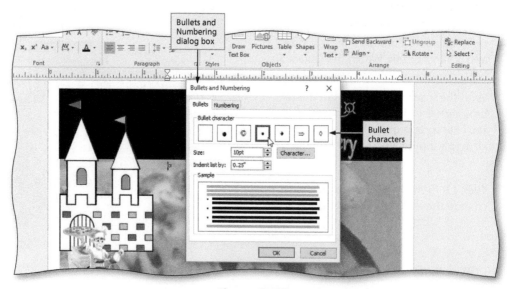

Figure 4–57

3

- Click the Character button (Bullets and Numbering dialog box) to display the Bullet Character dialog box.

- Click the Font arrow (Bullet Character dialog box) to display the Font list (Figure 4–58).

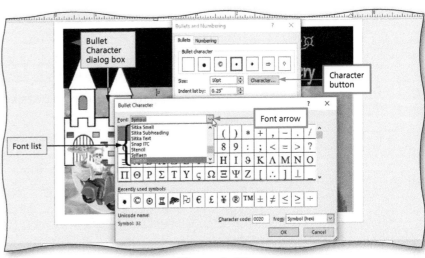

Figure 4–58

4

- Scroll as necessary and then click 'Segoe UI Symbol' in the list.

- Scroll as necessary in the list of symbols and then click the rook shape, character code 2656 (Figure 4–59).

Q&A Could I enter the character code to find the character faster?
Yes.

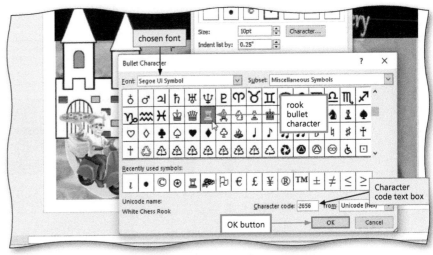

Figure 4–59

5

- Click the OK button (Bullet Character dialog box) to choose the symbol and return to the Bullets and Numbering dialog box.

- Click the Size up arrow until it says 16pt to enter the size.

- Click the 'Indent list by' up arrow twice to choose a .45" indentation (Figure 4–60).

Q&A What does pt stand for?
The letters pt stand for **point**, which is a physical measurement equal to approximately 1/72nd of an inch. Therefore, the bullet will be approximately .22 inches square.

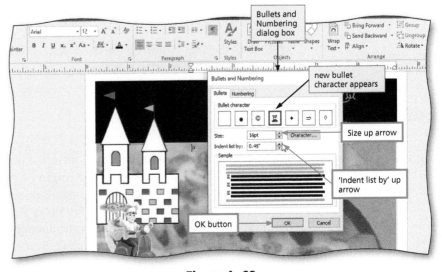

Figure 4–60

6

- Click the OK button (Bullets and Numbering dialog box) to apply the settings.

To Enter Text

The following steps enter bulleted text.

1 With the insertion point in the text box, click the Font Size arrow (Home tab | Font group) and then click 16 in the Font Size list.

2 Type the following text, pressing the ENTER key after every line but the last one.

```
Wednesday: $5 Pizza Night
Thursday: Unlimited Pizza and Salad Bar
Friday: Live Music 8:00 p.m. - 11:00 p.m.
Saturday: Table Trivia 8:00 p.m.
```

Q&A Do hyphens always change to a dash?

It depends on an AutoCorrect setting. You can look at the setting by clicking the Options tab in the Backstage view. Click Proofing (Publisher Options dialog box) and then click the AutoCorrect Options button. The AutoFormat As You Type tab displays the default settings.

3 If the text does not fit, drag the lower-center handle slightly downward, until you can see all of the text (Figure 4–61).

Figure 4–61

4 Click the Save button on the Quick Access Toolbar to save the file again with the same name and in the same location.

Advertisements

Publisher **advertisements** include a group of promotional templates used to market a product or service, including ads that might be placed in newspapers, attention getters, and coupons. Advertisements can be stand-alone publications or inserted as building block items in larger publications. The Pizza Palace will offer a coupon. A coupon is a promotional device used to market a product or service. Customers exchange coupons for discounts when purchasing a product. Some coupons offer rebates or free items to attract customers. Coupons often are distributed widely as small printed documents through mail, magazines, newspapers, and newsletters. More recently, however, they are distributed as electronic tags collected through preferred customer cards via the Internet and mobile devices, such as smartphones.

To Insert a Coupon

The following steps insert a coupon into the mailer. ***Why?*** *A coupon is an excellent marketing tool to help track who is reading your publications.*

1

- Deselect any selected object.
- Display the Insert tab.
- Click the Advertisements button (Insert tab | Building Blocks group) to display the Advertisements gallery (Figure 4–62).

Q&A Why does my gallery look different?
Your Advertisements gallery may or may not have an area of recently used items. If necessary, scroll down in the gallery to display the Coupons area.

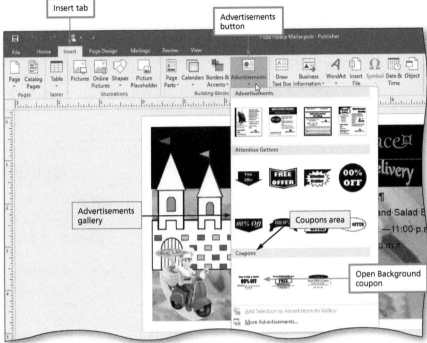

Figure 4–62

2

- In the Coupons area, click the Open Background coupon to insert it in the mailer.
- Drag the border of the inserted coupon to move it to the scratch area.
- Zoom to approximately 200% (Figure 4–63).

Q&A My coupon looks different. Did I do something wrong?
No, depending upon your printer and fonts, the coupon may be displayed slightly differently.

Figure 4–63

To Edit and Format the Coupon

The following steps edit the text boxes in the coupon.

1 Replace each text field as shown in Figure 4–64.

2 Change the font size of the Expiration Date to 6. Change the font size of the date to 6.

3 Drag around the coupon to select the entire coupon. Display the Drawing Tools Format tab.

4 Click the Shape Fill arrow (Drawing Tools Format tab | Shape Styles group) to display the Shape Fill gallery. Click 'Accent 2 (Gold)' in the Scheme Colors area.

Figure 4–64

To Resize, Move, and Duplicate the Coupon

The following steps resize the coupon, move it into the publication, and duplicate it so the mailer displays two coupons.

1 Drag around the outside of the coupon to select all of its parts.

2 SHIFT+drag the upper-left corner handle downward until the coupon is approximately 2.5 inches wide as shown on the status bar.

3 Click the 'Show Whole Page' button (Publisher status bar).

4 Move the coupon to a location in the lower-right corner of the mailer, snapping to the margins.

5 SHIFT+CTRL+drag the coupon to the left to create a duplicate positioned beside the original (Figure 4–65).

Figure 4–65

To Enter Other Text

The following steps draw a text box at the top of the publication that will contain the phone number and location.

1 Display the Home tab.

2 Click the 'Draw a Text Box' button (Home tab | Objects group) to select it.

3 Drag a text box just to the right of the blue flag in the logo, approximately 2 inches wide and .75 inches tall.

4 Change the font size to 14 and the font color to white.

5 Click the Bold button (Home tab | Font group).

6 Type `Call 205-555-FREE` and then press the ENTER key to finish the first line.

If instructed to do so, insert your phone number instead of the restaurant phone number.

7 Type `Route 40, Loman, ID` to finish the text (Figure 4–66).

Figure 4–66

To Check the Publication for Errors

The following steps check the publication for errors.

1 Press the F7 key to begin checking the publication for spelling errors. If Publisher flags any words, fix or ignore them as appropriate.

2 When Publisher displays a dialog box asking if you want to check the rest of your publication, click the Yes button.

3 When the spell check is complete, click the OK button.

4 Click File on the ribbon to open the Backstage view and, by default, the Info tab.

5 Click the 'Run Design Checker' button.

6 Ignore any errors related to the text boxes being partially of the page or pictures out of proportion. Both of those were intentional in this publication. If the Design Checker identifies any other errors, fix them as necessary.

7 Close the Design Checker task pane.

⑧ Print the mailer, if instructed to do so.

⑨ Click the Save button on the Quick Access Toolbar to save the file again with the same name and in the same location.

To Close a Publication without Exiting Publisher

The following steps close the publication without exiting Publisher.

① Click File on the ribbon to open the Backstage view.

② Click Close to close the publication without exiting Publisher and to return to the template gallery.

Using Customized Sizes, Schemes, and Building Blocks

Earlier in this module, you created a custom blank page for a 5 × 7 mailer, a customized font scheme, a customized color scheme, and a graphic that you stored as a building block. These customizations are meant to be used again. They also can be deleted if you no longer need them.

In the following sections, you will open and access the customizations as if you were going to create a second publication for the same company. You then will delete them.

To Open a Customized Blank Page

1 CUSTOMIZE PUBLICATION | 2 EDIT GRAPHICS | 3 USE BUILDING BLOCKS | 4 FORMAT TEXT | 5 USE WORDART
6 CREATE BULLETED LISTS | 7 INSERT COUPON | 8 APPLY CUSTOMIZATIONS | **9 DELETE CUSTOMIZATIONS**

The following steps open a customized blank page. **Why?** *The previously stored page size was stored in the custom area.*

• With Publisher running, if necessary, click File on the ribbon to open the Backstage view and then click New to display the New template gallery (Figure 4–67).

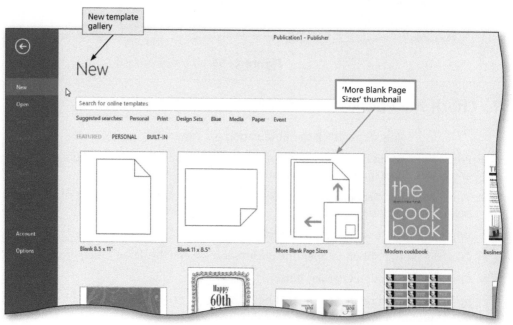

Figure 4–67

2

- Click the 'More Blank Page Sizes' thumbnail to view the Standard and Custom page sizes ('More Blank Page Sizes' gallery).

- Click the Mailer thumbnail in the Custom area to select it (Figure 4–68).

Q&A My thumbnails look different. Did I do something wrong?
No, you did not do anything wrong. The custom sizes on your computer will differ depending on the users and previous customizations.

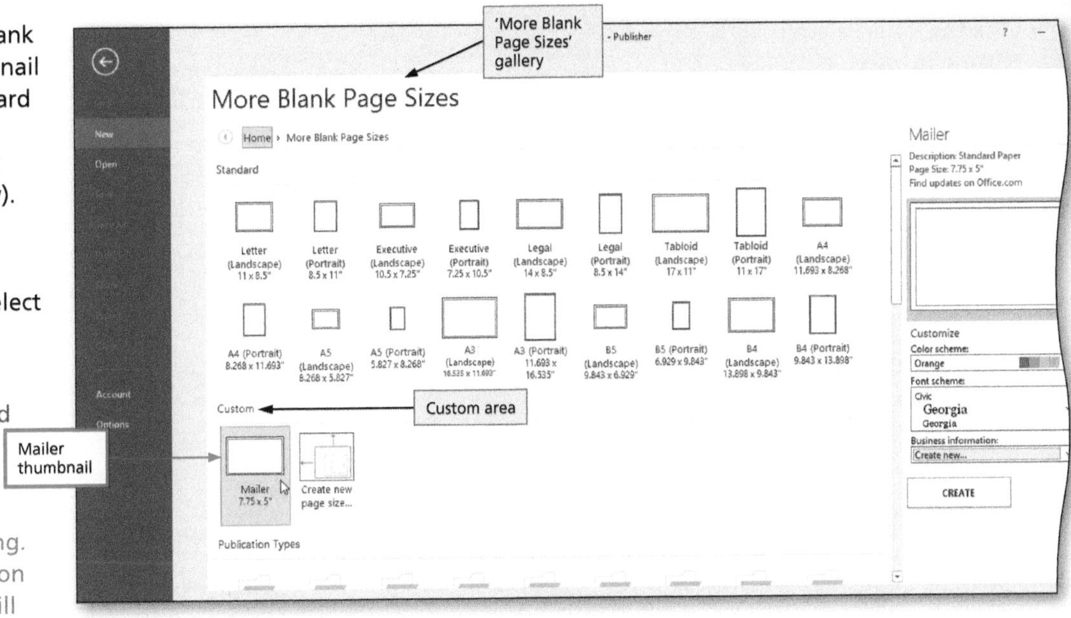

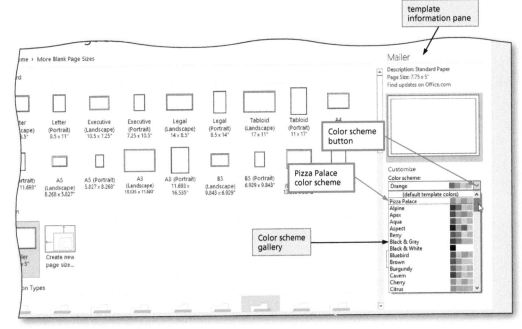

Figure 4–68

Other Ways

1. Click 'Choose Page Size' button (Page Design tab | Page Setup group), click custom size

To Apply Customized Color and Font Schemes

1 CUSTOMIZE PUBLICATION | 2 EDIT GRAPHICS | 3 USE BUILDING BLOCKS | 4 FORMAT TEXT | 5 USE WORDART
6 CREATE BULLETED LISTS | 7 INSERT COUPON | **8 APPLY CUSTOMIZATIONS** | **9 DELETE CUSTOMIZATIONS**

The following steps apply customized color and font schemes. *Why? Your publication colors and fonts need to adhere to company schemes.*

1

- Click the Color scheme button (template information pane), and then scroll to the top of the list (Figure 4–69).

Figure 4–69

- Click the Pizza Palace color scheme to select it.
- Click the Font scheme button (template information pane) and then scroll to the top of the list (Figure 4–70).

3

- Click the Pizza Palace font scheme to select it.
- Click the CREATE button (template information pane) to create the publication.

🔍 **Experiment**

- Type a few words and watch Publisher create a page-sized text box. Delete the text box after you are done.

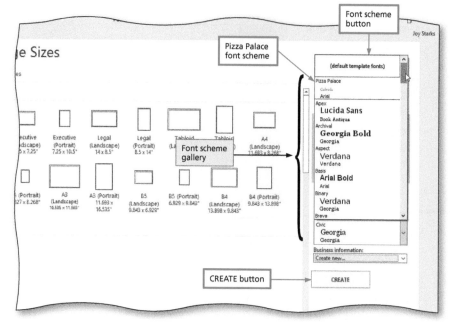

Figure 4–70

Other Ways

1. Click More button (Page Design tab | Schemes group), click custom color scheme
2. Click Scheme Fonts button (Page Design tab | Schemes group), click custom font scheme

TO INSERT A BUILDING BLOCK

If you wanted to insert a building block into another publication, you would perform the following steps

1. Display the Insert tab.
2. Click the Show Building Block Library Dialog Box Launcher (Insert tab | Building Blocks group) to display the Building Block Library dialog box.
3. Click the Page Parts folder (Building Block Library dialog box) to open it.
4. Double-click the desired building block to insert it into the publication.

Deleting Customizations

In laboratory environments, where many students work on the same computers throughout the day, it is a good idea to delete content you have created that is stored on the computer. You also might want to delete customization and content for companies with which you no longer do business.

To Delete Content from the Building Block Library

The following steps delete the Pizza Palace Logo from the Building Block Library. *Why? Many logos are proprietary or copyrighted. It is a good idea to delete them when you no longer need them.* Deleting from the library does not delete the graphics from saved publications.

1

- Display the Insert tab.

- Click the Show Building Block Library Dialog Box Launcher (Insert tab | Building Blocks group) to display the Building Block Library dialog box (Figure 4–71).

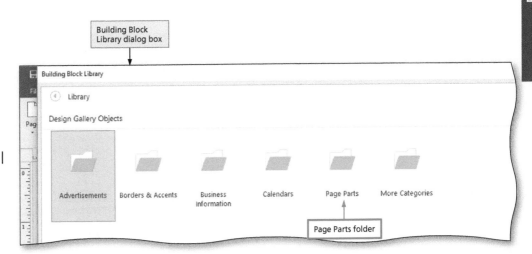

Figure 4–71

2

- Click the Page Parts folder (Building Block Library dialog box) to open it.

- Right-click the Pizza Palace Logo to display its shortcut menu (Figure 4–72).

🔍 **Experiment**

- Click Edit Properties on the shortcut menu and view the Edit Building Block Properties dialog box and its fields of information that Publisher saves. When finished, click the OK button to close the dialog box and then right-click again to display the graphic's shortcut menu.

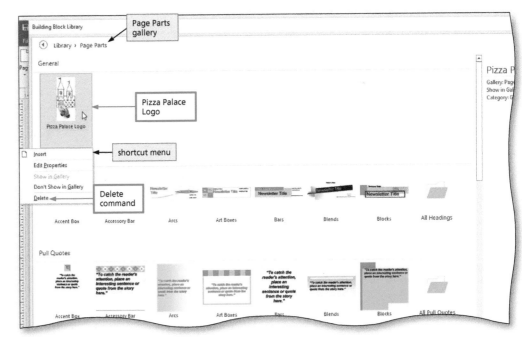

Figure 4–72

3

- Click Delete on the shortcut menu to delete the graphic.

- If Publisher displays a dialog box asking if you want to delete the building block permanently, click the Yes button.

- Click the Close button (Building Block Library dialog box) to close the dialog box.

To Delete the Custom Color Scheme

The following steps delete the Pizza Palace color scheme from Publisher's list of color schemes. *Why? If you are working in a lab environment, you should delete all custom schemes.* Deleting the color scheme does not change the colors in previously created publications.

● Display the Page Design tab to display the color schemes (Figure 4–73).

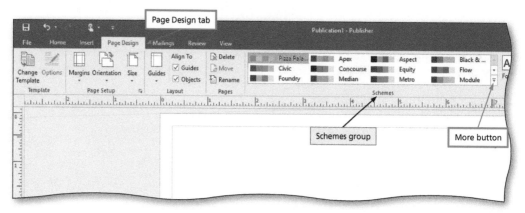

Figure 4–73

● Click the More button (Page Design tab | Schemes group) to display the Color Scheme gallery.

● Right-click the Pizza Palace color scheme in the Custom area to display the shortcut menu (Figure 4–74).

Q&A

How does the 'Add Gallery to Quick Access Toolbar' command work?

Recall that the Quick Access Toolbar appears above the ribbon on the Publisher title bar. It contains buttons for commonly used commands and settings, and it is customizable. Clicking the command will add a button on the right side of the toolbar. When you click that button, Publisher will set your color scheme automatically.

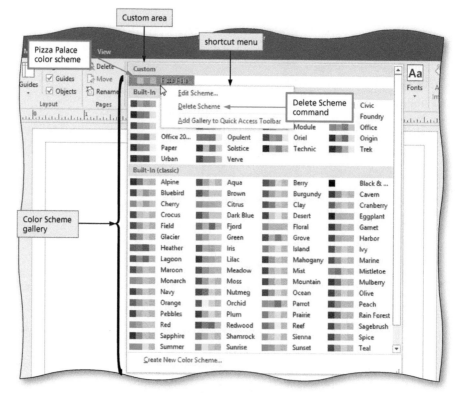

Figure 4–74

● Click Delete Scheme on the shortcut menu to delete the color scheme.

● When Publisher displays a dialog box asking if you want to delete the color scheme, click the Yes button.

Other Ways

1. Right-click custom scheme name (Page Design tab | Schemes group), click Delete Scheme on shortcut menu, click Yes button (Microsoft Publisher dialog box)

To Delete the Custom Font Scheme

The following steps delete the Pizza Palace font scheme from the list of font schemes. *Why? You no longer need to use the font scheme.* Deleting the font scheme does not change the fonts in previously created publications.

1

- Click the Scheme Fonts button (Page Design tab | Schemes group) to display the Scheme Fonts gallery.

- Right-click the Pizza Palace font scheme in the Scheme Fonts gallery to display the shortcut menu (Figure 4–75).

Q&A How does the 'Update Scheme from Publication Styles' command work?
If you change the font in some of your text boxes and like it better than the original one in the font scheme, you can click the command to change the font scheme permanently.

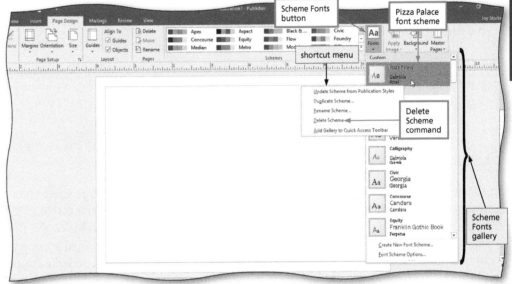

Figure 4–75

2

- Click Delete Scheme on the shortcut menu to delete the font scheme.

- When Publisher displays a dialog box asking if you want to delete the building block, click the Yes button.

To Delete the Custom Page Size

The following steps delete the customized blank page size named Mailer. Deleting the page size does not change the size of previously created publications. *Why? Publisher does not go back and change settings in a saved publication.*

1

- Click the 'Choose Page Size' button (Page Design tab | Page Setup group) to display the Choose Page Size gallery.

- Right-click Mailer to display the shortcut menu (Figure 4–76).

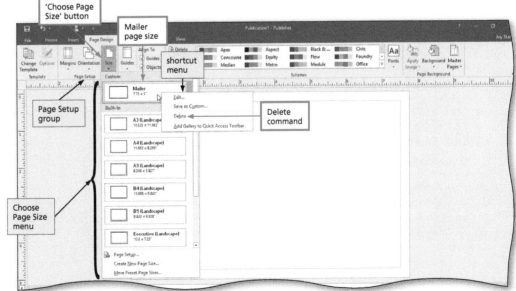

Figure 4–76

- Click Delete on the shortcut menu to delete the page size.
- When Publisher displays a dialog box asking if you want to delete the size permanently, click the Yes button.

- To exit Publisher, click the Close button on the right side of the title bar.
- If a Microsoft Publisher dialog box is displayed, click the Don't Save button so that any changes you have made to the current publication are not saved.

Other Ways

1. In template gallery, right-click custom template, click Delete on shortcut menu

---

Summary

In this module, you learned how to customize Publisher, creating new page sizes, color schemes, and font schemes. You edited graphics by rotating, flipping, changing the proportions, selecting a correction, and setting a transparent color. After you grouped several graphics, you added the graphic to the Building Block Library. You created a text box and formatted the text with a gradient. You created a WordArt object and a bulleted list with a custom bullet. You learned how to change the default line spacing. You added a coupon advertisement to the publication, formatting and duplicating it. Finally, you opened a blank publication and learned how to choose all of the customizations. You then learned how to delete customized building blocks, color schemes, font schemes, and page sizes.

CONSIDER THIS: PLAN AHEAD

What decisions will you need to make when creating your next custom publication?

Use these guidelines as you complete the assignments in this module and create your own publications outside of this class.

1. Decide on the customization.

    a) Create a custom page size.

    b) Create a custom color scheme.

    c) Create a custom font scheme.

2. Choose your graphics.

    a) Edit and format pictures and clip art to create custom graphics.

3. Save reusable graphics as building blocks.

4. Create headings and text.

    a) Change the line spacing as necessary.

    b) Wrap text.

    c) Apply text effects.

    d) Align and distribute objects.

    e) Create bulleted lists.

5. Use WordArt sparingly.

6. Insert shapes for emphasis and interest.

    a) Use color, gradient, and picture fills as necessary.

    b) Crop pictures to shapes as needed.

7. Delete customizations in lab settings.

Apply Your Knowledge

Reinforce the skills and apply the concepts you learned in this module.

Customizing for a Business

Note: To complete this assignment, you will be required to use the Data Files. Please contact your instructor for information about accessing the Data Files.

Instructions: Run Publisher. You are to create a page size, color scheme, font scheme, and building block for Boxes Galore, a local shipping and packing business. You produce the rack card publication shown in Figure 4–77.

Figure 4–77

Perform the following tasks:

1. Click the Blank 8.5 × 11 template.

2. To create a custom page size:

    a. Click the 'Choose Page Size' button (Page Design tab | Page Setup group) and then click 'Create New Page Size' on the Choose Page Size menu. In the Name text box (Create New Page Size dialog box), type **Boxes Galore** to name the custom size.

    b. Click the Layout type button and then click 'One page per sheet'.

    c. Set the width to 4 and the height to 8.5.

    d. One at a time, select the text in each of the four Margin guides text boxes and type **0.25** to change the margins on each side of the publication

    e. Click the OK button to save the page size and margins.

Continued >

Apply Your Knowledge *continued*

3. To create a custom color scheme:

a. Click the More button (Page Design tab | Schemes group) and then click 'Create New Color Scheme'.

b. Type **Boxes Galore** in the Color scheme name text box (Create New Color Scheme dialog box).

c. In the Scheme colors area, click the New button next to the Accent 1 and then click Orange.

d. Click the Accent 2, New button, and then click Sky Blue.

e. Click the Save button without changing any of the other colors.

4. To create a custom font scheme:

a. Click the Scheme Fonts button (Page Design tab | Schemes group) and then click 'Create New Font Scheme'.

b. Type **Boxes Galore** in the Font scheme name text box (Create New Font Scheme dialog box).

c. Select Arial as the heading font and Arial Rounded MT Bold as the body font.

d. Click the Save button without changing any of the other colors.

5. Click the Background button (Page Design tab | Page Background group). Click 'Accent 2 Vertical Gradient' in the Background gallery.

6. To create the heading:

a. Draw a text box across the top of the publication, snapping it to the left, top, and right margins. Make the text box approximately 1.4 inches tall.

b. Change the font size to 36. Click the Center and Bold buttons (Home tab | Font group). Type **Boxes** and then press the ENTER key. Type **Galore** to finish the text.

c. Select the text and then click the Stylistic Sets button (Text Box Tools Format tab | Typography group). Choose the second stylistic set.

d. Click the Font Color arrow (Home tab | Font group) and then click Fill Effects.

e. Click Gradient fill (Format Shape dialog box).

f. In the Gradient fill area, click the Preset gradients button and then click the 'Path Gradient - Accent 1' (Preset gradients gallery). Click the Direction button and then click From Center (Direction gallery).

g. Click the OK button to close the dialog box.

7. Create a text box in the center of the rack card, approximately 3.5 inches tall and snapped to the right and left margin guides. Format it as follows:

a. Set the font size to 18. Click the Line spacing button (Home tab | Paragraph group) and set the line spacing to 1.5.

b. Click the Bullets button (Home tab | Paragraph group). Click the Character button and then choose the Segoe UI Symbol font. Search for a scissors graphic or enter the character code 2700.

c. Change the size to 14pt.

d. Insert the bulleted text as shown in Figure 4–77.

8. Create a text box in the lower right portion of the rack card and enter the address and phone number shown in Figure 4–77.

9. If instructed to do so, change the address and phone number to your address and phone number.

10. Click the Online Pictures button (Insert tab | Illustrations group). Insert a picture of boxes similar to the one shown in Figure 4–77. If necessary, use the 'Set a Transparent Color' command in the Recolor gallery (Picture Tools Format tab | Adjust group) to remove any white background. Resize and position the graphic as necessary. Click the Corrections button (Picture Tools Format tab | Adjust group) and choose an appropriate correction. Right-click the edited graphic and save it as a building block named Boxes Galore. Use appropriate key words.

11. From the Data Files, insert the picture named, Apply 4–1 Bubble Wrap. Use the rotation handle to rotate the box to approximately 50°. Resize, position, and send the graphic backward as necessary.

12. Save the file with the file name, Apply 4–1 Boxes Galore, and submit it in the format required by your instructor.

13. For extra credit, create a second page that will print on the back of the rack card. Insert a coupon for free bubble wrap with the next shipped package.

14. Delete all customizations as described in the module.

15. ✸ Would adding more orange to the rack card reinforce the company colors or add to the look and feel of the rack card? How? What would you do differently?

Extend Your Knowledge

Extend the skills you learned in this module and experiment with new skills. You may need to use Help to complete the assignment.

Working with Windows Metafiles

Note: To complete this assignment, you will be required to use the Data Files. Please contact your instructor for information about accessing the Data Files.

Instructions: Run Publisher. Open the file named Extend 4–1 Hobby Express. Zoom to 150%. The local hobby shop, Hobby Express, would like you to create a logo for them. You produce the logo shown in Figure 4–78.

Figure 4–78

Continued >

Extend Your Knowledge *continued*

Perform the following tasks:

1. Use Help to read about formatting shapes.

2. To separate the parts of the graphic:

   a. Select the graphic and then click the Ungroup button (Picture Tools Format tab | Arrange group). When Publisher asks if you want to convert the picture to a Microsoft Office drawing object, click the Yes button (Microsoft Publisher dialog box).

   b. Right-click the drawing object and then click Ungroup on the shortcut menu.

   c. Click outside the graphic to deselect it. One at a time, select and delete each of the light blue lines that comprise the tracks, the smoke, and the railroad crossing sign.

   d. Drag around the remaining parts of the graphic and then click the Group button (Drawing Tools Format tab | Arrange group) to regroup the graphic.

3. Flip the graphic horizontally by using the Rotate button (Drawing Tools Format tab | Arrange group).

4. To save the graphic as a picture, right-click the grouped object and then click 'Save as Picture' on the shortcut menu. Save the file on your storage device with the file name, Extend 4–1 Engine. Delete the graphic from the publication.

5. To insert and format a shape:

   a. Click the Shapes button (Insert tab | Illustrations group).

   b. Click the Oval button in the Basic Shapes area of the Shapes gallery and then SHIFT+drag a circle approximately 2 inches by 2 inches.

   c. Click the Shape Fill arrow (Drawing Tools Format tab | Shape Styles group) and then click Picture in the Shape Fill gallery.

   d. Click the Browse button in the From a file area (Insert Pictures dialog box), navigate to your storage location, and then double-click the Extend 4–1 Engine graphic file.

   e. Click the Shape Outline arrow (Drawing Tools Format tab | Shape Styles group) and then click More Outline Colors. Choose a dark blue color on the Standard tab (Colors dialog box). Click the Shape Outline arrow (Drawing Tools Format tab | Shape Styles group) again, point to Weight, and then click 3pt in the list.

6. To create a text box:

   a. If necessary, zoom out and then draw a text box on the page approximately .75 inches tall, from margin to margin. Type the words, **Hobby Express**. Right-click the text and then click Best Fit on the shortcut menu.

   b. Click the Shape Fill arrow (Drawing Tools Format tab | Shape Styles group) and then choose a dark blue color.

   c. Select the text, and then click the Font Color arrow (Home tab | Font group). Choose a white color.

   d. Click the Wrap Text button (Drawing Tools Format tab | Arrange group) and then click Square.

7. To position the graphics:

   a. Zoom to Whole Page view. Drag the graphic to the top of the page approximately 2 inches from the left margin.

   b. Drag the text box up so the bottom of the text box roughly aligns with the bottom of the graphic.

   c. Click the Send Backward button (Drawing Tools Format tab | Arrange group).

8. If instructed to do so, insert a text box with your name and the date at the bottom of the page.

9. Save the file with the file name, Extend 4–1 Hobby Express Complete.

10. Submit the revised publication in the format specified by your instructor.

11. ✹ Why do you think the instructions ask you to save the graphic as a picture in Step 4? What other things would you add to the file to make it usable as letterhead? Why might you save the graphic and the text box as a building block?

Expand Your World

Choosing Colors

Instructions: Locate a picture with your school colors, or the web address (URL) of your school logo. The picture should be in the .gif, .png, or .jpg format. The web address might be something like www.myschool.edu/logo.gif. Run a browser and navigate to www.imagecolorpicker.com (Figure 4–79). The website may differ slightly.

Figure 4–79

Perform the following tasks:

1. If you have the web address of your school logo, type it in the 'URL to Image' text box. If you have a picture, click the 'Upload your image' button, browse to and open the image, and then click the Submit Query button (File upload dialog box).

2. When the image is displayed, click the main color of the image. Write down the RGB codes. Click two other prominent colors in the logo and write down their RGB codes.

Continued >

Expand Your World *continued*

3. Run Publisher and create a blank publication. Click the More button (Page Design tab | Schemes group) to display the Color Schemes gallery. Click 'Create New Color Scheme' in the Color Schemes gallery to display the Create New Color Scheme dialog box. Enter a name for your new color scheme.

4. Click the Accent 1 New button and then click the More Colors button to display the Colors dialog box. Click the Custom tab and enter the RGB numbers. Click the OK button (Colors dialog box).

5. Repeat Step 4 for the Accent 2 and Accent 3 colors.

6. Save the color scheme. Use the color scheme to create a shape, WordArt, or text fill.

7. Submit the assignment in the format specified by your instructor.

8. If you are working in a lab environment, delete any customizations.

9. ✹ In what other situations might you want to search for exact colors? Make a list of companies that probably copyright their logo and its colors. Do you know of any colors that commonly are referred to by a company name, such as "Facebook blue"?

In the Labs

Design, create, modify, and/or use a publication following the guidelines, concepts, and skills presented in this module. Labs 1 and 2, which increase in difficulty, require you to create solutions based on what you learned in the module; Lab 3 requires you to apply your creative thinking and problem-solving skills to design and implement a solution.

Lab 1: Creating a Recipe Card

Problem: You enjoy the Student Chef Club on campus. They are holding a recipe exchange at the next meeting, so you decide to create the recipe card shown in Figure 4–80. You plan to print 20 copies.

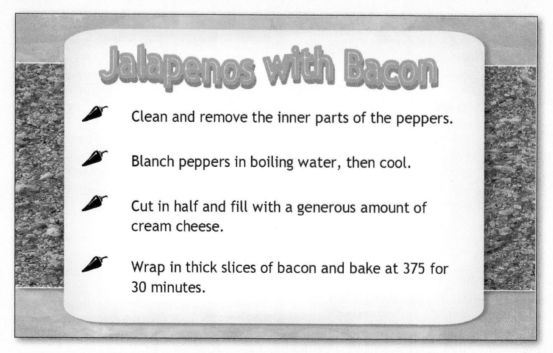

Figure 4–80

Perform the following tasks:

1. Run Publisher. Choose a blank 8.5 × 11 publication. Select the Desert color scheme and the Opulent font scheme. Create the publication.

2. Click the 'Choose Page Size' button (Page Design tab | Page Setup group). Create a new page size named 3 × 5 Recipe Card (Create New Page Size dialog box). Set the width to 5 inches and the height to 3 inches. Set all margins to zero. Click the Layout type arrow and then click 'Multiple pages per sheet' in the list. In the Options area, set the side and top margins to 1 inch. Click the OK button to close the Create New Page Size dialog box.

3. Click the Online Pictures button (Insert tab | Illustrations group) and search for the term, border. Choose a graphic with four sides and white space in the middle, similar to the one shown in Figure 4–80. If you cannot find the specific image, you may use another appropriate image. Make sure you review the license to ensure you can comply with any copyright restrictions.

4. Resize the graphic to fill the page layout.

5. Insert a WordArt object into the scratch area. Use the 'Fill - Light Orange, Outline - Orange' WordArt Style. Type the text, `Jalapenos with Bacon` as the title. Choose the Trebuchet MS font and font size 24.

6. If instructed to do so, click the Change WordArt Shape button (WordArt Tools Format tab | WordArt Styles group). Choose a new shape for the title.

7. Change the shape of the WordArt to 'Double Wave 1' and then drag the WordArt to a location across the top of the white area of the border graphic.

8. Draw a text box in the scratch area, approximately 4 inches wide and 2.25 inches tall. Create a custom bullet character using the pepper character (code 44) in the Webdings character set. Set the bullet character to be size 22. Select the text in the 'Indent list by' text box (Bullets and Numbering dialog box) and then type `.5` for the indenture.

9. In the text box, change the font size to 10. Enter the following lines of text, pressing the ENTER key after each line except the last:

   `Clean and remove the inner parts of the peppers.`

   `Blanch peppers in boiling water, then cool.`

   `Cut in half and fill with a generous amount of cream cheese.`

   `Wrap in thick slices of bacon and bake at 375 for 30 minutes.`

10. Drag the text box into the publication and align it relative to the margins.

11. Check the publication for spelling and design errors.

12. Save the publication on your storage device with the file name, Lab 4–1 Recipe Card.

13. If you are working in a lab situation, delete any customization.

14. Submit the file as directed by your instructor.

15. ✸ Are custom bullet characters distracting? Why or why not? How hard is it to find the character you want in the Bullet Character dialog box? Can you think of other ways to create or find custom bullets?

Lab 2: Designing an Advertisement

Note: To complete this assignment, you will be required to use the Data Files. Please contact your instructor for information about accessing the Data Files.

Problem: It is Mardi Gras time! The tourism board has asked you to create a newspaper advertisement about the Mardi Gras parade. In the broadsheet newspaper format, a 1/8-page advertisement would be 3 columns wide (approximately 5.25 inches) by 5 inches tall with 1/8-inch (or .125-inch) margins. You decide to start from scratch to create the ad shown in Figure 4–81. *Continued >*

In the Labs *continued*

Figure 4–81

Perform the following tasks:

1. Run Publisher. Choose a blank 8.5 × 11 publication

2. Click the Size button (Page Design tab | Page Setup group) and then click 'Create New Page Size'. Create a new page size named 1/8 Page Advertisement. Click the Layout type arrow and then click 'One page per sheet' (Create New Page Size dialog box). Set the width to 5.25 inches and the height to 5 inches. Set all margins to zero.

3. Click the More button (Page Design tab | Schemes group) and then click 'Create New Color Scheme' in the Color Scheme gallery. Create a custom color scheme named Mardi Gras with the Black as the main color and accent colors of violet, green, gold, and red.

4. Click the Scheme Fonts button (Page Design tab | Schemes group) and then click 'Create New Font Scheme' in the Scheme Fonts gallery. Create a custom font scheme named Mardi Gras with Jokerman as the heading font and Imprint MT Shadow as the body font.

5. Change the background to 10% tint of Accent 3.

6. Insert several images using the Online Pictures button (Insert tab | Illustrations group). Search for clip art related to Mardi Gras, beads, fleur-de-lis, and feathers. Choose clip art images similar to those shown in Figure 4–81. If you cannot find the specific image, you may use another appropriate image. Make sure you review the license to ensure you can comply with any copyright restrictions. Move the pictures to the scratch area.

7. Insert the Lab 4–2 Mask graphic from the Data Files.

8. Select the beads graphic. Click the Corrections button (Picture Tools Format tab | Adjust group), and choose a very light preview. Click the Recolor button (Picture Tools Format tab | Adjust group) and then click the 'Set Transparent Color' command in the Recolor gallery. Click the white background in the beads graphic to make that color transparent. Move the graphic into the page layout.

9. Ungroup the mask to create a Microsoft Office drawing object, and then ungroup to separate the graphic. Click away from the graphic to deselect its parts. Drag around half of the mask and recolor the selection. Drag around the other half of the mask and recolor it using a different color. Regroup the mask and then move it into the page layout.

10. Select the fleur-de-lis and recolor it. Click the Picture Effects button (Picture Tools Format tab | Picture styles group). Click Glow in the gallery and choose an appropriate glow. Use the gallery again to choose a reflection similar to Figure 4–81. Move the graphic into the page layout.

11. Recolor and rotate the feathers and move them into the page layout.

12. Create a text box in the scratch area, approximately 3.5 inches wide and 4 inches tall. Set the text wrapping on the text box to Through. Set the font size to 24. Press CTRL+E to center the text. Type the following text, pressing the ENTER key after each line except the last.

```
Mardi Gras Parade!
February 17
8:00 p.m.
17th & Main
to
38th & Main
```

13. If instructed to do so, add the name of your town as a new, last line in the text box.

14. Format the first line with the Jokerman font, and then move the text box into the page layout.

15. Save the file with the file name, Lab 4–2 Mardi Gras Advertisement.

16. If you are working in a lab environment, delete any customization.

17. Submit the file in the format specified by your instructor.

18. ✳ What are some differences between Text Fill effects and Picture effects? Why do you think the Picture Effects gallery has more options and settings? How many picture and fill effects are too many?

Lab 3: **Creating a Custom Building Block**

Problem: The American Sign Language Club has a module at your school, and they have asked for your help. They would like you to create a building block that includes the signs for the letters, A, S, and L. They plan to use the building block in several ways, including on their correspondence, website, and flyers.

Perform the following tasks:

Part 1:   Open a blank publication. Set the color scheme to Metro. Use Office.com Clip Art to look for graphics related to sign language. One at a time, insert the signs for A, S, and L into the publication. Recolor each one differently. Rotate the A and the L at 45-degree angles on either side of the letter S, creating a sort of triangle. Select the three graphics and group. Add the group to the Building Block Library. Save the publication. Remember to include a description and searchable keywords. If you create the building block on a lab computer, remember to delete it after submitting the assignment to your instructor.

Part 2:   Why do you think the assignment called for setting the color scheme? How did it affect required steps after that? What recolor options did you choose, and why?

5 Using Business Information Sets

Objectives

You will have mastered the material in this module when you can:

- Design a letterhead
- Create a logo
- Fill a shape with a picture and crop
- Create a business information set
- Insert business information fields into a publication
- Use the Measurement task pane to position and scale objects
- Create and apply a new text style
- Wrap text

- Apply the read-only attribute to a publication
- Insert an automatically updated date and time
- Add a numbered list and increase indent
- Create and print an envelope
- Create a certificate
- Create and print business cards
- Publish a portable PDF/XPS file
- Embed fonts in a publication

Introduction

Incorporating personal information unique to a business, organization, or individual user expands the possibilities for using Publisher as a complete application product for small businesses. Business information sets, which include pieces of information, such as a name, an address, a motto, or even a logo, can be inserted automatically and consistently across all publications. Publisher allows you to insert, delete, and save multiple business information sets and apply them independently.

Business information sets are just one way that people expand Publisher's capabilities. Some users create large text boxes and use Publisher like a word processor. Others create a table and perform mathematical and statistical operations or embed charts as they would with a spreadsheet. Still others create a database and use Publisher for mass mailings, billings, and customer accounts. Publisher's capabilities make it an efficient tool in small business offices — without the cost and learning curve of some of the high-end, dedicated application software.

CONSIDER THIS

How do you make decisions about letterhead components?

Work with the customer to design a letterhead that matches the color and font schemes of the company, if any. Decide on placement of vital information, page size, and white space. Discuss a plan for printing. Will the customer send the letterhead out for commercial printing or print copies themselves? Will users want to type directly on the Publisher letterhead? Define user-friendly features, such as an automatic date and an easy-to-use text box for typing letters.

Project — Letterhead and Business Cards

Storing permanent information about a business facilitates the customization of publications, such as letterhead, business cards, and other office-related publications. A **business information set** is a group of customized information fields about an individual or an organization that can be used to generate information text boxes across publications. Many of the Publisher templates automatically create business information text boxes to incorporate data from the business information set. Publications created from scratch also can integrate a business information set by including one or more pieces in the publication. For example, you can save your name, address, and telephone number in a business information set. Whenever you need that information, you can insert it in a publication without retyping it.

To illustrate some of the business features of Microsoft Publisher, this project presents a series of steps to create a business information set. You will use the business information set in a letterhead, envelope, certificate, and business card. You also will create a logo and a portable file for easy viewing and embed fonts in the Publisher file for editing on a different computer. The project creates publications for a business named Make My Smile Dentistry, as shown in Figure 5–1.

The following roadmap identifies general activities you will perform as you progress through this module:

1. CREATE a business letterhead and a LOGO.
2. Create and USE a BUSINESS INFORMATION SET.
3. USE the MEASUREMENT TASK PANE.
4. CREATE and apply a NEW STYLE.
5. CUSTOMIZE business LETTERHEAD for ease of use.
6. CREATE OTHER PUBLICATIONS, including an envelope, certificate, and business cards.
7. CREATE PORTABLE FILES.
8. EMBED FONTS.

Creating Letterhead

In many businesses, **letterhead** is preprinted paper with important facts about the company and blank space to contain the text of the correspondence. Letterhead, typically used for official business communication, is an easy way to convey company information to the reader and quickly establish a formal and legitimate mode of correspondence. The company information may be displayed in a variety of places — across the top, down the side, or split between the top and bottom of the page. Although most business letterhead is 8½ × 11 inches, other sizes are becoming more popular, especially with small agencies and not-for-profit organizations.

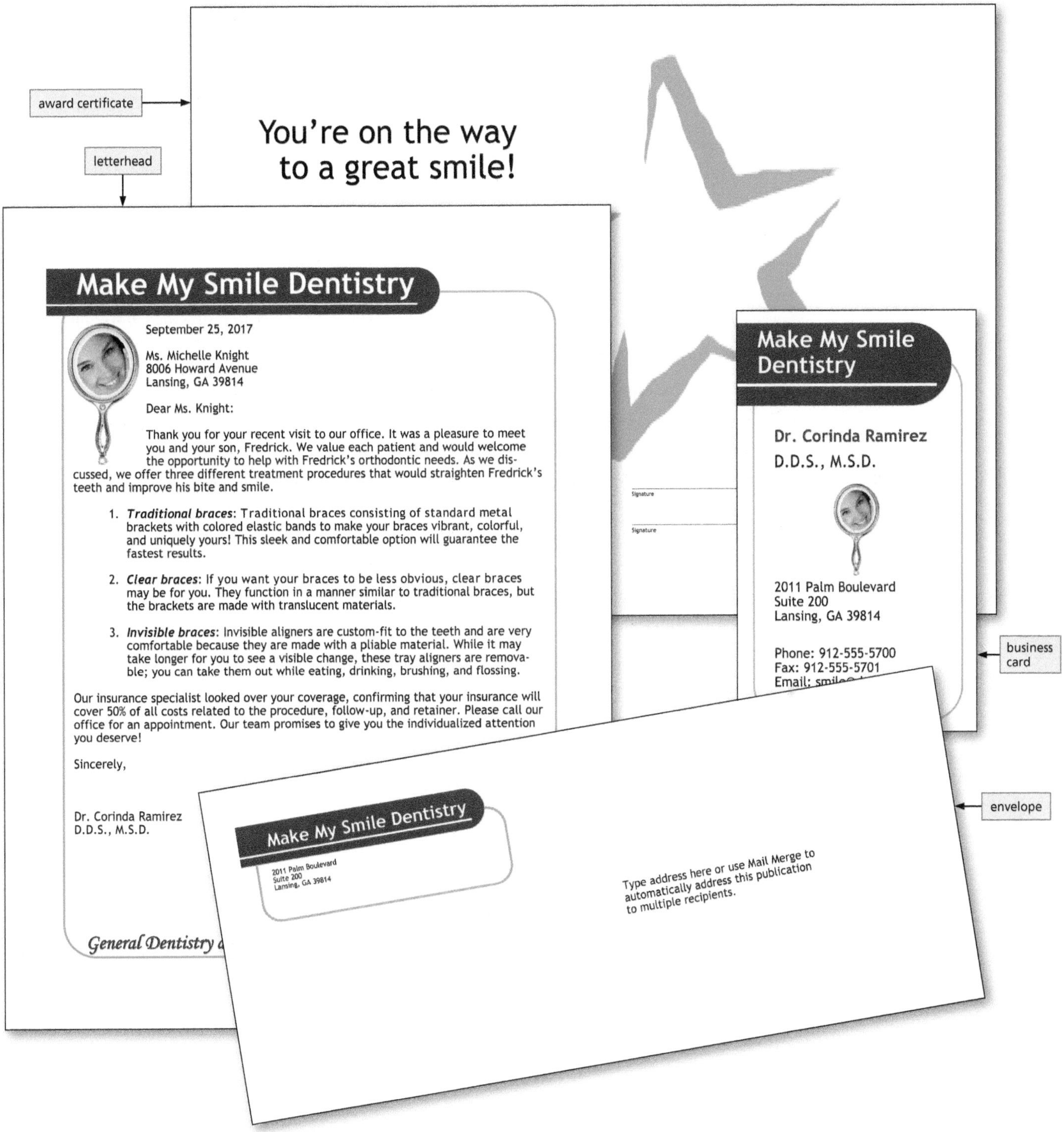

5K Flyer.pub – Publisher

File Home Insert Page Design Mailings Review View Format

Drawing Tools Text

award certificate

letterhead

You're on the way to a great smile!

Make My Smile Dentistry

September 25, 2017

Ms. Michelle Knight
8006 Howard Avenue
Lansing, GA 39814

Dear Ms. Knight:

Thank you for your recent visit to our office. It was a pleasure to meet you and your son, Fredrick. We value each patient and would welcome the opportunity to help with Fredrick's orthodontic needs. As we discussed, we offer three different treatment procedures that would straighten Fredrick's teeth and improve his bite and smile.

1. *Traditional braces*: Traditional braces consisting of standard metal brackets with colored elastic bands to make your braces vibrant, colorful, and uniquely yours! This sleek and comfortable option will guarantee the fastest results.

2. *Clear braces*: If you want your braces to be less obvious, clear braces may be for you. They function in a manner similar to traditional braces, but the brackets are made with translucent materials.

3. *Invisible braces*: Invisible aligners are custom-fit to the teeth and are very comfortable because they are made with a pliable material. While it may take longer for you to see a visible change, these tray aligners are removable; you can take them out while eating, drinking, brushing, and flossing.

Our insurance specialist looked over your coverage, confirming that your insurance will cover 50% of all costs related to the procedure, follow-up, and retainer. Please call our office for an appointment. Our team promises to give you the individualized attention you deserve!

Sincerely,

Dr. Corinda Ramirez
D.D.S., M.S.D.

General Dentistry

Signature

Signature

Make My Smile Dentistry

Dr. Corinda Ramirez
D.D.S., M.S.D.

2011 Palm Boulevard
Suite 200
Lansing, GA 39814

Phone: 912-555-5700
Fax: 912-555-5701
Email: smile@

business card

envelope

Make My Smile Dentistry

2011 Palm Boulevard
Suite 200
Lansing, GA 39814

Type address here or use Mail Merge to automatically address this publication to multiple recipients.

Figure 5–1

Generally, it is cost effective for companies to outsource the printing of their letterhead; however, designing the letterhead in-house and then sending the file to a commercial printer saves design consultation time, customization, and money. Black-and-white or spot-color letterhead is more common and less expensive than composite or process color. Businesses sometimes opt not to purchase preprinted letterhead because of its expense, color, or the limited quantity required. In those cases, companies design their own letterhead and save it as a file. In some cases, businesses print multiple copies of their blank letterhead and then, using application software, prepare documents to print on the letterhead paper.

To Open a Letterhead Template

The following steps open a letterhead template and apply color and font schemes.

1 Run Publisher.

2 In the template gallery, click BUILT-IN to display the BUILT-IN templates.

3 Scroll as necessary and then click the Letterhead thumbnail within the BUILT-IN templates to display the Letterhead templates.

4 In the section labeled, More Installed Templates, click the Radial thumbnail to choose the template.

5 Click the Color scheme button in the template information pane. Scroll as necessary then and click Paper to choose the color scheme.

6 Click the Font scheme button, scroll as necessary, and then click Virtual to choose the font scheme.

7 If necessary, click to display the check mark in the Include logo check box (Figure 5–2).

8 Click the CREATE button to create the publication based on the template settings.

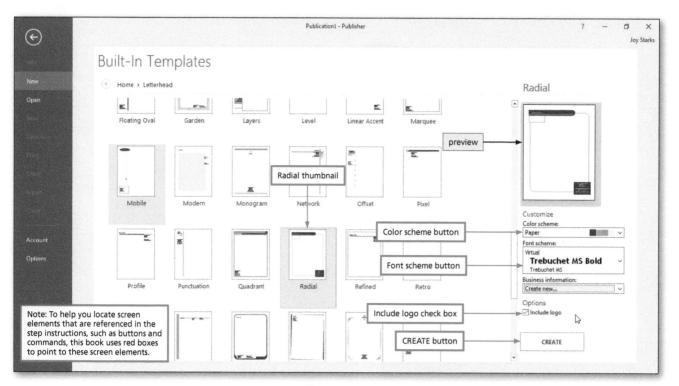

Figure 5–2

To Set Publisher Display Settings

The following steps display formatting marks and special characters and then hide the Page Navigation pane.

1 If the Publisher window is not maximized, click the Maximize button (Publisher title bar).

2 If the Special Characters button (Home tab | Paragraph group) is not selected already, click it to display formatting marks on the screen.

3 If the Page Navigation pane is displayed, click the Page Number button on the status bar to hide the Page Navigation pane, because this is a single page publication.

Creating a Logo

With the basic letterhead created, you now are ready to create a customized logo for the company. Recall that you created a logo in a previous module, grouping pictures and saving them as a building block. You also have drawn shapes and filled objects with colors, changed the outline color, and formatted with gradients. To create a logo for Make My Smile Dentistry, you now will crop a picture, save it, fill a shape with a picture, and then combine the pictures and save the logo. Many types of publications use logos to identify and distinguish the page. A **logo** is a recognizable symbol that identifies a person, business, or organization. A logo may be composed of a name, a picture, or a combination of text, symbols, and graphics.

1 CREATE LOGO | **2 USE BUSINESS INFORMATION SET** | **3 USE MEASUREMENT TASK PANE** | **4 CREATE NEW STYLE**

5 CUSTOMIZE LETTERHEAD | 6 CREATE OTHER PUBLICATIONS | 7 CREATE PORTABLE FILES | 8 EMBED FONTS

To Crop a Picture

The following steps open a picture and crop it. *Why? Cropping is an easy way to remove portions of a picture that you do not need in a publication.* To complete these steps, you will be required to use the Data Files. Please contact your instructor for information about accessing the Data Files.

1

- Display the Insert tab.

- Click the Pictures button (Insert tab | Illustrations group) to display the Insert Picture dialog box.

- Navigate to the Data Files and then insert the file named, Mirror. In the publication, drag the mirror to the scratch area, and resize it to be approximately 5 × 6.5 inches.

- Click the Crop button (Picture Tools Format tab | Crop group) to display the crop handles (Figure 5–3).

Q&A What are crop handles?
Crop handles are a set of six handles on the sides and corners of a picture that appear when you click the Crop button. They are similar to resizing handles, but when they are dragged, the edge of the picture is cropped.

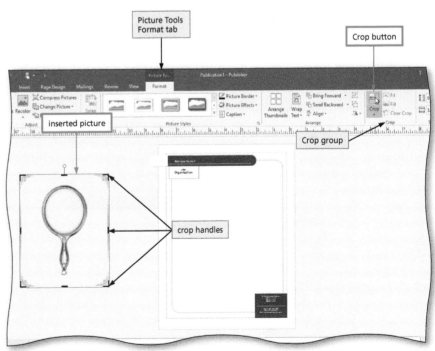

Figure 5–3

- Drag the upper-left corner crop handle toward the center until the border is removed and less white space appears at the top.

- Drag the lower-right corner crop handle toward the center until the border is removed and less white space appears at the bottom (Figure 5–4).

Q&A What is the purpose of the Fit and Fill buttons (Picture Tools Format tab | Crop group)?

The Fit and Fill buttons are used with picture placeholders. If your picture is larger or smaller than the placeholder, Publisher allows you quickly to resize the picture to fit (in the case of larger pictures) or fill (in the case of smaller pictures) the placeholder, while maintaining the original aspect ratio.

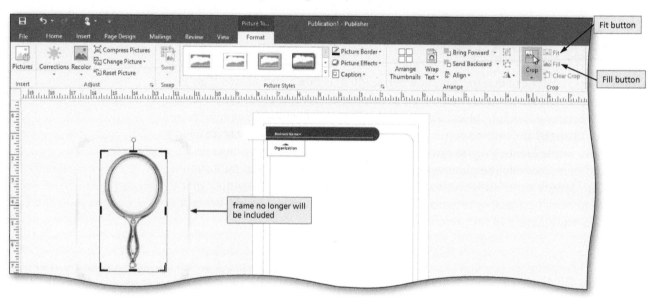

Figure 5–4

- Click the Crop button again, to turn off the crop handles and to display the cropped picture (Figure 5–5).

Experiment

- Click the Clear Crop button (Picture Tools Format tab | Crop group) to see what happens when you clear the crop. Click the Undo button (Quick Access Toolbar) to undo the Clear Crop command.

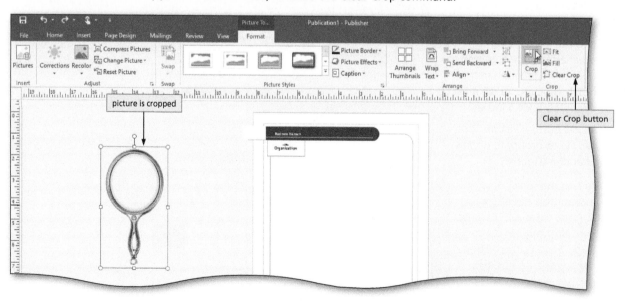

Figure 5–5

Shape Fills

Every shape in the Shapes gallery can be filled, except for the lines and braces. In the past, you have filled a shape with solid color, but you also can fill shapes with pictures and many other types of formatting. The Shape Styles gallery (Drawing Tools Format tab) displays many preset fills and outlines; however, the Shape Fill button (Drawing Tools Format tab | Shape Styles group) displays a gallery with various ways to customize the fill (Table 5–1).

Table 5–1 Ways to Fill a Shape

Shape Fill	Display	Result
Color	Displays Color gallery	Fills with a solid color
More Fill Colors	Displays Colors dialog box	Fills with chosen solid color
Tints	Displays Fill Effects dialog box	Fills with a tint or shade of a chosen color
Sample Fill Color	Changes the pointer to an eyedropper	Fills with color that is clicked
Picture	Displays Insert Pictures dialog box	Fills with a picture from storage or an online picture, clipped or cropped to the shape
Gradient	Displays Gradient gallery	Fills with chosen gradient
Texture	Displays Texture gallery	Fills with chosen texture
Pattern	Displays Format Shape dialog box	Fills with chosen pattern using foreground and background color
Crop to Shape	Accessed via the Crop arrow, displays Shape gallery	Crops or clips displayed picture to the desired shape

The Drawing Tools Format tab appears only when working with shapes, graphics, or clip art. It normally does not appear when you are working with a picture; however, another way to use shapes is to **crop to shape**, also called clipping. With **clipping**, you display the picture first and then crop it to the desired shape using the Crop arrow (Picture Tools Format tab | Crop group). You also can right-click a shape and insert text with the Add Text command on the shortcut menu. You will learn more about some of the shape fills in a later module.

To Fill a Shape with a Picture

1 CREATE LOGO | 2 USE BUSINESS INFORMATION SET | 3 USE MEASUREMENT TASK PANE | 4 CREATE NEW STYLE
5 CUSTOMIZE LETTERHEAD | 6 CREATE OTHER PUBLICATIONS | 7 CREATE PORTABLE FILES | 8 EMBED FONTS

The following steps create an oval shape and fill it with a picture. *Why? Filling is an easy way to change the shape of a rectangular picture.* To complete these steps, you will be required to use the Data Files. Please contact your instructor for information about accessing the Data Files.

1

- Display the Insert tab.

- Click the Shapes button (Insert tab | Illustrations group) to display the Shapes gallery (Figure 5–6).

Q&A How do I create a circle? I do not see one in the Shape gallery.

To create a circle, you must click the oval and then SHIFT+drag in the publication. To create a square, select a rectangle and then SHIFT+drag in the publication.

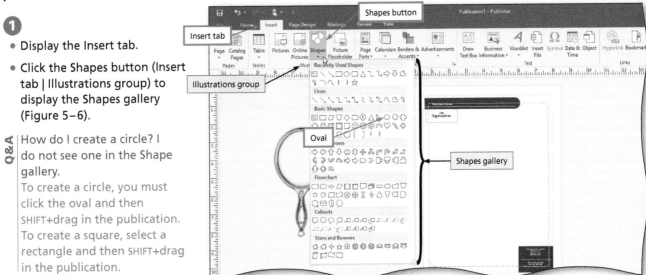

Figure 5–6

2

- Click the Oval shape in the Basic Shapes area.

- In the scratch area, drag downward to create a slightly oval shape, approximately 2 × 2.5 inches, as shown in Figure 5–7.

- If necessary, move the mirror to the left.

Q&A Why is the oval filled with dark green?
Publisher uses the Accent 1 color from the color scheme to fill shapes.

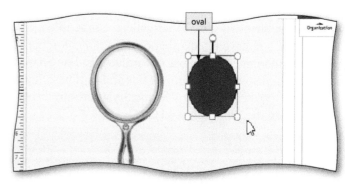

Figure 5–7

Experiment

- Click the More button (Drawing Tools Format tab | Shape Styles group) and point to several of the styles and watch how live preview changes the oval.

3

- Display the Drawing Tools Format tab, if necessary.

- Click the Shape Fill arrow (Drawing Tools Format tab | Shape Styles group) to display the Shape Fill gallery (Figure 5–8).

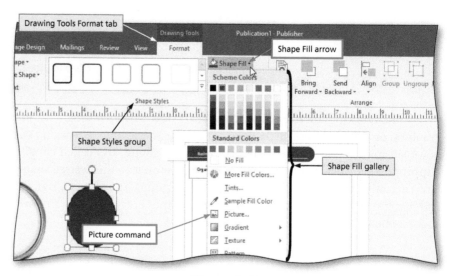

Figure 5–8

4

- Click Picture in the Shape Fill gallery to display the Insert Pictures dialog box.

- Click the Browse button (Insert Pictures dialog box) to display the Select Picture dialog box. Navigate to the Data Files and the Module 05 folder (Figure 5–9).

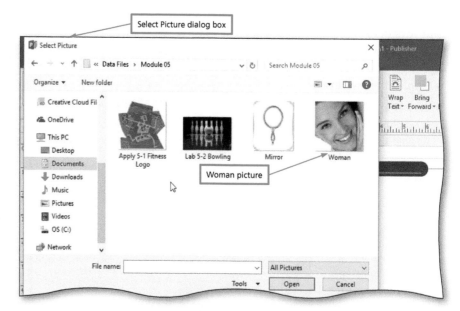

Figure 5–9

5

- Double-click the Woman picture to insert it into the shape (Figure 5–10).

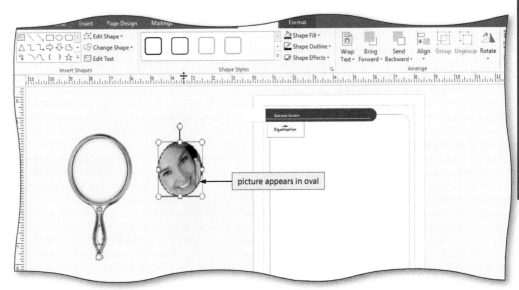

Figure 5–10

Other Ways

1. Insert picture, click Crop arrow (Picture Tools Format tab | Crop group), point to 'Crop to Shape' on Crop menu, select shape

---

To Group Objects

The following steps group the mirror with the oval.

1 Select the mirror and position it over the picture as shown in Figure 5–11.

2 If necessary, click the Bring Forward button (Picture Tools Format tab | Arrange group) so the mirror is in front of the oval.

3 If necessary, drag a corner handle of the mirror to resize it so that the oval picture fits within the frame.

4 Drag around both graphics to select them and then press CTRL+SHIFT+G to group.

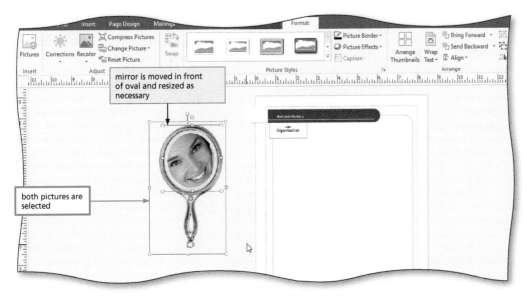

Figure 5–11

To Save as a Picture

The following steps save the grouped pictures as a new picture on your storage device. *Why? Saving them as a new picture allows you to use it in many other apps, in other Publisher publications, and in business information sets.*

- Right-click the grouped pictures to display the shortcut menu (Figure 5–12).

Q&A Are grouped graphics the only kind of object you can save as a picture?
No. You can save any object as a picture, including shapes, tables, text boxes, and clip art.

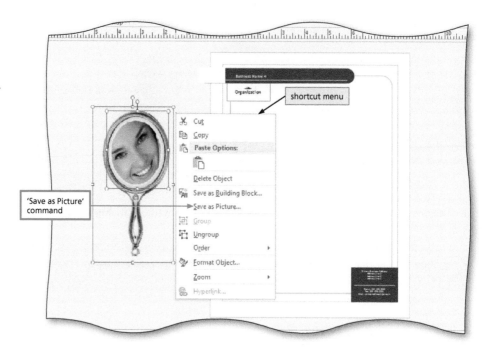

Figure 5–12

- Click 'Save as Picture' on the shortcut menu to display the Save As dialog box.
- Type `Make My Smile Logo` in the File name text box to name the file.
- Navigate to your storage device (Figure 5–13).

Experiment
- Click the 'Save as type' button (Save As dialog box) to see the different kinds of file formats that are available.

- Edit property tags as desired and then click the Save button (Save As dialog box) to save the graphic as a picture.
- Delete the grouped graphic from the scratch area.

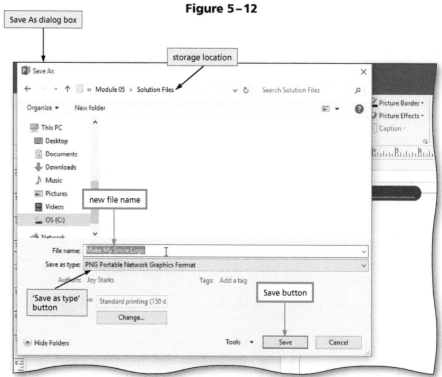

Figure 5–13

Business Information Sets

Business information sets store data about a company. This data then is used in publications whenever you need it or when a Publisher template incorporates it. For example, rather than typing the name of the company multiple times, you can insert the data from a field in the business information set. A **field** is a specific component in the set, such as an individual's name, job position or title, organization name, address, telephone and fax numbers, email address, tagline, or logo. When inserting a field, Publisher places a text box in your publication and supplies the text.

Publisher allows you to create and save as many different business information sets as you want. If you have more than one set saved, you can choose the set you need from a list. The sets are stored within the Publisher application files on your computer. When you create a new publication, the business information set used most recently populates the new publication. When Publisher first is installed, the business information is generic, with words such as Title and Business Name. In a laboratory situation, the business information set may be populated with information about your school, which was provided when Microsoft Office 2016 was installed.

If you edit a text box within a publication that contains personal information, you change the set for that publication only, unless you choose to update the set. To affect changes for all future publications, you edit the business information set itself. You can edit the stored business information set at any time — before, during, or after performing other publication tasks.

Table 5–2 displays the data for each of the fields in the business information set that you will create in this project.

Table 5–2 Data for the Business Information Set	
Fields	**Data**
Individual name	Dr. Corinda Ramirez
Job or position or title	D.D.S., M.S.D.
Organization name	Make My Smile Dentistry
Address	2011 Palm Boulevard Suite 200 Lansing, GA 39814
Phone, fax, and email	Phone: 912-555-5700 Fax: 912-555-5701 Email: smile@dentistry.biz
Tagline or motto	General Dentistry and Orthodontics
Business Information set name	Make My Smile

To Create a Business Information Set

1 CREATE LOGO | 2 USE BUSINESS INFORMATION SET | 3 USE MEASUREMENT TASK PANE | 4 CREATE NEW STYLE
5 CUSTOMIZE LETTERHEAD | 6 CREATE OTHER PUBLICATIONS | 7 CREATE PORTABLE FILES | 8 EMBED FONTS

The following steps create a business information set for Make My Smile Dentistry and apply it to the current publication, the Make My Smile Letterhead. You will enter data for each field. *Why? Entering the data fields and saving them will allow you to reuse the content in other publications.*

1

- Display the Insert tab.

- Click the Business Information button (Insert tab | Text group) to display the Business Information menu, which lists business information fields and commands (Figure 5–14).

Why does my screen look different?

If you have any saved business information sets on your computer, your menu may contain other data in each field.

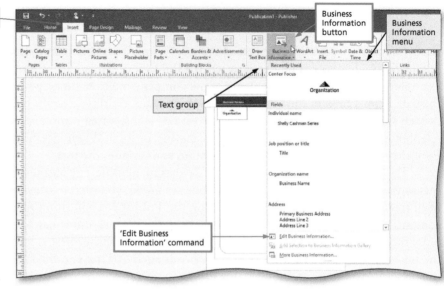

Figure 5–14

2

- Click 'Edit Business Information' on the Business Information menu to display the Create New Business Information Set dialog box (Figure 5–15).

Why does the Individual name text box already have a name in it?

The person or company that installed Publisher may have supplied data for the business information set. You will replace the data in the next step.

How do you use the other commands on the Business Information menu?

The 'Add Selection to Business Information Gallery' command allows you to add selected text and graphics as a Publisher building block. The 'More Business Information' command opens the Building Block Library from which you can add objects to your publication.

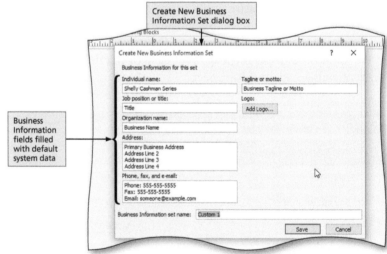

Figure 5–15

3

- Enter the data from Table 5–2, pressing the TAB key to advance from one field to the next (Figure 5–16).

How do I delete data once it is inserted in a field?

In the Create New Business Information Set dialog box, you can select the text in the field and then press the DELETE key. To remove a business information field while editing a publication, you simply delete the text box from the publication itself; however, this does not delete it permanently from the set. You can remove entire business information sets once they are stored; you will see how to do this later in this module.

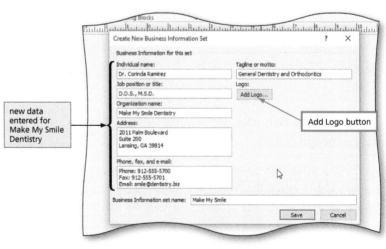

Figure 5–16

- Click the Add Logo button (Create New Business Information Set dialog box) to display the Insert Picture dialog box.
- Navigate to the storage location you used previously to save the Make My Smile Logo file.
- Double-click the desired file (in this case, the Make My Smile Logo file) (Insert Picture dialog box) to insert the logo (Figure 5–17).

Figure 5–17

- Click the Save button (Create New Business Information Set dialog box) to save the business information set and to display the Business Information dialog box (Figure 5–18).

Q&A Does saving the business information set also save the publication?
No, you are saving a separate, internal data file that contains only the data in the fields.

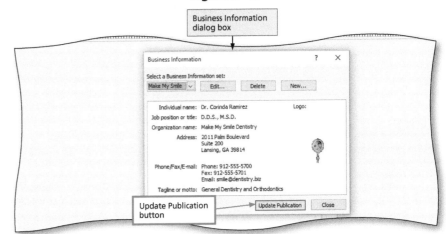

Figure 5–18

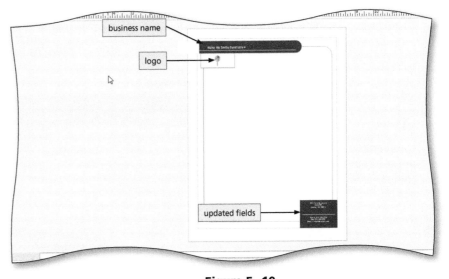

- Click the Update Publication button (Business Information dialog box) (Figure 5–19).

Experiment
- Zoom in and scroll to view all of the business information fields.

Q&A What is the white tab that appears to cross into the margin and scratch area at the top of the publication?
Publisher includes the white rectangular shape to cover the left part of the dark green oval, so the oval appears to have a flat end. The white shape will not cause any printing issues.

Figure 5–19

- Click the Save button on the Quick Access Toolbar. Browse to your storage location. Save the file with the file name, Make My Smile Letterhead.

Other Ways

1. In BUILT-IN templates, click Business Information button (Customize area | template information pane), click Create new on Business Information menu, enter field data

To Change the Business Information Set of an Existing Publication

If you wanted to apply a different business information set to a publication, you would perform the following tasks.

1. Open a publication.
2. Display the Insert tab.
3. Click the Business Information button (Insert tab | Text group) to display the Business Information menu.
4. Click 'Edit Business Information' on the Business Information menu to display the Business Information dialog box.
5. Click the leftmost button in the Select a Business Information set area to display the available business information sets.
6. Click the business information set you wish to use.
7. Click the Update Publication button (Business Information dialog box).

Break Point: If you wish to take a break, this is a good place to do so. Exit Publisher. To resume at a later time, run Publisher, open the file named Make My Smile Letterhead, and continue following the steps from this location forward.

To Insert a Business Information Field

1 CREATE LOGO | 2 USE BUSINESS INFORMATION SET | 3 USE MEASUREMENT TASK PANE | 4 CREATE NEW STYLE
5 CUSTOMIZE LETTERHEAD | 6 CREATE OTHER PUBLICATIONS | 7 CREATE PORTABLE FILES | 8 EMBED FONTS

When you insert an individual field, Publisher places either a text box with the information in the center of the screen with a preset font and font size, or a picture box with the logo. You then may position the field and format the text as necessary. *Why? Publisher uses the default formatting. Applied formatting affects the current publication only.* The following steps insert a field, in this case the tagline or motto, from the business information set into the current publication.

- Zoom to approximately 120%, scroll to the lower portion of the page layout, and display the Insert tab.
- Click the Business Information button (Insert tab | Text group) to display the Business Information menu (Figure 5–20).

Experiment

- Scroll through the various information fields and commands on the menu to see the kinds of fields and components that you might insert.

Q&A
When would I use the other components, such as those in the Content Information area?
Content Information components are similar to building block items that can be inserted as objects into the current publication. Content Information components are populated with appropriate business information fields from the current set.

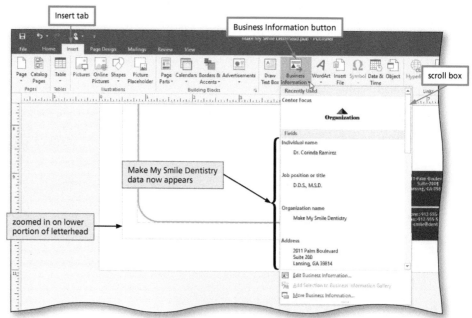

Figure 5–20

2

- Scroll as necessary and then click the desired field (in this case, the 'Tagline or motto' field) to insert it into the publication (Figure 5–21).

Q&A My field inserted in the middle of the letterhead. Did I do something wrong?
No. Publisher inserts business information fields in the center of the screen. You will adjust the position later in the module.

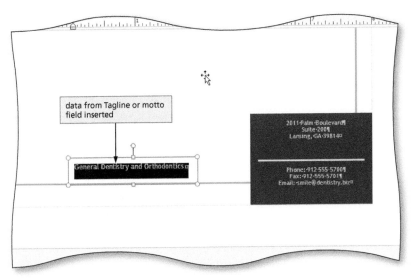

Figure 5–21

TO CREATE A BUSINESS INFORMATION SET FROM A PUBLICATION

If you have typed business information manually into a letterhead, you still can save it as a business information set. To do so, you would perform the following steps. If you currently are performing the steps in this module, do not perform these steps until you are finished, as creating a business information set from a publication overwrites the current business information set.

1. Choose a letterhead template and create the publication.
2. Click the text in the Business Name text box and then type the name of the business.
3. To add the field to the current business information set, which will overwrite the current information, click the information smart tag and then click 'Save to Business Information Set' to save the data.
4. Repeat Steps 2 and 3 for the address, phone, tagline (if it exists), and logo.

Using the Measurement Task Pane

To place and scale objects precisely, rather than estimating by dragging and resizing, you use the **Measurement task pane** to enter the exact values for the horizontal position, vertical position, width, and height of the object. The Measurement task pane not only sets the location and size of an object but also sets the angle of rotation. If the object is text, the Measurement task pane offers additional character spacing or typesetting options. The Measurement task pane is a floating toolbar with eight text boxes (Figure 5–22). Entries can be typed in each box by clicking the appropriate arrows. If no object is selected, the boxes will be disabled.

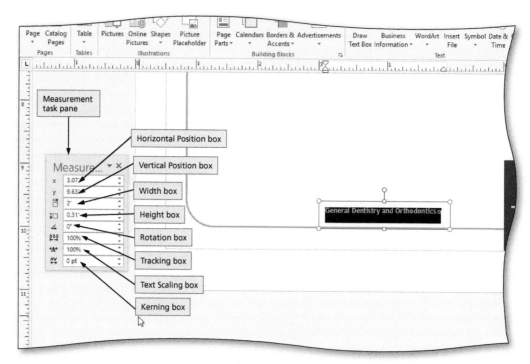

Figure 5–22

Table 5–3 lists the text boxes on the Measurement task pane that are used to edit the position, size, and rotation of an object. The first five text boxes edit the location and position of objects on the page layout. You will learn about the other text boxes in a later module.

Table 5–3 Measurement Task Pane Settings

Box Name	Specifies	Preset Unit of Measurement
Horizontal Position	Horizontal distance from the left edge of the page to the upper-left corner of the object	Inches
Vertical Position	Vertical distance from the top of the page to the upper-left corner of the object	Inches
Width	Width of the object	Inches
Height	Height of the object	Inches
Rotation	Rotation of the object counterclockwise from the original orientation	Degrees
Tracking	General spacing between all selected characters	Percentages
Text Scaling	Width of selected characters	Percentages
Kerning	Spacing between two selected characters to improve readability	Points

To Display the Measurement Task Pane

1 CREATE LOGO | 2 USE BUSINESS INFORMATION SET | 3 USE MEASUREMENT TASK PANE | 4 CREATE NEW STYLE
5 CUSTOMIZE LETTERHEAD | 6 CREATE OTHER PUBLICATIONS | 7 CREATE PORTABLE FILES | 8 EMBED FONTS

The following step displays the Measurement task pane. *Why? You can choose the exact size and location of any object using the Measurement task pane.*

- Display the Drawing Tools Format tab.

- Click the Measurement button (Drawing Tools Format tab | Size group) to display the Measurement task pane.

- If necessary, drag the task pane's title bar toward the status bar and let it snap into an anchored position (Figure 5–23).

Q&A Does the Measurement task pane always appear at the bottom of the workspace?
No. It is a floating toolbar and can be placed anywhere on the screen or docked to any of the four sides of the workspace.

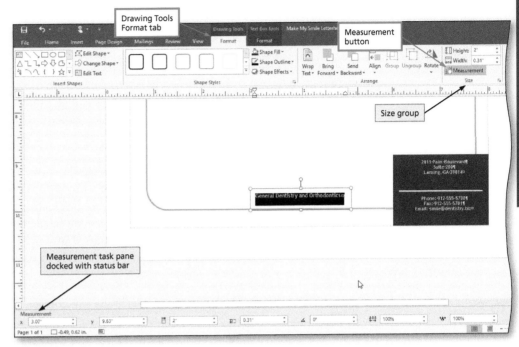

Figure 5–23

Other Ways

1. Click Object Position button on status bar   2. Click Object Size button on status bar

To Position Objects Using the Measurement Task Pane

1 CREATE LOGO | 2 USE BUSINESS INFORMATION SET | 3 USE MEASUREMENT TASK PANE | **4 CREATE NEW STYLE**
5 CUSTOMIZE LETTERHEAD | **6 CREATE OTHER PUBLICATIONS** | **7 CREATE PORTABLE FILES** | **8 EMBED FONTS**

The following step positions and scales the motto precisely using the Measurement task pane. *Why? The customer has asked that the Make My Smile tagline appear more prominently at the bottom of the letterhead.*

1

- With the Tagline or motto text box selected, on the Measurement task pane, select the text in the Horizontal Position box and then type 1.11 to replace it. Press the TAB key to advance to the next text box.

- Type 9.57 in the Vertical Position box and then press the TAB key.

- Type 4.6 in the Width box and then press the TAB key.

- Type .5 in the Height box and then press the ENTER key to finish editing the exact place and size of the object (Figure 5–24).

Q&A Should I change the value in the Rotation box?
No. A zero value is appropriate for an object that should appear straight up and down.

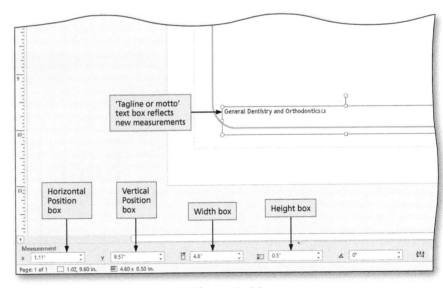

Figure 5–24

Creating a New Style

Publisher allows you to create a new formatting style from scratch or one based on a current style or text selection. A **style** is a named group of formatting characteristics, including font, font size, font color, character spacing, bullets, and shadows, among other attributes. The default style in Publisher is called the **Normal style**, which includes the body font from the current font scheme in a black font color with left-justified alignment.

Styles can be used as branding for a business; for example, many people recognize the James Bond font. It has become a brand for the movie series. Some companies even copyright their text styles or brands. Creating a new style is a good idea when you want to change those defaults or you have multiple text passages that must be formatted identically and the desired attributes are not saved as a current style. For this module, you will create and apply a new style to the tagline or motto.

To Sample a Font Color

The first step in creating a new style will be to choose a font color. You will sample the dark green color in the logo. *Why? The font color of your new style will match the dark green color in the publication.* When you **sample** a color, the pointer changes to an eyedropper; then, any color that you click in the publication is added to all color galleries, just below the color scheme palette. The following steps sample the font color.

- Double-click the text, General, to select it.
- Display the Text Box Tools Format tab, if necessary.
- Click the Font Color arrow (Text Box Tools Format tab | Font group) to display the Font Color gallery (Figure 5–25).

Q&A Does it make any difference whether I use the Font Color arrow on the Home tab or on the Text Box Tools Format tab?

You may use either one. Typically, when you select text, Publisher automatically displays the Text Box Tools Format tab, so that tab's Font Color arrow would be quicker to use.

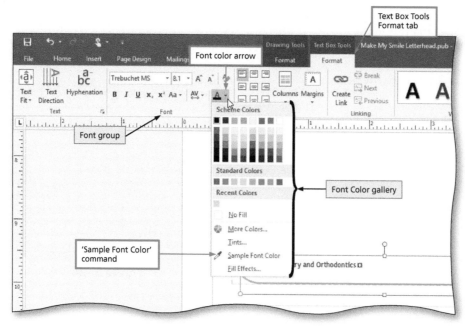

Figure 5–25

- Click 'Sample Font Color' in the Font Color gallery to display the eyedropper pointer (Figure 5–26).

Could I just click the dark green color in the color palette?

You could; however, sampling from the publication itself will assure no change to the style if someone changes the color scheme later.

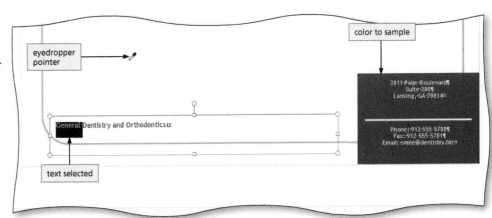

Figure 5–26

- Click the green color in the business information rectangle at the lower-right corner of the page to apply the sampled color to the selected text.

- Click outside the rectangle to deselect it and view the result (Figure 5–27).

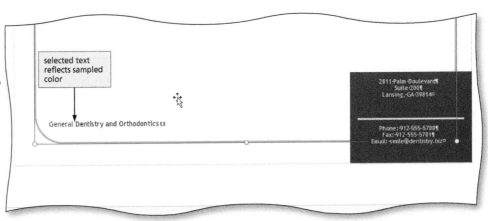

Figure 5–27

To Create a New Style

1 CREATE LOGO | 2 USE BUSINESS INFORMATION SET | 3 USE MEASUREMENT TASK PANE | 4 CREATE NEW STYLE
5 CUSTOMIZE LETTERHEAD | 6 CREATE OTHER PUBLICATIONS | 7 CREATE PORTABLE FILES | 8 EMBED FONTS

The following steps display the New Style Dialog box to create a new style. *Why? Using a style sometimes is easier than using the format painter.*

1

- Select the text, General, again.

- Display the Home tab.

- Click the Styles button (Home tab | Styles group) to display the Styles gallery (Figure 5–28).

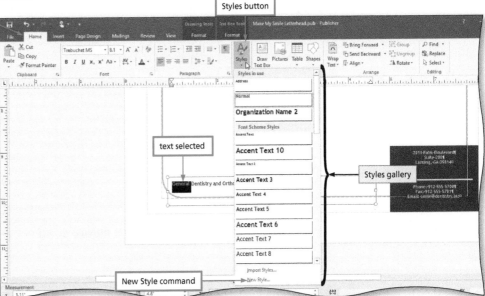

Figure 5–28

2

- Click New Style in the Styles gallery to display the New Style dialog box.

- In the 'Enter new style name' text box, type **Make My Smile** to name the style (Figure 5–29).

Q&A Why did the name also appear in the 'Style for the following paragraph' box? Publisher assumes you will want to use the same style for subsequent paragraphs. If you want to change that setting, you can click the 'Style for the following paragraph' arrow (New Style dialog box) and then click a different style.

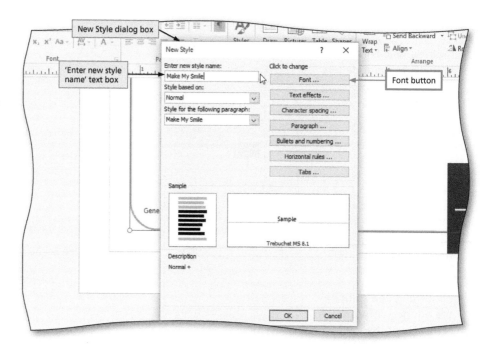

Figure 5–29

3

- Click the Font button (New Style dialog box) to display the Font dialog box.

- Click the Font arrow (Font dialog box) and then select the Monotype Corsiva font in the Font list.

- Click the Font style button and then click Bold Italic in the Font style list.

- Type **20** in the Font size box to set the font size (Figure 5–30).

⊘ Experiment

- Click the More Effects button (Font dialog box) to display the Format Text Effects dialog box. Explore the many settings. Close the Format Text Effects dialog box without changing the settings.

Q&A Why should I choose Monotype Corsiva? Monotype Corsiva is a nice contrasting font to the Trebuchet font in the font scheme. It displays swashes and glyphs making the letters flow from one to another.

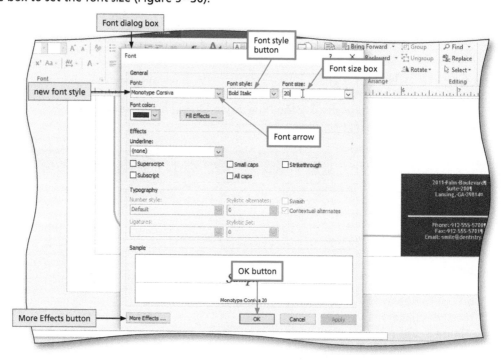

Figure 5–30

4

- Click the OK button (Font dialog box) to close the Font dialog box.

- Click the OK button (New Style dialog box) to close the New Style dialog box.

To Apply the New Style

New styles are stored in the publication in which they are created. ***Why?*** *Publisher assumes you will want to use the style again in the same publication; however, you can import styles from one publication to another.* The following steps apply the new style to the entire tagline.

1

- Select the entire text, General Dentistry and Orthodontics.

- Click the Styles button (Home tab | Styles group) to display the Styles gallery.

- Scroll to display the Make My Smile style (Figure 5–31).

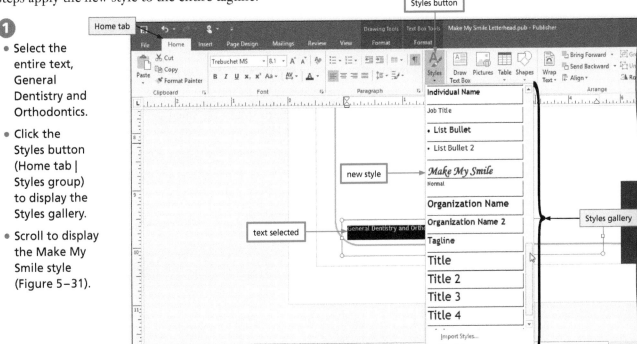

Figure 5–31

2

- Click the 'Make My Smile' style to apply it to the text.

- Click outside the selected text to view the change (Figure 5–32).

Q&A Could I use the format painter to copy the formatting attributes?
Yes, you can edit the formatting either way.

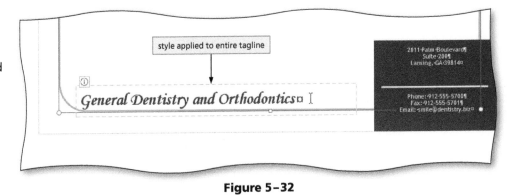

Figure 5–32

To Import Styles

Because styles are publication specific, if you want to use a style in a different publication, you would have to perform the following steps to import the style.

1. Click the Styles button (Home tab | Styles group) to display the Styles gallery.

2. Click Import Styles in the Styles gallery.

3. Navigate to the publication that contains the desired style (Import Styles dialog box).

4. When Publisher asks if you wish to make changes to the Normal style, click the No button (Microsoft Publisher dialog box).

5. As Publisher goes through each of the font styles, click the No button until you see the desired style. In that case, click the Yes button (Microsoft Publisher dialog box).

To Edit the Masthead

The following steps edit the masthead at the top of the letterhead.

1 Scroll to the top of the page and zoom to 100%.

2 Right-click the Business Name text box (Make My Smile Dentistry) to display the shortcut menu and then click Best Fit on the shortcut menu.

3 Select the green-bordered rectangle around the logo. Delete the rectangle.

4 Resize the logo as shown in Figure 5–33. If necessary, adjust the measurements in the Measurement task pane until the picture is proportionate.

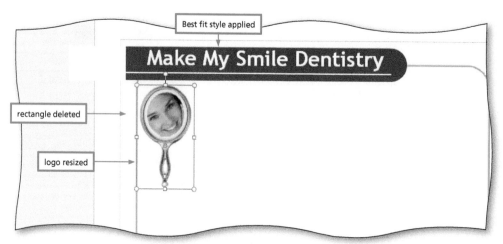

Figure 5–33

Customizing the Letterhead for Interactivity

When creating publications that are designed to be edited by others or publications with which users must interact, it is important to make the publication as user-friendly as possible. Prepare the publication with the novice user in mind. Always place the interactive components in the front, or on top, of other objects in the publication. Use updatable fields when possible, and insert blank lines or tabs to help users know where to type. In a later module, you also will learn how to create customized code to place the insertion point, turn on and off certain Publisher features, and create dialog box reminders for the user.

Why do I need to consider interactivity?

Your publications will be more beneficial to others if you make them as user-friendly as possible. Think about the times you have opened templates or files and had to find the pointer, navigate to a field, figure out the formatting, and worry about how to save the file. You should mitigate those problems as much as possible as you design templates and files that will be used over and over. Business sets, building blocks, updatable fields, interactive components, and preset margins, lines, and tabs will help users create their publications quickly and efficiently.

To Create a Text Box for Users

To make the letterhead more functional for the company, the following steps insert a large text box in which users can type their text.

1. Click the 'Show Whole Page' button on the status bar and then click the scratch area so that no object is selected.

2. Click the 'Draw a Text Box' button (Home tab | Objects group) to select it.

3. Drag to create a large rectangular text box that fills the center of the letterhead as shown in Figure 5–34. The text box will overlap the logo.

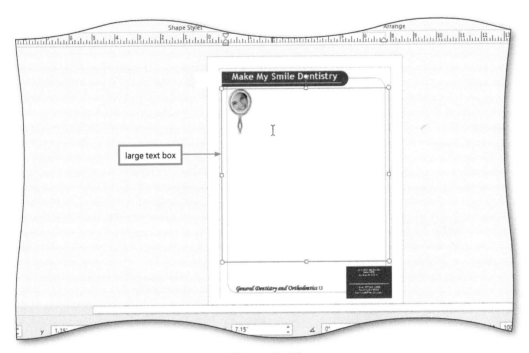

Figure 5–34

1 CREATE LOGO | 2 USE BUSINESS INFORMATION SET | 3 USE MEASUREMENT TASK PANE | 4 CREATE NEW STYLE
5 CUSTOMIZE LETTERHEAD | **6 CREATE OTHER PUBLICATIONS** | **7 CREATE PORTABLE FILES** | **8 EMBED FONTS**

To Use the Paragraph Dialog Box

The default settings for line and paragraph settings are determined by the font or style used; however, in general, the default line spacing for text boxes is greater than 1 because Publisher accommodates the largest character of the font family and adds an additional amount of space for the text box margin. The default spacing after paragraphs varies. The Paragraph dialog box allows you to change line spacing, indentation, and alignment with more settings than are available on the ribbon. Line spacing refers to the spacing before and after paragraphs, as well as the line spacing between lines. **Indentation** refers to how far the first line is from the margin; it does not change subsequent lines in the paragraph. Alignment refers to how paragraph text wraps at the margin.

The following steps change the font size to 12 and set the line spacing to insert no extra spacing when the user presses the ENTER key. *Why? Many business letters use a font size of 12. In addition, most users do not indent business letters, but press the ENTER key twice at the end of a paragraph.*

1.

- Press the F9 key to zoom the text box to 100%.

- Click the Font Size arrow (Home tab | Font group) and then click 12 in the Font Size gallery.

- Click the Paragraph
Settings Dialog Box
Launcher (Home
tab | Paragraph
group) to display the
Paragraph dialog box.
If necessary, click the
Indents and Spacing
tab (Figure 5–35).

 Experiment

- Click the Alignment
button (Paragraph
dialog box) and view
the various Alignment
styles. Click the
Preset button in the
Indentation area
and view the various
Indentation styles.

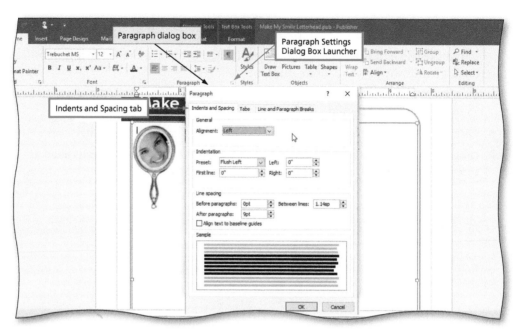

Figure 5–35

2

- If necessary, select the
text in the Between
lines box and then
type `1.14sp` to
enter the line spacing.

- Select the text in the
After paragraphs box.
Type `0` to change
the line spacing after
each paragraph
(Figure 5–36).

3

- Click the OK button
(Paragraph dialog
box) to save the
settings.

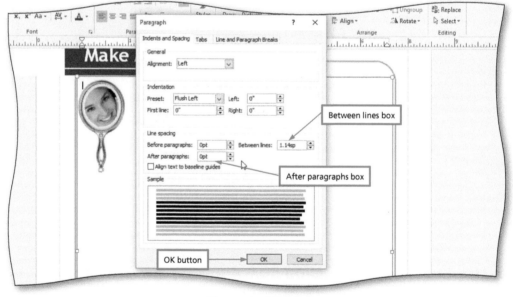

Figure 5–36

Other Ways

1. Right-click text, point to Change Text on shortcut menu, click Paragraph on Change Text
   submenu, enter settings, click OK button (Paragraph dialog box)

Text Wrapping

Wrapping refers to how objects wrap themselves around other objects on the
page. Typically, text wrapping is used when wrapping text boxes around pictures;
however, it also is used when wrapping text boxes with other text boxes and other
objects. Wrapping tightly means that not much space appears around the margins of the
object, allowing text to be placed very close. Wrapping loosely means more space appears
between the text and the object. Some pictures wrap differently than others. Some clip
art, for example, has internal **wrapping points** that create nonrectangular wraps when
you choose to wrap tightly. Table 5–4 defines the various Wrap Text options.

Table 5–4 Wrap Text Options

Option	Result
None	Text does not wrap. It is displayed either behind or in front of the graphic depending upon which object is in front.
Square	Text wraps around the graphic, creating a rectangular white border between the text and graphic.
Tight	Text wraps very closely around the graphic, creating a narrow white border between the text and graphic. Depending on the wrapping points of the graphic itself, the border may not be rectangular.
Top and Bottom	Text is displayed above and below the graphic, leaving horizontal white space across the text box on either side of the graphic.
Through	Depending on the type of graphic, text is displayed through the graphic, or around it based on wrapping points.
In Line with Text	Text is displayed above graphic. Subsequent lines of text are displayed in line with the bottom of the graphic, leaving horizontal white space across the text box.
Edit Wrap Point	Wrapping points are displayed for customized wrapping solutions.

To Set the Text Wrapping

1 CREATE LOGO | 2 USE BUSINESS INFORMATION SET | 3 USE MEASUREMENT TASK PANE | 4 CREATE NEW STYLE
5 CUSTOMIZE LETTERHEAD | **6 CREATE OTHER PUBLICATIONS** | 7 CREATE PORTABLE FILES | 8 EMBED FONTS

If you were to begin typing in the text box, the text would appear over the top of the logo. *Why? The default setting for pictures is no wrapping.* The following steps set the text wrapping of the logo so that text will appear to the side of the logo.

1

- With the text box selected, display the Drawing Tools Format tab.

- Click the Send Backward button (Drawing Tools Format tab | Arrange group) to send the text box behind the logo (Figure 5–37).

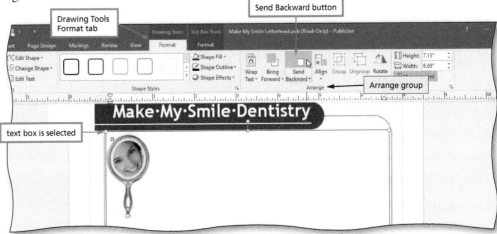

Figure 5–37

2

- Select the logo and then display the Home tab.

- Click the Wrap Text button (Home tab | Arrange group) to display the Wrap Text gallery (Figure 5–38).

Q&A I cannot select the logo. What should I do?
Click in the text box area and try sending it backward again.

Experiment

- Click 'Edit Wrap Points' in the Wrap Text gallery to view the wrapping points. Click the Undo button (Quick Access Toolbar) to undo the setting. Click the Wrap Text button again.

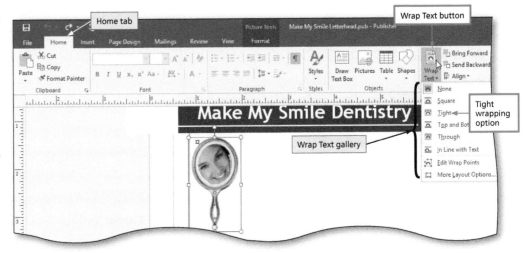

Figure 5–38

3

- Click Tight in the Wrap Text gallery to have the text wrap around the picture.

- Click the text box to display the insertion point (Figure 5–39).

Q&A What changed?
Because you have yet to type any text, the only thing that changed was the position of the insertion point.

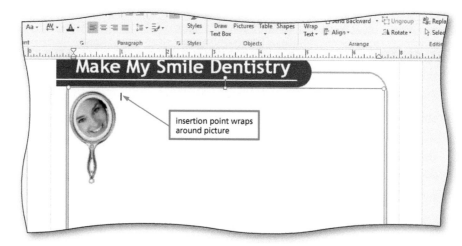

Figure 5–39

Other Ways

1. Click Wrap Text button (Picture Tools Format tab | Arrange group), click desired wrapping style	2. Click Format Text Box Dialog Box Launcher (Text Box Tools Format tab | Text group), click Layout tab, click desired wrapping style, click OK button (Format Text Box dialog box)	3. Right-click text, click 'Format Text Box' on shortcut menu, click Layout tab, click desired wrapping style, click OK button (Format Text Box dialog box)

To Insert an Automatic Date

1 CREATE LOGO | 2 USE BUSINESS INFORMATION SET | 3 USE MEASUREMENT TASK PANE | 4 CREATE NEW STYLE
5 CUSTOMIZE LETTERHEAD | 6 CREATE OTHER PUBLICATIONS | 7 CREATE PORTABLE FILES | 8 EMBED FONTS

Publisher and other Microsoft Office applications can access your computer's stored date and time. You can retrieve the current date and/or time and display it in a variety of formats. Additionally, you can choose to update the date and time automatically each time the file is accessed. *Why? Whenever the user opens the letterhead to prepare a new letter, the date will be current.* The following steps insert an automatic date.

1

- With the insertion point inside the text box, display the Insert tab.

- Click the 'Date & Time' button (Insert tab | Text group) to display the Date and Time dialog box (Figure 5–40).

Experiment

- Scroll in the Available formats list to view the various ways that Publisher can insert the date or time.

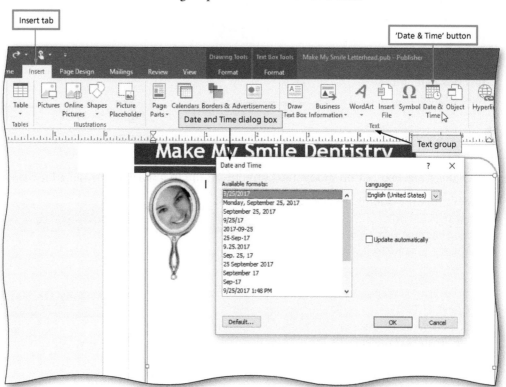

Figure 5–40

2

- Click the third format in the Available formats list to select it.

- Click the Update automatically check box so that it contains a check mark (Figure 5–41).

Q&A What does the Default button do?
When you click the Default button, the current settings for date and time are chosen automatically every time you insert the date or time.

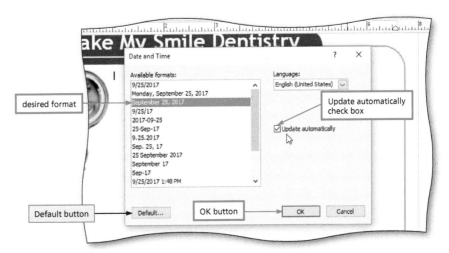

Figure 5–41

3

- Click the OK button (Date and Time dialog box) to close the dialog box.

- Press the ENTER key twice to create a blank line after the date (Figure 5–42).

Q&A Why is my date different?
Checking the Update automatically check box causes Publisher to access your computer's system date. The publication will display your current date.

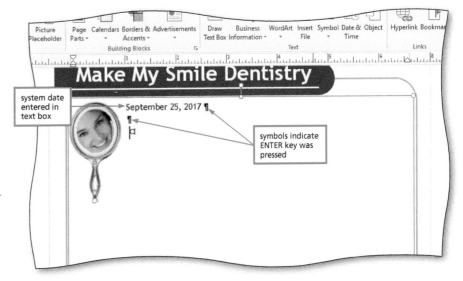

Figure 5–42

4

- Click the Save button on the Quick Access Toolbar to save the file with the same file name in the same location.

- Click File on the ribbon to open the Backstage view.

- Click Close to close the publication without exiting Publisher and to return to the template gallery.

To Set the Read-Only Attribute

1 CREATE LOGO | 2 USE BUSINESS INFORMATION SET | 3 USE MEASUREMENT TASK PANE | 4 CREATE NEW STYLE
5 CUSTOMIZE LETTERHEAD | 6 CREATE OTHER PUBLICATIONS | 7 CREATE PORTABLE FILES | 8 EMBED FONTS

Once a generic letterhead is created, it is a good idea to change the file's attribute, or classification, to read-only. With a **read-only** file, you can open and access the file normally, but you cannot make permanent changes to it. *Why? That way, users will be forced to save the publication with a new file name, keeping the original letterhead intact and unchanged for the next user.*

While you can view system properties in Publisher 2016, you cannot change the read-only attribute from within Publisher. Setting the read-only attribute is a function of the operating system. Therefore, the following steps turn on the read-only attribute using File Explorer and the Properties dialog box.

1

- Click the File Explorer button on the Windows 10 taskbar. Navigate to your storage location.

- Right-click the file named Make My Smile Letterhead to display the shortcut menu (Figure 5–43).

Q&A It shows multiple files named Make My Smile Letterhead. Which one should I choose?
Choose the top or most recent one in the list. It is possible that another person has created the file using your computer, which would result in multiple listings. Your file should be the most recent and appear at the top of the list, provided you saved the document recently.

Q&A Why is my shortcut menu different?
You may have different programs installed on your computer that affect the shortcut menu.

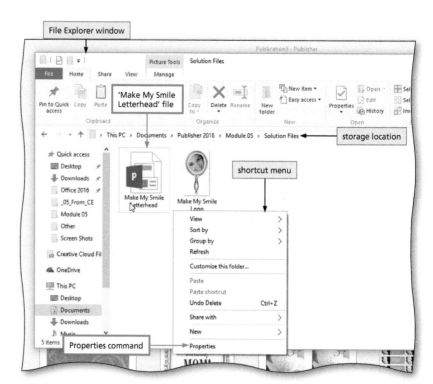

Figure 5–43

2

- Click Properties on the shortcut menu to display the Make My Smile Letterhead Properties dialog box.

- If necessary, click the General tab (Make My Smile Letterhead Properties dialog box) to display its settings.

- Verify that the file is the one you previously saved on your storage device by looking at the Location information.

- Click to place a check mark in the Read-only check box in the Attributes area (Figure 5–44).

Q&A What is the difference between applying a read-only attribute and creating a Publisher template?
Publisher templates do not prevent users from saving over the template with the same name, which would destroy the default settings and user text box features. The read-only attribute keeps the file unchanged and the same for every user.

3

- Click the OK button (Make My Smile Letterhead Properties dialog box) to close the dialog box and apply the read-only attribute.

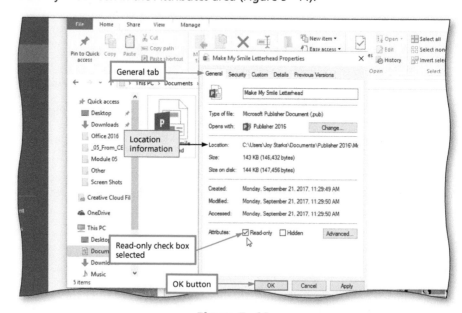

Figure 5–44

Break Point: If you wish to take a break, this is a good place to do so. Exit Publisher. To resume at a later time, run Publisher, and continue following the steps from this location forward.

Using the Custom Letterhead Template

In this project, employees will open the letterhead file in Publisher, type the text of their letter, and then save the finished product with a new file name — thus preserving the original letterhead file.

To Open a Publication from the Recent List

Recall that Publisher maintains a list of the last few publications that have been opened or saved on your computer. The following steps open the Make My Smile Letterhead publication from the Recent list.

1 If necessary, click the Publisher app button on the Windows 10 taskbar to return to Publisher and the template gallery.

2 Click the Open tab to display the recent publications.

3 Click the Make My Smile Letterhead file in the Recent Publications list to open the file.

4 Click the center of the letterhead to place the insertion point in the main text box (Figure 5–45).

5 Close the Measurement task pane by clicking its Close button, to give yourself more room in the workspace.

Q&A Can I position the insertion point automatically for the user?
Yes. In a later module, you will learn how to write a macro event to help streamline data entry.

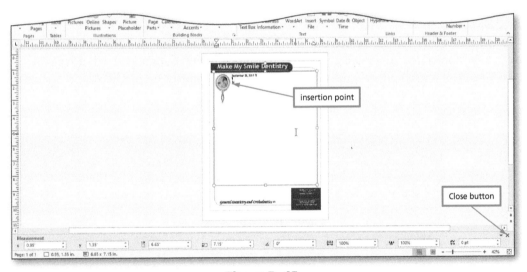

Figure 5–45

To Type the Beginning of the Letter

The following steps enter the text of a letter.

1 Zoom to 150% and scroll to the top of the letterhead, if necessary.

2 Type the first part of the letter as shown in Figure 5–46. Press the ENTER key only to complete a line in the address, to complete a paragraph, or to insert a blank line.

3 Insert a blank line after the paragraph.

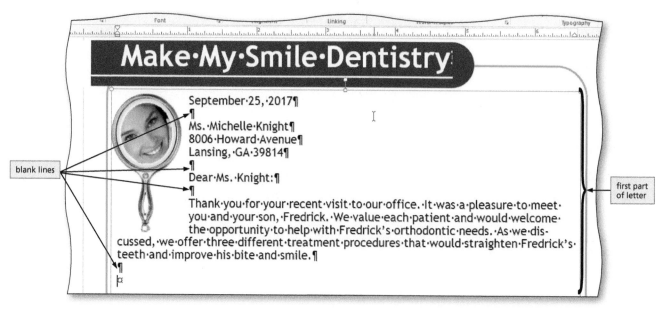

Figure 5–46

To Create a Numbered List

Numbered lists are paragraphs that begin with a number or letter followed by a separator character, such as a period or parenthesis. The following steps create a numbered list. *Why? Numbered lists make paragraphs stand out from the regular text and, thus, are more likely to catch a reader's attention.*

Recall that a hard return is created when you press the ENTER key. A hard return also causes a number to appear on the next line in a numbered list. To create a new line within a numbered item, you will use a **soft return** by pressing the SHIFT+ENTER keys. Neither hard returns nor soft returns print on hard copies.

1

- Click the Numbering button (Home tab | Paragraph group) to display the Numbering gallery (Figure 5–47).

Experiment

- Point to each of the formats and watch the live preview.

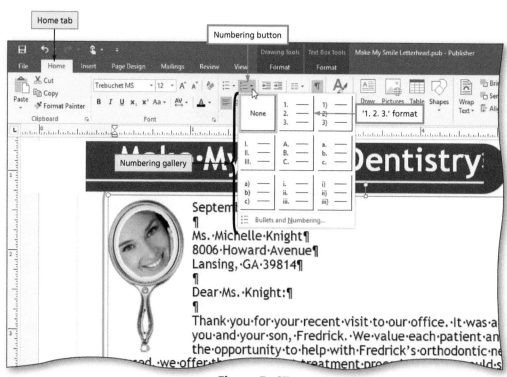

Figure 5–47

2

• Click the '1. 2. 3.' format to choose the formatting (Figure 5–48).

Q&A | What is the 'Bullets and Numbering' command?
That command displays the Bullets and Numbering dialog box where you can change the format, the separator, the number with which to start, and the indentation.

Figure 5–48

3

• Type the paragraphs shown in Figure 5–49. At the end of each paragraph, press SHIFT+ENTER and then press the ENTER key to create a blank, unnumbered line (Figure 5–49).

Q&A | How does SHIFT+ENTER differ when using numbers or letters?
Pressing SHIFT+ENTER creates a blank line without adding an extra number or letter to the blank line.

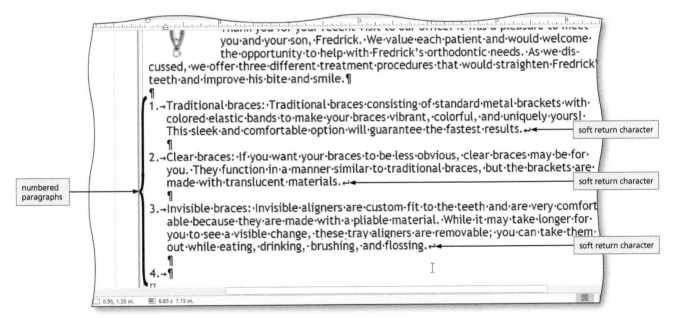

Figure 5–49

4

- Click the Numbering arrow (Home tab | Paragraph group) to display the Numbering gallery and then click None to turn off the numbering.

- Type the rest of the letter as shown in Figure 5–50. Press the ENTER key at the end of paragraphs. Press the ENTER key four times after the word, Sincerely, to leave room for a signature.

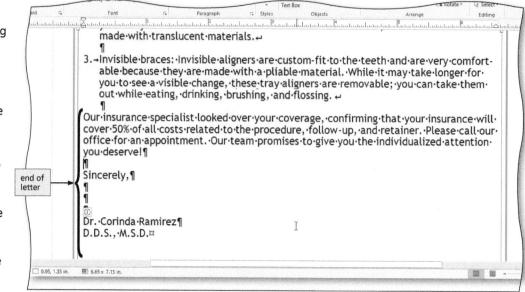

Figure 5–50

Other Ways

1. Type beginning number and separator, type text, press ENTER key to turn on numbering

To Increase the Indent

1 CREATE LOGO | 2 USE BUSINESS INFORMATION SET | 3 USE MEASUREMENT TASK PANE | 4 CREATE NEW STYLE
5 CUSTOMIZE LETTERHEAD | 6 CREATE OTHER PUBLICATIONS | 7 CREATE PORTABLE FILES | 8 EMBED FONTS

The 'Increase Indent Position' and 'Decrease Indent Position' buttons (Home tab | Paragraph group) move paragraphs further away or closer to the margin of the text box. The following step increases the indent for the numbered paragraphs. *Why? Indenting the paragraphs will further delineate them and make the three options easy to find on the page.*

1

- Select the three numbered paragraphs by dragging down the left margin of the text box.

- Click the 'Increase Indent Position' button (Home tab | Paragraph group) to indent the paragraphs (Figure 5–51).

Q&A How far does it indent the paragraphs?
By default, it moves the paragraph .5 inches every time you click the button.

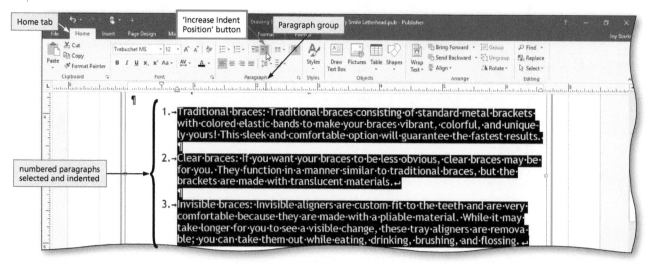

Figure 5–51

Other Ways

1. Select text, click 'Increase Indent Position' button on mini toolbar

2. Right-click text, point to Change Text on shortcut menu, click Paragraph on Change Text submenu, enter settings, click OK button (Paragraph dialog box)

The Format Painter

A convenient way to apply specific formatting is to copy the formatting from existing text or objects using the Format Painter button (Home tab | Clipboard group). The **format painter** copies formatting, such as color, border, font, font size, and special effects, from a **source** object (the object whose formatting you wish to copy) to a **destination** object (the object that will be reformatted to match the source). When using the format painter with objects, click anywhere in the source object, click the Format Painter button, and then click the destination object. When using the format painter with text, click the source text, click the Format Painter button, and then select the destination text. To apply formatting to multiple destinations, double-click the Format Painter button so that it stays on. In those cases, when you finish formatting, click the Format Painter button again to turn it off. While you are using the format painter, the button will appear selected and the pointer will display a paintbrush.

To Use the Format Painter

1 CREATE LOGO | 2 USE BUSINESS INFORMATION SET | 3 USE MEASUREMENT TASK PANE | 4 CREATE NEW STYLE
5 CUSTOMIZE LETTERHEAD | **6 CREATE OTHER PUBLICATIONS** | **7 CREATE PORTABLE FILES** | **8 EMBED FONTS**

When you make a change to the formatting of text, it is a good idea to use that formatting more than once. **Why?** *Using the formatting more than once keeps it from looking like a mistake and provides continuity in the publication.* The following steps apply formatting and copy it to other locations using the format painter.

1

- Select the text, Traditional braces, in the paragraph numbered 1.

- Press CTRL+B to bold the text. Press CTRL+I to italicize the text.

- Double-click the Format Painter button (Home tab | Clipboard group) to copy the formatting of the selected text (Figure 5–52).

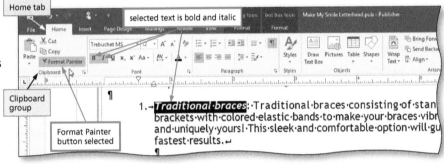

Figure 5–52

2

- Drag through the text, Clear braces, in the paragraph numbered 2 to apply the formatting.

- Drag through the text, Invisible braces, in the paragraph numbered 3 to apply the formatting.

- Click the Format Painter button (Home tab | Clipboard group) to turn it off.

- Deselect the text in order to view the formatting (Figure 5–53).

3

- Press the F7 key to check spelling. Correct any errors.

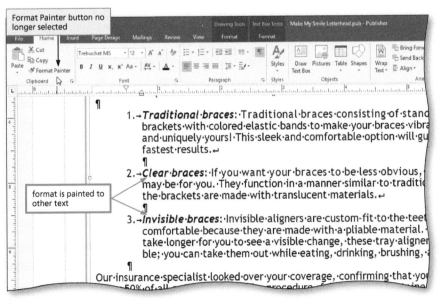

Figure 5–53

To Save the Letter

To illustrate the read-only properties of the letter, you will try to save the publication in the same place with the same file name, Make My Smile Letterhead. *Why? Because you have changed the publication to read-only, Publisher will generate an error message. You then will choose a new file name and save the file.* The following steps save the file with a new file name.

1

- Click the Save button on the Quick Access Toolbar to display the Save As dialog box. Do not navigate to another location.

- Click the Save button (Save As dialog box) to display the Confirm Save As dialog box (Figure 5–54).

Q&A What would happen if the file were not read-only?
Clicking the Save button would save the edited letter, replacing the custom template.

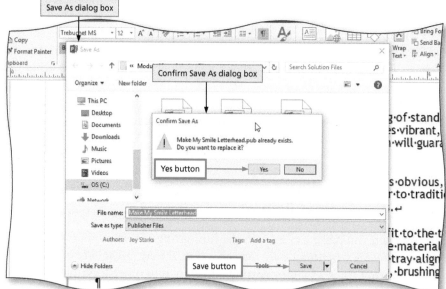

Figure 5–54

2

- Click the Yes button (Confirm Save As dialog box) to try to save the file. A Save As warning dialog box is displayed (Figure 5–55).

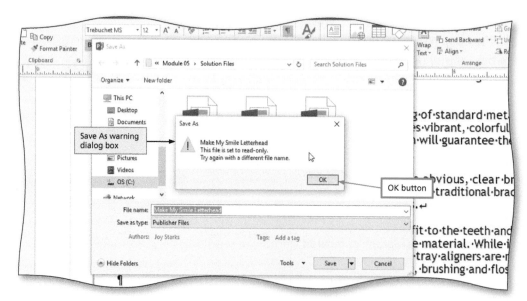

Figure 5–55

3

- Click the OK button to return to the Save As dialog box.

- Click the File name text box, delete the previous file name, and then type **Knight Letter** as the new file name.

- Click the Save button (Save As dialog box) to save the file with the new file name.

- Print a hard copy of the letter, if instructed to do so. When the printer stops, retrieve the hard copy (Figure 5–56).

Make My Smile Dentistry

September 25, 2017

Ms. Michelle Knight
8006 Howard Avenue
Lansing, GA 39814

Dear Ms. Knight:

Thank you for your recent visit to our office. It was a pleasure to meet you and your son, Fredrick. We value each patient and would welcome the opportunity to help with Fredrick's orthodontic needs. As we discussed, we offer three different treatment procedures that would straighten Fredrick's teeth and improve his bite and smile.

1. *Traditional braces*: Traditional braces consisting of standard metal brackets with colored elastic bands to make your braces vibrant, colorful, and uniquely yours! This sleek and comfortable option will guarantee the fastest results.

2. *Clear braces*: If you want your braces to be less obvious, clear braces may be for you. They function in a manner similar to traditional braces, but the brackets are made with translucent materials.

3. *Invisible braces*: Invisible aligners are custom-fit to the teeth and are very comfortable because they are made with a pliable material. While it may take longer for you to see a visible change, these tray aligners are removable; you can take them out while eating, drinking, brushing, and flossing.

Our insurance specialist looked over your coverage, confirming that your insurance will cover 50% of all costs related to the procedure, follow-up, and retainer. Please call our office for an appointment. Our team promises to give you the individualized attention you deserve!

Sincerely,

Dr. Corinda Ramirez
D.D.S., M.S.D.

2011 Palm Boulevard
Suite 200
Lansing, GA 39814

Phone: 912-555-5700
Fax: 912-555-5701
Email: smile@dentistry.biz

General Dentistry and Orthodontics

Figure 5–56

 ❹

- Click File on the ribbon to open the Backstage view.

- Click Close to close the publication without exiting Publisher and to return to the template gallery.

Other Ways

1. Press CTRL+S, click Save button (Save As dialog box), click Yes button (Confirm Save As dialog box), click OK button (Save As warning dialog box), navigate to storage location, enter new file name, click Save button (Save As dialog box)

Envelopes

Envelopes are manufactured in a variety of sizes and shapes. The most common sizes are #6 personal envelopes that measure $3\frac{5}{8} \times 6\frac{1}{2}$ inches and #10 business envelopes that measure $4\frac{1}{8} \times 9\frac{1}{2}$ inches. You can customize the page layout to instruct Publisher to print envelopes for invitations, cards, and mailers, or to merge an address list with an envelope template to avoid using labels.

Although the majority of businesses outsource the production of their preprinted envelopes, most desktop printers have an envelope-feeding mechanism that works especially well for business envelopes. Check your printer's documentation for any limitations on the size and shape of envelopes. For testing purposes, you can print the envelope on $8\frac{1}{2} \times 11$-inch paper, if necessary.

To Create an Envelope

1 CREATE LOGO | 2 USE BUSINESS INFORMATION SET | 3 USE MEASUREMENT TASK PANE | 4 CREATE NEW STYLE
5 CUSTOMIZE LETTERHEAD | 6 CREATE OTHER PUBLICATIONS | **7 CREATE PORTABLE FILES** | **8 EMBED FONTS**

The following steps use the template gallery to produce a business-sized envelope for Make My Smile Dentistry. *Why? The template automatically uses information from the business information set created earlier in this project.*

- With the template gallery still displayed, click BUILT-IN and then click Envelopes to display the available templates.
- Scroll down to the More Installed Templates area and then click the Radial thumbnail.
- If necessary, choose the Paper color scheme and the Virtual font scheme (Customize area).
- If necessary, click the Business information button and then click Make My Smile to select the business information set.
- Click the Page size button to display the list of page sizes (Figure 5–57).

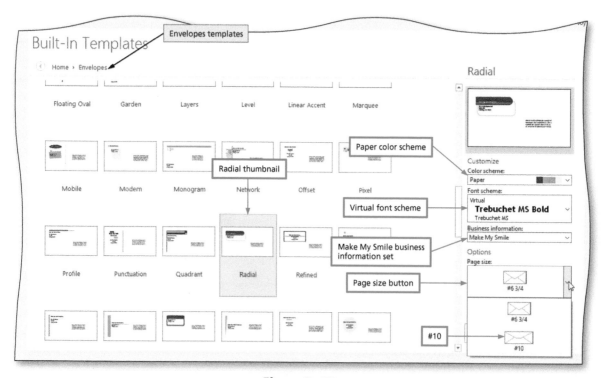

Figure 5–57

2

- Click #10 to choose a business-size envelope.

- If necessary, click to remove the check mark in the Include logo check box (Figure 5–58).

Q&A What if I want a different size envelope?
In the template gallery, scroll down to the Blank Sizes area and choose the size from the list. Otherwise, you could change the size using the Size button (Page Design tab | Page Setup group).

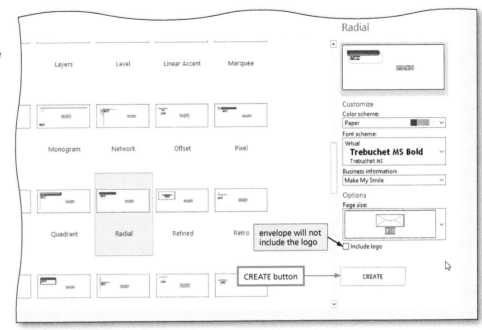

Figure 5–58

3

- Click the CREATE button.

- When Publisher displays the envelope, right-click the business name in the upper-left corner to display the shortcut menu and then click Best Fit to autofit the text (Figure 5–59).

Q&A Why does a different number appear on my title bar after the word, Publication?
Depending on how many publications you have opened or created during the current Publisher session, the number will vary.

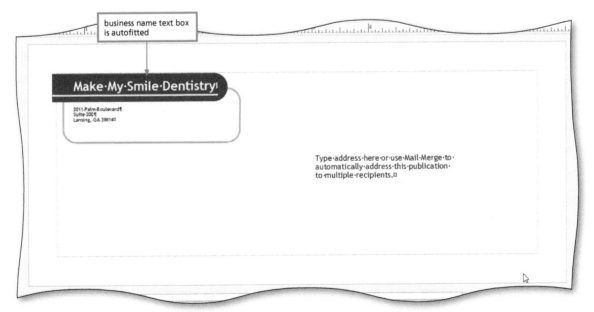

Figure 5–59

4

- Click the Save button on the Quick Access Toolbar. Browse to your storage location. Save the file with the file name, Make My Smile Envelope.

To Address the Envelope

The envelope is ready to use. The following steps fill in the name and address on this envelope.

1 Click the placeholder text in the address text box to select it.

2 Type the address as shown in Figure 5–60.

Type your name and address on the envelope if instructed to do so.

Q&A Could I use a mailing label instead of typing the address?
Yes, you can delete the text box and use a mailing label. In later modules, you will learn how to create both mailing labels and a mail merge for customers on a mailing list.

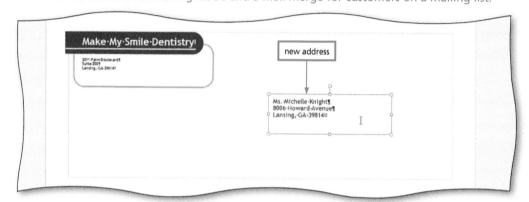

Figure 5–60

To Set Options and Print the Envelope

1 CREATE LOGO | 2 USE BUSINESS INFORMATION SET | 3 USE MEASUREMENT TASK PANE | 4 CREATE NEW STYLE
5 CUSTOMIZE LETTERHEAD | 6 CREATE OTHER PUBLICATIONS | **7 CREATE PORTABLE FILES** | 8 EMBED FONTS

The following steps print a hard copy of the envelope with special settings. *Why? Most of the time, you must adjust the settings when printing envelopes.*

- Open the Backstage view and then click the Print tab to display the Print gallery.

- Verify that the printer listed on the Printer Status button will print a hard copy of the publication.

- Click the Tiled button to display the options (Figure 5–61).

Q&A Why is the envelope displayed across two pages?
The default value for page settings is to place the publication on an 8½ × 11-inch piece of paper. The envelope will not fit, so Publisher tiles it until you change the setting.

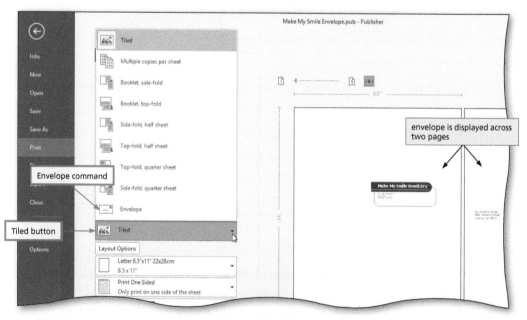

Figure 5–61

2

• Click Envelope in the list (Figure 5–62).

3

• If instructed to do so, click the Print button in the Print gallery to print the envelope on the currently selected printer. Otherwise, click Close to close the publication without saving and without exiting Publisher. If Publisher displays a dialog box that asks you to save the publication again, click the Save button to save the envelope print settings along with the envelope.

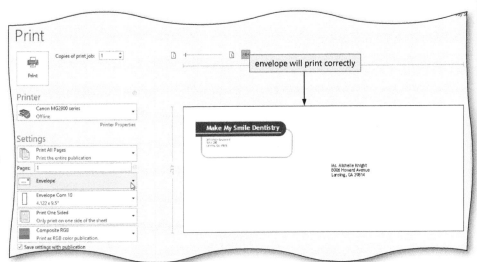

Figure 5–62

Award Certificates

Award **certificates** commonly are single-page publications presented in recognition of an achievement. Publisher has several certificate templates that are customized to the color scheme and font scheme. Many others are available online. The certificates have many uses, such as for attendance, for accomplishments, a gift certificate, or upon completion of a regimen or coursework.

To Create and Edit an Award Certificate

1 CREATE LOGO | 2 USE BUSINESS INFORMATION SET | 3 USE MEASUREMENT TASK PANE | 4 CREATE NEW STYLE
5 CUSTOMIZE LETTERHEAD | 6 CREATE OTHER PUBLICATIONS | **7 CREATE PORTABLE FILES** | **8 EMBED FONTS**

The following steps use the template gallery to produce an award certificate for Make My Smile Dentistry. *Why? Younger patients are given a certificate for taking good care of their braces since their last visit.*

1

• With the template gallery still displayed, click BUILT-IN and then click Award Certificates to display the available templates.

• Scroll down if necessary and then click the Star thumbnail.

• If necessary, choose the Paper color scheme and the Virtual font scheme (Customize area).

• If necessary, click the Business information button and then click 'Make My Smile' to select the business information set (Figure 5–63).

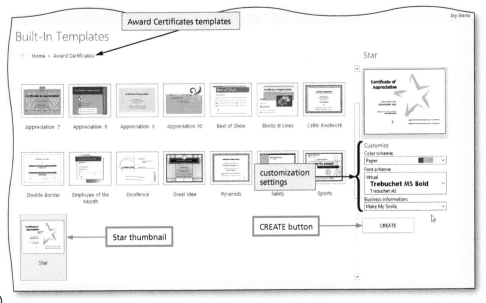

Figure 5–63

- Click the CREATE button.

- When Publisher displays the certificate, select the text in the Certificate of Appreciation text box. Type `You're on the way to a great smile!` to replace the text.

- Delete the recognition text box just above the Business Name text box.

- Right-click the business name in the lower part of the certificate to display the shortcut menu and then click Best Fit to autofit the text (Figure 5–64).

- Click the Save button on the Quick Access Toolbar. Browse to your storage location. Save the file with the file name, Make My Smile Certificate.

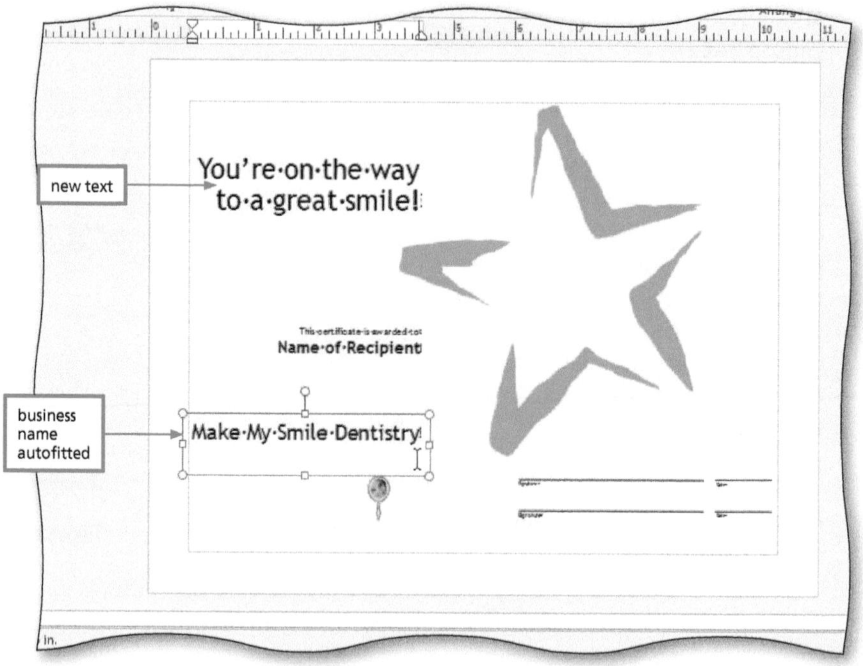

- Print the certificate if instructed to do so.

- Close the publication without exiting Publisher. If Publisher displays a dialog box that asks you to save the publication again, click the Don't Save button.

new text → You're·on·the·way to·a·great·smile!

This·certificate·is·awarded·to:
Name·of·Recipient

business name autofitted → Make·My·Smile·Dentistry

Figure 5–64

Break Point: If you wish to take a break, this is a good place to do so. Exit Publisher. To resume at a later time, run Publisher, and continue following the steps from this location forward.

Business Cards

Another way companies are reducing publishing costs is by designing their own business cards. A **business card** is a small publication, 3½ × 2 inches, typically printed on heavy stock paper. It usually contains the name, title, business, and address information for an employee, as well as a logo, distinguishing graphic, or color to draw attention to the card. Many employees want their telephone, cell phone number, and fax numbers on their business cards in addition to their email and web addresses, so that colleagues and customers can reach them quickly.

Business cards can be saved as files to send to commercial printers or to be printed by desktop color printers on perforated paper.

To Create a Business Card

1 CREATE LOGO | 2 USE BUSINESS INFORMATION SET | 3 USE MEASUREMENT TASK PANE | 4 CREATE NEW STYLE
5 CUSTOMIZE LETTERHEAD | 6 CREATE OTHER PUBLICATIONS | **7 CREATE PORTABLE FILES** | 8 EMBED FONTS

Because the business information set contains information about Make My Smile Dentistry and its orthodontist, using a Publisher business card template is the quickest way to create a business card. *Why? Not only does the template set the size and shape of a typical business card, it also presets page and printing options for easy production.*

The following steps use the template gallery to produce a business card for the orthodontist at Make My Smile Dentistry.

1

- With the template gallery still displayed, click BUILT-IN and then click the Business Cards thumbnail.
- Scroll down to the More Installed Templates area and then click the Radial thumbnail.
- If necessary, choose the Paper color scheme, the Virtual font scheme, and the Make My Smile business information set.
- Click the Page size button (Options area) and then click Portrait in the Page size list.
- If necessary, place a check mark in the Include logo check box (Figure 5–65).

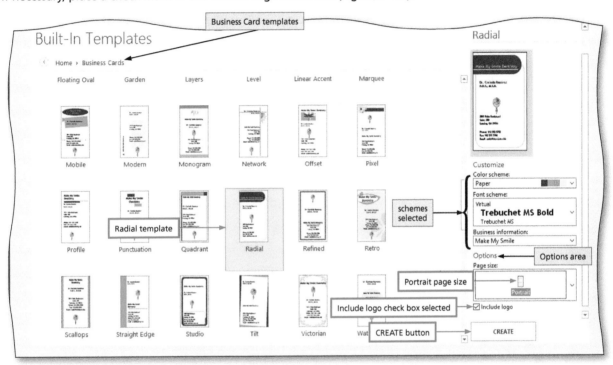

Figure 5–65

2

- Click the CREATE button to create the business card.
- Right-click the business name in the upper part of the business card to display the shortcut menu and then click Best Fit to autofit the text.
- Select the text in the name text box and change the font size to 10. Select the text in the title text box and change the font size to 10.
- Select the text in the address text box and change the font size to 8. Select the text in the phone/fax/email text box and change the font size to 8.
- Resize the logo to fix the vertical area between the title and the address (Figure 5–66).

3

- Click the Save button on the Quick Access Toolbar. Browse to your storage location. Save the file with the file name, Make My Smile Business Card.

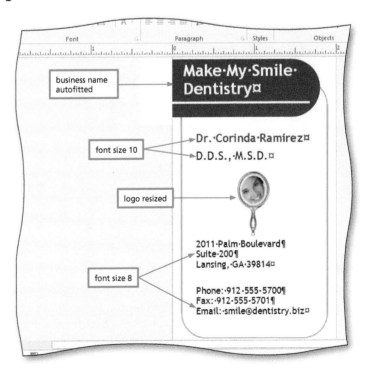

Figure 5–66

To Print the Business Card

The following steps change settings in the Print gallery. ***Why?*** *You have the choice of printing multiple business cards per sheet or only one card per sheet. Layout options allow you to set specific margins to match specialized business card paper.*

- Open the Backstage view and then click the Print tab to display the Print gallery.
- If necessary, verify that the printer shown on the Printer Status button will print a hard copy of the publication.
- If necessary, click the Pages button to display the Pages list, and then click 'Multiple copies per sheet' to select the option.
- If necessary, type   9   in the 'Copies of each page' box.
- Click the Layout Options button to display the Layout Options dialog box.
- Make sure your settings match those in Figure 5–67.

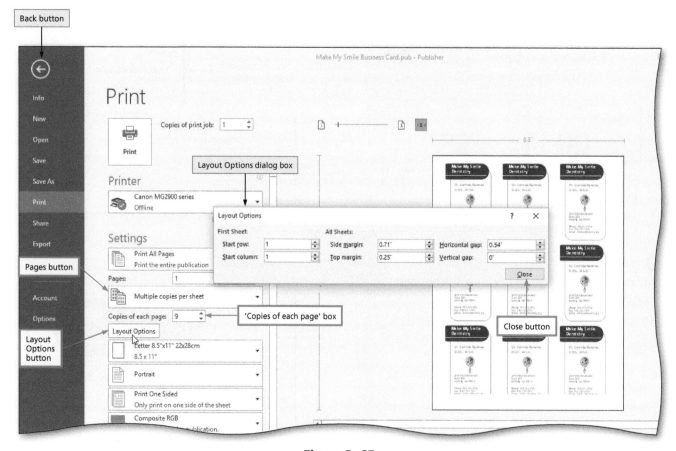

Figure 5–67

- Click the Close button (Layout Options dialog box) to close the dialog box.

If instructed to do so, click the Print button in the Print gallery to print the business cards on the currently selected printer (Figure 5–68). Otherwise, click the Back button (Backstage view) to return to the publication.

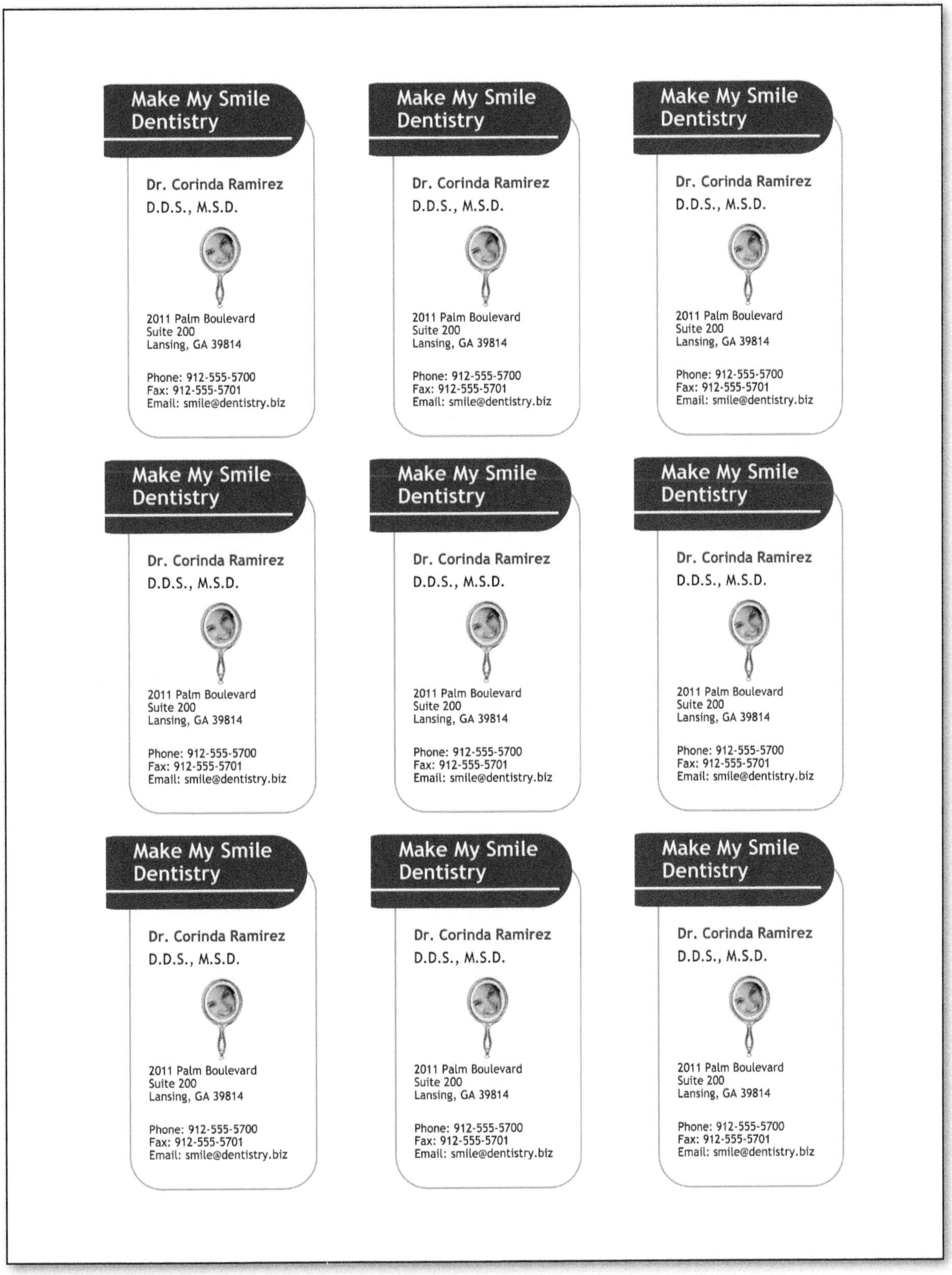

Figure 5–68

Other Ways

1. Press CTRL+P, set options in Print gallery, click Print button

To Set Publication Properties

Because you also plan to send the business cards to a commercial printer, it is important to set publication properties. Recall from the Office 2016 and Windows 10 module that publication properties are set in the Info gallery in the Backstage view. The following steps set publication properties.

1 Open the Backstage view and, by default, select the Info tab.

2 Click the Publication Properties button in the right pane of the Info gallery and then click Advanced Properties to display the properties dialog box for your publication. If necessary, click the Summary tab.

3 Type `Business Card` in the Title text box.

4 If necessary, type `Corinda Ramirez` in the Author text box. Or, if requested by your instructor, type your name to replace the text in the Author text box.

5 Type `Make My Smile Dentistry` in the Company text box (Figure 5–69).

6 Click the OK button (Publication Properties dialog box) to save the settings.

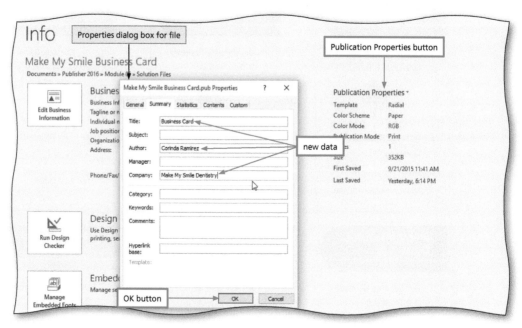

Figure 5–69

Creating Portable Files

The final step is to create a portable file of the business card for document exchange between computers. Publisher offers two choices: PDF or XPS. **PDF** stands for **Portable Document Format**, a flexible file format based on the PostScript imaging model that is cross-platform and cross-application. PDF files accurately display and preserve fonts, page layouts, and graphics. The content in a PDF file is not changed easily, but it can be viewed by everyone with a free viewer available on the web. **XPS** stands for **XML Paper Specification** and is also a format that preserves document formatting and enables file sharing. XPS is Microsoft's portable format similar to PDF. When the XPS file is viewed online or printed, it retains exactly the format that you intended. Like PDF files, the data in XPS files cannot be changed easily.

Why do I need to create portable files?

You might have to distribute your artwork in a variety of formats for customers, print shops, webmasters, and as email attachments. The format you choose depends on how the file will be used, but portability is always a consideration. The publication might need to be used with various operating systems, monitor resolutions, computing environments, and servers.

It is a good idea to discuss with your customer the types of formats he or she might need. It usually is safe to begin work in Publisher and then use the Save As command or Print command to convert the files. PDF is a portable format that can be read by anyone using a free reader, which is available on the web. The PDF format is platform- and software-independent. Commonly, PDF files are virus-free and safe as email attachments.

To Publish in a Portable Format

1 CREATE LOGO | 2 USE BUSINESS INFORMATION SET | 3 USE MEASUREMENT TASK PANE | 4 CREATE NEW STYLE

5 CUSTOMIZE LETTERHEAD | 6 CREATE OTHER PUBLICATIONS | **7 CREATE PORTABLE FILES** | **8 EMBED FONTS**

The following steps publish the business card in a portable format using high-quality settings and maintaining document properties. *Why? You might want to create a portable file for an outside printing service or to display your publication on the web. Publisher allows you to set additional options for quality, graphics, and document properties when creating portable files.*

- If necessary, open the Backstage view and then select the Export tab.
- If necessary, click the Create PDF/XPS Document tab.
- Click the 'Create PDF/XPS' button to display the Publish as PDF or XPS dialog box.
- If necessary, navigate to your storage device and appropriate folder (Figure 5–70).

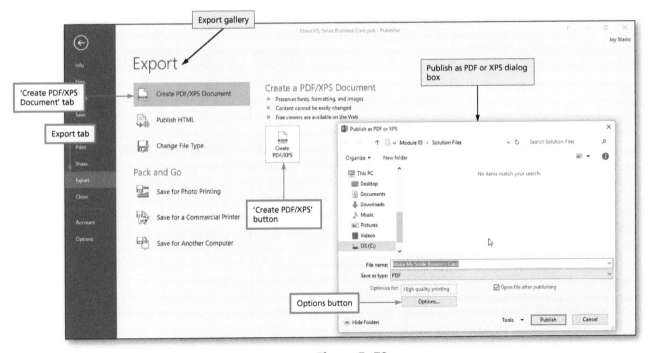

Figure 5–70

- Click the Options or Change button (Publish as PDF or XPS dialog box) to display the Publish Options dialog box.
- If necessary, in the Specify how this publication will be printed or distributed area, click 'High quality printing' (Publish Options dialog box).

- If necessary, in the Include non-printing information area, click both check boxes to select them.

- Do not change any of the other default values (Figure 5–71).

Experiment

- Click each choice in the 'Specify how this publication will be printed or distributed' box to view the description that displays below the box, along with other settings. When you are done, click 'High quality printing'.

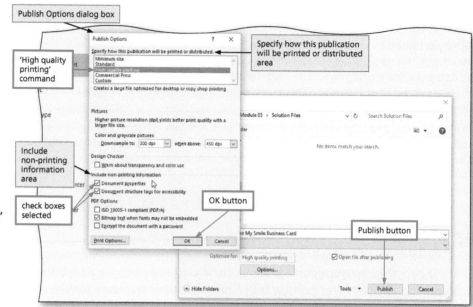

Figure 5–71

❸

- Click the OK button (Publish Options dialog box) to close the dialog box.

- Click the Publish button (Publish as PDF or XPS dialog box) to create the portable file.

- When the PDF file opens, maximize the window (Figure 5–72).

Q&A Why does my display look different?
Your computer may not have the same PDF reader installed. If no PDF reader is installed, the file may open with an XPS reader.

❹

- Click the Close button on the PDF or XPS title bar to close the display of the portable file.

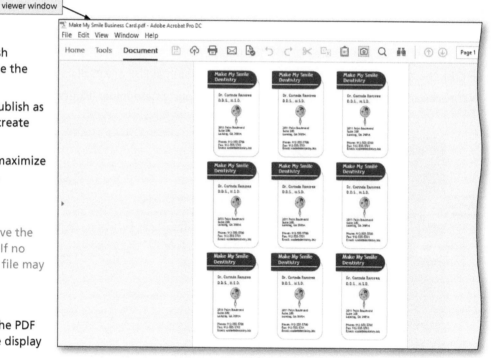

Figure 5–72

Other Ways

1. In Backstage view, click Save As button, specify save location, click 'Save as type' button (Save As dialog box), click PDF (*.pdf) in Save as type list, click Options or Change button, select options, click OK button (Publish Options dialog box), click Save button (Save As dialog box)

Embedding Fonts

If you plan to send the Publisher file to a professional printing service or to other users, they may or may not have the same fonts available on their computers as you do on yours. Thus, any fonts unique to your printer or new font styles that you created may have to be substituted. When the publication is opened, Publisher usually displays a dialog box that informs the user of the substitution. Publisher tries to find a similar font based on the text ornamentation, but your publication will not look exactly as it did. One option is to create a PDF or XPS as you did earlier in the module, which would maintain the look of the publication; however, the PDF or XPS user cannot make significant changes to the design. If you want to preserve your font settings and create a fully editable file, you should **embed** or save the fonts with the publication. Optionally, you can embed a **subset** of the font, which means that it will embed only the specific characters you used in the publication.

Most common fonts, such as Times New Roman, do not have to be embedded because most users already will have that font. In general, TrueType fonts can be embedded only if their licensing allows embedding; however, all of the TrueType fonts that are included in Publisher allow licensed embedding.

Embedded fonts increase the file size of your publication, so you may want to limit the number of fonts or subsets that you embed; however, embedding fonts is one of the best ways to ensure that a font is always available.

Table 5-5 displays some of Publisher's embedding options.

Table 5–5 Type of Embedding

Type of Embedding	Kinds of Fonts (If Any)	Advantages	Restrictions
Full Font Embedding		The recipient does not need the same font to view or edit the file.	You must own the embedded font by owning your printer or by purchasing the font. Fully embedded fonts create a large file size.
	Print and preview fonts	Viewable fonts are embedded in the publication.	The recipient cannot edit the publication.
	Licensed, installable fonts	Embedded fonts, licensed as installable, may be installed permanently for use in other publications and programs.	No restrictions exist.
	Licensed, editable fonts	Embedded fonts that are licensed as editable are available for use in other publications and programs.	The publication with the editable fonts must remain open in order for the recipient to use the font.
	TrueType fonts	TrueType fonts include permissions defined by the original publisher of the font that detail when and how the font may be embedded.	The TrueType fonts can be applied to a publication only if the embedded fonts are installed on the local computer.
Subset Font Embedding		The recipient does not have to own the font to view it.	Only the characters that you use in the publication are included in the font family. Subset font embedding creates a file that is larger than one with no embedding but smaller than one with full font embedding.
No Font Embedding		File size does not change.	The recipient needs to have the same fonts installed or accept a substitution.
Save as PDF or XPS		Fonts, layout, and design are maintained.	Recipient has limited editing capabilities.

To Embed Fonts

1 CREATE LOGO | 2 USE BUSINESS INFORMATION SET | 3 USE MEASUREMENT TASK PANE | 4 CREATE NEW STYLE
5 CUSTOMIZE LETTERHEAD | 6 CREATE OTHER PUBLICATIONS | 7 CREATE PORTABLE FILES | **8 EMBED FONTS**

The following steps embed the fonts with the business card. *Why? Because other workers at Make My Smile Dentistry may want to use this file to create their own business cards, you will embed all of the characters in the heading font, rather than just a subset.* You will not embed the common system fonts that most users have, in this case Times New Roman, in order to reduce the file size slightly.

- With the Make My Smile Business Card still displayed in the workspace, click the File tab to open the Backstage view and, by default, select the Info tab.

- Click the 'Manage Embedded Fonts' button to display the Fonts dialog box.

• Click to place a check mark in the 'Embed TrueType fonts when saving publication' check box (Fonts dialog box).

• If necessary, click to place a check mark in the 'Do not embed common system fonts' check box (Figure 5–73).

Q&A What will users see when they open the file?

A dialog box will verify that some fonts were embedded and allow the user to substitute those if necessary.

Q&A What does the Embed/Don't Embed button do?

If you own the font but do not want others to use it, you can click to select the specific font in the list and then click the Don't Embed button. In that case, the yes column changes to no, and the button changes to the Embed button. You must select a specific font in the list to enable the button.

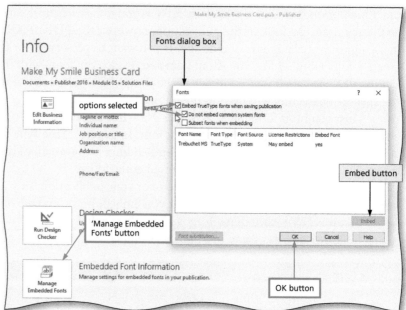

Figure 5–73

• Click the OK button (Fonts dialog box) to close the dialog box.

• Click the Back button (Backstage view) to return to the publication.

• Click the Save button (Quick Access Toolbar) to save the file again with the same file name.

To Delete the Business Information Set

1 CREATE LOGO | 2 USE BUSINESS INFORMATION SET | 3 USE MEASUREMENT TASK PANE | 4 CREATE NEW STYLE
5 CUSTOMIZE LETTERHEAD | 6 CREATE OTHER PUBLICATIONS | 7 CREATE PORTABLE FILES | 8 EMBED FONTS

The following steps delete the Make My Smile business information set. *Why? Others who work on your computer may not want to use the business information set. Deleting the business information set does not delete the information from saved publications.*

• Display the Insert tab.

• Click the Business Information button (Insert tab | Text group) to display the Business Information menu.

• Click 'Edit Business Information' on the Business Information menu to display the Business Information dialog box.

• If necessary, click the leftmost button in the Select a Business Information set area and then click 'Make My Smile' to select the set (Figure 5–74).

Q&A Should I delete the style that I created?

No, the style stays with the document rather than with the system.

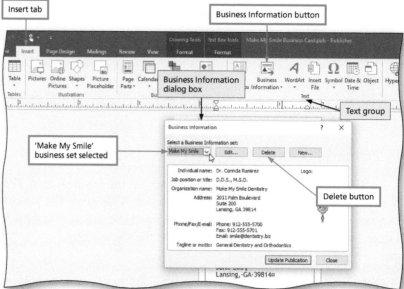

Figure 5–74

2

- Click the Delete button (Business Information dialog box) to delete the business information set (Figure 5–75).

Q&A Will this delete the fields from the current business card?
No. It will delete only the set. All publications containing that data will remain unchanged.

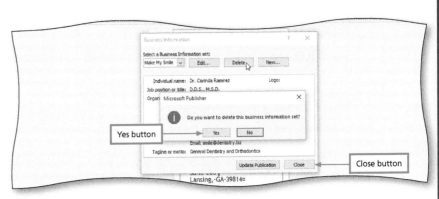

Figure 5–75

3

- When Publisher displays a dialog box asking you to confirm the deletion, click the Yes button.
- Click the Close button (Business Information dialog box) to close the dialog box.
- To exit Publisher, click the Close button on the right side of the title bar. If a Microsoft Publisher dialog box is displayed, click the Don't Save button so that any changes you have made are not saved.

Summary

In this module, you have learned how to create a logo, cropping and filling a shape with a picture. To personalize and customize the publication further, you created the business information set with its many components and then used the business information set to create a letterhead. You created a new style and applied it to text in the letterhead using the Measurement task pane for exact placement and scaling. After adding a customized text box with an automatic date, you saved the letterhead as a read-only file. As you prepared a letter using the new letterhead, you utilized a numbered list and the format painter. Finally, you used the business information set to create an award certificate, envelope, and business card. You created a portable file using the business card and embedded fonts in preparation for an outside printer.

What decisions will you need to make when creating your next business publications?
Use these guidelines as you complete the assignments in this module and create your own publications outside of this class.

1. Gather the business information from the customer.
   a) Create a business information set including appropriate fields and a logo, if applicable.
   b) Create any necessary text styles.
2. Create letterhead.
   a) Use business information fields or type business information text.
   b) Create an automatic date and a user-friendly text box for future use.
   c) Set the read-only attribute.
3. Create certificates.
   a) Choose an appropriate template.
   b) Edit text boxes as necessary.
4. Create envelopes.
   a) Use business information sets when possible.
   b) Include a location for addresses or future labels.
   c) Set publication properties.
5. Create business cards.
   a) Insert a tagline or motto.
   b) Set publication properties.
6. Publish portable files.
   a) Proofread and check the publication.
   b) Save in a PDF or XPS format.

CONSIDER THIS: PLAN AHEAD

Apply Your Knowledge

Reinforce the skills and apply the concepts you learned in this module.

Customizing Letterhead

Note: To complete this assignment, you will be required to use the Data Files. Please contact your instructor for information about accessing the Data Files.

Instructions: Run Publisher. Open the publication, Apply 5–1 Dakota Fitness Letterhead, from the Data Files for Students. The publication is a letterhead that contains default business information fields. You will create a new business information set, publish the file in a portable format, and create an envelope. Figure 5–76 shows the completed letterhead and envelope.

Figure 5–76

Perform the following tasks:

1. Click the Business Information button (Insert tab | Text group) and then click 'Edit Business Information' on the Business Information menu. Click the New button (Business Information dialog box).

2. Enter the information from Table 5–6 and then insert the logo file. The picture for the logo is available on the Data Files for Students. If instructed to do so, use your email address in the business information set.

3. Click the Save button (Create New Business Information Set dialog box) to save the business information set with the company's name, Dakota Fitness.

4. Click the Update Publication button (Business Information dialog box) to change the fields in the current letterhead.

5. Select the logo and then click the Measurement button (Drawing Tools Format tab | Size group) to display the Measurement task pane.

   a. Select the text in the Horizontal Position text box and then type **6.67** to replace it. Press the TAB key to advance to the next box.

   b. Type **.5** in the Vertical Position text box and then press the TAB key.

   c. Type **1.3** in the Width text box and then press the TAB key.

   d. Type **1.3** in the Height text box and then press the ENTER key.

   e. Close the Measurement task pane.

6. Zoom to 100% and then scroll to the bottom of the page. Click the Business Information button (Insert tab | Text group) to display the Business Information menu. Click Individual name and position it at the bottom of the letterhead. Repeat the process for the Job position or title field and the Tagline or motto field, as shown in Figure 5–76.

7. One at a time, apply the Heading 4 style to each of the three text boxes across the bottom of the page by selecting the text and then clicking the Styles button (Home tab | Styles group).

8. Open the Backstage view and then click Save As. Save the publication using the file name, Apply 5–1 Dakota Fitness Letterhead Complete.

9. To publish the letterhead as a PDF in order to send it to a commercial printer, open the Backstage view and then click the Export tab. Click the 'Create PDF/XPS' button in the Export gallery to display the Publish as PDF or XPS dialog box.

10. Navigate to your storage device and appropriate folder, if necessary.

11. Click the Options button (Publish as PDF or XPS dialog box) to display the Publish Options dialog box. If necessary, in the Specify how this publication will be printed or distributed area, click 'High quality printing' in the list. If necessary, in the Include non-printing information area, click both check boxes to select them. Do not change any of the other default values.

12. Click the OK button (Publish Options dialog box) to close the dialog box. Click the Publish button (Publish as PDF or XPS dialog box) to create the portable file. View the PDF (or XPS) file and then close the Adobe Reader (or XPS Reader) window.

13. Close the letterhead publication. Set the Read-only attribute using the File Explorer window as discussed in the module.

14. Run Publisher. Click BUILT-IN, click the Envelopes thumbnail, and then choose the Bars envelope template in size #10. Use the Aqua color scheme and the Modern font scheme. Click the CREATE button to display the publication in the Publisher workspace. If necessary, update the publication with the business information set.

15. Right-click the company name text box and then click Best Fit on the shortcut menu. Repeat the process for the company address text box.

16. Print the envelope with appropriate printer settings.

Table 5–6 Business Information Data	
Field Name	Company Data
Individual name	Devin Sturgis
Job position or title	Manager
Organization name	Dakota Fitness
Address	3177 Stanley Blvd. Munster, SD 57904
Phone, fax, and email	Phone: 605-555-2400 Fax: 605-555-2401 Email: devin@sturgis.biz
Business Information set name	Dakota Fitness
Tagline or motto	Fitness is a lifestyle!
Logo	Apply 5–1 Fitness Logo.png

Continued >

STUDENT ASSIGNMENTS

Apply Your Knowledge continued

17. Click the Business Information button (Insert tab | Text group) and then click 'Edit Business Information' on the business Information menu. Click the Delete button (Business Information dialog box) and then click the Yes button (Microsoft Publisher dialog box) to delete the Dakota Fitness business information set. Click the Close button (Business Information dialog box).

18. Save the envelope with the file name, Apply 5–1 Dakota Fitness Envelope, and then exit Publisher.

19. Submit the files as specified by your instructor.

20. ✳ When would it be more advantageous to send the letterhead out for printing, rather than just typing text in the template and printing it on a desktop printer? If a company uses preprinted letterhead, how do they create content? Would an advantage be gained by running the paper through the printer and just using a Publisher text box with proper dimensions? Or do you think most companies use a copy machine?

Extend Your Knowledge

Extend the skills you learned in this module and experiment with new skills. You may need to use Help to complete the assignment.

Adding Styles to the Quick Access Toolbar

Note: To complete this assignment, you will be required to use the Data Files. Please contact your instructor for information about accessing the Data Files.

Instructions: Open the publication Extend 5–1 Insurance Thank You from the Data Files for Students. You will add the Styles button to the Quick Access Toolbar, apply styles to the publication, and then remove the button from the Quick Access Toolbar.

Perform the following tasks:

1. Use Help to learn more about customizing the Quick Access Toolbar.

2. If necessary, click the Page Number button on the status bar to show the Page Navigation pane.

3. Right-click the Styles button (Home tab | Styles group) to display the shortcut menu.

4. Click 'Add to Quick Access Toolbar' on the shortcut menu to add the Styles button to the Quick Access Toolbar (shown in Figure 5–77).

5. Select the text on Page 1 of the thank you card. Click the Styles button on the Quick Access Toolbar and then choose the 'Pete Hayes Insurance' style.

6. Click the 'Page 2 and Page 3' thumbnail in the Page Navigation pane to display the inside pages in the Publisher workspace.

7. Select the text on Page 2 (in the upper portion of the page layout). Click the Styles button on the Quick Access Toolbar and then choose the Heading 4 style, if necessary.

8. Select the text on Page 3 (in the lower portion of the page layout). Click the Styles button on the Quick Access Toolbar and then choose the 'Body Text 5' style.

9. Click the Page 4 icon in the Page Navigation pane to display the back page in the Publisher workspace.

10. Select the text on Page 4 of the thank you card. Click the Styles button on the Quick Access Toolbar and then choose the 'Pete Hayes Insurance' style.

11. If instructed to do so, draw a text box and insert your name and address on Page 4.

12. Click the 'Customize Quick Access Toolbar' button on the right side of the Quick Access Toolbar to display the shortcut menu and then click More Commands to display the Publisher Options dialog box and, by default, the Quick Access Toolbar settings.

13. Click the Styles button in the Customize Quick Access Toolbar list (Figure 5–77).

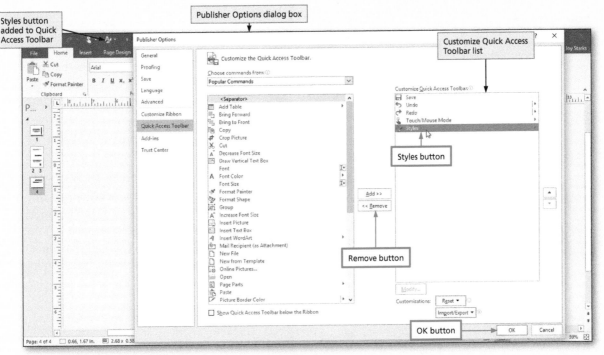

Figure 5–77

14. Click the Remove button (Publisher Options dialog box) to remove the Styles button from the Quick Access Toolbar. Click the OK button to return to the publication.

15. Save the revised publication with the file name, Extend 5–1 Insurance Thank You Complete, and then submit it in the format specified by your instructor.

16. Exit Publisher.

17. ✳ Would you consider adding the Styles button to the Quick Access Toolbar on a permanent basis? Why or why not? What other features do you use so often that you might want to add them to the Quick Access Toolbar?

Expand Your World

Create a solution that uses cloud and web technologies by learning and investigating on your own from general guidance.

Sharing Ideas

Problem: You work online from home as a desktop publisher for a business. You would like to discuss your ideas for a new company letterhead with a coworker, but it has become tedious and time-consuming sending files back and forth. You decide to try a free screen-sharing program.

Instructions:

1. Run a browser and navigate to http://join.me. Click the Start Meeting button, which requires a short download for the app to work. Double-click the downloaded app, join.me.

2. The join.me app will provide you with a nine-digit number to share with others.

3. Click the Share button (Figure 5–78) and then click Share screen.

4. Contact another student in your class or a friend, and ask him or her to navigate to the join.me website and click the Join Meeting button to enter the number. (No download is required for others to view your screen, just the nine-digit number.)

5. Once the user has joined you, run Publisher and demonstrate how to create a simple letterhead.

6. When you are finished, click the Exit button.

Continued >

Expand Your World *continued*

Figure 5–78

7. Write a paragraph about your experience with the screen-sharing program. Include several advantages and disadvantages for collaborating in this manner.

8. Submit the assignment in the format specified by your instructor.

9. ✳ What other screen-sharing programs have you heard about or used? What are the advantages to a web-based, free service, such as join. me? Do you think screen sharing is an important tool in business? Why or why not?

In the Labs

Design, create, modify, and/or use a publication following the guidelines, concepts, and skills presented in this module. Labs 1 and 2, which increase in difficulty, require you to create solutions based on what you learned in the module; Lab 3 requires you to apply your creative thinking and problem-solving skills to design and implement a solution.

Lab 1: **Creating a Business Card**

Problem: Your friend has just opened a clothing resale shop. She wants you to create a business card for her. You prepare the business card shown in Figure 5–79. Because this is the only publication she needs, it is not necessary to save the business information set.

Perform the following tasks:

1. Run Publisher. In the template gallery, click BUILT-IN and then click Business Cards.

2. Choose the Retro Business card, the Lilac color scheme, the Breve font scheme, and the Landscape page size option.

3. Select the text in the Business Name text box. Change the font to French Script MT and the font size to 20. Type **Trends Again** to change the name of the business.

4. Change the name to Amanda Renfro and, if necessary, change the position to Manager.

5. If instructed to do so, use your name instead of Amanda Renfro.

6. Change the address, phone, fax, and email as shown in Figure 5–79.

7. Delete the logo.

8. Draw a text box in the lower-right portion of the business card. Insert the text, Specializing in vintage clothing. Use the format painter to copy the formatting from the business name text box. Autofit the text. Resize the text box as necessary to ensure that the text is not cut off on the bottom.

9. Right-click the small flower picture over the business name to display the shortcut menu. Point to Change picture on the shortcut menu, click Change Picture on the submenu, and then use Bing Image Search to replace the picture with one related to the term, fashion. Delete the replaced file from the scratch area.

10. Embed the fonts and then save the publication using the file name, Lab 5–1 Trends Again Business Card, and then print a copy.

11. Submit the file as directed by your instructor, and exit Publisher.

12. ✸ With business cards being fairly inexpensive to have produced professionally and online, why do you think people still buy the business card paper and print them? What other kinds of paper do people buy to do their own desktop publishing? Is that a good use of their time and money?

Figure 5–79

Lab 2: **Formatting Paragraphs and Filling Shapes**

Problem: The local bowling alley wants to present gift certificates to nonleague players earning a score of 200 or higher. They have a certificate started, but they would like you to finish it. You add details and graphics to create the certificate shown in Figure 5–80.

Perform the following tasks:

1. Run Publisher. Open the file Lab 5–2 Bowling Certificate.

2. Display the Measurement task pane. Draw a text box with the following settings: x = 1.75, y = 6.5, Width = 5.5, and Height = 2.

3. Zoom to 100%. With the insertion point inside the text box, format it as follows:

   a. Click the Font Size arrow (Home tab | Font group) and then click 20 in the Font Size gallery.

   b. Click the Paragraph Settings Dialog Box Launcher (Home tab | Paragraph group) to display the Paragraph dialog box. If necessary, click the Indents and Spacing tab.

   c. If necessary, select the text in the Between lines box, and type **1.19sp** to enter the line spacing.

   d. Select the text in the After paragraphs text box. Type **0** to change the line spacing after each paragraph. Click the OK button (Paragraph dialog box) to save the settings.

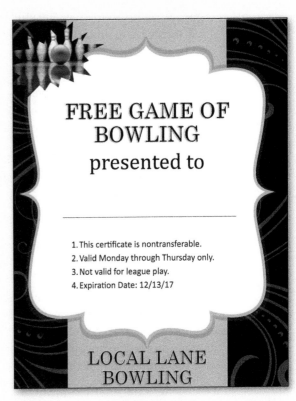

Figure 5–80

Continued >

In the Labs *continued*

4. Click the Numbering arrow (Home tab | Paragraph group) and then click '1. 2. 3.' in the Numbering gallery to choose the formatting. Type the following text (Publisher will apply the transferable numbers):

   `This certificate is nontransferable.`

   `Valid Monday through Thursday only.`

   `Not valid for league play.`

   `Expiration Date: 12/13/17`

5. Create a text box and use the format painter as follows:

   a. Draw a text box across the bottom of the screen in the yellow portion below the scalloped frame. Type **Local Lane Bowling** to enter the text.

   b. If instructed to do so, change the name of the bowling alley to the name of your favorite bowling alley or video arcade.

   c. Select the text, Free Game, and then click the Format Painter button (Home tab | Clipboard group). Drag through the text, Local Lane Bowling, with the format painter on.

   d. Right-click the text and then click Best Fit on the shortcut menu.

6. To create a graphic:

   a. Insert the picture, Lab 5–2 Bowling, and move it to the scratch area. Use the Measurement task pane to resize the picture to approximately 3 × 2.25 inches.

   b. Click the Crop button (Picture Tools Format tab | Crop group) and use the crop handles to remove most of the black around the edge of the picture. Do not crop the bowling ball, pins, or reflection. Deselect the picture.

   c. Click the Crop arrow (Picture Tools Format tab | Crop group) and then point to 'Crop to Shape' on the Crop menu. When Publisher displays the gallery, click the Explosion 2 shape in the Stars and Banners area.

   d. Move the graphic to the upper-left corner of the certificate.

7. Change the publication properties, as specified by your instructor. Save the publication with the file name, Lab 5–2 Bowling Certificate Complete.

8. Submit the publication in the format specified by your instructor, and exit Publisher.

9. ✷ How would you improve this publication to make it more user-friendly? How would you instruct the user of your publication to fill in the person's name? Do you think some text such as, <Type Name Here>, would be appropriate? Why or why not?

Lab 3: **Consider This: Your Turn**

Creating a New Style

Problem: The Baker's Dozen donut shop would like you to create a text style that employees can import into all of their current publications.

Perform the following tasks:

Part 1: Run Publisher. Using a blank page, create a text box with the name of the donut shop as text. Create a new style using the Harlow Solid Italic font or a decorative italic font on your computer. Use a 48-point, bright red font. Save the style with the name, Baker's Dozen. Create another text box with your name in it, and apply the new style. Embed all possible fonts and then save the publication for the donut shop to use. Print a copy for your instructor.

Part 2: ✷ Can you think of several companies that have distinct formatting for the business name? How is branding the text different from branding a logo? Search the web for third-party providers of specific font styles, such as the James Bond font or the IBM font. Write a brief report on your findings. Include information about the vendor, pricing, downloading, and copyrights.

6 | Working with Publisher Tables

Objectives

You will have mastered the material in this module when you can:

- Change page orientation
- Apply shape effects
- Create tables and enter data
- Apply table formats
- Select table rows, columns, and cells
- Insert and delete rows and columns in tables
- Merge, split, and divide cells diagonally
- Resize and align tables and cells

- Format tables with borders
- Create a multipage calendar
- Use the Master Page
- Edit BorderArt
- Embed an Excel table in a Publisher publication
- Use Excel tools on the Publisher ribbon to format a table

Introduction

A table is a good way to present a large amount of data in a small, organized space. Tabular data, or data that can be organized into related groups and subgroups, is presented best in rows and columns with appropriate headings. A well-defined, descriptive table will have three general characteristics. First, the data will be meaningful; it will relate closely to the purpose of the publication. The data in a table will support or provide evidence of any analyses or conclusions. Second, a table will be unambiguous — it will have clear labels, titles, headings, legends, or footnotes. The purpose of the table will be clear, and the scale will be well defined. Third, a table should be efficient so that the reader quickly can understand the data and its presentation, in order to draw conclusions and apply the data to a particular situation. An efficient table is formatted appropriately and read quickly.

While many tables are created using Microsoft Excel, Publisher tables are formatted easily and fit well in many kinds of publications. Readers can understand the purpose of a publication table and promptly retrieve the important information. As you also will learn in this module, many of Excel's features can be embedded for use in Publisher tables.

Project — Table, Calendar, and Excel Functionality

The decision to use a table in a publication is based on a need to organize a large amount of information in an easily recognizable format and to reduce the amount of text necessary to explain the situation. From tables of contents to bank rate tables to timetables, you may need to display text, graphics, dates, or color in many different tabular ways. Publisher allows you to create tables from scratch or use tables that already are organized for specific purposes.

In this project, you will create three different publications that incorporate tables for the Harris College Residential Services (HCRS) department, as shown in Figure 6–1. A four-year college with a diverse set of majors and programs, the mascot is the Greyhound, and the college colors are crimson and gray. With several dormitories and commuting students, they offer a variety of meal plans and ways to spend Greyhound dollars.

A WordArt object with shape effects will serve as a common element across publications. A table (Figure 6–1a) will show students and staff where they can use their prepaid cards. An academic calendar (Figure 6–1b) will present each month as a table. Finally, a letter to the food service managers (Figure 6–1c) will contain an embedded table with totals and formatting.

The following roadmap identifies general activities you will perform as you progress through this module:

1. EMPLOY REUSABLE PARTS, such as business information sets, building blocks, and logos.

2. APPLY SHAPE EFFECTS, such as glows, reflections, and 3-D effects.

3. INSERT and FORMAT TABLES.

4. CREATE a CALENDAR.

5. USE MASTER PAGES to insert objects that will appear on every page.

6. ADD BORDERART to help outline pages and tables.

7. EMBED or link a TABLE for advanced formatting.

8. USE EXCEL FUNCTIONALITY WITHIN PUBLISHER.

Reusable Parts

The manager at HCRS wants several publications, including a list of prepaid card options, a publicity calendar, and a letter to the food service managers. Certain objects will be repeated in all publications, including the color and font scheme, the business information set, and the name of the company in a WordArt object to serve as a recognizable branding of the school.

Harris College

Greyhound Dollars

Where

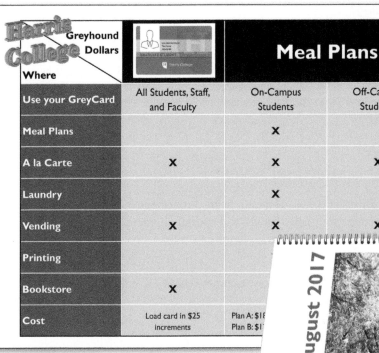

Meal Plans

Use your GreyCard	All Students, Staff, and Faculty	On-Campus Students	Off-Campus Students
Meal Plans		X	
A la Carte	X	X	X
Laundry		X	
Vending	X	X	X
Printing			
Bookstore	X		
Cost	Load card in $25 increments	Plan A: $18 Plan B: $1	

a) Formatted Table

b) Calendar with Graphics

Harris College

632 Michigan Street
Suite 501
Dugan, NH 03033

Phone: 603-555-3123
Fax: 603-555-3125
Email: hcrs@harrisc.edu

October 16, 2017

To All Managers:

Below you will see the Fall 2017 Meal Plan Enrollments. Note that we have 4 percent more students on meal plans than last year.

Please bring your comments to our next meeting on Oct. 23, 2017 at 10:00 a.m. in the HCRS conference room. I will have a copy of our new academic calendar to show you!

Sincerely,

Fredrick Brewster

HCRS Manager

HCRS Fall 2017 Meal Plan Enrollments	Reed Suites	Neely Hall	Wright Quad	Total
Meal Plan A	$ 185,000.00	$ 340,400.00	$ 606,800.00	$ 1,132,200.00
Meal Plan B	62,500.00	62,500.00	62,500.00	187,500.00
Total	$ 247,500.00	$ 402,900.00	$ 669,300.00	$ 1,319,700.00
Resident Count	150	276	492	918

c) Letter with Embedded Table

Figure 6–1

CONSIDER THIS

Why should I create reusable objects for branding?

Creating reusable components, such as business sets, logos, and a stylistic company name, helps create a positive perception of a company and creates identifiable branding. A brand identity should be communicated in multiple ways with frequency and consistency throughout the life of a business. Sometimes, a brand is as simple as golden arches; other times, it is a stylistic font that identifies a popular soda, no matter what the language. Developing and marketing a brand takes time and research. When desktop publishers are asked to help with brand recognition, they can suggest reusable colors, fonts, schemes, logos, business information sets, graphics, and other tools to assist the company in creating a customer-friendly, consistent brand.

To Select a Blank Publication and Adjust Settings

The following steps select an 8.5 × 11″ blank print publication, adjust workspace settings, such as the Page Navigation pane display and special characters, and choose schemes that will apply to the table for Harris College.

1. Run Publisher.

2. Click the Blank 8.5 × 11″ thumbnail in the New template gallery to create a blank publication in the Publisher window.

3. Collapse the Page Navigation pane.

4. If it is not selected already, click the Special Characters button (Home tab | Paragraph group) to display formatting marks.

5. Display the Page Design tab.

6. Click the Equity color scheme (Page Design tab | Schemes group) to choose a color scheme.

7. Click the Scheme Fonts button (Page Design tab | Schemes group) and then click Solstice to choose a font scheme.

To Change the Page Orientation

1 EMPLOY REUSABLE PARTS | 2 APPLY SHAPE EFFECTS | 3 INSERT & FORMAT TABLES | 4 CREATE CALENDAR
5 USE MASTER PAGES | 6 ADD BORDERART | 7 EMBED TABLE | 8 USE EXCEL FUNCTIONALITY

When a publication is in **portrait orientation**, the short edge of the paper is the top of the publication. You can instruct Publisher to lay out a publication in **landscape orientation**, so that the long edge of the paper is the top of the publication. The following steps change the page orientation of the publication from portrait to landscape.

1

• Click the 'Change Page Orientation' button (Page Design tab | Page Setup group) to display the Change Page Orientation menu (Figure 6–2).

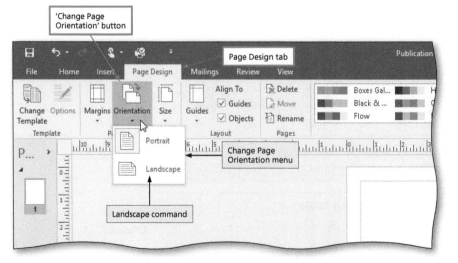

Figure 6–2

2

- Click Landscape on the Page Orientation menu to change the orientation of the page (Figure 6–3).

Q&A Could I have chosen a template with landscape orientation?
Yes, if you know in advance that you want landscape orientation, choose one of the landscape orientation templates. If you already have created objects, use the 'Change Page Orientation' button (Page Design tab | Page Setup group).

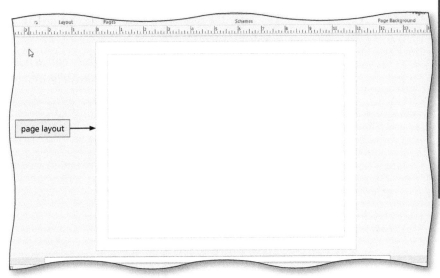

Figure 6–3

Creating a Business Information Set

Table 6–1 displays the data for each of the fields in the business information set that you will create in this project. Because you will be creating a graphical representation for the organization name/logo, you will leave those fields blank.

Table 6–1 Data for Business Information Fields	
Fields	**Data**
Individual name	Fredrick Brewster
Job position or title	HCRS Manager
Organization name	<none>
Address	632 Michigan Street Suite 501 Dugan, NH 03033
Phone, fax, and e-mail	Phone: 603-555-3123 Fax: 603-555-3125 Email: hcrs@harrisc.edu
Tagline or motto	Impacting the Future
Logo	<none>
Business Information set name	HCRS

To Create a Business Information Set

The following steps create a business information set for HCRS, which will be used in multiple publications.

1 Display the Insert tab.

2 Click the Business Information button (Insert tab | Text group) to display the Business Information menu.

3 Click 'Edit Business Information' on the Business Information menu. If Publisher displays the Business Information dialog box, click the New button (Business Information dialog box) to display the Create New Business Information Set dialog box.

④ Enter the data from Table 6–1, pressing the TAB key to advance from one field to the next (Figure 6–4).

⑤ Click the Save button (Create New Business Information Set dialog box).

⑥ Click the Update Publication button (Business Information dialog box).

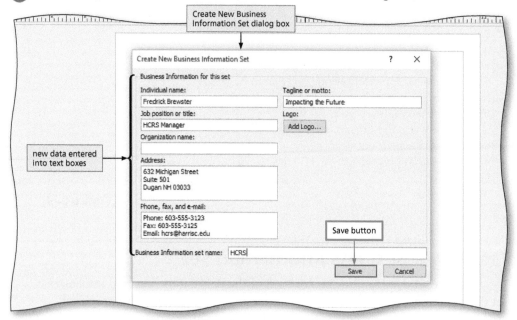

Figure 6–4

To Insert and Format a WordArt Object

The following steps insert a WordArt object to use as a brand.

① Zoom to 100% and, if necessary, display the Insert tab.

② Click the Insert WordArt button (Insert tab | Text group) to display the WordArt gallery.

③ Click the 'Fill - None, Outline - Red' preview in the Plain WordArt Styles area of the WordArt gallery to select it.

④ In the Text text box (Edit WordArt Text dialog box), type **Harris** and then press the ENTER key. Type **College** to finish the text.

⑤ Click the Font arrow (Edit WordArt Text dialog box) and then click Century Schoolbook or a similar font.

⑥ If necessary, click the Size arrow (Edit WordArt Text dialog box) and then click 36 to choose a 36-point font size.

⑦ Click the OK button (Edit WordArt Text dialog box) to close the dialog box and insert the WordArt object.

⑧ Click the Shape Fill arrow (WordArt Tools Format tab | WordArt Styles) and then click 'Accent 5 (White), Darker 25%' (eighth column, fourth row) to fill the WordArt with a gray color.

⑨ Click the Shape Outline arrow (WordArt Tools Format tab | WordArt Styles group) and then click Red in the Standard Colors area of the color palette to outline the WordArt with a red color.

⑩ Click the Shape Outline arrow (WordArt Tools Format tab | WordArt Styles group), point to Weight in the Shape Outline gallery to display the Weight submenu, and then click 2¼ pt on the Weight submenu to change the outline weight (Figure 6–5).

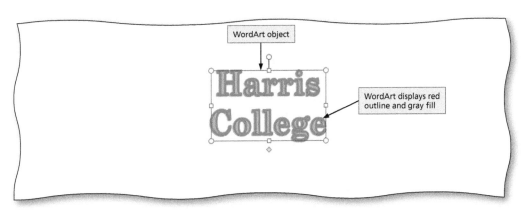

Figure 6-5

To Edit WordArt Alignment

1 EMPLOY REUSABLE PARTS | 2 APPLY SHAPE EFFECTS | 3 INSERT & FORMAT TABLES | 4 CREATE CALENDAR
5 USE MASTER PAGES | 6 ADD BORDERART | 7 EMBED TABLE | 8 USE EXCEL FUNCTIONALITY

Recall that in word processing applications, the right, center, and left alignment tools always refer to the current margins of the page. In desktop publication applications, the alignment tools refer to the object with which you are working. *Why? Each object has its own margins, independent from the page margins.* The following steps change the WordArt alignment from center to left align.

- If necessary, select the WordArt object and display the WordArt Tools Format tab.

- Click the Align Text button (WordArt Tools Format tab | Text group) to display the Align Text gallery (Figure 6-6).

Experiment

- Point to each of the alignments in the Align Text gallery and watch the WordArt change.

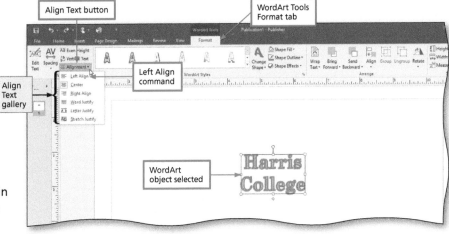

Figure 6-6

- Click Left Align in the Align Text gallery to change how Publisher aligns the object (Figure 6-7).

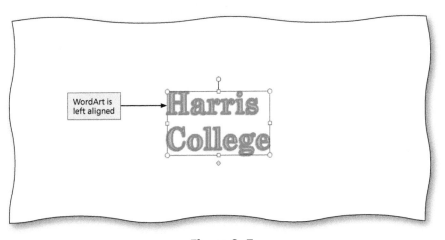

Figure 6-7

BTW
WordArt
Design experts recommend using WordArt sparingly. As a rule, use WordArt as decoration rather than to convey information. Use only one WordArt object per publication.

Shape Effects

Shape effects change the design and style of a shape or WordArt and other objects. Recall that text effects were used in a previous module to fill and outline text. Shape effects are applied in a similar way. Many new shape effects are available in Publisher 2016, including advanced shadows, reflections, glow, soft edges, bevels, and 3-D rotations, as shown in Table 6–2.

Table 6–2 Shape Effects			
Effect	**Description**	**Gallery Options**	**Adjustable Settings**
Shadow	A semitransparent shading is added to the shape to create the illusion of a shadow, giving the shape depth.	Outer Inner Perspective	Transparency Size Blur Angle Distance
Reflection	A replicated shadow with matching borders is added to the shape to create the appearance of a reflection.	Variations	Transparency Size Blur Distance
Glow	Color and shading is added around all sides of the shape so it seems to glow for decorative emphasis.	Glow Variations	Color Size Transparency
Soft Edges	Blurs the edges of a shape inward a certain amount to make the border less harsh.	point values	Size
Bevel	Shading and artificial shadows are used to emulate a 3-D beveled edge or contour, framing the shape.	Bevel	Top Bottom Depth Contour Material Lighting
3-D Rotation	Rotates and angles shape, backfilling with a shadow effect to apply parallel, perspective, and oblique 3-D effects.	Parallel Perspective	X Rotation Y Rotation Perspective

BTW
The Ribbon and Screen Resolution
Publisher may change how the groups and buttons within the groups appear on the ribbon, depending on the computer or mobile device's screen resolution. Thus, your ribbon may look different from the ones in this book if you are using a screen resolution other than 1366 x 768.

A Shape Effects button is available on both the Drawing Tools Format tab and the WordArt Tools Format tab. The Picture Tools Format tab displays a similar Picture Effects button. Each button displays a gallery and, when chosen, a dialog box or task pane with adjustable settings. You will use the 3-D Rotation tool in the next series of steps to add a 3-D effect to the WordArt.

To Apply a Shape Effect

1 EMPLOY REUSABLE PARTS | 2 APPLY SHAPE EFFECTS | 3 INSERT & FORMAT TABLES | 4 CREATE CALENDAR
5 USE MASTER PAGES | 6 ADD BORDERART | 7 EMBED TABLE | 8 USE EXCEL FUNCTIONALITY

The following steps format the WordArt with the 3-D Rotation shape effect. **Why?** *The 3-D effect provides the perception of depth and adds interest to the publication.*

• Scroll the workspace to the right so that objects on the screen will be visible when the gallery is open in the next step.

- If necessary, select the shape (in this case, the WordArt object) and then click the Shape Effects button (WordArt Tools Format tab | WordArt Styles group) to display the Shape Effects gallery (Figure 6–8).

 Experiment

- One at a time, click each of the commands and view the choices in each gallery.

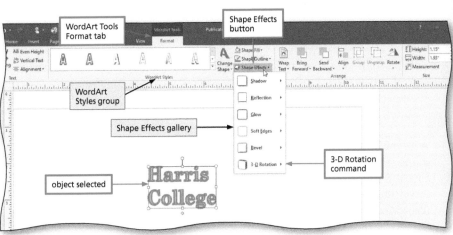

Figure 6–8

2

- Point to the desired shape effect (in this case, 3-D Rotation) to display the gallery (Figure 6–9).

 Experiment

- If you are using a mouse, point to various previews in the gallery and watch the WordArt change with live preview.

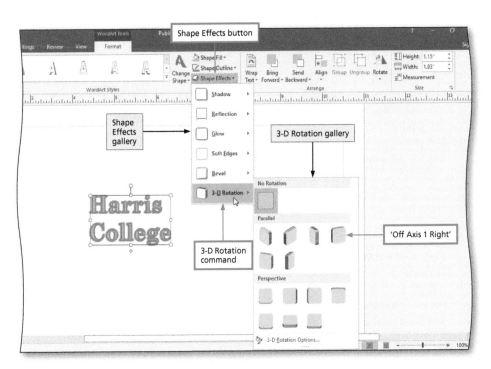

Figure 6–9

3

- Click 'Off Axis 1 Right' in the 3-D Rotation gallery to format the shape (Figure 6–10).

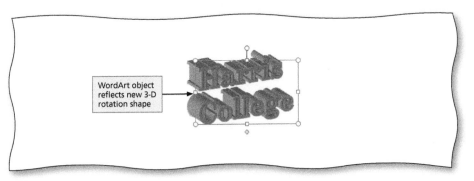

Figure 6–10

Other Ways

1. Click Format WordArt Dialog Box Launcher (WordArt Tools Format tab | WordArt Styles group), click Shape Effects button (Colors and Lines tab) (Format Shape dialog box), click desired effect, click Presets button, click desired thumbnail, click OK button (Format Shape dialog box), click OK button (Format Object dialog box)

To Fine-Tune a Shape Effect

The following steps make changes to the shape effect by adjusting specific settings. *Why? In this case, you have decided that the 3-D effect is too thick and you want to reduce its depth.*

1

- With the WordArt shape still selected, click the Shape Effects button (WordArt Tools Format tab | WordArt Styles group) to display the Shape Effects gallery.

- Point to 3-D Rotation to display its gallery (Figure 6–11).

Q&A What is the difference between Parallel and Perspective rotations in the gallery?

Parallel rotations adjust from side to side. Perspective rotations adjust from top to bottom.

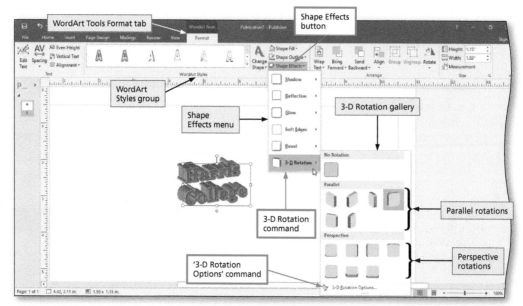

Figure 6–11

2

- Click '3-D Rotation Options' in the gallery to display the Format Shape dialog box for this shape.

- If necessary, drag the title bar of the dialog box to position it so that it does not cover the WordArt shape (Figure 6–12).

Experiment

- Scroll through the choices in the Format Shape dialog box and click various effects to look at their settings.

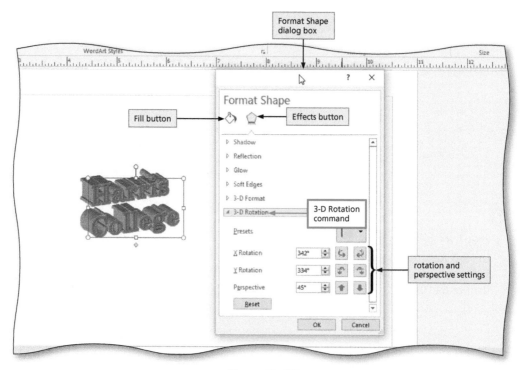

Figure 6–12

Q&A What does the Fill button do at the top of the Format Shape dialog box?

The Fill button causes Fill settings to appear. The default value is a gray, solid fill for the 3-D effect. You can change the color, type of fill, and apply gradients.

3

- Click 3-D Format (Format Shape dialog box) to display the settings.

- Select the text in the Depth Size text box and then type 12 to enter a value smaller than the default setting (Figure 6–13).

Q&A What does a smaller value do to the shape?
The smaller the value, the thinner the shadowing behind the object, creating the illusion of a more narrow 3-D depth.

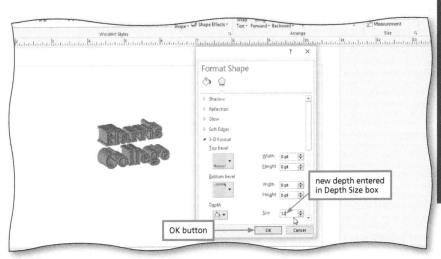

Figure 6–13

4

- Click the OK button (Format Shape dialog box) to change the depth of the 3-D shape (Figure 6–14).

Q&A What other options might I change when using a 3-D Rotation shape effect?
In the 3-D rotation area, the X Rotation text box changes the width of the rotation; the Y Rotation text box changes the height of the rotation. The Perspective option makes a change only if you chose one of the perspective preset styles.

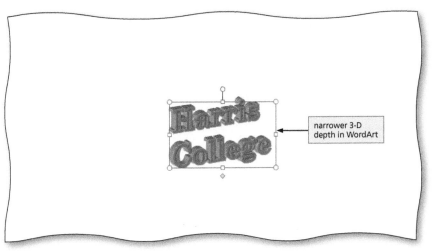

Figure 6–14

Other Ways

1. Click Format WordArt Dialog Box Launcher (WordArt Tools Format tab | WordArt Styles group), click Shape Effects button (Colors and Lines tab) (Format Shape dialog box), click desired effect, choose desired settings, click OK button (Format Shape dialog box), click OK button (Format Object dialog box)

To Add an Object to the Building Block Library

The following steps add the formatted WordArt object to the Building Block library, so that you can use it in multiple publications.

1 Right-click the WordArt object to display the shortcut menu and then click 'Save as Building Block' on the shortcut menu to display the Create New Building Block dialog box.

2 Type **Harris College** to replace the text in the Title text box.

3 Press the TAB key to move to the Description text box and then type **WordArt brand to use in all publications** to insert a description.

4 Click the Keywords text box and then type **logo, brand, Harris** to enter keywords.

5 Accept all other default settings and then click the OK button (Create New Building Block dialog box) to close the dialog box.

6 To prepare for inserting a table on the page, drag the WordArt object to the scratch area.

7 Save the publication on your desired save location using the file name, Greyhound Dollars Table.

When should you use a table?
Use tables to present numeric and tabular information in an easy-to-digest format. Work with the customer to design a table that is clear and concise. Make sure the overall heading and the row and column headings employ standard wording and measurements. Format the table for easy reading. Work with the customer to design a table that is clear and concise. Use recognizable labels for each row and column. Use standard scales and measures. Make sure the reader does not have to spend a lot of time to identify the purpose of the table and grasp the data they are seeking. Use borders, colors, fonts, and alignment to delineate each row and/or column.

Using Tables

BTW
Touch Screen Differences
The Office and Windows interfaces may vary if you are using a touch screen. For this reason, you might notice that the function or appearance of your touch screen differs slightly from this module's presentation.

The next step in creating the publication is to place a table listing the locations for card use and people (shown in Figure 6–1a). A Publisher **table** is a collection of contiguous text boxes that are displayed in rows and columns. The intersection of a row and a column is called a **cell**, and cells are filled with text or graphical data. Within a table, you easily can rearrange rows and columns, change column widths and row heights, merge or divide cells, and insert diagonal lines. You can format the cells to give the table a professional appearance, using elements such as preset formats, shading, and cell diagonals. You also can edit the inner gridlines and outer border of a table. For these reasons, many Publisher users create tables rather than using large text boxes with tabbed columns. Tables allow you to enter data in columns as you would for a schedule, price list, resume, or table of contents.

The first step in creating a table is to insert an empty table in the publication. When inserting a table, you must specify the number of columns and rows you expect to use. The number of columns and rows is called the **dimension** of the table. In Publisher, the first number in a dimension is the number of columns, and the second is the number of rows. For example, in Publisher, a 2 × 1 table (pronounced "two by one") consists of two columns and one row.

To Insert an Empty Table

1 EMPLOY REUSABLE PARTS | 2 APPLY SHAPE EFFECTS | 3 INSERT & FORMAT TABLES | 4 CREATE CALENDAR
5 USE MASTER PAGES | 6 ADD BORDERART | 7 EMBED TABLE | 8 USE EXCEL FUNCTIONALITY

When you click the 'Add a Table' button (Insert tab | Tables group), Publisher presents a grid of rows and columns from which you can choose, as well as the Insert Table command. The following steps insert an empty table with five columns and eight rows. **Why?** *The numbers are an estimate of how many you will need. If necessary, you can add more columns and insert more rows after creating the table.*

1

- Display the View tab and then click the Whole Page button (View tab | Zoom group) to display the entire page.

- Display the Insert tab.

- Click the 'Add a Table' button (Insert tab | Tables group) to display the Add a Table gallery (Figure 6–15).

Q&A What does Publisher show in the Add a Table gallery?
The gallery displays a grid of clickable squares. Each square represents the number of columns and rows.

Where will the table be inserted?
Publisher inserts the table in the center of the workspace window.

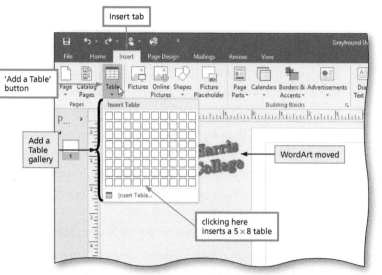

Figure 6–15

Experiment

- If using a mouse, point to various cells on the grid to see a preview of various table dimensions in the publication window.

2

- In the grid, click the '5 × 8' cell to create a table with five columns and eight rows as shown in Figure 6–16.

Q&A What are the small symbols in the table cells?

Each table cell has an **end-of-cell mark,** which is a formatting mark that assists you with selecting and formatting cells. Recall that formatting marks do not print on a hard copy. The end-of-cell marks currently are left-aligned, that is, positioned at the left edge of each cell.

Other Ways

1. Click 'Add a Table' button (Insert tab | Tables group), click Insert Table in Add a Table gallery, enter number of columns and rows (Create Table dialog box), click OK button

---

To Apply a Table Format

1 EMPLOY REUSABLE PARTS | 2 APPLY SHAPE EFFECTS | 3 INSERT & FORMAT TABLES | 4 CREATE CALENDAR
5 USE MASTER PAGES | 6 ADD BORDERART | 7 EMBED TABLE | 8 USE EXCEL FUNCTIONALITY

You may have noticed that the ribbon now displays two new tabs. *Why? When working with tables, the Table Tools Layout tab offers buttons and commands that help you in inserting, deleting, merging, and aligning rows, columns, and cells; the Table Tools Design tab provides formatting, borders, and alignment options.*

The Table Format gallery (Table Tools Design tab | Table Formats group) allows you to format a table with a variety of colors and shading. The following steps apply a table format to the table in the publication.

1

- If necessary, click the table to select it and then click the Table Tools Design tab (Figure 6–16).

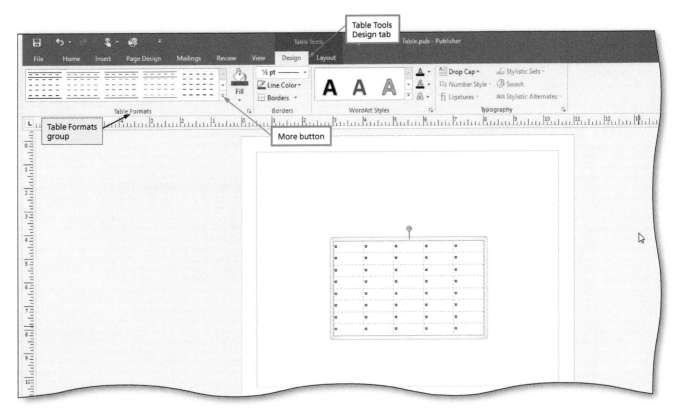

Figure 6–16

2

• Click the More button in the Table Formats gallery (Table Tools Design tab | Table Formats group) to expand the gallery (Figure 6–17).

Q&A My gallery is different. Did I do something wrong?
No. Depending on your screen resolution, your gallery choices may differ.

🔍 **Experiment**

• If you are using a mouse, point to various table styles in the Table Formats gallery and watch the format of the table change in the publication window.

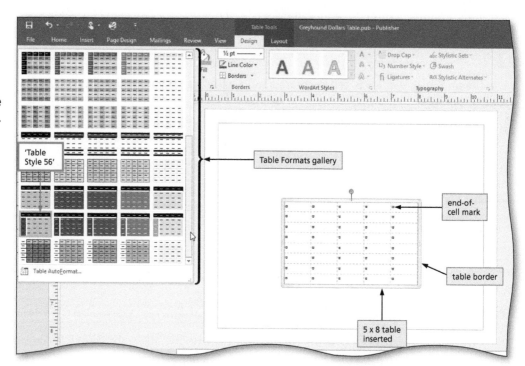

Figure 6–17

3

• Click 'Table Style 56' in the Table Format gallery to apply the selected style to the table (Figure 6–18).

Q&A How does the table style adjust when I add rows and columns?
Some table styles replicate the pattern correctly when you add a column, but do not alternate colors when you add a row. If you add rows or columns, you may need to reapply the table style.

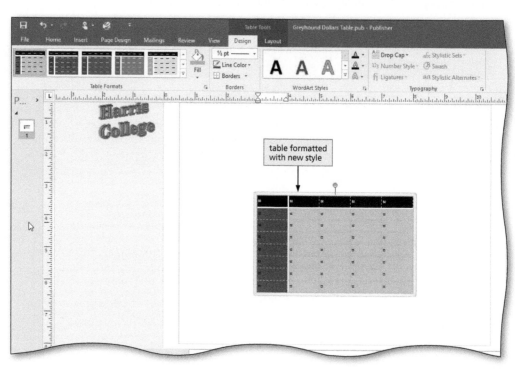

Figure 6–18

Other Ways

1. Click More button in Table Formats gallery (Table Tools Design tab | Table Formats group), click Table AutoFormat, select table format, click OK button (Auto Format dialog box)

Selecting Table Contents

When working with tables, you may need to select the contents of cells, rows, columns, or the entire table. Table 6–3 identifies ways to select various items in a table.

Table 6–3 Selecting Items in a Table	
Item to Select	**Action**
Cell	If you are using a mouse, point to the upper-left edge of the cell and click when the pointer changes to a small, solid, upward-angled pointing arrow. Or, position the insertion point in the cell, click the Select Table button (Table Tools Layout tab | Table group), and then click Select Cell in the Select Table gallery. Or, right-click the cell, point to Select on the shortcut menu, click Select Cell on the Select submenu.
Column	If you are using a mouse, point above the column and click when the mouse pointer changes to a small, solid, downward-pointing arrow. Or, position the insertion point in the column, click the Select Table button (Table Tools Layout tab | Table group), and then click Select Column in the Select Table gallery. Or, right-click the column, point to Select on the shortcut menu, click Select Column on the Select submenu.
Row	If you are using a mouse, point to the left of the row and click when the pointer changes to a right-pointing block arrow. Or, position the insertion point in the row, click the Select Table button (Table Tools Layout tab | Table group), and then click Select Row in the Select Table gallery. Or, right-click the row, point to Select on the shortcut menu, click Select Row on the Select submenu.
Multiple cells, rows, or columns adjacent to one another	Drag through cells, rows, or columns. Or, select first cell and then hold down the SHIFT key while selecting the next cell, row, or column.
Next cell	Press the TAB key.
Previous cell	Press SHIFT+TAB.
Table	Click somewhere in the table, click the Select Table button (Table Tools Layout tab | Table group), and then click Select Table on the Select Table gallery. Or right-click the table, point to Select on the shortcut menu, click Select Table on the Select submenu.

To Delete a Column

1 EMPLOY REUSABLE PARTS | 2 APPLY SHAPE EFFECTS | 3 INSERT & FORMAT TABLES | **4 CREATE CALENDAR**
5 USE MASTER PAGES | 6 ADD BORDERART | 7 EMBED TABLE | 8 USE EXCEL FUNCTIONALITY

The following steps delete the fifth column. *Why? You previously estimated how many columns you would need. You now realize that you need only four columns.* Deleting a column also deletes any text in the column cells.

- If necessary, position the insertion point anywhere in the column that you wish to delete (in this case, column five).
- Click Table Tools Layout on the ribbon to display the Table Tools Layout tab.

- Click the 'Delete Rows or Columns' button (Table Tools Layout tab | Rows & Columns group) to display the Delete Rows or Columns menu (Figure 6–19).

Q&A

How would I delete just the data in the column?

Drag to select the cells in the column and then press the DELETE key. Or, right-click the selection and then click Delete Text on the shortcut menu.

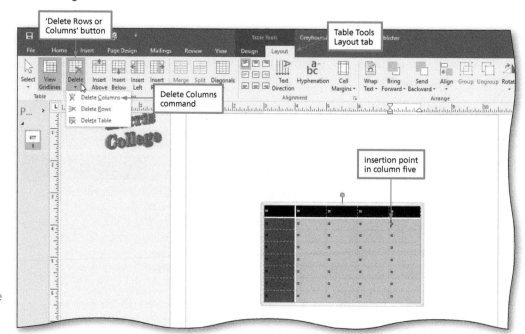

Figure 6–19

 ②

- Click Delete Columns on the Delete Rows or Columns menu to delete the current column (Figure 6–20).

Q&A

How would I delete more than one column?

You could delete them one at a time, or select multiple cells, rows, and columns. Once they are selected, you use the 'Delete Rows or Columns' button to delete them.

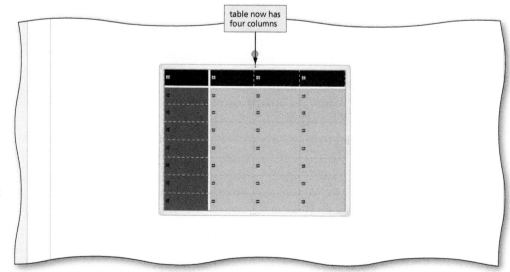

Figure 6–20

Other Ways

1. Right-click cell, point to Delete on shortcut menu, click Delete Columns (Delete submenu)

TO DELETE A ROW

If you wanted to delete a row in a table rather than a column, you would perform the following steps.

1. Position the insertion point in the row that you want to delete.
2. Click the 'Delete Rows or Columns' button (Table Tools Layout tab | Rows & Columns group) and then click Delete Rows; or, right-click cell, point to Delete on the shortcut menu, and then click Delete Rows on the Delete submenu.

To Insert Rows

The next step is to insert two new rows. You can insert a row at the end of a table by positioning the insertion point in the bottom-right corner cell and then pressing the TAB key. You cannot use the TAB key to insert a row at the beginning or middle of a table. Instead, you use the 'Insert Rows Above' or 'Insert Rows Below' buttons. Where you place the insertion point is important before making a decision to insert above or below the current location. *Why? A new row takes on the formatting of the row that contains the insertion point.* For example, you might want to insert a new row in the Greyhound Dollars table between the first and second rows. If you place the insertion point in row 1 and choose to insert below, the new row will be formatted as a header row (in this instance, with a black background and white text). If you place the insertion point in row 2 and choose to insert above, the new row will be formatted to match the data cells (in this case, with a light gray background and black text).

The following steps insert two new rows in the table using the ribbon.

1

- Position the pointer somewhere in the first row of the table, because you want to insert a row above this row.

- Click the 'Insert Rows Above' button (Table Tools Layout tab | Rows & Columns group) to add a new heading row.

- Click elsewhere in the table to remove the selection of the new row (Figure 6–21).

Experiment

- On the Table Tools Layout tab, point to each of the buttons in the Rows & Columns group to view the ScreenTips. In addition, look at the pictures on the buttons themselves, which will help you identify each function.

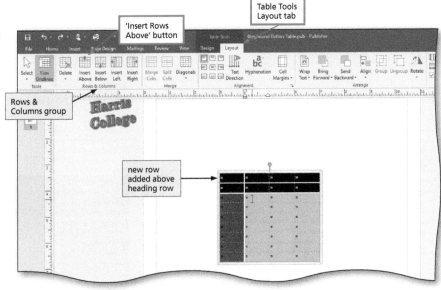

Figure 6–21

2

- Click in the last row of the table and then click the 'Insert Rows Below' button (Table Tools Layout tab | Rows & Columns group) to insert a similarly styled detail row.

- Click elsewhere in the table to remove the selection of the new row (Figure 6–22).

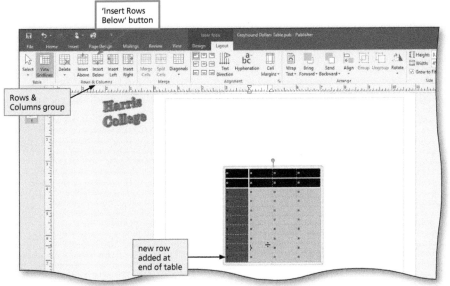

Figure 6–22

Other Ways

1. Right-click row, click Insert on shortcut menu, click appropriate Insert command

To Insert a Column

If you wanted to insert a column in a table rather than a row, you would perform the following steps.

1. Position the insertion point in the column to the left or right of where you want to insert the column.

2. Click the 'Insert Columns to the Left' button (Table Tools Layout tab | Rows & Columns group) to insert a column to the left of the current column, or click the 'Insert Columns to the Right' button (Table Tools Layout tab | Rows & Columns group) to insert a column to the right of the current column. Or, you could right-click the column, point to Insert on the shortcut menu, and then click Insert Left or Insert Right on the Insert submenu.

To Resize the Table

1 EMPLOY REUSABLE PARTS | 2 APPLY SHAPE EFFECTS | 3 INSERT & FORMAT TABLES | **4 CREATE CALENDAR**
5 USE MASTER PAGES | 6 ADD BORDERART | 7 EMBED TABLE | 8 USE EXCEL FUNCTIONALITY

The following step resizes the table. *Why? Making the table as large as possible allows for more information in each of the cells and accommodates larger font sizes that are appropriate for publications intended for posting.*

- Drag the border of the table up and left, until it snaps to the upper-left corner margins.

- Using the mouse, point to the lower-right corner of the table border. When the pointer changes to a double-headed arrow, drag down and to the right until the table border snaps to the lower-right corner margin guides.

- Zoom to approximately 60% (Figure 6–23).

Q&A
What do I do if I have no mouse?
You can resize the table by using the Measurement toolbar. Tap the Object Size button on the status bar to display the Measurement task pane and then enter 10" and 7.5" in the Width and Height text boxes, respectively.

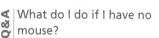

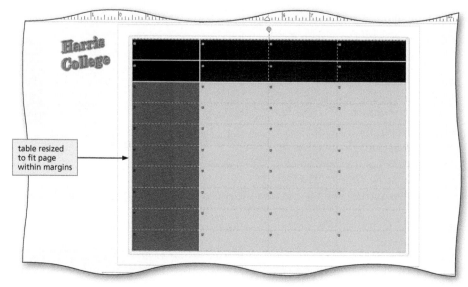

Figure 6–23

Other Ways

1. Right-click table, click Format Table on shortcut menu, enter size of table in Size and rotate area on Size tab (Format Table dialog box), click OK button

To Merge Cells

1 EMPLOY REUSABLE PARTS | 2 APPLY SHAPE EFFECTS | 3 INSERT & FORMAT TABLES | **4 CREATE CALENDAR**
5 USE MASTER PAGES | 6 ADD BORDERART | 7 EMBED TABLE | 8 USE EXCEL FUNCTIONALITY

The cells in the heading area need to be changed in order to allow the desired content, in a process called merging. *Why? The area will hold the table title and a graphic.* The following steps merge multiple cells into a single cell.

1

- Drag to select the third and fourth cells in rows 1 and 2 (Figure 6–24).

Q&A Why did the cells turn white?

In Publisher, the selection highlight reverses the color scheme. Because the cells have a black background, the selection appears white.

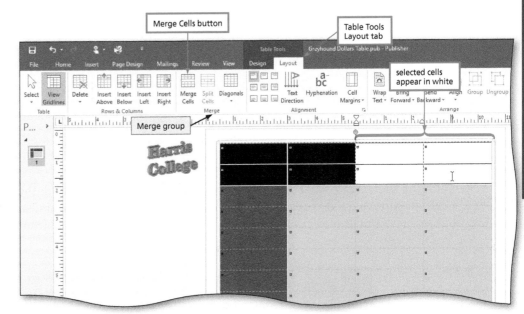

Figure 6–24

2

- Click the Merge Cells button (Table Tools Layout tab | Merge group) to merge the four cells into one cell.

- Click elsewhere in the table to view the merged cells (Figure 6–25).

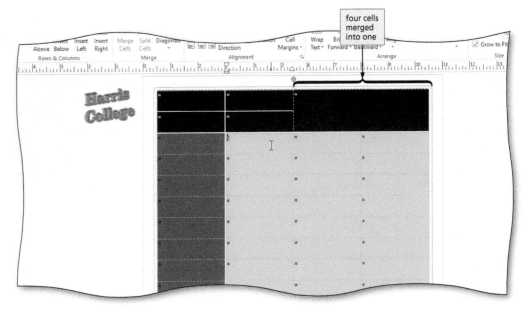

Figure 6–25

3

- Drag to select the first and second cell in column 1.

- Click the Merge Cells button (Table Tools Layout tab | Merge group) to merge the two cells into one cell.

- Repeat the process to merge the first and second cell in column 2.

- Click elsewhere in the table to view the merged cell (Figure 6–26).

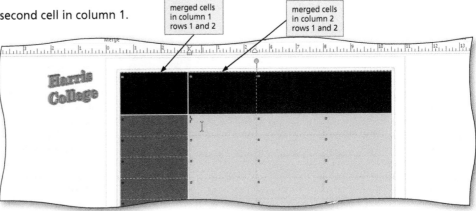

Figure 6–26

TO SPLIT CELLS

Sometimes, you may want to split a merged cell back into multiple cells. If you wanted to split cells, you would perform the following steps.

1. Position the insertion point in the cell to split.
2. Click the Split Cells button (Table Tools Layout tab | Merge group).

To Create a Cell Diagonal

The following steps create a cell diagonal to accommodate a heading for both the column and row in the same cell. A **cell diagonal** is a line that splits the cell diagonally, creating two triangular text boxes. Commonly used for split headings or multiple entries per cell, the cell diagonal can be slanted from either corner.

- Click the merged cell in column 1, row 1 of the table.

- If necessary, display the Table Tools Layout tab.

- Click the Diagonals button (Table Tools Layout tab | Merge group) to display the Diagonals menu (Figure 6–27).

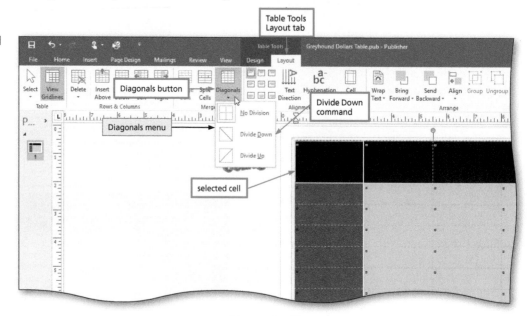

Figure 6–27

- Click Divide Down on the Diagonals menu to create a diagonal in the cell.

- Click outside the table to deselect the cell (Figure 6–28).

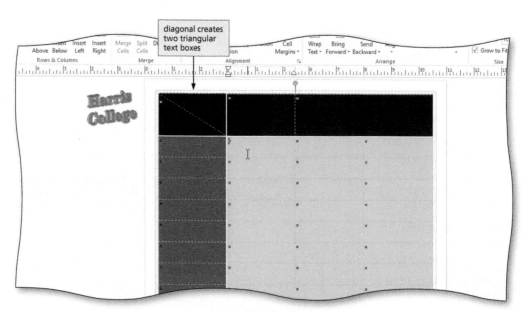

Figure 6–28

To Remove a Diagonal

Sometimes, you may want to remove a previously placed diagonal in a cell. If you wanted to remove the diagonal, you would perform the following steps.

1. Position the insertion point in either side of the diagonal cell.
2. Click the Diagonals button (Table Tools Layout tab | Merge group) to display the Diagonals menu and then click No Division on the Diagonals menu.

Table Borders

In addition to applying a table style and changing columns and rows, you can customize your table by adding borders. A **border** is the line that displays along the edge of a cell, row, column, or table. It is good practice to format and create borders in the following order:

1. Make your selection. Publisher allows you to add borders to individual cells, rows, columns, or the entire table.
2. Set the weight of the border. The default value is ½ pt, but you can change the weight to various point values; the higher the point value, the thicker the border.
3. Set the color of the border. The shades of the color scheme colors display in a palette, but all colors are available.
4. Set the borders, choosing individual borders, inside or outside borders on multiple cells, cell diagonals, all borders, or no border at all. The default value is no borders for an unformatted table. When you click the Borders button (Table Tools Design tab | Borders group), as opposed to the Borders arrow, all weight and color settings are applied.

To Select a Table

1 EMPLOY REUSABLE PARTS | 2 APPLY SHAPE EFFECTS | 3 INSERT & FORMAT TABLES | 4 CREATE CALENDAR
5 USE MASTER PAGES | 6 ADD BORDERART | 7 EMBED TABLE | 8 USE EXCEL FUNCTIONALITY

The following steps select the table in preparation for adding a border on the outside of the table. *Why? A border defines the edges, especially when multiple background colors exist.*

- Click to position the insertion point in the table.
- If necessary, display the Table Tools Layout tab.
- Click the Select Table button (Table Tools Layout tab | Table group) to display the Select Table menu (Figure 6–29).

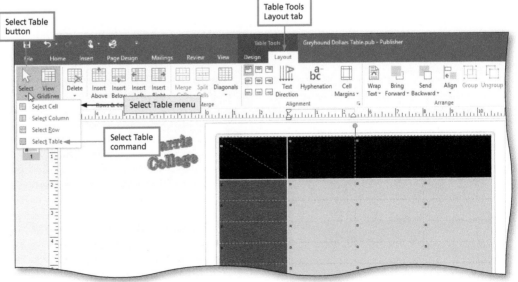

Figure 6–29

• Click Select Table to select the table (shown in Figure 6–30).

Other Ways

1. Right-click table, point to Select on shortcut menu, click Select Table on Select submenu

---

To Change the Line Weight

The following steps change the weight of the border on all cells in the table. *Why? A thicker border will be more visible if the table is printed or posted online.*

• Display the Table Tools Design tab.

• With the desired portions of the table selected (in this case, the entire table), click the Line Weight button (Table Tools Design tab | Borders group) to display the Line Weight menu (Figure 6–30).

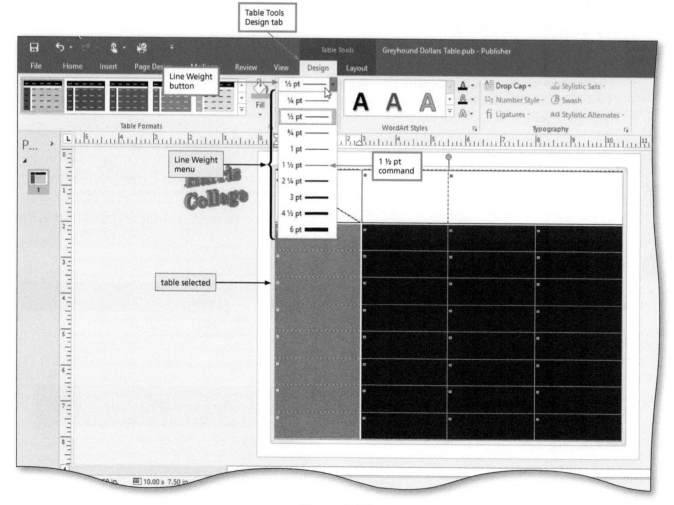

Figure 6–30

- Click the 1 ½ pt line weight on the Line Weight menu to increase the size of the border.

◄
Q&A |Nothing seemed to happen. Did I do something wrong?
The default setting is No borders, so your weight setting will not be visible until you choose to add borders in subsequent steps.

Other Ways

1. Right-click table, click Format Table on shortcut menu, click Colors and Lines tab (Format Table dialog box), click desired border preset, enter weight in Width text box, click OK button

To Change the Border Color

1 EMPLOY REUSABLE PARTS | 2 APPLY SHAPE EFFECTS | 3 INSERT & FORMAT TABLES | **4 CREATE CALENDAR**
5 USE MASTER PAGES | **6 ADD BORDERART** | **7 EMBED TABLE** | **8 USE EXCEL FUNCTIONALITY**

The following steps change the border color. **Why?** *The default color is gray; black will make the borders stand out more.*

①

- With the desired portions of the table selected (in this case, the entire table), click the Line Color button (Table Tools Design tab | Borders group) to display the Line Color gallery (Figure 6–31).

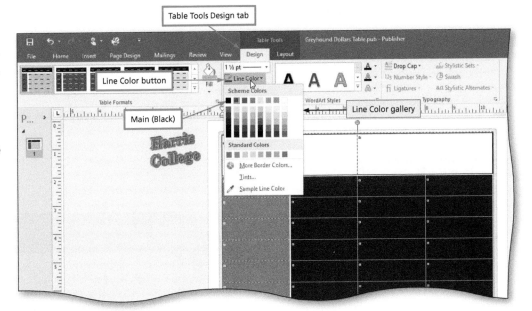

Figure 6–31

②

- Click Main (Black) in the Line Color gallery to choose black as the color (shown in Figure 6–33).

Other Ways

1. Right-click table, click Format Table on shortcut menu, click Colors and Lines tab (Format Table dialog box), click desired border preset, click Color button in Line area, select color, click OK button

To Add Borders

1 EMPLOY REUSABLE PARTS | 2 APPLY SHAPE EFFECTS | 3 INSERT & FORMAT TABLES | **4 CREATE CALENDAR**
5 USE MASTER PAGES | **6 ADD BORDERART** | **7 EMBED TABLE** | **8 USE EXCEL FUNCTIONALITY**

The following steps add a border to the cell edges. **Why?** *Adding the border to the table will cause the previous setting changes to display.*

1

- With the desired portions of the table selected (in this case, the entire table), click the Borders arrow (Table Tools Design tab | Borders group) to display the Borders menu (Figure 6–32).

What happens if I click the Borders button instead of the Borders arrow? If you click the Borders button, Publisher applies the previous border setting to the current selection. If you point to the button, Publisher displays the current settings as a ScreenTip.

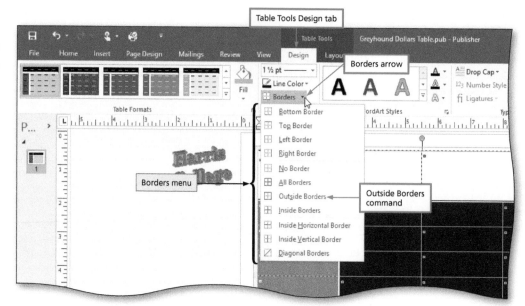

Figure 6–32

2

- Click Outside Borders on the Borders menu to add an outside border to the selection.
- Click outside the table to view the borders (Figure 6–33).

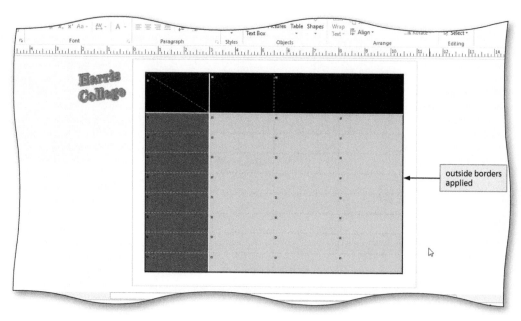

Figure 6–33

Other Ways

1. Right-click table, click Format Table on shortcut menu, click Colors and Lines tab (Format Table dialog box), click desired border preset, click OK button

Changing Row and Column Widths

When you first create a table, all of the columns have the same width and all of the rows have the same height. To change the column width, drag the right border of the column. To change the row height, drag the bottom border of a row. When you drag a border, the current column or row changes size; all of the other columns or rows remain the same, increasing or decreasing the overall size of the table. If you SHIFT+DRAG a border, the table remains the same size; the rows or columns on either side of the border change size. The only limitation is when changing the row height; you can decrease the height only down to the current font size.

To Select a Row

1 EMPLOY REUSABLE PARTS | 2 APPLY SHAPE EFFECTS | 3 INSERT & FORMAT TABLES | 4 CREATE CALENDAR
5 USE MASTER PAGES | 6 ADD BORDERART | 7 EMBED TABLE | 8 USE EXCEL FUNCTIONALITY

The following step selects the first row. *Why? The row needs to be selected before applying formatting.*

1

- Point to the left of the first row in the table until the pointer displays a solid, black arrow.

- Click to select the row (Figure 6–34).

🔍 **Experiment**

- Point to the outside of other rows and columns. When the pointer changes to a solid arrow, click to select the row or column. Select the first row again.

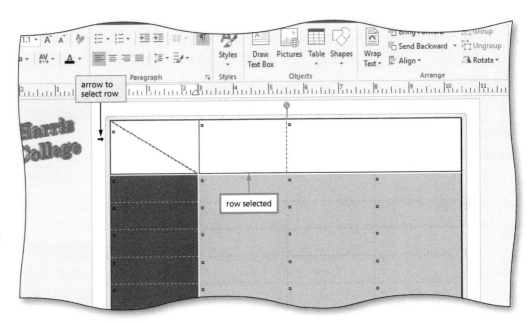

Figure 6–34

To Format Inside Borders

The following steps format the inside borders of the heading row. Note that these steps will not change the diagonal. You will format that cell later in the module.

1 With the row still selected, click the Line Color button (Table Tools Design tab | Borders group) and then click 'Accent 5 (White)' in the Line Color gallery to choose the border color.

2 Click the Borders arrow (Table Tools Design tab | Borders group) to display the Borders menu and then click Inside Borders on the Borders menu to add an inside border to the selection (in this case, the first row).

③ Click outside the table to view the borders (Figure 6–35).

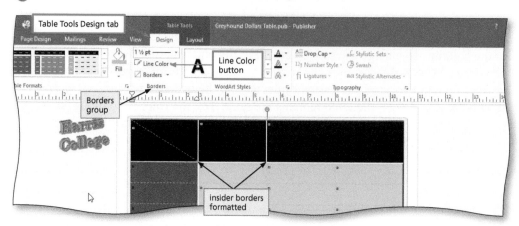

Figure 6–35

To Change the Fill and Font Color

The following steps change the fill color of the diagonal cell to white. **Why?** *Changing the fill color will provide additional delineation for the diagonal headings.* You also will change the font color to black

①

- Drag to select both halves of the diagonal cell.

- Click the Fill arrow (Table Tools Design tab | Table Formats group) to display the Fill gallery (Figure 6–36).

Q&A Are the Fill button and Fill arrow different?

Yes. The upper half of the selected area is the button. If you click the button, Publisher applies the previous settings. If you click the arrow, Publisher displays the gallery.

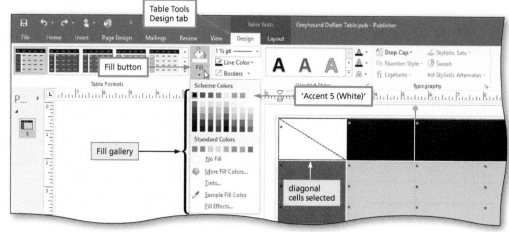

Figure 6–36

②

- Click 'Accent 5 (White)' in the Fill gallery to change the fill color of the selection.

- Click the Font Color arrow (Home tab | Font group) and then click Main (Black) in the Font Color gallery to change the font color.

- Click outside the selection to view the fill color (Figure 6–37).

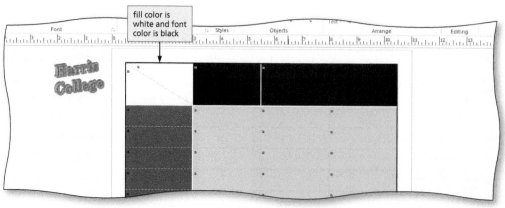

Figure 6–37

To Format the Diagonal Border

The following steps format the diagonal border.

1 Drag to select both sides of the diagonal cell.

2 Click the Line Color button (Table Tools Design tab | Borders group) and then click Main (Black) on the Line Color menu to choose black as the color.

3 Click the Borders arrow (Table Tools Design tab | Borders group) to display the Borders menu and then click Diagonal Borders to add a diagonal border to the selection.

4 Click outside the selection to view the borders (Figure 6–38).

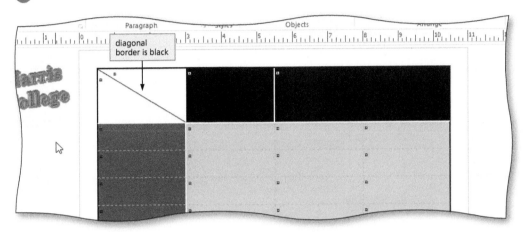

Figure 6–38

To Edit Cell Alignment

1 EMPLOY REUSABLE PARTS | 2 APPLY SHAPE EFFECTS | 3 INSERT & FORMAT TABLES | 4 CREATE CALENDAR
5 USE MASTER PAGES | 6 ADD BORDERART | 7 EMBED TABLE | 8 USE EXCEL FUNCTIONALITY

As with text box alignment, Publisher offers nine options for aligning text within a cell, both vertically and horizontally. The Alignment group on the Table Tools Layout tab also includes options for changing the text direction, applying hyphenation, and specifying cell margins. The following step edits the cell alignment. *Why? Aligning the text properly will make the table easier to read.*

1

- Click the left side of the diagonal cell to position the insertion point.

- Display the Table Tools Layout tab.

- Click the 'Align Bottom Left' button (Table Tools Layout tab | Alignment group) to position the insertion point in the lower-left corner of the cell (Figure 6–39).

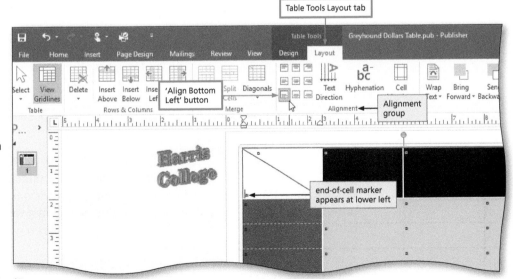

Figure 6–39

Q&A How can I tell if it worked?
Notice the end of cell marker positioned in the lower-left corner of the cell. This indicates that text will appear at that position.

To Align Other Cells

The following steps align the other cells in the table.

1 Click the right side of the diagonal cell to position the insertion point.

2 Click the 'Align Center Right' button (Table Tools Layout tab | Alignment group) to position the text centered and right-aligned.

3 Click the rightmost cell in the first row to select it and then click the Align Center button (Table Tools Layout tab | Alignment group).

4 Select all of the medium gray cells in column 1 and change the alignment to align center left.

5 Select all of the light gray cells in columns 2 through 4, rows 2 through 9, and change the alignment to center (Figure 6–40).

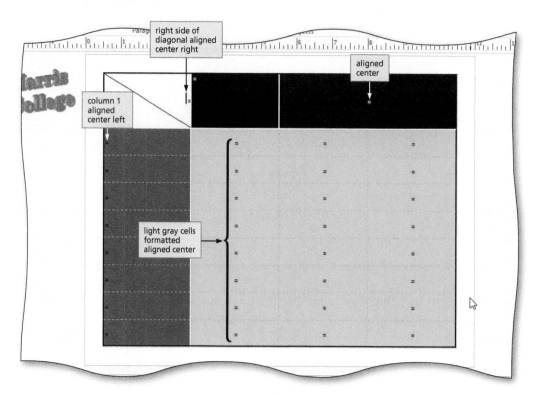

Figure 6–40

Entering Data in Tables

The next step is to enter text and graphics in the table cells. To place text in a cell, you click the cell and then type. To advance rightward from one cell to the next, press the TAB key. When you are at the rightmost cell in a row, press the TAB key to move to the first cell in the next row. To move up or down within the table, use the arrow keys, or simply click the desired cell.

Because each cell in a Publisher table is a text box, graphics, including photos, clip art, and WordArt, cannot be placed directly into Publisher tables. Graphics are layered in front of locations on the table; however, they print and display on the web correctly, as if they were in the table cell.

To Enter Data in a Table

The following steps enter data in the table. As you enter data, be careful when using the ENTER key. *Why?* *The ENTER key is used to begin a new paragraph within a cell. You cannot add new rows or columns by using the ENTER key. Pressing SHIFT+ENTER creates a new line within the cell without the extra spacing adding for a new paragraph.*

1

- Click the left side of the diagonal cell.
- Zoom the table to 130% magnification.
- Change the font size to 18.
- Type `Where` to complete the text.
- Press the TAB key to move to the next cell.
- Change the font size to 18. Click the Bold button (Home tab | Font group) to bold the text.
- Type `Greyhound` and then press SHIFT+ENTER to create a soft return.
- Type `Dollars` to finish the column heading (Figure 6–41).

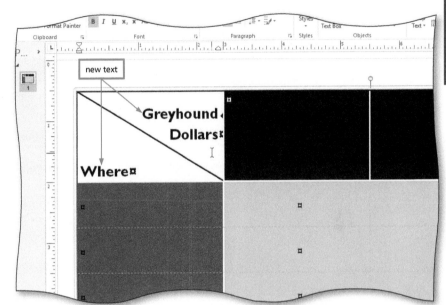

Figure 6–41

Q&A How do I edit cell contents if I make a mistake?
Click in the cell and then correct the entry.

I cannot see the soft return. Did I do something wrong?
No. Because the cell is small due to the diagonal, the soft return in the narrow cell margin may not be visible.

2

- Press the TAB key twice to move to the rightmost cell in row 1.
- Change the font size to 36.
- Type `Meal Plans` to complete the heading (Figure 6–42).

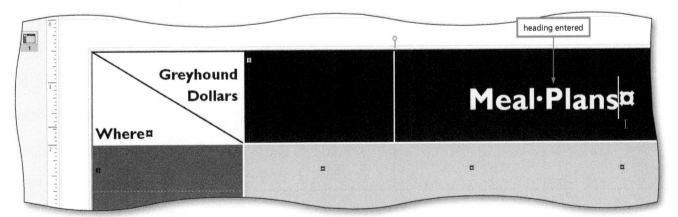

Figure 6–42

Q&A How common is it to perform the formatting before entering the text?
Formatting first saves keystrokes. You do not have to go back and select to add the formatting.

- Finish typing the columns headings as shown in Figure 6–43.
- Use a font size of 18. Use the TAB key to advance the insertion point. Press SHIFT+ENTER as indicated, to create multiple lines in the cells.

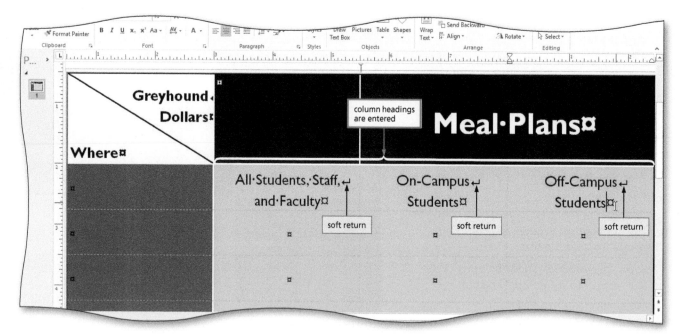

Figure 6–43

Q&A | Can I set all of those cells to a font size of 18 at one time?
Yes. Select the cells and then type 18 in the Font Size box (Home tab | Font group).

- Select the remaining cells in column 1. Change the font size to 18. Change the font color to 'Accent 5 (White)'.

- Enter the row headings as shown in Figure 6–44. Zoom and scroll as necessary.

Q&A | Why are my row headings bold?
The table format you selected includes bold headings.

What if I have more data than will fit in a cell?
By default, the data you enter in a cell wraps just as text wraps between the margins of a text box. You can turn off that feature by clicking to remove the check mark in the 'Grow to Fit Text' check box (Table Tools Layout tab | Size group).

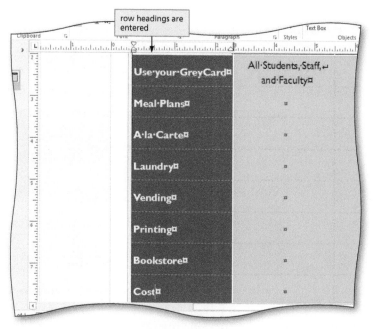

Figure 6–44

5
- Select the remaining cells in row 9. Change the font size to 14.
- Enter the text as shown in Figure 6–45. Zoom and scroll as necessary.
- If instructed to do so, change the word Greyhound to the name of your school's mascot in both of the locations in the table.

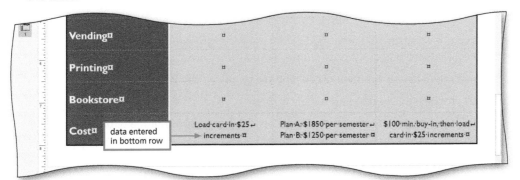

Figure 6–45

Deleting Table Data

To delete the contents of a cell, select the cell contents and then press the DELETE or BACKSPACE key. You also can drag and drop or cut and paste the contents of cells. To delete an entire table, select the table, click the 'Delete Rows or Columns' button (Table Tools Layout tab | Rows & Columns group), and then click Delete Table on the Delete Rows or Columns menu.

To Insert a Graphic in a Table Cell

The following steps insert a picture and move it to the table. To complete these steps, you will be required to use the Data Files. Please contact your instructor for information about accessing the Data Files.

1 Display the Insert tab and then zoom to display the entire table.

2 Click the Pictures button (Insert tab | Illustrations group). Navigate to the Data Files and the Module 06 folder. Double-click the file named ID Card to insert the graphic.

3 Resize the graphic to approximately 2 inches wide and 1.3 inches tall.

4 Move the graphic to a position over the empty cell in Row 1 (Figure 6–46).

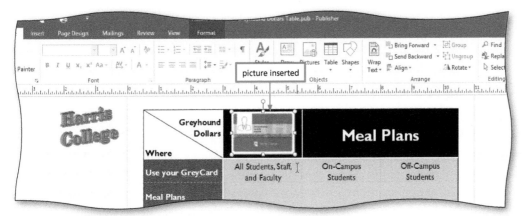

Figure 6–46

To Finish the Table

The following steps complete the table by placing an X in appropriate cells, applying white, inner borders, and checking the publication for errors.

1 Select all empty cells and change the font size to 18. If necessary, press CTRL+B to bold the cells. Place an uppercase X in each of the cells shown in Figure 6–47.

2 Select rows 2 through 9. Apply a white inside border to the cells.

3 Drag the WordArt object to the top-left corner of the table. If necessary, click the Bring Forward button (WordArt Tools Format tab | Arrange group).

4 Press the F7 key to run spell check. Choose to ignore the word, GreyCard.

5 Run the Design Checker and fix any errors.

6 Click the Save button on the Quick Access Toolbar to save the file with the same file name in the same location.

7 If instructed to do so, print the publication.

8 Click File on the ribbon to open the Backstage view and then click Close to close the publication without exiting Publisher and return to the template gallery.

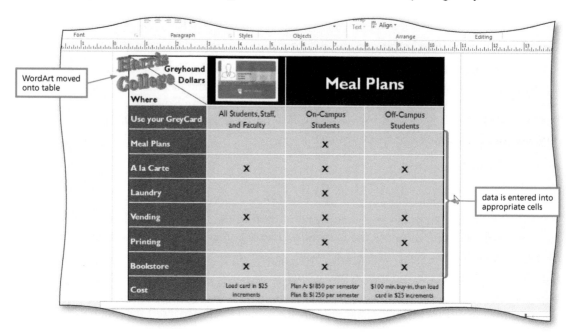

Figure 6–47

Break Point: If you wish to take a break, this is a good place to do so. Exit Publisher. To resume at a later time, run Publisher and continue following the steps from this location forward.

Calendars

The next series of steps creates a calendar. A **calendar** is a specialized table or set of tables that Publisher can format with any combination of months and year. Calendar cells, like table cells, can be formatted with colors, borders, text, and styles. You can create calendars as independent, stand-alone publications, or insert them as building blocks into other publications. Calendars are used for many purposes other than just presenting the date. Information that changes from day to day can be presented as text in a calendar, such as school lunches, practice schedules, homework assignments, or appointments and meetings. Colors and graphics are used in calendars to display holidays, special events, reminders, and even phases of the moon.

Why do companies create promotional pieces?
A **promotional piece**, or **promo**, is an inclusive term for a publication or article that includes advertising and marketing information for a product or service known to and purchased by customers and clients. Companies create promotional pieces that will increase company recognition. Make sure that promotional pieces are useful to customers and not just gimmicky. Remember that calendars date promotional material.

Including calendars in a publication dates the material, because the publication may not be useful after the calendar date has passed. Companies should consider carefully whether to include calendars in publications.

To Create a Calendar

1 EMPLOY REUSABLE PARTS | 2 APPLY SHAPE EFFECTS | 3 INSERT & FORMAT TABLES | 4 CREATE CALENDAR
5 USE MASTER PAGES | 6 ADD BORDERART | 7 EMBED TABLE | 8 USE EXCEL FUNCTIONALITY

The following steps create a 10-month academic calendar that Harris College will use as a promotional piece.

- Click BUILT-IN in the New template gallery (Backstage view) to display the built-in templates.
- Click the Calendars thumbnail to display the calendar templates.
- Click the Varsity calendar template to select it.
- If necessary, click the Color scheme button in the Customize area and then click Equity in the list to choose a color scheme.
- If necessary, click the Font scheme button and then click Solstice in the list to choose a font scheme.
- If necessary, click the Business information button and then click HCRS to select it.
- If necessary, scroll to display the remaining settings (Figure 6–48).

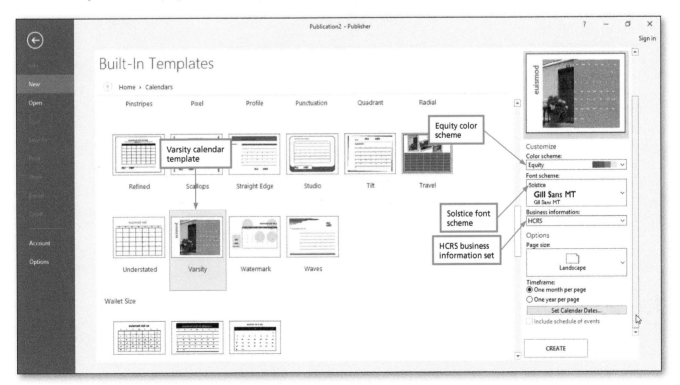

Figure 6–48

2

- If necessary, click the Page size arrow in the Options area and then click Landscape in the list to choose a landscape orientation.

- If necessary, click the 'One month per page' option button to select it.

- Click the 'Set Calendar Dates' button to display the Set Calendar Dates dialog box.

- Click the Start date button (Set Calendar Dates dialog box) to display the list of months (Figure 6–49).

Q&A How can I create a one-month calendar?

To create just one month on one page, use the same month and year in both the Start date and End date boxes (Set Calendar Dates dialog box).

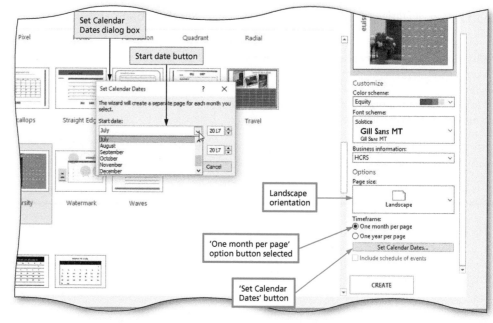

Figure 6–49

3

- Scroll as necessary and click August to select the starting month.

- If necessary, click the up or down arrow on the Start date year box (Set Calendar Dates dialog box) until 2017 is displayed.

- Click the End date button, and then click May to choose the ending month.

- If necessary, click the up or down arrow on the End year box until 2018 is displayed (Figure 6–50).

Q&A What kind of object is the year box with the up and down arrows?

Microsoft refers to this as a numerical up and down box. It commonly is used for fixed data in a sequential list from which the user can choose. You also can type in a numerical up and down box.

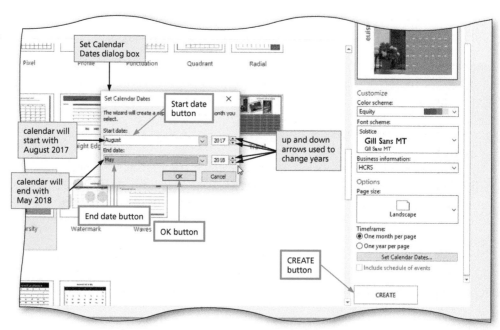

Figure 6–50

④

- Click the OK button (Set Calendar Dates dialog box) to set the dates and close the dialog box.

- Click the CREATE button to create the calendar (Figure 6–51).

Q&A Why do so many thumbnails appear in the Page Navigation pane?
Because you selected August through May, Publisher created 10 pages, one for each month.

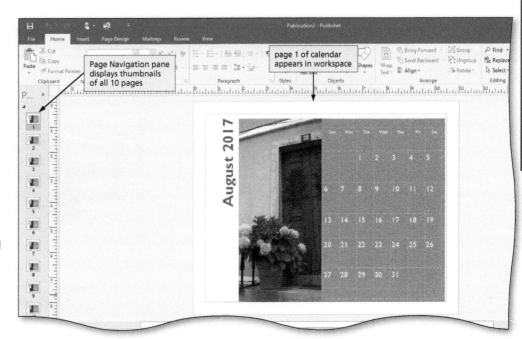

Figure 6–51

⑤

- Save the publication on your desired save location using the file name, Calendar.

Master Pages

A **master page** is a background area that is repeated across all pages of a publication. Similar to the header and footer area in traditional word processing software, you have to enter the information or insert the objects only once to synchronize them across all pages. The master page is the ideal place for a watermark, a page border, or repeating graphics. When accessing the master page, Publisher displays a new tab (shown in Figure 6–53).

Each publication starts with one master page. If you have a multipage publication, you can choose to use two different master pages for cases such as facing pages in a book; in those circumstances, you might want different graphics in the background of each page. If you want to display master page objects only on certain pages, the Apply To button (Master Page tab | Master Page group) provides several options. This is useful for cases such as background images on every page except the title page in a longer publication, or a watermark on the inside of a brochure but not on the front. In the calendar publication, you will create a page border and use the building block you created earlier in the module.

To View the Master Page

1 EMPLOY REUSABLE PARTS | 2 APPLY SHAPE EFFECTS | 3 INSERT & FORMAT TABLES | 4 CREATE CALENDAR
5 USE MASTER PAGES | 6 ADD BORDERART | 7 EMBED TABLE | 8 USE EXCEL FUNCTIONALITY

The following steps view the master page. **Why?** *The master page is a special page that cannot be accessed via the Page Navigation pane.*

- Click View on the
  ribbon to display
  the View tab
  (Figure 6–52).

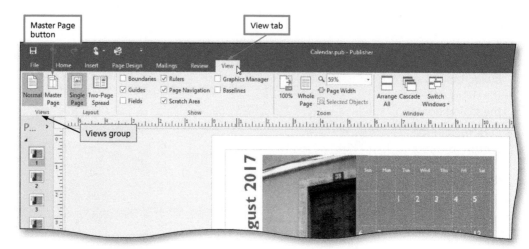

Figure 6–52

2

- Click the Master Page button (View tab | Views group) to access the master page (Figure 6–53).

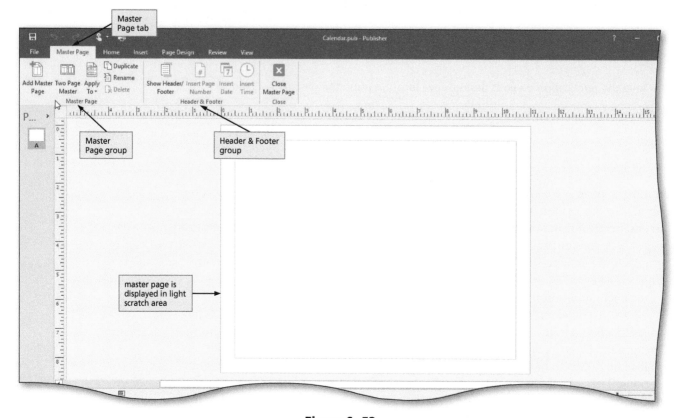

Figure 6–53

Q&A Why is the scratch area a different color?
Publisher uses a different color to remind you that you are not in the regular publication window. It helps you to
remember to close the master page before continuing with the other objects in the publication.

Other Ways

1. Click Master Pages button (Page Design tab | Page Background group), click 'Edit Master Pages' on Master Pages menu

2. Press CTRL+M

BorderArt

BorderArt is a group of customizable graphical borders, such as crosses, hearts, apples, balloons, or decorative shapes, which can be added as an edge or border to a shape, a text box, or the entire page. BorderArt makes the page margins stand out and adds interest to the page. Placing BorderArt on a master page causes the border to display on every page of the publication.

To Add BorderArt

1 EMPLOY REUSABLE PARTS | 2 APPLY SHAPE EFFECTS | 3 INSERT & FORMAT TABLES | 4 CREATE CALENDAR
5 USE MASTER PAGES | **6 ADD BORDERART** | **7 EMBED TABLE** | **8 USE EXCEL FUNCTIONALITY**

The following steps create a rectangle shape on the master page and apply BorderArt. *Why? BorderArt creates a page border for each page of the calendar.*

- Display the Insert tab.
- Click the Shapes button (Insert tab | Illustrations group) and then click the Rectangle shape.
- Drag to draw a rectangle that fills the area within the margins.
- Right-click the shape to display the shortcut menu (Figure 6–54).

Q&A Should I allow for a margin around the rectangle?
No. The company will send this publication out for professional printing and binding. Most professional printers can print right to the edge of the page.

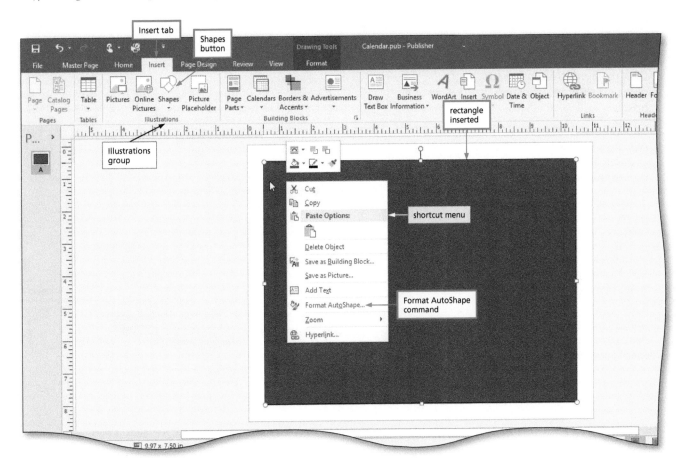

Figure 6–54

- Click Format AutoShape on the shortcut menu to display the Format AutoShape dialog box.

- If necessary, click the 'Colors and Lines' tab (Format AutoShape dialog box). Click the Color arrow in the Fill area to display the Color gallery (Figure 6–55).

Q&A Can I apply a border directly to the margin of the page?
No. Borders must be attached to a shape, picture, text box, or table.

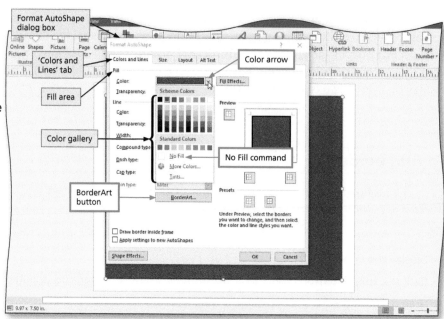

Figure 6–55

- Click No Fill in the Color gallery to create a shape without any fill color.

- Click the BorderArt button to display the BorderArt dialog box.

- Scroll as necessary in the Available Borders area and then click the 'Push Pin in Note 2' border to select it.

- If necessary, click the 'Stretch pictures to fit' option button to select it (Figure 6–56).

Experiment

- Scroll to view all of the available borders in the list. Notice some are repeating square elements and others use special corners.

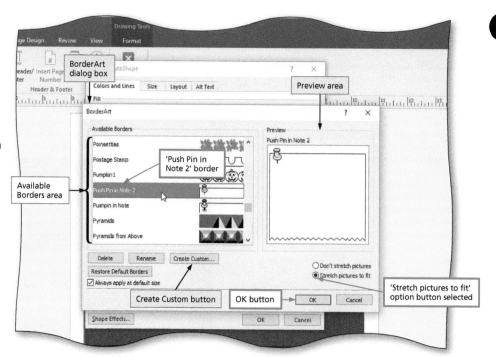

Figure 6–56

4

- Click the OK button (BorderArt dialog box) to return to the Format AutoShape dialog box.

- Click the Color arrow in the Line area and then choose the 'Accent 2 (RGB (155, 45, 31))' color.

- Select the text in the Width text box, and then type **30 pt** to enter the width (Figure 6–57).

Q&A How is the Color gallery organized?

The upper half of the Color gallery includes the accent colors related to the chosen color scheme and displays RGB numbers in the ScreenTip. Colors in the Standard Color area, shown in Figure 6-55, display color names only when you point to them.

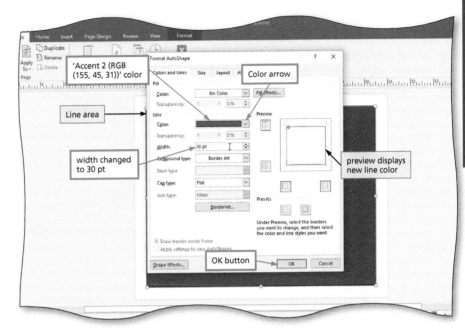

Figure 6–57

5

- Click the OK button (Format AutoShape dialog box) to apply the border (Figure 6–58).

Q&A Could I use one of my own pictures as BorderArt?

Yes, you can click the Create Custom button, shown in Figure 6–56, and then navigate to your storage location.

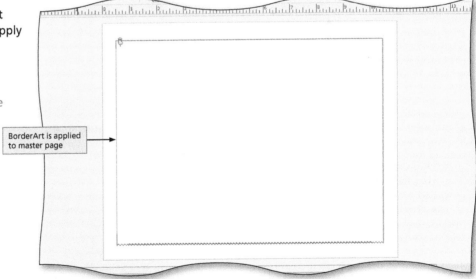

Figure 6–58

Other Ways

1. Select shape, click Format Shape Dialog Box Launcher (Drawing Tools Format tab | Shape Styles group), click BorderArt button (Format AutoShape dialog box), select border, click OK button (BorderArt dialog box), click OK button (Format AutoShape dialog box)

To Insert a Building Block

The following steps insert a building block on the master page.

1 Display the Insert tab.

2 Click the Page Parts button (Insert tab | Building Blocks group) to display the Page Parts gallery.

3 Click the Harris College graphic in the Page Parts gallery to insert the graphic on the master page.

4 Drag the graphic to the lower-left corner of the master page (Figure 6–59).

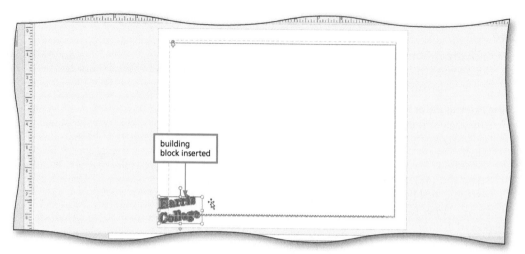

building block inserted

Figure 6–59

To Close the Master Page

1 EMPLOY REUSABLE PARTS | 2 APPLY SHAPE EFFECTS | 3 INSERT & FORMAT TABLES | 4 CREATE CALENDAR
5 USE MASTER PAGES | 6 ADD BORDERART | **7 EMBED TABLE** | 8 USE EXCEL FUNCTIONALITY

The following steps close the master page and return to the regular page layout and Publisher workspace. *Why?* *You are finished with the background elements and need to work on the calendar pages themselves.*

1

• Display the Master Page tab (Figure 6–60).

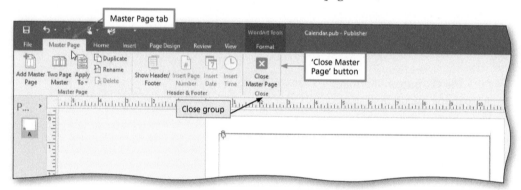

Master Page tab

'Close Master Page' button

Close group

Figure 6–60

2

• Click the 'Close Master Page' button (Master Page tab | Close group) to close the master page (Figure 6–61).

Q&A What else could I add to the master page?
You could add a background effect, headers, footers, page numbers, or any text or graphics that you want to appear on every page of the publication.

border appears in page layout

Figure 6–61

Other Ways

1. Click Normal button (View tab | Views group)   2. Press CTRL+M

To Insert Clip Art

The following steps insert clip art images on page 1. To complete these steps, you will be required to use the Data Files. Please contact your instructor for information about accessing the Data Files.

1 Display the Insert tab and zoom to display the entire calendar.

2 Click the Pictures button (Insert tab | Illustrations group) to display the Insert Picture dialog box. Browse to the location of the Data Files and the Module 06 folder. SHIFT+CLICK the files named Football, Campus, Greyhound, and Books to select them all. Click the Insert button (Insert Picture dialog box). Click the scratch area to deselect.

3 Point to the campus picture. When the swap icon appears, drag the swap icon to a location over the current picture in the calendar. When the picture displays the pink border, release the mouse button.

4 One at a time, drag the other graphics to locations in the calendar as shown in Figure 6–62. Resize the graphics as necessary.

5 Delete the original picture that was swapped to the scratch area.

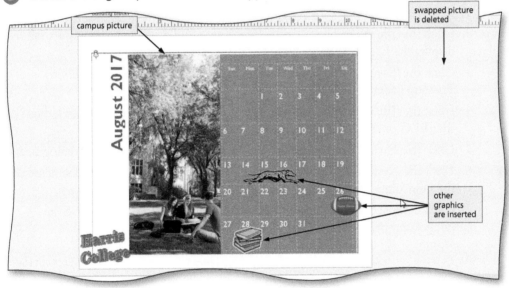

Figure 6–62

To Edit Other Pages in the Calendar

The following steps edit the rest of the pages in the calendar. You will replace the graphic on each page. As you choose graphics using the Bing Image Search, read the specific license for any image you plan to use, even for educational purposes, to ensure you have the right to use the image.

1 Click the next page in the Page Navigation pane.

2 Click the graphic to select the picture placeholder. Use the shortcut menu to change the picture. Search for a picture related to the month displayed on the page or use pictures related to colleges and campuses.

3 Repeat Steps 1 and 2 to change each page in the calendar.

4 Click the Save button on the Quick Access Toolbar to save the file with the same file name in the same location.

5 Close the file without exiting Publisher.

BTW
Conserving Ink and Toner
If you want to conserve ink or toner, you can instruct Publisher to print draft quality documents by clicking File on the ribbon to open the Backstage view, clicking the Options tab in the Backstage view to display the Publisher Options dialog box, clicking Advanced in the left pane (Publisher Options dialog box), scrolling to the Print area in the right pane, placing a check mark in the 'Use draft quality' check box, and then clicking the OK button. Then, use the Backstage view to print the document as usual.

TO PRINT THE CALENDAR

If you wanted to print the calendar, you would perform the following steps.

1. Click the Print tab in the Backstage view to display the Print gallery.
2. Verify that the printer listed on the Printer Status button will print a hard copy of the publication. If necessary, click the Printer Status button to display a list of available printer options and then click the desired printer to change the currently selected printer.
3. Click the Print button in the Print gallery to print the publication on the currently selected printer.
4. When the printer stops, retrieve the hard copy. The calendar will print on 10 pages of paper.

TO SAVE THE CALENDAR PAGES AS IMAGES

If you wanted to send the calendar or other publication to a professional printer with each page as a separate image, you would perform the following steps.

1. Save the file as usual on your storage location.
2. Click the File tab to open the Backstage view and then click the Export tab to display the Export gallery.
3. Click the 'Save for Photo Printing' button to display the Save for Photo Printing gallery.
4. Click the 'JPEG Images for Photo Printing' button and then choose either the JPEG or the TIFF file format.
5. Click the 'Save Image Set' button to display the Choose Location dialog box.
6. Click the New folder button (Choose Location dialog box). Type the name of the new folder, such as Calendar Pages, and then press the ENTER key.
7. Click the Select Folder button (Choose Location dialog box) to save the publication pages as images.

Break Point: If you wish to take a break, this is a good place to do so. Exit Publisher. To resume at a later time, run Publisher and continue following the steps from this location forward.

Using Excel Tables

BTW
Distributing a Document
Instead of printing and distributing a hard copy of a document, you can distribute the document electronically. Options include sending the document via email; posting it on cloud storage (such as OneDrive) and sharing the file with others; posting it on social media, a blog, or other website; and sharing a link associated with an online location of the document. You also can create and share a PDF or XPS image of the document, so that users can view the file in Acrobat Reader or XPS Viewer instead of in Publisher.

In Module 2, you learned how to edit a story using Microsoft Word from within Publisher. In this module, you will learn how to integrate Microsoft Excel when you create a Publisher table. An **Excel-enhanced table** is one that uses Excel tools to enhance Publisher's table formatting capabilities, and one that adds table functionality to enhance your tables with items such as totals, averages, charts, and other financial functions. You can paste, create, or insert an Excel-enhanced table into your Publisher publication. Two types of Excel-enhanced tables are available: embedded and linked.

An **embedded** table uses Excel data and can be manipulated with some Excel functionality; however, the data becomes part of the Publisher publication and must be edited with Publisher running. Publisher displays Excel tabs on the ribbon to help you edit an embedded table. Alternately, a **linked** table is connected permanently to an Excel worksheet; it is updated automatically from the Excel worksheet. When you edit a linked table, you actually are working in Excel, with full functionality. You can edit a linked table in Excel or Publisher. If you edit in Excel, the table is updated automatically the next time you open the Publisher publication. In either case, the data you use from the Excel file is called the **source** document. Publisher is the **destination** document.

The actual process of integrating an Excel table can be performed in one of three ways. You can create an embedded table from scratch, you can paste an embedded or linked table, or you can insert an embedded or linked table from a file.

In this project, you will create a letter and insert an embedded table. You then will format the Excel-enhanced table.

How should you make the decision whether to embed a table or link a table?

The decision on which type of table to use depends on the data. You would embed a table when you want a static or unchanging table that you edit in Publisher. For example, a table from last year's sales probably is not going to change; thus, if you paste it into a Publisher brochure about the company's sales history, it will look the same each time you open the publication. You would link a table when the data is likely to change, and you want to make sure the publication reflects the current data in the Excel file. For example, suppose you link a portion or all of an Excel worksheet to a Publisher investment statement and update the worksheet quarterly in Excel. With a linked table, any time you open the investment statement in Publisher, the latest update of the worksheet will be displayed as part of the investment statement; in other words, the most current data always will appear in the statement.

To Create the Letterhead

The following steps create a letterhead that Harris College will use to send a letter and table to the HCRS managers.

1 Click BUILT-IN in the New template gallery (Backstage view) to display the built-in templates.

2 Click the Letterhead thumbnail to display the letterhead templates.

3 If necessary, click the Arrows template to select it.

4 If necessary, click the Color scheme button in the Customize area and then click Equity in the list to choose a color scheme.

5 If necessary, click the Font scheme button and then click Solstice in the list to choose a font scheme.

6 If necessary, click the Business information button and then click HCRS to select it.

7 If necessary, click to remove the check mark in the Include logo check box.

8 Click the CREATE button to create the letterhead (shown in Figure 6–63).

To Insert the Building Block

The following steps insert the Harris College building block into the publication.

1 Display the Insert tab.

2 Click the Page Parts button (Insert tab | Building Blocks group) and then click the Harris College graphic to insert it into the publication.

3 Resize the graphic to approximately 2.25 inches wide and 1.5 inches tall.

4 Drag the object to the upper-left corner of the page.

5 Zoom to 150% and scroll to the top of the page.

6 Select the text in the address text box and change the font size to 10.

7 Select the text in the phone, fax, email text box, and change the font size to 10. If necessary, drag the right-center sizing handle so that the email notation appears on one line (Figure 6-63).

8 Save the publication on your desired save location using the file name, HCRS Manager Letter.

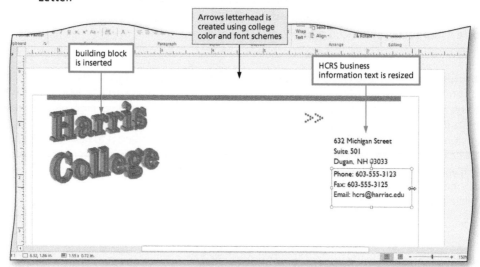

Figure 6-63

To Type the Letter

The following steps create a text box and enter text for the body of the letter.

1 Zoom to 120% and scroll to the middle of the page.

2 Click the 'Draw a Text Box' button (Insert tab | Text group) and then drag to create a text box below the upper objects on the page, approximately 7.25 inches wide and 4 inches tall.

3 Change the font to Calibri and the font size to 12 pt.

4 Type the text shown in Figure 6-64.

If instructed to do so, use your name and today's date in the letter.

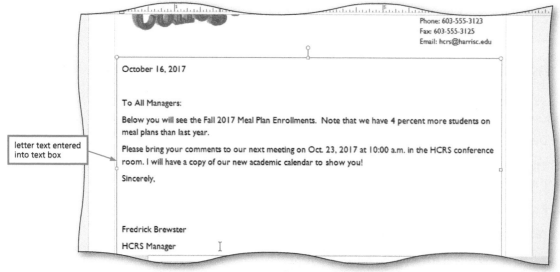

Figure 6-64

To Create an Embedded Table

Recall that embedding means using a copy of a source document in a destination document, without establishing a permanent link. Embedded objects can be edited; however, changes do not affect the source document. For example, if a business embedded an Excel worksheet into its Publisher electronic newsletter that contained updatable fields, users viewing the publication in Publisher could enter their personal data into the embedded table and recalculate the totals. Those users would not need access to the original Excel worksheet. *Why? Publisher embeds the necessary Excel commands.*

The following steps create an embedded table showing meal plan purchases by dormitory. You will retrieve the values from an Excel file. To complete these steps, you will be required to use the Data Files. Please contact your instructor for information about accessing the Data Files.

1

- Zoom to whole page and then scroll to the right of the page layout to display more of the scratch area in the Publisher workspace.

- Display the Insert tab.

- Click the Object button (Insert tab | Text group) to display the Insert Object dialog box (Figure 6–65).

Q&A Why should I insert the table in the scratch area?
It is easier to work with tables outside of the publication and then move them to the page layout after editing.

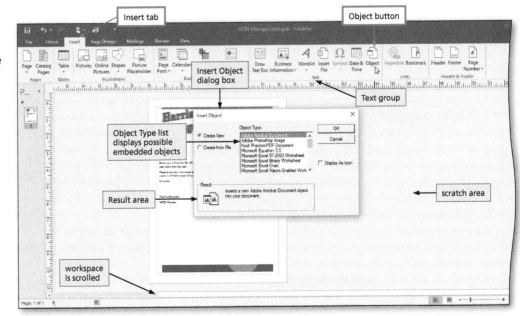

Figure 6–65

- Scroll through the list of object types to view the different kinds of documents and graphics that you can embed. Click the object types to read a description in the Result area.

2

- Click the 'Create from File' option button to select it (Insert Object dialog box) (Figure 6–66).

Q&A What does the Create New option button do?
You would click the Create New option button if you wanted to create an embedded table or other object from scratch.

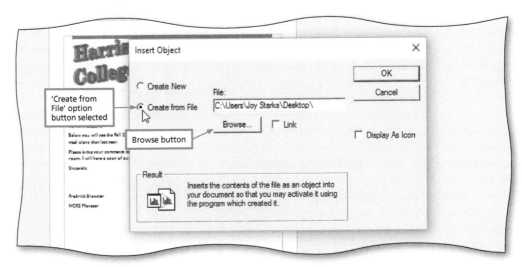

Figure 6–66

• Click the Browse button to display the Browse dialog box.

• Navigate to the location of the Data Files on your computer.

• Double-click the Excel file named Meal Plan Purchases (Browse dialog box) to select the file and return to the Insert Object dialog box.

• Click the OK button (Insert Object dialog box) to embed the data from the Excel file. If your system opens an Excel window, click the Close button on the Excel title bar.

• If necessary, drag the border of the embedded table so it does not overlap the page layout (Figure 6–67).

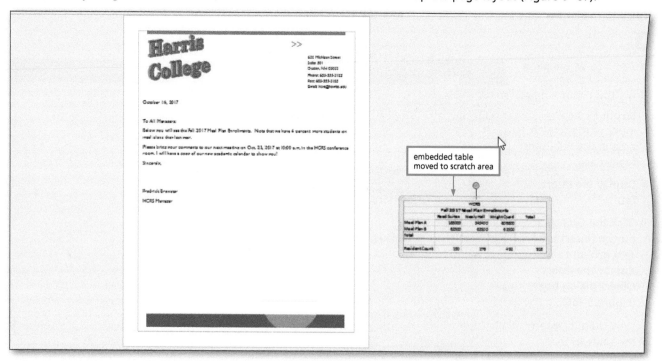

Figure 6–67

To Create an Embedded Table from Scratch

If you wanted to create an embedded table from scratch, you would perform the following steps.

1. In Publisher, display the Insert tab.
2. Click the Object button (Insert tab | Text group).
3. Click the Create New option button (Insert Object dialog box).
4. In the Object Type list, click 'Microsoft Excel Worksheet'.
5. Click the OK button (Insert Object dialog box) to insert the table.
6. Double-click the table and insert data into each cell.

To Insert a Linked Table

If you wanted to create a linked table, you would perform the following steps.

1. In Publisher, display the Insert tab.
2. Click the Object button (Insert tab | Text group).
3. Click the 'Create from File' option button (Insert Object dialog box) and then click to display a check mark in the Link check box.

4. Click the Browse button to display the Browse dialog box.

5. Navigate to your storage location or the location of the Data Files on your computer and then double-click the desired Excel file (Browse dialog box).

6. Click the OK button (Insert Object dialog box) to link the data from the Excel file.

TO COPY AND PASTE AN EMBEDDED TABLE

If you wanted to copy and paste from an Excel worksheet to create an embedded table, you would perform the following steps.

1. Run Microsoft Excel 2016.

2. Select the cells to include in the embedded table and then press CTRL+C to copy them.

3. Run Microsoft Publisher 2016.

4. Click the Paste arrow (Home tab | Clipboard group), and then click Paste Special in the gallery.

5. Click the Paste option button (Paste Special dialog box) and then click New Table in the As box.

6. Click the OK button (Paste Special dialog box) to embed the table.

TO COPY AND PASTE A LINKED TABLE

If you wanted to copy and paste from an Excel worksheet to create a linked table, you would perform the following steps.

1. Run Microsoft Excel 2016.

2. Select the cells to include in the embedded table and then press CTRL+C to copy them.

3. Run Microsoft Publisher 2016.

4. Click the Paste arrow (Home tab | Clipboard group) and then click Paste Special in the gallery to display the Paste Special dialog box.

5. Click the Paste Link option button.

6. Click the OK button (Paste Special dialog box) to link the table.

To Format an Embedded Table

1 EMPLOY REUSABLE PARTS | 2 APPLY SHAPE EFFECTS | 3 INSERT & FORMAT TABLES | 4 CREATE CALENDAR
5 USE MASTER PAGES | 6 ADD BORDERART | 7 EMBED TABLE | **8 USE EXCEL FUNCTIONALITY**

When you double-click an embedded object, Publisher activates a subset of the source application commands on a ribbon that appears in the destination application. *Why? The embedded features allow you to edit the object without running the source app.*

Excel cell references in the following steps represent the intersection of the column (indicated by a capital letter) and the row (indicated by a number). For example, the first cell in column A is cell A1, the third cell in column B is cell B3, and so forth.

Specifically, in the following steps you will use Excel commands to format the first and last rows of numerical data with the Accounting Number Format that includes a dollar sign ($), commas where necessary, and two decimal places. You will format other dollar figures with just a comma and two decimal places using the Comma Style format.

- Zoom in on the table.

- Double-click the table to display the Excel tabs on the Publisher ribbon.

- Drag through cells B4 through E4 to select them (Figure 6–68).

Q&A What happened to the File tab and the other Publisher tabs?
Publisher displays Excel functionality while you are working on an embedded table. When you click outside the table, the Publisher tabs will reappear.

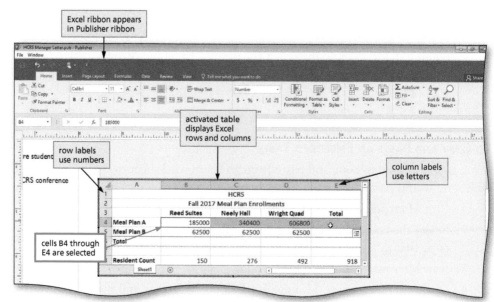

Figure 6–68

- Click the 'Accounting Number Format' button (Excel Home tab | Number group) to apply dollar signs to the cells (Figure 6–69).

Q&A The formatting is not showing up in cell E4. Did I do something wrong?
No. The formatting will show up as soon as you enter a value or sum in the cell in the next series of steps. Excel allows you to format empty cells.

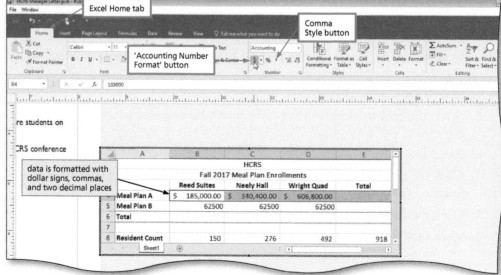

Figure 6–69

- Repeat Steps 1 and 2 for the range B6 through E6.

- Select the range, B5 through E5. Click the Comma Style button (Excel Home tab | Number group) to apply the comma style to the cells (shown in Figure 6–70).

To Sum in an Embedded Table

1 EMPLOY REUSABLE PARTS | 2 APPLY SHAPE EFFECTS | 3 INSERT & FORMAT TABLES | 4 CREATE CALENDAR
5 USE MASTER PAGES | 6 ADD BORDERART | 7 EMBED TABLE | 8 USE EXCEL FUNCTIONALITY

The following steps sum the columns of the embedded table. You will use the Sum button (Excel Home tab | Editing group) to create a total. *Why? Publisher does not have a Sum command, so you must use the Excel function.* When you click the Sum button, the values to add appear in a **marquee**, or dotted flashing border. After a sum is created, you can repeat the pattern and duplicate the procedure in a process called **replication**. Excel displays a special fill handle to help with replication.

1

- Click cell B6 to position the insertion point.
- Click the Sum button (Excel Home tab | Editing group) to sum the cells, and then click the Enter button on the formula bar to display the total (Figure 6–70).

Q&A What other math operations can I perform?

You can type any formula in the formula bar using real numbers or cell references. You also can click the Microsoft Office Excel Help button on the ribbon to learn about many mathematical functions that will help you with formulas that are more complex.

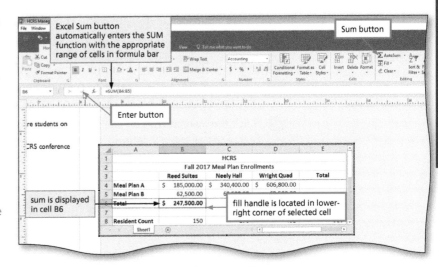

Figure 6–70

2

- Drag the fill handle in the lower-right corner of cell B6 across and through cells C6 through E6 to replicate the sum across the columns (Figure 6–71).

Q&A How does the fill handle replicate the sum?

When you drag to the right, the sum is adjusted to include the same number of cells above the total line in each column. When you drag down, the sum is adjusted to include cells to the left in each row.

What is the button that appears after replicating the function?

That is the 'Auto Fill Options' button. If you click the button, you have the choice to fill with or without formatting.

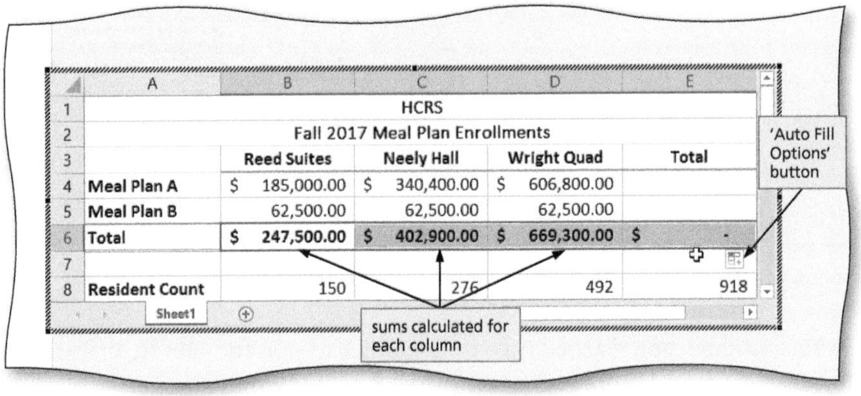

Figure 6–71

3

- Click cell E4 to select it.
- Click the Sum button (Excel Home tab | Editing group) to sum the cells and then click the Enter button on the formula bar to display the total.
- Drag the fill handle in the lower-right corner of cell E4 down through cell E5 to replicate the sum.
- Apply the Comma Style format to cell E5, if necessary (Figure 6–72).

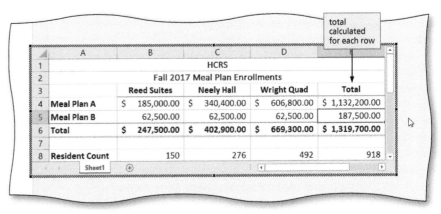

Figure 6–72

Other Ways

1. Double-click Sum button (Excel Home tab | Editing Group)

2. To sum, press ALT+=

3. To replicate, click Fill button (Excel Home tab | Editing group), click desired fill direction

To Move and Position the Table

The following steps move and reposition the embedded table.

1 Click outside the table to display the table border.

2 Zoom to 80%. Scroll as necessary to view both the letter and the table.

3 Drag the border of the table to position the table in the lower portion of the letter. Resize the table as necessary to fill the area as shown in Figure 6–73.

4 Click the Save button on the Quick Access Toolbar to save the file with the same file name in the same location.

5 Check the publication for spelling errors and design errors. If instructed to do so, print the publication.

6 Click the Close button on the Publisher title bar to exit Publisher.

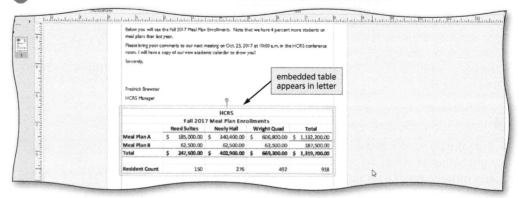

Figure 6–73

Summary

In this module, you learned how to use tables to present data in efficient and meaningful ways. First, you formatted a WordArt object to assist in branding a company name. Next, you created and formatted tables and data, including the use of table styles, merging, and cell diagonals. Next, you created a calendar with a page border on the master page. Finally, you embedded data from Excel into a Publisher publication and used the Excel-enhanced tools to format the table and perform calculations.

CONSIDER THIS: PLAN AHEAD

What decisions will you need to make when creating your next custom publication?
Use these guidelines as you complete the assignments in this module and create your own publications outside of this class.

1. Choose reusable objects.
    a) Use business information sets.
    b) Use building blocks.
    c) Create new objects.
2. Apply shape effects sparingly.
3. Create tables.
    a) Create and format a table.
    b) Enter data.
    c) Add table borders.
4. Create a calendar.
5. Use the master page for repeating items across pages.
6. Apply BorderArt to make pages or tables stand out.
7. If you need added functionality, embed an Excel table.
    a) Embed tables for static data edited in Publisher.
    b) Link tables when you want both Publisher and Excel to change and to use the full functionality of Excel.

Apply Your Knowledge

Reinforce the skills and apply the concepts you learned in this module.

Formatting a Table

Note: To complete this assignment, you will be required to use the Data Files. Please contact your instructor for information about accessing the Data Files.

Instructions: Run Publisher. Open the publication, Apply 6-1 Monthly Expenses, from the Data Files. The publication is a table of monthly expenses for statewide meetings of the Alpha Omega Sorority. Figure 6–74 shows the formatted table.

Perform the following tasks:

1. Click the table. Click the More button (Table Tools Design tab | Table Formats group). Click 'Table Style 24' to apply the format to the table.

2. Click the Select Table button (Table Tools Layout tab | Table group) and then click Select Table in the gallery to select the entire table. Display the Home tab. Change the font size to 20.

3. Click anywhere in the first row of the table. Click the 'Insert Rows Above' button (Table Tools Layout tab | Rows & Columns group) to insert a row above row 1.

Alpha Omega Sorority Monthly Meeting Expenses			
Expense Month	January	February	March
Hall Rental	120.00	120.00	120.00
Postage	65.90	62.90	69.91
Computer and Wi-Fi	117.29	118.50	119.12
Paper Supplies	46.57	41.67	48.70
Food/Beverages	122.04	99.88	100.00
Awards	50.00	50.00	50.00
Total	521.80	492.95	507.73

Figure 6–74

4. With the new row still selected, click the Merge Cells button (Table Tools Layout tab | Merge group) to merge the cells in the new row. Type **Alpha Omega Sorority Monthly Meeting Expenses** to enter a title. Format the font size to be 28. If necessary, format the text to be white.

5. Center the title. For each of the column headings, click the 'Align Center Right' button (Table Tools Layout tab | Alignment group). Right-align the numeric data.

6. Click the first cell in the second row. Click the Diagonals button (Table Tools Layout tab | Merge group) and then click Divide Down in the gallery to create a cell with a diagonal. Type **Expense** in the left side of the split cell and then click the 'Align Bottom Left' button (Table Tools Layout tab | Alignment group) to change the heading alignment. Drag the bottom border of the second row down, until all of the text appears. In the right side of the split cell, type **Month** and then click the 'Align Center Right' button (Table Tools Layout tab | Alignment group) to change the heading alignment. Change both headings to font size 20.

7. Select both halves of the diagonal cell. Click the Line Weight button (Table Tools Design tab | Borders group) and then choose 2 ¼ pt in the gallery. Click the Line Color button (Table Tools Design tab | Borders group) and then click 'Accent 5 (White)' in the gallery to choose white as the color. Click the Borders arrow (Table Tools Design tab | Borders group) to display the Borders gallery and then click Diagonal Borders to add a white, diagonal border to the selection.

8. Select the first two rows of the table. Click the Line Weight button (Table Tools Design tab | Borders group) and choose a 2¼ pt line. Click the Line color button (Table Tools Design tab | Borders group) and choose the 'Accent 5 (White)' color. Click the Borders arrow (Table Tools Design tab | Borders group) and choose All Borders.

9. Select rows 3 through 9. Click the Line Weight button (Table Tools Design tab | Borders group) and choose a 2¼ pt line. Click the Line color button (Table Tools Design tab | Borders

Continued >

Apply Your Knowledge *continued*

group) and choose 'Accent 3 (RGB (204,153,204))' as the line color. Click the Borders arrow (Table Tools Design tab | Borders group) and then choose All Borders.

10. Click the border of the table and then drag to align the table centered both horizontally and vertically, relative to the margins. *Hint*: Click the Align button (Table Tools Layout tab | Arrange group) and make choices from there.

11. If directed to do so by your instructor, draw a text box in the lower-right corner of the page and enter your name, and make other formatting decisions.

12. Open the Backstage view and then click Save As to display the Save As dialog box. Save the publication on your storage device using the file name, Apply 6-1 Monthly Expenses Complete.

13. Check the publication for spelling errors and design errors. Print the publication with appropriate printer settings.

14. Submit the file as specified by your instructor.

15. ✸ Look at the totals in the table. Are you sure they are correct? How do you know? If the table were embedded or linked to Excel, what tools, commands, or functions would you have used to enhance or check the table?

Extend Your Knowledge

Extend the skills you learned in this module and experiment with new skills. You may need to use Help to complete the assignment.

Adding an Excel Chart to a Publication

Note: To complete this assignment, you will be required to use the Data Files. Please contact your instructor for information about accessing the Data Files.

Instructions: Open the publication, Extend 6-1 IT Majors Table, from the Data Files. You will add a 3-D Column chart to the publication so that it appears as shown in Figure 6–75.

Perform the following tasks:

1. Use Help to learn more about adding an Excel chart to a Publisher publication.

2. Zoom to 40%. Double-click the table so that the Excel tabs appear on the Publisher ribbon.

3. Drag the lower-center sizing handle of the table down, to fill the page.

4. If directed by your instructor to do so, change the major in cell B1 to your major and change the major in cell C1 to a friend's major.

5. Drag to select cells A1 through D5. Do not include the totals row.

6. Display the Excel Insert tab. Click the 'Insert Column or Bar Chart' button (Excel Insert tab | Charts group) to display the gallery and then click the 3-D Column preview to add the chart to the publication.

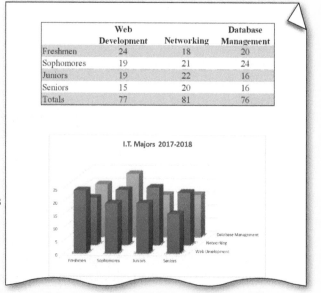

Figure 6–75

7. Click the scratch area to return to Publisher. Zoom to 120% and, if necessary, scroll to center the chart in the workspace.

8. Double-click the chart to enable the Excel tabs on the Publisher ribbon. Point to each part of the chart, labels, data columns, and legend to identify the various parts of the chart.

9. Display the Excel Chart Tools Design tab. Click the Style 5 button (Chart Tools Design tab | Chart Styles group).

10. Click to select the legend and then press the DELETE key to delete the legend.

11. Select the text in the Chart Title and then type `I.T. Majors 2017-2018` to replace the text.

12. Drag one of the top or bottom sizing handles on the chart to resize the chart to approximately 18 rows high. Drag a side sizing handle to increase the width of the chart to approximately six inches as measured on the horizontal ruler. Do not drag close to the edge of the workbook object.

13. Click the table above the chart. Display the Excel View tab. Click to remove the check mark in the Gridlines check box (Excel View tab | Show group).

14. Click outside the table to display the Publisher tabs on the ribbon. Check the publication for spelling errors and design errors.

15. Save the revised publication with the file name, Extend 6-1 Majors Table Complete. Print the publication and then submit it in the format specified by your instructor.

16. Exit Publisher.

17. ✷ In reviewing the available types of charts and graphs, what other type of chart might make sense for the data in the table? Why would a pie chart be a poor choice?

Expand Your World

Create a solution that uses cloud and web technologies by learning and investigating on your own from general guidance.

Uploading a Publication to Flickr

Instructions: You would like to upload one of your publications to Flickr to show your friends, but Flickr does not accept the .pub format. You decide to investigate saving the publication as a TIFF or TIF file.

Perform the following tasks:

1. Run Publisher and open a single-page publication you have created. Click File on the ribbon to open the Backstage view and then click Save As. Browse to your storage location.

2. Click the 'Save as type' button (Save As dialog box), and then click 'Tag Image File Format (*.tif)' in the list. Click the Save button. Exit Publisher. If Publisher asks you to save the publication again, click the Don't Save button.

3. Run a browser and navigate to http://flickr.com (Figure 6–76). If you have a Yahoo! account, click the Sign In button at the top of the page (or the 'Sign up with Yahoo' button). If you do not have an account, click the Sign Up button at the top of the page and then fill in the appropriate fields for a free account.

Figure 6–76

Source: flickr.com

Continued >

Expand Your World *continued*

4. Once you are signed in, click the Upload command on the menu bar. When the Upload window appears, click the 'Choose photos and videos to upload' button. Navigate to the location of your .tiff or .tif file and then double-click the file to upload it. Add a short description.

5. Click the 'Upload 1 Photo' button in the upper-right portion of the window and then click the 'Upload to Photostream' button when prompted to finish the upload process.

6. Right-click the image in the Flickr window and then click Copy shortcut on the shortcut menu to copy the web address to the clipboard.

7. Paste the image address in an email to your instructor.

8. Write a paragraph about your experience with the Flickr program. Include several advantages and disadvantages of collaborating in this manner.

9. Submit the assignment in the format specified by your instructor.

10. ✺ What other photo sharing programs have you heard about or used? What are the advantages to a web-based, free service such as Flickr?

In the Labs

Design, create, modify, and/or use a publication following the guidelines, concepts, and skills presented in this module. Labs 1 and 2, which increase in difficulty, require you to create solutions based on what you learned in the module; Lab 3 requires you to apply your creative thinking and problem-solving skills to design and implement a solution.

Lab 1: Creating a Logo

Problem: The Pub Hub restaurant would like to brand its name. The company has asked you to use your knowledge of shape effects to create a logo. Prepare the publication shown in Figure 6–77.

Figure 6–77

Perform the following tasks:

1. Run Publisher. In the template gallery, click the Blank 11 × 8.5" thumbnail. Use the Page Design tab to set the font scheme to Metro and the color scheme to Metro.

2. Insert a WordArt object. Click the 'Gradient Fill - Orange, Shadow, Circular' preview in the WordArt Transform Styles area of the WordArt gallery to select it. Change the font to Consolas and the font size to 48. Type a space and then type **Pub Hub** in the Edit WordArt Text dialog box. Click the OK button (Edit WordArt Text dialog box) to insert the WordArt object on the page.

3. Use the Measurement toolbar to resize the WordArt to approximately 6 × 6 inches.

4. Click the Shape Effects button (WordArt Tools Format tab | WordArt Style group), click 3-D Rotation, and then click 3-D Rotation options to display the Format Shape dialog box. Change the X Rotation to 340 degrees.

5. Click the Shape Effects button (WordArt Tools Format tab | WordArt Styles group) and then click Bevel to display the Shape Effects gallery. Click 3-D Options in the Shape Effects gallery to display the Format Shape dialog box. If necessary, click 3-D Format to display the settings. Enter the values as shown in Table 6–4.

Table 6–4 3-D Format Settings

SETTING	VALUE
Top bevel button	Angle
Top bevel Width box	12
Top bevel Height box	12
Bottom bevel Width box	0
Bottom bevel Width box	0
Depth Size box	48
Contour Size box	0
Material button	Plastic
Lighting button	Bright Bottom

6. Click the Shape Effects button (WordArt Tools Format tab | WordArt Styles group), and then click Glow to display the Glow Gallery. Click the 'Accent 4, 18 pt glow' preview to apply a glow effect.

7. Click the Shape Outline button (WordArt Tools Format tab | WordArt Styles) and then click No Outline in the gallery.

8. If instructed to do so, create a small text box in the upper-right corner of the publication and insert your name and class number.

9. Save the publication with the file name, Lab 6-1 Pub Hub Logo.

10. Submit the file as directed by your instructor.

11. Exit Publisher.

12. ✳ Did the chosen color scheme affect the WordArt Styles? How do you know? What is the best way to change the color of WordArt? Why?

Lab 2: **Using BorderArt on a Calendar**

Problem: Your nephew's third grade teacher wants a calendar for next month. She will add events and assignments to the calendar, but she wants you to help with its initial design. She reminds you to use a decorative border around the calendar (Figure 6–78).

Perform the following tasks:

1. Run Publisher. In the template gallery, choose the Pinstripes calendar from the built-in calendar templates. Choose the Citrus color scheme and the Casual font scheme. Choose a landscape orientation.

Figure 6–78

Continued >

2. Choose a One month per page timeframe, and set the calendar dates to begin and end in October 2017 so that Publisher creates a single page with a single month's calendar.

3. If directed by your instructor to do so, choose the current month.

4. Create the publication. Change the picture to one that represents October and then delete the caption. Delete the picture in the scratch area.

5. Right-click the colored rectangle in the background and then click Format AutoShape on the shortcut menu.

6. When Publisher displays the Format AutoShape dialog box, click the BorderArt button to display the BorderArt dialog box. Choose the Candy Corn border art in the Available Borders list. Click the OK button (BorderArt dialog box).

7. In the Format AutoShape dialog box, set the width to size 24 pt. Click the OK button (Format AutoShape dialog box).

8. Drag a sizing handle to increase the size of the rectangle slightly.

9. If necessary, adjust the size of fonts in the table. Save the publication with the file name, Lab 6-2 Grade School Calendar.

10. Submit the publication in the format specified by your instructor.

11. Exit Publisher.

12. ✷ What kinds of formats could you apply to the cells in the calendar table to help the teacher enter data at a later date? Would you consider enlarging the table and reducing the size of the picture or omitting the picture? Why or why not?

Lab 3: **Consider This: Your Turn**

Using a Master Page

Problem: The Jupiter City Parks and Recreation Department would like you to create a master page that they can use as a background for an upcoming brochure.

Perform the following tasks:

Part 1:   Create a blank 11 × 8.5" publication. Go to the master page. Add a rectangle with a light blue gradient background that fills the page. Choose an appropriate BorderArt. Create a WordArt object with a 3-D Rotation shape effect that contains the word, Jupiter. Right-click the WordArt object and then click Format WordArt on the shortcut menu to display the Format WordArt dialog box. Change the transparency to 75%. Close the WordArt dialog box. Return to the publication. Create a table of four columns and five rows. Select an appropriate table style. Insert June, July, and August as the column headings for columns 2 through 4. For row headings, enter the names of summer programs offered in your city. Insert a row with an overall heading and format it appropriately. Save the publication.

Part 2: ✷ What kind of publications might use a master page? Which items from a business information set might be appropriate for a master page? Which items would have to stay in the foreground? Why?

7 Advanced Formatting and Merging Publications with Data

Objectives

You will have mastered the material in this project when you can:

- Create a watermark
- Explain character spacing techniques
- Kern and track characters
- Use the Measurement task pane to edit character spacing
- Differentiate among tab styles
- Set a tab stop and enter tabbed text
- Produce a main publication to be used as a form letter
- Use the Mail Merge Wizard to create form letters

- Create and edit a data source
- Use grouped field codes
- Select, sort, and filter records in a data source
- Insert individual field codes and preview results
- Recolor and compress graphics
- Merge a publication with an Excel database
- Print selected records

Introduction

Whether you want individual letters sent to everyone on a mailing list, personalized envelopes for a mass mailing, an invoice sent to all customers, or a printed set of mailing labels to apply to your brochures, you can use Publisher to maintain your data and make the task of mass mailing and merged publication creation easier.

Merged publications, such as form letters, should be timely and professional looking, yet at the same time personalized. Used regularly in both business and personal correspondence, a **form letter** has the same basic content no matter to whom it is sent; however, items such as name, address, city, state, and ZIP code change from one form letter to the next. Thus, form letters are personalized to the addressee. An individual is more likely to open and read a personalized letter or email than a standard Dear Sir or Dear Madam message. With word processing and database techniques, it is easy to generate individual, personalized documents for a large group and include features unique to desktop publishing. A **data source** or **data file** is a file that may contain a list of names and addresses, or it also may include paths to pictures, product part numbers, postal bar codes, customer purchase history, amount due, accounts receivable, email addresses, and a variety of additional data that you may use in a merged publication.

Project — Merging Form Letters and Tickets

The project in this module begins with letterhead from the Rocketroad Drag Racing racetrack and creates a form letter with merged fields for each addressee from a Publisher mailing list, as shown in Figure 7–1. The letter, formatted with a graphic watermark (Figure 7–1a), will be mailed with enclosed tickets (Figure 7–1b) that displays individual seat numbers.

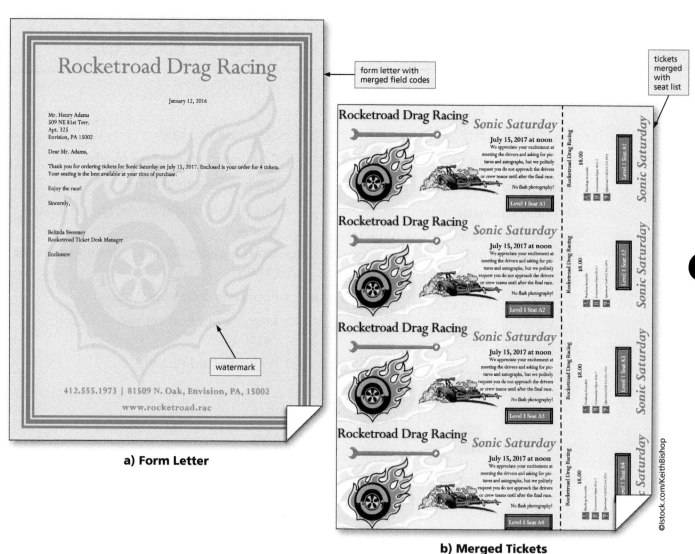

a) Form Letter

b) Merged Tickets

Figure 7–1

The following roadmap identifies general activities you will perform as you progress through this module:

1. CREATE a WATERMARK.
2. CHANGE the CHARACTER SPACING, such as tracking, kerning, and scaling.
3. SET and use TABS.

4. USE the MAIL MERGE WIZARD to create a data source.

5. INSERT FIELD CODES in a form letter.

6. EDIT the DATA SOURCE and sort.

7. ADJUST GRAPHICS by editing the color brightness, contrast, and compression.

8. Create tickets to MERGE with an EXCEL LIST.

To Run Publisher and Open a File

The following steps run Publisher and open a file. To complete these steps, you will be required to use the Data Files. Please contact your instructor for information about accessing the Data Files.

1 Run Publisher. Click 'Open Other Publications' in the left pane of the Publisher gallery to display the Open gallery.

2 Click the Browse button and then navigate to the location of the file to be opened (in this case, CIS 101/Publisher/Data Files/Module 07).

3 Double-click the file named Racetrack Letterhead to open the selected publication in the Publisher window.

4 If the Publisher window is not maximized, click the Maximize button on the Publisher title bar to maximize it.

5 If the Special Characters button (Home tab | Paragraph group) is not selected already, click it to display formatting marks on the screen.

6 If the Page Navigation pane is displayed, click the Page Number button on the status bar to hide the Page Navigation pane, because this is a single-page publication (Figure 7–2).

BTW

The Ribbon and Screen Resolution
Publisher may change how the groups and buttons within the groups appear on the ribbon, depending on the computer or mobile device's screen resolution. Thus, your ribbon may look different from the ones in this book if you are using a screen resolution other than 1366 × 768.

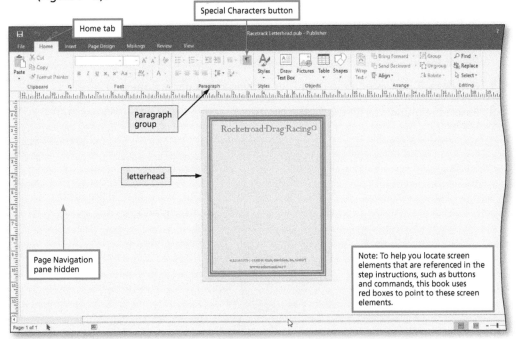

Figure 7–2

Watermarks

A **watermark** is a semitransparent graphic that is visible in the background on a printed page. In Publisher, you create watermarks by placing text or graphics on the master page. Recall that the master page is a background area similar to the header and footer area in traditional word processing software. Each publication starts with one master page. If you have a multipage publication, you can choose to use two different master pages for cases such as facing pages in a book; you might want different graphics in the background of each page. If you want to display master page objects only on certain pages, the Apply To button (Master Page tab | Master Page group) provides several options. This is useful for cases in which background images appear on every page, except the title page in a longer publication, or a watermark that appears on the inside of a brochure but not on the front.

How do you use watermarks?

As a graphic visible in the background on some publications, watermarks may be translucent; others can be seen on the paper when held up to the light. Other times the paper itself has a watermark when it is manufactured. Watermarks are used as both decoration and identification, as well as to provide security solutions to prevent document fraud. Creating watermarks on the master page causes the watermark to repeat on each page of the publication. A master page can contain anything that you can put on a publication page, as well as headers, footers, page numbers, date and time, and certain layout guides that can be set up only on a master page.

To Insert and Place the Watermark Graphic

The following steps insert the graphic that will be used for the watermark on the master page. To complete these steps, you will be required to use the Data Files. Please contact your instructor for information about accessing the Data Files.

1 Press CTRL+M to access the master page.

2 Display the Insert tab.

3 Click the Pictures button (Insert tab | Illustrations group) to display the Insert Picture dialog box.

4 If necessary, navigate to the Data Files and insert the picture named Flame.

5 Resize the graphic to fill the page horizontally within the margins (Figure 7–3).

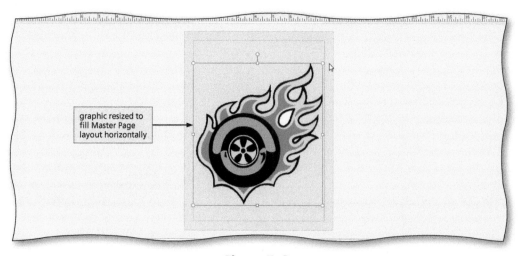

graphic resized to fill Master Page layout horizontally

Figure 7–3

To Change the Transparency of a Graphic

The following steps change the transparency of the graphic. *Why? The downloaded graphic is too dark for a watermark; text inserted over the graphic would be difficult to read.* You also will save the publication.

1

- Right-click the graphic to display the shortcut menu (Figure 7–4).

Figure 7–4

2

- Click Format Picture on the shortcut menu to display the Format Picture dialog box.

- In the Transparency area, drag the Transparency slider to 95% (Figure 7–5).

Q&A

What does the transparency percentage mean?
A 100% transparency appears white. A 0% transparency displays the picture in its original, full-color state.

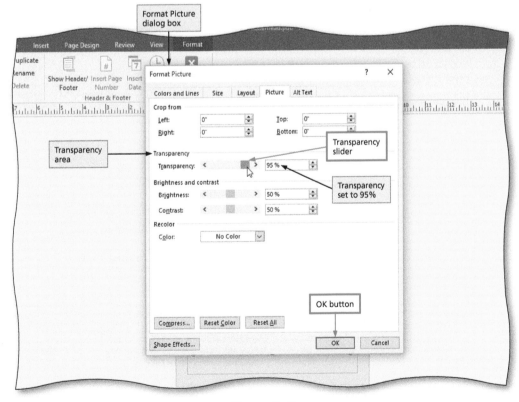

Figure 7–5

- Click the OK button (Format Picture dialog box) to close the dialog box and apply the transparency to the graphic (Figure 7–6).

 Q&A

What else could I add to the master page?

You could add a background effect, headers, footers, or any text or graphics that you want to appear on every page of the publication.

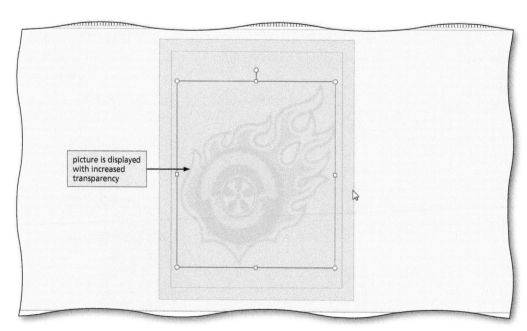

picture is displayed with increased transparency

Figure 7–6

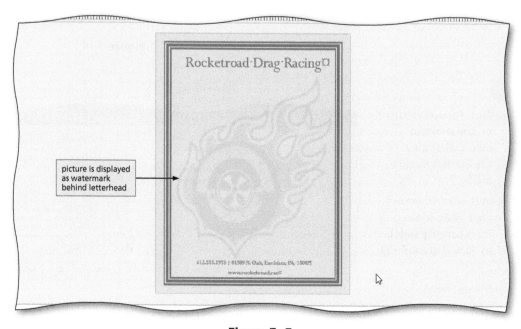

- Press CTRL+M to close the master page.
- Click the File tab to display the Backstage view and then click Save As. Browse to your storage location. Save the file with the file name, Racing Letter (Figure 7–7).

Rocketroad·Drag·Racing

picture is displayed as watermark behind letterhead

412.555.1973 | 81509 N. Oak, Envision, PA, 15082
www.rocketroadrac

Figure 7–7

Other Ways

1. Click Recolor button (Picture Tools Format tab | Adjust group), click 'Picture Color Options' on Recolor menu, set Transparency slider (Format Picture dialog box), click OK button

2. Click Corrections button (Picture Tools Format tab | Adjust group), click 'Picture Corrections Options' in the Corrections gallery, set Transparency slider (Format Picture dialog box), click OK button

3. Click Format Shape Dialog Box Launcher (Picture Tools Format tab | Picture Styles group), click Picture tab (Format Picture dialog box), set Transparency slider, click OK button

Spacing between Characters

Sometimes, you need to fine-tune the spacing between characters on the page. For instance, you may want to spread characters apart for better legibility. Other times, you may want to move characters closer together for space considerations without changing the font or font size. Or, you may be using a font that employs **proportional spacing**, or different widths for different characters. For example, in a proportionally spaced font, the letter i is narrower than the letter m. This book uses a proportionally spaced font, as do most books, newspapers, and magazines.

The opposite of proportional spacing is **monospacing**, where every letter is the same width. Older printers and monitors were limited to monospaced fonts because of the dot matrix used to create the characters. Now, almost all printers, with the exception of line printers, are capable of printing with either proportionally spaced or monospaced fonts. Because most fonts use proportional spacing, the scaling, tracking, and kerning features in Publisher allow you many ways to make very precise character spacing adjustments.

Scaling, or **text scaling**, refers to the process of shrinking or stretching text. It changes the width of individual characters in text boxes. Scaling can be applied to any text box by using the Measurement task pane.

Tracking, or **character spacing**, refers to the adjustment of the general spacing between selected characters. Tracking text compensates for the spacing irregularities caused when you make text much larger or much smaller. For example, smaller type is easier to read when it has been tracked loosely, meaning more space appears between characters. Tracking maintains the original height of the font and overrides adjustments made by justification of the margins. Tracking is available only if you are working on a print publication. It is not available with web publications.

Kerning, or **track kerning**, is a form of tracking related to pairs of characters that can appear too close together or too far apart, even with standard tracking. Kerning can create the appearance of even spacing and is used to fit text into a given space or adjust line breaks. For instance, certain uppercase letters, such as T, V, W, and Y, have a wider top than bottom and often are kerned when preceded or followed by a lowercase a, e, i, o, or u. With manual kerning, Publisher lets you choose from normal, expanded, and condensed kerning for special effects. Text in smaller point sizes usually does not need to be kerned, unless the font contains many serifs.

You can adjust the spacing between characters and the size of characters using the lower three boxes on the Measurement task pane as described in Table 7–1. Some spacing specifications also can be applied using the ribbon or through dialog boxes.

Table 7–1 Character Spacing Tools in the Measurement Task Pane		
Box Name	**Specifies**	**Preset Unit of Measurement**
Tracking	General space between characters	Percent
Text Scaling	Width of characters	Percent
Kerning	Subtle space between paired characters	Point size

In the following sections, you will track and kern text that appears at the top and bottom of the letterhead.

To Kern Character Pairs

The following steps kern character pairs in the heading on the page. ***Why?*** *Some letters look better and are easier to read when kerned, especially when using large font sizes.* You can use kerning to move characters closer together or further apart.

- Click the Rocketroad Drag Racing textbox and then press the F9 key to zoom to 100%.

- Click the Object Size button on the taskbar to display the Measurement task pane. If necessary, drag the Measurement task pane so that it floats on the left of the page.

- Drag to select the letters, tr, in the word, Rocketroad (Figure 7–8).

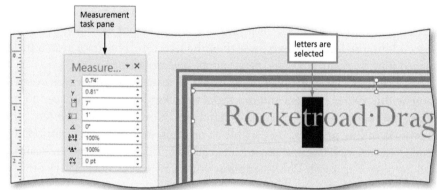

Figure 7–8

- Drag through the text in the Kerning box in the Measurement task pane, type 2 to replace the value, and then press the ENTER key to move the letters further apart (Figure 7–9).

Q&A How is kerning measured?
When you enter a value in the Kerning box (Measurement task pane), it changes the points between characters. Recall that a point is approximately equal to 1/72 of an inch. The higher the number, the further apart the characters will appear. A negative number will move the characters closer together.

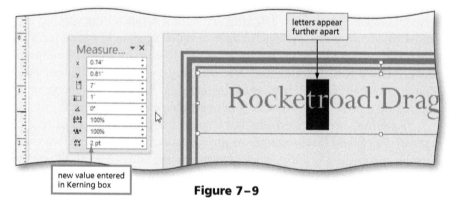

Figure 7–9

❸

- Select the letters, Ro, in the word, Rocketroad.

- Drag through the text in the Kerning box (Measurement task pane), type -2 as the new value, and then press the ENTER key to move the letters closer together (Figure 7–10).

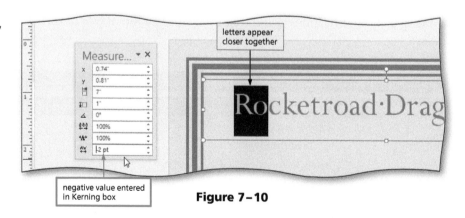

Figure 7–10

Other Ways

1. Right-click selected text, point to Change Text on shortcut menu, click Character Spacing on Change Text submenu, enter kerning settings (Character Spacing dialog box), click OK button

2. To increase kern, press CTRL+SHIFT+RIGHT BRACKET (])

3. To decrease kern, press CTRL+SHIFT+LEFT BRACKET ([)

To Track Characters

The following steps track the small text at the bottom of the page more loosely. *Why? Small text is harder to read when the letters are very close together.* Publisher has five predefined tracking sizes that include Very Tight, Tight, Normal, Loose, and Very Loose.

1

- Scroll to the bottom of the page, click the text in the text box, and then press CTRL+A to select all of the text.

- Click the Character Spacing button (Home tab | Font group) to display the Character Spacing gallery (Figure 7–11).

Experiment

- Point to each of the choices in the Character Spacing gallery and watch how the text changes.

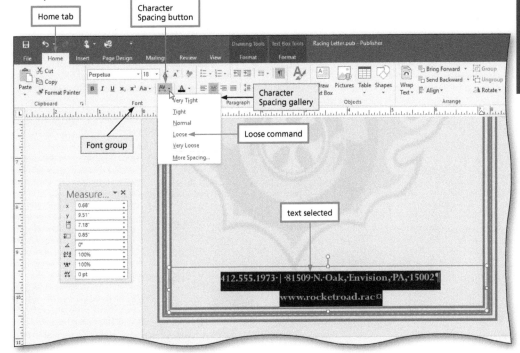

Figure 7–11

2

- Click Loose in the Character Spacing gallery to track the text more loosely (Figure 7–12).

Q&A

How can I tell if the text changed?
You can click the Undo button (Quick Access Toolbar) and then click the Redo Button (Quick Access Toolbar) to see the before and after effects of tracking.

How is tracking measured?
Tracking is a percentage of how much space is inserted between characters. Tight tracking reduces the percentage. Loose tracking increases the percentage. For example, when you choose Very Loose, the text is tracked 125%.

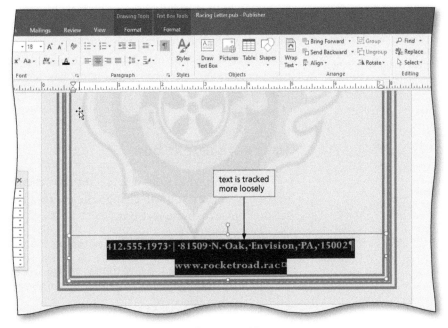

Figure 7–12

Other Ways

1. Enter setting in Tracking box in Measurement task pane

2. Right-click text, point to Change Text on shortcut menu, click Character Spacing on Change Text submenu, enter tracking settings (Character Spacing dialog box), click OK button

The Character Spacing Dialog Box

The Character Spacing dialog box (Figure 7–13) displays more ways to customize the spacing between characters and the width of the characters themselves. To access the Character Spacing dialog box, you can click the Character Spacing button (Home tab | Font group) and then click More Spacing in the Character Spacing gallery. Alternately, you can right-click the selected text, point to Change Text on the shortcut menu, and then click Character Spacing on the Change Text submenu.

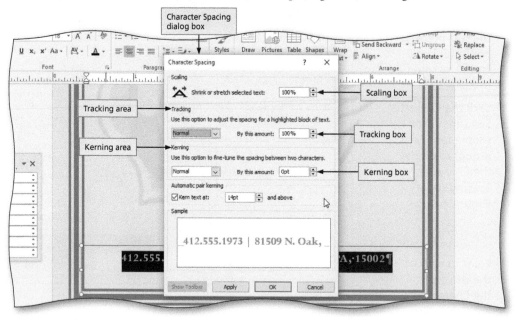

Figure 7–13

Using the dialog box, you can make precise changes to the scaling, tracking, and kerning of selected text. In the Tracking area, you can adjust the tracking by using one of the five predefined adjustments as described earlier, or you can specify an exact percentage. In the Kerning area, you can adjust the tracking by using one of three predefined kerns: Normal, Expand, and Condense. If you prefer, you can specify an exact percentage. If a pair of characters is selected, you can apply a kern to a specific font size.

To Create a Text Box

The following steps create a text box that will contain the body text of the letter itself. In addition, you will change the paragraph spacing as you did in Module 5 and set the font size in the text box.

1 Click the 'Show Whole Page' button on the status bar to display the whole page.

2 Display the Home tab and then click the 'Draw a Text Box' button (Home tab | Objects group). Drag to draw a large text box in the middle of the page.

3 Set the font size to 12.

④ Click the Paragraph Settings Dialog Box Launcher (Home tab | Paragraph group) to display the Paragraph dialog box. If necessary, click the Indents and Spacing tab to display the Indents and Spacing sheet.

⑤ In the Line spacing area (Paragraph dialog box), select the text in the After paragraphs box and then type 0 to replace the text. Click the OK button to change the settings and close the dialog box.

⑥ Use the Measurement task pane to enter the following settings: Horizontal Position 1", Vertical Position 2", Width 6.5", and Height 7.25" (Figure 7–14).

⑦ Close the Measurement task pane.

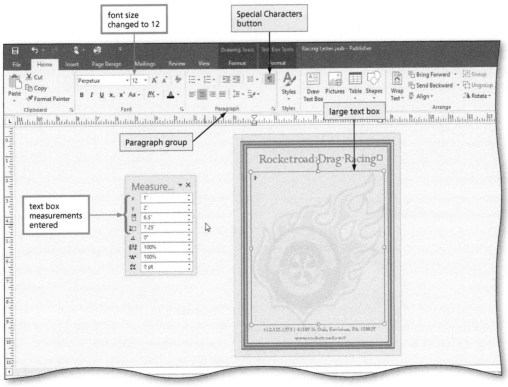

Figure 7–14

BTW
Leader Tabs
A **leader tab** is a special type of right tab in which the blank space to the left of the text is filled with a specific character. Customized via the Tabs dialog box, a leader repeats the character from the previous text or tab stop to fill in the tabbed gap. For example, a printed musical program might contain the name of the composition on the left and the composer on the right. Using a leader tab, that space in between could be filled by dots or periods to help the viewer's eye follow across to the corresponding composer.

BTW
Displaying Rulers
To turn the rulers on or off, press CTRL+R or click the Rulers check box (View tab | Show group).

BTW
Units of Measurement
If you want to change the unit of measurement on the ruler, open the Backstage view, and then click the Options tab to display the Publisher Options dialog box. Click Advanced in the left pane and then click the 'Show measurements in units of' arrow. Choose the preferred unit of measurement and then click the OK button (Publisher Options dialog box).

Working with Tabs and the Ruler

The **ruler** appears above the Publisher workspace and contains buttons, markers, margins, and measurements to help you place text and objects. Publisher uses tabs and markers to help position tab stops, margins, and indentures within text boxes. A **tab**, or **tab stop**, is a horizontal location inside a text box designated by a tab stop marker on the Publisher ruler. A **tab stop marker** appears darkened on the ruler as a straight line, an L-shaped marker, or a T-shaped marker. A **margin marker** appears as either a gray pentagon or gray rectangle on the ruler. Margin markers set and indicate margins on the left and right of a text box. A special **First-Line Indent marker** allows you to change the left margin for only the first line in a paragraph. The typing area within the text box boundaries appears in white on the ruler; the rest of the ruler is gray. Numbers on the ruler represent inches, but inches can be changed to centimeters, picas, pixels, or points. The **tab selector** is located at the left end of the ruler. It displays an icon representing the alignment of the text at the tab stop (Figure 7–15).

BTW
Special Characters
Recall that the Special
Characters button (Home
tab | Paragraph group)
shown in Figure 7–14
makes special nonprinting
characters visible to help
you format text passages,
including tab characters (→),
end-of-paragraph marks (¶),
and end-of-frame marks (□).

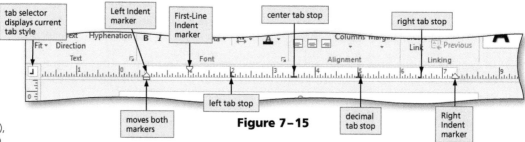

Figure 7–15

Table 7–2 explains the functions of the markers and buttons on the ruler, as well as how to modify them.

Table 7–2 Ruler Tools

Tool Name	Description	How to Change	Other Ways
First-Line Indent marker	A downward-pointing pentagon that indicates the position at which paragraphs begin	Drag to desired location	Double-click margin marker, enter location in First line box (Paragraph dialog box)
Left Indent marker	An upward-pointing pentagon that indicates the left position at which text wraps	Drag to desired location	Double-click margin marker, enter location in Left box (Paragraph dialog box)
Move both markers	A small rectangle used to move both the Left Indent marker and the First-Line Indent marker at the same time	Drag to desired location	Right-click text box, click 'Format Text Box', click Text Box tab (Format Text Box dialog box), enter text box margins
Object margins	Gray indicates the area outside the object margin; white indicates the area inside the object margin	Resize object	Right-click text box, click 'Format Text Box', click Size tab (Format Text Box dialog box), enter height and width
Right Indent marker	An upward-pointing pentagon that indicates the rightmost position at which text wraps to the next line	Drag to desired location	Double-click margin marker, enter location in Right box (Paragraph dialog box)
Tab selector	Displays the current alignment setting: left, right, center, or leader	Click to toggle choice	Double-click tab stop marker, select alignment (Paragraph dialog box)
Tab stop marker	Displays the location of a tab stop	Click to create; drag to move	Double-click ruler, set tab stop location (Paragraph dialog box)

BTW
Zero Point
You also can CTRL+drag or
CTRL+click the tab selector
to change the publication's
zero point or **ruler origin**.
The zero point is the position
of 0 inches on the ruler. It
is useful for measuring the
width and height of objects
on the page without having
to add or subtract from a
number other than zero.
To change the ruler back,
double-click the tab selector.

You can drag markers to any place on the ruler within the text box boundaries. You can click a marker to display a dotted line through the publication, which allows you to see in advance where the marker will be set. Markers are paragraph specific, which means that when you set the tabs and indents, they apply to the current paragraph. Once the tabs and indents are set, however, pressing the ENTER key while typing carries the markers forward to the next paragraph.

Setting Tabs

Publisher offers two ways to set tabs. With a text box selected, you can choose the type of tab you want by clicking the tab selector button until the appropriate icon is displayed. You then can click at the desired tab location on the ruler to place the icon.

A second way to set tabs in a text box is by using the Tabs sheet in the Paragraph dialog box (Figure 7–16). You can access the Paragraph dialog box by double-clicking the ruler or by clicking the Paragraph Settings Dialog Box Launcher (Home tab | Paragraph group).

BTW
Tab Stop Alignment
The tab stop alignment can
be changed by clicking the
Paragraph Settings Dialog
Box Launcher (Home tab |
Paragraph group), by double-
clicking an existing marker,
or by clicking the tab selector
until it displays the type of
tab that you want.

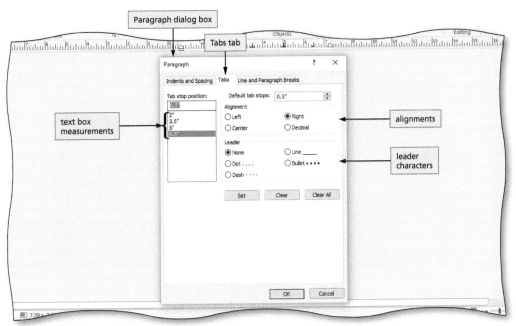

Figure 7–16

BTW

Default Tabs
Default tabs are set every .5 inches in a text box; default tabs do not display markers.

BTW

Leader Tab Characters
Available leader tab character styles include None, Dot, Dash, Line, and Bullet.

With tab stops, you can align text to the left, right, center, or at a decimal character. Additionally, Publisher can insert special leading characters before a tab, such as dashes, dots, or lines. Table 7–3 lists the types of tab alignments and their common uses.

Table 7–3 Types of Tab Alignments

Name	Icon	Action	Purpose
Left tab	L	Text begins at tab stop and is inserted to the right	Used for most tabbing
Right tab	⌐	Text begins at tab stop and is inserted to the left	Used for indexes, programs, and lists
Center tab	⊥	Text is centered at the tab stop as it is typed	Used to center a list within a column
Decimal tab	⊥	Aligns numbers only, based on a decimal point, independent of the number of digits	Used for aligning currency amounts in a list
Leader tab	⊥	Text begins at tab stop and is inserted to the left; space preceding the tab is filled with chosen character: dot, dash, line, or bullet	Used for tables of contents, printed programs, bulletins, etc.

The tab stop alignment can be changed by using the Paragraph dialog box, by double-clicking an existing marker, or by clicking the tab selector until it displays the type of tab that you want. The leader character can be changed only through the Paragraph dialog box.

To Set a Tab Stop

The following step uses the horizontal ruler to set, or insert, a tab stop at the 3.25" position in the form letter text box. *Why? The standard modified block format of letter writing displays the date beginning at the center of the letter, horizontally.*

- With the insertion point located in the main text box of the form letter, press the F9 key to zoom to 100%.

- Click the horizontal ruler at the 3.25" mark to create a left tab stop. Move the pointer to view the tab stop marker (Figure 7–17).

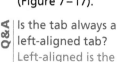 Is the tab always a left-aligned tab?
Left-aligned is the default tab setting. If you want to change the tab type, click the tab selector until you see the tab type you want and then click the ruler at the tab stop location.

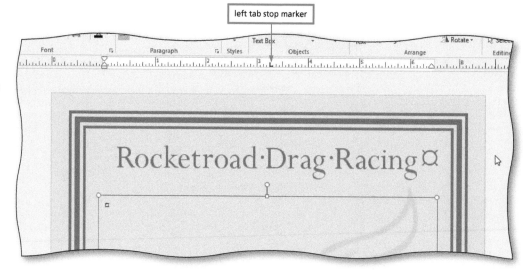

Figure 7–17

Experiment

- Click the Paragraph Settings Dialog Box Launcher (Home tab | Paragraph group) and then click the Tabs tab to view the tab setting. Click the Close button (Paragraph dialog box).

Other Ways

1. Click Paragraph Settings Dialog Box Launcher button (Home tab | Paragraph group), click Tabs tab (Paragraph dialog box), enter tab stop position in Tab stop position text box, click OK button

To Enter Tabbed Text

1 CREATE WATERMARK | 2 CHANGE CHARACTER SPACING | 3 SET TABS | **4 USE MAIL MERGE WIZARD**
5 INSERT FIELD CODES | 6 EDIT DATA SOURCE | 7 ADJUST GRAPHICS | 8 MERGE EXCEL LIST

The following steps enter tabbed text. *Why? Pressing the TAB key will move the insertion point to the center of the letter, so that the date can be entered.*

- Press the TAB key to move the insertion point to the tab stop (Figure 7–18).

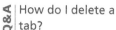 How do I delete a tab?
To delete a tab, click the Paragraph Settings Dialog Box Launcher (Home tab | Paragraph group) and then click the Tabs tab (Paragraph dialog box). Select the tab stop location and then click the Clear button.

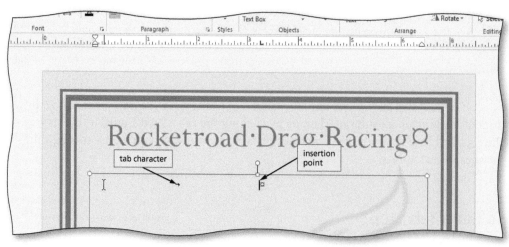

Figure 7–18

2

- Display the Insert tab on the ribbon.
- Click the 'Date & Time' button (Insert tab | Text group) to display the Date and Time dialog box.
- Click the third available format and then click the Update automatically check box to place a check mark in it (Figure 7–19).

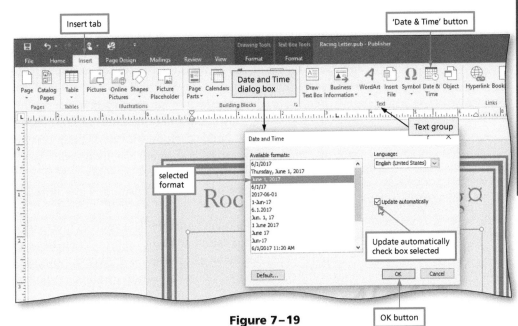

Figure 7–19

3

- Click the OK button (Date and Time dialog box) to insert the current date at the tab stop.
- Press the ENTER key twice to insert a blank line (Figure 7–20).

Q&A Why is my date different?
Publisher inserts the current date; your display should reflect the current date (the date you create this publication).

Rocketroad·Drag·Racing

June·1,·2017

Figure 7–20

4

- Click the Save button on the Quick Access Toolbar to overwrite the previously saved file.

Break Point: If you wish to take a break, this is a good place to do so. Exit Publisher. To resume at a later time, run Publisher, open the file named Racing Letter, and then continue following the steps from this location forward.

Merging Data into Publications

The process of generating an individualized publication for mass mailing involves creating a main publication and a data source. The main publication contains the constant or unchanging text, punctuation, space, and graphics, embedded with variables or changing values from the data source. A data source or database is a file

BTW

Tabs vs. Indents
Sometimes it is difficult to determine whether to use tab stops or indents. Use tab stops when you want to indent paragraphs as you go, or when you want a simple column. When the tab stop is positioned for a long passage of text, using the TAB key to indent the first line of each paragraph is inefficient, because you must press it each time you begin a new paragraph. In these cases, it is better to use an indent because it automatically carries forward when you press the ENTER key.

BTW

Main Publications
When you open a main publication, Publisher attempts to open the associated data source file, too. If the data source is not in exactly the same location (i.e., drive and folder) as when it originally was merged and saved, Publisher displays a dialog box indicating that it cannot find the data source. When this occurs, click the 'Find Data Source' button to display the Open Data Source dialog box, and locate the data source file yourself.

where you store all addresses or other personal information for customers, friends and family, or merchants with whom you do business. The term **database** generically describes a collection of data, organized in a manner that allows easy access, retrieval, and use of that data. **Merging** is the process of combining the contents of a data source with a main publication.

Personalized contact with your customers can result in increased revenue. Addressing customers by name and remembering their preferences is the kind of personal attention that builds customer loyalty. When retail establishments keep close track of customers' interests, customers usually respond by returning and spending more time and money there. When you include content in a mailing that addresses your customers' specific interests, the customers are more likely to pay attention and respond.

Publisher allows users to create data sources internally, which means using Publisher as both the creation and editing tool. Publisher creates a database that can be edited independently by using Microsoft Access; however, you do not need to have Microsoft Access or any database program installed on your system to use a Publisher data source.

If you plan to **import**, or bring in data, from another application, Publisher can accept data from a variety of other formats, as shown in Table 7–4.

Table 7–4 Data Formats	
Data-Creation Program	**File Extension**
Any text files, such as those generated with WordPad, TextPad, or Notepad, where tabs or commas separate the columns and paragraph marks separate the rows	.txt, .prn, .csv, .tab, and .asc
Microsoft Access	.ade, .adp, .mdb, .mde, .accdb, and .accde
Microsoft Data Access and OLE DB provider for Oracle	.dbf
Microsoft Data links	.udl
Microsoft Data Links	.od
Microsoft Excel	.xls and .xlsx
Microsoft Office Address Lists	.mdb
Microsoft Office List Shortcuts	.ols
Microsoft Outlook Contacts list	.pst
Microsoft Publisher Address Lists	.mdb
Microsoft Word	.doc, .docx, and .docm
ODBC file DSNs	.dsn
SQL Server and Office Database Connections	.odc
Web Pages	.htm, .html, .asp, .mht, .mhtml

Creating a Data Source

A data source is a file that contains the data that changes from one merged publication to the next. As shown in Figure 7–21, a data source often is shown as a table that consists of a series of rows and columns. Each row is called a **record**. The first row of a data source is called the **header row** or **header record** because it identifies the name of each column. Each row below the header row is called a **data record**. Data records contain the text that varies in each copy of the merged publication. The data source for this project contains five data records; each data record identifies a different person who has purchased tickets for a race. Thus, five form letters will be generated from this data source.

Each column in the data sources is called a **data field**. A data field represents a group of similar data. Each data field must be identified uniquely with a name, called a **field name**. For example, First Name is the name of the data field (column) that contains the first names of those who purchased tickets. In this project, the data source contains nine data fields with the following field names: Title, First Name, Last Name, Address Line 1, Address Line 2, City, State, ZIP Code, and Number of Tickets.

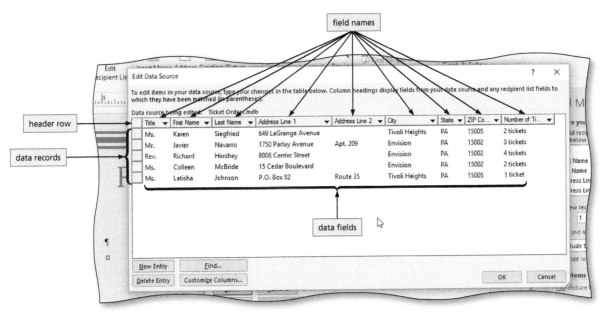

Figure 7–21

How do you know what to include in a data source?

When you create a data source, you will need to determine the fields it should contain. That is, you will need to identify the data that will vary from one merged publication to the next. Following are a few important points about fields:

- For each field, you may be required to create a field name. Because data sources often contain the same fields, some programs create a list of commonly used field names that you may use.

- Field names must be unique; that is, no two field names may be the same.

- Fields may be listed in any order in the data source. That is, the order of fields has no effect on the order in which they will print in the main publication.

- Organize fields so that they are flexible. For example, break the name into separate fields: title, first name, and last name. This arrangement allows you to customize letters.

In Publisher, data sources sometimes are called **recipient lists** or **address lists**. Publisher allows you to create as many data sources as you like, providing a customizable interface in which to enter the data.

To Use the Mail Merge Wizard

1 CREATE WATERMARK | 2 CHANGE CHARACTER SPACING | 3 SET TABS | 4 USE MAIL MERGE WIZARD
5 INSERT FIELD CODES | 6 EDIT DATA SOURCE | 7 ADJUST GRAPHICS | 8 MERGE EXCEL LIST

A **wizard** is a tool that guides you through the steps of a process or task by asking a series of questions or presenting options. The following steps begin the process of creating a data source by using the Mail Merge Wizard. *Why? The Mail Merge Wizard displays a task pane with steps to create the data source and the form letter.*

1

• Click Mailings on the ribbon to display the Mailings tab.

• Click the Mail Merge arrow (Mailings tab | Start group) to display the Mail Merge menu (Figure 7–22).

Q&A What is the difference between a mail merge and an email merge?
An email merge uses fields common to email correspondence, such as To, From, and Subject, whereas a mail merge uses fields such as address, city, and state. Both need to connect to recipient lists or data files.

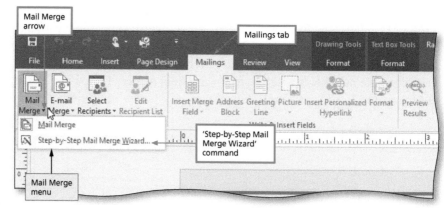

Figure 7–22

2

• Click 'Step-by-Step Mail Merge Wizard' on the Mail Merge menu to display the Mail Merge task pane.

• Click the 'Type a new list' option button (Mail Merge task pane) to select it (Figure 7–23).

Q&A My task pane looks different. Did I do something wrong?
No. Your task pane may display a different font or resolution.

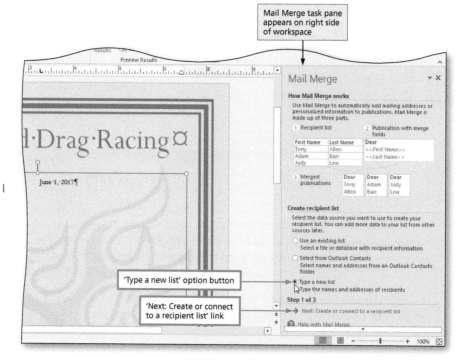

Figure 7–23

3

• Click the 'Next: Create or connect to a recipient list' link at the bottom of the task pane to display the New Address List dialog box (Figure 7–24).

Q&A Can I use other tabs and ribbon commands while the Mail Merge task pane is open?
Yes, the task pane will remain open in the workspace while you edit the form letter.

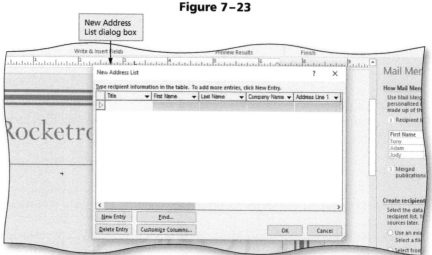

Figure 7–24

To Customize Data Source Fields

As you create a data source, Publisher provides a list of 13 commonly used field names; you can create and user others as well. This project uses 8 of the 13 field names supplied by Publisher: Title, First Name, Last Name, Address Line 1, Address Line 2, City, State, and ZIP Code. This project does not use the other five field names supplied by Publisher: Company Name, Country or Region, Home Phone, Work Phone, and E-mail Address. Thus, you will delete those field names and create a new field named Number of Tickets. *Why? As you create the letter, you will need to reference the number of tickets for each customer.*

The following steps customize the fields in the New Address List dialog box.

1

- With the New Address List dialog box displayed, click the Customize Columns button (New Address List dialog box) to display the Customize Address List dialog box.
- Click Company Name in the Field Names area to select it (Figure 7–25).

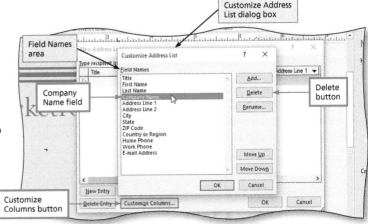

Figure 7–25

2

- Click the Delete button (Customize Address List dialog box) to delete the field. When Publisher displays a dialog box asking if you are sure you want to delete the field, click the Yes button (Microsoft Publisher dialog box) (Figure 7–26).

Q&A What other options do I have for customization?
You can add a new field, rename a field to better describe its contents, or move fields up and down to place the fields in the desired order.

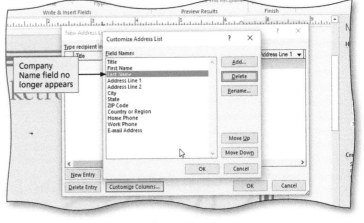

Figure 7–26

3

- Select, delete, and confirm the deletion of the Home Phone, Work Phone, and E-mail Address fields.
- Click 'Country or Region' in the list of Field Names, and then click the Rename button to display the Rename Field dialog box.
- Type **Number of Tickets** in the To text box (Figure 7–27).

Q&A Can I delete multiple fields at one time?
No, you must select them and delete them individually.

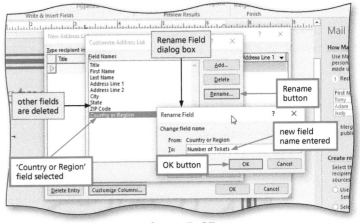

Figure 7–27

• Click the OK button (Rename Field dialog box) to close the dialog box and return to the Customize Address List dialog box (Figure 7–28).

🔎 **Experiment**

• Experiment with moving the fields to different locations by selecting individual fields and then clicking the Move Up button or the Move Down button.

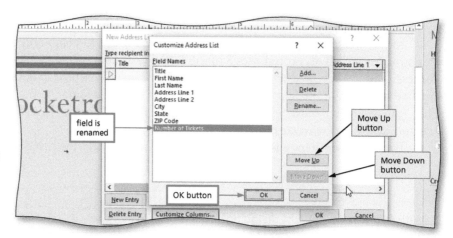

Figure 7–28

• Click the OK button (Customize Address List dialog box) to close the dialog box and return to the New Address List dialog box.

• Scroll to the right to see the new fields (Figure 7–29).

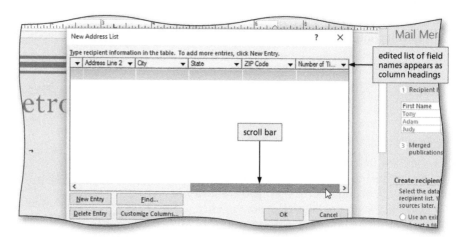

Figure 7–29

Entering Data in the Data Source

Table 7–5 displays the customer data for five people who bought tickets to the race.

Table 7–5 Ticket Data								
Title	**First Name**	**Last Name**	**Address1**	**Address2**	**City**	**State**	**ZIP Code**	**Number of Tickets**
Ms.	Karen	Siegfried	649 LaGrange Avenue		Tivoli Heights	PA	15005	2 tickets
Mr.	Javier	Navarro	1750 Parlay Avenue	Apt. 209	Envision	PA	15002	3 tickets
Rev.	Richard	Hershey	8006 Center Street		Envision	PA	15002	4 tickets
Ms.	Colleen	McBride	15 Cedar Boulevard		Envision	PA	15002	2 tickets
Ms.	Latisha	Johnson	P.O. Box 82	Route 35	Tivoli Heights	PA	15005	1 ticket

Notice that some customers have no Address Line 2. For those customers, you will leave that field blank. As you enter data, do not press the SPACEBAR at the end of the field. Extra spaces can interfere with the display of the merged fields.

To Enter Data in the Data Source File

The following steps enter the first record into the data source file, using the information from Table 7–5. You will use the TAB key to move from field to field. *Why? Like a Publisher table, the TAB key automatically moves to the next cell for data entry.*

- With the New Address List dialog box displayed, scroll as necessary to click the box in the first row, below the Title heading.
- Type **Ms.** in the Title box and then press the TAB key.
- Type **Karen** in the First Name box and then press the TAB key.
- Type **Siegfried** in the Last Name box and then press the TAB key (Figure 7–30).

Q&A What if the data is wider than the entry field?
Publisher will allow up to 256 characters in each entry field and move the text to the left, out of site, as you type. While not visible, the text still will be saved with the rest of the data.

What does the Find button do?
When you click the Find button, Publisher displays the Find Entry dialog box. In this dialog box, you can look for specific pieces of data that have been typed so far in the data source. The Find Entry dialog box lets you search the entire list or specific fields.

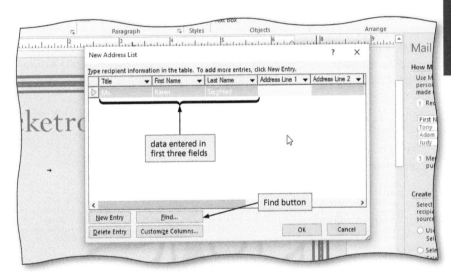

Figure 7–30

②

- Continue to enter data from Table 7–5. Press the TAB key to advance to each new entry field. Press the TAB key twice to leave a field empty. Do not press the TAB key at the end of the last row (Figure 7–31).

Q&A What do the other buttons do?
You can use the New Entry button (New Address List dialog box) instead of the TAB key to move to the next line and create a new entry. The Delete Entry button deletes the entry at the location of the insertion point.

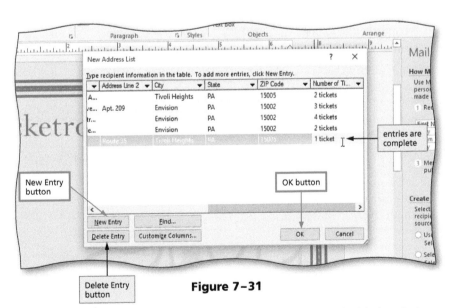

Figure 7–31

Experiment

- Position the pointer in between the Address1 and Address2 field. When the pointer changes to a double-headed arrow, drag to increase the width of Address1 so that you can see the entire address. Change other column widths as necessary.

To Save the Data Source

The following steps save the data source file with the file name, Ticket Orders. *Why? You must save the data source in order to merge it with the form letter.* It is best to save the form letter and the data source in the same directory.

● Click the OK button (New Address List dialog box) to display the Save Address List dialog box.

● Type **Ticket Orders** in the File name box. Do not press the ENTER key.

● Navigate to the same save location on which you saved the Racing Letter file (Figure 7–32).

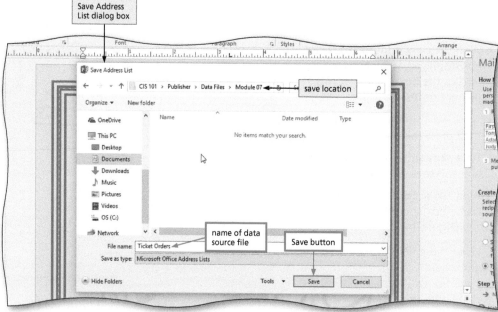

Figure 7–32

● Click the Save button (Save Address List dialog box) to save the file and to display the Mail Merge Recipients dialog box (Figure 7–33).

Q&A What kinds of tasks can I perform using the Mail Merge Recipients dialog box?
You can select specific recipients, add new recipients, filter, sort, or create a new list. You will learn more about the Mail Merge Recipients dialog box later in the module.

Did the field order change?
Yes, Publisher now displays the Last Name field first; however, the data itself is not sorted.

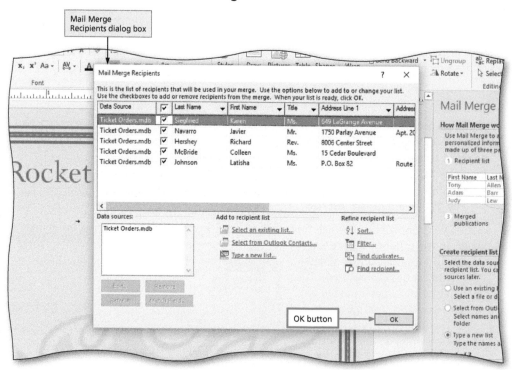

Figure 7–33

● Click the OK button (Mail Merge Recipients dialog box) to close the dialog box.

Inserting Field Codes

A publication designed for merging not only must be connected to its data source but also must contain form fields, sometimes called field codes, in the publication. A **field code** is placeholder text in the publication that shows Publisher where to insert the information from the data source. Once the publication is merged with the address list, the field codes are replaced with unique information. For example, a form letter may say, Thank you for your business, to every customer, but follow it with the individual customer's name, such as John. In this case, you would type the words, Thank you for your business, insert a comma, and then insert the field code, First Name, from the data source. Publisher would insert the customer's name so that the letter would read, Thank you for your business, John.

You can format, copy, move, or delete a field code just as you would regular text. Field codes need to be spaced and punctuated appropriately. For instance, if you want to display a greeting such as Dear Katie, you need to type the word, Dear, followed by a space before inserting the First Name field code. You then would type a comma or a colon after the field code to complete the greeting.

To insert a field code from the Mail Merge task pane, you either can position your insertion point in the publication and click the field code, or drag the field code from the task pane to the publication and then drop it at the appropriate location.

Publisher allows you to insert field codes from the address list into the main publication one field at a time or in predefined groups. Grouped field codes appear in the More items area of the Mail Merge task pane, or can be accessed using the appropriate grouped field button on the Mailings tab. For example, if you wanted to display the amount due from an address list, you would choose that one field from the task pane. To use predefined groups, you would use a **grouped field code**, which is a set of standard fields, such as typical address fields or salutation fields, preformatted and spaced with appropriate words and punctuation. For example, instead of entering the field codes for Title, First Name, Last Name, Company Name, Address Line 1, and so on, you can choose the grouped field named Address Block, which includes all the fields displayed correctly.

BTW

Empty Fields
If your data source contains empty or blank fields, Publisher will omit the field when the publication is merged. For instance, if no second address line exists, Publisher will move up the other fields during the print process in order to fill the gap.

1 CREATE WATERMARK | 2 CHANGE CHARACTER SPACING | 3 SET TABS | 4 USE MAIL MERGE WIZARD
5 INSERT FIELD CODES | **6 EDIT DATA SOURCE** | **7 ADJUST GRAPHICS** | **8 MERGE EXCEL LIST**

To Insert Grouped Field Codes

The following steps insert grouped field codes for the address block and greeting line in the form letter. *Why? The grouped field codes contain the correct fields, spaced and formatted appropriately.*

- Click in the text box to ensure that the insertion point is positioned two lines below the date in the publication and then zoom to 130%.

- In the Mail Merge task pane, click the Address block link to display the Insert Address Block dialog box.

- If necessary, click each of the enabled check boxes so that they contain check marks.

- If necessary, click the format 'Mr. Joshua Randall Jr.' in the Insert recipient's name in this format list.

- If necessary, click the Previous button in the Preview area until the first recipient in the data source is displayed (Figure 7–34).

Q&A What is the difference between an Address block and Address fields?

The Address block link will include fields in the current data source. If you choose Address fields, Publisher displays a list of typical address fields that could be matched with different data sources. That way, if you are sending a form letter to two different address lists, Publisher will try to match the fields consistently. For example, one address source might include a middle initial or company name, while another one might not.

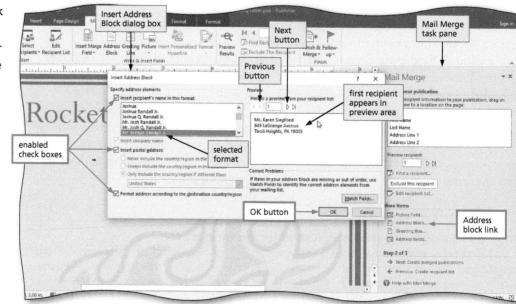

Figure 7–34

Experiment

- One at a time, click the different formats in the Insert recipient's name in this format list. View the changes in the preview. Click the Next button to view other entries from the address list. When you are finished, click the format shown in Figure 7–34.

2

- Click the OK button (Insert Address Block dialog box) to insert the address block into the form letter.

- Click at the end of the Address Block grouped field code to position the insertion point (Figure 7–35).

Q&A What do the chevron symbols represent?

Each field code displays chevrons to let you know that it is not actual text.

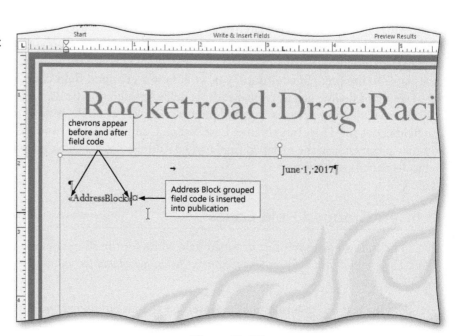

Figure 7–35

③

- Press the ENTER key twice and then click the Greeting line link in the Mail Merge task pane to display the Insert Greeting Line dialog box.
- If necessary, choose the various settings shown in Figure 7–36.

🔍 Experiment

- One at a time, click the box arrows to view the various kinds of greeting formats. Notice how the preview changes with each selection.

Q&A ◁ What is the purpose of the Match Fields button?

Unique to grouped fields, the Match Fields button displays a dialog box where you can choose which individual fields to use in the group. If you had renamed the Title field, for example, you would have to match your new field name with the one that Publisher automatically places in the group.

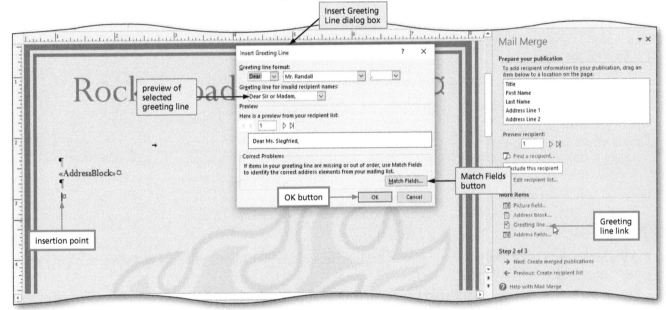

Figure 7–36

④

- Click the OK button (Insert Greeting Line dialog box) to insert the Greeting Line field code into the publication.
- Click after the Greeting Line field code and then press the ENTER key twice to move the insertion point in the publication (Figure 7–37).

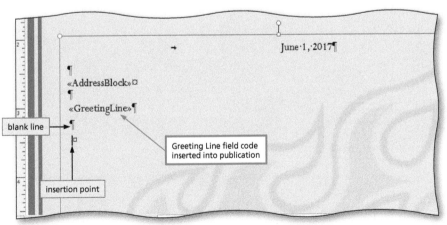

Figure 7–37

Other Ways

1. Click appropriate grouped field code button (Mailings tab | Write & Insert Fields group)

To Insert Individual Field Codes

The following steps insert individual field codes as you type the body of the form letter. ***Why? Using*** *individualized data in the body of the letter helps personalize the form letter.* You will finish the merge process later in this module.

- With the insertion point positioned two lines below the greeting line (shown in Figure 7–37), type **Thank you for ordering tickets for Sonic Saturday on July 15, 2017.** and then press the SPACEBAR key.

- Type **Enclosed is your order for** and then press the SPACEBAR key (Figure 7–38).

Figure 7–38

- In the Mail Merge task pane, scroll in the list of fields as necessary and then click 'Number of Tickets' to insert the field code into the publication.

- Type a PERIOD (.) and then press the SPACEBAR key to finish the sentence (Figure 7–39).

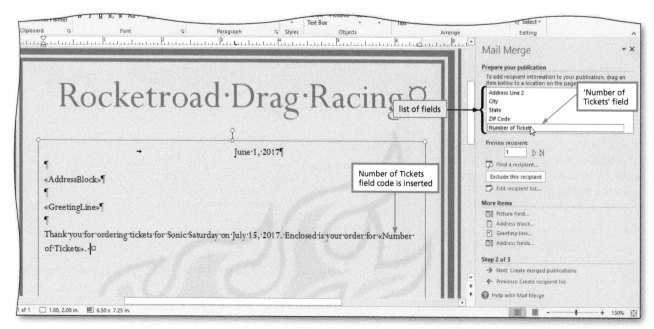

Figure 7–39

Real:

3

- Type `Your seating is the best available at your time of purchase.` to complete the sentence.
- Press the ENTER key twice to insert a blank line.

Q&A Why did my line wrap differently?
Subtle differences in the width of the text box can create a big difference in where wordwrap occurs. Your line may wrap at a different location.

- Type `Enjoy the race!` and then press the ENTER key twice.
- Type `Sincerely,` and then press the ENTER key four times to leave room for a signature.
- Type `Belinda Sweeney` and then press the ENTER key.
- Type `Rocketroad Ticket Desk Manager` and then press the ENTER key twice.
- Type `Enclosure` to finish the letter (Figure 7–40).

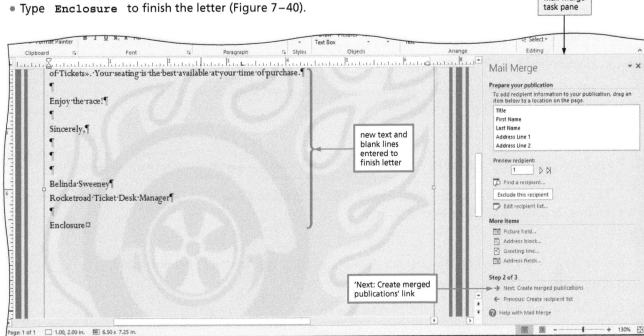

Figure 7–40

4

- Click the 'Next: Create merged publications' link at the bottom of the Mail Merge task pane to create the merged publication.

Other Ways

1. Click 'Insert Merge Field' button (Mailings tab | Write & Insert Fields group), select field (Insert Merge Field menu)   2. Drag field from Mail Merge task pane into publication

How do you merge the data source to create the form letters?
Merging is the process of combining the contents of a data source with a main publication. You can print the merged letters on the printer or place them in a new publication, which you later can edit or save. You also have the options of merging all data in a data source or merging just a portion of it by performing a filter or sort.

CONSIDER THIS

BTW
Distributing a
Document
Instead of printing and
distributing a hard copy of a
document, you can distribute
the document electronically.
Options include sending the
document via email; posting
it on cloud storage (such as
OneDrive) and sharing the
file with others; posting it
on social media, a blog, or
other website; and sharing a
link associated with an online
location of the document.
You also can create and
share a PDF or XPS image of
the document, so that users
can view the file in Acrobat
Reader or XPS Viewer instead
of in Publisher.

Managing Merged Publications

You have several choices in previewing, saving, printing, and exporting merged publications. Table 7–6 describes the merged publication options.

Table 7–6 Merged Publication Options

Option	Description
Print	Print all pages with merged data, one at a time
Print preview	Preview each page of the merged pages
Merge to a new publication	Create a new publication with the merged pages, which you can edit further, print, or save
Add to existing publication	Add the merged pages to the end of the existing publication
Print recipient list	Create a hard copy of the recipient list for your records, including filters or sorts
Save a shortcut to recipient list	Create a shortcut to the address list used in the current merge
Export recipient list to new file	Create a new file based on the filtered or sorted address list used in the current merge
Preview Results group on Mailings tab	Traverse through each page of the merged pages; find and exclude data

To Preview the Form Letters

The following steps preview the form letters. **Why?** *It is always a good idea to preview the result of the merge before printing the letters in the event an error occurred.*

• Click the Preview Results button (Mailings tab | Preview Results group) to display the first record.

• Scroll up in the letter to view the address block (Figure 7–41).

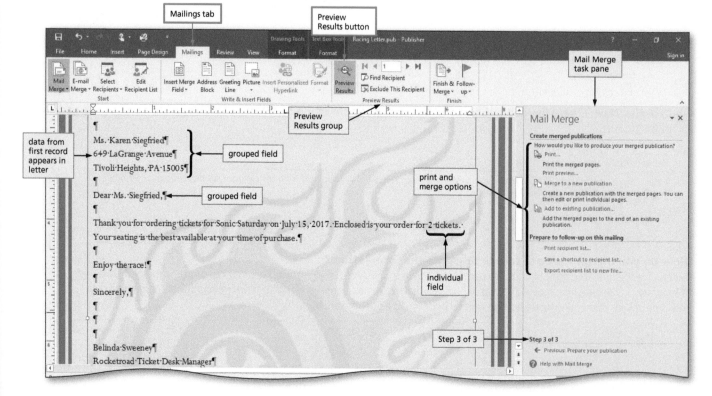

Figure 7–41

②

- Click the Next Record button (Mailings tab | Preview Results group) to display the next letter (Figure 7–42).

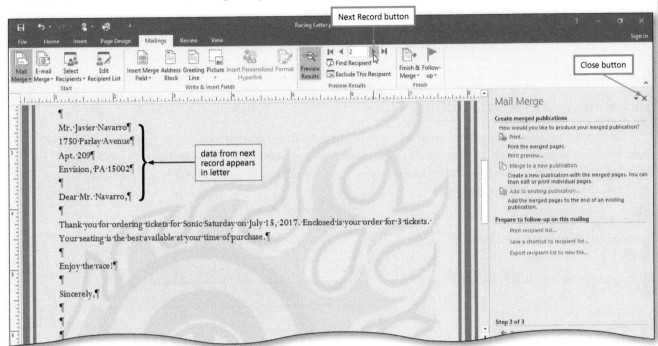

Figure 7–42

To Print Merged Pages

If you wanted to print the merged publication, you would perform the following steps.

1. Ready the printer. Click the Print link in the Mail Merge task pane.
2. When Publisher opens the Backstage view, verify that the selected printer that appears on the Printer Status button will print a hard copy of the publication. If necessary, click the Printer Status button to display a list of available printer options and then click the desired printer to change the currently selected printer.
3. Click the Print button to print the merged pages.
4. Retrieve the printouts.

To Close the Mail Merge Task Pane

The following steps close the Mail Merge task pane and close the file.

① Click the Close button on the Mail Merge task pane title bar (shown in Figure 7–42) to close the task pane.

② Click the Save button on the Quick Access Toolbar to overwrite the previously saved file.

③ Open the Backstage view and then click Close to close the publication without exiting Publisher.

Break Point: If you wish to take a break, this is a good place to do so. Exit Publisher. To resume at a later time, run Publisher and continue following the steps from this location forward.

Editing a Merged Publication

When you open a file with a connected data source, Publisher will ask you to reconnect to the database, especially if the form file or the data source file has been moved. Once you are connected, if you want to edit, filter, or sort the recipient list, you must use the Mailings tab.

To Connect with a Data Source

1 CREATE WATERMARK | 2 CHANGE CHARACTER SPACING | 3 SET TABS | 4 USE MAIL MERGE WIZARD
5 INSERT FIELD CODES | 6 EDIT DATA SOURCE | 7 ADJUST GRAPHICS | 8 MERGE EXCEL LIST

The save location is very important when opening a publication with a connected data source. *Why? Publisher searches for the connected data source in its original location, relative to the publication you are opening; if you move either file, the link is broken.* The following steps open the letter file and connect it with the data source, in this case, the Ticket Orders data file.

1

- Open the Publisher file named Racing Letter (Figure 7–43).

Q&A Why did Publisher display a dialog box?

Anytime a publication has been saved while connected to a data source, Publisher alerts you and verifies the connection when you open the file again.

Figure 7–43

2

- Click the Yes button (Microsoft Publisher dialog box).
- If the Racing Letter publication is displayed, proceed to Step 6.

Q&A What happens if I click the No button?
The publication will open with no connection to data.

3

- When Publisher displays a dialog box because the data source file is not in the expected storage location, click the 'Try to reconnect to the data source' option button to select it (Figure 7–44).

Q&A What happens if I click the 'Work without connection' option button?
The publication will open with no connection to data. The field names will appear, but you cannot preview any results.

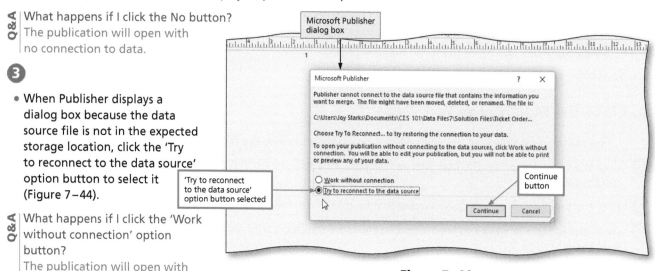

Figure 7–44

4

- Click the Continue button (Microsoft Publisher dialog box).

- When Publisher displays the Select Data Source dialog box, navigate to the location of your data source file (in this case, Ticket Orders).

- Click the file to select it (Figure 7–45).

Q&A What is the purpose of the New Source button?

When you click the New Source button, Publisher starts a Data Connection Wizard that allows you to choose from a variety of database options, including files on different servers with possible tables, network connections, passwords, and access restrictions.

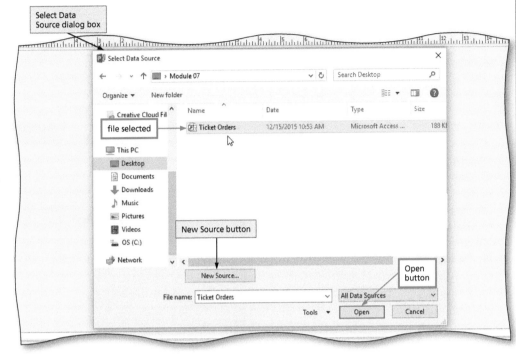

Figure 7–45

5

- Click the Open button (Select Data Source dialog box) to open the data source and connect the file.

6

- Zoom in on the address block to verify the merge (Figure 7–46).

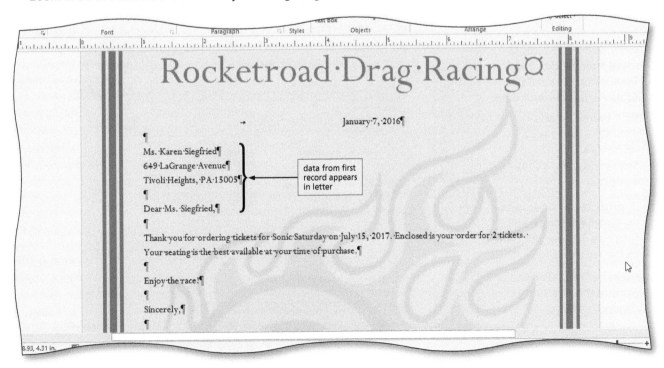

Figure 7–46

To Edit the Data Source

The following steps edit the data source to add a new recipient. You also will sort the recipients by last name. *Why? The list currently is not sorted; data commonly is sorted by last name.*

• Display the Mailings tab.

• Click the 'Edit Recipient List' button (Mailings tab | Start group) to display the Mail Merge Recipients dialog box.

• In the Data sources area, click the name of the data file to select it (Figure 7–47).

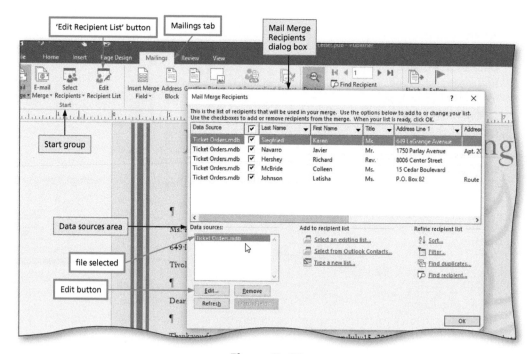

Figure 7–47

• Click the Edit button (Mail Merge Recipients dialog box) to display the Edit Data Source dialog box.

• Click the New Entry button (Edit Data Source dialog box) to create a new entry.

• Enter the following information for the new entry. Use the TAB key to move from field to field. Do not press the TAB key after the last piece of data.

```
Mr. Henry Adams
509 NE 81st Terr.
Apt. 325
Envision, PA 15002
4 Tickets
```

• If instructed to do so, add your name, address, and a fictitious number of tickets to the recipient list.

• Click the OK button to confirm the new entry (Figure 7–48).

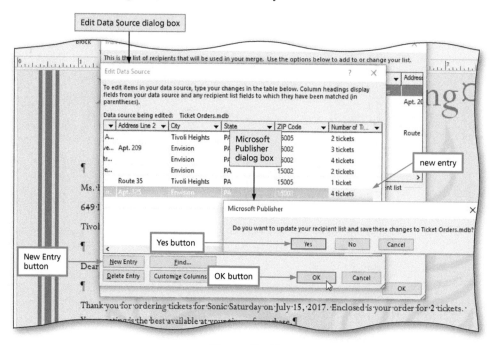

Figure 7–48

3

- Click the Yes button (Microsoft Publisher dialog box) to update the recipient list.
- Click the Sort link (Mail Merge Recipients dialog box) to display the Filter and Sort dialog box.
- Click the Sort by arrow (Filter and Sort dialog box) to display the field names (Figure 7–49).

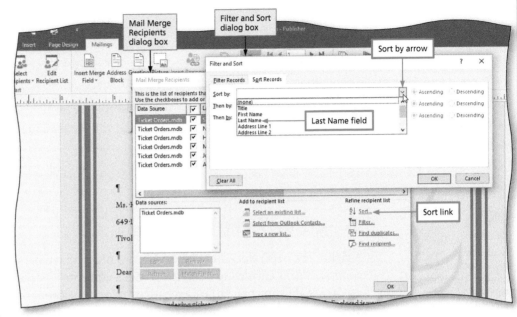

Figure 7–49

4

- Click Last Name in the Sort by list and then, if necessary, click to select the Ascending option button (Figure 7–50).

Q&A What is the purpose of the Then by boxes?
You can perform a secondary sort on the data. For example, if several customers had the same last name, you could further sort by first name.

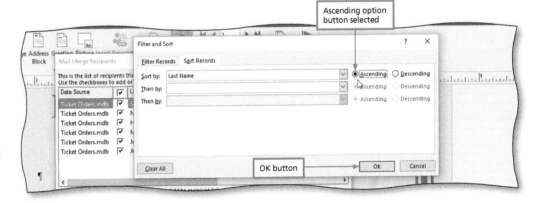

Figure 7–50

5

- Click the OK button (Filter and Sort dialog box) to close the dialog box and sort the data (Figure 7–51).

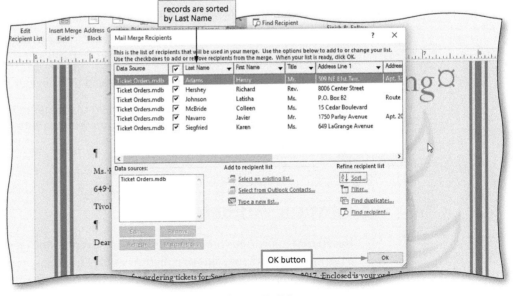

Figure 7–51

- Click the OK button (Mail Merge Recipients dialog box) to close the dialog box.
- Check the spelling of the publication and run the Design Checker. Fix any issues.
- Click the Save button on the Quick Access Toolbar to overwrite the previously saved file.
- Open the Backstage view and then click Close to close the publication without exiting Publisher.

Break Point: If you wish to take a break, this is a good place to do so. Exit Publisher. To resume at a later time, run Publisher and continue following the steps from this location forward.

Creating Tickets

A **ticket** is a paper document or voucher to prove that a person has paid for admission or is entitled to a service. Tickets come in all sizes and are used for events, establishments, raffles, exchanges, or even as proof of receipt. Tickets may be numbered and may identify certain seating, dates, times, and charges. Tickets sometimes have a tear-off or ticket stub that is detached once the service is rendered.

The people who purchased tickets will receive the tickets along with the form letter. The racetrack has a database of seat numbers that you will merge with the ticket publication to produce a ticket for each seat in the stadium. The database is stored in a Microsoft Excel worksheet. This time, you will merge and insert field codes manually rather than through the wizard.

To Copy the Data Source File

Publisher recommends that the publication and its data source reside in the same folder location; therefore, the following steps copy the Microsoft Excel worksheet file from the Data Files to your storage location. To complete these steps, you will be required to use the Data Files. Please contact your instructor for information about accessing the Data Files. If you already have downloaded the Data Files to the same storage location that you are using to create files in this module, you can skip these steps.

1. Click the File Explorer button on the Windows taskbar to open a File Explorer window.

2. Navigate to the location of the Data Files.

3. In the Module 07 folder, right-click the Seat List file to display the shortcut menu and then click Copy on the shortcut menu to copy the file.

4. Navigate to the location on which you saved the previous files created in this module.

5. Right-click a blank part of the right pane in the folder to display the folder's shortcut menu and then click Paste on the shortcut menu to paste the file.

6. Close the File Explorer window.

Graphic Adjustments

Recall that in previous modules you inserted graphics or pictures into publications, set a transparent color, and added a picture style. The Adjust group on the Picture Tools Format tab provides other ways to edit graphics other than by changing size, position, and style (Figure 7–52).

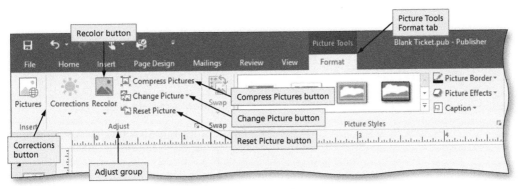

Figure 7–52

The Corrections button includes settings for brightness, contrast, and transparency. **Brightness** is the percentage of black or white added to a main color. The higher the brightness percentage, the more white the image contains. **Contrast** is the saturation or intensity of the color. The higher the contrast percentage, the more intense the color. In addition, using a command in the Corrections gallery, you can change the transparency or opacity of a graphic.

When you **recolor** a graphic, you make a large-scale color change; the color applies to all parts of the graphic, with the option of leaving the black parts black. It is an easy way to convert a color graphic to a black and white line drawing so that it prints more clearly. The reverse also is true; if you have a black and white graphic, you can convert it to a tint or shade of any one color.

The Change Picture button allows you to change the picture while maintaining the placement and size of the graphic in the publication. **Resetting** discards all of the formatting changes you might have made to the picture.

Compress means to reduce the storage size of a publication by changing the internal size of the picture. When you click the Compress Pictures button, Publisher displays the Compress Pictures dialog box. Table 7–7 describes the compression settings.

BTW
Spot Colors
You can use the Recolor command to create a spot color, which is an extra color added to a page. For example, many newspapers print only black and white in their news sections, but use one color for the masthead, called a spot color. Occasionally a fifth color is added to CMYK publications to match an exact brand color or to add a specialized finish or sheen, such as metallic. Adding a fifth spot color is more expensive, but sometimes is desirable.

Table 7–7 Compress Pictures Settings

Setting	Description
Current combined image size	Displays the current combined size of all pictures in the publication.
Estimated combined image size after compression	Displays the estimated combined size of all pictures in the publication after compression settings.
'Delete cropped areas of pictures' check box	Deletes the pixel information that normally is stored for cropped areas of pictures.
'Remove OLE data' check box	Removes the internal part of a graphic that is used when the graphic is linked or embedded. While the picture itself appears the same, you no longer are able to open that picture by using the software in which it was created originally.
Resample pictures check box	Makes a resized picture smaller by deleting the residual data from the picture's original size. You should avoid making the picture larger after resampling.
'Convert to JPEG where appropriate' check box	Converts the picture to a JPEG file.
Commercial Printing option button	Compresses pictures to 300 pixels per inch (ppi). This option does not compress JPEG files.
Desktop Printing option button	Compresses pictures to 220 ppi and a 95 JPEG quality level.
Web option button	Compresses pictures to 96 dots per inch (dpi) and a 75 JPEG quality level.
'Apply to all pictures in the publication' option button	Applies the compression settings to all of the pictures in the publication.
'Apply to selected pictures only' option button	Applies the compression settings to only the selected picture or pictures.

To Open a File and Insert Graphics

The following steps open the Blank Ticket file. To complete these steps, you will be required to use the Data Files. Please contact your instructor for information about accessing the Data Files.

1 With Publisher running, open the Blank Ticket file from the Data Files.

2 Insert the following pictures from the Data Files: Flame, Info Graphic, Racecar, and Wrench.

3 Click the scratch area to deselect the inserted graphics (Figure 7–53).

Q&A Why are my graphics in a different location?
Publisher places them in the area with the most room while maintaining the orientation of your publication. Yours may differ.

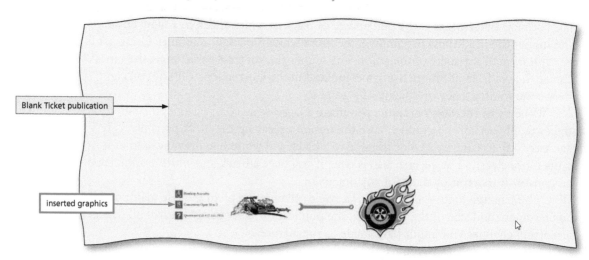

Figure 7–53

To Recolor a Picture

1 CREATE WATERMARK | 2 CHANGE CHARACTER SPACING | 3 SET TABS | 4 USE MAIL MERGE WIZARD
5 INSERT FIELD CODES | 6 EDIT DATA SOURCE | 7 ADJUST GRAPHICS | 8 MERGE EXCEL LIST

The following steps recolor the picture. *Why? The downloaded graphic is too dark; text inserted over the graphic would be difficult to read.*

1

- CTRL+drag the Flame graphic from the scratch area to the lower-left corner of the ticket, creating a copy.

- Resize the graphic to fill approximately half of the ticket (Figure 7–54).

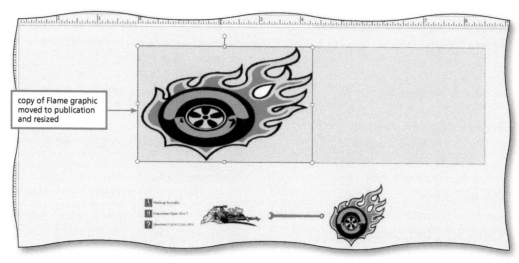

Figure 7–54

2

- If necessary, with the picture selected, display the Picture Tools Format tab.

- Click the Recolor button (Picture Tools Format tab | Adjust group) to display the Recolor gallery (Figure 7–55).

🔍 **Experiment**

- Point to each option in the Recolor gallery and watch the picture change.

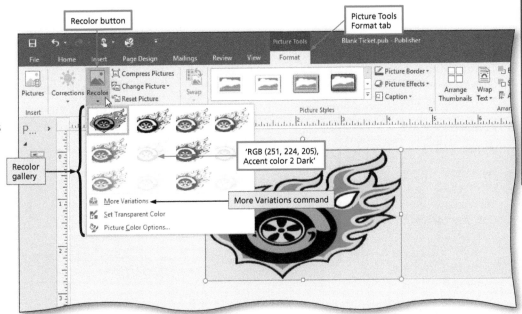

Figure 7–55

3

- Click 'RGB (251, 224, 205), Accent color 2 Dark' to change the picture to a light orange (Figure 7–56).

Q&A What does the More Variations command in the Recolor gallery do?
It displays the Scheme Colors gallery, where you can choose different colors than those displayed in the Recolor gallery.

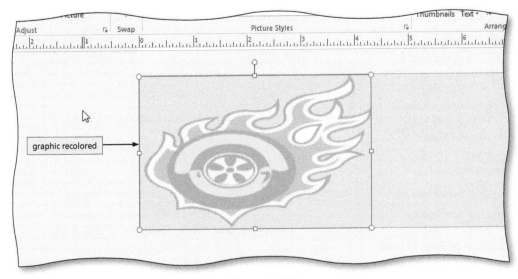

Figure 7–56

Other Ways

1. Click Recolor button (Picture Tools Format tab | Adjust group), click 'Picture Color Options' in Recolor gallery, click Color button (Format Picture dialog box | Picture tab), select color

To Edit the Brightness and Contrast

1 CREATE WATERMARK | 2 CHANGE CHARACTER SPACING | 3 SET TABS | 4 USE MAIL MERGE WIZARD
5 INSERT FIELD CODES | 6 EDIT DATA SOURCE | **7 ADJUST GRAPHICS** | **8 MERGE EXCEL LIST**

The following steps edit the brightness and contrast of the picture. *Why? Adjusting the brightness and contrast will make the features stand out, even as a watermark.* You also will move and crop the picture.

1

- With the picture selected, click the Corrections button (Picture Tools Format tab| Adjust group) to display the Corrections gallery (Figure 7–57).

What does the 'Picture Corrections Options' command do?
If you click 'Picture Corrections Options' in the Corrections gallery, Publisher will display the Format Picture dialog box where you can edit exact settings for brightness, contrast, and transparency.

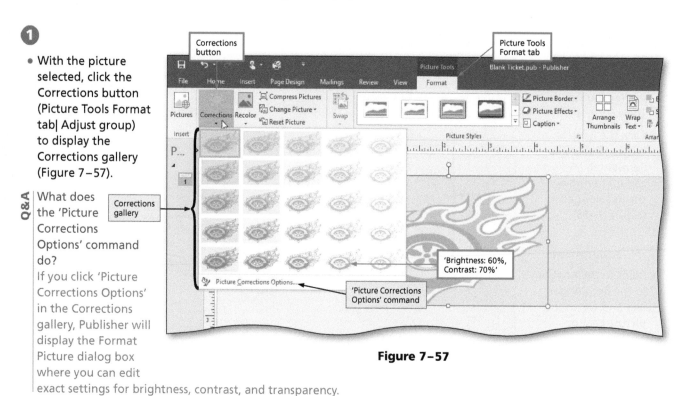

Figure 7–57

2

- Click 'Brightness: 60%, Contrast: 70%' in the Corrections gallery to change the brightness and contrast (Figure 7–58).

- (icon) **Experiment**

- Click the Reset Picture button (Picture Tools Format tab | Adjust group) to view the picture in its original coloring, contrast, and proportion. Press CTRL+Z to undo the reset.

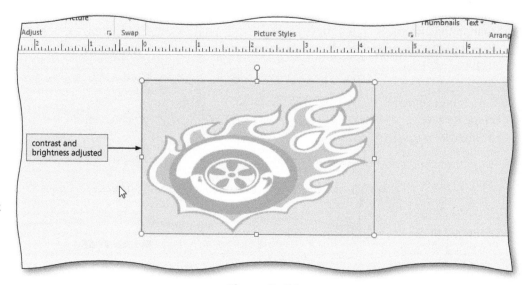

Figure 7–58

My gallery looks different. Did I do something wrong?
No. Depending on your screen resolution and other settings, the size of the gallery will differ as well as the placement of the gallery choices. Point to the gallery choices to verify you are using the 'Brightness: 60%, Contrast: 70%' correction.

3

- Drag the graphic slightly off the page, down and to the left.
- Click the Crop button (Picture Tools Format tab | Crop group).

- Drag the lower-left crop handle up to the edge of the ticket (Figure 7–59).

4

- Click the Crop button (Picture Tools Format tab | Crop group) again to crop the picture (shown in Figure 7–60).

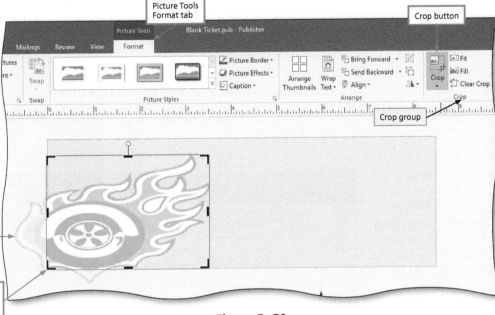

Figure 7–59

Other Ways

1. Click Corrections button (Picture Tools Format tab | Adjust group), click 'Picture Corrections Options' in Corrections gallery, drag Brightness or Contrast sliders (Format Picture dialog box | Picture tab), click OK button

2. Right-click graphic, click Format Picture on shortcut menu, drag Brightness or Contrast sliders (Format Picture dialog box | Picture tab), click OK button

To Place Other Graphics

The following steps move the other graphics to the page layout and bring them forward, in front of the recolored graphic.

1 Drag the flame graphic from the scratch area to the center of the recolored graphic. Click the Bring Forward button (Picture tools Format tab | Arrange group).

2 Drag the racecar graphic to a location to the right of the flame graphic. Bring the graphic forward.

3 Drag the info graphic to the right side of the ticket.

4 Drag the wrench graphic to a location above the flame, and bring it forward. Resize it as necessary.

5 Zoom to Whole Page view (Figure 7–60).

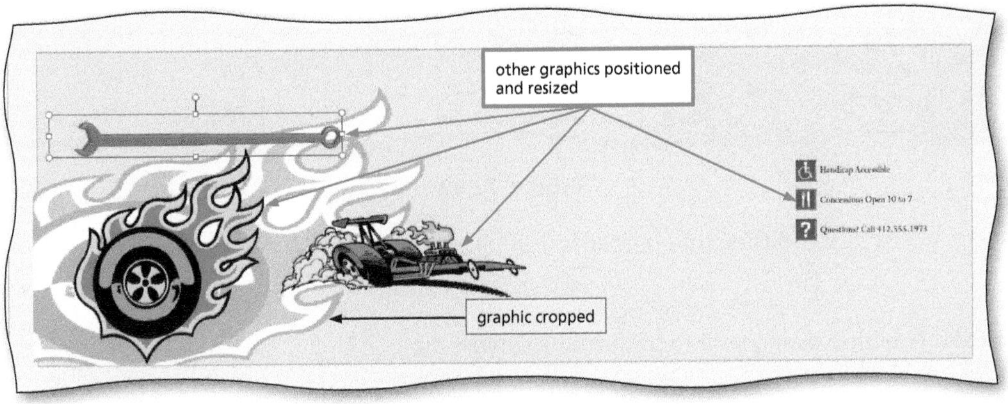

BTW

Recoloring Graphics
You can recolor most pictures inserted into Publisher. This procedure does not apply to pictures that are in Encapsulated PostScript (EPS) format, however. EPS is a graphic file format that is created using the PostScript page description language. EPS graphics are designed to be printed on PostScript compatible printers and cannot be recolored.

Figure 7–60

To Compress Pictures

The following steps compress the pictures. *Why? When you have many graphics or pictures in a publication, the physical size of the stored file increases.* To reduce the file size, you will compress the pictures. You may be familiar with Windows file compression, or zipping. In Publisher, compression includes deleting cropped areas, changing graphic file types and resolutions where necessary, and removing any extraneous data stored with the pictures.

- With any picture selected, click the Compress Pictures button (Picture Tools Format tab | Adjust group) to display the Compress Pictures dialog box.

- Click the Desktop Printing option button in order to compress the picture for desktop printing.

- If necessary, click the 'Apply to all pictures in the publication' option button to compress all of the pictures (Figure 7–61).

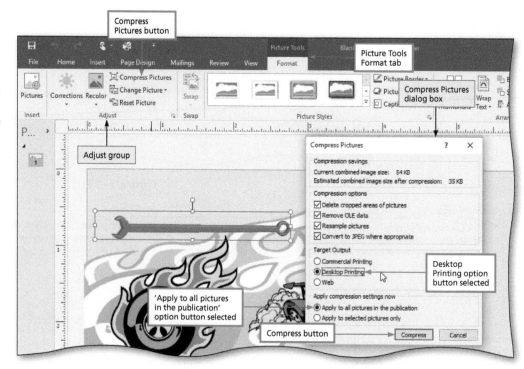

Figure 7–61

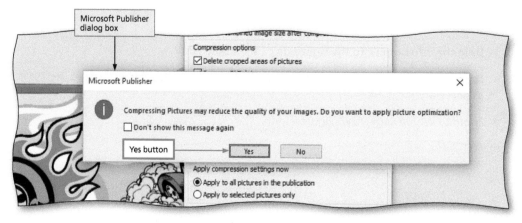

- Click the Compress button (Compress Pictures dialog box) to begin the compression process and to display a Microsoft Publisher dialog box (Figure 7–62).

Q&A | What is picture optimization?
Picture optimization replaces the original high-resolution pictures with a compressed version that is smaller in storage size and easier to print.

Figure 7–62

- Click the Yes button (Microsoft Publisher dialog box) to confirm the compression.

To Insert Text

The following steps add several text boxes to the ticket. Use the Measurement task pane to help you place objects, if necessary.

1 Click the 'Draw a Text Box' button (Home tab | Objects group). Drag to create a text box in the upper-left corner of the publication, approximately 4 inches wide. If necessary, change the font type to Perpetua. Set the font size to 28. Type `Rocketroad Drag Racing` to complete the text. If the word, Rocketroad, displays a red wavy line, right-click the word and then click Ignore All on the shortcut menu.

2 Select the text and then click the Text Effects button (Text Box Tools Format tab | WordArt Styles group). Point to Shadow (Text Effects menu) and then click Offset Left in the Shadow gallery.

3 Create another text box to the right and slightly below the first one, approximately 2.3 inches wide. Change the font size to 28 and the font color to Dark Red. Right-align the text. Type `Sonic Saturday` to complete the text. Bold and italicize the text.

4 Create a text box below the Sonic Saturday text box, approximately 2.1 inches wide and 1.5 inches tall. The text box will overlap the racecar. Change the font size to 14 and the font color to Automatic (Black). Right-align the text. Type `July 15, 2017 at noon` and then press the ENTER key. Bold the text.

5 Change the font size to 10. Type `We appreciate your excitement at meeting the drivers and asking for pictures and autographs, but we politely request you do not approach the drivers or crew teams until after the final race.` and then press the ENTER key.

6 Type `No flash photography!` to finish the text.

7 Move the racecar up or down as necessary so that it does not overlap the text (Figure 7–63).

new text is entered

Figure 7–63

To Draw a Line

The following steps draw a line. *Why? A vertical line will separate the ticket and the ticket stub.*

- Click the Shapes button (Insert tab | Illustrations group) and then click the Line shape. SHIFT+drag a vertical line from the top of the publication to the bottom, at approximately the 6-inch marker on the horizontal ruler.

- Click the Shape Outline arrow (Drawing Tools Format tab | Shape Styles group) and then point to Dashes (Shape Outline gallery) to display the Dashes gallery (Figure 7–64).

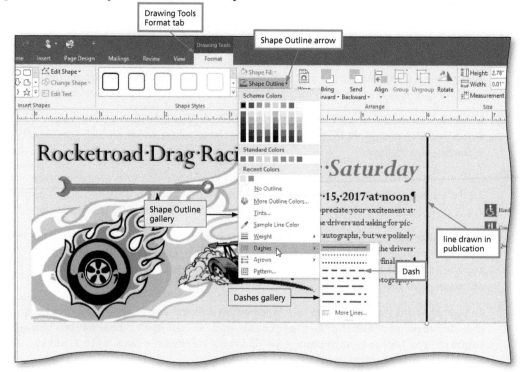

Figure 7–64

- Click Dash in the Dashes gallery to create a dashed line (Figure 7–65).

Figure 7–65

To Change the Text Direction

The following steps create a text box on the ticket stub and change the text direction. *Why? It is common for tickets stubs to be printed sideways on the ticket for easy tear-off and reading by those who seat the attendees.*

1

- Draw a text box to the right of the dashed line filling the area from the top of the ticket to the bottom, approximately .65 inches wide.

- Click the Text Direction button (Text Box Tools Format tab | Text group) to change the direction of the text (Figure 7–66).

Q&A Which direction did Publisher rotate the text?
The text box rotated 90 degrees clockwise.

Figure 7–66

2

- Drag the rotation handle of the text box straight down to invert the box 180 degrees (Figure 7–67).

Figure 7–67

To Edit the Ticket Stub Further

The following steps edit the ticket stub.

1 With the insertion point in the ticket stub text box, change the font to size 12, and then press CTRL+E to center the text.

2 Type **Rocketroad Drag Racing** and then press the ENTER key to enter the first line of the ticket stub.

3 Type **$8.00** to complete the text.

④ Right-click the red, Sonic Saturday text box and then click Copy on the shortcut menu. Paste the text box in the publication, move it to the ticket stub, and then rotate it as shown in Figure 7–68.

⑤ Select the Info graphic. Click the Rotate Objects button (Picture Tools Format tab | Arrange group) and then click 'Rotate Left 90°' in the Rotate Objects gallery. Use the pink layout guides to help you move the graphic and align it on the left with the Sonic Saturday text box.

⑥ Open the Backstage view and then click Save As. Navigate to your storage location and then save the file with the file name, Racing Ticket.

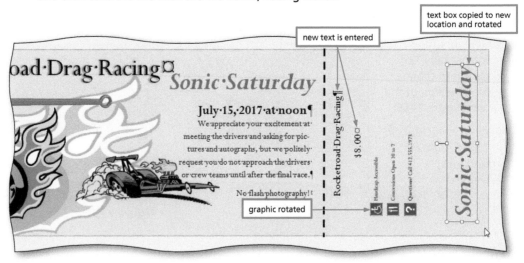

Figure 7–68

Merging with Excel

Earlier in this module, you used the Mail Merge Wizard to help you create a recipient list saved as a database file with the extension, .mdb (Microsoft Database). While Publisher saves its data in the .mdb format, it can accept or read databases in other formats when merging. In the following sections, you will connect manually with a database stored in the Excel format. Excel files are stored with the .xlsx or .xls extension.

To Select Recipients

1 CREATE WATERMARK | 2 CHANGE CHARACTER SPACING | 3 SET TABS | 4 USE MAIL MERGE WIZARD
5 INSERT FIELD CODES | 6 EDIT DATA SOURCE | 7 ADJUST GRAPHICS | 8 MERGE EXCEL LIST

The following steps select recipients from the Microsoft Excel worksheet that you copied to your save location earlier. *Why? The file contains the ticket numbers, seats, and rows for the race.* This time you will use the ribbon rather than the wizard.

①

- Click Mailings on the ribbon to display the Mailings tab.

- Click the Select Recipients button (Mailings tab | Start group) to display the Select Recipients menu (Figure 7–69).

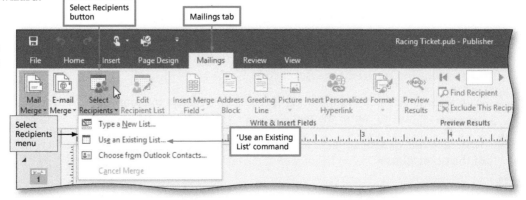

Figure 7–69

2

- Click 'Use an Existing List' on the Select Recipients menu to display the Select Data Source dialog box.

- If necesary, navigate to the location to which you copied the Seat List file (Figure 7–70).

Figure 7–70

3

- Double-click the Seat List file to display the Select Table dialog box.

- If necessary, click the appropriate table in the list (in this case, Stadium$).

- If necessary, click to display a check mark in the 'First row of data contains column headers' check box (Figure 7–71).

Q&A Does the Microsoft Excel worksheet contain multiple tables?

No, but the Select Table dialog box displays for you to choose different sheets when using an Excel file, should it contain multiple tables.

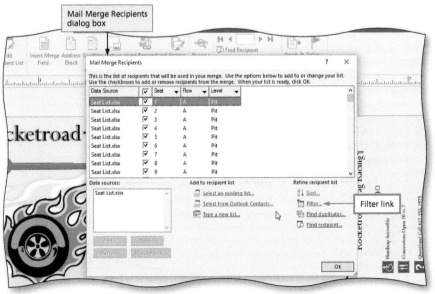

Figure 7–71

4

- Click the OK button (Select Table dialog box) to select the table and display the Mail Merge Recipients dialog box (Figure 7–72).

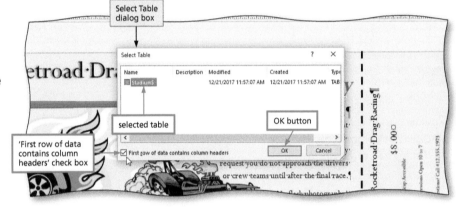

Figure 7–72

To Filter Data

The following steps filter the data so that no tickets will be issued for the Pit level. *Why? Pit level tickets are reserved for members of the racing crew and their families and are not for sale to the general public.*

1

- Click the Filter link (Mail Merge Recipients dialog box) to display the Filter and Sort dialog box.

- If necessary, click the Filter Records tab (Filter and Sort dialog box) and then click the Field arrow to display its list (Figure 7–73).

 Q&A What is the difference between filter and sort?

Filtering examines all records and displays only those that meet specific criteria that you specify. Sorting merely rearranges the records in a specific order, but displays them all.

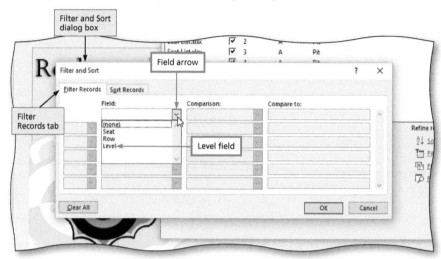

Figure 7–73

2

- Click Level in the list to filter by level.

- Click the Comparison arrow to display its list (Figure 7–74).

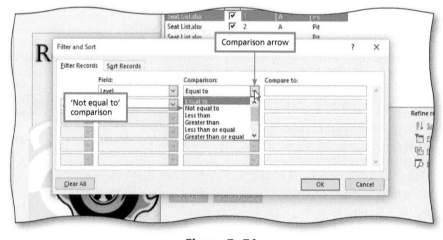

Figure 7–74

3

- Click 'Not equal to' in the Comparison list to filter or display levels that are not equal to Pit.

- Press the TAB key to advance to the Compare to box and then type **Pit** to insert the Compare to value (Figure 7–75).

Q&A Will the filter delete all the Pit tickets?

No. It changes only which tickets will be used in the merge. The filter and sort links do not change the data source or mail merge permanently.

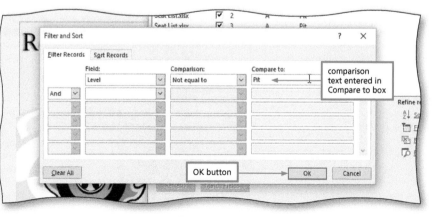

Figure 7–75

④

- Click the OK button (Filter and Sort dialog box) to accept the filter and return to the Mail Merge Recipients dialog box (Figure 7–76).

Q&A How did the recipient list change? Compare Figure 7–72 to Figure 7–76. Notice the ticket levels now begin with Level 1. Pit level tickets have been filtered out.

🔎 **Experiment**

- Scroll in the list to see all seats for all levels.

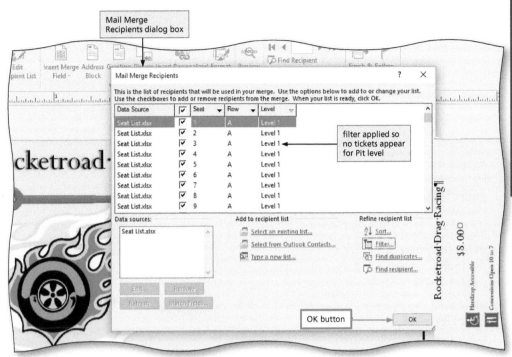

Figure 7–76

⑤

- Click the OK button (Mail Merge Recipients dialog box) to close the dialog box.

To Add Text to a Shape

1 CREATE WATERMARK | 2 CHANGE CHARACTER SPACING | 3 SET TABS | 4 USE MAIL MERGE WIZARD
5 INSERT FIELD CODES | 6 EDIT DATA SOURCE | 7 ADJUST GRAPHICS | **8 MERGE EXCEL LIST**

The following steps create a shape with text. ***Why?*** *The shape will display the ticket number on both the ticket and the stub.*

①

- Click the Shapes button (Insert tab | Illustrations group) to display the Shapes gallery (Figure 7–77).

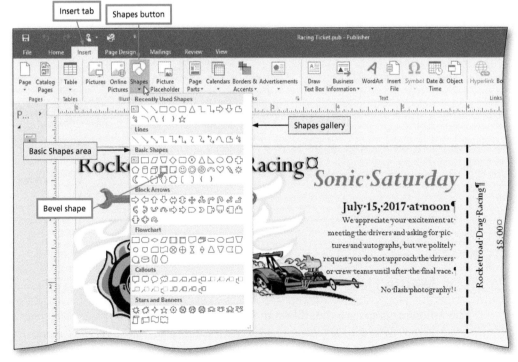

Figure 7–77

2

- In the Basic Shapes area, click the Bevel shape (Shape gallery) to select it.

- In the publication, drag to create a bevel shape approximately 1.25 inches wide and 0.4 inches tall just below the text in the ticket.

- Right-click the shape to display the shortcut menu (Figure 7–78).

  Where did the shape get its coloring?
Shapes are filled with colors from the color scheme assigned to the Blank Ticket data file.

Figure 7–78

3

- Click Add Text on the shortcut menu to position the insertion point in the shape.

- Change the font color to 'Accent 5 (White)'. Change the font size to 12. Do not click outside the shape (Figure 7–79).

Figure 7–79

To Insert Merge Field Codes

1 CREATE WATERMARK | 2 CHANGE CHARACTER SPACING | 3 SET TABS | 4 USE MAIL MERGE WIZARD
5 INSERT FIELD CODES | 6 EDIT DATA SOURCE | 7 ADJUST GRAPHICS | **8 MERGE EXCEL LIST**

The following steps use the ribbon to insert merge field codes. *Why? Sometimes using the buttons on the Mailings tab on the ribbon is easier than using the wizard, especially if the data file has been created already.*

1

- With the insertion point positioned in the shape, click the 'Insert Merge Field' button (Mailings tab | Write & Insert Fields group) to display the menu (Figure 7–80).

Q&A What is the purpose of the Picture button (Mailings tab | Write & Insert Fields group)?
If your database has a field with pictures in each record, you can insert that as a field code. Publisher will display the picture in the merged file.

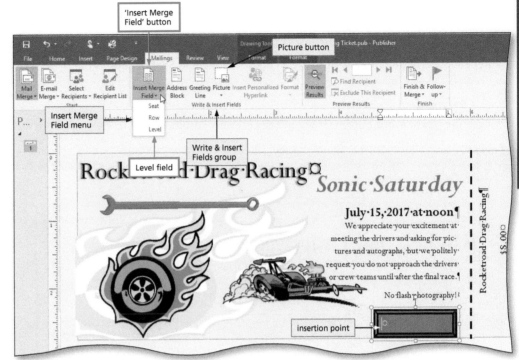

Figure 7–80

2

- Click Level on the Insert Merge Field menu to insert the field and then press the SPACEBAR.
- If necessary, click the Preview Results button (Mailings tab | Preview Results group) to enable it (Figure 7–81).

Figure 7–81

③

- Type `Seat` and then press the SPACEBAR key.
- Repeat Steps 1 and 2 to insert the field codes for Row and Seat (Figure 7–82).

ⓟ Experiment

- Click the Next Record button (Mailings tab | Preview Results group) to view subsequent tickets.

Q&A My row and seat numbers do not appear. Did I do something wrong?
It may be your font size is too large for the shape size. Right-click the text inside the shape and then click Best Fit on the shortcut menu.

Figure 7–82

To Copy the Shape to the Ticket Stub and Check the Publication

The following steps copy the previously created bevel shape with its field codes to the ticket stub.

① CTRL+drag the shape to the ticket stub.

② Rotate the shape and move it to a location centered near the Sonic Saturday text box (shown in Figure 7–83).

③ Check the spelling of the publication and run the Design Checker. Fix any issues.

To Print a Page of Tickets

1 CREATE WATERMARK | 2 CHANGE CHARACTER SPACING | 3 SET TABS | 4 USE MAIL MERGE WIZARD
5 INSERT FIELD CODES | 6 EDIT DATA SOURCE | 7 ADJUST GRAPHICS | **8 MERGE EXCEL LIST**

The following steps print one page of tickets. *Why? The data source has many numbered tickets. Printing one page as a test will assure that the merge executed properly.* If desired, you can insert special ticket paper or a heavy card stock paper in the printer to produce the tickets.

1

- Click the 'Finish & Merge' button (Mailings tab | Finish group) to display the Finish and Merge menu (Figure 7–83).

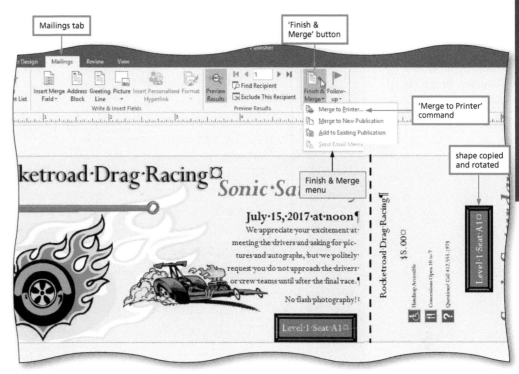

Figure 7–83

2

- Click 'Merge to Printer' on the Finish and Merge menu to display the Print gallery in the Backstage view.

- Click the Records text box and then type 1-4 to print the first four tickets (Figure 7–84).

Q&A Why do all of the tickets display the same number?
The 'Merge to Print' command repeats one record per page. You will change that setting in the next step.

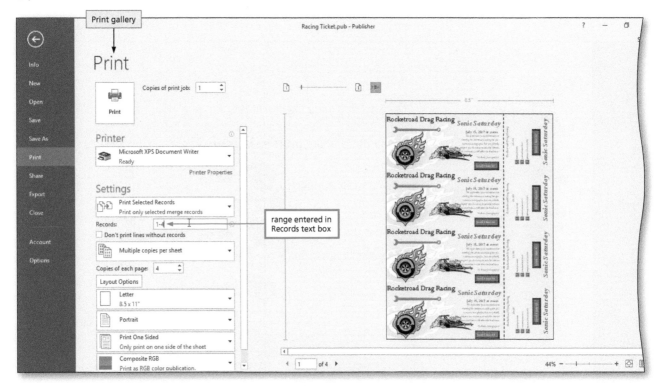

Figure 7–84

3

- Click the 'Multiple copies per sheet' button to display its list (Figure 7–85).

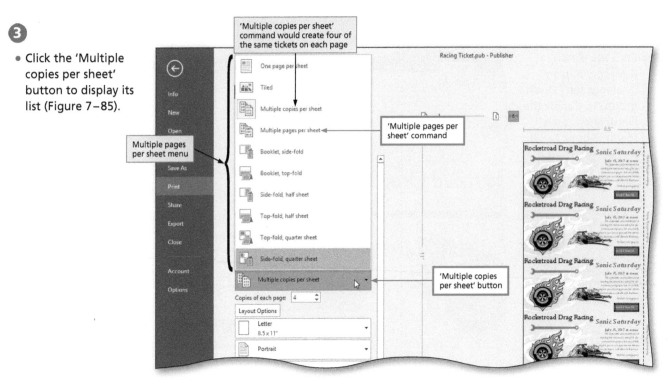

Figure 7–85

4

- Click 'Multiple pages per sheet' to choose the option.

- Verify that other settings match those shown in Figure 7–86.

 Q&A What is the difference between 'Multiple copies per sheet' and 'Multiple pages per sheet'?

When you print more than one copy per page, the 'Multiple copies per sheet' command repeats the record data on all the copies on your printed page. The 'Multiple pages per sheet' command does not repeat the data; each ticket on the printed page has a different row, seat, and level number.

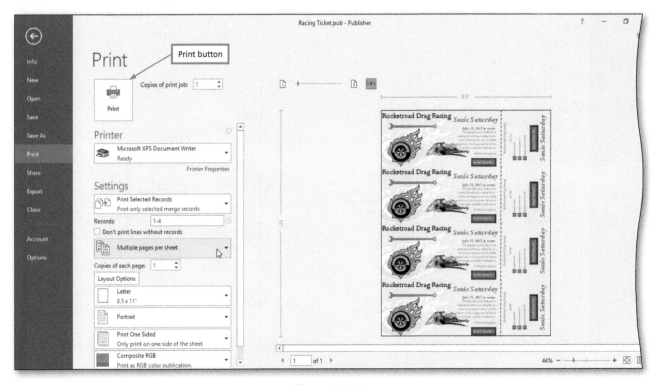

Figure 7–86

5

- Click the Print button in the Print gallery to print the publication on the currently selected printer.
- When the printer stops, retrieve the hard copy.

To Save and Exit

The following steps save the file and exit Publisher.

1 Save the file on your storage location in the same folder as the data source.

2 To exit Publisher, click the Close button on the right side of the title bar.

3 If a Microsoft Publisher dialog box is displayed, click the Don't Save button.

Summary

In this module, you learned how to merge data files with publications. First, you created a form letter with a watermark and applied special character formatting, such as kerning and tracking. You inserted and formatted tabs. Then, you created a Publisher data source, customizing the fields. Next, you merged the form letter with the data source, inserting both grouped and individual field codes, and filtering the data. Finally, you created a ticket, made graphic adjustments, drew a line, and used a Microsoft Excel data file to merge fields manually using the ribbon. You printed one page of tickets.

CONSIDER THIS: PLAN AHEAD

What decisions will you need to make when creating your next business publication?

Use these guidelines as you complete the assignments in this module and create your own publications outside of this class.

1. Use a master page to place repeating objects.
2. Create a watermark.
    a) Use recoloring, brightness, and contrast techniques to fade necessary graphics while retaining detail.
3. To make text easier to read, use character spacing, tracking, and kerning techniques.
4. Set necessary tab stops.
    a) Use leader tabs to fill tabbed areas, if necessary.
    b) Use decimal tabs for dollars and cents.
5. Determine the data source.
    a) Use Access, Excel, or other files as data sources.
    b) Create new data sources as necessary.
6. Create the main publication.
    a) Use fields codes and grouped field codes to insert changing parts of the publication.
    b) Filter and sort the data as necessary.
7. Merge the main publication and the data source.
    a) Proofread and check a merged copy of the publication.

Apply Your Knowledge

Reinforce the skills and apply the concepts you learned in this module.

Creating Merged Invoices

Note: To complete this assignment, you will be required to use the Data Files. Please contact your instructor for information about accessing the Data Files.

Instructions: Run Publisher. If necessary, copy the data source file, Apply 7–1 Address List, from the Data Files to your storage location and appropriate folder. Review the section in this module entitled, To Copy the Data Source File, for instructions on copying and pasting the file from one folder to another. The data will be merged with an invoice to produce billing information for a fitness club. You are to kern characters, set tabs, edit the address list, and then merge and print. The first merged invoice is shown in Figure 7–87.

Figure 7–87

Perform the following tasks:

1. Open the publication named Apply 7–1 Victory Fitness Invoice from the Data Files. Save the publication on your storage location in the same folder as the Apply 7–1 Address list with the file name, Apply 7–1 Victory Fitness Invoice Complete.

2. Drag to select the letters, Vi, in the company name. Press the F9 key to zoom to 100%. Click the Object Size button on the Publisher status bar to display the Measurement task pane. In the Kerning box, type **-3** to move the two letters closer together. Close the Measurement task pane.

3. Click the text box for Invoice Date, Customer ID, and Due Date. Press CTRL+A to select all of the text. Click the 1.5" mark on the horizontal ruler to set a left tab. In the text box, click after the words, Invoice Date, and then press the TAB key. Type **Oct. 6, 2017** at the tab stop to enter the Invoice Date. Repeat the process for the Due Date and then type **Nov. 1, 2017** at the tab stop.

4. Display the Mailings tab. Click the Mail Merge arrow (Mailings tab | Start group) and then click 'Step-by-Step Mail Merge Wizard' on the Mail Merge menu.

5. In the Mail Merge task pane, if necessary, click the 'Use an existing list' option button to select it and then click the 'Next: Create or connect to a recipient list' link. When Publisher displays the Select Data Source dialog box, navigate to your storage location and then double-click the file name, Apply 7–1 Address List.

6. In the Mail Merge Recipients dialog box, select the file name, Apply 7–1 Address List.mdb, in the Data sources box and then click the Edit button (Mail Merge Recipients dialog box) to display the Edit Data Source dialog box.

7. Click the New Entry button (Edit Data Source dialog box) and then create a fictitious customer number and dollar amount.

8. If requested by your instructor, enter your name and address as a new record.

9. Click the OK button (Edit Data Source dialog box). When Publisher asks if you want to update and save the list, click the Yes button. When the Mail Merge Recipients dialog box again is displayed, click the OK button.

10. In the publication, select the three lines of placeholder text in the Bill To text box. In the Mail Merge task pane, select the Address block group field code, and then choose an appropriate address style in the Insert Address Block dialog box. Click the OK button (Insert Address Block dialog box) to close the dialog box.

11. In the publication, click in the Invoice text box to the right of the words, Customer ID. Press the TAB key to move the insertion point to the tab stop. Insert the Customer Number field from the Mail Merge task pane.

12. Click the table cell below the column heading, Amount Due. After the dollar sign, insert the Amount Due field from the Mail Merge task pane.

13. Save the publication again, using the same file name, on your storage location.

14. Submit the files as specified by your instructor.

15. ✲ What kind of data source files would you expect to find with invoice generation? Do you think most small businesses use Access or Excel to store their invoice data? If you were asked about database options, what would you recommend for use with Publisher?

Extend Your Knowledge

Extend the skills you learned in this module and experiment with new skills. You may need to use Help to complete the assignment.

Filtering and Sorting a Recipient List

Note: To complete this assignment, you will be required to use the Data Files. Please contact your instructor for information about accessing the Data Files.

Instructions: If necessary, copy the data source file, Extend 7–1 Recipient List, from the Data Files to your storage location and appropriate folder. Review the section in this module entitled, To Copy the Data Source File, for instructions on copying and pasting the file from one folder to another. Open the publication, Extend 7–1 First America Bank Envelope, from the Data Files.

    In this assignment, you will filter an address list for recipients living in two specific cities. Next, you will sort the list by last name and then by first name to create an alphabetical listing. Finally, you will apply the merged address block to an envelope publication.

Perform the following tasks:

1. Use Help to learn more about printing, exporting, filtering, sorting, and saving recipient lists.

2. Save the publication with the name, Extend 7–1 First America Bank Envelope Complete.

3. To prevent any changes to the return address and logo, move them to the master page as follows: select all (CTRL+A) and then cut (CTRL+X). Go to the master page and paste (CTRL+V) all objects to the master page. Close the master page.

4. Access the Mail Merge task pane. Use the list named Extend 7–1 Recipient List from your storage location.

5. In the Mail Merge Recipients List dialog box, click the Filter link. Choose to filter the list with the City field equal to Eden. Click the And box arrow (Filter and Sort dialog box) and then click Or in the list to add a second filter with the City field equal to Griffith.

Continued >

Extend Your Knowledge *continued*

6. In the Mail Merge Recipients dialog box, click the Sort link. Sort the list alphabetically first by last name and then by first name, in ascending order (Figure 7–88).

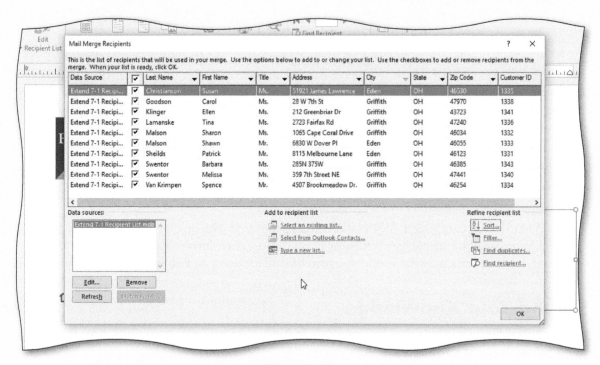

Figure 7–88

7. If instructed to do so, add your name as a new record in the file. Click the OK button (Mail Merge Recipient dialog box).

8. In the Mail Merge task pane, if necessary, click the 'Next: Create or connect to a recipient list' link. Select the grouped field named Address block. Choose an appropriate address style. When Publisher displays the text box, autofit, resize, and reposition the text box so that it creates an appropriate envelope address.

9. Return to the Mail Merge task pane and proceed to the next wizard step. Click the 'Export recipient list to a new file' link (Mail Merge task pane) and then save the filtered list with the file name, Extend 7–1 Eden and Griffith Residents.

10. Click the 'Print recipient list' link (Mail Merge task pane) and include only the First Name, Last Name, Address, City, State, and Zip Code fields. Submit the copies to your instructor.

11. Save the envelope file again and submit it to your instructor as directed.

12. ✹ List two other ways you could generate envelopes if you do not have access to a printer with an envelope feed.

Expand Your World

Create a solution that uses cloud and web technologies by learning and investigating on your own from general guidance.

Creating a Watermark

Instructions: You would like to create a watermark from a picture you have taken. You decide to try a web tool named PicMarkr (Figure 7–89).

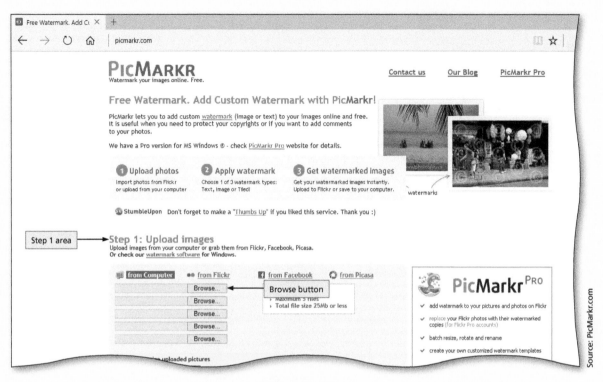

Figure 7–89

Perform the following tasks:

1. Run a browser and navigate to PicMarkr.com.
2. Click the Browse button in Step 1: Upload images section and navigate to a picture that you have taken. When you are finished uploading, scroll down and click the 'Ok! Go to Step2' button.
3. When PicMarkr displays Step 2, enter your name in the Text to display box in the Text watermark section and then choose a placement in the Watermark align area.
4. Click the Continue button.
5. When PicMarkr is finished, download the pictures and then insert them into a publication. Submit the assignment in the format specified by your instructor.
6. ✳ How does PicMarkr compare to creating a watermark in Publisher? What steps would you have to take in Publisher to create the same effect?

In the Labs

Design, create, modify, and/or use a publication following the guidelines, concepts, and skills presented in this module. Labs 1 and 2, which increase in difficulty, require you to create solutions based on what you learned in the module; Lab 3 requires you to apply your creative thinking and problem-solving skills to design and implement a solution.

Lab 1: **Creating an Address List**

Problem: Your company had a booth at the Home Show last month. Many visitors to the show stopped by and filled out cards of interest about your products. Your boss has asked you to enter them into an address list for future mailings.

Continued >

In the Labs *continued*

Perform the following tasks:

1. Run Publisher and open a blank 8.5 × 11" publication.
2. Access the Step-by-Step Mail Merge Wizard and click the 'Type a new list' option button.
3. Click the 'Next: Create or connect to a recipient list' link at the bottom of the Mail Merge task pane. When the New Address List dialog box is displayed, click the Customize Columns button (New Address List dialog box) and then delete all columns that do not appear in Table 7–8. When you are finished, click the OK button (Customize Address List dialog box) to return to the New Address List dialog box.

Table 7 – 8 College Recipient List

Title	First Name	Last Name	Address	City	State	Zip Code
Mr.	Dang	Chou	764 Clay Street	Liberty	NE	68504
Ms.	Doreen	Anderson	267 Green Way	Liberty	NE	68504
Mr.	Raphael	Garcia	345 Norton Ave.	Liberty	NE	68504
Mr.	Patrick	See	1422 88th St.	Liberty	NE	68504

4. Enter the data from Table 7–8.
5. If requested by your instructor, enter your name as a fifth record to the address list.
6. Save the list. When Publisher asks you to name the address list, navigate to your storage location and save the file with the file name, Lab 7–1 Home Show Interest Cards.
7. Sort the list by last name.
8. Click the OK button (Mail Merge Recipients dialog box). If Publisher asks to update the data, click the Yes button.
9. Click the 'Next: Create merged publications' link in the Mail Merge task pane. Click the link, 'Print recipient list' to display the Print List dialog box (Figure 7–90).

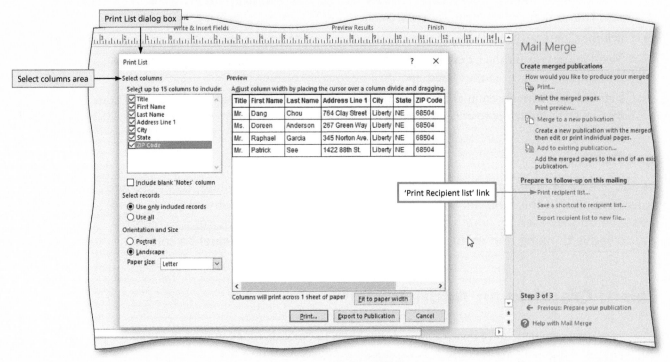

Figure 7–90

10. In the Select columns area, select all of the check boxes so they are included in the address list. Click the Use all option button. Click the Landscape option button. Adjust the columns as necessary in the Preview area.

11. Click the Print button and then print the list. Exit Publisher without saving the publication. Submit the data source file, Lab 7–1 Home Show Interest Cards, or the printout, as directed by your instructor.

12. ✸ What other fields of data might a company include on interest cards? How could Publisher make use of that data?

Lab 2: **Watermarks, Tabs, and Kerning**

Note: To complete this assignment, you will be required to use the Data Files. Please contact your instructor for information about accessing the Data Files.

Problem: The School of Music is planning to implement a new concert series called A Song with Lunch. Vocal majors get performance experience while the audience brings a sack lunch. The Dean's office has given you a publication with a list of songs and a graphic. They have asked you to apply the finishing touches. You decide to change the graphic to a watermark, add leader tabs, and check the kerning and tracking. The completed publication is shown in Figure 7–91.

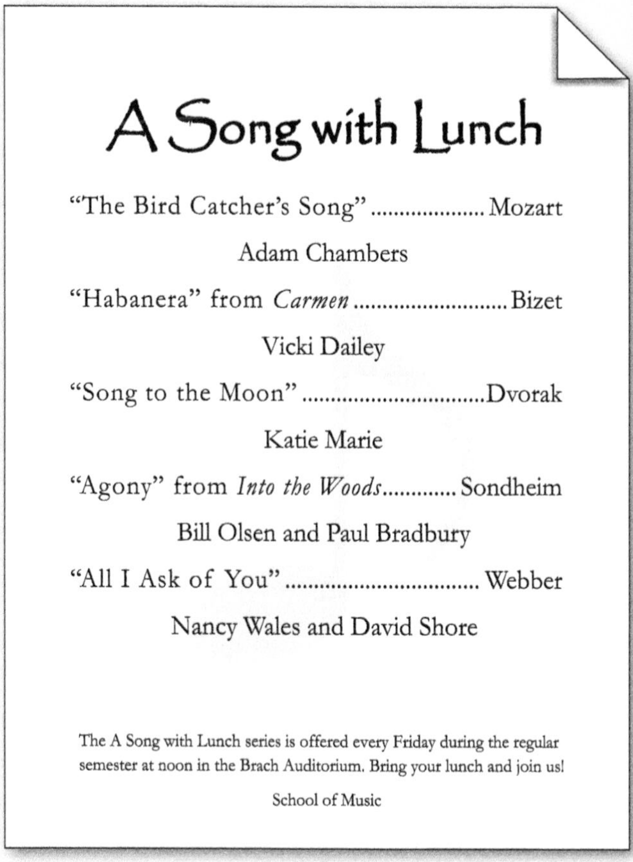

Perform the following tasks:

1. Run Publisher. Open the file named Lab 7–2 Song List. Save the file on your storage location with the file name, Lab 7–2 Program Complete.

2. Do the following to create the watermark:
   a. Press CTRL+M to view the master page.
   b. Move the graphic to the center of the page layout.
   c. Right-click the graphic and then click Format Picture on the shortcut menu. Change the transparency to 95%.
   d. Close the master page.

3. Do the following to create a dot leader tab:
   a. Select the first line of text in the list of songs text box.
   b. Click the Paragraph Settings Dialog Box Launcher (Home tab | Paragraph group) to display the Paragraph dialog box. Click the Tabs tab.
   c. Clear all of the current tabs.
   d. Set a right tab with a dot leader at the 4.75" mark on the ruler.
   e. Click the OK button (Paragraph dialog box) to accept the tabs.
   f. In the text, delete the comma and the space after it. Insert a tab to create the dot leader.
   g. Use the format painter to copy the formatting to all of the titles.

A Song with Lunch

"The Bird Catcher's Song" .... Mozart
Adam Chambers

"Habanera" from *Carmen* .... Bizet
Vicki Dailey

"Song to the Moon" .... Dvorak
Katie Marie

"Agony" from *Into the Woods* .... Sondheim
Bill Olsen and Paul Bradbury

"All I Ask of You" .... Webber
Nancy Wales and David Shore

The A Song with Lunch series is offered every Friday during the regular semester at noon in the Brach Auditorium. Bring your lunch and join us!

School of Music

Figure 7–91

Continued >

In the Labs continued

4. Do the following to create a center tab:

   a. In the text box, click at the beginning of the second line.

   b. Click the Paragraph Settings Dialog Box Launcher (Home tab | Paragraph group) to display the Paragraph dialog box. Click the Tabs tab.

   c. Clear all of the current tabs.

   d. Set a center tab at the 2.5" mark on the ruler and then click the OK button (Paragraph dialog box).

   e. In the text box, insert a tab at the beginning of the second line.

   f. Copy the formatting to each performer's name.

   g. If instructed to do so, change the name of one of the performers to yours and change the song and composer to one of your choosing.

5. Do the following to format the song titles:

   a. Select the first song title. Click the Character Spacing button (Home tab | Font group) and then click Loose on the Character Spacing menu.

   b. Repeat Step 5a for each of the other song titles.

   c. Format each of the titles with quotation marks and italics as shown in Figure 7–91.

6. Kern in the title by doing the following:

   a. Select the letters Lu in the program title.

   b. Open the Measurement task pane.

   c. In the Kerning box, type -7 to move the u closer to the L.

7. Save the publication and submit the file as directed by your instructor.

8. ✳ What would have happened if you had selected all of the songs and performers and then set both tabs at the same time? Explain why you had to set them individually.

Lab 3: **Consider This Your Turn**

Merging with an Excel File

Note: To complete this assignment, you will be required to use the Data Files. Please contact your instructor for information about accessing the Data Files.

Problem: A club on your campus is sponsoring a lecture on the Baader-Meinhof phenomenon. Baader-Meinhof is the phenomenon where a person hears about some obscure piece of information — often an unfamiliar word or name — and soon afterward encounters the same topic again, sometimes repeatedly. The club has asked you to create a ticket for the lecture.

Part 1: From scratch, create a ticket with the name of the lecture, the lecturer, and the location. If instructed to do so, change the location of the lecture to your classroom building and room number. Create a text box with appropriate tabbing to display the section, row, and seat. The college has given you an Excel spreadsheet that contains the seat numbers; however, due to construction, only the center section is available for the lecture. The spreadsheet, located in the Data Files, is named Lab 7–3 Ticket Seat Numbers. If necessary, copy and paste the file to your storage location. Merge the publication with the data source, filter the data, and then place appropriate fields. Save the merged publication.

Part 2: ✳ How can you be sure that the tickets will print correctly? What are the advantages and disadvantages of buying prescored paper to create tickets? What are the advantages and disadvantages of sending the tickets out for publication?

8 | Generating Data-Driven Catalogs

Objectives

You will have mastered the material in this module when you can:

- Insert headers and footers
- Duplicate a master page
- Apply alternating master pages
- Use textures and number styles
- Format a picture by cropping to shape and adding a reflection
- Create catalog pages

- Use the catalog merge area
- Turn on boundaries and align objects
- Find entries
- Preview and merge catalogs
- Work with the Graphics Manager
- Translate text

Introduction

As most businesses keep track of their inventory, data, and statistics in electronic databases, it is efficient to use that data to build custom marketing pieces, such as catalogs for print media or for e-commerce applications on the web. A publication directly populated and updated from a database is considered a **data-driven publication**.

As you learned in the previous module, data-driven publications can include form letters, documents with individualized data, such as tickets and envelopes, and documents linked to other applications that contain data, such as Excel data imported to Publisher tables. In this module, you will learn another way to create data-driven publications using the catalog tool. Many businesses customize Publisher catalogs and use customer profiling to target certain markets. While publishing a large, full-color catalog can be a significant marketing investment due to production, printing, and distribution costs, with desktop publishing, even small businesses can create external and internal publications about products, personnel, or services.

Project — Intern Directory

Figure 8–1 displays a directory about the new interns hired at a large B2B company in the technology industry. **B2B** stands for business-to-business and refers to a situation where one business conducts a commercial transaction with another. Transactions between companies usually are made for production purposes, operational services,

or for direct goods. Recently, the Mills-Deck Corporation has hired a new set of interns. To introduce them to the rest of the company, the corporation would like a directory with pictures of the interns, background descriptions, and other pieces of data in which employees might be interested. The directory contains eight half-pages, printed on both sides of two, 8.5 × 11-inch pieces of paper, and then folded.

Figure 8–1

This directory will be created using Publisher's catalog merge, which differs from its mail merge in two distinctive ways. The catalog merge is designed with graphics or pictures in mind. It is easy to incorporate pictures into the merge process — pictures that change from record to record. Secondly, a catalog merge includes all records in one longer booklet publication, rather than separate pages like form letters. Toward that end, Publisher provides a unique **merge area** that desktop publishers use to design their presentation with fields that change from record to record, and layout that does not.

The following roadmap identifies general activities you will perform as you progress through this module:

1. FORMAT ALTERNATING MASTER PAGES with graphics, headers, footers, and page numbers.

2. USE textures and NUMBER STYLES.

3. FORMAT a PICTURE by cropping to shape and adding a reflection.

4. CREATE and format CATALOG PAGES, inserting nonrepeating text and graphics.

5. CONNECT with a DATA SOURCE.

6. INSERT picture and text MERGE FIELDS.

7. MANAGE GRAPHICS.

8. TRANSLATE TEXT as necessary.

9. MERGE to a printed publication.

Catalogs and Directories

A **catalog** is a collection of pictures and descriptive details, representing items for sale, services offered, or any data list. A **directory** is a type of catalog that usually provides details about individuals, products, or organizations, sorted alphabetically. A directory is intended as an in-house reference, while a catalog commonly is more of an external marketing tool.

Publisher has catalog templates to assist you in designing catalogs and directories. In addition, Publisher provides a catalog merge that quickly and easily populates the publication. A catalog merge is the process of combining information from a data source with a template or original publication, to create pages that display multiple records per page.

Typically, a Publisher catalog template creates eight pages of content with replaceable graphics and text boxes. You easily can add more pages. You can select the page size, font scheme, and color scheme of the catalog, just as you do with other publications. Furthermore, with catalogs, you can choose the content layout of specific pages, selecting the number of columns, forms, calendars, featured items, or table of contents for those pages. Alternately, you can create a catalog or directory from scratch, designing your pages one at a time, or by using a blank catalog template, as you will do in this project.

CONSIDER THIS

How do you plan the layout of a catalog or directory?

Due to the graphical, full-color nature of these publications and the high-quality paper that commonly is used, planning is essential to keep a catalog project on schedule and within budget. You must identify resource requirements and formulate strategies that drive business growth. Typically, a business can reuse and repurpose catalog content for other forms of advertisements, such as seasonal promotion publications. Many companies store pictures and data together in database files, ready to populate catalogs, directories, brochures, and websites. Here are some general rules when you are planning your layout:

- Create your publication in a common size. It will be less costly at both the printer and the post office.
- Use an even number of pages to avoid blank pages in your catalog or directory. Check ahead of time to find out how many records of data are in the data source.
- Alternate headers and footers as necessary to create outside edge page numbers.
- Create a layout that will attract your audience. A business-to-business (B2B) catalog is different from a business-to-consumer (B2C) catalog. Catalogs for young people will have a different look than a catalog for older people. Make the style of your catalog match the style preferences of your audience.
- Repeat layout designs or use alternating pages for consistency. Do not make the customer look for information in two places. For example, keep your prices in approximately the same place in each repeating element.
- Repeat some objects to provide consistency. Use headers and footers or a background to create a cohesive unit.
- Keep the name of the product close to any pictures or graphics.
- Limit the fonts to two or three, and use WordArt sparingly.

To Create a Two-Page Spread

1 FORMAT ALTERNATING MASTER PAGES | 2 USE NUMBER STYLES | 3 FORMAT PICTURE | 4 CREATE CATALOG PAGES
5 CONNECT DATA SOURCE | 6 INSERT MERGE FIELDS | 7 MANAGE GRAPHICS | 8 TRANSLATE TEXT | 9 MERGE

The following steps choose a blank catalog template and set the font and color schemes for the catalog. Publisher will offer to create multiple pages, using a two-page spread. *Why? Publisher recognizes this file as a catalog template.* A **two-page spread**, or simply a **spread**, refers to the way inner pages appear as two adjacent, facing pages in a book, catalog, magazine, or other publication.

1

- Run Publisher.
- In the New Template gallery, click BUILT-IN and then click Catalogs to view the available templates.
- Scroll to the middle portion of the gallery to display the Blank Sizes area.
- Click the '1/2 Letter Booklet 5.5 × 8.5"' template to select it.
- In the Customize area, select the Oriel color scheme and the Casual font scheme.
- Click the CREATE button to display the Microsoft Publisher dialog box (Figure 8–2).

Q&A

My publication was created with a previous business information set. What should I do?

If you do not need to keep the business information set, click the Business Information button (Insert tab | Text group), click 'Edit Business Information' on the Business Information menu, click the Delete button (Business Information dialog box), click the Yes button (Microsoft Publisher dialog box), and then click the Close button (Business Information dialog box).

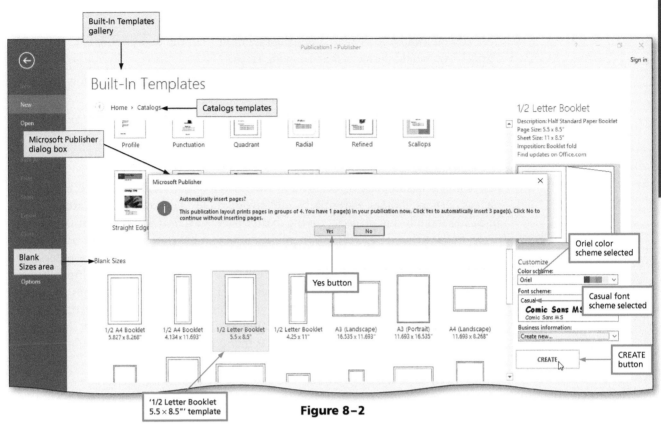

Built-In Templates gallery

Built-In Templates

Home › Catalogs

Catalogs templates

Microsoft Publisher dialog box

Profile   Punctuation   Quadrant   Radial   Refined   Scallops

1/2 Letter Booklet
Description: Half Standard Paper Booklet
Page Size: 5.5 x 8.5"
Sheet Size: 11 x 8.5"
Imposition: Booklet fold
Find updates on Office.com

Microsoft Publisher   ✕

Automatically insert pages?

This publication layout prints pages in groups of 4. You have 1 page(s) in your publication now. Click Yes to automatically insert 3 page(s). Click No to continue without inserting pages.

Yes   No

Straight Edge

Blank Sizes area

Blank Sizes

Yes button

Oriel color scheme selected

Customize
Color scheme:
Oriel

Font scheme:
Casual
Comic Sans MS
Comic Sans MS

Casual font scheme selected

Business information:
Create new...

Options

1/2 A4 Booklet   1/2 A4 Booklet   1/2 Letter Booklet   1/2 Letter Booklet   A3 (Landscape)   A3 (Portrait)   A4 (Landscape)
5.827 x 8.268"   4.134 x 11.693"   5.5 x 8.5"   4.25 x 11"   16.535 x 11.693"   11.693 x 16.535"   11.693 x 8.268"

CREATE

CREATE button

'1/2 Letter Booklet 5.5 × 8.5"' template

Figure 8–2

2

- Click the Yes button (Microsoft Publisher dialog box) to have Publisher create an even number of pages in the publication.

- If the rulers do not appear, press CTRL+R.

- If the Page Navigation pane does not appear, click the Page Number button on the status bar.

- If the Page Navigation pane is collapsed, click the 'Expand Page Navigation Pane' button at the top of the Page Navigation pane.

- If necessary, click the Special Characters button (Home tab | Paragraph group).

- Display the Page Design tab.

- Click the Adjust Margins button (Page Design tab | Page Setup group) and then click Narrow on the Adjust Margins menu to create a narrow margin (Figure 8–3).

Q&A Why did Publisher display three icons in the Page Navigation pane?
The front and back of a catalog are single pages. Pages 2 and 3 appear as a two-page spread.

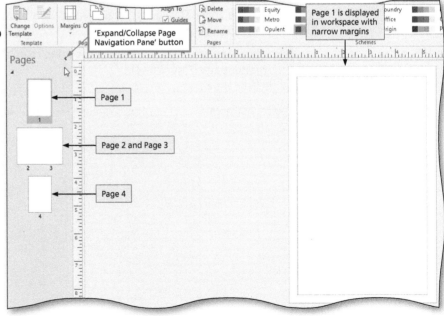

Change Template   Options   Margins

Align To   ☑ Guides

Delete   Move   Rename

Equity   Metro   Opulent

Foundry   Office   Origin

Page 1 is displayed in workspace with narrow margins

Template   Pages   Schemes

'Expand/Collapse Page Navigation Pane' button

Pages

Page 1

Page 2 and Page 3

Page 4

Figure 8–3

To View Single Pages

If you wanted to display single pages, rather than the two-page spread for pages 2 and 3, you would perform the following steps.

1. Right-click the 'Page 2 and Page 3' thumbnail in the Page Navigation pane to display the shortcut menu.
2. Click 'View Two-Page Spread' on the shortcut menu to turn off the setting.

BTW
The Ribbon and Screen Resolution
Publisher may change how the groups and buttons within the groups appear on the ribbon, depending on the computer or mobile device's screen resolution. Thus, your ribbon may look different from the ones in this book if you are using a screen resolution other than 1366 x 768.

Alternating Master Pages

Recall that a master page is background area used to create repeatable elements, such as headers, footers, watermarks, and layout guides. You created a watermark in an earlier module and placed it on the master page, so that it would appear on every page of your printed publication. In publications that have more than one page, you can create multiple, alternating master pages for a more versatile publication design. For example, in publications that use a spread, it is common to create multiple master pages for verso (left) and recto (right) pages, or for the front and back pages.

In Publisher, the default is Normal view. **Normal view** is the view where you perform most of the tasks while creating a publication. **Master Page view** shows you the page or pages that contain the elements that you want to repeat on multiple pages.

To Create the Background on Master Page A

The following steps create a shape to use on Master Page A, which will appear on the first and last page of the booklet.

1 Press CTRL+M to view the publication in Master Page view. In the Page Navigation pane, click 'Master Page A' to select it, if necessary.

2 Display the Insert tab and then, using the Shapes button (Insert tab | Shapes group), insert a rectangle and resize it to fill the left hand or verso side of Master Page A within the margins.

3 Use the Shape Fill arrow (Drawing Tools Format tab | Shape Styles group) to fill the rectangle with the 'Accent 2 (RGB (254, 134, 55))' color.

4 Use the Shape Outline arrow (Drawing Tools Format tab | Shape Styles group) to outline the rectangle with the 'Accent 3 (RGB (117, 152, 217))' color and with a weight of 6 pt.

5 CTRL+drag the shape to create a copy and then place the copy on the recto side of the master page (Figure 8–4).

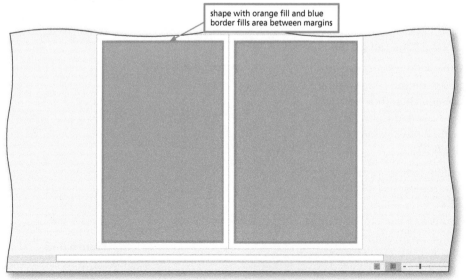

shape with orange fill and blue border fills area between margins

Figure 8–4

Headers and Footers

A **header** is text and graphics that print at the top of each page in a publication. Similarly, a **footer** is text and graphics that print at the bottom of every page. In Publisher, headers print one-half inch from the top margin of every page, and footers print one-half inch from the bottom margin of every page. In addition to text and graphics, headers and footers can include document information, such as the page number, current date, current time, and author's name.

The 'Show Header/Footer' button (Master Page tab | Header & Footer group) toggles between the header and footer areas, displaying a text box in which you can insert text elements. If you want to use a graphic, you must insert the graphic and drag it to the header or footer area.

To Create a Header

1 FORMAT ALTERNATING MASTER PAGES | **2 USE NUMBER STYLES** | **3 FORMAT PICTURE** | **4 CREATE CATALOG PAGES**
5 CONNECT DATA SOURCE | **6 INSERT MERGE FIELDS** | **7 MANAGE GRAPHICS** | **8 TRANSLATE TEXT** | **9 MERGE**

The following steps create a header that will repeat across all pages of the publication. **Why?** *A repeating header will provide consistency and brand the look and feel of the publication.* You will add text to the header area and insert a graphic to complete the header for the verso page (left side) of Master Page A. To complete these steps, you will be required to use the Data Files. Please contact your instructor for information about accessing the Data Files.

1

- Click the rectangle shape on the verso page and then display the Master Page tab, if necessary.

- Click the 'Show Header/Footer' button (Master Page tab | Header & Footer group) to display the Header text box.

- Move the header down slightly, on top of the shape, and resize the height of the header text box to be approximately 0.5 inches tall (Figure 8–5).

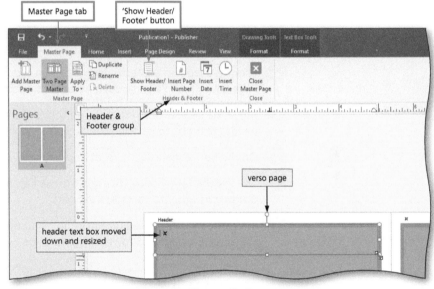

Figure 8–5

2

- Click the 1.25" mark on the horizontal ruler to place a tab stop.

- With the insertion point positioned in the Header text box, change the font size to 18 and then press the TAB key.

- Type **Mills-Deck Corporation** to complete the text (Figure 8–6).

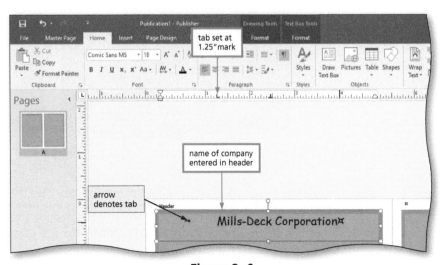

Figure 8–6

- Display the Insert tab.

- Click the Pictures button (Insert tab | Illustrations group) to display the Insert Picture dialog box.

- Navigate to the Data Files and then insert the picture named Left Graphic.

- Drag the graphic to the upper-left corner of the page, as shown in Figure 8–7.

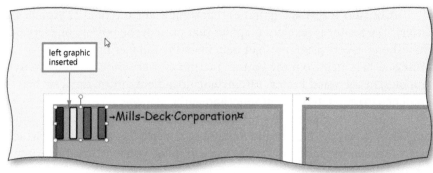

Figure 8–7

Other Ways

1. Click Insert Header button (Insert Tab | Header & Footer group), type header text

To Create a Mirrored Header

The following steps create a mirrored header for the recto (right) pages.

1 Scroll to display the right side of Master Page A, which will be the recto pages in the booklet. Display the Master Page tab.

2 Click the shape on the recto page and then click the 'Show Header/Footer' button (Master Page tab | Master Page group) if necessary to display the Header text box for the recto page.

3 Move the header down slightly, on top of the shape, and resize the height of the header text box to be approximately 0.5 inches tall.

4 On the horizontal ruler, click at approximately the 7/8" mark to create a tab.

5 Change the font size to 18, press the TAB key, and then type **Mills-Deck Corporation** to complete the text.

6 Insert the picture named Right Graphic and then drag the graphic to the upper-right corner of the page as shown in Figure 8–8.

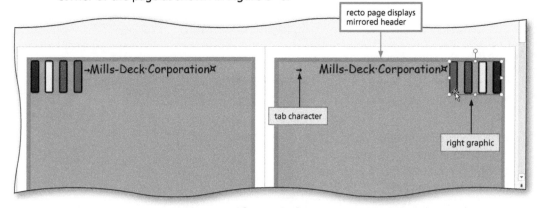

Figure 8–8

To Duplicate a Master Page

1 FORMAT ALTERNATING MASTER PAGES | 2 USE NUMBER STYLES | 3 FORMAT PICTURE | 4 CREATE CATALOG PAGES
5 CONNECT DATA SOURCE | 6 INSERT MERGE FIELDS | 7 MANAGE GRAPHICS | 8 TRANSLATE TEXT | 9 MERGE

The following steps create a second master page. *Why? You will use different features on the back and front of the booklet versus the inside pages; thus, you will need a second master page.*

1

- Display the Master Page tab.

- Click the Duplicate button (Master Page tab | Master Page group) to display the Duplicate Master Page dialog box.

- With the Description text selected, type **Inside Pages** to describe the duplicate master page (Figure 8–9).

Q&A Could I use the 'Add a Master Page' button (Master Page tab | Master Page group)?
The 'Add a Master Page' button will create a blank page. In this booklet, you would like to copy some of the features from Master Page A.

How does Publisher use the description that I entered?
The description appears in a ScreenTip when you point to the master page thumbnail in the Page Navigation pane.

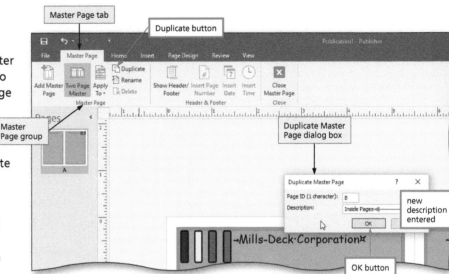

Figure 8–9

2

- Click the OK button (Duplicate Master Page dialog box) to close the dialog box and create the duplicate master page.

Other Ways

1. In Master Page view, right-click Master Page in Page Navigation pane, click 'Insert Duplicate Page' on shortcut menu, right-click duplicate page, click Rename on shortcut menu, enter description (Rename Master Page dialog box), click OK button

TO RENAME A MASTER PAGE

If you wanted to rename a master page, you would perform the following steps.

1. In Master Page view, right-click the desired page in the Page Navigation pane, such as Master Page A, to display a shortcut menu.
2. Click Rename on the shortcut menu to display the Rename Master Page dialog box.
3. In the Description text box, enter a new name, such as Front and Back.
4. Click the OK button (Rename Master Page dialog box).

To Remove Colored Background Shapes from Master Page B

The following steps remove the shapes from Master Page B, as the inside pages will use a different background.

1 On Master Page B, click the shape on the verso page to select it. Press the DELETE key to delete the shape.

2 Click the shape on the recto page to select it. Press the DELETE key to delete the shape (Figure 8–10).

BTW
Touch Screen Differences
The Office and Windows interfaces may vary if you are using a touch screen. For this reason, you might notice that the function or appearance of your touch screen differs slightly from this module's presentation.

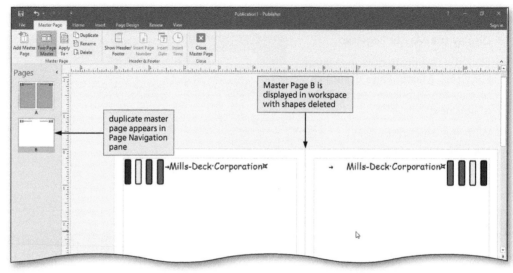

Figure 8–10

To Insert a Texture

1 FORMAT ALTERNATING MASTER PAGES | 2 USE NUMBER STYLES | 3 FORMAT PICTURE | 4 CREATE CATALOG PAGES
5 CONNECT DATA SOURCE | 6 INSERT MERGE FIELDS | 7 MANAGE GRAPHICS | 8 TRANSLATE TEXT | 9 MERGE

You have learned that Shape fills and Background fills include color, tints, pictures, gradients, textures, and patterns. In previous modules, you have used colors, pictures, and gradients to fill the background of publications. Now you will use a texture. Recall that a texture is a combination of color and patterns without gradual shading. Publisher's Texture gallery includes 24 images that you can use as a fill; many websites also have downloadable textures for Publisher. These textures create repeating rectangles across the page in a tiled fashion. After choosing a texture and setting a transparency if necessary, you can select an offset. An **offset**, or **tiling option**, determines the scaling factor for the texture fill. Table 8–1 displays the offset options used to customize a texture fill.

Table 8–1 Offset Options	
Setting	**Purpose**
Offset X	Shifts the fill to the left (negative numbers) or the right (positive numbers).
Offset Y	Shifts the fill up (negative numbers) or down (positive numbers).
Scale X	Specifies horizontal scaling of the fill by a percentage.
Scale Y	Specifies vertical scaling of the fill by a percentage.
Alignment	Specifies the anchor position where the picture tiling begins, such as top left or bottom right.
Mirror type	Specifies that alternating horizontal or vertical tiles should display mirrored or flipped with every other tile, horizontally, vertically, or both.

The following steps add a texture to the master page. *Why? In a published directory, catalog, or booklet, a texture background will soften the look of a plain white background.*

1

- Display the Page Design tab and then click the Background button (Page Design tab | Page Background group) to display the Background gallery (Figure 8–11).

 Experiment

- Point to each of the backgrounds and watch the live preview.

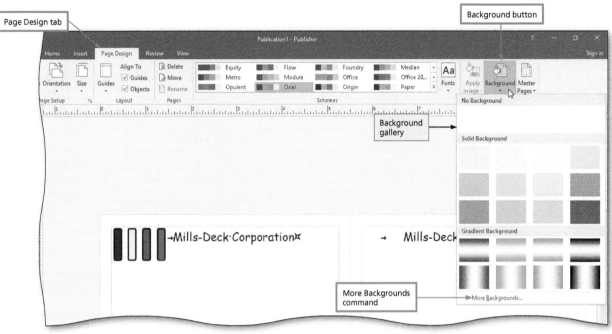

Figure 8-11

②

- Click More Backgrounds in the Background gallery to display the Format Background dialog box.

- Click the 'Picture or texture fill' option button (Format Background dialog box) to display the available settings.

- Drag the Transparency slider to 65% to increase the transparency of the texture.

- Click the Texture button to display the Texture gallery (Figure 8-12).

Experiment

- Point to each of the textures to display the texture name in a ScreenTip.

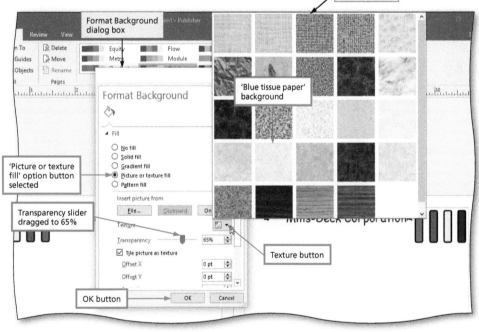

Figure 8-12

③

- Click the 'Blue tissue paper' texture in the Texture gallery to select it.

Experiment

- Click the various offset boxes (Format Background dialog box) to look at the choices for tiling options.

- Click the OK button (Format Background dialog box) to apply the background to the master page (Figure 8-13).

Q&A Could I have created the background in Normal view?

Yes, but it would have applied only to the current page. Creating the background in Master Page view applies it to all pages.

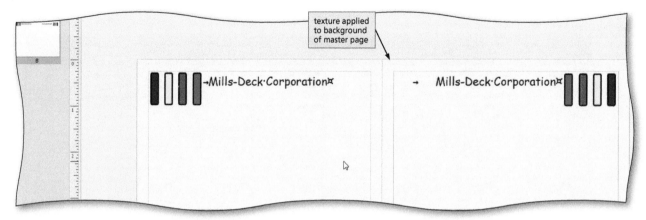

Figure 8–13

To Insert Alternating Footers

1 FORMAT ALTERNATING MASTER PAGES | 2 USE NUMBER STYLES | 3 FORMAT PICTURE | 4 CREATE CATALOG PAGES
5 CONNECT DATA SOURCE | 6 INSERT MERGE FIELDS | 7 MANAGE GRAPHICS | 8 TRANSLATE TEXT | 9 MERGE

The master page for the front and back of the directory will not display a footer. *Why? The first and back pages in a booklet rarely display a page number.* The inside pages will display a footer with a page number and the company's web address.

In many publications that contain facing pages, the page number is located on the outside edges of the pages. In Publisher, you accomplish this task by specifying one type of footer for verso pages and another type for recto pages, a technique called **alternating footers**. The following steps create alternating footers for the inside pages.

- Display the Master Page tab.

- With Master Page B still selected, click the 'Show Header/Footer' button (Master Page tab | Header & Footer group) and then click the button again to move to the verso footer area.

- Zoom to 150% (Figure 8–14).

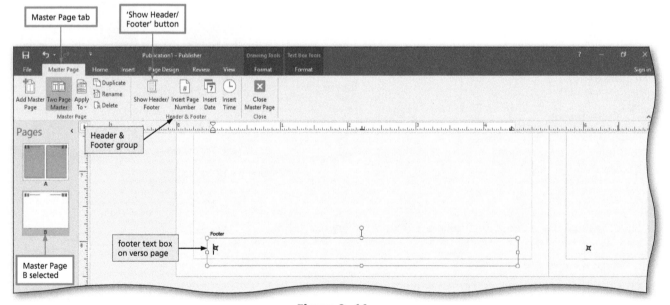

Figure 8–14

2

- Move the footer text box up slightly, on top of the shape, and resize the height of the header text box to be approximately 0.5 inches tall.

- Type **Page** and then press the SPACEBAR.

- Click the 'Insert Page Number' button (Master Page tab | Header & Footer group) to enter the page number placeholder (Figure 8–15).

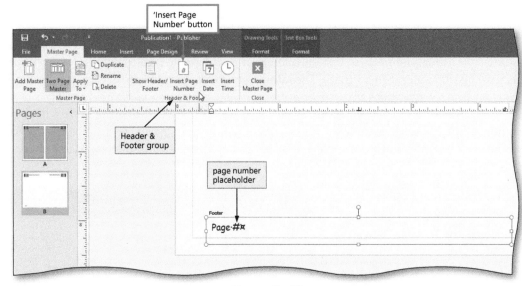

Figure 8–15

Q&A Could I have just typed the # symbol?
No. The symbol that Publisher inserts is a field code that automatically is populated with the page number when you return to Normal view.

3

- Press the TAB key twice to move to the right side of the footer.

- Type **www.mills-deck.com** to enter the web address (Figure 8–16).

Q&A Were tab stops created automatically?
Yes, the footer text box has a center tab and a right tab because most users place footer information at one of those two locations or at the left margin.

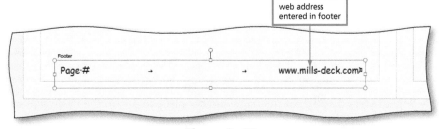

Figure 8–16

4

- Click the bottom of the recto page in the two-page spread to display the footer text box for the alternating footer.

- Type **www.mills-deck.com** to enter the web address. If Publisher capitalizes the first letter, click the AutoCorrect Options button and then click 'Undo Automatic Capitalization' on the menu.

- Press the TAB key twice. Type **Page** and then press the SPACEBAR.

- Click the 'Insert Page Number' button (Master Page tab | Header & Footer group) to enter the page number placeholder.

- Move the recto footer text box up slightly, on top of the shape, and increase its height to approximately 0.5 inches (Figure 8–17).

Q&A What else can I insert into a header or footer?
You can type any text, insert any picture, or add an automatic date or time using the ribbon.

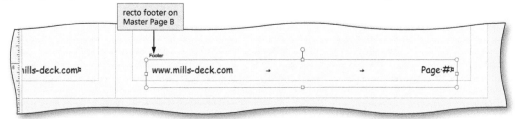

Figure 8–17

To Apply a Number Style

Along with stylistic sets, Publisher has several styles of numbers from which you may choose. The **proportional lining** style formats numbers so that the number of pixels used to create a number is proportional; for example, a 0 (zero) may be wider than a 1 (one). The **tabular style** formats numbers so each number is the same width. *Why? Numbers with the same width are better for aligned numbers, such as those used with decimal tabs, or for tables of numbers.*

Each of those two number styles has a stylistic alternative: the **lining style** will align the bottom of all numbers; the **old-style** setting will allow certain numbers, such as 3, to drop below the baseline of the other numbers. The following steps apply a number style to the page numbers on Master Page B.

1

- Select the page number placeholder.

- Display the Text Box Tools Format tab.

- Click the Number Style button (Text Box Tools Format tab | Typography group) to display its menu (Figure 8–18).

2

- Click 'Proportional Old-style' to select the number style.

Q&A

Should I see a difference?
No. You will see the number change when you leave Master Page view.

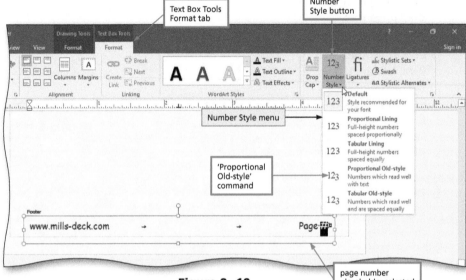

Figure 8–18

3

- Repeat Steps 1 and 2 for the page number placeholder on the verso side of Master Page B.

- Click outside of the footer to deselect.

To Apply Master Pages

The following steps apply Master Page B (with footers) to all pages in the catalog and then change the first and last page to Master Page A (without footer). *Why? The directory will not display a page number on the cover page or on the back page.* You can apply a master page from either Master Page view or from the Page Navigation pane shortcut menu in Normal view.

1

- With Master Page B still selected in the Page Navigation pane, click the Apply To button (Master Page tab | Master Page group) to display the Apply To menu (Figure 8–19).

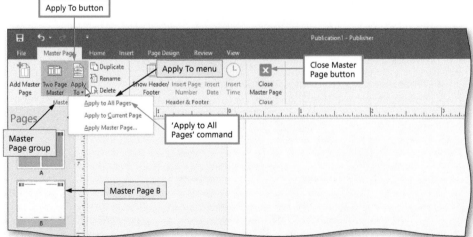

Figure 8–19

②

- Click 'Apply to All Pages' on the Apply To menu to apply Master Page B with its alternating footers to all pages in the catalog.

- Click the 'Close Master Page' button (Master Page tab | Close group) to return to Normal view.

- If necessary, navigate to page 2 and page 3 to view the page number (Figure 8–20).

Q&A My two-page spread did not change. Did I do something wrong?
No. Publisher sometimes separates Page 2 and Page 3 because they have different footers. You can right-click Page 2 and Page 3 in the Page Navigation pane and then click 'View Two-Page Spread' on the shortcut menu if you want to turn on the view.

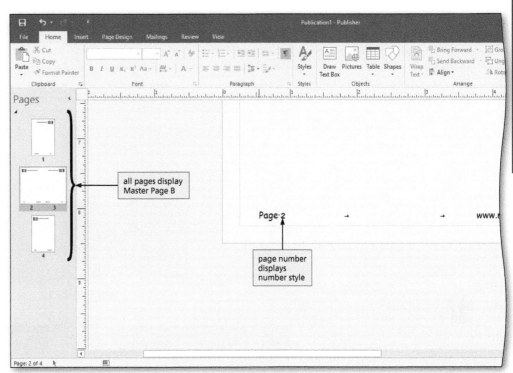

Figure 8–20

③

- In the Page Navigation pane, right-click Page 1 to display the shortcut menu and then point to Master Pages to display the Master Pages submenu (Figure 8–21).

Q&A What is the purpose of the 'Apply Master Page' command?
The 'Apply Master Page' command displays the Apply Master Page dialog box, where you can make additional choices about which master page to use.

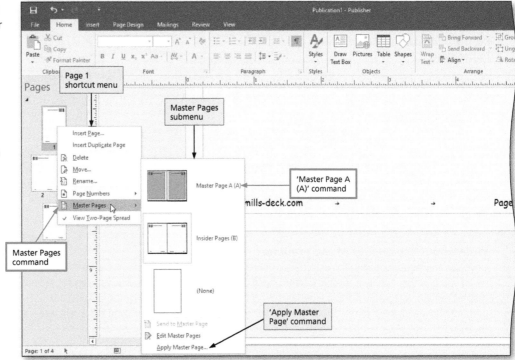

Figure 8–21

4

- Click 'Master Page A (A)' on the Master Pages submenu to apply it to page 1 of the catalog (Figure 8–22).

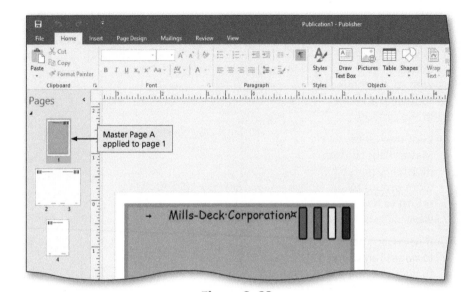

Figure 8–22

5

- Repeat Steps 3 and 4 to apply Master Page A to Page 4 of the publication.

- Click the Save button on the Quick Access Toolbar. Click the Browse button (Backstage view). Navigate to your desired save location and then save the file using the file name, Mills-Deck Intern Directory (Figure 8–23).

Experiment

- Click each of the thumbnails in the Page Navigation pane, and view the headers, footers, and number style.

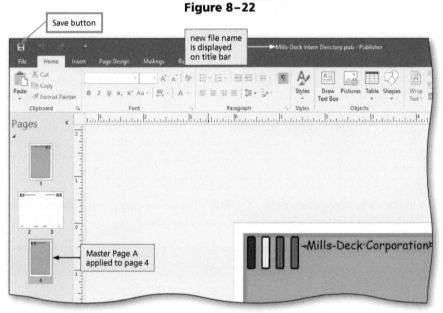

Figure 8–23

Creating the Front Cover

You have created master pages that will serve as the background in the directory. In the next sections, you will add graphics and text to page 1. You will crop a picture to a shape and format it with a reflection.

What about the quality of the graphics?

Catalogs are more appealing to customers when they use high-quality, color pictures and graphics. Use a picture or photograph when you want to display a specific person, place, or thing. Use a graphic, such as clip art, when you do not have a photograph or when you are describing a general concept or service. Consult a graphics specialist to help choose high-resolution graphics; however, keep in mind that the images will require more memory and storage space.

To Insert a Picture

The following steps insert a picture on page 1, which will serve as the cover of the directory. To complete these steps, you will be required to use the Data Files. Please contact your instructor for information about accessing the Data Files.

1 Click Page 1 in the Page Navigation pane and then click the 'Show Whole Page' button on the status bar.

2 Display the Insert tab. Click the Pictures button (Insert tab | Illustrations group) to display the Insert Picture dialog box.

3 Navigate to the location of the file to be opened (in this case, the Module 08 folder of the Data Files).

4 Double-click the file, Front Cover, to insert it into the publication.

5 If necessary, resize the graphic to approximately 2.50 by 2.50 and move it to the upper center of the page as shown in Figure 8–24.

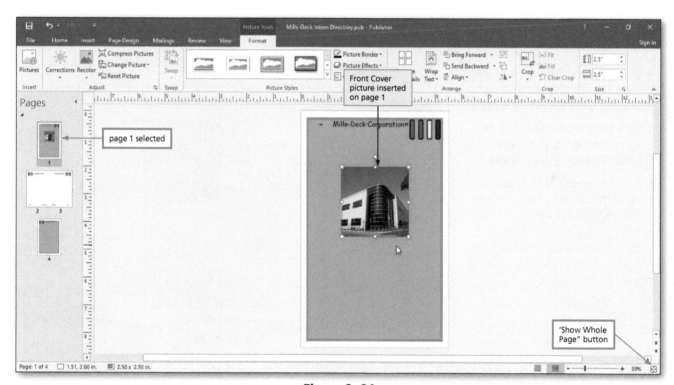

Figure 8–24

To Crop to Shape

1 FORMAT ALTERNATING MASTER PAGES | 2 USE NUMBER STYLES | 3 FORMAT PICTURE | **4 CREATE CATALOG PAGES**
5 CONNECT DATA SOURCE | 6 INSERT MERGE FIELDS | 7 MANAGE GRAPHICS | 8 TRANSLATE TEXT | 9 MERGE

The following steps crop a picture to fit within a certain shape. *Why? The company wants a softer look than the square corners of the current picture.* When you choose the 'Crop to Shape' command, Publisher displays the Basic Shapes gallery where you can choose the way the picture should be cropped.

1

- With the picture selected, click the Crop arrow (Picture Tools Format tab | Crop group) to display its menu and then point to 'Crop to Shape' to display the Crop To gallery (Figure 8–25).

Q&A What is the difference between the Crop button and the Crop arrow?

If you click the Crop button, which is the upper half of the button/arrow combination, Publisher will display the picture with cropping handles and assume you want square corners. The Crop arrow, which is the lower-half of the button/arrow combination, will display a menu.

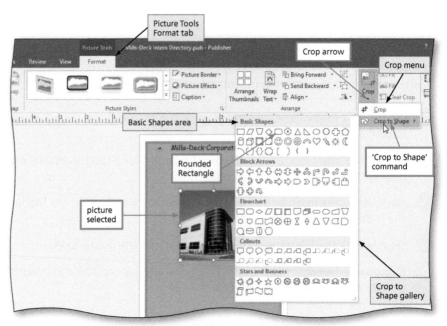

Figure 8–25

2

- Click Rounded Rectangle in the Basic Shapes area in the Crop to Shape gallery to crop to shape.

- Click the Crop button (Picture Tools Format tab | Crop group) to finish the crop (Figure 8–26).

Q&A Could I use one of the picture styles (Picture Tools Format tab | Picture Styles group)?

You could, but none of those styles matches the desired output exactly. In this case, it is easier to crop to a shape.

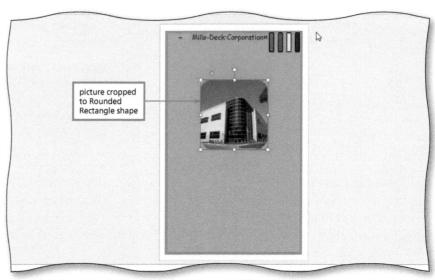

Figure 8–26

To Format the Border

The following steps format the border of the picture by sampling the purple color in the header graphic and by setting the weight.

1 With the picture still selected, click the Picture Border arrow (Picture Tools Format tab | Picture Styles group) to display the Picture Border menu. Click 'Sample Line Color' on the menu to display the eyedropper pointer.

2 Click the purple color on the right side of the header graphic to sample it and apply the border color.

3 Click the Picture Border arrow (Picture Tools Format tab | Picture Styles group) again, point to Weight to display the Weight gallery, and then click 3 pt to change the weight of the line.

4 Click outside of the graphic to view the formatting (Figure 8–27).

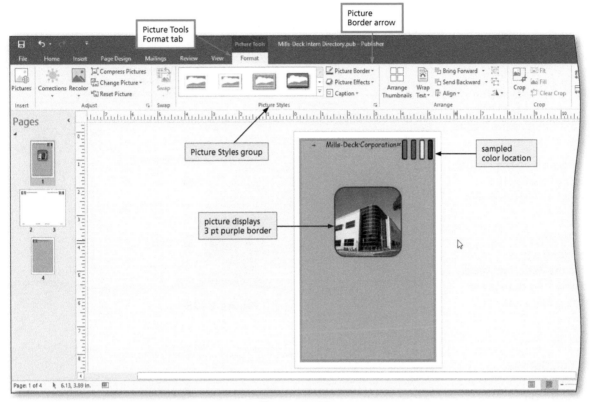

Figure 8–27

1 FORMAT ALTERNATING MASTER PAGES | 2 USE NUMBER STYLES | 3 FORMAT PICTURE | **4 CREATE CATALOG PAGES**
5 CONNECT DATA SOURCE | 6 INSERT MERGE FIELDS | 7 MANAGE GRAPHICS | 8 TRANSLATE TEXT | 9 MERGE

To Create a Reflection

Recall that shape and picture effects are similar, with options to add a bevel, glow, 3-D, and rotation, among others. In Publisher, a **reflection** is a mirrored image of the original graphic, with matching borders, to create the appearance of a partial reflection. A reflection reproduces the details of a picture or shape as opposed to a shadow, which is usually a solid color, such as gray. The Reflection gallery has many preset reflections. Table 8-2 describes other reflection settings.

Table 8–2   Reflection Settings

Setting	Description
Transparency	A percentage related to how much you see through the graphic to the background
Size	A percentage of how much of the graphic to include in the reflection
Blur	A point measurement of how much detail you can see in the reflection (a very high blur is a shadow)
Distance	A point measurement of the distance between the original graphic and its reflection (a low distance may touch the original graphic)

The following steps format the picture with a reflection. *Why? A reflection will add depth and interest to the front cover of the directory.*

● Select the picture and display the Picture Tools Format tab, if necessary.

● Click the Picture Effects button (Picture Tools Format tab | Picture Styles group) to display the Picture Effects menu.

● Point to Reflection on the Picture Effects menu to display the Reflection gallery (Figure 8–28).

Experiment

● Point to each of the preset reflections in the Reflection gallery, and watch how they change the picture in the publication.

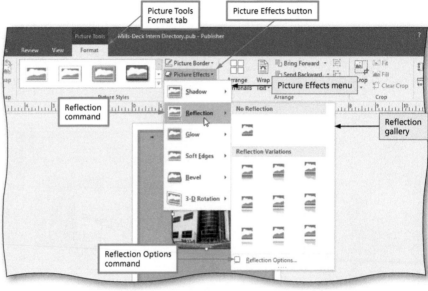

Figure 8–28

● Click Reflection Options (Reflection gallery) to display the Format Shape dialog box.

● Enter the numbers as shown in Figure 8–29 to create a reflection with 50% transparency, a reduced size of 50% of the original, a 0.5 point blur, and a distance location 10 points away from the original.

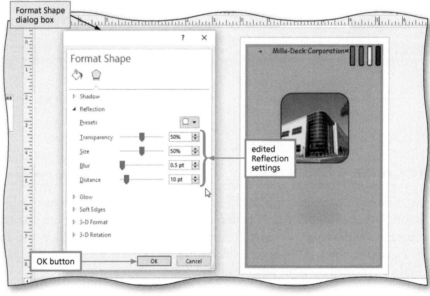

Figure 8–29

● Click the OK button (Format Shape dialog box) to apply the reflection settings to the picture (Figure 8–30).

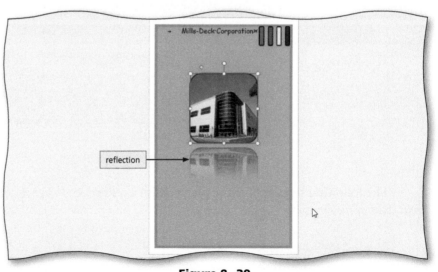

Figure 8–30

To Create a Title Graphic

The following steps create a title graphic in the lower portion of the front page of the directory. You also will save the publication.

1 Insert a rounded rectangle shape. Resize it to fit the bottom of page 1, approximately 1 inch tall.

2 Change the fill color of the shape to reflect the same purple color you sampled earlier.

3 Right-click the shape and then click Add Text on the shortcut menu.

4 Click the Font Size box (Text Box Tools Format tab | Font group). Type **30** to change the font size. Change the font color to white.

4 Type **Meet Our 2017 Interns** to complete the text.

5 Center the text within the shape.

6 Press CTRL+S to save the publication again (Figure 8–31).

Figure 8–31

Break Point: If you wish to take a break, this is a good place to do so. Exit Publisher. To resume at a later time, run Publisher, open the file named Mills-Deck Intern Directory, and then continue following the steps from this location forward.

Generating the Catalog Merge

Recall that the merge process requires a main publication and a data source. The main publication contains the constant or unchanging text, punctuation, space, and graphics, embedded with variables or changing values from the data source. The data source is a file with fields of information that will change for each record. Catalog merges include pictures and all records commonly merged into a single publication.

The data source for Publisher's catalog merge is a called a **product list** — even if the data is not a list of products. Normally, it is a table of data that includes information about the product or service, unique product numbers or ID numbers, and paths to pictures you want to use in the catalog. A **path** is the route Publisher must take through your computer's stored files to find the picture file and the file name. For

BTW
Product Lists vs. Address Lists
A product list data source differs from an address list data source in that it may contain a unique field and path to a graphic file.

example, if a .jpg picture file named Dog is located on the USB (E:) storage device in a folder named Pictures, the path would be E:\Pictures\Dog.jpg. If the file is located in the same folder as the merged publication, however, the path is simply the file name; thus, in the previous example, the path would be Dog.jpg.

Generally, for classroom purposes you should keep the main publication and the data source in the same folder on the same storage device. If you are using the Data Files, these data sources may be stored in a different location from the location where you saved your completed publications; thus, they should be copied to your preferred storage location.

To Copy the Data Source Files

Publisher recommends that the publication and its data source reside in the same folder location; therefore, the following steps copy a folder named Interns from the Data Files to your save location. To complete these steps, you will be required to use the Data Files. Please contact your instructor for information about accessing the Data Files.

If you already have downloaded the Data Files to the same location that you are using to create and save files in this module, you can skip these steps.

1 Click the File Explorer button on the Windows taskbar to open a File Explorer window.

2 In the File Explorer window, navigate to the location of the Data Files.

3 In the Module 08 folder, right-click the Interns folder to display its shortcut menu, and then click Copy on the shortcut menu to copy the file.

4 Navigate to your preferred storage location, in this case, the folder in which you saved the Mills-Deck Intern Directory publication.

5 Right-click a blank part of the folder to display the folder's shortcut menu and then click Paste on the shortcut menu to paste the folder.

6 Close the File Explorer window.

Catalog Pages

Catalog pages contain a unique merge area for positioning text and pictures. The **catalog merge area**, also called the **repeatable area**, is a box in the publication into which you can insert field codes. Recall that field codes are placeholders inserted in the main publication that correspond with fields from the data source. The merge area repeats for each record in the file, because a catalog merge will merge all records to a single publication.

You start the catalog merge by clicking the Catalog Pages button (Insert tab | Pages group). If you start from scratch, you must insert catalog pages. Publisher then automatically adds a page or pages to your publication and inserts a catalog merge area. The merge area can be resized and adjusted for multiple records per page. You can format fields or objects added to the merge area using normal formatting techniques.

When the merge is complete, data from the data source will populate each field, and the catalog merge area will repeat to display multiple records.

To Insert Catalog Pages

The following step inserts catalog pages. *Why? Because you started with a blank template, no catalog pages were created automatically; you must insert them.*

1

• Click the 'Page 2 and Page 3' thumbnail in the Page Navigation pane, and show the whole page if necessary.

• Display the Insert tab (Figure 8–32).

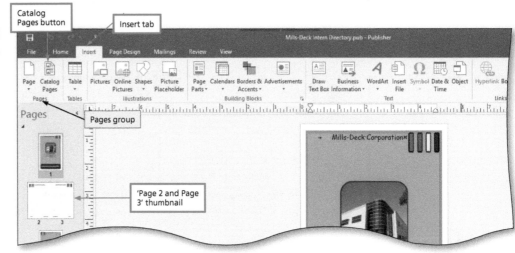

Figure 8–32

2

• Click the Catalog Pages button (Insert tab | Pages group) to insert catalog pages (Figure 8–33).

Q&A What are the new objects that appeared? Publisher's catalog merge area is displayed in the page layout. New catalog pages are displayed in the Page Navigation pane. While you are working on catalog pages, the ribbon displays the Catalog Tools Format tab.

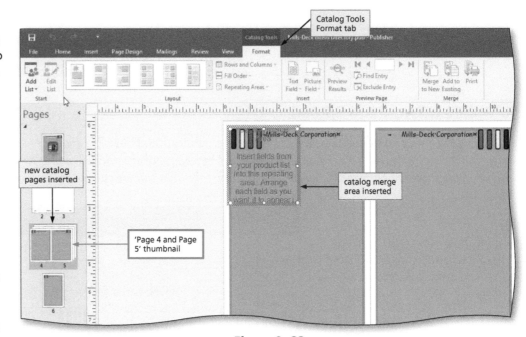

Figure 8–33

To Format the Catalog Pages

The following steps assign Master Page B to the catalog pages and resize the merge area.

1 Right-click the 'Page 4 and Page 5' thumbnail in the Page Navigation pane. Point to Master Pages on the shortcut menu to display the Master Pages submenu and then click Inside Pages (B) to assign the master page to the catalog pages.

2 In the publication, select the catalog merge area. Move the catalog merge area down below the header.

③ Resize the catalog merge area to fill the area between margins and between the header and footer as shown in Figure 8–34.

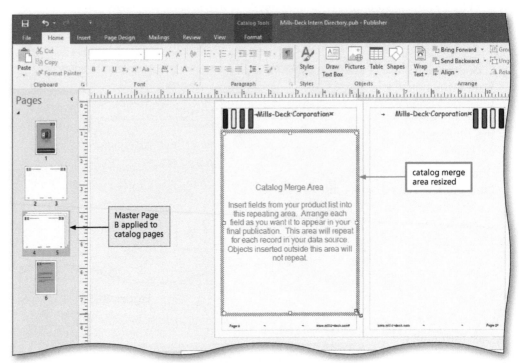

Figure 8–34

To Delete a Two-Page Spread

The following steps delete pages 2 and 3 in the publication. **Why?** *The Publisher template that you used earlier in the module created a blank page 2 and page 3. Now that you have inserted catalog pages and formatted them with the appropriate master page, you no longer need those pages. You will use only the front, back, and catalog pages in the publication.*

①

• Right-click the 'Page 2 and Page 3' thumbnail in the Page Navigation pane to display the shortcut menu (Figure 8–35).

Q&A

Why does Publisher include pages that are not part of the catalog merge?

In some publications, you may want an index page or introduction to the catalog. All pages in catalogs must be in groups of two for the publication to print correctly.

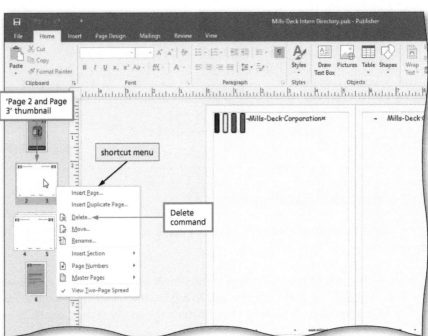

Figure 8–35

2

- Click Delete on the shortcut menu to display the Delete Page dialog box.

- If necessary, click the Both pages option button to select it (Figure 8–36).

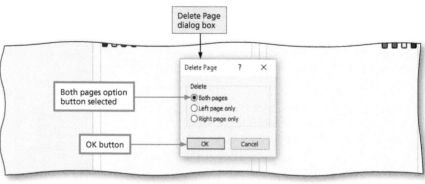

Figure 8–36

3

- Click the OK button (Delete Page dialog box) to delete the pages (Figure 8–37).

Q&A Did Publisher renumber the pages?

Yes. The catalog pages were moved to the page 2 and page 3 position; however, once you merge with the data source, extra pages will be created as needed depending on the number of records in your data source. Notice the pages appear in 3-D in the Page Navigation pane.

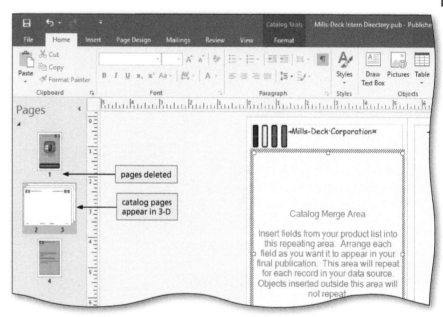

Figure 8–37

To Select the Data Source

1 FORMAT ALTERNATING MASTER PAGES | 2 USE NUMBER STYLES | 3 FORMAT PICTURE | 4 CREATE CATALOG PAGES
5 CONNECT DATA SOURCE | 6 INSERT MERGE FIELDS | 7 MANAGE GRAPHICS | 8 TRANSLATE TEXT | 9 MERGE

The following steps select an existing data source. *Why? You must choose a data source to complete the merge.* The data source is located in the folder that you copied to your storage location earlier in the module.

1

- With the catalog page still selected, display the Catalog Tools Format tab.

- Click the Add List button (Catalog Tools Format tab | Start group) to display the Add List menu (Figure 8–38).

Q&A What if I want to create a new list?

You would choose the 'Type a New List' command. A dialog box would be displayed similar to the New Address List dialog box that you have seen. You then could customize fields and insert data just as you did in Module 7.

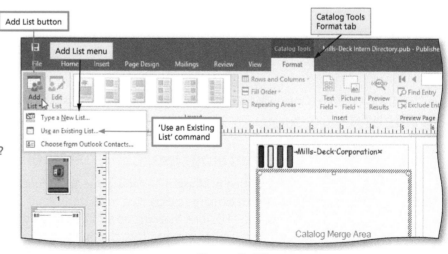

Figure 8–38

2

- Click 'Use an Existing List' to display the Select Data Source dialog box.

- Navigate to your storage location and then double-click the folder named Interns (Figure 8–39).

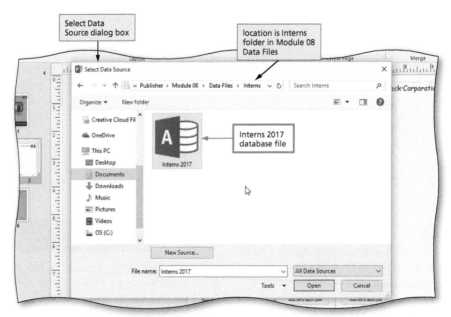

Figure 8–39

3

- Double-click the Interns 2017 file to display the Catalog Merge Product List dialog box (Figure 8–40).

Experiment

- Scroll to the right or resize the dialog box to see all of the fields and records.

Q&A Do the commands in this dialog box work the same as the commands when performing a mail merge?
Yes. All of the commands in the Catalog Merge Product List dialog box work the same as the ones in the Mail Merge List dialog box described in Module 7. For example, if you want the interns to appear in alphabetical order by last name, you can click the Last_Name button.

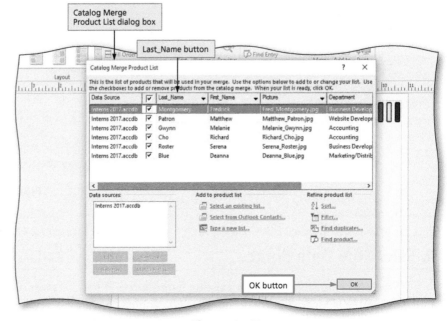

Figure 8–40

4

- Click the OK button (Catalog Merge Product List dialog box) to close the dialog box and connect the data source to the publication.

The Catalog Tools Format Tab

When performing a catalog merge, Publisher displays the Catalog Tools Format tab, which contains specialized formatting tools for catalog pages and merging (Figure 8–41). The Start group includes an Add List button used to specify or create a product list and connect it to the publication. The Edit List button is used to make changes to the catalog list once it is connected to the publication.

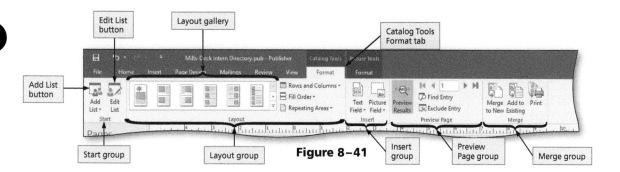

Add List
button

Edit List
button

Layout gallery

Catalog Tools
Format tab

Start group

Layout group

Figure 8–41

Insert
group

Preview
Page group

Merge group

The Layout group contains a gallery of preset page layouts, formatted to a single column per page; however, Publisher has a button to create rows and columns that can be used for large catalogs. In that case, records from the database are preformatted to run across, then down. You can change that setting with the Fill Order button. The Repeating Areas button allows you to specify a custom layout by row or column.

The Insert group is used to insert text and pictures manually from the data source. The Preview Page and Merge groups are similar to those on the Mailings tab that you learned about in Module 7.

If you choose not to use a preset layout, the merge area can be resized and adjusted for one or multiple records per page. You can format fields or objects added to the merge area using normal formatting techniques, as you will do in this module.

To Insert a Picture Field

1 FORMAT ALTERNATING MASTER PAGES | 2 USE NUMBER STYLES | 3 FORMAT PICTURE | 4 CREATE CATALOG PAGES
5 CONNECT DATA SOURCE | 6 INSERT MERGE FIELDS | **7 MANAGE GRAPHICS** | 8 TRANSLATE TEXT | 9 MERGE

The following steps insert the picture from the data source or product list into the catalog merge area. *Why? Fields or objects inserted in the catalog merge area will repeat for each record in the data source. Objects outside the area will not repeat.* You can format, resize, and reposition objects in the catalog merge area.

1
• With the catalog merge area selected, click the Picture Field button (Catalog Tools Format tab | Insert group) to display the Picture Field menu (Figure 8–42).

Q&A
What does the 'More Picture Options' command do?
The 'More Picture Options' command will display the Insert Picture dialog box. It is used when you have multiple picture fields in your database.

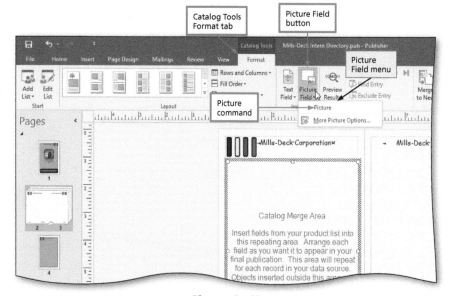

Catalog Tools
Format tab

Picture Field
button

Picture
Field menu

Picture
command

Figure 8–42

2

- Click Picture on the Picture Field menu to insert the Picture field.

- If necessary, click the Preview Results button (Catalog Tools Format tab | Preview Page group) to display the picture (Figure 8–43).

🔎 **Experiment**

- Click the More button (Catalog Tools Format tab | Layout group) to view the possible preset formats. One at a time, click each of the buttons in the Layout group to view their choices and commands.

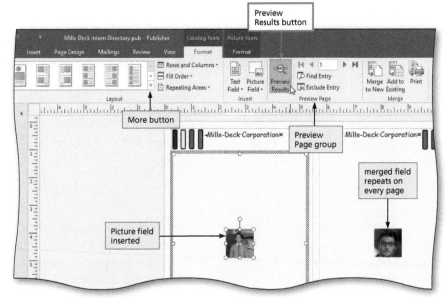

Figure 8–43

My picture does not appear. Did I do something wrong?

No. To conserve memory resources on your computer, Publisher may not display the pictures until the file is ready to preview or print.

Other Ways

1. Choose preset layout (Catalog Tools Format tab | Layout group), click picture placeholder, click Picture field, click OK button (Insert Picture Field dialog box)

To View Boundaries

1 FORMAT ALTERNATING MASTER PAGES | 2 USE NUMBER STYLES | 3 FORMAT PICTURE | 4 CREATE CATALOG PAGES
5 CONNECT DATA SOURCE | 6 INSERT MERGE FIELDS | **7 MANAGE GRAPHICS** | 8 TRANSLATE TEXT | 9 MERGE

The following step turns on the boundaries display. ***Why?*** *Boundaries will assist you in placing the other fields in the catalog merge area.* Recall that a boundary is the gray, dotted line surrounding a selected object. Boundaries are useful when you want to move or resize objects on the page.

1

- Display the View tab.

- Click to display a check mark in the Boundaries check box (View tab | Show group) (Figure 8–44).

🔎 **Experiment**

- Click other check boxes in the Show group on the View tab to see what objects are displayed. When you are finished, check the boxes as shown in Figure 8–44.

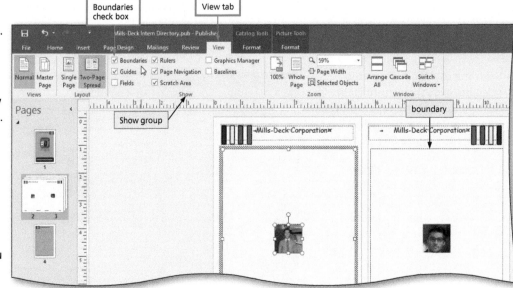

Figure 8–44

Other Ways

1. Press CTRL+SHIFT+O

To Move and Resize the Picture Field

The following steps resize the picture field and move it to the top of the page. You will place it more precisely in later steps.

1 With the picture field selected, drag the picture field to the upper-left portion of the catalog merge area.

2 SHIFT+drag the lower-right sizing handle down and to the right until the picture is approximately 3.25 inches square (Figure 8–45).

Figure 8–45

1 FORMAT ALTERNATING MASTER PAGES | 2 USE NUMBER STYLES | 3 FORMAT PICTURE | 4 CREATE CATALOG PAGES
5 CONNECT DATA SOURCE | 6 INSERT MERGE FIELDS | **7 MANAGE GRAPHICS** | 8 TRANSLATE TEXT | 9 MERGE

To Insert Text Fields

The following steps insert the other fields from the data source. You will create text boxes, insert fields, and then format the fields as you enter them. *Why? Formatting fields in the first merge area will apply the same formatting across all pages in the publication.* Use the Measurement task pane and the rulers as necessary to help you draw the text boxes. You will align the objects on the page in a later set of steps.

1

- Zoom to 150% and then scroll to the lower half of page 2.

- Display the Home tab.

- Click the 'Draw a Text Box' button (Home tab | Objects group) and then draw a text box below the picture, approximately 3/8 inch high and 4 inches wide.

- Display the Catalog Tools Format tab. Click the Preview Results button (Catalog Tools Format tab | Preview Page group) to turn off the display so that you can see field codes as you insert them.

- With the insertion point positioned in the new text box, click the Text Field button (Catalog Tools Format tab | Insert group) to display the Text Field menu (Figure 8–46).

Q&A Could I use the Picture field and insert the picture from this list?
No. This list contains text field codes. If you insert the text field code named Picture, Publisher would insert the data from the text field itself, not the picture. You would see the words, Fred_Montgomery.jpg, in the merge.

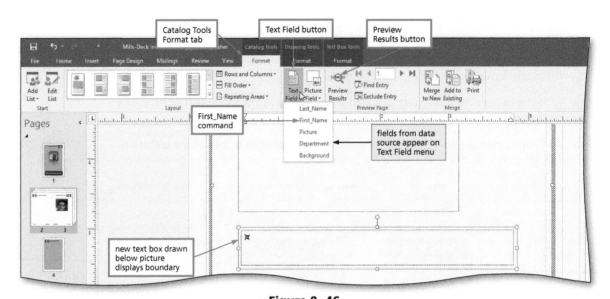

Figure 8–46

②

- Click First_Name on the menu to insert the First_Name field code into the text box (Figure 8–47).

Q&A How are the field codes ordered in the list?
The field codes appear in the order in which they are stored in the database.

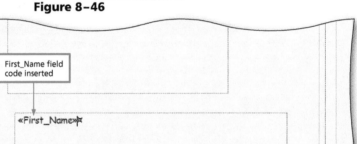

Figure 8–47

③

- Press the SPACEBAR to insert a space and then click the Text Field button (Catalog Tools Format tab | Insert group) to display the menu again.

- Click Last_Name on the Text Field menu to insert the Last_Name field code into the text box.

- Select all of the information in the text box, right-click the selection, and then use the mini toolbar to change the font size to 18 (Figure 8–48).

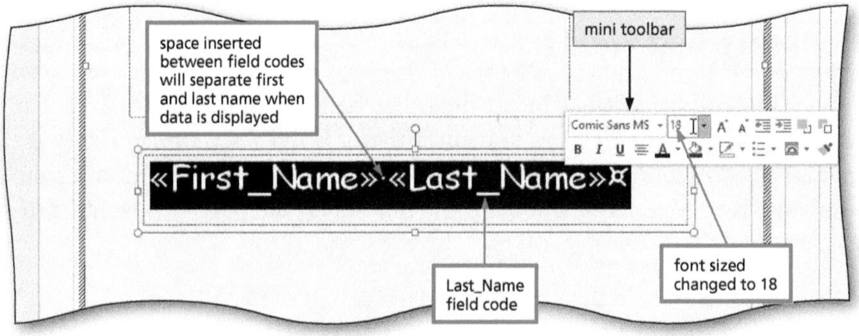

Figure 8–48

To Insert Other Text Fields

The following steps create text boxes and insert the Department and Background fields into the catalog merge area.

1 Draw a text box below the previous text box, approximately the same size.

2 With the insertion point inside the text box, change the font size to 18 and then insert the Department field using the Text Field button (Catalog Tools Format tab | Insert group).

3 Create a third text box in the lower portion of the catalog merge area, 4.5 inches wide and 1 inch tall. Use the Measurement task pane to set the width and height, if necessary.

4 With the insertion point inside the text box, change the font size to 10 and then insert the Background field (Figure 8–49).

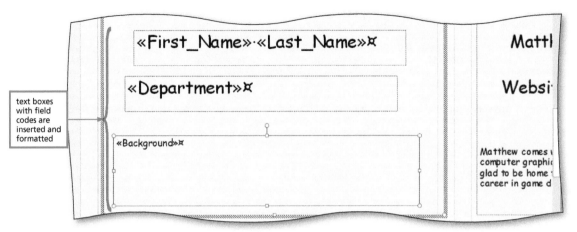

Figure 8–49

To Align Objects

1 FORMAT ALTERNATING MASTER PAGES | 2 USE NUMBER STYLES | 3 FORMAT PICTURE | 4 CREATE CATALOG PAGES
5 CONNECT DATA SOURCE | 6 INSERT MERGE FIELDS | **7 MANAGE GRAPHICS** | 8 TRANSLATE TEXT | 9 MERGE

Recall that in desktop publication applications, the Home tab alignment tools refer to the text box in which you are working; however, in most cases, you also can align objects with each other or relative to the margins on the page. In the following steps, you will align the picture using the pink layout guide and then align the text boxes using tools on the ribbon, such as align top, align middle, align bottom, align left, align center, or align right. *Why? Using an align command will guarantee correct placement.*

Another option when you are working on pages outside of the catalog merge area is to **distribute** objects, which means to equalize the space between three or more objects vertically or horizontally.

The following steps align objects and then save the publication.

1

• Click the 'Show Whole Page' button on the status bar.

• On page 2, select the picture placeholder and then and drag it until the pink layout guide appears to align it within the center of the catalog merge area (Figure 8–50).

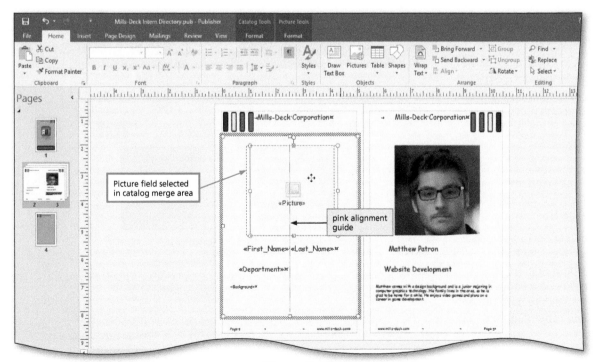

Figure 8–50

● Deselect the picture and then, if necessary, display the Home tab.

● Beginning just above and to the left of the name text box, drag down and right to select all three text boxes in the catalog merge area.

● Click the Align Objects button (Home tab | Arrange group) to display the Align Objects menu (Figure 8–51).

Q&A I am having trouble selecting the text boxes by dragging. Can I select them using a different method?
Yes, you can select one of the text boxes and then, one at a time, SHIFT+click the other two boxes.

Why is the 'Relative to Margin Guides' command dimmed?
The text boxes you are working with are in the catalog merge area and will be aligned relative to that container rather than the margins.

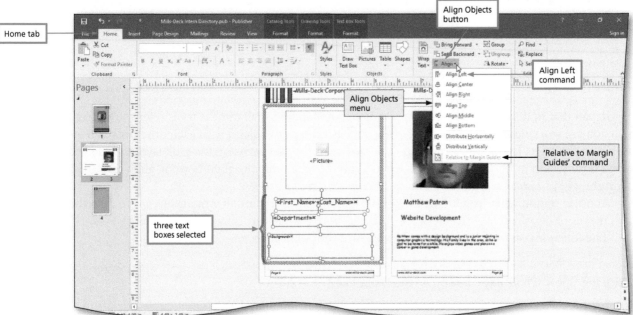

Figure 8–51

3

● Click Align Left on the Align Objects menu to left align the three objects.

Q&A How does Publisher decide the left position?
Publisher aligns all objects with the object that is the furthest left on the page.

● If necessary, use the ARROW keys to move the selected text boxes slightly away from the edge of the catalog merge area.

● Display the Catalog Tools Format tab and then click the Preview Results button (Catalog Tools Format tab | Preview Page group) to display the data rather than the field codes (Figure 8–52).

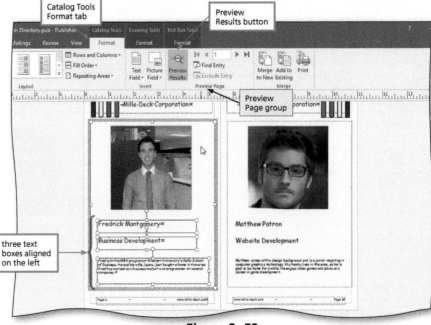

Figure 8–52

4

● Click the Save button on the Quick Access Toolbar to overwrite the previously saved file.

Break Point: If you wish to take a break, this is a good place to do so. Exit Publisher. To resume at a later time, run Publisher, open the file named Mills-Deck Intern Directory, and then continue following the steps from this location forward.

To Find Entries

1 FORMAT ALTERNATING MASTER PAGES | 2 USE NUMBER STYLES | 3 FORMAT PICTURE | 4 CREATE CATALOG PAGES
5 CONNECT DATA SOURCE | 6 INSERT MERGE FIELDS | **7 MANAGE GRAPHICS** | 8 TRANSLATE TEXT | 9 MERGE

Publisher provides a special method for finding information in catalog entries. *Why? The merged publication is not searchable via regular means unless you merge it to a new file.* Using the Find Entry button (Catalog Tools Format tab | Preview Page group), Publisher looks through the data source for the keyword(s) and then navigates to that page in the catalog publication.

The following steps find an entry based on keywords. In this case, you want to determine if any of the interns have experience in event management.

1
- On any catalog page, click outside any object so that nothing is selected.
- Click the Find Entry button (Catalog Tools Format tab | Preview Page group) to display the Find Entry dialog box.
- In the Find text box, type **event management** to enter the search term (Figure 8–53).

Experiment
- Click the This field arrow to display the list of searchable fields.

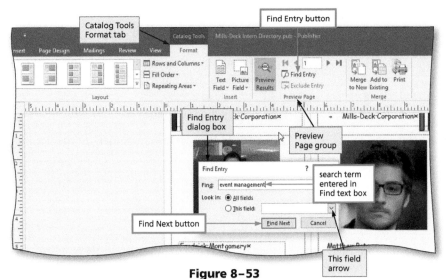

Figure 8–53

2
- Click the Find Next button (Find Entry dialog box) to search for the keywords (Figure 8–54).

Q&A What would happen if Publisher could not locate the search term? In those cases, Publisher would display a dialog box stating it could not find the search term you entered. Publisher then would return you to the Find Entry dialog box to enter a new search term.

Is the search term highlighted? No. Publisher does not highlight the search term when working with data from the data source.

Figure 8–54

3
- Click the Cancel button (Find Entry dialog box) to close the dialog box.

BTW

**Conserving Ink
and Toner**

If you want to conserve ink
or toner, you can instruct
Publisher to print draft quality
documents by clicking File
on the ribbon to open the
Backstage view, clicking the
Options tab in the Backstage
view to display the Publisher
Options dialog box, clicking
Advanced in the left pane
(Publisher Options dialog
box), scrolling to the Print
area in the right pane,
placing a check mark in the
'Use draft quality' check
box, and then clicking the
OK button. Then, use the
Backstage view to print the
document as usual.

TO EXCLUDE ENTRIES

If you wanted to exclude an entry from your data source, you would perform the following steps.

1. Navigate to the record that you wish to exclude either by using the Find Entries button (described in the previous steps), or by clicking the 'Next Catalog Page' button or the 'Previous Catalog Page' button (Catalog Tools Format tab | Preview Page group).

2. When the desired record is displayed, if necessary, click the catalog merge area around that entry to select it.

3. Click the Exclude Entry button (Catalog Tools Format tab | Preview Page group) to exclude the record.

To Turn Off Boundaries

Because you are finished with the page layout, the following steps turn off the boundaries so that Publisher displays a more realistic preview.

1 Display the View tab.

2 Click to remove the check mark in the Boundaries check box (View tab | Show group).

To Preview the Merge

1 FORMAT ALTERNATING MASTER PAGES | 2 USE NUMBER STYLES | 3 FORMAT PICTURE | 4 CREATE CATALOG PAGES
5 CONNECT DATA SOURCE | 6 INSERT MERGE FIELDS | **7 MANAGE GRAPHICS** | 8 TRANSLATE TEXT | 9 MERGE

The following step previews the merged publication. *Why? Previewing allows you to look for anomalies in the merge, such as unusual hyphenation or large fields that overlap.*

1

- If necessary, zoom to whole page.
- Display the Catalog Tools Format tab.
- Click the 'First Catalog Page' button (Catalog Tools Format tab | Preview Page group) to display the first page of the merge (Figure 8–55).

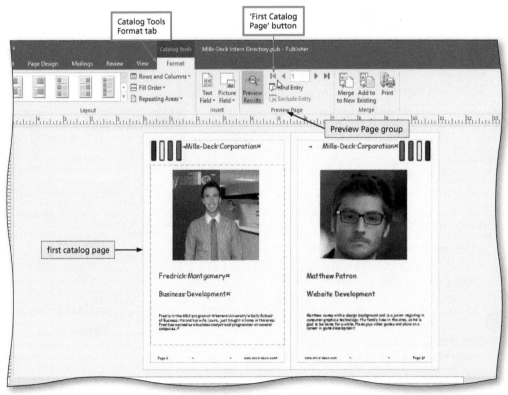

Figure 8–55

- Click the 'Next Catalog Page' button.

- If the Background description displays incorrect hyphenation, click the 'First Catalog Page' button (Catalog Tools Format tab | Preview Pages group). Assure that the font is Comic Sans MS, the font size is 10, and the text box is 4.5 inches wide by 1 inch tall. If necessary, adjust the width of the text box slightly, and check all pages.

Q&A Why are all of the pages numbered 2 and 3?

Publisher makes multiple copies of the catalog pages — enough to handle all of the records in the data source. When you merge to the printer, the pages will be renumbered and printed correctly.

Experiment

- Click the 'Next Catalog Page' button and the 'Previous Catalog Page' button (Catalog Tools Format tab | Preview Page group) to display other pages of the catalog.

The Graphics Manager

The Graphics Manager helps you manage and display all the pictures you have inserted into your publication, such as embedded pictures or linked pictures. You can change the display of the pictures so that quicker editing is possible and fewer system resources are consumed by controlling display options. You can view all the pictures related to a publication, or you can see only those pictures that are missing or have been modified since the last time you saved the publication. The Graphics Manager can display thumbnails of all graphics in the publication using the Graphics Manager task pane. You can order the pictures in the Graphics Manager task pane by file name, page number, extension, or size, showing the details about each one.

You can use the Graphics Manager to check the status of each picture, such as whether a picture is linked or embedded, whether it has been modified, or whether a link to an external picture is missing.

If you have many pictures in a publication with multiple pages, you can navigate quickly to a particular picture by pointing to it in the Graphics Manager task pane, clicking the arrow to the right of the picture, and then clicking 'Go to this Picture' on the menu.

BTW

Graphics
A file with many graphics and merged pages sometimes refreshes more slowly on the screen. If you move to a new page, or edit the data source, it may take several moments to open. Use the Previous Sheet button and Next Sheet button (Catalog Tools Format tab | Preview Page group) to view each record. Consider using the Graphics Manager to turn off the display of graphics and minimize the Page Navigation pane. Sometimes, it is better to edit the database outside of the publication, so that you do not have to wait for the updated screens.

To Work with the Graphics Manager

1 FORMAT ALTERNATING MASTER PAGES | 2 USE NUMBER STYLES | 3 FORMAT PICTURE | 4 CREATE CATALOG PAGES
5 CONNECT DATA SOURCE | 6 INSERT MERGE FIELDS | **7 MANAGE GRAPHICS** | **8 TRANSLATE TEXT** | 9 MERGE

The following steps open the Graphics Manager task pane. *Why? You will view information about each of the pictures.*

- Navigate to page 1 of the publication and then display the View tab.

- Click to display a check mark in the Graphics Manager check box (View tab | Show group) and to display the Graphics Manager task pane.

- Click the Sort by arrow in the Display options area in the Graphics Manager task pane to display the list of picture details (Figure 8–56).

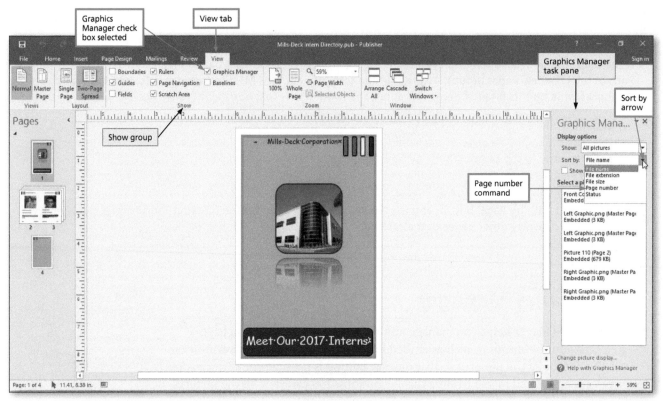

Figure 8–56

②

• Click Page number in the list to view the pictures sorted by page number (Figure 8–57).

Q&A

Why is the intern picture named differently?

The name represents all of the pictures from the database. It is a random name that Publisher assigns to indirect pictures, those that are not directly inserted using the Insert Picture button on the ribbon.

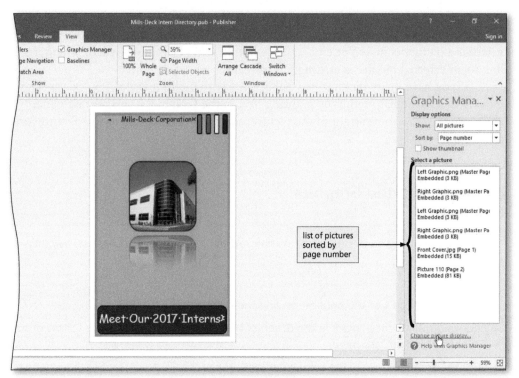

Figure 8–57

3
- Point to 'Front Cover.jpg (Page 1)' to display the picture's arrow.
- Click the arrow to display actions you can perform related to the picture (Figure 8–58).

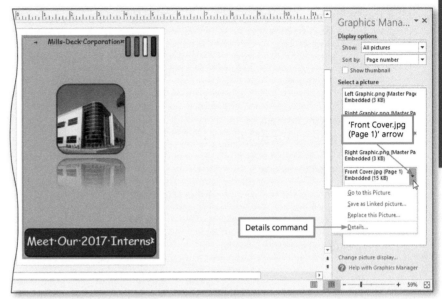

Figure 8–58

4
- Click Details to display the Details dialog box (Figure 8–59).

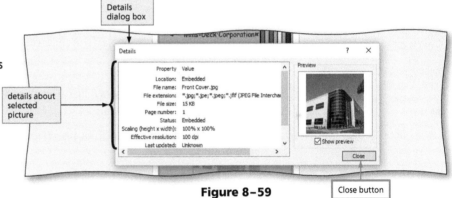

Figure 8–59

5
- Click the Close button (Details dialog box) to close the dialog box.
- In the lower portion of the Graphics Manager task pane, click the 'Change picture display' link to display the Picture Display dialog box.
- Click the Hide pictures option button to select it (Figure 8–60).

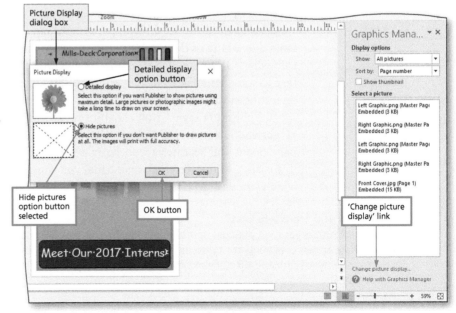

Figure 8–60

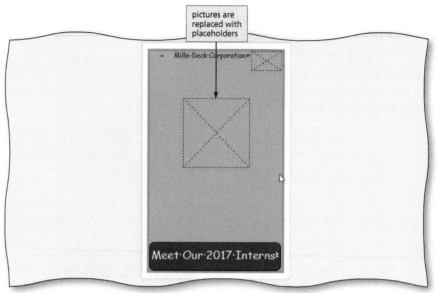

Figure 8–61

• Click the OK button (Picture Display dialog box) to hide the pictures in the display (Figure 8–61).

Experiment

• Click each of the thumbnails in the Page Navigation pane to see how quickly the pages are displayed when pictures are hidden.

To Redisplay the Pictures and Close the Graphics Manager Task Pane

The following steps redisplay the pictures throughout the publication and close the Graphics Manager task pane.

1 Click the 'Change picture display' link (Graphics Manager task pane) to display the Picture Display dialog box.

2 Click the Detailed display option button (Picture Display dialog box) (shown in Figure 8–60) to select it.

3 Click the OK button to close the dialog box.

4 Click the Close button in the Graphics Manger task pane to close it.

Translating Text

Publisher can translate phrases, paragraphs, and individual words to a different language. Many of the modern languages are installed automatically when you install Publisher. Other languages require installation the first time you use them. To translate text to some languages, such as right-to-left languages, you may need to satisfy certain operating system requirements.

Publisher's translation capability requires web access. When you click the 'Translate Selected Text' button (Review tab | Language group), the Research task pane opens and accesses a web-based service, such as World Lingo or Microsoft Translator. In the Research task pane, you can set the language from which and to which you wish to translate. The translated text appears in the task pane.

When should you translate text?
Use the Translation tool for short passages of text or individual words in your publications. If the entire publication needs to be translated, use a professional translator. While the translation tool is not a substitute for learning the language and knowing how tone and sentence structure affect the meaning, it may be appropriate for those times when you need to look up short phrases or translate a single word.

CONSIDER THIS

To Enter Text

The following steps create a text box on the last page in the catalog and then enter a phrase in English. In addition, you will center the text box horizontally and vertically, relative to the margin guides.

1 Navigate to page 4 in the publication and then display the Home tab.

2 Click the 'Draw a Text Box' button (Home tab | Objects group) and then drag to draw a text box approximately 4.4 inches wide and 2.75 inches tall.

3 Change the font size to 18 pt.

4 Type **Mills-Deck Corporation is an equal opportunity affirmative action employer.** and then press the ENTER key twice.

5 Type **Visit us at www.mills-deck.com.** and then press the ENTER key twice.

6 Type **For information in Spanish please call 1-800 555-8784.** to finish the text.

7 Display the Home tab, click the Align button (Home tab | Arrange group), and then click 'Relative to Margin Guides' on the Align menu.

8 Click the Align button (Home tab | Arrange group) again and then click Align Center on the Align menu.

9 Click the Align button (Home tab | Arrange group) again and then click Align Middle on the Align menu (Figure 8–62).

If requested by your instructor, create another text box across the bottom of the back page. In the text box, type **Directory created by** and then type your name and the date.

BTW

Translating
If the Research task pane cannot find a translation for your word or phrase, click the Translation options link in the middle of the Research task pane. Publisher will display the Translation Options dialog box. In the lower text box, choose your language pair and then tap or click the translation service arrow to choose a different service.

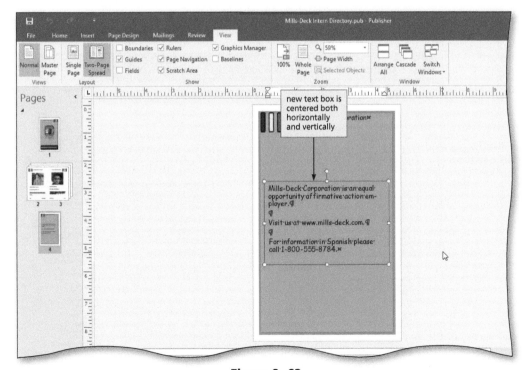

Figure 8–62

To Translate and Insert Text

The following steps translate part of the text to Spanish. *Why? The company wants to attract Spanish-speaking college students as interns.* You must have a web connection to perform these steps.

- Drag to select the last sentence in the text box, excluding the phone number.

- Display the Review tab.

- Click the 'Translate Selected Text' button (Review tab | Language group) to display the Translate Selected Text dialog box (Figure 8–63).

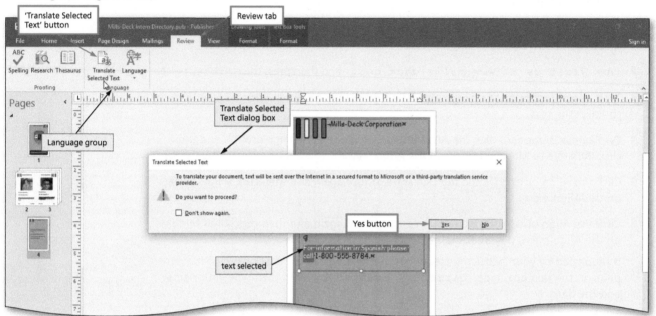

Figure 8–63

- Click the Yes button (Translate Selected Text dialog box) to continue and to open the Research task pane.

- In the Translation area of the Research task pane, if necessary, click the From arrow to display the list of languages (Figure 8–64).

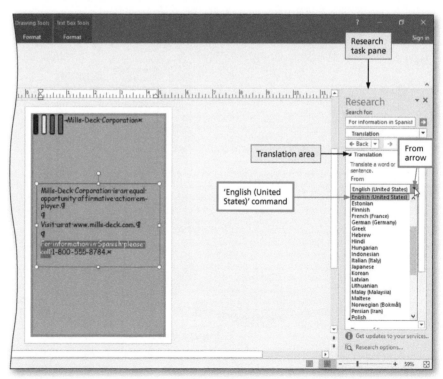

Figure 8–64

3

- Click the desired language you wish to translate from, in this case, 'English (United States)' in the list.

- Click the To arrow to display the list of languages and then click the desired language you wish to translate to, in this case Spanish (Spain) (Figure 8–65).

🔍 **Experiment**

- Click the To arrow and then choose other languages and view the translations. When you are finished, click the To arrow and then click Spanish (Spain).

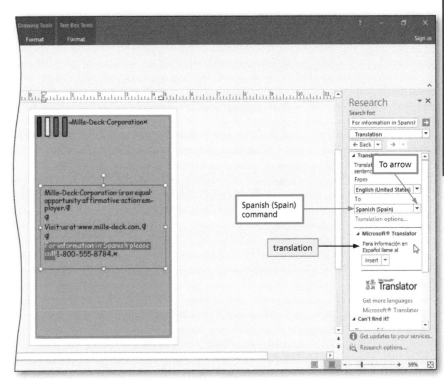

Figure 8–65

4

- Click the Insert button (Research task pane) to insert the translated text (Figure 8–66).

Q&A My task pane does not show an Insert button. What should I do?
If a translation appears, copy and paste it into your publication. If no translation appears, see your instructor for ways to install the translation feature.

5

- In the text box, insert a comma after the word, Español.

- Click the Close button in the Research task pane to close the task pane.

Q&A Why is the comma inserted afterward?
The translation service works better without punctuation.

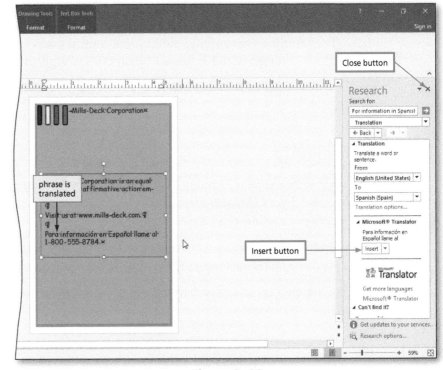

Figure 8–66

Other Ways

1. To translate single word, ALT+click word, click Insert button (Research task pane)

BTW
Distributing a Document
Instead of printing and distributing a hard copy of a document, you can distribute the document electronically. Options include sending the document via email; posting it on cloud storage (such as OneDrive) and sharing the file with others; posting it on social media, a blog, or other website; and sharing a link associated with an online location of the document. You also can create and share a PDF or XPS image of the document, so that users can view the file in Acrobat Reader or XPS Viewer instead of in Publisher.

To Ignore Flagged Words and Check the Publication

The following steps ignore the flagged Spanish words on the last page.

1 Right-click the first flagged word on the back page to display the shortcut menu and then click Ignore All to remove the flag.

2 Repeat Step 1 for each flagged word.

3 Press the F7 key to run the spell checker program. Fix any errors. Note that you will not be able to spell check merged fields.

4 Run the Design Checker from the Backstage view, and fix any errors. Note that Master Page A may have empty footer text boxes; those are not errors. Close the Design Checker task pane.

5 Click the Save button on the Quick Access Toolbar to overwrite the previously saved file.

Merging Catalogs

You have three choices in finalizing the merge. You can merge the pages and create a new document using the 'Merge to New Publication' button (Catalog Tools Format tab | Merge group). In that new document, the merged pages will not need a preview and you will not need the database connection. You will be able to edit the merged text and graphics; all eight pages will show in the Page Navigation pane. Another choice is to add the pages to another publication using the 'Add to Existing Publication' button (Catalog Tools Format tab | Merge group). This option is useful when you have created catalog pages independent of any template and want to add them into another publication. A third option is to print the document using the Print button (Catalog Tools Format tab | Merge group), which retains the merged nature of the catalog.

To Merge to a Printer

1 FORMAT ALTERNATING MASTER PAGES | 2 USE NUMBER STYLES | 3 FORMAT PICTURE | 4 CREATE CATALOG PAGES
5 CONNECT DATA SOURCE | 6 INSERT MERGE FIELDS | 7 MANAGE GRAPHICS | 8 TRANSLATE TEXT | **9 MERGE**

The following steps merge the catalog to the printer. *Why? The merge preview will display the collated contents of the Mills-Deck Intern Directory file correctly.*

- Click the 'Page 2 and Page 3' thumbnail in the Page Navigation pane to display the Catalog Tools Format tab.

- Click the 'First Catalog Page' button (Catalog Tools Format tab | Preview Page group).

- If necessary, click the 'Show Whole Page' button on the status bar and then display the Catalog Tools Format tab (Figure 8–67).

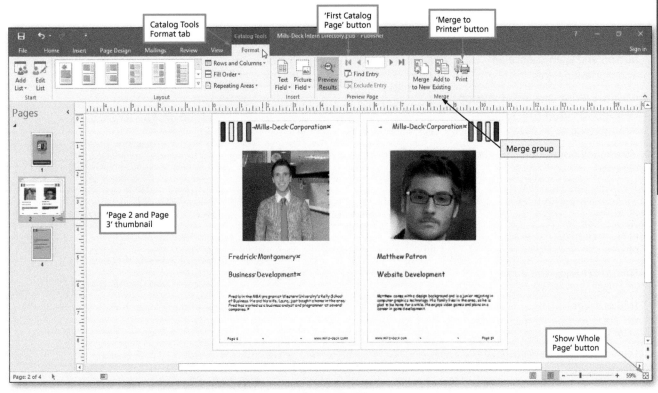

Figure 8–67

2

- Click the 'Merge to Printer' button (Catalog Tools Format tab | Merge group) to display the Print gallery in the Backstage view (Figure 8–68).

Q&A How are the pages displayed in Page Preview?

The pages are displayed as they will print on the paper. Once the printed pages are printed, folded, and collated correctly, they will appear in the correct order.

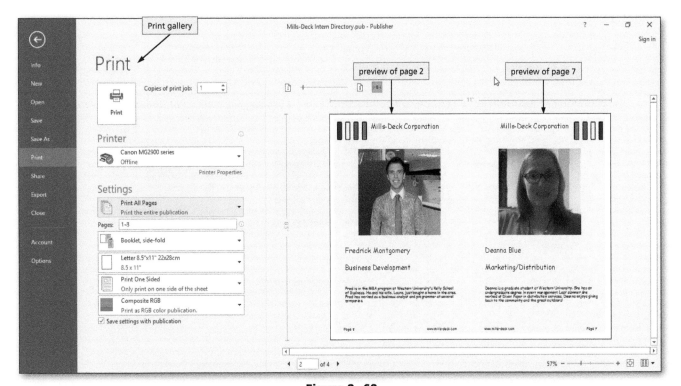

Figure 8–68

- If necessary, click the Printer button and then choose an appropriate printer.
- Click the 'Print One Sided' button to display your printer's duplex settings (Figure 8–69).

 How many pages does the catalog contain?

The directory contains eight pages. Printed on both sides, the entire catalog can be printed using two pieces of 8.5 × 11" paper.

Should I change the page size, orientation, or booklet fold settings?

No. Because you started with a blank catalog template, many of the settings in the Print gallery are preset for you.

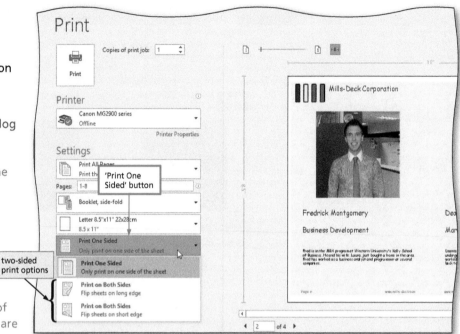

Figure 8–69

④

- If you have the choice, click the 'Print on Both Sides' option. If you do not have the option, choose an appropriate option (Figure 8–70).

What are the new buttons at the bottom of the Print gallery preview area?

If you choose duplex or two-sided printing, you will see a Front button and a Back button, allowing you to preview exactly how the pages will be collated or arranged.

🔍 **Experiment**

- To preview the pages, click the Next Sheet button. Click the Front button. Click the Back button. Click the Previous Sheet button.

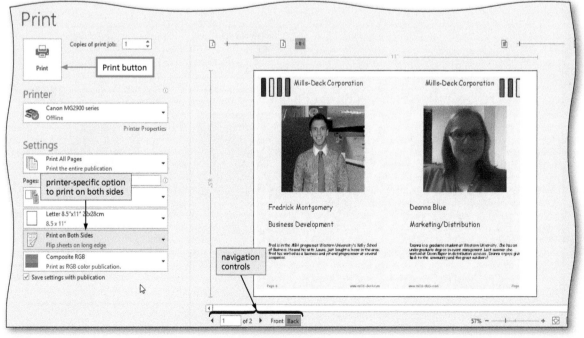

Figure 8–70

5

- Click the Print button in the Print gallery to print the document on the currently selected printer.

- When the printer stops, retrieve the hard copy.

Q&A My printing was very slow or stopped completely. What did I do wrong?

Older printers may not have enough printer memory to handle the many graphics included in the catalog. Wait a few moments. If your printer does not continue, right-click the printer icon on the taskbar and then click your printer name to open its dialog box, right-click the file name of the document being printed, and then click Cancel on the shortcut menu. Try printing the catalog on a different printer.

Other Ways

1. Click Print in Backstage view, choose settings, click Print button

---

To Exit Publisher

This project is complete. The following steps exit Publisher.

1 To exit Publisher, click the Close button on the right side of the title bar.

2 If a Microsoft Publisher dialog box is displayed, click the Don't Save button so that any changes you have made are not saved.

Reopening Catalogs

When you close and then reopen a catalog, Publisher will try to reconnect to the data source and display a dialog box. If you click the No button, Publisher will open the catalog with no connected data, and the catalog pages will be blank. If you click the Yes button, Publisher will open the catalog and connect to the data; however, if the data source is not in its original location, or you have moved the entire folder, Publisher will prompt you to reconnect. You then will need to browse to the location of the data source. For more information, review the section entitled Editing a Merged Publication in Module 7.

Summary

In this module, you learned how to create a data-driven catalog. First, you created alternating master pages with headers and footers. You applied a texture to the background of a duplicate master page and then formatted the page number with a number style. As you created catalog pages with a merge area, you inserted field codes, for both text and graphics from the product list data source. You aligned objects, searched for specific data, and previewed the catalog merge. Using the Graphics Manager, you learned how to manage and display pictures. On the back page, you created a text box and translated a phrase using the translation feature in Publisher. Finally, you merged the catalog and printed it.

What decisions will you need to make when creating your next catalog?

Use these guidelines as you complete the assignments in this module and create your own publications outside of this class.

1. Gather the database, text, and pictures from the customer.

2. Create a catalog publication using a catalog template or blank template.

    a) Add extra pages as necessary.

3. Create two sets of master pages.

    a) One master page will be used for the front and back of the catalog; a different master page will be used for inside pages.

    b) Use headers and footers with mirrored styles for inner pages.

    c) Consider adding a background for catalog pages so that they are not stark white.

4. Insert text and graphics for front and back pages.

5. Create the merge.

    a) Connect to the data source and filter as necessary.

    b) Choose a layout for the merge area.

    c) Insert fields and format them.

6. Use the Graphics Manager to verify graphics.

7. Translate any necessary phrases to user languages.

8. Merge to a printer or a file.

Apply Your Knowledge

Reinforce the skills and apply the concepts you learned in this module.

Using a Catalog Template

Note: To complete this assignment, you will be required to use the Data Files. Please contact your instructor for information about accessing the Data Files.

Instructions: Copy the folder, Apply 8-1 Homes, from the Data Files to your storage location as explained in the module. You are to create a catalog of home for sale as shown in Figure 8–71.

Perform the following tasks:

1. If instructed to do so, take a picture of your house. Save the file in the .jpg format, and name it Home1.jpg. Copy the picture to the Apply 8-1 Homes folder, replacing the Home1.jpg that is already there.

2. Run Publisher. Click BUILT-IN and then click Catalogs in the list of publication types. Select the Checkers catalog design, the Field color scheme, and the Versatile font scheme. Create the publication.

3. Look through the pages to see what kinds of pages Publisher includes in template catalogs.

4. Delete pages 4, 5, 6, and 7 in order to make room for new catalog pages. Save the file in the same folder as the database using the file name, Apply 8-1 Homes Complete.

5. To edit page 1:

    a. Click page 1 in the Page Navigation pane.

    b. In the Business Name text box at the top of the page, change the name to Village Reality. Delete the Date text box.

    c. Select the title. Type **Homes for Sale** and press the ENTER key. Type **Lakeside Village** to finish the text.

    d. Replace the picture with the picture named Home6 in the Apply 8-1 Homes folder. Click the scratch area to deselect the pictures. Delete the original picture from the scratch area.

Woodsy Dutch Colonial

3 bedrooms, 2 baths
Agent: Sarah Brown

$275,000

Offshore Craftsman

4 bedrooms, 3 baths, garage
Agent: Joe Cable

$375,900

Lake A-frame

2 bedrooms, 1.5 baths
Agent: Marion Peru

$325,000

Unusual Lakeside

3 bedrooms, 2 baths
Agent: Julie LaVerne

$742,000

Expanded Cape Cod

4 bedrooms, 2.5 baths, garage
Agent: Helen Chow

$395,500

Lakefront Lodge

4 bedrooms, 4 baths
Agent: Bill Calhoun

$685,400

Page 4   Call Village Realty at 555-LAKE

(b) Catalog Pages

Village Realty

Homes for Sale Lakeside Village

Fall 2017

(a) Front Page

Figure 8–71

Continued >

Apply Your Knowledge *continued*

    e. Select the picture on page 1. Click the Crop arrow (Picture Tools Format tab | Crop group), point to 'Crop to Shape' on Crop menu, and then click Pentagon in the Block Arrows area of the Crop to Shape gallery.

    f. To create a reflection, click the Picture Effects button (Picture Tools Format tab | Picture Styles group) to display the Picture Effects menu, and then point to Reflection to display the Reflection gallery. Click the 'Half Reflection, 8 pt offset' style in the Reflection Variations area.

    g. Delete the Sidebar Heading text box. Select the text in the Catalog Subtitle text box and then type **Fall 2017** to replace it.

6. Go to the two-page spread of pages 2 and 3. At the bottom of the pages, delete the page number text boxes, the Business Name text box, and the 'To Order Call' text box. Select the checkerboard at the bottom of the page and copy it to the clipboard. Delete both checkerboards.

7. To create an alternating master page:

    a. Press CTRL+M to go to the master page. Paste the checkerboard at the bottom of each page.

    b. Click the 'Show Header/Footer' button twice to display the footer text box. On the verso page, drag the footer text box above the checkerboard.

    c. In the text box, change the font size to 10, if necessary. Type **Page** to enter the text. Press the SPACEBAR and then insert the page number field code.

    d. Press the TAB key twice and then type **Call Village Realty at 555-LAKE** to enter the text.

    e. Select the page number field code and then click the Number Style button (Text Box Tools Format tab | Typography group). Choose the Proportional Lining style.

    f. Repeat Steps 7b through 7e for the recto page, but alternate the order of the two parts of the text box.

    g. Close the master page.

8. In the Page Navigation pane, right-click page 1, point to Master Pages, and then click None on the Master Pages submenu. Repeat the process for page 4.

9. To create catalog pages:

    a. With page 4 still selected, click the Catalog Pages button (Insert tab | Pages group).

    b. Delete all content at the bottom of the catalog pages. In the Page Navigation pane, right-click the catalog pages and apply the master page.

    c. Click the Add List button (Catalog Tools Format tab | Start group), click 'Use an Existing List' on the Add List menu, and then navigate to the Apply 8-1 Homes folder. Double-click the Apply 8-1 Home Database file. Look through the data and then click the OK button (Catalog Merge Product List dialog box).

    d. Click the '3 entries, picture on left' layout (Catalog Tools Format tab | Layout group) to choose a layout for the catalog merge area.

    e. In the top corner of the catalog merge area, click the picture placeholder and then click Picture in the list. Click the OK button (Insert Picture Field dialog box).

    f. Click the placeholder text below the picture to select it. Click the Text Field button (Catalog Tools Format tab | Insert group) and then click the Price field on the Text Field menu.

    g. To the right of the picture, click the 'Name of product or service' text to select it. Insert the Type field to replace the text.

    h. Select the rest of the text below the new Type field. Press the ENTER key and then insert the Description field. Pres the ENTER key again. Type **Agent:** to enter the text. Press the SPACEBAR and then insert the Agent field.

    i. Preview the results.

10. Click the 'Page 2 and Page 3' thumbnail in the Page Navigation pane. Note that the verso page is intentionally blank. Edit the table of contents on the recto page to include the following:

Woodsy Dutch Colonial	4
Lake A-frame	4
Expanded Cape Cod	4
Offshore Craftsman	5
Unusual Lakeside	5
Lakefront Lodge	5

11. Go to the last page. Delete the organization logo if one is displayed.

12. If requested by your instructor, change the business data to your name, address, and phone number.

13. Save the file again and then submit the file as directed by your instructor.

14. ✳ What other kinds of publications might benefit from a catalog merge? Describe what you would have to do to make a flyer showing the six homes in the database using catalog pages. Would that be easier than trying to insert the pictures and details manually?

Extend Your Knowledge

Extend the skills you learned in this module and experiment with new skills. You may need to use Help to complete the assignment.

Using Translation Services

Note: To complete this assignment, you will be required to use the Data Files. Please contact your instructor for information about accessing the Data Files.

Instructions: Open the publication named Extend 8-1 Welcome Home Poster from the Data Files. In this assignment, you will investigate different translation services and compare the results, creating a final poster as shown in Figure 8–72.

Perform the following tasks:

1. Use Help to learn more about choosing translation services.

2. Save the publication with the file name, Extend 8-1 Welcome Home Poster Complete.

3. One at a time, select each of the Welcome words, then click the Translate Selected Text button (Review tab | Language group) to open the Research task pane. Each time, choose a different language from the To list.

4. For two of the languages, click the Translation options link just below the To button to display the Translation Options dialog box. In the Available language pairs area, scroll to one of the other language pairs and then click the translation service arrow. If you have access to different languages translation services, choose a different one and compare the translation.

5. If available, click the Insert button in the Research task pane to insert the new translation into the poster.

6. Format each of the text boxes for Best Fit.

7. If instructed to do so, create a text box with your name and course number in the lower-left corner of the page.

8. Save the publication again, and print a copy for your instructor.

Continued >

Figure 8–72

9. ☀ Do you feel comfortable allowing Publisher to translate single words as is done in this exercise? Would you use Publisher to translate longer phrases or entire paragraphs? What kinds of translation issues arise with machine translation? In which cases would you use a human translator? Why?

Expand Your World

Create a solution that uses cloud and web technologies by learning and investigating on your own from general guidance.

Creating a Flipbook

Instructions: Flipdocs offers one free conversion of a publication into an electronic flipbook with pages you can turn online. You decide to convert one of your catalogs into a flipbook.

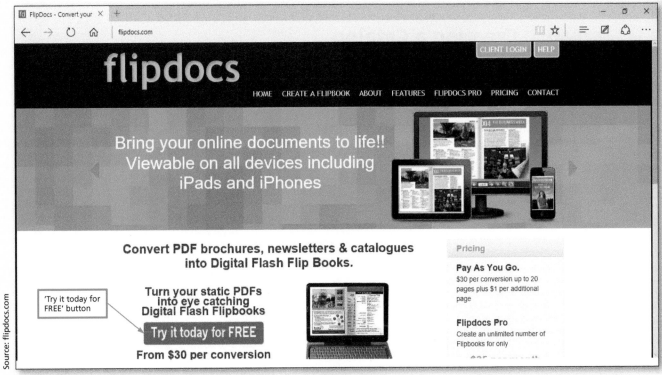

Source: flipdocs.com

Figure 8–73

Perform the following tasks:

1. Run Publisher and open one of your catalog publications.

2. Click the 'Merge to New Publication' button (Catalog Tools Format tab | Merge group) to create a merged file with all of the pages in order. Click File on the ribbon to open the Backstage view and then click the Export tab. Click the 'Create PDF/XPS' button in the Export gallery and then publish the file on your storage location.

3. Run a browser and navigate to http://www.flipdocs.com (Figure 8–73). Click the 'Try it today for FREE' button.

4. In the Upload your PDF here area, enter the required information, including the location of the PDF file. Click the Create Flipbook button.

5. When Flipdocs is finished creating the file, click the Continue button. On the FlipBook Review screen, click the 'Click here to view your Flipbook' link.

6. ✺ Does your flipbook look as you expected it to? What issues do you have? How can you resolve them?

In the Labs

Design, create, modify, and/or use a publication following the guidelines, concepts, and skills presented in this module. Labs 1 and 2, which increase in difficulty, require you to create solutions based on what you learned in the module; Lab 3 requires you to apply your creative thinking and problem-solving skills to design and implement a solution.

Continued >

In the Labs *continued*

Lab 1: **Creating a Catalog**

Note: To complete this assignment, you will be required to use the Data Files. Please contact your instructor for information about accessing the Data Files.

Problem: A local specialty food store would like a small brochure or catalog describing the wide variety of peppers that they sell. The manager has provided some information and pictures. You decide to try Publishers catalog merge to create a catalog of hot peppers as shown in Figure 8–74.

Courtesy of Joy Starks

Figure 8–74

Perform the following tasks:

1. Run Publisher. Copy the folder, Lab 8-1 Peppers, from the Data Files to your storage location as explained in this module.

2. Choose the built-in blank catalog template named 1/2 Letter Booklet, 5.5 × 8.5" as the page layout. In the Customize area, select the Foundry color scheme and the Foundry font scheme. Create the publication and click the Yes button when Publisher displays a dialog box asking if you want to add pages.

3. Press CTRL+M to go to the master page. Click the Background button (Page Design tab | Page Background group) and then click More Backgrounds in the Background gallery. Click the 'Picture or texture fill' option button (Format Background dialog box) and then click the Texture button. Choose the Parchment background. Change the transparency to 75%. Click the OK button to close the Format Background dialog box.

4. Duplicate the Master Page. Select Master Page B. Click the 'Show Header/Footer' button (Master Page tab | Header & Footer group) twice to navigate to the footer. On the verso page, insert the word, Page, at the left margin. Press the SPACEBAR and then click the 'Insert Page Number' button (Master Page tab | Header & Footer group). Repeat the process at the right margin of the recto page. Press CTRL+M to return to the publication pages.

5. To edit page 1:

   a. Click the Online Pictures button (Insert tab | Illustrations group). Search for a picture related to the search term, peppers, similar to the one shown in Figure 8–74. Resize the picture to be approximately 5.5 inches wide and 3.25 inches tall. Drag the picture to the top of the page and center it between the margin guides.

   b. Use WordArt or the text gradient fill, 'Gradient Fill - Red, Outline - Red', to create the first line of the title, Some Like. Create a second line with the same style with the words, 'em Hot! Position them as shown in Figure 8–74.

   c. Draw a text box at the bottom of the page and center the text. Type **Your guide** and then press the ENTER key. Type **to the** and then press the ENTER key. Type **HOTTEST peppers!** to finish the text. Center the text and change the font size to 18.

6. To create and then select a data source:

   a. Click the Catalog Pages button (Insert tab | Pages group) to insert catalog pages.

   b. Click the Add List button (Catalog Tools Format tab | Start group) and then click 'Use an Existing List' on the Add List menu.

   c. Navigate to the location of the copied folder, Lab 8-1 Peppers. Double-click the folder and then double-click the Lab 8-1 Peppers.accdb file to display the Catalog Merge Product List dialog box.

   d. Because you will use all eight records in this database, click the OK button (Catalog Merge Product List dialog box) to connect to the database. Navigate to the catalog pages if necessary.

7. Choose a preset layout by clicking the '1 entry, picture' layout (Catalog Tools Format tab | Layout group).

8. To complete the catalog pages:

   a. Turn on boundaries.

   b. Click the Picture field icon and then, if necessary, click Picture in the list (Insert Picture Field dialog box). Click the OK button to close the dialog box. Click the catalog merge area outside of the picture field to deselect it. If necessary, click the Preview Results button (Catalog Tools Format tab | Preview Page group) to view the picture.

Continued >

In the Labs *continued*

c. Draw a text box that fills the top of the page above the picture. Change the font to Rockwell Extra Bold, black font color, and size 36 pt. Click the Text Field button (Catalog Tools Format tab | Insert group) and insert the 'Name of Pepper' field.

d. Use the Pictures button (Insert tab | Illustrations group) to insert the thermometer picture from the Data Files. Position it below and to the right of the data source picture as shown in Figure 8–74.

e. Delete the text in the first text box that Publisher included on the page. Resize the text box to approximately 3 inches wide and 0.35 inches tall. In the text box, type `Scoville heat index:` and then press the SPACEBAR. Click the Text Field button (Catalog Tools Format tab | Insert group) and insert the Scoville Rating field. Right-align the text in the box.

f. Delete the text in the second text box that Publisher included on the page. Click the Text Field button (Catalog Tools Format tab | Insert group) and insert the Description field.

g. One at a time, SHIFT+click the Description field text box and the Name field text box to select them. Click the Align button (Drawing Tools Format tab | Arrange group) and then click Align Left on the Align menu.

9. Delete the blank pages, 4 and 5.

10. If directed to do so by your instructor, create a text box on the back page and write a short paragraph (real or fictional) about your experience with hot peppers.

11. Select a catalog page in the Page Navigation pane. Press CTRL+M to go to the master page. Click Master Page B in the Page Navigation pane. Click the Apply To button (Master Page tab | Master Page group) and then click 'Apply to Current Page' on the Apply To menu to apply Master Page B to the catalog pages.

12. Display the Graphics Manager and order the graphics by name. Sort the pictures by page number. Display the details about one of the pictures. In the lower portion of the Graphics Manager task pane, click the 'Change picture display' link and hide the pictures. Redisplay the pictures.

13. Merge to the printer to preview the results and then save the file in the same folder as your data source using the file name, Lab 8-1 Hot Peppers Catalog.

14. Turn off boundaries.

15. Submit the files as specified by your instructor.

16. ✺ What other pieces of information would you expect to be in a catalog about hot peppers? Would a paragraph describing the Scoville heat index be a good idea? Would you add such a paragraph on a catalog page or other page? Why?

Lab 2: **Creating a Product List from Scratch**

Problem: A travel agency has asked you to create a product list about popular National Parks, which the agency can merge into several different publications.

Perform the following tasks:

1. Create a new folder on your storage device and name it Lab 8-2 National Parks.

2. One at a time, go to each of the websites listed in the first column of Table 8–3. Right-click the picture at the top of the website, just below the navigation links, and then click 'Save Picture As' on the shortcut menu. The pictures on the National Park Service website are considered to be in the public domain. They may be copied as permitted by applicable law. Save the picture on your storage location in the folder created in Step 1. Save each picture with the file name shown in the second column of Table 8–3.

Table 8–3 National Park Service Photos	
Web Address	**Picture Name**
http://www.nps.gov/acad/index.htm	Acadia.jpg
http://www.nps.gov/grca/index.htm	Grand Canyon.jpg
http://www.nps.gov/yose/index.htm	Yosemite.jpg
http://www.nps.gov/yell/index.htm	Yellowstone.jpg
http://www.nps.gov/romo/index.htm	Rocky Mountain.jpg
http://www.nps.gov/havo/index.htm	Hawaii Volcanoes.jpg

3. Run Publisher and create a blank 8.5 × 11" publication with the default color and font schemes.

4. Click the Catalog Pages button (Insert tab | Page group) to display the Catalog Tools Format tab.

5. Click the Add List button (Catalog Tools Format tab | Start group) and then click 'Type a New List' on the Add List menu to display the New Product List dialog box.

6. Click the Customize Columns button (New Product List dialog box) and then rename the columns to match the column headings in Table 8–4. Add new columns as necessary.

Table 8–4 National Parks Database						
Name	**Location**	**Acreage**	**Description**	**Established**	**Web Address**	**Picture**
Acadia National Park	Bar Harbor, Maine	47,000	Acadia National Park has mountains, national coastline, and plenty of historic sites. Visit the Bass Harbor Head lighthouse, and take a boat cruise to learn about wild sea life.	1901	http://www.nps.gov/acad/	Acadia.jpg
Grand Canyon National Park	Grand Canyon, Arizona	1,218,375	Grand Canyon National Park is one mile deep and easily is accessed by the South Rim. Attend ranger programs, visit the Museum, or you can even hike the mile down to the canyon's bottom. Beware, though; it is hard to get back up!	1919	http://www.nps.gov/grca/	Grand Canyon .jpg
Yosemite National Park	Yosemite National Park, California	747,956	Yosemite National Park is home to giant sequoias, waterfalls, and vast amounts of wilderness. Hike, climb rock walls, camp, and see plenty of wildlife.	1890	http://www.nps.gov/yose/	Yosemite.jpg
Yellowstone National Park	Yellowstone National Park, Wyoming	2,221,776	See the most wildlife in one place! Yellowstone boasts bears, wolves, elk, and buffalo. It is also home to the most geothermal activity in the U.S.	1872	http://www.nps.gov/yell/	Yellowstone .jpg
Rocky Mountain National Park	Estes Park, Colorado	265,800	John Denver sang about a Rocky Mountain high for a good reason. Visit Rocky Mountains National Park. Go from 8,000 feet to over 14,000 feet multiple times within one park. See nature in all its splendor.	1915	http://www.nps.gov/romo/	Rocky Mountain.jpg
Hawaii Volcanoes	Hawaii Island, Hawaii	333,000	Hawaii Volcanoes displays the results of 70 million years of volcanism, migration, and evolution. The park highlights two of the world's most active volcanoes and offers insights on the birth of the Hawaiian Islands.	1916	http://www.nps.gov/havo/	Hawaii Volcanoes.jpg

Continued >

In the Labs *continued*

7. Click the OK button (Customize Product List dialog box). Enter the fields of data from Table 8–4 (Figure 8–75) in the New Product List dialog box. Resize the dialog box as necessary.

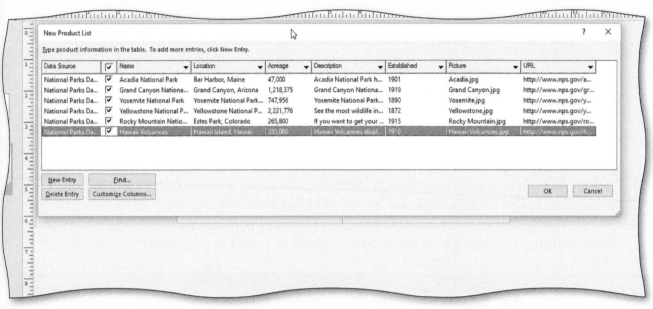

Figure 8–75

8. If instructed to do so, add another national park that you have visited or would like to visit.

9. When you are finished, click the OK button (New Product List dialog box) to display the Save Address List dialog box. Navigate to the folder you created in Step 1. Name the file Lab 8-2 National Parks Database and then click the OK button (Save Address List dialog box).

10. Close the publication without saving.

11. If instructed to do so, send the Lab 8-2 National Park Database.accdb file to your instructor as an email attachment.

12. ✺ What other fields could you add to the database that might be helpful to potential visitors? Describe the process of how to add another column and data to the file, using Publisher 2016.

Lab 3: **Consider This: Your Turn**

Translating a Menu

Note: To complete this assignment, you will be required to use the Data Files. Please contact your instructor for information about accessing the Data Files.

Problem: Your friend is having a party with a French theme and has sent you a copy of the menu she is planning. You do not have a strong background in French, so you decide to use Publisher's translation feature to find out what foods you will be served.

Perform the following tasks:

Part 1: Open the file named Lab 8-3 French from the Data Files. Translate and replace as many of the menu items as you can find in the translation service. Save the file with the file name, Lab 8-3 English Menu.

Part 2: ✺ Search the web for free translation services. Try translating some of the French terms using the service. What differences did you notice? Are the web translation services easier to use than Publisher's translation services? Why or why not? When would you use which?

9 | Sharing and Distributing Publications

Objectives

You will have mastered the material in this module when you can:

- Select and format an email newsletter template
- Change the size of an email newsletter
- Set the email newsletter background using a pattern
- Fit pictures in picture placeholders
- Insert symbols and special characters
- Use the Research task pane
- Create a cited definition

- Insert a hyperlink, hot spot, and a mailto hyperlink
- Choose options for the Design Checker
- Preview an email newsletter using Publisher
- Send an HTML-enabled email newsletter
- Send a postcard as an email attachment
- Create and print greeting cards
- Use design accents

Introduction

Publisher makes it easy to share and distribute publications. Sending email messages and newsletters, attaching publications to email messages, using publications with social media, and uploading publications to websites are among the ways that desktop publishers can market and correspond electronically with customers, business associates, and friends.

Email, short for electronic mail, is a popular form of communication used to transmit messages and files via a computer network. For businesses, email can be an efficient and cost-effective way to keep in touch with customers and interested parties. Email is used in ways similar to traditional mail. With it, you can send correspondence, business communications, and other types of publications. An email may display traditional correspondence-related text and graphics and may include hyperlinks similar to a webpage, as well as attachments. Many email messages sent from companies or organizations include a way for recipients to unsubscribe from the mailing list. When recipients **unsubscribe**, they remove their names and addresses from the mailing list.

Publications that sometimes are attached to an email message (or more traditionally are mailed using a postal service) include graphics, postcards, and greeting cards, among others.

Project — Distributed Publications

You may find the need to share and distribute Publisher files with others electronically. To ensure that others can read and/or open the files successfully, Publisher presents a variety of formats and tools to assist with sharing documents. In this module, you will create and send several publications, including an email newsletter, a postcard, and a greeting card. Figure 9–1a displays an email newsletter sent to residents of the city of Gentry, Alabama. Figure 9–1b displays a postcard sent to people who have participated in Park District programs. Figure 9–1c displays a holiday greeting card to be sent via the postal service. The publications include colorful headings, graphics, and directions for obtaining more information.

When you send an email message, recipients can read it using HTML-enabled email programs, such as Gmail, Yahoo! Mail, or the current versions of Microsoft Outlook and Windows Mail. **HTML-enabled email** allows the sender to include formatted text and other visuals to improve the readability and aesthetics of the message. The majority of Internet users can access HTML-enabled email. Recipients do not need to have Publisher installed to view email newsletters, because the page you send will be displayed as the body of the email newsletter. Sending a one-page publication by email to a group of customers or friends is an efficient and inexpensive way to deliver a message.

Publisher provides several ways to create an email newsletter. You can use a template or create an email publication from scratch. Publisher's email templates are preformatted and use placeholder text and graphics that download quickly and are suitable for the body of an email newsletter.

A second way to create an email publication is to send a single page of another publication. This expands the use of your existing content, although you may need to adjust the width of your publication in order for it to fit in an email newsletter.

Another way is to send an entire Publisher publication as an attachment; however, this requires that the recipient have Microsoft Publisher 2002 or a later version installed to view it. When the recipient opens the attached file, Publisher automatically runs and opens the publication. Unless you convert a multipage publication into a single-page email publication, it must be sent as an email attachment.

Finally, you can create an **email merge** when you want to send a large number of messages that mostly are identical, but you also want to include some unique or personalized information in each message. An email merge, which uses the same merge techniques that you learned about in Module 7, creates personalized content for each recipient on a mailing list.

The type of publication you choose depends on the content and the needs of the recipients. Table 9–1 describes specific audiences and the appropriate kinds of email publications.

Table 9–1 Publisher Email Types			
Audience Characteristic	**Email Message**	**Email Merge**	**Email Attachment**
Recipients definitely have Publisher installed.			X
Recipients may not have Publisher installed.	X	X	
Recipients need to read and print the content in its original format.			X
Recipients may not have HTML-enabled email.	X	X	
Recipients need personalized messages.		X	

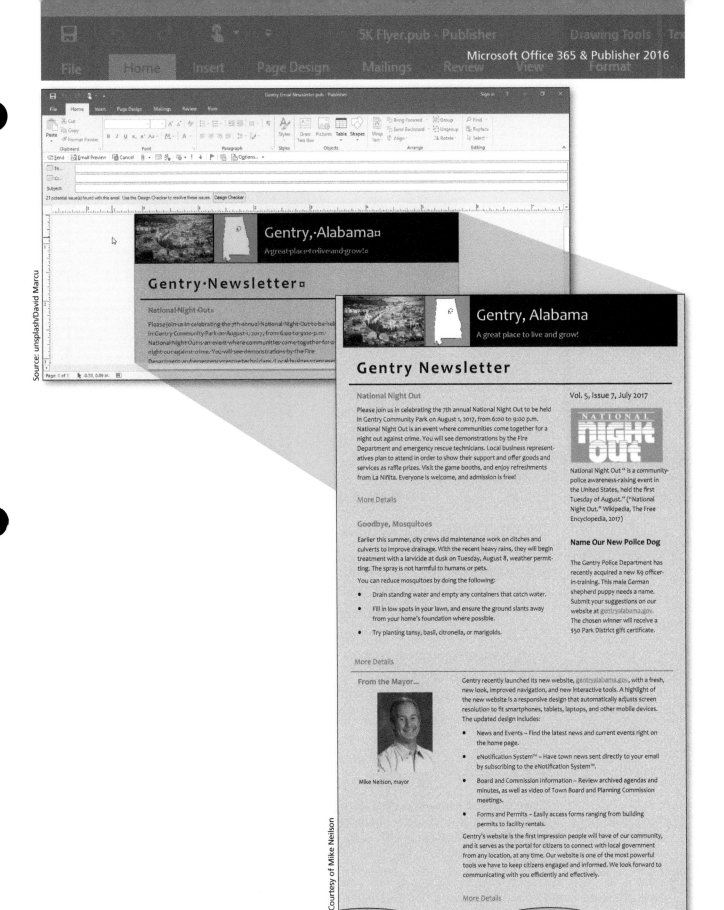

(a) Email Newsletter

Figure 9–1 (Continued)

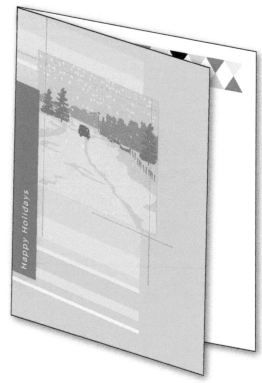

(b) Postcard   **(c) Greeting Card**

Figure 9–1

The following roadmap identifies general activities you will perform as you progress through this module:

1. CREATE an EMAIL PUBLICATION, such as a newsletter.
2. INSERT SYMBOLS, patterns, and special characters.
3. USE the RESEARCH TASK PANE, and create a citation.
4. CREATE HYPERLINKS and hot spots.
5. DISTRIBUTE EMAIL publications.
6. CREATE a POSTCARD.
7. CREATE a GREETING CARD.
8. USE DESIGN ACCENTS as appropriate.

Email Templates

Each of Publisher's design sets features several email templates, so you can create and send email that is consistent in design with the rest of the business communication and marketing materials that you create using Publisher. Table 9–2 lists the types of email templates and their purpose.

What should I keep in mind when designing an email newsletter?

Be sure to start with a Publisher email template, or resize your publication to fit standard email newsletter sizes. When using a template, choose one that matches the purpose of the email, as Publisher will supply many of the necessary elements, such as text, graphics, and links. Use graphics sparingly, keeping in mind the download time. If you use a wallpaper or stationery, keep it simple or a solid color.

Table 9–2 Types of Email Templates

Type	Purpose
Event/Activity	A notice of a specific upcoming activity or event containing a combination of pictures, dates, times, maps, agenda, and the ability to sign up
Event/Speaker	A notice of a specific upcoming event that includes a speaker and usually contains pictures, dates, times, and a map
Featured Product	A publication that provides information about a company and a specific product or service, including graphics and webpage links for more information
Letter	A more personalized document to correspond with one or more people, including specific information on a single topic
Newsletter	Informs interested clientele about an organization or business with stories, dates, contact information, and upcoming events
Product List	A sales-oriented publication to display products, prices, and special promotions including webpage links for more information

To Select an Email Template

The following steps select an email template from the template gallery and choose color and font schemes. You do not have to be connected to the Internet or have an email program on your computer in order to create the email. You can create and save the email newsletter on any storage location rather than send it via email.

1 Run Publisher. In the template gallery, click BUILT-IN to display the BUILT-IN templates.

2 Scroll as necessary and then click the E-mail thumbnail in the BUILT-IN templates to display the E-mail templates.

3 Scroll down to the section labeled More Installed Templates and then scroll to the Newsletter templates, near the end of the gallery.

4 Click the Floating Oval thumbnail to choose the template.

5 In the Customize area, choose the Prairie color scheme and the Concourse font scheme (Figure 9–2).

BTW

Email Templates
Email templates contain text boxes, logos, hyperlinks, and graphics. To customize the email message, you replace the placeholder text and graphics with your own content, just as you would in any other template publication.

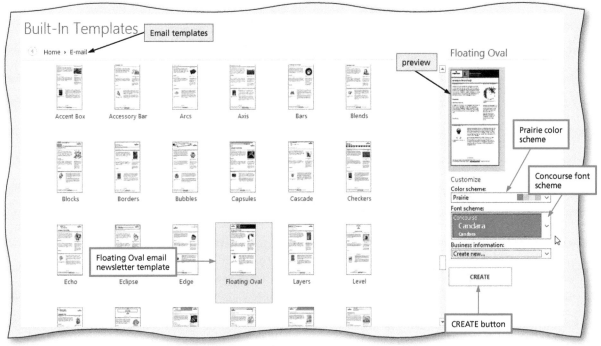

Figure 9–2

To Create the Publication and Customize the Workspace

The following steps customize the workspace.

1 Click the CREATE button in the Customize area to create the publication with the chosen settings.

2 Display the View tab. If necessary, click to display a check mark in the Boundaries check box (View tab | Show group).

3 Display the Home tab. If necessary, click the Special Characters button (Home tab | Paragraph group) to display paragraph marks and special characters.

4 Close the Page Navigation pane (Figure 9–3).

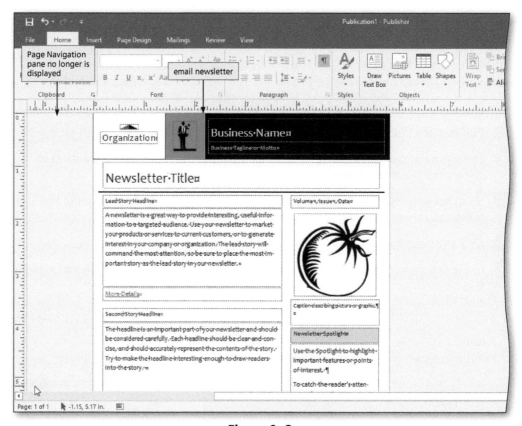

Figure 9–3

To Change the Email Newsletter Page Size

1 CREATE EMAIL PUBLICATION | 2 INSERT SYMBOLS | 3 USE RESEARCH TASK PANE | 4 CREATE HYPERLINKS
5 DISTRIBUTE EMAIL | 6 CREATE POSTCARD | 7 CREATE GREETING CARD | 8 USE DESIGN ACCENTS

Publisher has two length settings for email newsletters. The Large setting is 66 inches long. The Short setting is 11 inches long. The following steps change the length of the email newsletter to the Short setting. *Why? The Gentry city officials have chosen a shorter length, as most people who read emails prefer not to scroll through longer pages.*

1

- Display the Page Design tab.

- Click the 'Choose Page Size' button (Page Design tab | Page Setup group) to display the Choose Page Size gallery.

- If necessary, scroll to the bottom of the Choose Page Size gallery (Figure 9–4).

Q&A My list of sizes is different. Did I do something wrong?
No. Your list may differ depending on page sizes that have been saved previously.

Could I click the Page Setup Dialog Box Launcher to customize the page size?
Yes, you can set the margins and choose various paper sizes and layouts in the Page Setup dialog box. The email sizes include the standard width of 5.818 inches but differing lengths, including a long email (up to 66 inches), a short email (up to 11 inches), or a custom size.

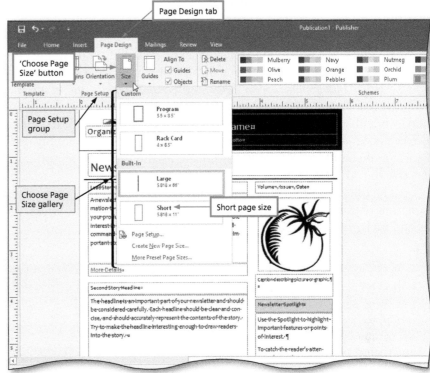

Figure 9–4

2

- Click Short in the Choose Page Size gallery to choose a short page format (Figure 9–5).

Q&A My email newsletter has a different business name listed in the publication. Did I do something wrong?
No, your computer may be using a different business information set, or it may have an installed school or company name. You will edit the boxes later in the module.

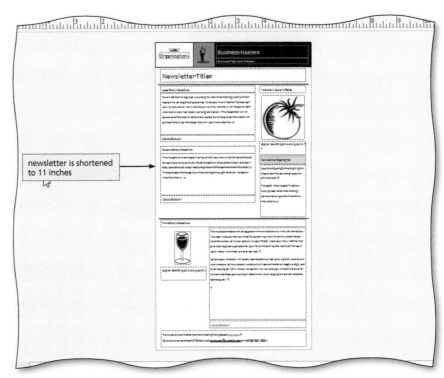

Figure 9–5

To Set the Email Background Using a Pattern

You can add a background to an email or web publication in the same way you do for other publications, by applying a color, gradient, picture, texture, or pattern; however, a web background should not be detailed or busy. **Why?** *Backgrounds appear behind the text and graphics and should not detract from reading the text.* People include email backgrounds, also called **wallpaper** or **stationery**, to add interest to their email messages, to convey or enhance the message, to grab the reader's attention, or to emulate business letterhead. A background also can make your email newsletter stand out from those who simply use black text on a white background. Publisher especially is useful for those email programs that do not offer wallpaper. Backgrounds usually do not increase the download time.

The following steps choose a pattern background for the email page. Recall that patterns include variations of repeating designs, such as lines, stripes, checks, and bricks. Publisher uses a foreground color and a second background color when creating a pattern.

1

- Click the Background button (Page Design tab | Page Background group) to display the Background gallery and then click More Backgrounds to display the Format Background dialog box.

- Click the Pattern Fill option button (Format Background dialog box) and then scroll down to display the settings (Figure 9–6).

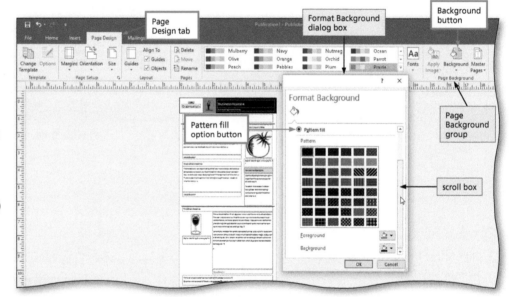

Figure 9–6

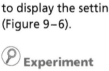 **Experiment**

- Point to each of the thumbnails in the Pattern area to view each pattern name in a ScreenTip.

Q&A | My patterns are different. Did I do something wrong?
No. Someone may have changed the foreground and background colors. The patterns are the same.

2

- Click the 40% pattern and then click the Foreground button to display the scheme colors (Figure 9–7).

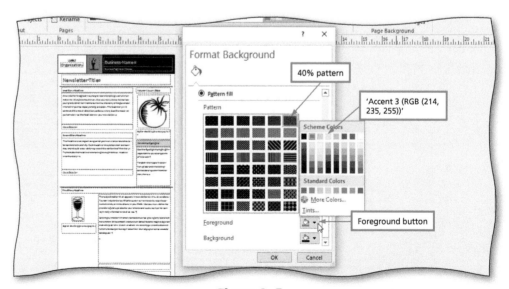

Figure 9–7

③
- Click 'Accent 3 (RGB (214, 235, 255))' to choose a light blue foreground color.
- Click the Background button to display the scheme colors (Figure 9–8).

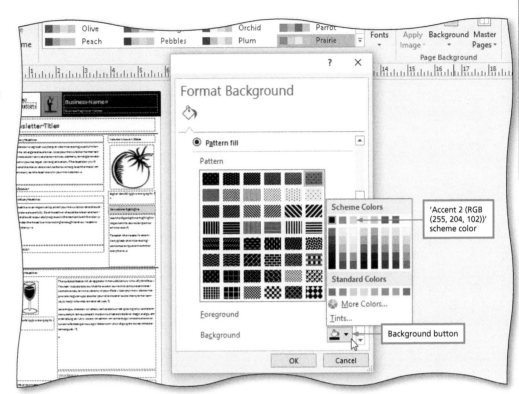

Figure 9–8

④
- Click 'Accent 2 (RGB (255, 204, 102))' to choose a very light orange background (Figure 9–9).

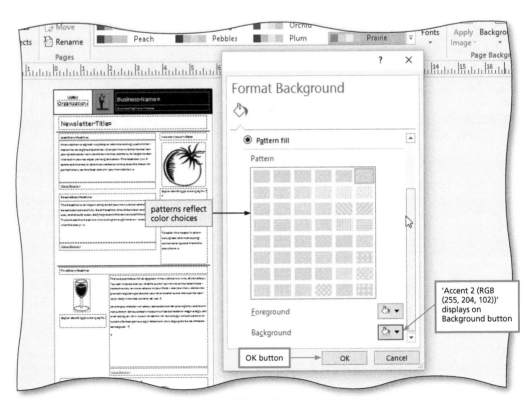

Figure 9–9

⑤
- Click the OK button (Format Background dialog box) to apply the background.

- Zoom to 150% and then scroll to the top of the page (Figure 9–10).

Figure 9–10

Reading Online

As with printed newsletters, when creating an email newsletter, you should pay attention to readability. A few things, however, become very important when users are reading online. First, repetition is very important. Use the same font and font size for all headings and all stories. Do not use more than three different fonts or font sizes on the page. Do not choose a third-party font that you may have downloaded. Some browsers change unknown fonts, which can cause your text to be harder to read. Use standard font sizes. In this module, you will use the Candara font, which is a common Microsoft font, and font sizes of 8, 10, and 20. Make sure you have some repeated elements, such as links for more details, repeated lines, or repeated colors. In this module, you will have all three. Using an element only once can look like an error. Try to use three or four colors at most.

Even though repetition is the most important consideration, make sure the color and font scheme you choose, as well as any graphics you include, provide some contrast. For example, use the most contrasting color in the scheme for headings versus stories and for shapes versus the background. You might want to include a very bright graphic that includes a small amount of repetitive color but lots of bright contrasting colors.

Keep related objects together; for example, if you have graphics, keep them close to the story and keep any caption close to the picture. Keep a More Details link close enough to the story so the reader will not be confused as to what details they expect to see when clicking the link. All links should be underlined and use the standardized medium blue color.

Finally, alignment is important. Every object in your email should be aligned with something — either another object or the margin. Try to align both vertically and horizontally. The templates help you get started, but as you resize and move elements, keep alignment in mind.

To Edit the Heading

The following steps edit the heading of the newsletter.

1 Select the text, Newsletter Title, at the top of the page. Type `Gentry Newsletter` to replace the text.

2 Select the text again, change the font size to 20, and then press CTRL+B to bold the text.

3 Click the Object Size button on the taskbar to display the Measurement task pane. Change the tracking to 120% to spread the letters of the heading.

4 Click the text to remove the selection (Figure 9–11).

5 Click the Close button on the Measurement task pane to close it.

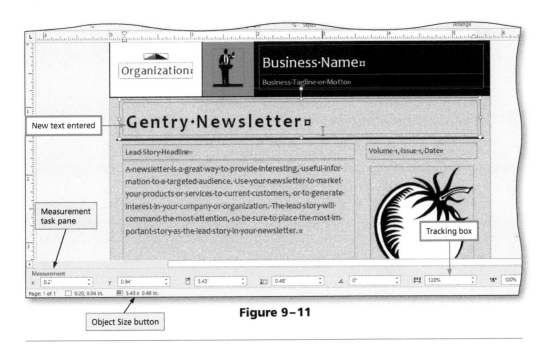

Figure 9–11

To Edit Other Text Boxes at the Top of the Page

The following steps edit the text boxes in the upper portion of the email newsletter.

1 Select the text in the Business Name text box and then type `Gentry, Alabama` to replace the text.

2 Select the text in the 'Business Tagline or Motto' text box, change the font size to 10, and then type `A great place to live and grow!` to replace the text.

3 Click to select the text in the volume text box, change the font size to 10, and then type `Vol. 5, Issue 7, July 2017` to replace the text (Figure 9–12).

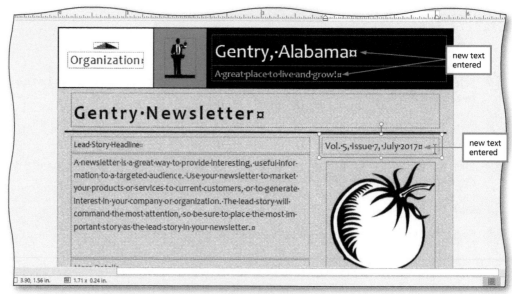

Figure 9–12

To Complete the Lead Story

The following steps edit the headline and text for the lead story. To complete these steps, you will be required to use the Data Files. Please contact your instructor for information about accessing the Data Files.

As you import this and other stories into the email newsletter, if the story is too long, Publisher will create a second page with a new text box to continue the story. If that happens, press CTRL+Z to undo the import, resize the current text box, and then import the file again.

After importing the first story, you will need to hyphenate due to the way the text wraps. Check all your stories for the need to hyphenate. You will run spell check at the end of the module.

1 Click to select the Lead Story Headline placeholder text. Change the font size to 10, bold the text, and then type **National Night Out** to replace the text.

2 Click the text in the story text box below the headline to select it.

3 Display the Insert tab.

4 Click the Insert File button (Insert tab | Text group) to display the Insert Text dialog box. Navigate to the Data Files and then double-click the file named First Story to insert it in the publication.

5 Display the Text Box Tools Format tab.

6 Click the Hyphenation button (Text Box Tools Format tab | Text group) to display the Hyphenation dialog box.

7 Click to remove the check mark in the 'Automatically hyphenate this story' check box. Click the Manual button (Hyphenate Dialog box) to begin hyphenating the story.

8 When Publisher recommends hyphenating the word, National, click the No button because it is part of a title.

9 When Publisher recommends hyphenating the word, Department, click the No button because it is part of a name.

10 When Publisher recommends hyphenating the word, representatives, click the Yes button (Figure 9–13).

11 If Publisher displays a Microsoft Publisher dialog box, click the OK button.

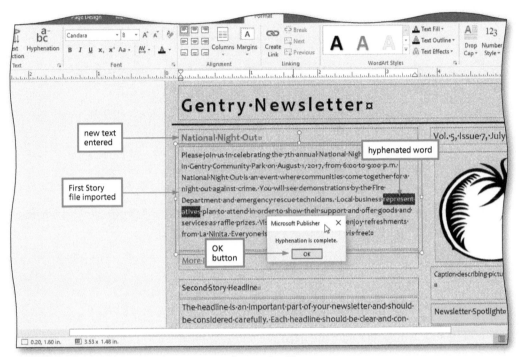

Figure 9–13

To Complete the Second Story

The following steps edit the headline and text for the second story. Because the second story is long, you will move and resize text boxes before importing the story. To complete these steps, you will be required to use the Data Files. Please contact your instructor for information about accessing the Data Files.

1 Click to select the Second Story Headline placeholder text. Change the font size to 10, bold the text, and then type `Goodbye, Mosquitoes` to replace the text.

2 Select the More Details text box below the second story. SHIFT+drag the border of the More Details text box to move it straight down to a location just above the separator line.

3 Resize the second story text box to be approximately 2 inches tall.

4 Click the text in the story text box to select it.

5 Click the Insert File button (Insert tab | Text group) to display the Insert Text dialog box. Navigate to the Data Files and then double-click the file named Second Story to insert it in the publication.

6 Select the last three paragraphs and apply bullets (Figure 9–14).

7 If necessary, hyphenate the story, as described in the previous steps.

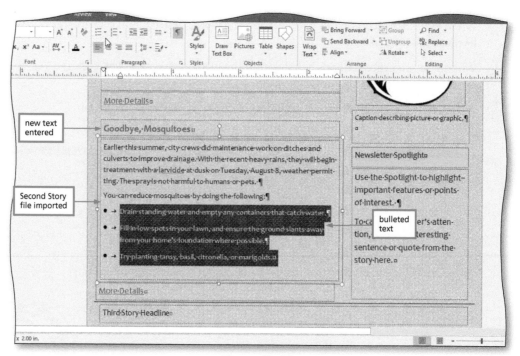

Figure 9–14

To Complete the Third Story

The following steps edit the headline and text for the third story. Because the third story is long, you also will resize the text box before importing the story. To complete these steps, you will be required to use the Data Files. Please contact your instructor for information about accessing the Data Files.

1 Click to select the Third Story Headline placeholder text. Change the font size to 10, bold the text, and then type **From the Mayor…** to replace the text.

2 Click the text box beside the headline to select it. To resize the text box, drag the upper-middle sizing handle upward, until the text box aligns with the top of the heading. Some overlapping will occur but will not affect either text box. The story text box will be approximately 3.5 inches tall.

3 Select the text.

4 Click the Insert File button (Insert tab | Text group) to display the Insert Text dialog box. Navigate to the Data Files and then double-click the file named Third Story to insert it into the publication.

5 Select paragraphs 2 through 5 and apply bullets (Figure 9–15).

6 If necessary, hyphenate the story, as described earlier in the module.

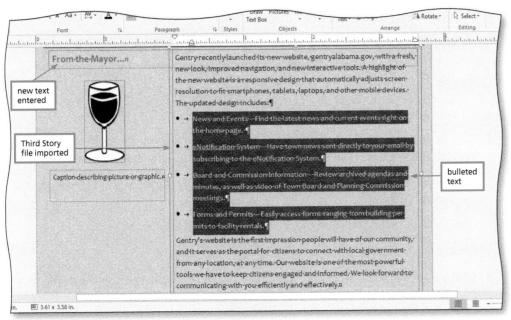

Figure 9–15

To Edit the Comment Text Box

The following steps edit the last text box on the page.

1 Scroll as necessary to the bottom of the page.

2 Click the email placeholder text to select it and then type **news@gentryalabama.gov** to replace the text.

3 Select the phrase after the email address and then type **or call 205-555-4900.** to replace the text (Figure 9–16).

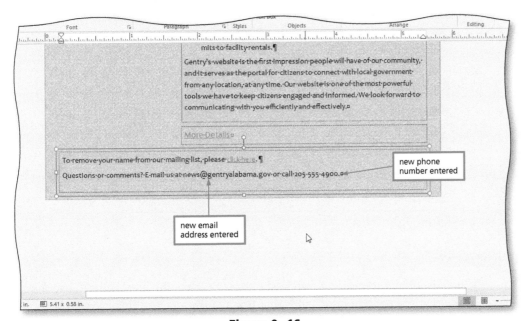

Figure 9–16

To Complete the Sidebar

The following steps edit the headline and text for the sidebar. To complete these steps, you will be required to use the Data Files. Please contact your instructor for information about accessing the Data Files.

1 Scroll to the center of the page.

2 Click to select the Newsletter Spotlight headline in the sidebar. Change the font size to 10, bold the text, and then type **Name Our New Police Dog** to replace the text.

3 If necessary, drag the upper-middle sizing handle upward so that all of the text in the headline is displayed.

4 Click the text in the story text box below the headline to select it.

5 Display the Insert tab.

6 Click the Insert File button (Insert tab | Text group) to display the Insert Text dialog box. Navigate to the Data Files and then double-click the file named Sidebar Story to insert it in the publication (Figure 9–17).

7 If necessary, hyphenate the story, as described earlier in the module.

8 Save the publication on your desired save location using the file name, Gentry Email Newsletter.

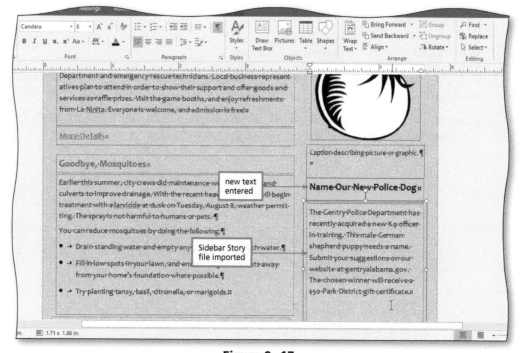

Figure 9–17

Pictures

When using pictures on the web, make sure you have the legal right to use the pictures and that the owner understands that the picture will be transmitted over the web via email. Some people who do not object to their pictures being used in print are opposed to having their pictures distributed electronically.

Pictures or images used on webpages or in email newsletters should be used to draw attention, trigger emotions, and, most importantly, enhance or add meaning to the story. Do not use pictures just to "dress up" the email. If the owner of the email or website has a logo, use it. Logos help brand the publication and let users know they are on the right page.

Check your images for quick display. Despite the kind of graphic or picture you include, lower ppi (points per inch) will load faster. Use the Graphics Manager and compression techniques, when necessary.

Finally, use real people and real pictures when possible. Research has shown that clip art is not as effective in electronic publications. Publisher's email feature does not support animated graphics.

To Insert Pictures

The following steps insert pictures in the email newsletter. To complete these steps, you will be required to use the Data Files. Please contact your instructor for information about accessing the Data Files.

1 Scroll to the top of the page.

2 If Publisher displays a logo placeholder or picture placeholder in the upper-left corner of the email newsletter, right-click the object and then click Delete Object on the shortcut menu.

3 Click the Pictures button (Insert tab | Illustrations group), browse to the location of the Data Files, and then insert the graphic named Town.

4 Drag the picture to the upper-left corner of the email newsletter and resize it, as shown in Figure 9–18.

5 Delete the picture in the blue rectangle. Insert another picture named Alabama. Resize the picture and place it in the blue rectangle at the top of the page (Figure 9–18).

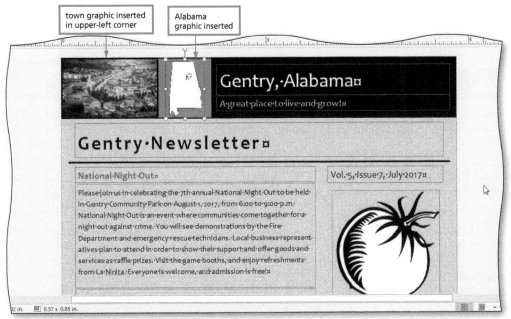

Figure 9–18

To Fit a Picture

When you replace a picture in a template, you may get either excessive white space, empty space, or part of the picture may not display. *Why? The new picture fills the picture placeholder. If the new picture is a different size, Publisher may adjust the picture, but you always should double-check it.* The following steps use the Fit button to make the picture fit the picture placeholder. You then can crop any extra white space and resize. To complete these steps, you will be required to use the Data Files. Please contact your instructor for information about accessing the Data Files.

- Right-click the picture placeholder below the volume and issue text box and then point to Change Picture on the shortcut menu. Click Change Picture on the Change Picture submenu to display the Insert Pictures dialog box.
- Click the Browse button (Insert Pictures dialog box) and then navigate to the Data Files. Insert the graphic named National Night Out.
- Click the scratch area to deselect the original picture and its replacement. Delete the original picture from the scratch area.
- Click the new picture to select it and then zoom to 150% (Figure 9–19).

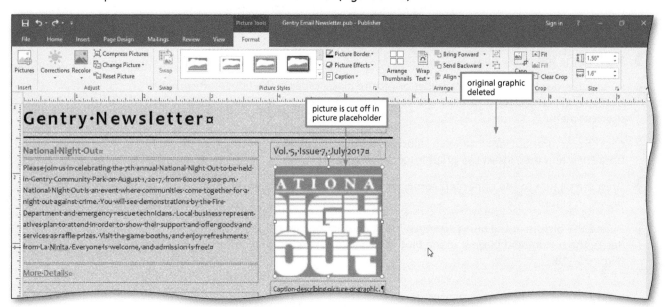

Figure 9–19

- Click the Fit button (Picture Tools Format tab | Crop group) to fit the picture in the picture placeholder (Figure 9–20).

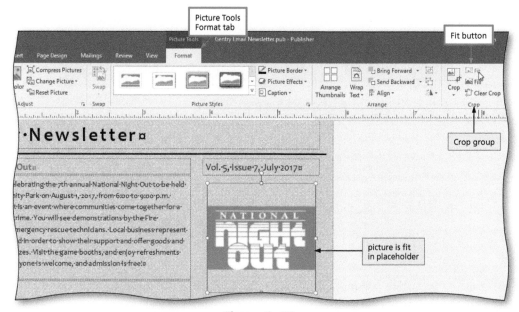

Figure 9–20

3

- Click the Crop button (Picture Tools Format tab | Crop group) and then drag the top and bottom crop lines toward the middle to crop the blank space (Figure 9–21).

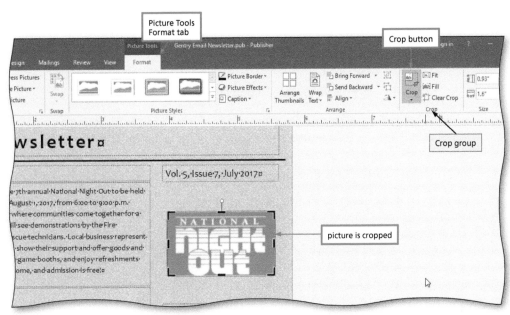

Figure 9–21

4

- Click the Crop button (Picture Tools Format tab | Crop group) again to turn off the cropping feature.

- Move the picture up and center-align it with the volume and issue text box as shown in Figure 9–22.

Figure 9–22

To Insert and Fit Another Picture

The following steps insert and fit another picture, positioned lower on the page. To complete these steps, you will be required to use the Data Files. Please contact your instructor for information about accessing the Data Files.

1 Scroll down as necessary to display the picture placeholder on the left side of the page, just below the 'From the Mayor…' text box.

2 Right-click the picture placeholder and then point to Change Picture on the shortcut menu. Click Change Picture on the Change Picture submenu and then navigate to the Data Files. Insert the graphic named Mayor.

3 Deselect the pictures and then delete the original picture from the scratch area.

4 Zoom to 150% and select the new picture.

5 Click the Fit button (Picture Tools Format tab | Crop group) to fit the picture in the picture placeholder.

6 Crop the blank space. SHIFT+drag a corner sizing handle to resize the picture to fill the space below the headline. Center-align the picture with the headline (Figure 9–23).

7 Select the caption text and then type `Mike Neilson, mayor` as the new caption.

8 Save the publication again.

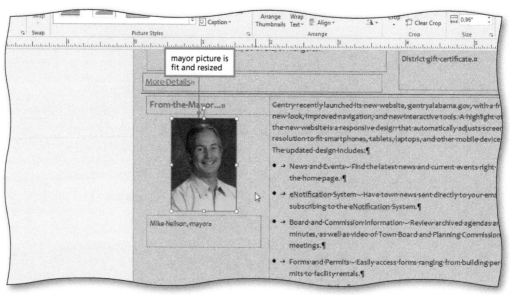

Figure 9–23

Break Point: If you wish to take a break, this is a good place to do so. Exit Publisher. To resume at a later time, run Publisher, open the file named Gentry Email Newsletter, and then continue following the steps from this location forward.

Symbols and Special Characters

In Publisher, a **symbol** is a character that is not on your keyboard, such as ½ and ©, or **special characters**, such as an em dash (—) or ellipsis (…). Some special symbols use ASCII characters or Unicode characters. **ASCII** and **Unicode** are coding systems that represent text and symbols in computers, communications equipment, and other devices that use text.

CONSIDER THIS

Should you use symbols, hyperlinks, and hot spots?
Limit the use of symbols and special characters in emails, as some may not be displayed correctly. Make sure you check for terms that may need copyright, trademark, and registration symbols. Double-check all hyperlinks for purpose and type. Create **hot spots**, or nontext hyperlinks, around graphics as necessary. Use mailto hyperlinks to help the recipient respond via email.

To Insert a Symbol from the Symbol Dialog Box

1 CREATE EMAIL PUBLICATION | 2 INSERT SYMBOLS | 3 USE RESEARCH TASK PANE | 4 CREATE HYPERLINKS
5 DISTRIBUTE EMAIL | 6 CREATE POSTCARD | 7 CREATE GREETING CARD | 8 USE DESIGN ACCENTS

In the email newsletter, the lowercase letter, n, in the word Ninita should display a tilde. *Why? The Spanish word, Niñita, contains a tilde, or diacritical mark, used in many written languages to be punctuated correctly.* The following steps insert the letter n with a tilde symbol in the text of the email newsletter.

1

- Scroll to the top of the page and zoom to 200%.
- In the first story, select the lowercase n in the middle of the word Ninita.
- Display the Insert tab.
- Click the 'Insert a Symbol' button (Insert tab | Text group) to display the Insert a Symbol gallery (Figure 9–24).

Q&A What if the symbol I want to insert already appears in the Insert a Symbol gallery?
You can click any symbol shown in the Insert a Symbol gallery to insert it in the document.

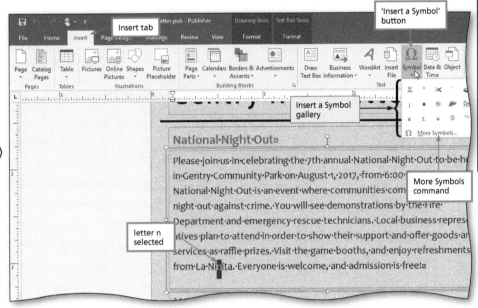

Figure 9–24

2

- Click More Symbols in the Insert a Symbol gallery to display the Symbol dialog box.

🔍 **Experiment**

- Click the Font arrow to display the list of available fonts.

Q&A Which font should I choose?
When you are unsure where the special character you need might be located, it is a good idea to choose the current font and start looking at the top of the list.

- Scroll as necessary in the list and then click the desired symbol (in this case, ñ) to select it (Figure 9–25).

Q&A Does the symbol have a special name?
Publisher uses the name, Latin Small Letter N With Tilde, to identify the symbol. Publisher also references a Unicode number, 00F1, to reference the ñ symbol.

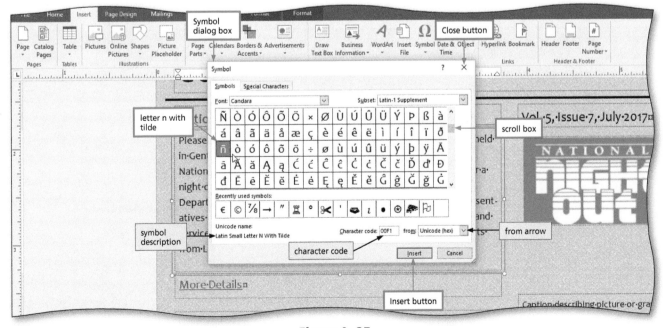

Figure 9–25

- Click the Insert button (Symbol dialog box) to place the selected symbol in the publication at the current location.
- Click the Close button (Symbol dialog box) to close the dialog box (Figure 9–26).

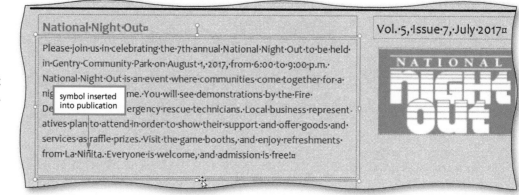

Figure 9–26

Other Ways

1. Click 'Insert a Symbol' button (Insert tab | Text group), click More Symbols in Insert a Symbol gallery, enter Unicode number in Character code box (Symbol dialog box), click Insert button, click Close button

To Insert a Special Character Using the Symbol Dialog Box

1 CREATE EMAIL PUBLICATION | 2 INSERT SYMBOLS | 3 USE RESEARCH TASK PANE | 4 CREATE HYPERLINKS
5 DISTRIBUTE EMAIL | 6 CREATE POSTCARD | 7 CREATE GREETING CARD | 8 USE DESIGN ACCENTS

The following steps insert a trademark special character, ™, using the Symbol dialog box. *Why? This special character is not on the keyboard.*

- Navigate to the third story. Position the insertion point after the first occurrence of the phrase, eNotification System, and before the space and hyphen.
- Click the 'Insert a Symbol' button (Insert tab | Text group) to display the Insert a Symbol gallery.
- Click More Symbols in the Symbol gallery to display the Symbol dialog box.
- Click the Special Characters tab (Symbol dialog box) to display the list of special characters.
- Click the desired special character (in this case, the ™ Trademark symbol) in the list of special characters (Figure 9–27).

Q&A Does the insertion point have to be inside a text box before I insert a special character?
Yes, Publisher uses text boxes to display text, unlike word processing programs. Unless you have the symbol as a separate graphic file or can find it in clip art, you need to draw a text box first and then insert it.

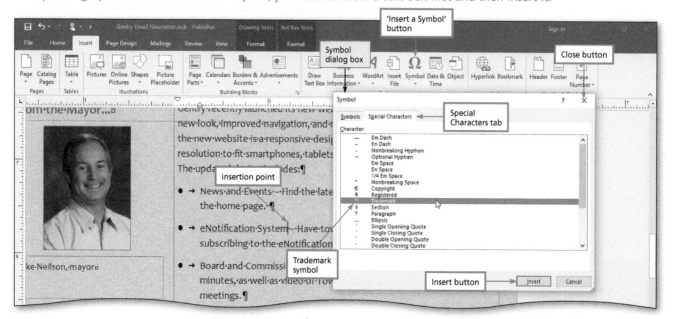

Figure 9–27

2

- Click the Insert button (Symbol dialog box) to place the selected special character in the publication.

- Click the Close button (Symbol dialog box) to close the dialog box (Figure 9–28).

Q&A What is the difference between a symbol and a special character?
The special character list is a subset of symbols that are used often in professional typing tasks.

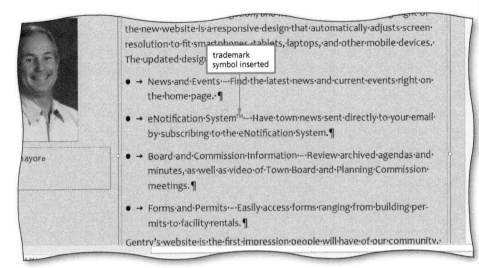

Figure 9–28

3

- Position the insertion point after the second occurrence of the phrase, before the period.

- Repeat the process in Steps 1 and 2 to insert another trademark symbol (Figure 9–29).

Q&A Could I just copy and paste the other trademark symbol?
Yes, although sometimes it is difficult to select small symbols in the text.

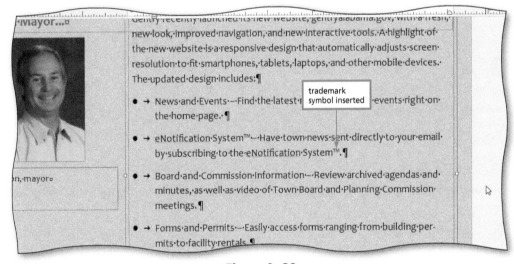

Figure 9–29

Research Task Pane

From within Publisher, you can search various forms of reference information. Services include a dictionary and, if you are connected to the web, an encyclopedia, a search engine, and other websites that provide information, such as historical data, stock quotes, news articles, and company profiles.

Publisher's research options usually are broken down into two areas: reference books and research sites. Depending on your installation and your connection to the web, your list of reference books may include books such as the Encarta dictionary and various thesauruses. Research sites may include Bing, Factiva Works, and other search engines. The Research options link at the bottom of the Research task pane allows you to add other books and sites to your list.

To Use the Research Task Pane

You decide to include a definition of National Night Out in the email newsletter. The following steps use the Research task pane to look up a definition. You must be connected to the Internet to perform these steps. *Why? The Research tool relies on web-based dictionaries, encyclopedias, and search engines.*

1

- Scroll to the caption location below the National Night Out graphic.
- Resize the caption text box to fill the area between the picture and the next heading.
- Click the text to select it and then change the font size to 8 (Figure 9–30).

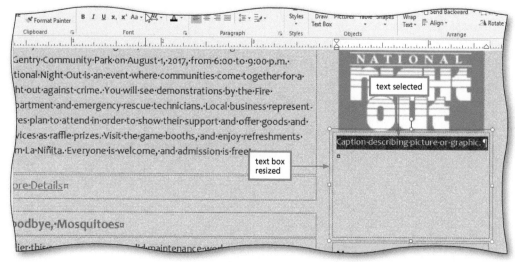

Figure 9–30

2

- Type **National Night Out "** to begin the caption.
- Select the text and then display the Review tab.
- Click the Research button (Review tab | Proofing group) to open the Research task pane (Figure 9–31).

Experiment

- Click the arrow next to the word, Bing. Notice all of the different locations in which you can search.

Q&A How do I choose the search location?

If the term you want to research is one that you think might be in a dictionary or encyclopedia, click the arrow next to the word, Bing, and then click 'All Reference Books'. If the term is more of a cultural item or a phrase, you may want to use Bing.

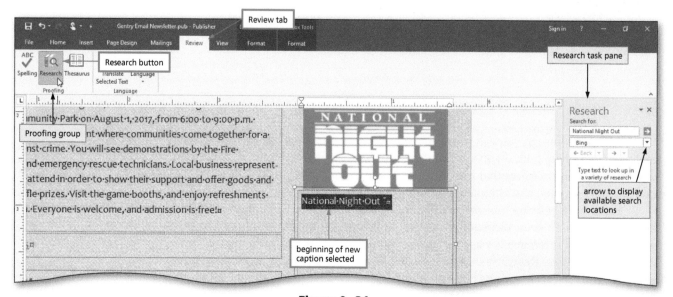

Figure 9–31

③

- Click the Start searching button (Research task pane) to display the results from a Bing search (Figure 9–32).

🔍 **Experiment**

- Scroll through the list to display the various sites related to the search term.

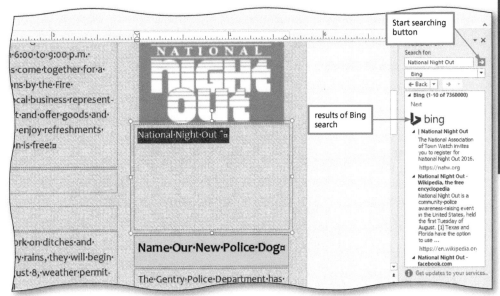

Figure 9–32

Other Ways

1. ALT+click desired word

To Create a Cited Reference

1 CREATE EMAIL PUBLICATION | 2 INSERT SYMBOLS | 3 USE RESEARCH TASK PANE | 4 CREATE HYPERLINKS
5 DISTRIBUTE EMAIL | 6 CREATE POSTCARD | 7 CREATE GREETING CARD | 8 USE DESIGN ACCENTS

The following steps copy and paste a reference from the Research task pane into the caption text box and create a citation. *Why? You always should include quotes and a citation when copying and pasting.*

①

- In the Research task pane, select the text in the second reference, beginning with the word, is, and continuing to the end of the sentence.

- Press CTRL+C to copy the definition (Figure 9–33).

 Is Wikipedia an acceptable source? In this case, the definition is usable. If you are citing a historical fact or a quotation, verify your information with several reputable and verifiable sources.

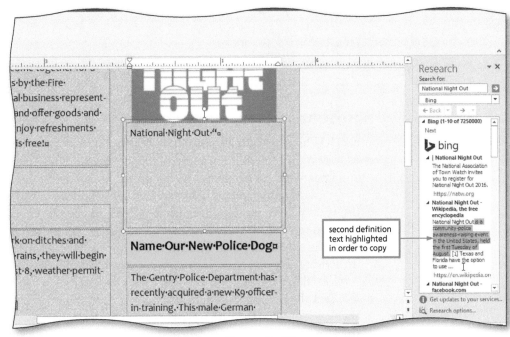

Figure 9–33

2

- Position the insertion point after the quotation mark in the caption, and then press CTRL+V to paste the definition.

- Type   **"**   to complete the quote and then press the SPACEBAR key.

- Type   **("National Night Out." Wikipedia, The Free Encyclopedia, 2017)**   to complete the citation.

- If the word, community is hyphenated on the first line (other than the hyphen at the end of the word), enlarge the text box slightly by dragging the right-center sizing handle (Figure 9–34).

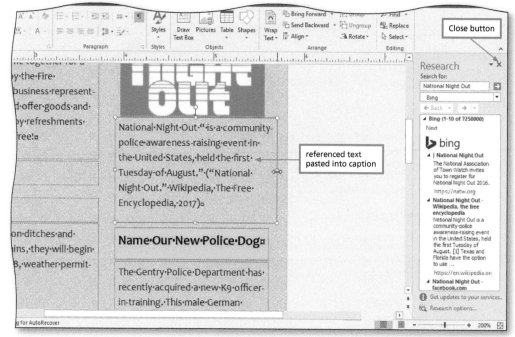

Figure 9–34

Q&A

Could I manually hyphenate the text?
You could; however, because the word, community, is on the first line, it should not be hyphenated at all. Moving it to the next line would leave a large gap on the first line. The text box is aligned on the left with other text boxes; extending it to the right is not a problem. Because this is not a print publication, you can place objects very close to the edge of the page.

What kind of citation am I using?
The citation uses an in-text reference in **APA style**, a standard citation style in technology fields.

3

- Click the Close button in the Research task pane.

- Save the publication again.

Research Task Pane Options

When you install Publisher, it selects a series of services (reference books and websites) that it searches when you use the Research task pane. You can view, modify, and update the list of services at any time.

Clicking the Research options link at the bottom of the Research task pane displays the Research Options dialog box, where you can view or modify the list of installed services. You can view information about any installed service by clicking the service in the list and then clicking the Properties button (Research Options dialog box). To activate an installed service, click the check box to its left. Likewise, to deactivate a service, click the check box to remove the check mark. To add a particular website to the list, click the Add Services button, enter the web address in the Address text box, and then click the Add button (Add Services dialog box). To update or remove services, click the Update/Remove button, select the service in the list, click the Update (or Remove) button (Update or Remove Services dialog box), and then click the Close button. You also can install parental controls through the Parental Control button (Research Options dialog box), for example, if you want to restrict web access for minors who use Publisher.

Creating Hyperlinks and Hot Spots

Email newsletters can contain hyperlinks just as webpages do. A hyperlink is usually colored and underlined text that you click to navigate to a file, a location in a file, a webpage, or an email address; but hyperlinks also can be a graphic, picture, button, or shape. When the hyperlink is not text, it is called a hot spot.

Typically, when you insert a hyperlink or hot spot, you must enter the webpage address, called a URL. **URL** stands for **uniform resource locator** and identifies the location of the file on the Internet.

To Insert a Hyperlink

1 CREATE EMAIL PUBLICATION | 2 INSERT SYMBOLS | 3 USE RESEARCH TASK PANE | 4 CREATE HYPERLINKS
5 DISTRIBUTE EMAIL | 6 CREATE POSTCARD | 7 CREATE GREETING CARD | 8 USE DESIGN ACCENTS

In the body of the email newsletter template, the words, More Details, should be a hyperlink to open the city's webpage. *Why? In an email message, users expect to click words, such as More Details.* The following steps insert a hyperlink into the publication.

- Display the Insert tab and zoom to 150%.
- Select the first occurrence of More Details, just below the lead story.
- Click the 'Add a Hyperlink' button (Insert tab | Links group) to display the Insert Hyperlink dialog box.
- If necessary, click the 'Existing File or Web Page' button in the Link to bar.
- Type **www.gentryalabama.gov** in the Address box (Figure 9–35).

Q&A Why did Publisher already list an address in the Address box?
Publisher may prefill the Address box with the most recent entry. You can replace that address as necessary.

Why did Publisher insert http:// before the web address?
The default prefix, or **protocol**, for websites is http://. While newer browsers do not require the protocol, to make sure all users can navigate to your webpage, Publisher inserts the protocol.

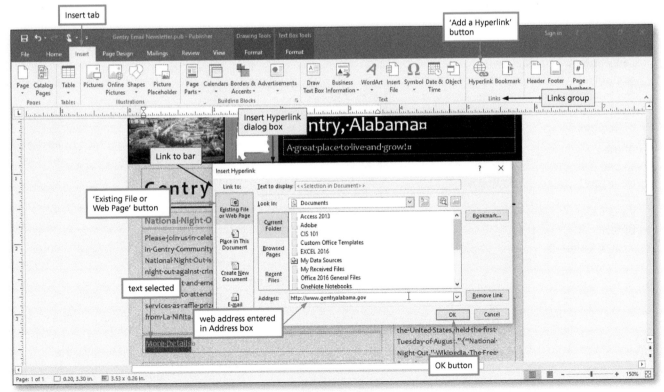

Figure 9–35

②

- Click the OK button (Insert Hyperlink dialog box) to apply the hyperlink.

③

- Repeat Steps 1 and 2 for the other two occurrences of the words, More Details, in the newsletter and the words, gentryalabama.gov, in the sidebar story and last story.

Q&A

How do I know for sure that the hyperlink works?
When you send the email message, users can click the link. Within Publisher, you would need to press CTRL+click to display the webpage.

Should the text use the www prefix?
You could add that to the text; however, many websites can be accessed either way. For example, the web addresses, facebook.com and www.facebook.com, both work to display the Facebook page.

Other Ways

1. Select text, press CTRL+K, click 'Existing File or Web Page' on Link to bar (Insert Hyperlink dialog box), enter web address, click OK button

To Insert a Mailto Hyperlink

1 CREATE EMAIL PUBLICATION | 2 INSERT SYMBOLS | 3 USE RESEARCH TASK PANE | 4 CREATE HYPERLINKS
5 DISTRIBUTE EMAIL | 6 CREATE POSTCARD | 7 CREATE GREETING CARD | 8 USE DESIGN ACCENTS

When clicked, a **mailto** hyperlink runs the user's email program. The following steps insert a mailto hyperlink using the words, click here, in the final text box at the bottom of the page. *Why? That way, when users click the link, an email window will open, allowing them to send a message to the recipient.*

①

- In the text box at the bottom of the page, select the text, click here.

- Click the 'Add a Hyperlink' button (Insert tab | Links group) to display the Insert Hyperlink dialog box.

- In the Link to bar, if necessary, click the E-mail Address button (Figure 9–36).

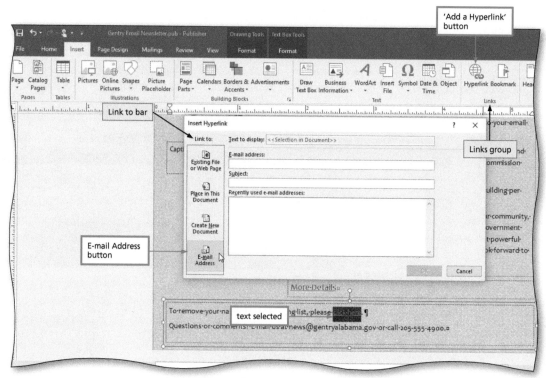

Figure 9–36

2

- In the E-mail address text box, type **unsubscribe@ gentryalabama .gov** to enter the address.

- In the Subject textbox, type **Unsubscribe to Newsletter** to enter a subject for the email (Figure 9–37).

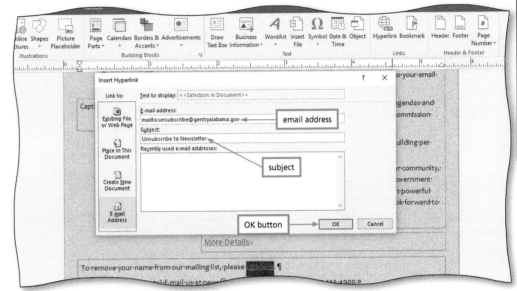

Figure 9–37

Q&A
Why did Publisher add the word, mailto, to the email address?
Because you clicked the E-mail Address button in the Link to bar, Publisher knows you want to create a mailto hyperlink and automatically creates the prefix for you.

How will Publisher use the text in the Subject text box?
When the user clicks the mailto link, Publisher will open an email message and fill in the Subject line of the email newsletter automatically with the entered text. That way, the recipient of the email will know that the request to unsubscribe came from an email newsletter rather than from the website or other mechanism.

3

- Click the OK button (Insert Hyperlink dialog box) to close the dialog box.

- Select the text, news@ gentryalabama.gov.

- Press CTRL+K to display the Insert Hyperlink dialog box.

- If necessary, click the E-mail Address button in the Link to bar (Insert Hyperlink dialog box).

- In the E-mail address text box, type **news@gentryalabama .gov** as the entry.

  If instructed to do so, enter your email address in the E-mail address text box.

- In the Subject text box, type **Inquiry from Website** as the entry (Figure 9–38).

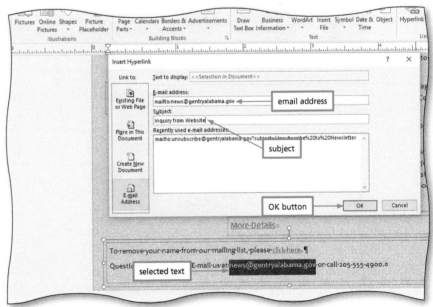

Figure 9–38

4

- Click the OK button (Insert Hyperlink dialog box) to create the mailto hyperlink.

Q&A
Will viewers of the email newsletter see the mailto prefix?
If users position the pointer over the link, the mailto prefix, colon, and email address may appear on their status bar.

Other Ways

1. Press CTRL+K, click E-mail Address button on Link to bar (Insert Hyperlink dialog box), enter email address, click OK button

To Create a Hot Spot

1 CREATE EMAIL PUBLICATION | 2 INSERT SYMBOLS | 3 USE RESEARCH TASK PANE | 4 CREATE HYPERLINKS
5 DISTRIBUTE EMAIL | 6 CREATE POSTCARD | 7 CREATE GREETING CARD | 8 USE DESIGN ACCENTS

The following steps turn the Alabama state outline graphic into a hot spot. *Why? City officials want the graphic to take readers to the city website.*

1

- Select the graphic that you wish to use as a hot spot (in this case, the state outline graphic at the top of the page).
- Click the 'Add a Hyperlink' button (Insert tab | Links group) to display the Insert Hyperlink dialog box.
- Click the 'Existing File or Web Page' button in the Link to bar.
- Click the Address arrow to display a list of recently used websites (Figure 9–39).

Q&A
What does the Address arrow do?
When you click the Address arrow, Publisher displays a list of previously used hyperlinks and hot spots. You can click from the list to save time.

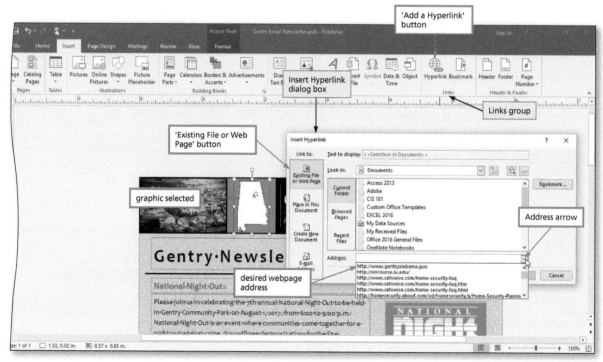

Figure 9–39

2

- Click http://www
.gentryalabama.gov
to select it
(Figure 9–40).

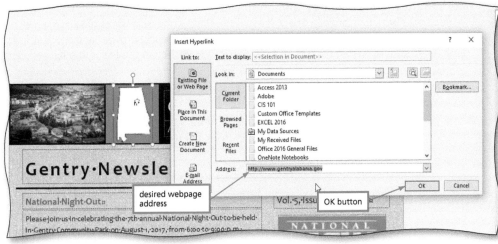

3

- Click the OK button
(Insert Hyperlink
dialog box) to create
the link.

Figure 9–40

Other Ways

1. Press CTRL+K, click 'Existing File or Web Page' button (Insert Hyperlink dialog box), enter address, click OK button

---

Design Issues in Email

Because email newsletters are generated electronically and are displayed in the user's email program, you must keep in mind several design issues. As with webpages, you want to make sure that the spacing, text, fonts, and hyperlinks are displayed correctly. HTML5, which is the most recent version of the scripting language, recommends that hyperlinks display in medium blue. Not all Publisher templates consistently apply that color; therefore, you may want to edit the color.

The Design Checker offers some specific checks for email publications that it does not perform with print publications. Table 9–3 displays the checks that Publisher uses to evaluate email publications.

Table 9–3 Design Issues

Object	Check Performed
HTML fragment	Looks for any HTML code fragment that is partially off the page
Hyperlink	Looks for instances in which a hyperlink on one webpage links to another page in a publication
Overlapping text	Looks for any object that is on top of a text box
Object	Looks for any object that is partially off a publication page
Object with text	Looks for any object that contains text and has been rotated
Shape with hyperlink	Looks for any shape that has a hyperlink on top of it
Table borders	Looks for instances in which a table has borders that are less than .75 point thick
Text box with zero margins	Looks for any text box that has a margin that is set to zero
Hyphenation	Looks for any hyphens in the text
Cell diagonal	Looks for text that is located in a diagonal table cell
Font	Looks for text that is not formatted in a web-safe font
Text overflow	Looks for any text box in which the text is too big
Vertical text	Looks for any text box that contains vertically rotated text

CONSIDER THIS

How should you check the email newsletter?
Proofread the newsletter carefully. Check the spelling. Check for design issues specific to email newsletters, including overlapping, hyphenation, fonts, and links. Preview the email publication in a browser and check all links. Consider sending the email newsletter to yourself first so that you can see how it will look before sending it to other recipients.

You can specify which checks Publisher will use when evaluating emails and other types of publications using the Design Checker Options dialog box.

To Edit the Color Scheme

1 CREATE EMAIL PUBLICATION | 2 INSERT SYMBOLS | 3 USE RESEARCH TASK PANE | 4 CREATE HYPERLINKS
5 DISTRIBUTE EMAIL | 6 CREATE POSTCARD | 7 CREATE GREETING CARD | 8 USE DESIGN ACCENTS

The following steps edit the color for hyperlinks. *Why? Using standard hyperlink colors help people recognize the links in your publication.* To change the colors, you will need to create a custom scheme.

 1

- Display the Page Design tab.

- Click the More button (Page Design tab | Schemes group) (visible in Figure 9–42) to display the Schemes gallery (Figure 9–41).

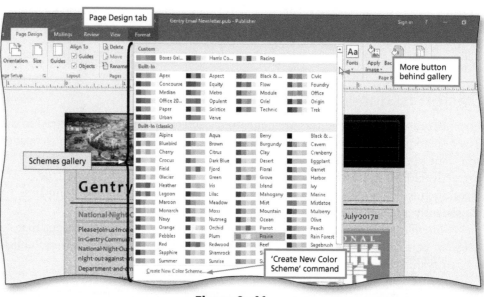

Figure 9–41

 2

- Click 'Create New Color Scheme' in the Schemes gallery to display the Create New Color Scheme dialog box.

- Click the Hyperlink arrow to display the color gallery and then click Blue to select the color (Figure 9–42).

Q&A
Should I change the followed hyperlink color or the name of the color scheme?
You can. The colors will stay with the document once it is saved. The name of the color scheme does not matter.

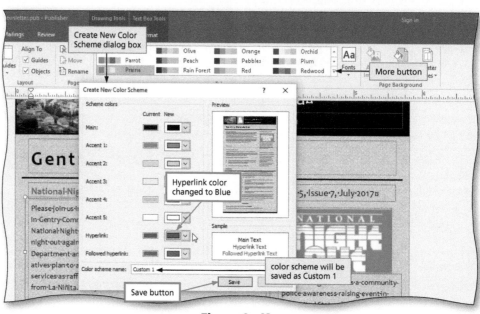

Figure 9–42

③

- Click the Save button (Create New Color Scheme dialog box).

⊘ Experiment

- Scroll through the email newsletter and look at the hyperlinks to verify their new color.

To Choose Design Checker Options

The following steps display the Design Checker dialog box. *Why? You should verify which Design Checker options will be used for email publications.*

①

- Click File on the ribbon to open the Backstage view.

- If necessary, click the Info tab and then click the 'Run Design Checker' button to open the Design Checker task pane.

- Click the 'Design Checker Options' link (Design Checker task pane) to display the Design Checker Options dialog box (Figure 9–43).

⊘ Experiment

- Click the Sort by button (Design Checker Options dialog box) and notice the options for sorting design issues.

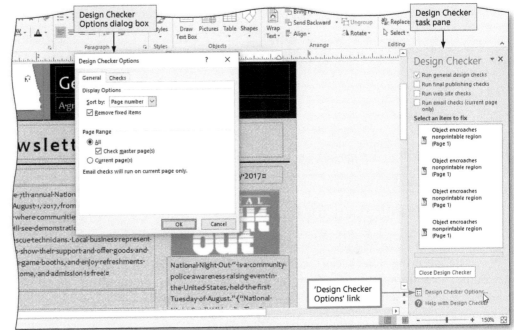

Figure 9–43

②

- Click the Checks tab (Design Checker Options dialog box) to view a list of all checks for all types of publications.

- Click the Show button to view the subcategories of checks (Figure 9–44).

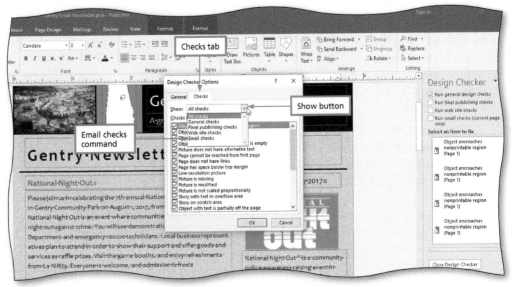

Figure 9–44

- Click Email checks to view the design issues that Publisher looks for in email publications.

- If necessary, click any check box that does not contain a check mark (Figure 9–45).

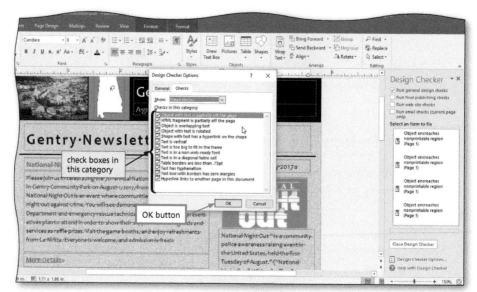

Figure 9–45

- Click the OK button (Design Checker Options dialog box) to apply the checks.

To Check a Publication for Email Design Errors

1 CREATE EMAIL PUBLICATION | 2 INSERT SYMBOLS | 3 USE RESEARCH TASK PANE | 4 CREATE HYPERLINKS
5 DISTRIBUTE EMAIL | 6 CREATE POSTCARD | 7 CREATE GREETING CARD | 8 USE DESIGN ACCENTS

The following step checks the publication for design errors specifically related to emails. You will encounter a common font error. Some email programs may not display the Vivaldi font correctly. *Why? The font may not be installed on the user's computer.* Therefore, Publisher will convert the font to a graphic so that the unique script font will be displayed correctly.

- With the Design Checker task pane still open, click to display a check mark in the 'Run email checks (current page only)' check box.

- Remove any other check marks in the task pane to display issues related only to emails (Figure 9–46).

Experiment

- Click the 'Help with Design Checker' link and read about the different kinds of design issues.

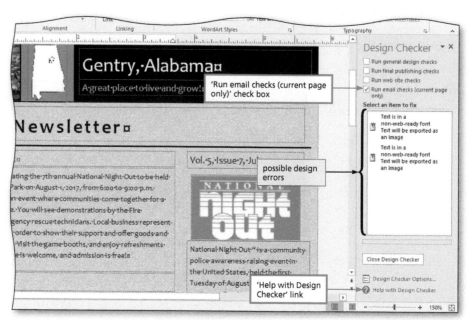

Figure 9–46

Troubleshooting Design Errors

Several kinds of errors may be displayed when running the Design Checker for email publications, such as an email newsletter. You may not see the same kind or number of errors as shown in the module figures, due to minor typing differences and resizing of objects. Table 9–4 displays some common errors in email design, possible resolutions, and pros and cons.

Table 9–4 Email Design Checker Errors			
Error Message	**Possible Resolution**	**Making the Change – Pros**	**Making the Change – Cons**
Text is too big to fit in the frame Text will be exported as an image	Click the error message arrow and then click the 'Fix: Reduce font size of text to fit' command.	The page will open slightly faster when someone views the email.	Reducing the font size will reduce readability slightly and may introduce many different fonts sizes, making the publication look sloppy.
Test is in a non-web-ready font Text will be exported as an image	Change the font scheme to include more popular web fonts, such as Arial, Helvetica, Times New Roman, Times, or Courier.	Publisher will not change any of the text to images.	In newer browsers and email viewers, the fonts will not be changed to images unless the font is extreme. Even, in that case, the fonts may be important to the branding of the company or the look and feel of the email.
Text has hyphenation Gaps may appear in some email viewers	Run a manual hyphenation check on the text box and choose not to hyphenate any words.	You never will have an unusual gap in the text of the email due to hyphenation.	Most email viewers can handle hyphens. You may have some unusual gaps if you do not hyphenate.
Object partially off page	Move the object to a location totally on the page or decide to delete it.	You should make the change.	The email will not be displayed correctly and may not even send correctly.
Object isn't visible	Go to the item and decide to bring it forward or delete it.	The email will be displayed faster.	The item will never be seen unless you bring it forward.

None of the issues listed in this publication is serious enough to elicit a change. If you want to make changes, click the arrow next to the issue, click 'Go to this Item' on the menu, and then perform the steps in the Possible Resolution column of Table 9–4. Other errors are described when you click the 'Help with Design Checker' link at the bottom of the Design Checker task pane.

To Check for Spelling Errors

The following steps check the publication for spelling errors.

1. If necessary, close the Design Checker task pane.

2. Press the F7 key to start the spelling check.

3. If necessary, correct any problems noted in the Check Spelling dialog box.

4. When Publisher asks if you want to check the rest of the publication, click the Yes button.

5. When Publisher notifies you that the spelling check is complete, click the OK button in the dialog box.

6. Save the publication again.

BTW
Hyperlink Colors
When hyperlink colors become standardized, the W3C (World Wide Web Consortium) that sponsors HTML5 will publish exact colors, such as the proposed blue with a hexadecimal number of #0000EE, or RGB (0, 0, 238).

Sending an Email Newsletter Using Publisher

Email publications can be sent to one or more people. Many organizations create a **listserv**, which is a list of interested people with email addresses who want to receive news and information email newsletters about the organization. A listserv email sends one email newsletter to everyone on the list. Listserv email newsletters always should contain an unsubscribe link that allows recipients to remove their names from the list to prevent receiving future email newsletters.

When you choose to send a publication, such as a newsletter, via email, Publisher displays special text boxes to allow you to enter the email addresses and subject line. Publisher also displays special buttons for email options (Figure 9–47).

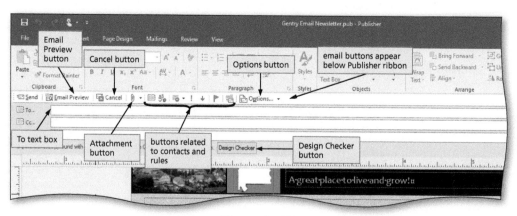

Figure 9–47

Before you send an email publication, you always should proofread it and then check it for design errors and spelling errors, as you did in the previous steps. With email publications, you also should preview the publication.

To Preview an Email Newsletter

1 CREATE EMAIL PUBLICATION | 2 INSERT SYMBOLS | 3 USE RESEARCH TASK PANE | 4 CREATE HYPERLINKS
5 DISTRIBUTE EMAIL | **6 CREATE POSTCARD** | **7 CREATE GREETING CARD** | **8 USE DESIGN ACCENTS**

The following steps describe how to preview an email newsletter. *Why? You want to see how it will look on the user's computer.*

- Click File on the ribbon to open the Backstage view.
- Click the Share tab to view the Share gallery.
- Click Email Preview in the Share gallery (Figure 9–48).

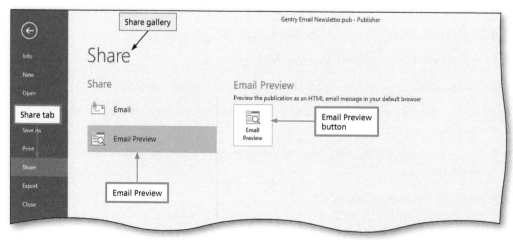

Figure 9–48

2

- Click the Email Preview button in the right pane to preview the email publication in your default browser. If necessary, double-click the browser title bar to maximize the window (Figure 9–49).

Q&A My publication did not appear. Did I do something wrong?
Your default browser may not be compatible with Publisher. Try using Internet Explorer or Chrome.

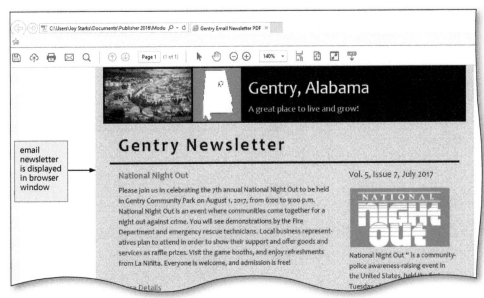

email newsletter is displayed in browser window

Figure 9–49

 Experiment

- Scroll through the email newsletter and try clicking the other hyperlinks. The city's website is fictional and will not be displayed, but the 'click here' hyperlink will display an email dialog box if your system is configured with an email program, such as Microsoft Outlook.

3

- Close all browser windows.

To Send an Email Newsletter Using Publisher

1 CREATE EMAIL PUBLICATION | 2 INSERT SYMBOLS | 3 USE RESEARCH TASK PANE | 4 CREATE HYPERLINKS
5 DISTRIBUTE EMAIL | **6 CREATE POSTCARD** | **7 CREATE GREETING CARD** | **8 USE DESIGN ACCENTS**

The following steps send an email newsletter using Publisher's Send Email command. *Why? Sending an email using Publisher saves the extra steps of running an email program and copying and pasting the newsletter in the message.* You do not actually have to send the email newsletter, nor do you have to be connected to the Internet to perform the steps.

1

- Click File on the ribbon to open the Backstage view.

- Click the Share tab to view the Share gallery.

- If necessary, click Email in the Share gallery (Figure 9–50).

Q&A What is the purpose of the 'Send as PDF' and 'Send as XPS' buttons?
Depending on which button you click, Publisher converts the current document to either the PDF or XPS format and then attaches the PDF or XPS document to the email newsletter.

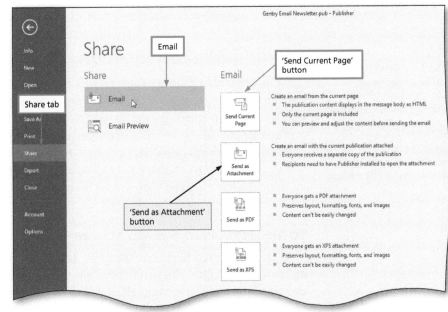

Figure 9–50

Q&A Do most people prefer to receive a publication as an email attachment?
It is not necessarily better to use attachments. For immediate viewing, such as an announcement, letter, or card, it is better to send a single page in the body of an email newsletter. If you do send an attachment, the person receiving your email newsletter must have Publisher installed on his or her computer in order to open and view the publication. Additionally, with a large attachment, you may run the risk of the email newsletter being blocked by firewalls and filters at the receiving end.

2

- Click the 'Send Current Page' button (Share gallery) to display the boxes and buttons used for emailing (Figure 9–51).

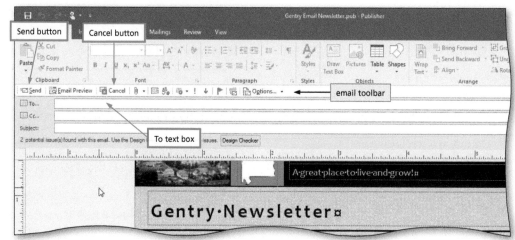

Figure 9–51

Q&A What if my computer wants to configure Outlook to send an email newsletter?
If you are not sure how to configure your computer for email, or you do not want to check your email via an email program, click the Cancel button on the email toolbar. Configuring your computer with an email program is not complicated, however. Windows 10 asks for your name, your email address, and your password. It then determines the kind of email program and connection you need.

3

- If you want to send the email newsletter, type your email address in the To text box, enter a subject in the Subject text box, and then click the Send button on the email toolbar. Otherwise, to cancel the request, click the Cancel button on the email toolbar.

Q&A What if I want to send an email newsletter to someone who does not have Publisher installed?
Email newsletters appear in the body of the email and do not require Publisher. If you are sending an attachment and are worried that your recipient may not have Publisher installed on his or her computer, you can send your publication in a different format. Publisher can create PDF files or XPS files, which have free or inexpensive viewers. Once converted, the files then can be attached to an email.

BTW
Mailto Hyperlinks
A mailto hyperlink communicates with the operating system to discover the default email program. Publisher then creates the underlying code to make the hyperlink run the program when a user clicks the link.

Sending Print Publications as Email Newsletters

In general, it is better to start with an email publication template, such as an email letter or email newsletter. If, however, you want to send a page of another publication as an email newsletter, you may need to modify the width and margins to ensure that the message will be displayed attractively for email recipients. The typical page size of an email newsletter is 5.818 by 11 inches, which ensures the recipients will not need to scroll horizontally to view the entire width of the message. Publisher allows only one page at a time sent as an email.

TO MODIFY THE PAPER SIZE AND MARGINS

If you wanted to change the page design settings of a print publication to create an email publication, you would perform the following steps. It is a good idea to send the email publication to yourself first, so that you can view the publication and look for problems.

1. Click the Page Setup Dialog Box Launcher (Page Design tab | Page Setup group) to display the Page Setup dialog box.
2. Click the Layout type button (Page Setup dialog box) and then click Email in the list.
3. Enter the new width and height measurements in the Width and Height boxes.
4. Click the OK button.

To Save and Close the Publication

The email newsletter is complete. The following steps save and close the publication.

1 Click the Save button on the Quick Access Toolbar to overwrite the previously saved file.

2 Open the Backstage view.

3 Click the Close button in the Backstage view. If Publisher offers to save the publication again, click the Don't Save button.

Break Point: If you wish to take a break, this is a good place to do so. Exit Publisher. To resume at a later time, run Publisher, and continue following the steps from this location forward.

Postcards

A **postcard** is a rectangular piece of mail intended for writing and sending without an envelope. People use postcards for greetings, announcements, reminders, and business contacts. Most postcards are rectangular, at least 3½ inches high and 5 inches long — some are larger. A common size is 4 inches by 6 inches.

What should I consider when deciding to attach a Publisher file to an email message?
Publications created for print must be attached as a separate file when using email, especially when converting the publication is not possible. Remember that users must have Publisher installed in order to open a publication. If you are unsure, save the publication in the PDF or XPS format and attach it. For large publications and multipage publications, consider compressing the file.

Many times, a postcard is an effective marketing tool used to generate prospective leads at a low cost. Businesses and organizations produce a postcard with a photo, graphic, advertisement, or postcard. Some postcards, such as picture postcards, leave space on one side to write a brief message. People purchase picture postcards to mail to friends or to serve as reminders of their vacation. Sometimes, a picture postcard is mailed to attract attention and direct people to websites or business locations. A postcard must portray its message or theme clearly in an eye-catching manner, keeping in mind the relevant audience.

Publisher has several postcard templates, including postcards for marketing, calendars, and real estate, as well as many blank templates to create postcards from scratch. In the past, postcards typically have been mailed using a postal service; however, many companies and individuals are sending **e-postcards**, or electronic postcards, electronically as attachments. An **attachment** is an electronic file sent along with an email newsletter; however, the recipient must perform some steps to open the file — it does not display within the body of the email newsletter. Table 9–5 displays some of the best practices for attachments.

BTW
Email Marketing
Using email for marketing purposes has many benefits, including low cost, immediate communications, interactivity, and the ability to contact multiple customers. It makes it easy to track positive and negative responses, visits to webpages, and increases in specific product sales. Considerate and thoughtful email marketing can reinforce positive interactions with your business.

Table 9–5 Best Practices for Attachments

Practice	Reasoning
Post or publish large attachments.	It is better to post large files on the web or on a shared resource, when possible.
Limit your attachments to under 5 megabytes.	Check with your Internet service provider (ISP) to verify the maximum allowable size of attachments.
Send multiple attachments using several email newsletters.	Some email programs have per-message limits.
Use compressed graphic file formats.	Smaller graphics are more likely to be opened and viewed.
Employ a file compression utility.	File compressing, sometimes called zipping, reduces the file size and keeps files together.
Review your Sent Items folder.	Emails and attachments take up room in the sender's email as well as the recipient's. Delete older sent items as necessary.

To Open a Postcard Template

The following steps open a postcard template.

1. In the template gallery, click BUILT-IN to display the BUILT-IN templates.

2. Scroll as necessary and then click the Postcards thumbnail in the BUILT-IN templates to display the Postcards templates.

3. Click the All Marketing folder.

4. Scroll down to the section labeled More Installed Templates and then scroll to the Special Offer templates.

5. Click the Floating Oval thumbnail to choose the template.

6. If necessary, click the Color scheme button and choose Prairie.

7. If necessary, click the Font scheme button and choose Concourse.

8. Click the CREATE button to create the publication using the selected template (Figure 9–52).

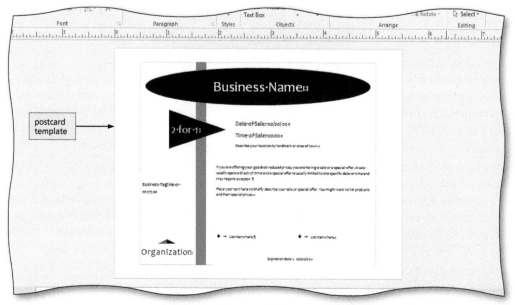

Figure 9–52

To Edit a Postcard

The following steps edit the text fields and graphics in the postcard. To complete these steps, you will be required to use the Data Files. Please contact your instructor for information about accessing the Data Files.

1. Select the Business Name placeholder text at the top of the page. Type `Gentry Park District` to replace the text. Select the text again and then press CTRL+B to bold the text.

2. Delete the first three text boxes below the heading.

3. Select the text in the description text box. Type `As a frequent participant in our Park District programs, you are invited to bring a friend the next time you register for free. Bring this postcard with you.` and then press the ENTER key. Type `Call 205-555-1725 or visit our website at gentryalabama.gov/parkdistrict` to enter the last line of text.

4. Underline the words, for free.

5. Right-click the text and then click Best Fit on the shortcut menu. Hyphenate the text if necessary.

6. Delete the text box that displays the bulleted items.

7. Replace the expiration date with the date, 12/31/2017.

8. Select the placeholder text in the Business Tagline or Motto text box. Type `A great place to live and grow!` to replace the text.

9. Delete the organization logo (Figure 9–53).

10. Save the publication on your desired save location using the file name, Park District Postcard.

BTW

Email Service Providers

Many email service providers use a browser interface, so setting up an email program is not necessary. Corporate and business communications commonly use the Microsoft Outlook email program, which allows access to email addresses for everyone in the company, along with tools to manage other forms of communication and scheduling.

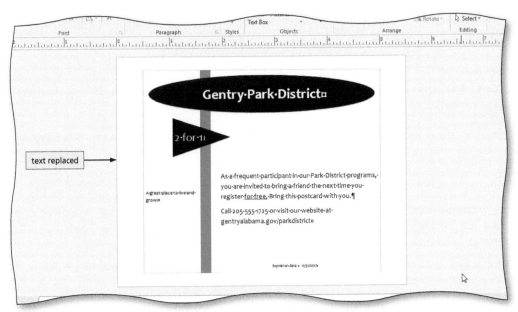

Figure 9–53

To Send a Postcard as an Attachment

The following steps send the postcard as an attachment to an email message. *Why? That way, users can download the attachment and print the postcard as a coupon.* You do not have to be connected to the Internet or have an email program installed on your computer in order to perform these steps.

1

- Open the Backstage view.

- If necessary, click the Share tab and then click Email.

- Click the 'Send as Attachment' button (shown in Figure 9–50) to open the Untitled Message (HTML) window (Figure 9–54).

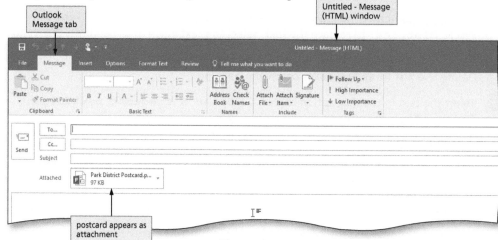

Figure 9–54

Q&A Publisher asked me to set up a user profile. Should I do that?
On your computer, you may not have a default email program as Publisher expects. You do not have to set up a user profile; you can close the publication and proceed to the next set of steps.

2

- In the To text box, type **listserv@ gentryalabama .parkdistrict .gov** to enter the name of the Park District's mailing list.

- In the Subject text box, type **Join us again at the Gentry Park District** to enter the subject.

- Click the message area. Type **Hello friends,** and then press the ENTER key twice.

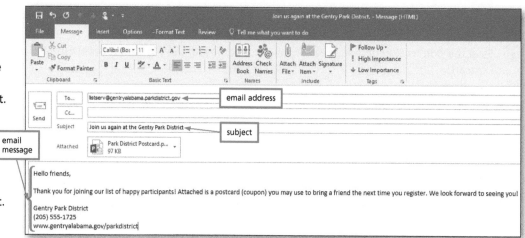

Figure 9–55

- Type **Thank you for joining our list of happy participants! Attached is a postcard (coupon) you may use to bring a friend the next time you register. We look forward to seeing you!** and then press the ENTER key twice.

- Type **Gentry Park District** and press the ENTER key. Type **(205) 555-1725** and press the ENTER key. Type **www.gentryalabama.gov/parkdistrict** to finish the message (Figure 9–55).

3

- If you want to send the email attachment, replace the email address with your own and then click the Send button to send the email message along with its attachment and to close the email window. Otherwise, close the Untitled Message (HTML) window without saving.

- Close the publication without exiting Publisher.

Break Point: If you wish to take a break, this is a good place to do so. Exit Publisher. To resume at a later time, run Publisher, and continue following the steps from this location forward.

Greeting Cards

A **greeting card** is a folded card, usually with pictures or illustrations that conveys an expression of friendship, holiday greetings, or other sentiment. Greeting cards can be mailed using a postal service, or they can be sent as e-cards using web services or email. In Publisher, the greeting card templates include categories such as birthdays, holidays, special occasions, and thank-yous. The greeting cards can be folded in half or in quarters and may contain a variety of layouts, in addition to the usual color and font schemes. Publisher also contains blank greeting card templates.

Creating a greeting card is no different from creating other publications. You need only to be mindful of how the pages and folds are organized. In the Publisher workspace, page 1 is the front of the card, pages 2 and 3 are the inside of the card, and page 4 is the back of the card. When you print using a standard paper size, all four pages will print on a single side of one piece of paper. The inside of the card will print upside down in comparison to the front and the back; however, folding remedies that. Your other option is to purchase special greeting card paper and direct Publisher to print pages 1 and 4 on the front and pages 2 and 3 on the back. These choices are available in the Print gallery in the Backstage view.

In this module, you will create a holiday card to be sent out from the mayor's office.

To Customize a Greeting Card Template

1 CREATE EMAIL PUBLICATION | 2 INSERT SYMBOLS | 3 USE RESEARCH TASK PANE | 4 CREATE HYPERLINKS
5 DISTRIBUTE EMAIL | 6 CREATE POSTCARD | **7 CREATE GREETING CARD** | **8 USE DESIGN ACCENTS**

The following steps open a greeting card template and make changes to the layout. *Why? Publisher offers several different layouts for each kind of greeting card. Selecting a different layout will create a unique card.*

1

- In the New template gallery, click BUILT-IN and then click the Greeting Cards thumbnail.

- Click the All Holidays folder.

- Scroll to the Holiday area and then click the Holiday 5 thumbnail in the list of templates.

- If necessary, click the Color scheme button and choose Prairie.

- If necessary, click the Font scheme button and choose the Concourse font scheme (Figure 9–56).

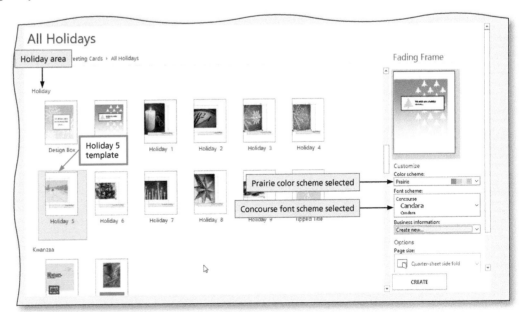

Figure 9–56

• Scroll in the
Customize area,
and then click
the Layout
button
(Figure 9–57).

⊘ Experiment

• One at a time,
click each of the
layouts. Notice
the changes in
the thumbnails
and preview.
Click the Layout
button again.

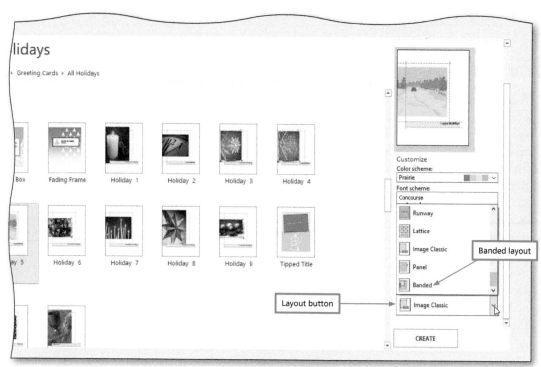

Figure 9–57

• Click the
Banded
layout
(Figure 9–58).

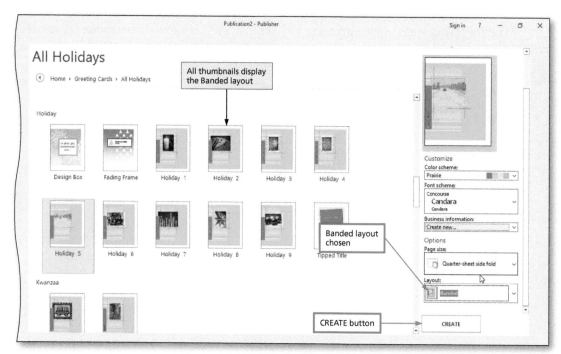

Figure 9–58

4

- Click the CREATE button.

- Click the Page Number button on the Publisher taskbar to display the Page Navigation pane (Figure 9–59).

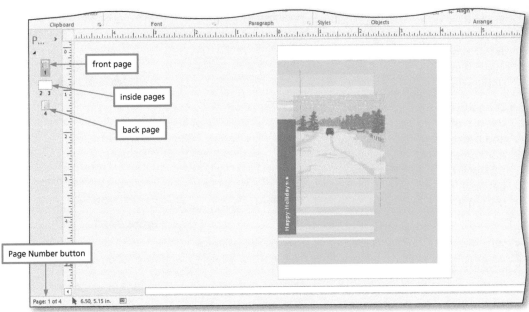

Figure 9–59

To Insert a Design Accent

1 CREATE EMAIL PUBLICATION | 2 INSERT SYMBOLS | 3 USE RESEARCH TASK PANE | 4 CREATE HYPERLINKS
5 DISTRIBUTE EMAIL | 6 CREATE POSTCARD | 7 CREATE GREETING CARD | **8 USE DESIGN ACCENTS**

Recall that you have applied borders to tables and to pages in earlier modules. The Borders & Accents gallery, part of the Building Block library, contains even more choices for your publications. A design **accent** is a graphic added for emphasis or flair, such as a bar, box, line, frame, or pattern. Unlike other graphics, accents are meant to fill the area; for example, line and bar accents increase the number of pattern repetitions as they are resized. Accents will display the same color scheme as your publication.

Accents are used as headers, mastheads, and in other places in a publication where the page may need some delineation or highlighting. The following steps insert a design accent on page 3. *Why? The page is rather plain and does not accentuate the town colors.*

1

- Navigate to the two-page spread for pages 2 and 3 and then display the Insert tab.

- Click the 'Borders & Accents' button (Insert tab | Building Blocks group) to display its gallery (Figure 9–60).

🔎 **Experiment**

- Scroll through the selections in the Borders & Accents gallery to see the different types of borders and accents.

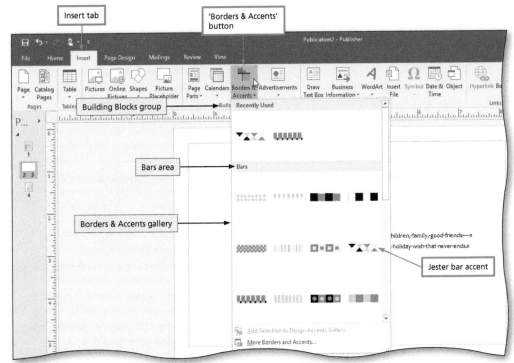

Figure 9–60

2
- In the Bars area, double-click the Jester accent to insert it into the publication.
- Drag the accent to the top of page 3 and resize it horizontally to fill the area between margins (Figure 9–61).

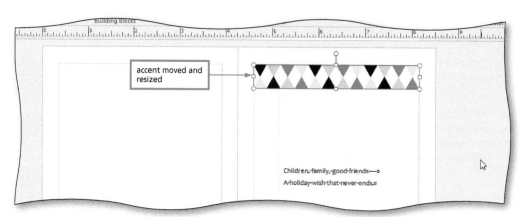

Figure 9–61

Q&A Why did the number of triangles in the pattern increase?

Accents such as the Jester bar are repeating patterns built specifically to fill and repeat.

To Edit Text on Page 3

The following steps insert text on page 3 of the greeting card.

1 Click the lower text box on page 3 and position the insertion point at the end of the current text.

2 Press the ENTER key three times.

3 Type **Mayor Mike Neilson** to enter the text, press the ENTER key, and then type **Gentry, Alabama** (Figure 9–62).

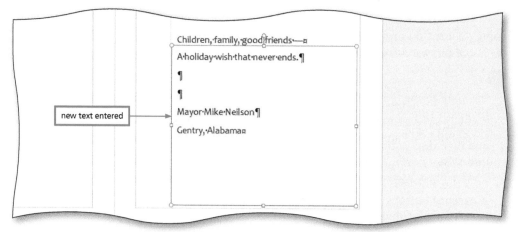

Figure 9–62

BTW
Emails from Print Publications
In the Backstage view, you can click the Share tab to share the current print publication as an email message. Publisher 2016 sends one print page at a time. If a print publication is multiple pages, it is better to include it as a Publisher or PDF attachment.

To Edit Text on Page 4

The following steps insert text on page 4 of the greeting card.

1 Navigate to page 4 and zoom to 140%.

2 Select the text in the last text box on page 4 and then type **the office of Mike Neilson** to replace the text (Figure 9–63).

If instructed to do so, insert your name in the text box rather than the text in Step 2.

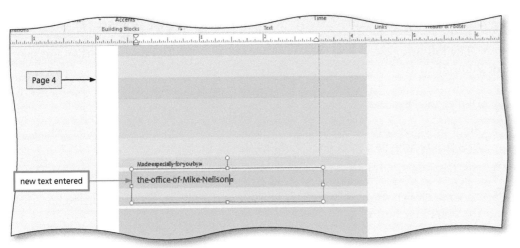

Figure 9–63

③ Save the publication on your desired save location using the file name, Mayor Holiday Card.

To Print a Folded Publication

The following steps print the greeting card using a single sheet of 8.5 × 11-inch paper. *Why? Unless you have special greeting card paper, an 8.5 × 11-inch piece of paper is the easiest way to print all four pages and fold them for a greeting card.*

①

- Open the Backstage view and then click the Print tab to display the Print gallery.

- Make sure your printer is displayed as the current printer.

- If necessary, click the first button in the Settings area and then click 'Print All Pages'.

- If necessary, type **1-4** in the Pages text box.

- If necessary, click the second button in the Settings area and then click 'Side-fold, quarter sheet' (Figure 9–64).

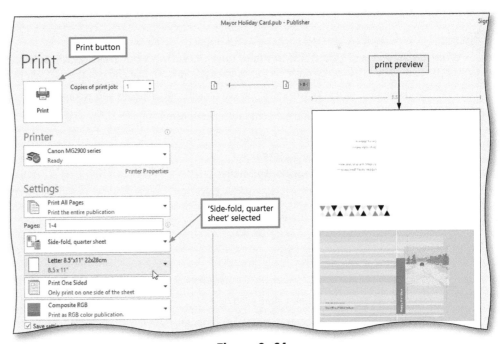

Figure 9–64

Experiment

- Click the 'Side-fold, quarter sheet' button to view the other printing possibilities.

②

- Click the Print button to print the publication.

- Retrieve the printout and fold the card.

To Delete the Custom Color Scheme and Exit Publisher

The following steps delete the custom color scheme you created earlier and then exit Publisher.

1 Display the Page Design tab.

2 Right-click the Custom 1 color scheme (Page Design tab | Schemes group) and then click Delete Scheme on shortcut menu.

3 When Publisher displays a dialog box asking if you are sure, click the Yes button.

4 Click the Close button on the Publisher title bar. If Publisher displays a dialog box, click the Don't Save button.

Summary

In this module, you learned how to create an email newsletter. First you selected and formatted an email template. Then you learned how to edit the background, text boxes, and graphics in an email publication. Next, you learned how to insert a symbol and special character. You created hyperlinks, hot spots, and mailto hyperlinks. After checking the publication for design errors and previewing the email newsletter, you sent the publication as an email newsletter. You also created a postcard and learned how to send a publication as an attachment. Finally, you created a publication for regular mail distribution as you designed and printed a greeting card with an accent.

CONSIDER THIS: PLAN AHEAD

What decisions will you need to make when creating your next email publication?
Use these guidelines as you complete the assignments in this module and create your own publications outside of this class.

1. Decide on the purpose of the email publication and gather stories and pictures.

2. Choose an appropriate template, font, and color scheme.

    a) Adjust the page length as necessary.

    b) Choose an appropriate background.

3. Use consistent styles for headings and stories.

4. Resize and fit pictures to fill the appropriate areas.

5. If necessary, insert special characters and symbols.

6. Cite any quoted materials.

7. Insert hyperlinks, hot spots, and mailto hyperlinks.

8. Use design checks geared toward email publications.

9. Preview the email publication before sending it.

10. Attach publications, such as postcards, when appropriate.

11. When creating greeting cards, customize the template.

    a) Choose an appropriate layout.

    b) Use a design accent where appropriate.

Apply Your Knowledge

Reinforce the skills and apply the concepts you learned in this module.

Editing an Email Newsletter

Note: To complete this assignment, you will be required to use the Data Files. Please contact your instructor for information about accessing the Data Files.

Instructions: Run Publisher and open the file named Apply 9–1 Family Newsletter from the Data Files. You are to add a page background and insert pictures, hyperlinks, and a symbol to create the email publication shown in Figure 9–65.

Perform the following tasks:

1. Save the publication with the file name, Apply 9–1 Family Newsletter Complete, on your storage location.

2. Zoom to 150% and scroll to the top of the page.

3. Click the 'Choose Page Size' button (Page Design tab | Page Setup group) to display the Choose Page Size gallery and then click Short in the gallery to choose a short page format.

4. Click the Background button (Page Design tab | Page Background group), and then click More Backgrounds in the gallery to display the Format Background dialog box.

5. Click the Pattern Fill option button and then choose the Dotted diamond pattern. Change the foreground color to 'Accent 2 (RGB (254,134, 55)) Lighter 80%', and change the background color to 'Accent 5 (White)'. Click the OK button to close the Format Background dialog box.

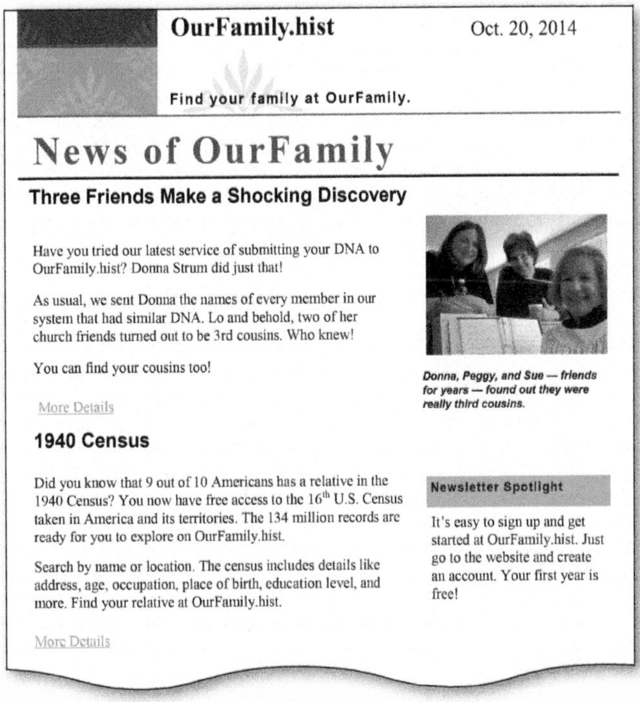

Figure 9–65

6. Right-click the picture at the upper-right side of the email newsletter and then use the Change Picture command to insert the Cousins.jpg graphic from the Data Files. Delete the original picture from the scratch area.

7. Click the Fit button (Picture Tools Format tab | Crop group) to fit the picture in the picture placeholder. Crop the top and bottom of the picture to remove the extra white space. Resize the picture to fit the area.

8. In the caption of the picture, select the first hyphen. Click the 'Insert a Symbol' button (Insert tab | Text group). Click the More Symbols command to display the Symbol dialog box. Click the Special Characters tab (Symbol dialog box), and then click 'Em Dash (—)' in the list. Click the Insert button and then click the Close button.

9. Repeat Steps 5 through 7 to replace the other picture with the picture named Daisy Malson. Resize the picture to fit the area.

10. Select the first occurrence of the placeholder text, More Details. Click the 'Add a Hyperlink' button (Insert tab | Links group) to display the Insert Hyperlink dialog box.

Continued >

11. If necessary, click the 'Existing File or Web Page' button in the Link to bar (Insert Hyperlink dialog box) and then type `OurFamily.hist` in the Address box.

12. Repeat Steps 10 and 11 for each occurrence of the words, More Details.

13. In the text box at the bottom of the page, select the text, click here. Press CTRL+K to display the Insert Hyperlink dialog box. In the Link to bar, click the E-mail Address button. In the E-mail address text box, type `unsubscribe@OurFamily.hist`. In the Subject text box, type `Unsubscribe to Newsletter`. Click the OK button to close the dialog box.

14. In the text box at the bottom of the page, select the text, questions@OurFamily.hist. Repeat the process in Step 13 to create a mailto hyperlink with `questions@OurFamily.hist` as the email address and `Inquiry from Newsletter` as the subject.

15. If instructed to do so, enter your email address in the E-mail address text box.

16. Open the Backstage view. If necessary, click the Info tab and then click the 'Run Design Checker' button to open the Design Checker task pane.

17. Click the 'Design Checker Options' link in the Design Checker task pane. Click the Checks tab (Design Checker Options dialog box) and then click the Show button. Click Email checks to view the design issues that Publisher looks for in email publications. If necessary, click any check box that does not contain a check mark. Click the OK button.

18. In the Design Checker task pane, click to display a check mark in the 'Run email checks (current page only)' check box. Remove any other check marks in the task pane. Correct any problems listed and then close the Design Checker task pane.

19. Open the Backstage view and then click the Share tab. Click Email Preview in the Share gallery and then click the Email Preview button. When you are done previewing, close the browser window.

20. Save the email publication again with the same file name and then exit Publisher.

21. If you have permission, send the publication to your instructor as an email newsletter.

22. ✳ People who read email newsletters do so because of topical or visual interest. What changes could you make to the top portion of this email to make it more striking and encourage readers to open it? What words would you use in the subject line?

Extend Your Knowledge

Extend the skills you learned in this module and experiment with new skills. You may need to use Help to complete the assignment.

Creating Links Using Bookmarks

Note: To complete this assignment, you will be required to use the Data Files. Please contact your instructor for information about accessing the Data Files.

Instructions: Run Publisher. Open the publication, Extend 9-1 Vehicle Diagnostics Email, from the Data Files. You will edit the email newsletter that uses the Long page design by creating links that help the viewer move down the page to inserted bookmarks (Figure 9–66).

Perform the following tasks:

1. Use Help to learn more about inserting bookmarks in Publisher.

2. Click the Bookmark button (Insert tab | Links group) to display the Bookmark dialog box.

3. Type `Vehicle Maintenance` in the Bookmark name text box to assign a name to the bookmark and then click the Add button (Bookmarks dialog box) to close the dialog box.

4. When Publisher displays the bookmark symbol as an object in the publication, drag the symbol to the correct location in the publication, in this case, beside the Vehicle Maintenance heading as shown in Figure 9–66.

5. Deselect the Bookmark.

6. Repeat Steps 2 through 5 for each of the other headings: Vehicle Diagnostics, Vehicle History, ConnectNow, and Dealer Location.

7. With the bookmarks assigned and positioned, scroll to the top of the page.

8. Select the text, Vehicle Maintenance, in the In this report area, and then press CTRL+K to display the Insert Hyperlink dialog box.

9. In the Link to bar (Insert Hyperlink dialog box), click the 'Place in This Document' button. *Hint:* If a plus sign appears beside any of the places listed in the Select a place in this document box, click the plus sign to display the embedded locations. Click Vehicle Maintenance in the Select a place in this document box and then click the OK button to close the dialog box.

10. Repeat Steps 8 and 9 for the other four links at the top of the page: Vehicle Diagnostics, Vehicle History, ConnectNow, and Dealer Location.

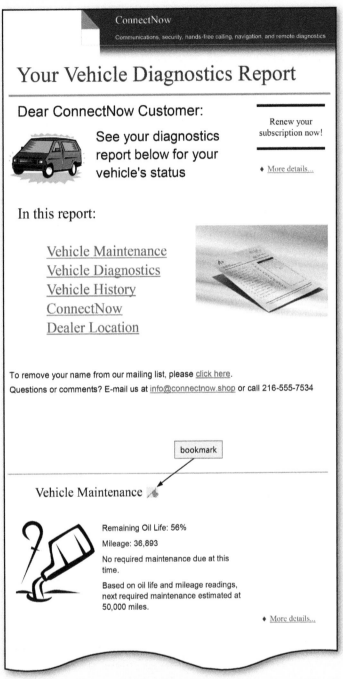

Figure 9–66

11. If instructed to do so, draw a text box and create a hyperlink with your email address.

12. Save the publication with the file name, Extend 9–1 Vehicle Diagnostics Email Complete.

13. Check the publication for design errors related to email newsletters. Save the revised publication and then send it as an attachment to your instructor.

14. Exit Publisher.

15. ✷ How is a bookmark within a Publisher document different from a same page hyperlink on the web? Same page hyperlinks, such as those on an FAQ page, are popular on the web. Make a list of some uses for same page hyperlinks.

Expand Your World

Create a solution that uses cloud and web technologies by learning and investigating on your own from general guidance.

Attaching a Word Cloud

Note: To complete this assignment, you will be required to use the Data Files. Please contact your instructor for information about accessing the Data Files.

Instructions: Open the publication, Expand 9–1 Module Terms from the Data Files. You have decided to make an interactive word cloud about the terms in this module. A word cloud, or tag cloud, is a visual representation of words taken from lists, documents, or websites. An interactive word cloud allows you to click words within the graphic to generate definitions or searches. You create the graphic shown in Figure 9–67 using Tagxedo.com. You must have Silverlight installed on your system to run Tagxedo. Most browsers already have Silverlight; if yours does not, see your instructor for ways to access Silverlight.

Perform the following tasks:

1. Click in the list and then press CTRL+A to select all of terms. Press CTRL+C to copy all of the terms.

2. Run a browser and then navigate to http://www.tagxedo.com/app.html.

3. Click the Start button.

4. On the left navigation bar, click the Load button, click the Enter Text box (Load menu dialog box), and then press CTRL+V to paste the terms. Click the Submit button.

5. One at a time, click each of the arrows: Theme, Font, Orientation, and Shape, and then choose a setting from the menu.

6. Point to any of the words in your word cloud to watch what happens.

7. Click the Save | Share button, and then click the Web tab. Enter your name and a title for your interactive word cloud. Click the Submit button.

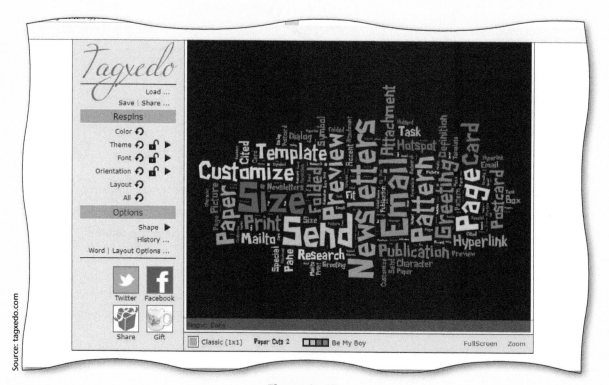

Source: tagxedo.com

Figure 9–67

8. Copy the web address of your interactive word cloud and send it as directed to your instructor.

9. Click one of the social media buttons in the lower-left corner of the Tagxedo window and send the graphic to your favorite social media.

10. Run a browser and paste the web address in the address bar. When your interactive word cloud appears, click a term and watch the search or definition appear.

11. ✳ Make a list of various reasons you might want to create an interactive word cloud. What kind of word lists might you use? Think of other documents or websites that you might use to create a word cloud.

In the Labs

Design, create, modify, and/or use a publication following the guidelines, concepts, and skills presented in this module. Labs 1 and 2, which increase in difficulty, require you to create solutions based on what you learned in the module; Lab 3 requires you to apply your creative thinking and problem-solving skills to design and implement a solution.

Lab 1: **Creating an Email Featured Product List**

Problem: You work for a company that sells music on the web. Your boss wants you to send an email newsletter to all previous customers advertising the newest songs. You decide to use a Publisher Email Featured Product template to design the email newsletter shown in Figure 9–68.

Perform the following tasks:

1. Run Publisher. Choose the Watermark Featured Product Email template (Choose E-mail from the BUILT-IN templates, scroll down to More Installed Templates, and then choose Watermark from the Featured Product templates). Select the Metro color scheme and the Foundry font scheme and then create the publication.

2. On the Page Design tab, choose the Short page size in the Choose Page Size gallery.

Figure 9–68

Continued >

STUDENT ASSIGNMENTS

In The Labs *continued*

3. Add a background to the email newsletter by clicking the Background button (Page Design tab | Page Background group) and then choosing a solid background of 10% tint of Accent 1.

4. Replace the Business Name placeholder with the words, Web Songs. Use the phrase, Our web songs are safe and spyware free!, as the tag line text.

5. Replace the logo graphic by using Bing search using the keyword, media. Review the specific license for any image you plan to use, even for educational purposes, to ensure you have the right to use the image.

6. Replace the logo text with the words, Web Songs.

7. Replace the large graphic with the data file named Lab 9–1 Band. If necessary, click the Fit button (Picture Tools Format tab | Crop group). Crop any blank space from the picture and resize as shown in Figure 9–68.

8. Search for a graphic using the keyword, portable device, and insert it toward the bottom of the page, above and to the right of the 'To remove your name' text box.

9. Describe your favorite artist or song in the lower text boxes.

10. Edit the hyperlink at the bottom to reflect your email address.

11. If instructed to do so, change the phone number in the middle of the page to your phone number.

12. Check the publication for spelling and design errors.

13. Save the publication with the file name, Lab 9–1 Web Songs Email. Preview the email.

14. If you have permission, send the publication to your instructor as an email newsletter. Include an appropriate subject line in the Subject text box.

15. ✸ How do the Email Featured Product templates differ from the Email Newsletter templates? Examine some of the other categories and make a list of distinguishing features of each kind.

Lab 2: **Using Symbols and the Research Task Pane**

Note: To complete this assignment, you will be required to use the Data Files. Please contact your instructor for information about accessing the Data Files.

Problem: A local company has asked you to apply formatting to their job advertisement flyer. You will use symbols, patterns, and the Research task pane. You also will insert a picture and fit it to the picture placeholder. The edited advertisement appears in Figure 9–69.

Perform the following tasks:

1. Run Publisher. Open the file, Lab 9–2 Advertisement. Save the file with the name Lab 9–2 Advertisement Complete.

2. Add a pattern background to the publication using the 70% pattern, an orange foreground, and a light orange background.

3. Replace the picture placeholder with the data file named Lab 9–2 Girl. Fit the picture, crop the blank areas, and then resize as shown in Figure 9–69.

4. Use the Symbol dialog box to insert an inverted question mark before the word, Se, in the Spanish phrase. In the word, ingles, change the e to an é. In the word, espanol, change the letter n to a ñ.

Figure 9–69

5. Use the Research task pane to look up a definition for the word, job. Then create a text box and summarize the definition in your own words. Resize the text and the text box to fit the area to the right of the word, JOB.

6. If instructed to do so, send the publication to your instructor as an email attachment. Include an appropriate subject line with your name and assignment number.

7. ✺ Native speakers of languages other than English use standard computer keyboards. How do you think they enter all of the diacritical marks used in their language? Do you think they rely on the Symbol dialog box? Why or why not?

Lab 3: **Consider This: Your Turn**

Creating a Greeting Card

Problem: In your position as an intern for a hospitality firm, you have been asked to create some sample greeting cards that the owner can send out to clients. You decide to investigate the greeting card templates in Publisher.

Perform the following tasks:

Part 1:   Look through the greeting card templates in Publisher's New template gallery. Choose four different templates with different kinds of messages. For each, choose a different color and font scheme. Create one as a half-page side fold, one as a half-page top fold, one as a quarter-page side fold, and one as a quarter-page top fold. Save each one with a descriptive file name. Print and fold the greeting cards. Choose your favorite, open it again, and tailor it to a specific person, event, gift, or holiday. Include a picture. On the back page, create a text box with the words, Custom created by, and then include your name.

Part 2:   ✺ Which of the greeting cards seems more professional-looking? Why?

10 | Editing Large-Scale Publications

Objectives

You will have mastered the material in this module when you can:

- Insert, collapse, expand, and merge sections
- Specify starting page numbers and their associated formats
- Remove page numbers from specific pages
- Set text box and cell margins
- Use preset guide patterns
- Duplicate pages

- Link text boxes across pages
- Use the Clipboard task pane
- Find and replace text
- Replace a word using the thesaurus
- Use the 'Go to Page' command
- Navigate through a publication
- Create breaks and bookmarks

Introduction

Large-scale publications — those consisting of 10 pages or more — require special techniques in editing, formatting, and printing. Planning and maintaining a consistent style is imperative. Large-scale publications require judicious use of sections, headers, footers, tables of contents, front matter, end matter, appendices, cover pages, graphics, styles, headings, and additional formatting considerations.

Examples of large-scale publications include books, booklets, magazines, catalogs, journals, and conference proceedings, among others.

Project — Creating a Short Story Booklet

The project in this module creates a 16-page booklet containing a short story. The front and back pages of the booklet have a blue background. The front (cover) displays WordArt, a graphic, and text. The inside pages have features such as pictures, author bio, sidebars, linked text boxes, headings, and page numbers (Figure 10–1).

Figure 10–1

The following roadmap identifies general activities you will perform as you progress through this module:

1. Design the layout and CREATE SECTIONS.
2. INSERT PAGE NUMBERS.
3. ADJUST CELL MARGINS and text box margins.
4. DISPLAY RULER GUIDES to help place objects on the page.
5. PREPARE PAGES for content and specify page numbers.
6. USE the CLIPBOARD TASK PANE to copy and paste.
7. USE FIND and REPLACE along with the thesaurus as necessary.
8. NAVIGATE WITH BOOKMARKS and hyperlinks through long publications.

To Select a Blank Publication and Adjust Settings

The following steps select an 8.5 × 11" blank print publication, choose schemes, and adjust workspace settings, such as the Page Navigation pane display and special characters.

1 Run Publisher.

2 Click the Blank 8.5 × 11" thumbnail in the New template gallery to create a blank publication in the Publisher window.

③ If necessary, press CTRL+SHIFT+Y to display special characters.

④ Display the Page Design tab.

⑤ Click the Scheme Fonts button (Page Design tab | Schemes group) and then scroll as necessary to click 'Office Classic 1' in the Scheme Fonts gallery.

⑥ To change the color scheme, click the More button (Page Design tab | Schemes group) and then click Office in the list of color schemes, if necessary.

⑦ Display the View tab.

⑧ If necessary, click the appropriate check boxes to display check marks for Boundaries, Guides, Rulers, Page Navigation, and the Scratch Area (View tab | Show group).

⑨ If the Page Navigation pane is expanded, click the 'Collapse Page Navigation Pane' button to collapse it (Figure 10–2).

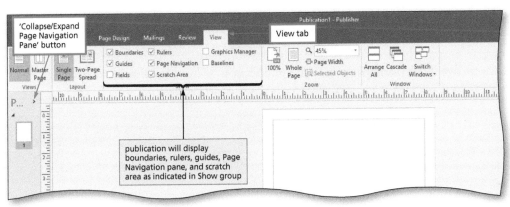

Figure 10–2

Designing the Layout

Recall that a layout is the way pages, component parts, or individual items are arranged in a publication. In the past, you used template layouts for your pages; or, you created objects on a blank page, thereby designing your own layout. When working with a large-scale publication, you need to plan for the cover, the back, the inside of the front and back covers, as well as the inner pages, which sometimes are called **content pages** or **body copy**. A publication also may contain sectional elements such as front matter and end matter. **Front matter** is a term that refers to content at the beginning of a book or publication that is neither a cover page nor content page, such as a forward, preface, or table of contents. **End matter** includes appendices, an index, reference pages, glossaries, or other lists. In the booklet in this module, you will make page-numbering decisions on front matter and content pages. Finally, you will need to decide on the layout of content pages, such as sidebars, headings, and tables of contents, among other elements.

BTW
Touch Screen Differences
The Office and Windows interfaces may vary if you are using a touch screen. For this reason, you might notice that the function or appearance of your touch screen differs slightly from this module's presentation.

CONSIDER THIS

What sections should you include in a large-scale publication?

Large-scale publications should contain some or all of the following sections:

- Cover page: A cover page should contain the complete title and name of the author, along with graphics or colors to encourage the reader to open the publication.

- Inside front cover page: Normally, the inside cover page is blank, but some books use the space for author comments, references, or other ancillary material.

- Front matter: Front matter includes a table of contents, notes from the editor or author, publication data, and other information to guide users through the content.

- Content pages: The content pages contain all of the text and graphics that constitute the book's contents, minus the front matter and end matter.

- End matter: The end matter may contain appendices, an index, reference pages, glossaries, or other lists.

- Inside back cover page: Like the inside front cover page, the inside back cover page normally is blank, but it may contain the last page of the content, reference material, or additional information about the text or author.

- Back cover page: The back cover page may contain only graphics or color, or it may contain additional information about the content, such as a summary, online content, ISBN numbers, bar codes, and references to other pertinent publications.

To Insert Pages

1 CREATE SECTIONS | 2 INSERT PAGE NUMBERS | 3 ADJUST CELL MARGINS | 4 DISPLAY RULER GUIDES
5 PREPARE PAGES | 6 USE CLIPBOARD TASK PANE | 7 USE FIND & REPLACE | 8 NAVIGATE WITH BOOKMARKS

The following steps insert five more blank pages into the publication. **Why?** *Unless you have chosen a template with the exact number of pages you wish to use, you will have to insert or delete pages.*

1

- Right-click page 1 in the Page Navigation pane to display the shortcut menu (Figure 10–3).

 Q&A Can I make the Pane Navigation bigger without expanding it to full size?
Yes, you can drag the right border of the Pane Navigation pane to change its size.

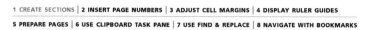

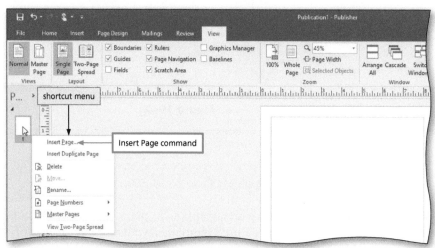

Figure 10–3

2

- Click Insert Page on the shortcut menu to display the Insert Page dialog box.

- In the 'Number of new pages' text box, type **5** to insert the number of pages.

- If necessary, click the 'After current page' option button to select it (Figure 10–4).

Q&A Could I choose to create a new text box on the next page?
The 'Create one text box on each page' option creates one large text box that fills the page, with no page formatting. It would not be appropriate for this module.

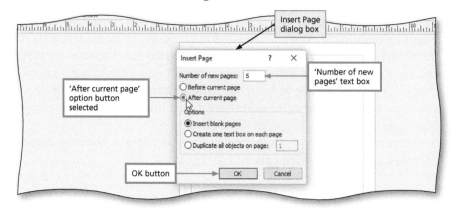

Figure 10–4

3

- Click the OK button (Insert Page dialog box) to insert the pages into the publication (Figure 10–5).

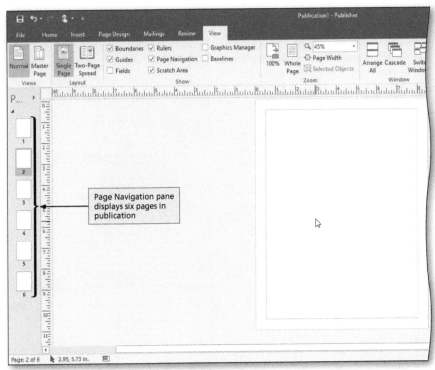

Page Navigation pane displays six pages in publication

Figure 10–5

Other Ways

1. Click 'Insert Blank Page' arrow (Insert tab | Pages group), click Insert Page on Insert Blank Page menu, enter desired number of pages (Insert Page dialog box), click OK button

2. Press CTRL+SHIFT+N for each new page

To Create Sections

1 CREATE SECTIONS | 2 INSERT PAGE NUMBERS | 3 ADJUST CELL MARGINS | 4 DISPLAY RULER GUIDES
5 PREPARE PAGES | 6 USE CLIPBOARD TASK PANE | 7 USE FIND & REPLACE | 8 NAVIGATE WITH BOOKMARKS

The cover page and back page of the booklet will have a blue background. The front matter and content pages will contain different layouts and page numbering. Publisher uses **sections**, or dividers, in the Page Navigation pane. *Why? Sections assist with pagination and organization and are used to separate the pages logically.* When you create a section, Publisher adds a section break above the page in the Page Navigation pane. Each break contains a section button that appears as a small arrow. You click the button to expand or collapse a section. The following steps create sections for the front of the booklet, for the front matter, for the content section, and for the back of the booklet — a total of four sections.

1

Right-click page 2 in the Page Navigation pane to display the shortcut menu (Figure 10–6).

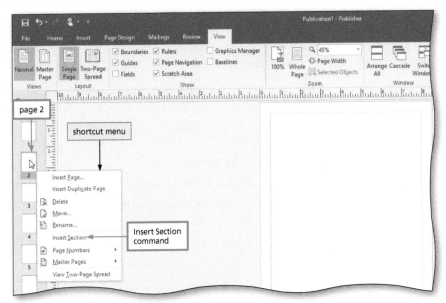

page 2

shortcut menu

Insert Section command

Figure 10–6

2

- Click Insert Section on the shortcut menu to create a section in the Page Navigation pane for the cover page (Figure 10–7).

Q&A

Can I name the sections?
Publisher has no functionality to give each section a unique name.

Does the section break arrow have a name?
Yes, it is called a Collapse Section button.

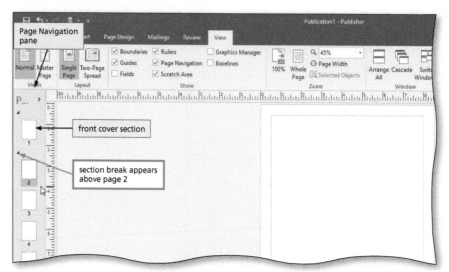

Figure 10–7

3

- Right-click page 5 of the publication and then click Insert Section on the shortcut menu to create a section for the front matter.

- Right-click page 6 of the publication and then click Insert Section on the shortcut menu to insert a section for content pages (Figure 10–8).

Experiment

- Right-click one of the Collapse Section buttons to view the commands related to sections.

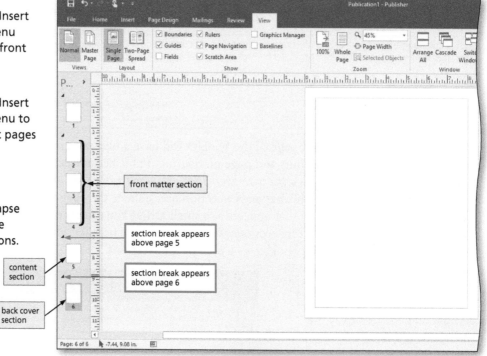

Figure 10–8

TO MERGE SECTIONS

If you wanted to merge sections, you would perform the following steps.

1. In the Page Navigation pane, right-click the Collapse Section button to display the shortcut menu.

2. Click 'Merge with Previous Section' on the shortcut menu to merge the sections.

Pagination

Pagination refers to the way a publication applies page numbers, including the location, whether the cover will be included in the page numbering system, and the number with which you wish to start. When inserting page numbers in a large-scale publication, it is common for the cover and back cover pages not to be numbered. If the front matter contains many pages, the pages in that section are numbered sequentially using lowercase Roman numerals. Page number 1 begins after the front matter.

How are pages numbered in booklets?

Using the correct pagination helps readers navigate through the sections of a booklet or large-scale publication. Decide which pages should not display page numbers, such as title pages, cover pages, and blank pages. Use lowercase Roman numerals for front matter. Use numerals for content pages. Appendices sometimes use pages numbered with letters of the alphabet. Be consistent; page numbers that change locations or styles within a publication are disconcerting to readers.

As you learned in a previous module, you can use headers and footers to place page numbers using the master page; however, you also can insert page numbers using the Insert tab on the ribbon. The information ultimately is stored on a master page, but the advantage of using the ribbon is that you can specify what number you wish to use as a starting page number, an especially useful technique for modules and sections of books. Additionally, using the ribbon, you can insert page numbers in text boxes other than the header and footer.

BTW

Page Navigation
When you have a multipage publication, you can move quickly between pages using the Next or Previous buttons at the bottom of the scroll bar on the right of the screen.

To Insert Page Numbers

1 CREATE SECTIONS | 2 INSERT PAGE NUMBERS | 3 ADJUST CELL MARGINS | 4 DISPLAY RULER GUIDES
5 PREPARE PAGES | 6 USE CLIPBOARD TASK PANE | 7 USE FIND & REPLACE | 8 NAVIGATE WITH BOOKMARKS

The following steps insert a page number at the bottom center of each page. *Why? When used with a table of contents, page numbers help guide the reader through the booklet.*

- If necessary, click page 5 in the Page Navigation pane.
- Display the Insert tab.
- Click the Page Number button (Insert tab | Header & Footer group) to display the Page Number gallery (Figure 10–9).

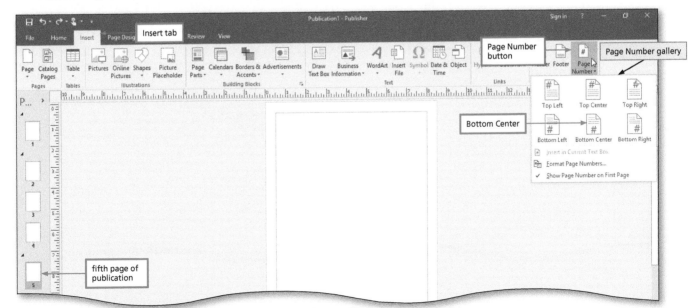

Figure 10–9

- Click Bottom Center in the Page Number gallery to insert page numbers at the bottom center of each page.
- Zoom to 150% and scroll to the bottom of the page to view the page number (Figure 10–10).

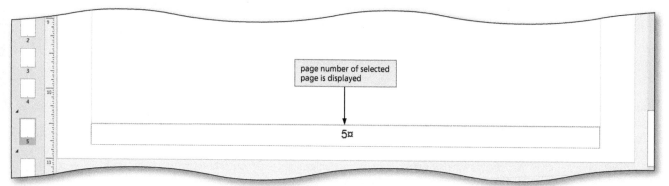

page number of selected page is displayed

5¤

Figure 10–10

Other Ways

1. Right-click page in Page Navigation pane, point to Page Numbers on shortcut menu, click desired location on Page Numbers submenu

To Specify a Starting Page Number Using the Ribbon

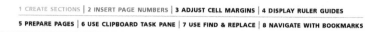

1 CREATE SECTIONS | 2 INSERT PAGE NUMBERS | 3 ADJUST CELL MARGINS | 4 DISPLAY RULER GUIDES

5 PREPARE PAGES | 6 USE CLIPBOARD TASK PANE | 7 USE FIND & REPLACE | 8 NAVIGATE WITH BOOKMARKS

The booklet's front matter will appear beginning with the inside cover page. The following steps specify a starting page number, i, which will appear on the second page of the publication. *Why? It is common for front matter to use lowercase Roman numerals.*

- In the Page Navigation pane, select the second page of the publication.
- Click the Page Number button (Insert tab | Header & Footer group) to display the Page Number gallery (Figure 10–11).

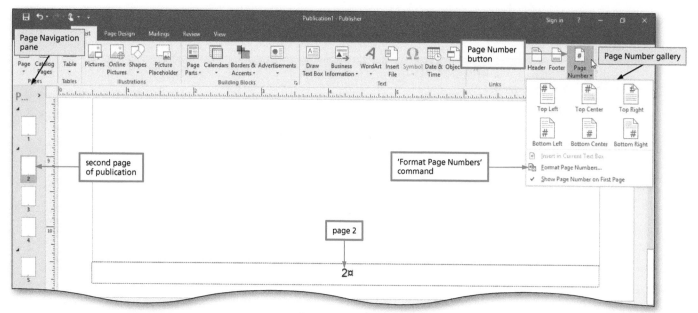

Figure 10–11

2

- Click 'Format Page Numbers' in the Page Number gallery to display the Page Number Format dialog box.

- Click the Number format arrow to display the available formats (Figure 10–12).

Experiment

- Scroll through the Number format list and view the different kinds of page numbering formats, including cardinal numbers, Roman numerals, letters, ordinal numbers, or spelled out numbers (i.e., one, two, three).

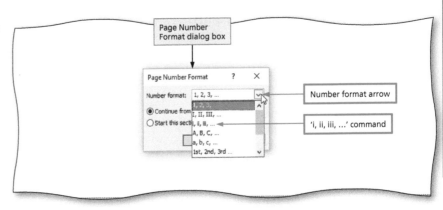

Figure 10–12

3

- Click 'i, ii, iii, …' in the Number format list.

- Click the 'Start this section with' option button to select it.

- Select the text in the 'Start this section with' text box and then type 1 to specify the starting page number (Figure 10–13).

Q&A Why should I type the numeral, 1, when I want to start with page i?
The 'Start this section with' box requires an integer. The page number is page 1 of the section; the page number format is lowercase Roman numerals. You would type a numeral 1 even if you were instructing Publisher to use letters on each page.

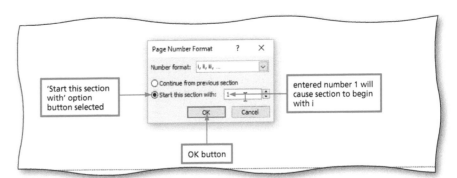

Figure 10–13

4

- Click the OK button (Page Number Format dialog box) to apply the page number format (Figure 10–14).

Experiment

- Click different pages in the Page Navigation pane to view the page numbers on each page.

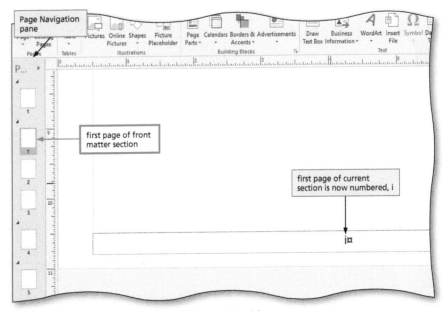

Figure 10–14

To Specify a Starting Page Number Using the Page Navigation Pane

The following steps apply the number, 1, to the fifth page of the publication. *Why? The fifth page of the publication is the beginning of the section for content pages.*

- In the Page Navigation pane, right-click the fifth page of the publication, which appears as the first page in the third section.

- Point to Page Numbers on the shortcut menu to display the Page Numbers submenu (Figure 10–15).

Q&A How can I tell which page I am working on?
The status bar always displays a number representing the current sequential page of the overall publication. Within each section, the pages are numbered in the Page Navigation pane.

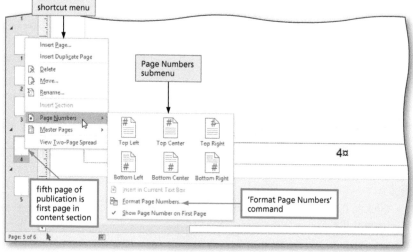

Figure 10–15

- Click 'Format Page Numbers' on the Page Numbers submenu to display the Page Number Format dialog box.

- If necessary, click the Number format arrow to display its list and then scroll as necessary to click '1, 2, 3, …' in the list.

- Click the 'Start this section with' option button to select it.

- Select the text in the 'Start this section with' text box and then type   1   to replace it (Figure 10–16).

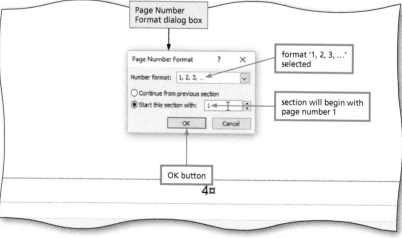

Figure 10–16

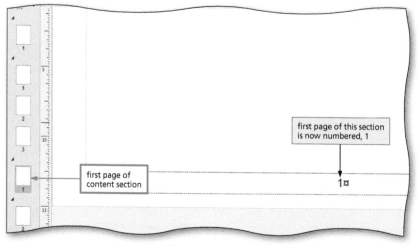

- Click the OK button (Page Number Format dialog box) to apply the page number format to the page (Figure 10–17).

Figure 10–17

To Remove Page Numbering from Specific Pages

The final step in paginating this publication is to remove page numbers from the first and last sections of the publication. *Why? Cover pages and back pages usually do not have page numbers.* Because page numbers and their formats are saved internally in a master page, the following steps remove page numbering by choosing to apply no master page to the specific pages in the publication.

- In the Page Navigation pane, right-click the first page of the publication to display the shortcut menu and then point to Master Pages on the shortcut menu to display the Master Pages submenu (Figure 10–18).

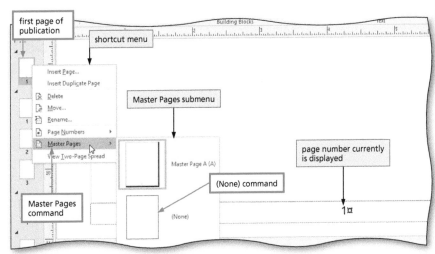

Figure 10–18

- Click (None) on the Master Pages submenu to remove the master page and, thus, remove page numbering from the page (Figure 10–19).

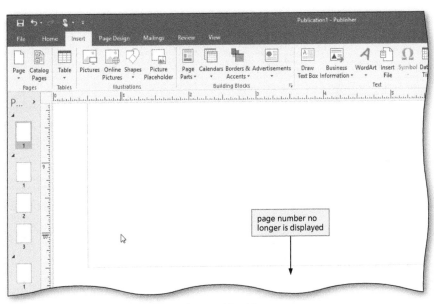

Figure 10–19

- Repeat Steps 1 and 2 for the last page of the publication, so that page numbering will not appear on that page.
- Save the publication on your desired save location using the file name, Graduation Short Story.

Break Point: If you wish to take a break, this is a good place to do so. Exit Publisher. To resume at a later time, run Publisher, open the file named Graduation Short Story, and then continue following the steps from this location forward.

To Apply a Background

The following steps insert a solid blue background on the first and last pages of the booklet.

1 Select the first page of the publication, zoom to whole page, and display the Page Design tab.

2 Click the Background button (Page Design tab | Page Background group) to display the Background gallery.

3 Click '30% tint of Accent 1' in the Solid Background area in the Background gallery.

4 Repeat Steps 1 through 3 for the last page of the publication (Figure 10–20).

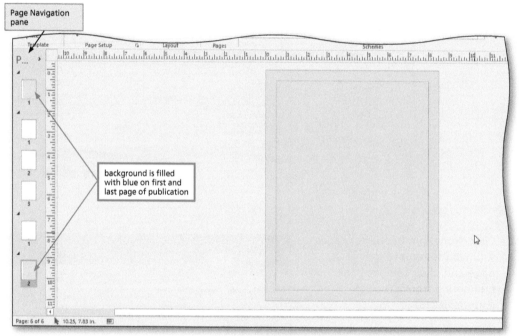

Figure 10–20

To Create the Title

The following steps create a WordArt title for the booklet.

1 Select the first page of the publication in the Page Navigation pane.

2 Display the Insert tab.

3 Click the Insert WordArt button (Insert tab | Text group) and then click 'Fill - White, Outline - Blue' in the Insert WordArt gallery.

4 When Publisher displays the Edit WordArt Text dialog box, type **Graduation** to change the text. Change the font to Maiandra GD or a similar font and then click the OK button (Edit WordArt Text dialog box).

5 Resize the WordArt object to approximately 6.5 inches wide and 1.5 inches tall.

6 Move the WordArt object to the top of the page, aligned at the top margin.

7 Click the Align Objects button (WordArt Tools Format tab | Arrange group) and then click 'Relative to Margin Guides' on the Align Objects menu. Click the button again and then click Align Center (Figure 10–21).

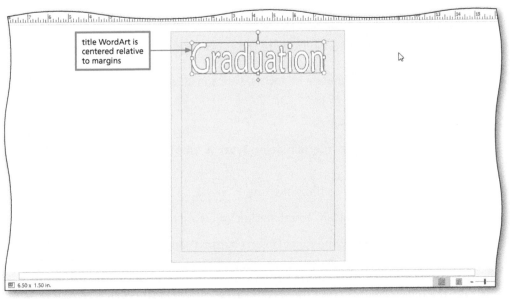

Figure 10–21

To Insert a Graphic

The following steps insert a graphic on the front page. To complete these steps, you will be required to use the Data Files. Please contact your instructor for information about accessing the Data Files.

1 Insert the graphic named Front Cover from the Data Files.

2 Move the graphic to a location below the WordArt.

3 Click the Align Objects button (Picture Tools Format tab | Arrange group) and then click Align Center (Figure 10–22).

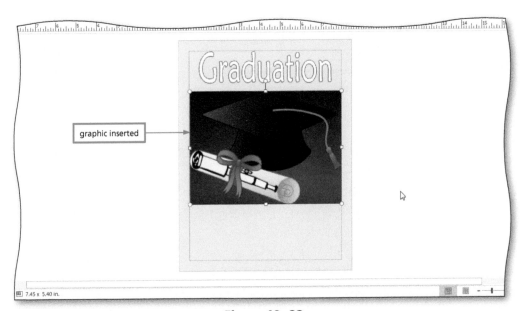

Figure 10–22

To Enter the Subtitle

The following steps add a subtitle to the cover page of the booklet.

1 Insert a text box approximately 7.5 inches wide and 2.5 inches tall at the bottom of the page.

2 Change the font size to 48.

3 Press CTRL+E to center the insertion point. Type **A short story by** and then press the ENTER key.

4 Type **Todd Outcalt** to finish the text.

5 Right-click the name, Outcalt, and then click Ignore All on the shortcut menu.

6 Center the text box using the Align Objects button (Home tab | Arrange group).

7 Drag around both text boxes and the graphic on the page to select all three objects.

8 Click the Align Objects button (Home tab | Arrange group) and then click Distribute Vertically.

9 Click the scratch area to deselect the objects (Figure 10–23).

BTW
Expand/Collapse Section Shortcut Menu
A section title bar runs the width of the Page Navigation pane. You can right-click anywhere in that area to display the Expand/Collapse Section shortcut menu.

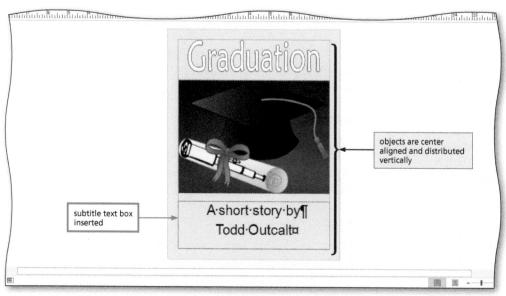

Figure 10–23

To Collapse Sections

1 CREATE SECTIONS | 2 INSERT PAGE NUMBERS | 3 ADJUST CELL MARGINS | 4 DISPLAY RULER GUIDES
5 PREPARE PAGES | 6 USE CLIPBOARD TASK PANE | 7 USE FIND & REPLACE | 8 NAVIGATE WITH BOOKMARKS

The front and back pages of the booklet are complete. The following steps collapse those pages in the Page Navigation pane. *Why? Collapsing complete sections helps reduce the size of the Page Navigation pane and allows you to focus on pages that need to be edited.*

1

• Select the second page of the publication.

• In the Page Navigation pane, click the Collapse Section button above the first page of the publication to collapse the front cover section (Figure 10–24).

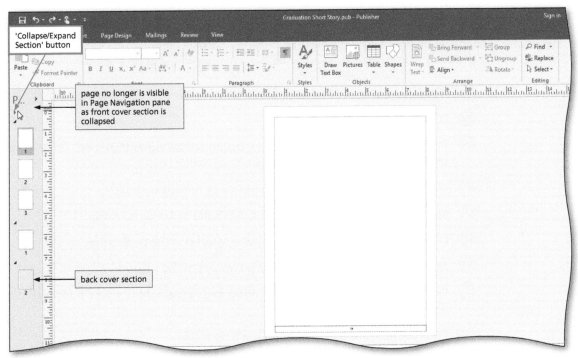

Figure 10–24

2

• Click the Collapse Section button above the last page in the Page Navigation pane to collapse the back cover section (Figure 10–25).

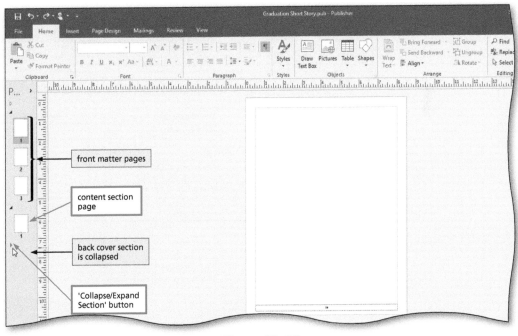

Figure 10–25

3

• Click the Save button on the Quick Access Toolbar to overwrite the previously saved file.

To Create a Page Border

The following steps insert a table of contents building block on the first page of the front matter to serve as a border for a picture of the author and his bio.

① If necessary, click the first page of the front matter with the page number, i.

② Display the Insert tab.

③ Click the Show Building Block Library Dialog Box Launcher (Insert tab | Building Blocks group) to display the Building Block Library dialog box.

④ Click the Page Parts folder (Building Block Library dialog box).

⑤ Scroll as necessary and then click the 'All Tables of Contents' folder.

⑥ Double-click the Tilt table of contents to insert it in the publication.

⑦ Move the building block to the top left corner of the page.

⑧ Drag the lower-right sizing handle down and to the right until the building block fills the page.

⑨ Press CTRL+SHIFT+G to ungroup the building block.

⑩ Delete the table object in the center of the building block.

⑪ Delete the text box in front of the light blue rectangle at the top of the page (Figure 10–26).

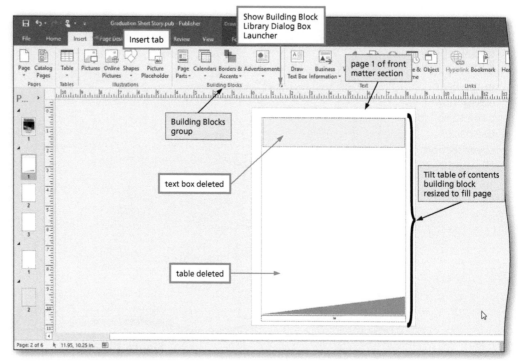

Figure 10–26

To Insert Author Information

The following steps insert a picture of the author and his bio. To complete these steps, you will be required to use the Data Files. Please contact your instructor for information about accessing the Data Files.

① Display the Insert tab.

② Insert the picture named Author from the Data Files.

③ SHIFT+drag a corner handle to resize the picture to be approximately 4.5 inches tall. Center the picture relative to the margins and just below the light blue graphic at the top of the page.

④ Draw a text box below the picture, approximately 7.5 inches wide and 2.5 inches tall.

⑤ With the insertion point inside the text box, click the Insert File button (Insert tab | Text group). Navigate to the Data Files and insert the file named Author Bio.

⑥ Select all of the text and then change the font size to 16.

⑦ Click the border of the text box to select it. Click the Align Objects button (Drawing Tools Format tab | Arrange group) and then click 'Relative to Margin Guides' on the Align Objects menu. Click the button again and then click Align Center to center the text box relative to the margins (Figure 10–27).

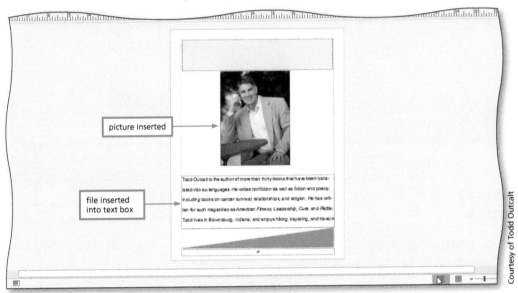

picture inserted

file inserted into text box

Courtesy of Todd Outcalt

Figure 10–27

Cell and Text Box Margins

Like page margins, you can adjust the margins within table cells and within text boxes. The default margin for a text box and for a cell is approximately 0.04 inches. In some cases, that may place the text too close to the edge or border. To improve readability, you will change the margin in the table of contents cells for the booklet so that the page numbers are farther away from the margin and its border.

To Create a Table of Contents

The following steps insert a table of contents building block on the second page of the front matter.

① Click the second page of the front matter with the page number, ii.

② Display the Insert tab.

③ Use the Show Building Block Library Dialog Box Launcher (Insert tab | Building Blocks group) to insert the Tilt table of contents in the publication.

④ Resize the table of contents to fill the page (Figure 10–28).

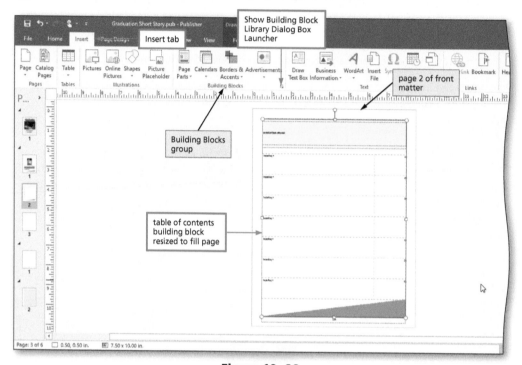

Figure 10–28

To Change Cell Margins

1 CREATE SECTIONS | 2 INSERT PAGE NUMBERS | 3 ADJUST CELL MARGINS | 4 DISPLAY RULER GUIDES
5 PREPARE PAGES | 6 USE CLIPBOARD TASK PANE | 7 USE FIND & REPLACE | 8 NAVIGATE WITH BOOKMARKS

The following steps increase the right margin of the cells in the second column. *Why? By changing the cell margin, the page number will not appear so close to the border.*

1

- Drag through the second column of the table to select the cells.

- Display the Table Tools Layout tab.

- Click the Cell Margins button (Table Tools Layout tab | Alignment group) to display the Cell Margins gallery (Figure 10–29).

 Experiment

- Click each of the cell margin choices in the Cell Margins gallery and watch the margins change in the table.

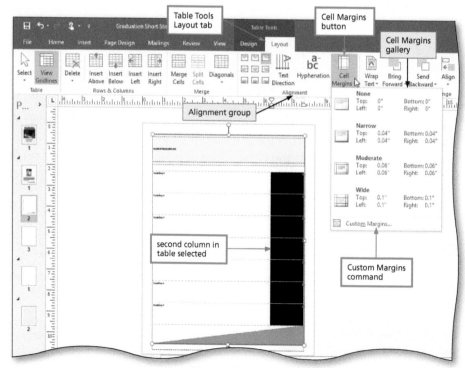

Figure 10–29

2

- Click Custom Margins in the Cell Margins gallery to display the Format Table dialog box. If necessary, click the Cell Properties tab.

- Select the text in the Right box and then type **.3** to change the right margin (Figure 10–30).

Q&A Could I use the numerical up and down buttons in the Right box?
Yes, those buttons change the text in the box by .1 inch each time you click them.

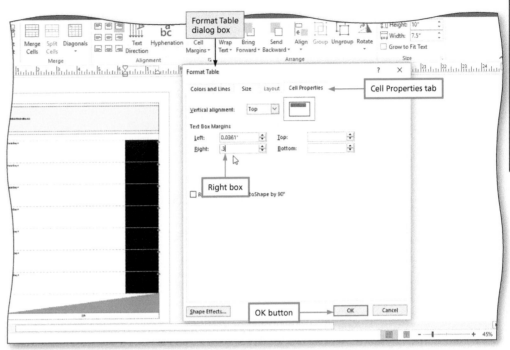

Figure 10–30

3

- Click the OK button (Format Table dialog box) to apply the new margin to the cells.

- Click outside the table to deselect the cells (Figure 10–31).

Q&A Should I enter new text in the table of contents?
No, you will update the table of contents later in the module, after you complete all pages.

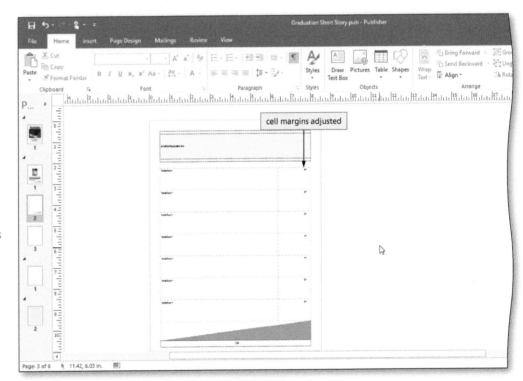

Figure 10–31

Other Ways

1. Right-click cell, click Format Table on shortcut menu, click Cell Properties tab (Format Table dialog box), enter cell margin, click OK button

TO CHANGE TEXT BOX MARGINS

If you wanted to change the margins of a text box, rather than a cell, you would perform the following steps.

1. Select the text box by clicking its boundary.

2. If necessary, display the Text Box Tools Format tab.

3. Click the Margins button (Text Box Tools Format tab | Alignment group) and then either choose a preset value from the Margins gallery, or click Custom Margins and enter the margin values (Format Text Box dialog box).

To Collapse the Front Matter Section

The following steps collapse the front matter section in the Page Navigation pane.

1 In the Page Navigation pane, click the first page of the content section with the page number 1.

2 Click the Collapse Section button above that page to collapse the section (Figure 10–32).

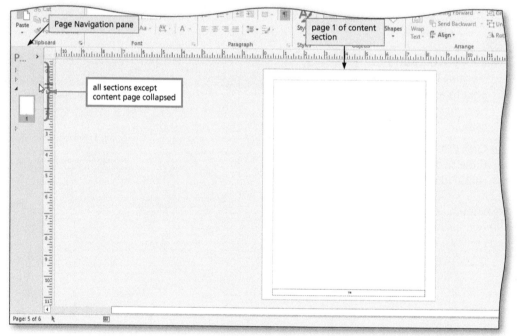

Figure 10–32

Ruler Guides

Recall that you have created individual ruler guides — green, dotted, nonprinting lines — by dragging from the rulers to help you align objects and provide visual reference. You also can choose sets of built-in ruler guides. These ruler guides are preset to contain headings, columns, and grids. Along with margin guides that are blue, the ruler guides also provide straight edges and snapping capabilities.

In the booklet, you will choose a set of ruler guides in order to display areas for text, headings, and sidebars.

To Select Ruler Guides

The following steps select a set of built-in ruler guides for page 1, a recto page. *Why? Ruler guides help you create objects in consistent places across pages.* After drawing a text box on page 1, you also will create a second page with a mirrored set of ruler guides and a text box for page 2, a verso page.

1

- If necessary, select the single page in the content section of the Page Navigation pane with the page number 1.

- Display the Page Design tab.

- Click the Guides button (Page Design tab | Layout group) to display the Guides gallery (Figure 10–33).

Q&A What does the Ruler Guides command do?
The command allows you to place ruler guides at specific measured locations.

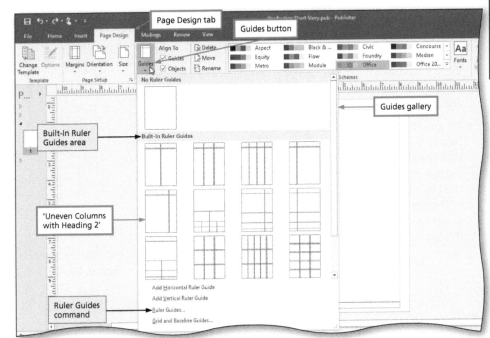

Figure 10–33

 **Experiment**

- Scroll in the Guides gallery to view other guides.

2

- In the Built-In Ruler Guides area, click 'Uneven Columns with Heading 2' to apply it to this recto page.

- Display the Home tab and then draw a text box filling the lower-left area within the guides and margins (Figure 10–34).

Q&A Can I use a different built-in ruler guide?
The 'Uneven Columns with Heading 2' ruler guide is meant to be used on recto pages. It has room on the left for a large amount of text that will appear close to the booklet binding. The outside margin provides room for sidebars.

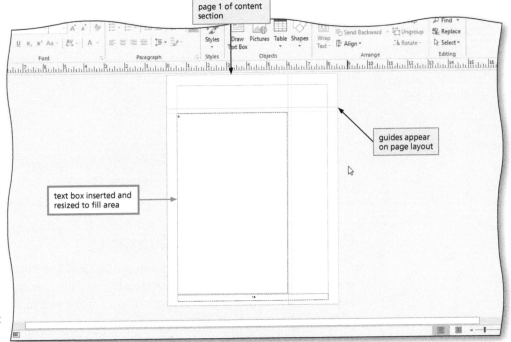

Figure 10–34

- In the Page Navigation pane, right-click the page and then click Insert Page on the shortcut menu. When Publisher displays the Insert Page dialog box, click the OK button to accept the settings and insert the page.

- Display the Page Design tab and then click the Guides button (Page Design tab | Layout group) to display the Guides gallery (Figure 10–35).

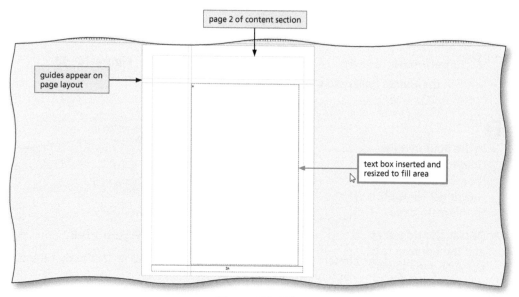

Figure 10–35

- Click 'Uneven Columns with Heading 1' to apply it to this verso page.

- Display the Home tab and then draw a text box filling the lower-right area within the ruler guides and margins (Figure 10–36).

Figure 10–36

Preparing Pages for Content

Once your page numbers, layout guides, and text boxes are prepared for content, you are ready to prepare the correct number of pages for content. The number of pages is directly related to the length of your story, so you should try to create plenty of room; however, if you underestimate the number of necessary pages, Publisher will create new ones for you at the end of the publication.

The following sections duplicate pages, rearrange them as necessary, and change the view. Finally, you will link text boxes across pages so the story will flow correctly from beginning to end once you import it.

To Duplicate a Page

The following steps duplicate page 1, including all objects — in this case, the guides and text box. *Why? It is easier to duplicate the page than to recreate all of its elements.*

1

- Right-click page 1 in the Page Navigation pane to display the shortcut menu (Figure 10–37).

Q&A Where will the duplicate page be placed?
The default setting is to place the page directly after the original page.

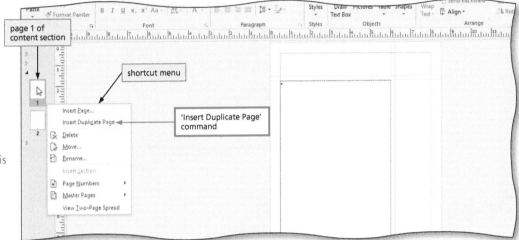

Figure 10–37

2

- Click 'Insert Duplicate Page' on the shortcut menu to create a duplicate page (Figure 10–38).

Q&A All of my sections expanded. Did I do something wrong?
No. You can collapse them again by clicking the appropriate Collapse Section buttons.

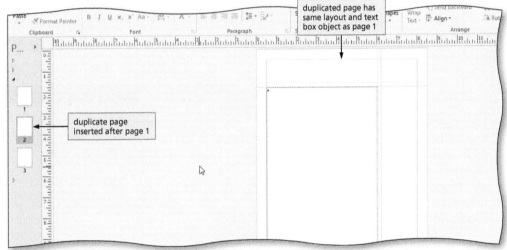

Figure 10–38

Experiment

- Click each page in the content section of the Page Navigation pane. Notice that the duplicate page is now page 2 and contains the same contents as page 1.

Other Ways

1. Click 'Insert Blank Page' arrow (Insert tab | Pages group), click 'Insert Duplicate Page' on Insert Blank Page menu   2. Press CTRL+SHIFT+N

To Rearrange Pages

You can use the Page Navigation pane to rearrange pages. The following steps move the newly duplicated page to position number 3 in the content section. *Why? The duplicated page is a recto page and needs to follow a verso page.*

- In the Page Navigation pane, drag page 2 down below the next page until Publisher displays a horizontal bar (Figure 10–39).

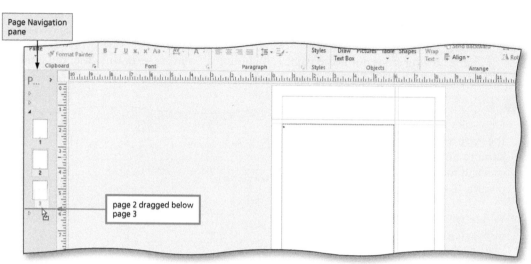

Figure 10–39

- Release the mouse button to move the page.

To View a Two-Page Spread

1 CREATE SECTIONS | 2 INSERT PAGE NUMBERS | 3 ADJUST CELL MARGINS | 4 DISPLAY RULER GUIDES
5 PREPARE PAGES | 6 USE CLIPBOARD TASK PANE | 7 USE FIND & REPLACE | 8 NAVIGATE WITH BOOKMARKS

The following step views the two-page spread of pages 2 and 3. *Why? Viewing the two-page spread allows you to verify the guides and text box placement.* Changing the view also expands all sections so that you can see how the pages fit into the booklet.

- Display the View tab.

- Click the 'Two-Page Spread' button (View tab | Layout group) to show pages 2 and 3 together in the workspace (Figure 10–40).

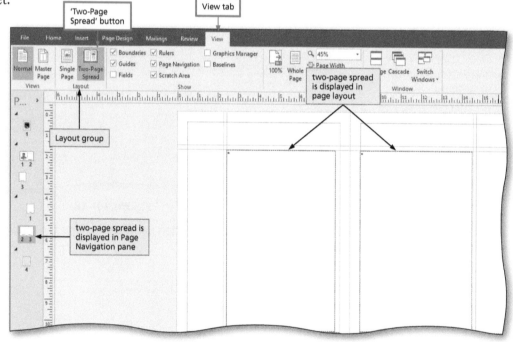

Figure 10–40

To Duplicate the Two-Page Spread

1 CREATE SECTIONS | 2 INSERT PAGE NUMBERS | 3 ADJUST CELL MARGINS | 4 DISPLAY RULER GUIDES
5 PREPARE PAGES | 6 USE CLIPBOARD TASK PANE | 7 USE FIND & REPLACE | 8 NAVIGATE WITH BOOKMARKS

The following steps duplicate the two-page spread four times. *Why? You need a total of 11 pages for the story — page 1 followed by five sets of two page spreads.* As you duplicate a two-page spread, Publisher attempts to create an even number of pages per section; you sometimes need to move a page to keep the two-page spread together. In that case, Publisher will warn you of an uneven page count.

1

- In the Page Navigation pane, right-click the page 2 and page 3 two-page spread to display the shortcut menu (Figure 10–41).

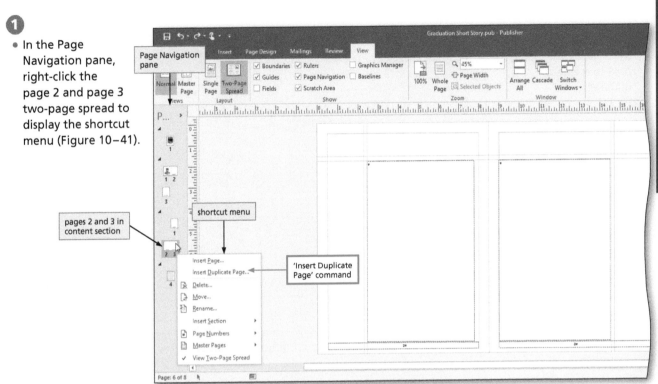

Figure 10–41

2

- Click 'Insert Duplicate Page' on the shortcut menu to display the Duplicate Page dialog box.

- If necessary, click the 'Insert duplicate of both pages' option button to select it (Figure 10–42).

Q&A Could I use the Insert Page command and request eight more pages?
You could, but all of the pages would be recto pages. Using the Insert Duplicate Page command creates a verso and recto page.

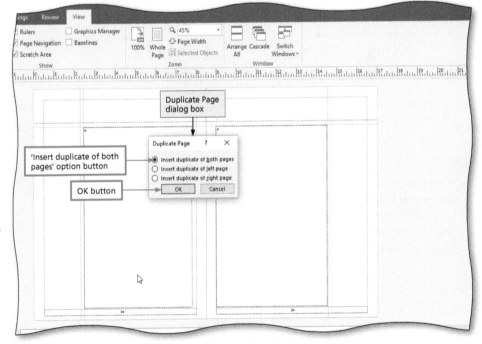

Figure 10–42

3

- Click the OK button (Duplicate Page dialog box) to create the duplicate.

- In the Page Navigation pane, drag page 6 above page 5 until the green bar is displayed (Figure 10–43).

Q&A Why did Publisher split the two-page spread?
Publisher tried to make an even number of pages per section. Dragging the page corrects the problem.

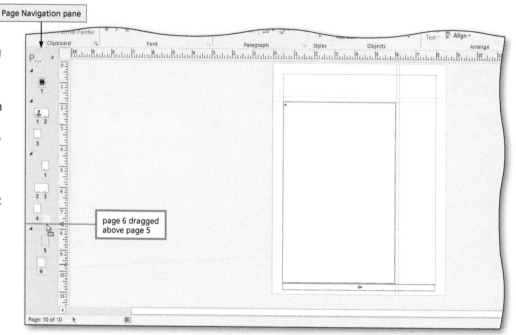

Figure 10–43

4

- Release the mouse button to move the page (Figure 10–44).

Q&A Why did Publisher display a warning message?
Moving the page up to a new section leaves a single page in the back cover section. Publisher warns you that the back cover section will be uneven.

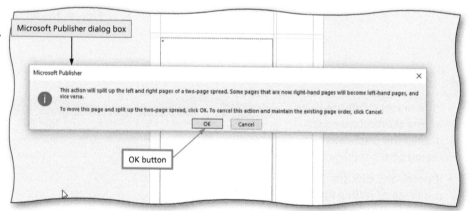

Figure 10–44

5

- Click the OK button (Microsoft Publisher dialog box) to accept the repagination (Figure 10–45).

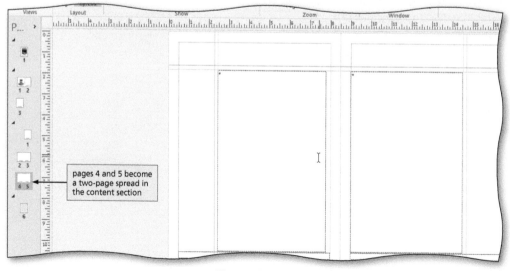

Figure 10–45

6

• In the Page Navigation pane, right-click the page 2 and page 3 two-page spread again and then click 'Insert Duplicate Page' on the shortcut menu.

• When Publisher displays the Duplicate Page dialog box, click the OK button.

7

• Repeat Step 6 two more times to create a total of 11 content pages (Figure 10–46).

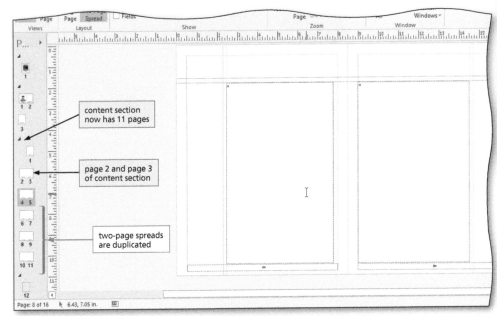

Figure 10–46

Q&A In the Page Navigation pane, my page 11 was not part of a two-page spread. Did I do something wrong?
If you copied the page 2 and page 3 two-page spread, it should have been displayed correctly. If your page 11 is displayed individually, drag it up into the previous section, just below page 10.

To Link Text Boxes Using the Menu

1 CREATE SECTIONS | 2 INSERT PAGE NUMBERS | 3 ADJUST CELL MARGINS | 4 DISPLAY RULER GUIDES
5 PREPARE PAGES | 6 USE CLIPBOARD TASK PANE | 7 USE FIND & REPLACE | 8 NAVIGATE WITH BOOKMARKS

In an earlier module, you linked a story from one text box to another after inserting text. Recall that you used the 'Text in Overflow' button when the story did not fit in the first text box. The following steps link text boxes using the ribbon, so that text inserted later will flow from one to the other. *Why? If you link text boxes before importing or typing the text, the Text Box Tools Format tab contains several tools to help you create, break, and move between linked text boxes.*

1

• In the Page Navigation pane, click page 1 in the content section.

• Click the text box and then display the Text Box Tools Format tab.

• Click the Create Link button (Text Box Tools Format tab | Linking group) to start the linking process.

• Move the pointer over the text box (Figure 10–47).

Q&A Why does my pointer look like a bucket?
Recall that Publisher uses a bucket icon to indicate a link is about to take place. The bucket is upright when you move over the original text box. The bucket will tip when you move over any other text box, as if it is pouring in the text.

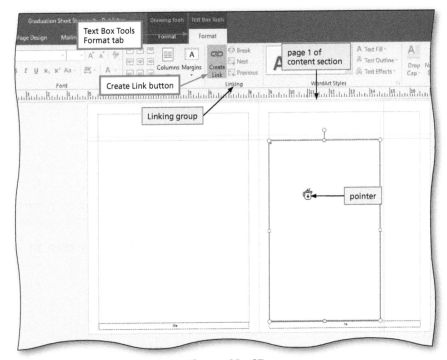

Figure 10–47

- In the Page Navigation pane, click the next page (in this case, the page 2 and page 3 spread).
- Move the pointer over the text box on the verso page (page 2 of the content section) (Figure 10–48).

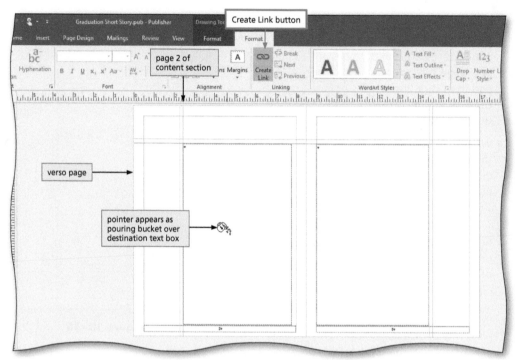

Figure 10–48

3

- Click the text box to link it (Figure 10–49).

Q&A

How can I be sure that I have linked correctly?

If you have linked correctly, Publisher will display a Previous button on the text box border and also will enable the Previous button on the ribbon.

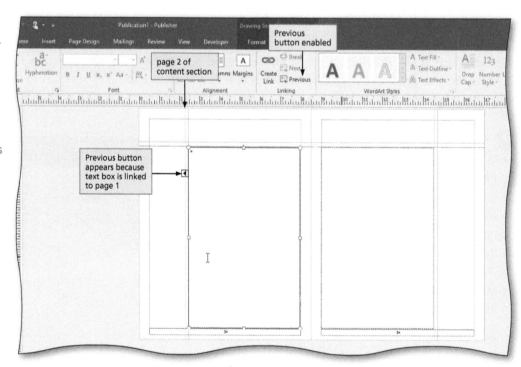

Figure 10–49

4

- To link page 2 to page 3, with the page 2 text box still selected, click the Create Link button (Text Box Tools Format tab | Linking group) and then click the recto page text box to link the two text boxes (Figure 10–50).

5

- Repeat the process to link all pages up to and including page 11.

- To verify the connections, begin at page 1 and click the Next button located on the lower-right border of the text box. Repeat on each page until you get to page 11.

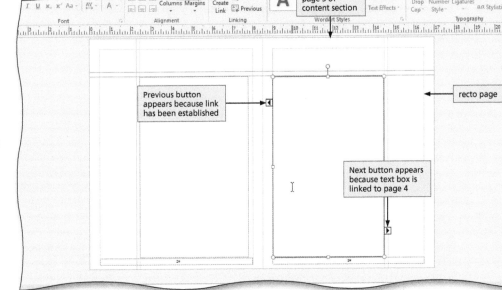

page 3 of content section

Previous button appears because link has been established

recto page

Next button appears because text box is linked to page 4

Figure 10–50

Q&A Is an easier way available to connect boxes for really long publications?
The only other way is to import the text first. Publisher will create extra pages with connected text boxes. You then would have to format the pages, create guides, and resize the text boxes on each page.

Adding Content

Recall that content for publications such as newsletters, catalogs, emails, and booklets may come from a variety of sources. For the Graduation Short Story booklet, the text is in one Word file. You already have linked the text boxes across the content pages, so importing a single file will be convenient. After importing the text file, you then will use the Clipboard task pane to help you keep track of objects as you insert them across pages. Some pages will display a picture. All of the verso pages will display a sidebar with the name of the story. As you place pictures, text will wrap around the pictures. Later in the module, some content pages will need a section heading, similar to a chapter heading.

BTW
Clipboard Options
You can turn on a shortcut key to display the Office Clipboard. Click the Options button at the bottom of the Clipboard task pane and then click 'Show Office Clipboard When CTRL+C Clicked Twice.' You then can access the Clipboard while copying by pressing CTRL+C twice.

To Import Text

The following steps import a text file into the booklet. To complete these steps, you will be required to use the Data Files. Please contact your instructor for information about accessing the Data Files.

1 Navigate to page 1 of the content section.

2 Display the Insert tab.

3 Click in the text box on page 1 of the content section.

④ Click the Insert File button (Insert tab | Text group), browse to the location of the Data Files, and then insert the file named Short Story to insert it into the publication (Figure 10–51).

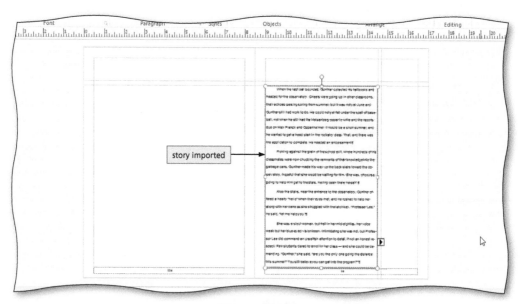

story imported

Figure 10–51

To Use the Clipboard Task Pane

1 CREATE SECTIONS | 2 INSERT PAGE NUMBERS | 3 ADJUST CELL MARGINS | 4 DISPLAY RULER GUIDES
5 PREPARE PAGES | 6 USE CLIPBOARD TASK PANE | **7 USE FIND & REPLACE** | **8 NAVIGATE WITH BOOKMARKS**

The **Clipboard task pane** allows you to cut and paste multiple items from the Office Clipboard. Recall that the Office Clipboard holds 24 items and is different from the Windows Clipboard, which holds only one. The following steps use the Clipboard task pane to copy the WordArt title for use on other pages. *Why? Using the Clipboard task pane to store the WordArt allows you to paste conveniently across pages, while making other edits.*

①

• Navigate to the first page of the publication and display the Home tab.

• Click the Clipboard Dialog Box Launcher to open the Clipboard task pane. If any previously copied items appear in the Click an Item to Paste area, click the Clear All button (Clipboard task pane) (Figure 10–52).

Experiment

• Click the Options button (Clipboard task pane) to view the choices regarding the display of the task pane. Click the scratch area to close the menu.

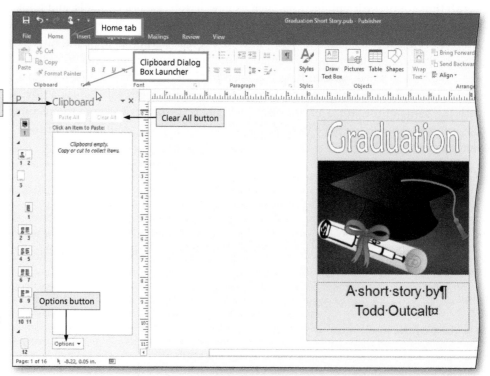

Figure 10–52

2

- Right-click the WordArt title, Graduation, and then click Copy on the shortcut menu to copy the WordArt to the Clipboard task pane (Figure 10–53).

Q&A What is the purpose of the yellow box that was displayed briefly when I pasted?

Publisher displays a yellow status box when pasting to the Clipboard task pane. It reminds you how many paste items you still have room for on the clipboard.

If I am going to paste the object in the next step, do I have to use the Clipboard task pane?

If you are sure that you will make no other edits until you paste the object, then you do not need to use the Clipboard task pane; however, if you are making changes to various pages, it is a good idea to keep the task pane open so that you do not lose the copy.

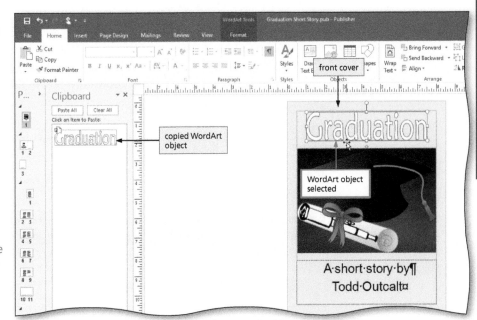

Figure 10–53

To Paste from the Clipboard Task Pane

1 CREATE SECTIONS | 2 INSERT PAGE NUMBERS | 3 ADJUST CELL MARGINS | 4 DISPLAY RULER GUIDES
5 PREPARE PAGES | 6 USE CLIPBOARD TASK PANE | **7 USE FIND & REPLACE** | **8 NAVIGATE WITH BOOKMARKS**

The following step pastes from the clipboard task pane. **Why?** *Pasting from the clipboard allows you to preview what will be pasted.*

1

- In the Page Navigation pane, navigate to page 2 in the content section. Collapse all other sections, if necessary.
- Click the copied item in the Clipboard task pane to paste it into the publication (Figure 10–54).

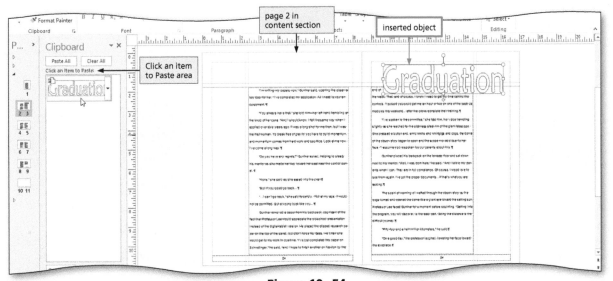

Figure 10–54

Other Ways

1. Click button next to item on Clipboard task pane, click Paste on menu

To Edit the WordArt

The following steps rotate, move, resize, and fill the WordArt to create a sidebar.

1 With the pasted WordArt still selected, click the Rotate Objects button (Home tab | Arrange group) and then click 'Rotate Left 90°' in the Rotate Objects gallery.

2 Display the WordArt Tools Format tab.

3 Click the Shape Fill arrow (WordArt Tools Format tab | WordArt Styles group) and then click 'Accent 1 (RGB (91, 155, 213))' to apply a medium blue color.

4 SHIIFT+drag a corner sizing handle to resize the WordArt object to approximately 5.5 by 1.25 inches.

5 Move the WordArt object to a location left of the text box on page 2. For horizontal alignment, place the left edge of the WordArt object at 0.75 inches. For vertical alignment, use the pink alignment guide to center it with the text box (Figure 10–55).

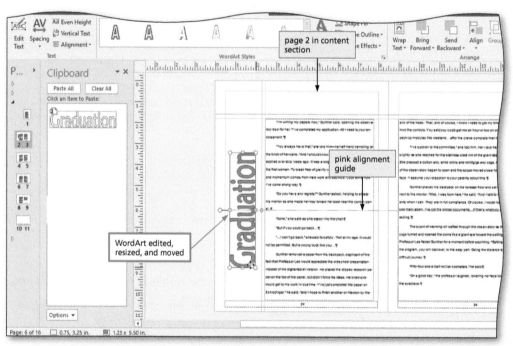

Figure 10–55

To Copy and Paste the Sidebar

BTW
Show Office
Clipboard Icon
While using the Office Clipboard, the Windows 10 taskbar displays a Clipboard icon. Right-clicking the icon displays a shortcut menu with commands to help you manage the Clipboard. If you do not see it, click the Options button (Clipboard task pane) and then click 'Show Office Clipboard Icon on Task Bar.' Alternately, you may need to click the 'Show hidden icons' button (Windows taskbar).

The following steps copy the sidebar and paste it to each of the verso pages in the content section. Pasting from the clipboard keeps the exact size, shape, and location of the object for each page.

1 With the filled WordArt object still selected, press CTRL+C to copy it to the Clipboard task pane.

2 Navigate to page 4.

3 On the Clipboard task pane, click the newly pasted object to paste it on the page.

4 Repeat the process for pages 6, 8, and 10, even though page 10 currently has no text (Figure 10–56).

5 Close the Clipboard task pane.

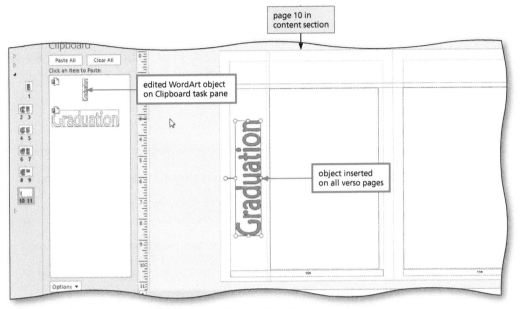

page 10 in content section

edited WordArt object on Clipboard task pane

object inserted on all verso pages

Figure 10–56

To Insert a Picture

The following steps insert a picture from the Data Files on page 3 and then move and resize it. Please contact your instructor for information about accessing the Data Files.

1 Navigate to page 3 of the content section.

2 Click the Pictures button (Insert tab | Illustrations group). When Publisher displays the Insert Picture dialog box, navigate to the Data Files, and then double-click the Observatory file.

3 SHIFT+drag a corner handle to resize the picture to approximately 4.25 inches wide.

4 Move the picture to the upper right corner of page 3 as shown in Figure 10–57.

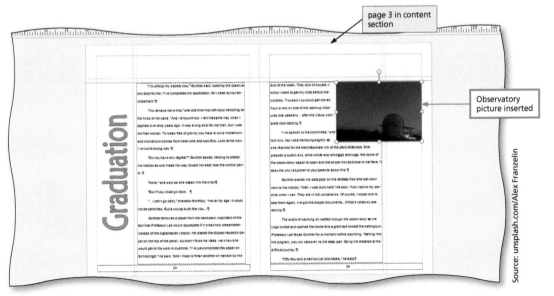

page 3 in content section

Observatory picture inserted

Source: unsplash.com/Alex Franzelin

Figure 10–57

To Insert More Pictures

The following steps insert pictures from the Data Files on the other recto pages. As you resize and move the pictures, use the Measurement task pane as necessary. Please contact your instructor for information about accessing the Data Files.

1 Navigate to page 5 and insert the picture named Galaxy.

2 SHIFT+drag a corner handle to resize the picture to approximately 4.25 inches wide.

3 Move the picture to the right margin and approximately 3.25 inches from the top of the page.

4 Navigate to page 7 and insert the picture named Mechanism.

5 SHIFT+drag a corner handle to resize the picture to approximately 4.25 inches wide.

6 Move the picture to the right margin and approximately 4.25 inches from the top of the page.

7 Navigate to page 9 and insert the picture named Stars.

8 SHIFT+drag a corner handle to resize the picture to approximately 4.25 inches wide.

9 Move the picture to the right margin and approximately 5 inches from the top of the page.

10 Navigate to page 11 and insert the picture named Earth.

11 SHIFT+drag a corner handle to resize the picture to approximately 4.25 inches wide.

12 Move the picture to the lower-right corner of the page, aligned with the margins.

To Change Text Wrapping Options

Recall that you have used the Text Wrap gallery to change how text wraps around a picture, including options such as tight, top and bottom, and square wrapping. In the following steps, you will increase the distance between the text and picture using text wrapping layout options. *Why? With large pictures and small text, the normal wrapping distance may seem too close.*

1

- Navigate to page 3 and select the Observatory picture.

- Click the Wrap Text button (Picture Tools Format tab | Arrange group) to display the Wrap Text gallery (Figure 10–58).

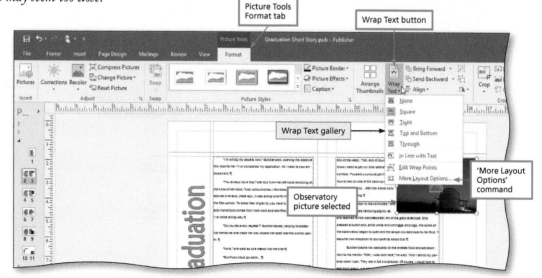

Figure 10–58

2

- Click 'More Layout Options' in the Wrap Text gallery to display the Format Picture dialog box.

- In the Distance from text area on the Layout tab, click to remove the check mark from the Automatic check box.

- Click the Bottom up arrow to increase the distance to 0.14 inches.

- Click the Left up arrow to increase the distance to 0.14 inches (Figure 10–59).

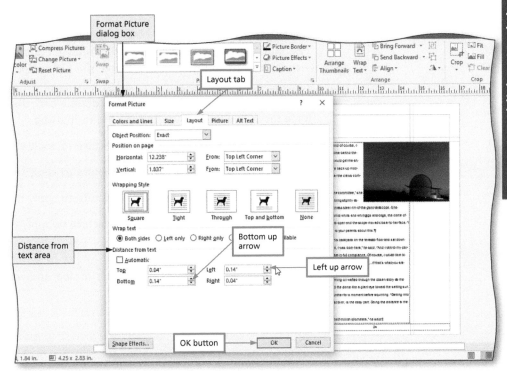

Figure 10–59

3

- Click the OK button (Format Picture dialog box) to apply the setting (Figure 10–60).

🔍 **Experiment**

- Click the Undo button on the Quick Access Toolbar to view the text wrapping before the change. Click the Redo button to compare the text wrapping.

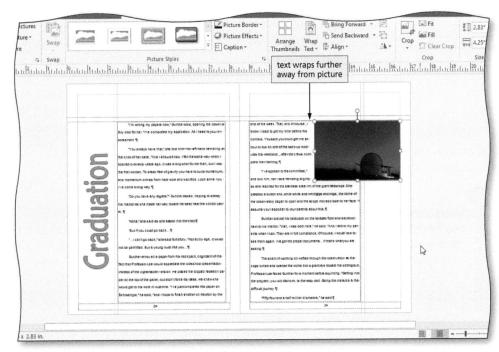

Figure 10–60

To Copy the Wrapping Style

The following steps use the format painter to copy the text wrapping format to the other pictures. In addition, you will save the file again.

1 With the picture on page 3 still selected, double-click the Format Painter button (Home tab | Clipboard group) to copy the formatting.

2 Navigate to page 5 and then click the picture to apply the formatting.

3 Navigate to page 7 and then click the picture to apply the formatting.

4 Navigate to page 9 and then click the picture to apply the formatting.

5 Navigate to page 11 and then click the picture to apply the formatting.

6 Click the Format Painter button (Home tab | Clipboard group) again to deselect it.

7 Click the Save button on the Quick Access Toolbar to overwrite the previously saved file.

Break Point: If you wish to take a break, this is a good place to do so. You can exit Publisher now. To resume at a later time, run Publisher, open the file called Graduation Short Story, and continue following the steps from this location forward.

Find and Replace

Many kinds of applications provide you the capability to find or search for specific characters. Most also allow you to search for and then replace text. Publisher's Find and Replace commands use a task pane to help you determine search parameters and how the replacement will be made. For example, you can search for matches that use whole words only or occurrences that match in case. You also can search forward or backward through the publication, as well as searching the publication in its entirety. In Publisher, you have to find the search string one occurrence at a time. The Replace command offers a choice between replacing one occurrence at a time or replacing all occurrences.

What are global tools?

Publisher tools that help you locate information in large-scale publications are called global tools. Use find and search techniques to make consistent corrections. Replace overused words, or find better terms with synonyms from the built-in thesaurus. Create manual page breaks to make content flow better and keep paragraphs together. Insert bookmarks at logical locations that you may need to locate frequently. Bookmarks are discussed later in the module.

CONSIDER THIS

You can search for individual characters, symbols, spaces, formatting marks, or entire words and phrases. Table 10–1 displays some of the wildcard and formatting marks for which you can search. A **wildcard** is a character that may be substituted for any possible characters when searching. Publisher uses the ? (question mark) as a wildcard character.

Table 10–1 Wildcard and Format Searching

Search Characters	Searches For	Example	Finds
?	wildcard	s?t	sat, sit, subset, stalwart, etc.
^^	caret	^^	next occurrence of ^
^?	question mark	^?	next occurrence of a question mark
^n	soft return	^n	next occurrence of a soft return
^(number)	search for ASCII character	^233	next occurrence of é
^p	hard return	^pTo	new line that begins with the word To, Today, etc.
^t	tab character	^t^t	two tabs together
^w	white space	^w	next occurrence of any kind of white space, including tabs

To Use the Find Command

1 CREATE SECTIONS | 2 INSERT PAGE NUMBERS | 3 ADJUST CELL MARGINS | 4 DISPLAY RULER GUIDES
5 PREPARE PAGES | 6 USE CLIPBOARD TASK PANE | 7 USE FIND & REPLACE | **8 NAVIGATE WITH BOOKMARKS**

Sometimes, you may want to find an occurrence of a certain character or phrase in a long publication. *Why? Using the Find feature in Publisher is faster than reading through the entire publication and attempting to locate the text manually.* The following steps use the Find command to locate the word, scope.

1

- Navigate to page 1 of the content section.
- Display the Home tab.
- Click the Find button (Home tab | Editing group) to open the Find and Replace task pane.
- In the Search for box, type **scope** to enter the search term (Figure 10–61).

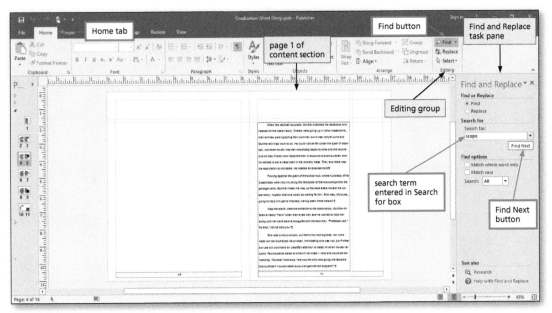

Figure 10–61

2

- Click the Find Next button.
- Press the F9 key to zoom to 100% (Figure 10–62).

Q&A

Why did Publisher find the word, telescope?
With none of the check boxes selected in the Find and Replace task pane, Publisher is looking for any sequence of the letters, scope. For example, it also would find periscope or scopes, with any combination of lowercase and uppercase letters.

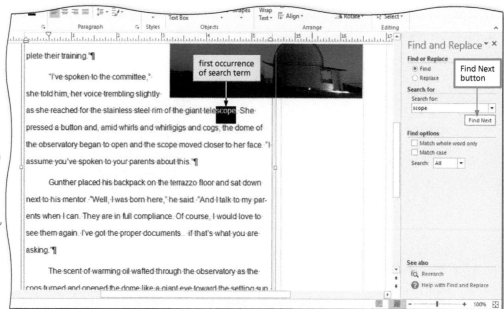

Figure 10–62

3

- Click the Find Next button several times to find other occurrences of the search term (Figure 10–63).

Experiment

- Enter some of the examples from Table 10–1 to look for formatting characters and to use wildcards.

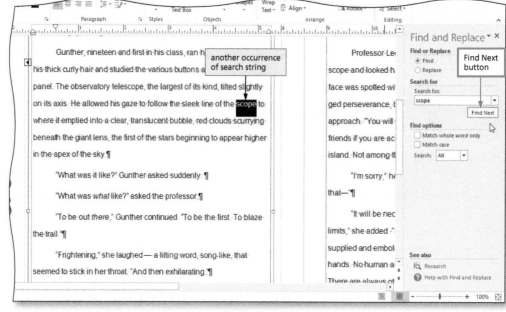

Figure 10–63

Other Ways

1. Press CTRL+F, enter characters to find in Find and Replace task pane, click Find Next button

To Find Whole Words Only

The following step uses the Find command to locate the whole word, test. *Why? Searching for the whole word will omit any of its other forms, such as testing or greatest.*

1

- Select the current text in the Search for text box (Find and Replace task pane) and then type **test** to enter the new search term.

- Click to display a check mark in the 'Match whole word only' check box.

- Click the Find Next button (Figure 10–64).

Q&A Do I need to start at the first page of my publication?
No, Publisher will search from the current location and continue searching all text boxes on all pages.

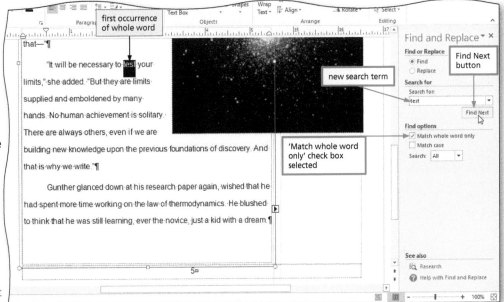

Figure 10–64

Source: unsplash.com/NASA

To Use the Replace Command

Sometimes, you may want to make changes to a character or set of characters across multiple locations in a publication. *Why? A date or place may change and you need to make sure you locate and change all of the occurrences.* In the Graduation short story, the author has decided to change the name of the character from Gunther to Gordon. The following steps use the Replace command.

1

- In the Find and Replace task pane, click the Replace option button to display the Replace with settings.

- Select the current text in the Search for text box and then type **Gunther** to enter the new search term.

- Press the TAB key to move to the Replace with text box.

- Type **Gordon** in the Replace with text box to specify the replacement term.

- If necessary, click to place a check mark in the 'Match whole word only' check box. Click to place a check mark in the Match case check box.

- Click the Find Next button (Figure 10–65).

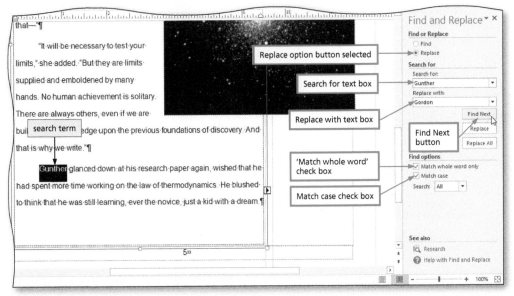

Figure 10–65

2

- Click the Replace button to replace the current selection and to move to the next occurrence (Figure 10–66).

Q&A What does the Match case check box do?
When you select the Match case check box, Publisher will find only the exact capitalization of the occurrence. For example, it would differentiate between School and school.

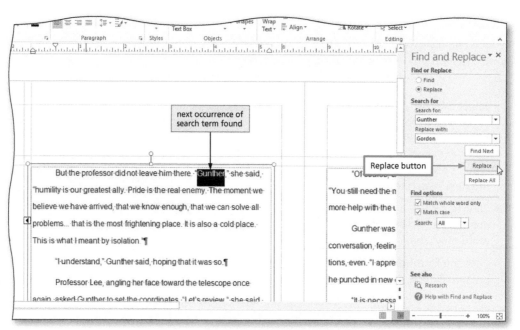

Figure 10–66

3

- Click the Replace All button to replace all of the other occurrences (Figure 10–67).

Q&A Can I always use the Replace All button?
No. You must be extremely careful about specifying exact text and parameters in the Find and Replace task pane. Do not click the Replace All button unless you absolutely are sure that your search term will not be misinterpreted.

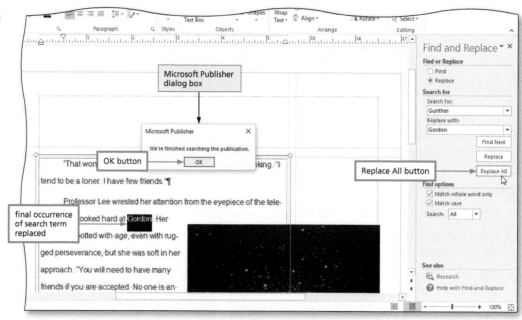

Figure 10–67

4

- When Publisher finishes replacing the text, click the OK button (Microsoft Publisher dialog box) to close the dialog box.

Other Ways

1. Press CTRL+H, enter characters to find, enter characters to replace, click Replace button in Find and Replace task pane

2. Click Replace button (Home tab | Editing group), enter characters to find, enter characters to replace, click Replace button in Find and Replace task pane

Thesaurus

When writing, you may discover that you used the same word in multiple locations or that a word you used was not quite appropriate. In these instances, you will want to look up a **synonym** or a word similar in meaning to the duplicate or inappropriate word. A **thesaurus** is a book of synonyms. Publisher provides a thesaurus so that you have a tool to assist you in creating your publications.

To Use the Thesaurus

In this project, you would like to find a synonym for the word, waning, in the third paragraph on page 7 of the content section. ***Why?*** *You would like to find a more suitable and modern term.* The following steps show how to find an appropriate synonym.

- Search for the word, waning.
- Click the Close button in the Find and Replace task pane.
- Display the Review tab.
- With the word, waning, selected, click the Thesaurus button (Review tab | Proofing group) to open the Thesaurus task pane (Figure 10–68).

⊘ Experiment

- Scroll in the Thesaurus task pane to display more synonyms.

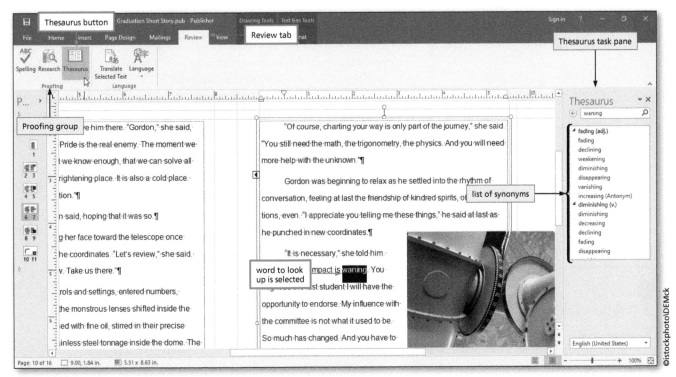

Figure 10–68

2

- Point to the word, diminishing, to display the arrow and then click the arrow to display the list of options (Figure 10–69).

Q&A | What if the synonyms list does not display a suitable word?

The Thesaurus task pane displays many listings; however, if you do not find a suitable word, you can click any word in the task pane to look up other synonyms. You also can look up an **antonym**, or a word with an opposite meaning.

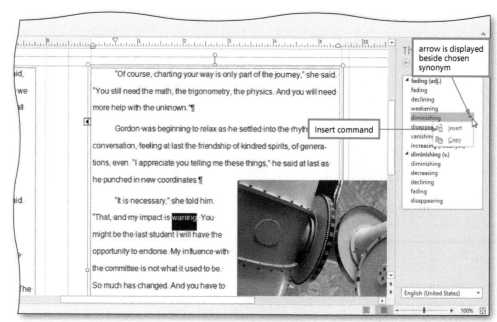

Figure 10–69

3

- Click Insert to replace the word, waning, in the document with the word, diminishing (Figure 10–70).

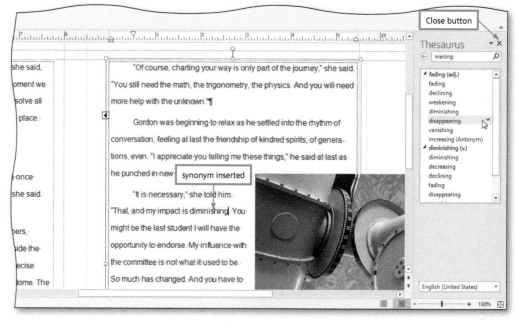

Figure 10–70

4

- Click the Close button on the Thesaurus task pane title bar to close the task pane.

Other Ways

1. Select word, press SHIFT+F7
2. Right-click word, click Look Up on shortcut menu, click synonym in Thesaurus task pane

Navigating through a Large-Scale Publication

To make it easier to navigate through a large publication and check pagination, Publisher provides commands that help both designers and viewers of the publication. The 'Go to Page' command allows you to move quickly to a given page number to edit or read the information.

By breaking a large publication into sections, chapters, or modules, you also make it easier for readers to find their way through the publications. You can insert breaks in connected text boxes to move text to the next page. Breaks sometimes are used to delineate chapters or sections of text. In this module, you will create breaks to indicate sections of the book. Those sections, with new headings, will be used in the table of contents.

To Use the 'Go to Page' Command

1 CREATE SECTIONS | 2 INSERT PAGE NUMBERS | 3 ADJUST CELL MARGINS | 4 DISPLAY RULER GUIDES
5 PREPARE PAGES | 6 USE CLIPBOARD TASK PANE | 7 USE FIND & REPLACE | **8 NAVIGATE WITH BOOKMARKS**

In longer publications, you may find the Page Navigation pane cumbersome, especially if you have to scroll through many sections and pages. The 'Go to Page' command displays a dialog box that allows you to enter the desired page number in the publication; however, you must use sequential page numbers related to the overall publication. *Why? Many publications will have duplicate page numbers, such as a page 1 for each section; therefore, you must use the page number as shown on the Publisher status bar.*

The following steps use the 'Go to page' command to move quickly to the sixth page of the publication.

- Display the Home tab.

- Click the Find arrow (Home tab | Editing group) to display the Find menu (Figure 10–71).

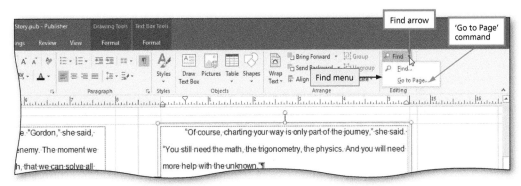

Figure 10–71

- Click 'Go to Page' on the Find menu to display the Go To Page dialog box.

- Type **6** to replace the text in the 'Go to page' text box (Figure 10–72).

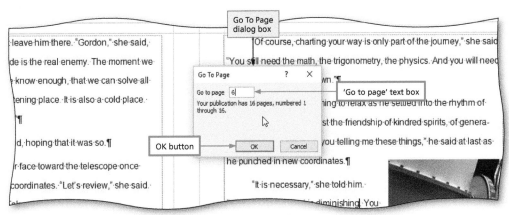

Figure 10–72

- Click the OK button (Go To Page dialog box) to go to the desired page.

- Scroll to the bottom of the page (Figure 10–73).

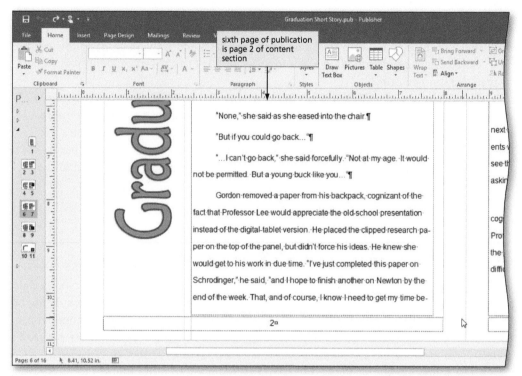

Figure 10–73

Other Ways

1. Press CTRL+G, enter page number, click OK button (Go To Page dialog box)

Page Breaks

It is important to look at large-scale publications with an eye for appropriate page or column breaks. You do not want a heading to display without its subordinate content. In some booklets, such as a schedule, you may want mornings, afternoons, or days all on the same page. You may decide a column should not break in the middle of a short paragraph.

Widow and orphan control is turned on automatically for connected text boxes. A **widow** is the last line of a paragraph appearing by itself at the top of a page. An **orphan** is the first line of a paragraph appearing by itself at the bottom of a page. For other pagination issues, you may need to manually break a page or column to force material to the next page. In Publisher, you can make decisions about keeping paragraphs together, such as bulleted lists; keeping lines together, such as for extended quotes; or forcing text to go to the next text box, which is similar to a page break.

To Create a Text Break

1 CREATE SECTIONS | 2 INSERT PAGE NUMBERS | 3 ADJUST CELL MARGINS | 4 DISPLAY RULER GUIDES
5 PREPARE PAGES | 6 USE CLIPBOARD TASK PANE | 7 USE FIND & REPLACE | **8 NAVIGATE WITH BOOKMARKS**

The author of the short story has identified four places in the text that would be better positioned as new sections. The following steps use the Paragraph dialog box to force text to go to the next text box, which in this case is the next page. *Why? Forcing text to the next page creates a kind of page break as you create sections within the short story.*

1

- Position the insertion point at the beginning of the last paragraph on the page (in this case, before the phrase that begins, Gordon removed a paper from his backpack) (Figure 10–74).

Q&A Will the setting apply before or after the insertion point?
The setting applies to the entire paragraph at the position of the insertion point, in this case following the insertion point.

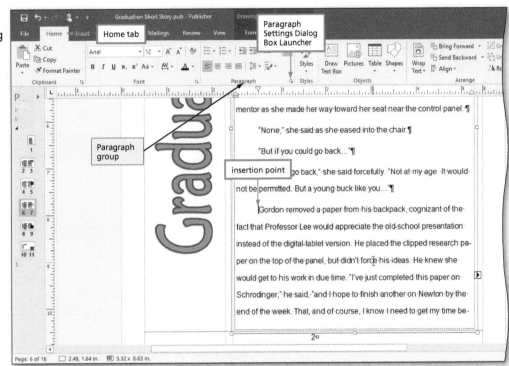

Figure 10–74

2

- Click the Paragraph Settings Dialog Box Launcher (Home tab | Paragraph group) to display the Paragraph dialog box.

- Click the 'Line and Paragraphs Breaks' tab to display the commands related to breaks.

- Click to display a check mark in the 'Start in next text box' check box (Figure 10–75).

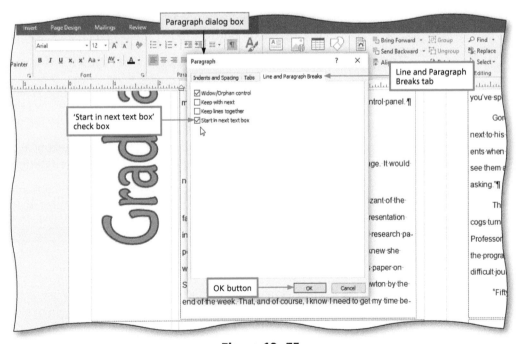

Figure 10–75

Q&A Could I press CTRL+ENTER to insert a section or page break as I do in word processing programs?
Pressing CTRL+ENTER inserts a new page and a break in the publication. In this case, you only want to move the paragraph to the next text box.

3

• Click the OK button (Paragraph dialog box) to apply the setting.

• Zoom to whole page to view the pagination (Figure 10–76).

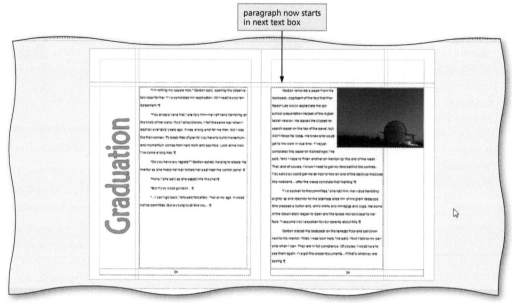

paragraph now starts in next text box

Figure 10–76

To Insert Other Breaks

The following steps create two more sections within the short story by using the Paragraph dialog box.

1 Press CTRL+G to display the Go To Page dialog box. Type **10** in the 'Go to page' text box. Click the OK button (Go To Page dialog box) to navigate to page 10.

2 Click just before the last paragraph that begins with the phrase, Gordon adjusted controls and settings.

3 Click the Paragraph Settings Dialog Box Launcher (Home tab | Paragraph group) and then click the Line and Paragraph Break tab to display the commands related to breaks.

4 Click to display a check mark in the 'Start in next text box' check box and then click the OK button (Paragraph dialog box) to apply the setting.

5 Repeat Steps 1 through 4 on the 12th page of the publication, inserting a break before the fourth paragraph that begins with the phrase, He smiled at the thought of being admitted to the program.

To Create a Section Heading

The following steps create a shape with text to use as a section heading.

1 Navigate to page 1 of the content section.

2 Insert a rectangle shape and move it to the top of the page. Resize it to fit the blank area between the margin guides as shown in Figure 10–77.

3 If necessary, fill the rectangle with the 'Accent 1 (RGB (91, 155, 213))' color.

4 If necessary, add a black shape outline.

5 Right-click the shape and then click Add Text on the shortcut menu.

6 Change the font size to 36, and if necessary, change the font color to black.

7 Type **Phase 1** to enter the text (Figure 10–77).

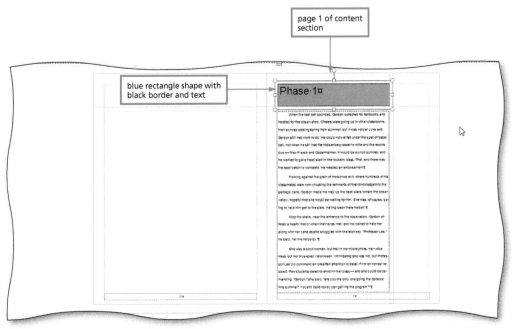

Figure 10-77

To Copy and Paste the Section Heading

The following steps copy the section heading to other pages.

1 Click the border of the section heading on page 1 to select the entire shape.

2 If desired, open the Clipboard task pane. Press CTRL+C to copy the shape.

3 Navigate to page 3 of the content section and paste the heading. Change the text to Phase 2.

4 Navigate to page 7 of the content section and paste the heading. Change the text to Phase 3.

5 Navigate to page 9 of the content section and paste the heading. Change the text to Phase 4 (Figure 10-78).

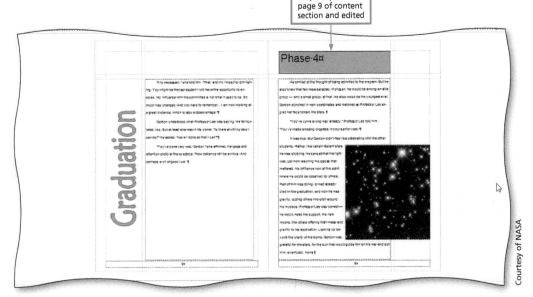

Courtesy of NASA

Figure 10-78

Updating the Table of Contents

Table 10–2 displays the table of contents for the story, based on the breaks you inserted.

Table 10–2 Table of Contents	
Item	**Page Number**
Phase 1	1
Phase 2	3
Phase 3	7
Phase 4	9

To Update the Table of Contents

The following steps update the table of contents on the third page of the publication.

1 Press CTRL+G to display the Go To Page dialog box.

2 Type **3** in the Go to page box (Go To Page dialog box), zoom to approximately 80%, and then scroll to the top of the page.

3 In the top row of the table, select the text, change the font size to 36 pt, and then type **PHASES** to replace the text.

4 Zoom and scroll as necessary while you enter the information from Table 10–2 to replace the placeholder text in the table.

5 Delete the unused rows.

6 In the table, select all cells except the PHASES heading and then change the font size to 20 pt.

7 Click outside the table to remove the selection.

8 Click the Save button on the Quick Access Toolbar to overwrite the previously saved file (Figure 10–79).

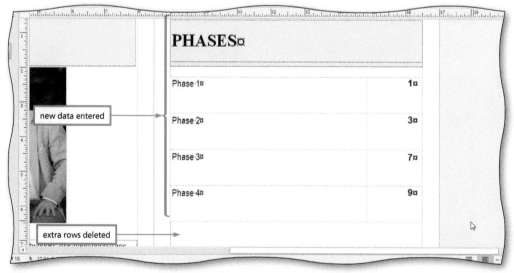

Figure 10–79

Break Point: If you wish to take a break, this is a good place to do so. You can exit Publisher now. To resume at a later time, run Publisher, open the file called Graduation Short Story, and continue following the steps from this location forward.

Bookmarks

A **bookmark** is a physical location in a publication that you name for reference purposes. Used to organize large publications, a named bookmark allows you to display its associated text quickly, instead of scrolling through the publication pages to locate an object or text. Bookmarks display as small flags in page layout only; they do not print in print publications. Bookmarks are saved, however, when the publication is saved. They serve as a searchable reference when viewing the publication online and can be referenced as a hyperlink within the Publisher publication and when converting the publication to the PDF format.

To Create a Bookmark

1 CREATE SECTIONS | 2 INSERT PAGE NUMBERS | 3 ADJUST CELL MARGINS | 4 DISPLAY RULER GUIDES
5 PREPARE PAGES | 6 USE CLIPBOARD TASK PANE | 7 USE FIND & REPLACE | **8 NAVIGATE WITH BOOKMARKS**

The following steps create a bookmark for Phase 1. *Why? When you link the table of contents to that part of the publication, bookmarks will help.*

- Navigate to page 1 in the content section.
- Display the Insert tab.
- Click the Bookmark button (Insert tab | Links group) to display the Bookmark dialog box.
- Type **Phase 1** in the Bookmark name text box (Figure 10–80).

Q&A What is the best way to navigate to page 1 of the content section? It depends on your personal preference. You can use the Page Navigation pane or press CTRL+G to display the Go To Page dialog box. If you use the dialog box, remember to enter the page number related to the entire publication, not the content section page number.

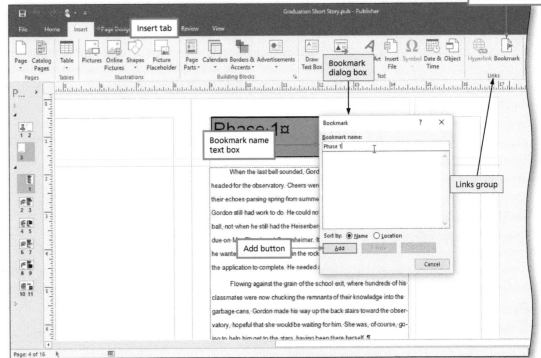

Figure 10–80

• Click the Add button (Bookmark dialog box) to insert the bookmark in the publication.

• Drag the bookmark to a location just to the left of the heading (Figure 10–81).

Q&A
Can I edit a bookmark?
You can double-click a bookmark to return to the Bookmark dialog box. From there, you can add, delete, sort, rename, or navigate to other bookmarks.

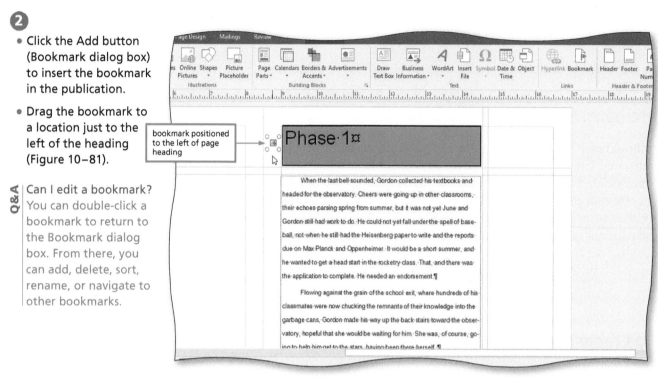

bookmark positioned to the left of page heading

Figure 10–81

To Create More Bookmarks

The following steps create additional bookmarks for each portion of the publication that is referenced in the table of contents.

1. Navigate to page 3 in the content section.

2. Click the Bookmark button (Insert tab | Links group) to display the Bookmark dialog box. Type **Phase 2** in the Bookmark name text box and then click the Add button (Bookmark dialog box) to insert the bookmark.

3. Drag the bookmark to a location just left of the heading.

4. Repeat Steps 1 through 3 to add bookmarks for Phase 3 on page 7 and Phase 4 on page 9 of the content section.

To Use Bookmarks to Create Hyperlinks

1 CREATE SECTIONS | 2 INSERT PAGE NUMBERS | 3 ADJUST CELL MARGINS | 4 DISPLAY RULER GUIDES
5 PREPARE PAGES | 6 USE CLIPBOARD TASK PANE | 7 USE FIND & REPLACE | **8 NAVIGATE WITH BOOKMARKS**

The following steps create hyperlinks in the table of contents that connect to the bookmarks in the publication. **Why?** *Using hyperlinks and bookmarks together provide quick navigation through long publications.*

1

• Navigate to the table of contents and then drag to select the text, Phase 1.

• Press CTRL+K to display the Insert Hyperlink dialog box.

• Click the 'Place in This Document' button in the Link to bar.

• Scroll in the Select a place in this document area and then click Phase 1 to choose the desired bookmark (Figure 10–82).

Q&A

What is the purpose of the Change Title button?

Each page of a publication has an internal bookmark initially named Page Title. You can edit that name by selecting the Page Title in the list and then clicking the Change Title button. That bookmark name also would appear in the title bar of a browser should the publication be used on the web.

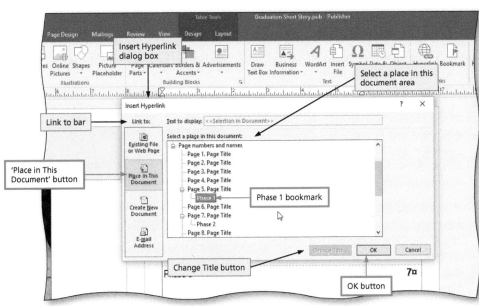

Figure 10–82

2

- Click the OK button (Insert Hyperlink dialog box) to create the hyperlink (Figure 10–83).

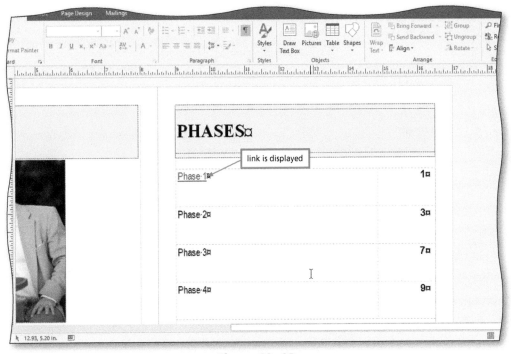

Figure 10–83

3

- Repeat Steps 1 and 2 for each of the phases in the table of contents. Link each item to its corresponding bookmark name in the Insert Hyperlink dialog box.

Other Ways

1. Select text, click 'Add a Hyperlink' button (Insert tab | Links group), click 'Place in This Document' button (Insert Hyperlink dialog box), select bookmark, click OK button

To Test a Hyperlink

The following step tests one of the hyperlinks. **Why?** *You always should test your hyperlinks to make sure they navigate to the correct location.*

1

• In the table of contents, CTRL+click the Phase 3 hyperlink to jump to the bookmark (Figure 10–84).

If instructed to do so, navigate to the end of the story. Click in the last text box and press the ENTER key twice. Type **Prepared by** and then type your name.

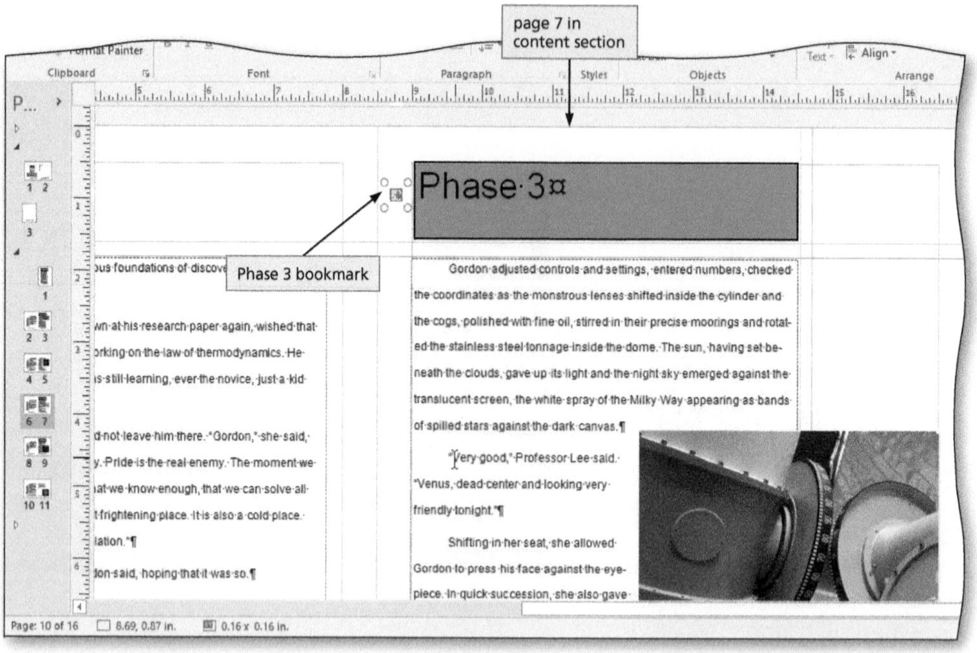

Q&A | Why did the pointer shape change to a hand when I pressed the CTRL key?
When positioned over a hyperlink, the pointer changes to a hand as soon as you press the CTRL key.

page 7 in content section

Phase 3¤

Phase 3 bookmark

Gordon·adjusted·controls·and·settings,·entered·numbers,·checked· the·coordinates·as·the·monstrous·lenses·shifted·inside·the·cylinder·and· the·cogs,·polished·with·fine·oil,·stirred·in·their·precise·moorings·and·rotat- ed·the·stainless·steel·tonnage·inside·the·dome.·The·sun,·having·set·be- neath·the·clouds,·gave·up·its·light·and·the·night·sky·emerged·against·the· translucent·screen,·the·white·spray·of·the·Milky·Way·appearing·as·bands· of·spilled·stars·against·the·dark·canvas.¶

"Very·good,"·Professor·Lee·said.· "Venus,·dead·center·and·looking·very· friendly·tonight."¶

Shifting·in·her·seat,·she·allowed· Gordon·to·press·his·face·against·the·eye- piece.·In·quick·succession,·she·also·gave·

Page: 10 of 16   8.69, 0.87 in.   0.16 x 0.16 in.

Figure 10–84

Experiment

• Return to the table of contents and check the other hyperlinks.

To Hyphenate the Publication

Long stories connected across text boxes need to be checked for proper hyphenation. While you should apply all of the hyphenation rules, you particularly should check the publication to avoid hyphenating the first or last line of paragraphs.

The following steps check the publication for spelling and design errors.

1 Navigate to page 1 of the content section and click in the text box.

2 Press CTRL+SHIFT+H to display the Hyphenation dialog box.

3 Remove the check mark in the 'Automatically hyphenate this story' check box.

4 Click the Manual button (Hyphenate dialog box) to begin the hyphenation. Go through the story following the hyphenation rules as outlined in Module 3.

To Check the Publication for Spelling and Design Errors

The following steps check the publication for spelling and design errors and then save it.

1 Press the F7 key to start checking the spelling. Choose to ignore names and acronyms.

2 When Publisher asks if you want to check the rest of the publication, click the Yes button and finish checking the spelling. If necessary, close the Master Page view.

3 Run the Design Checker. Ignore any design errors related to too much space at a margin or objects that may approach a nonprintable region.

4 Fix any other errors found by the Design Checker.

5 Close the Design Checker task pane.

6 Click the Save button on the Quick Access Toolbar to overwrite the previously saved file.

To Save in the PDF Format

To review and test the hyperlinks in a different application, the following steps save the Publisher file in the PDF format.

1 Click File on the ribbon to open the Backstage view.

2 Click the Export tab and then click the 'Create PDF/XPS' button in the right pane to display the Publish as PDF or XPS dialog box.

3 Navigate to the desired save location.

4 If necessary, type **Graduation Short Story** in the File name text box to change the file name.

5 Click the Publish button (Publish as PDF or XPS dialog box) to save the publication in the PDF format.

To Navigate with Bookmarks in a PDF File

1 CREATE SECTIONS | 2 INSERT PAGE NUMBERS | 3 ADJUST CELL MARGINS | 4 DISPLAY RULER GUIDES

5 PREPARE PAGES | 6 USE CLIPBOARD TASK PANE | 7 USE FIND & REPLACE | **8 NAVIGATE WITH BOOKMARKS**

The bookmarks and hyperlinks you created in the Publisher file automatically are created in the PDF file. Recall that PDF files open using an application such as Adobe Reader or Adobe Acrobat. The following steps open the PDF file and display the table of contents in the PDF file. *Why? The table of contents retains the hyperlinks you created in Publisher.*

1

• Open a File Explorer window and navigate to the location of your saved files.

• Double-click the PDF file named Graduation Short Story to open it.

• Zoom to view the entire page (Figure 10–85).

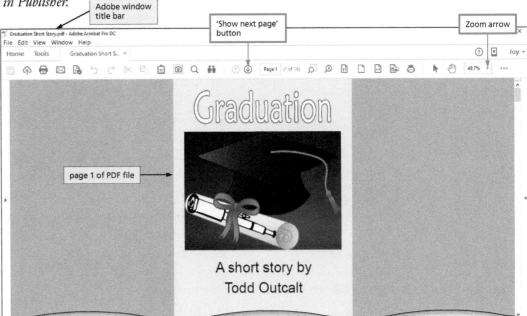

Figure 10–85

Q&A My reader does not have a 'Show next page' button. What is the best way to navigate in the PDF file?

Your application may use the RIGHT ARROW key to move down through the document, page by page.

- Navigate to page 3 in the 16-page publication (Figure 10–86).

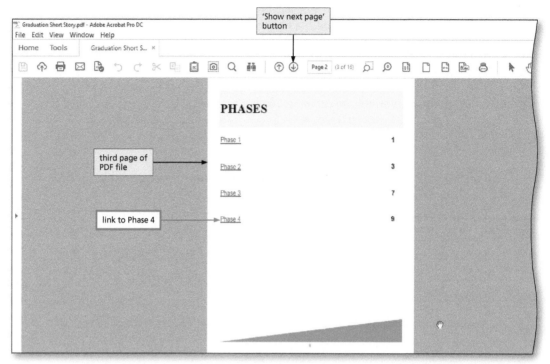

Figure 10–86

- Click the Phase 4 link to navigate to that page in the booklet (Figure 10–87).

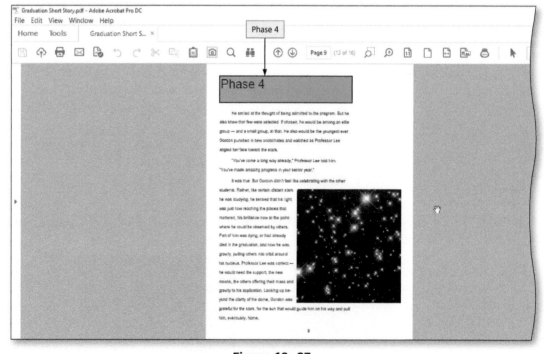

Figure 10–87

④

- Click the Close button on the viewer's title bar to exit the program.
- Click the Close button on the Publisher title bar to exit Publisher. If Publisher displays a dialog box, click the Don't Save button.

Summary

In this module, you worked with large-scale publications by inserting and duplicating pages, assigning page number formatting, set beginning page numbers, and paginating page parts. You learned how to create and work with sections in the Page Navigation pane. After inserting the front matter, you created ruler guides and linked text boxes for the content pages of the booklet. Next, you used global editing tools, such as find and replace, the thesaurus, and the 'Go to page' command. You created breaks in the publication. Finally, you created bookmarks and hyperlinks to help viewers navigate from the table of contents to various pages.

What decisions will you need to make when creating your next catalog?
Use these guidelines as you complete the assignments in this chapter and create your own publications outside of this class.

1. After deciding on the purpose and audience of a large-scale publication, design the layout, insert pages, and create sections.

2. Use appropriate pagination and be consistent in its placement.

   a) Use lowercase Roman numeral for the front matter.

   b) Use standard Arabic numerical for the main content.

   c) Decide on page numbering for any end matter material.

3. Apply BorderArt sparingly and purposefully.

4. Ruler guides may be used to help alignment of objects on each page.

5. Insert content and thoroughly proofread.

6. Employ the Find and Replace commands to make consistent changes throughout the publication.

7. Use the thesaurus as necessary.

8. Create bookmarks and hyperlinks to help with navigation.

9. Proofread again and use the Design Checker.

10. Convert to a PDF file, if necessary.

Apply Your Knowledge

Reinforce the skills and apply the concepts you learned in this module.

Paginating a Large-Scale Publication

Note: To complete this assignment, you will be required to use the Data Files. Please contact your instructor for information about accessing the Data Files.

Instructions: Run Publisher. Open the file, Apply 10–1 Book Template, from the Data Files. You are to add sections, page numbering, and a border to the template. Table 10–3 displays the sections to create and the page numbering formats.

Table 10–3 Pagination for Apply 10–1 Book Template Edited		
Publication Pages	**Section**	**Page Numbering**
1–2	front cover	none
3–6	front matter	i, ii, iii, …
7–15	content	1, 2, 3, …
16–18	end matter	continuing 1, 2, 3, …
19–20	back cover	none

A sample two-page spread is shown in Figure 10–88, along with the Page Navigation pane.

Continued >

Apply Your Knowledge *continued*

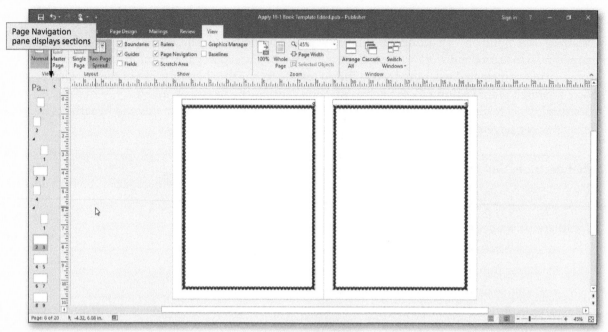

Figure 10–88

Perform the following tasks:

1. Click File on the ribbon and then click Save As to display the Save As gallery. Save the publication with the file name, Apply 10–1 Book Template Complete on your storage location.

2. If necessary, turn on boundaries, rulers, guides, page navigation, and the scratch area by clicking the appropriate check boxes (View tab | Show group).

3. To create sections:

    a. To create a section for the cover page and inside cover page, right-click page 3 in the Page Navigation pane, and then click Insert Section on the shortcut menu.

    b. To create a section for the four pages of front matter, right-click page 7 in the Page Navigation pane and then click Insert Section on the shortcut menu.

    c. To create a section for the nine pages of content, right-click page 16 in the Page Navigation pane and then click Insert Section on the shortcut menu.

    d. To create a section for the three pages of end matter, right-click page 19 in the Page Navigation pane and then click Insert Section on the shortcut menu.

4. To insert page numbers on every page:

    a. Display the Insert tab.

    b. Click the Page Number button (Insert tab | Header & Footer group) and then click Top Right to insert page numbers.

    c. Zoom to 100% and, if necessary, scroll to view the page numbers.

    d. Double-click the page number and format it to be bold and use a font size of 16.

    e. If necessary, press CTRL+M to close Master Page view.

5. To format page numbers for the front matter:

    a. Right-click page 3 in the Page Navigation pane, point to Page Numbers on the shortcut menu, and then click 'Format Page Numbers' on the Page Numbers submenu to display the Page Number Format dialog box.

    b. Click the Number format arrow (Page Number Format dialog box) and then click 'i, ii, iii, …' in the Number format list.

    c. Click the 'Start this section with' option button (Page Number Format dialog box) and then type **1** as the starting page number.

    d. Click the OK button (Page Number Format dialog box) to apply the page number formatting.

6. To format page numbers for the content pages:

    a. Right-click Page 7 in the Page Navigation pane, click Page Numbers on the shortcut menu, and then click 'Format Page Numbers' to display the Page Number Format dialog box.

    b. Click the Number format arrow (Page Number Format dialog box), and then click '1, 2, 3, …' in the list.

    c. Click the 'Start this section with' option button (Page Number Format dialog box) and then type **1** as the starting page number.

    d. Click the OK button (Page Number Format dialog box) to apply the page number formatting.

7. To remove page numbers from the front cover section and back cover section:

    a. Right-click the first page in the Page Navigation pane, click Master Pages on the shortcut menu, and then click None.

    b. Right-click the second page in the Page Navigation pane, click Master Pages on the shortcut menu, and then click None.

    c. Right-click the next-to-the-last page in the Page Navigation pane, click Master Pages on the shortcut menu, and then click None.

    d. Right-click the last page in the Page Navigation pane, click Master Pages on the shortcut menu, and then click None.

8. Press CTRL+M to access Master Page view. If necessary, click the 'Show Whole Page' button on the Publisher status bar.

9. Click the Duplicate button (Master Page tab | Master Page group) and name the page, BorderArt. Click the OK button (Duplicate Master Page dialog box).

10. To create a border for the content pages:

    a. Display the Insert tab. Click the Shapes button (Insert tab | Illustrations group) and then click the Rectangle shape.

    b. Drag the pointer to draw a rectangle that fills the entire page from the upper-left margin to the lower-right margin. Do not include the page number area.

    c. Right-click the rectangle and then click Format AutoShape on the shortcut menu.

    d. Click the BorderArt button (Format AutoShape dialog box) and then scroll as necessary to select the Zig Zag border.

    e. Click the OK button (BorderArt dialog box) to select the border.

    f. In the Line area, change the color to a dark blue.

    g. Click the OK button (Format AutoShape dialog box) to apply the border.

11. Press CTRL+M to close the master page.

12. Collapse all sections and then expand the third section that includes the content pages.

13. In the Page Navigation pane, right-click the first page in the content section, point to Master Pages on the shortcut menu, and then click BorderArt (B) on the Master Pages submenu.

14. Repeat Step 13 for each of the nine pages in the content section.

15. If instructed to do so, create a text box on the title page and enter your name, course number, and date.

Continued >

Apply Your Knowledge *continued*

16. Save the publication again with the same file name.

17. If you have permission, send the publication to your instructor as an email message attachment.

18. ❋ What are some advantages to creating a template like this one? What other features might you add to make the template even more useful?

Extend Your Knowledge

Extend the skills you learned in this module and experiment with new skills. You may need to use Help to complete the assignment.

Using Baseline Guides

Note: To complete this assignment, you will be required to use the Data Files. Please contact your instructor for information about accessing the Data Files.

Instructions: Run Publisher. Open the publication, Extend 10–1 Baseline Guides, from the Data Files. You will edit the publication to align the text in the two text boxes (Figure 10–89).

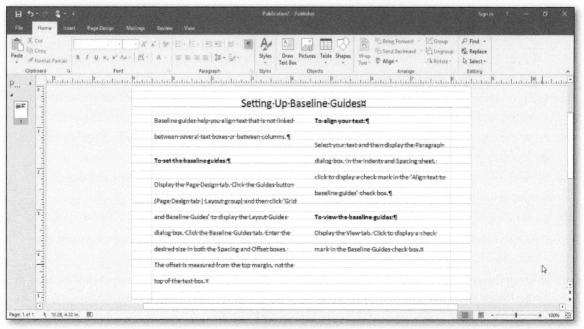

Figure 10–89

Perform the following tasks:

1. Use Help to learn more about Baseline Guides in Publisher.

2. To set the baseline guides:

   a. Display the Page Design tab.

   b. Click the Guides button (Page Design tab | Layout group) and then click 'Grid and Baseline Guides' in the Guides gallery to display the Layout Guides dialog box.

   c. Click the Baseline Guides tab. Enter **14** in both the Spacing and Offset boxes.

3. To align the text:

   a. Select the text in the left text box.

   b. Display the Paragraph dialog box and click the Indents and Spacing tab.

c. Click to display a check mark in the 'Align text to baseline guides' check box. Click the OK button (Paragraph dialog box).

d. Select the text in the right text box. Repeats Steps 3b and 3c.

4. To view the baseline guides:

a. Display the View tab.

b. Click to display a check mark in the Baselines check box (View tab | Show group).

5. If instructed to do so, create a third text box on the page. Write a few sentences about what you found when researching Publisher Help about baseline guides.

6. Save the publication with the file name, Extend 10–1 Baseline Guides Complete.

7. Submit the file in the format specified by your instructor.

8. ✹ Describe a publication that would need to use baseline guides. When would it be better to create linked text boxes? Why?

Expand Your World

Create a solution that uses cloud and web technologies by learning and investigating on your own from general guidance.

Publishing Online

Instructions: You would like to put your publication online for your friends and colleagues to see. You notice that most web services require a PDF file, so you decide to publish the PDF file you created in this module. If you did not complete the module, see your instructor for an appropriate file to use.

Perform the following tasks:

1. Run a browser and navigate to the issuu.com website.

2. Click the 'PUBLISH ON ISSUU' button (shown in Figure 10–90a).

a) Opening Screen on issuu.com

Figure 10–90a

Continued >

Expand Your World *continued*

3. On the next screen, click the 'See Our Plans' button.

4. On the next screen, click the GET STARTED button in the Basic Free area.

5. If necessary, create a free account for the service.

6. Click the 'Select a file to get started' button, navigate to the location in which you stored the files for this module, and then double-click the PDF file named Graduation Short Story.

7. If desired, enter a description of the story in the Description text box and enter the current date (Figure 10–90b).

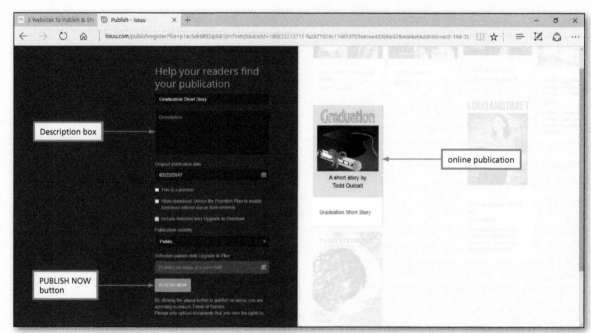

b) Publish Screen on issuu.com

Figure 10–90b

8. Click the PUBLISH NOW button to publish your pdf file online.

9. If instructed to do so, click the 'Share it socially' link and copy the web address. Send the web address to your instructor.

10. Double-click the story in the right pane of issuu.com. Flip through the pages.

11. Exit the browser.

12. ✳ What are the advantages of sharing a publication via a web service like issuu.com? Could friends and customers navigate through the publication easier than if it were emailed or posted on a social media site? What are the disadvantages?

In the Labs

Design, create, modify, and/or use a publication following the guidelines, concepts, and skills presented in this module. Labs 1 and 2, which increase in difficulty, require you to create solutions based on what you learned in the module; Lab 3 requires you to apply your creative thinking and problem-solving skills to design and implement a solution.

Lab 1: **Formatting Cell Margins, Vertical Text, and Tints**

Problem: You decide to keep track of your expenses for the spring semester as shown in Table 10–4.

Table 10–4 Spring Semester Expenses					
	Dorm	**Food**	**Locker**	**Phone**	**Miscellaneous**
January	448.77	166.89	15.00	32.53	55.00
February	448.77	127.44	15.00	27.33	68.00
March	448.77	112.55	15.00	22.86	57.00
April	448.77	100.89	15.00	30.97	73.00
May	448.77	102.85	15.00	26.55	51.00

The final copy of your monthly expenses table appears in Figure 10–91.

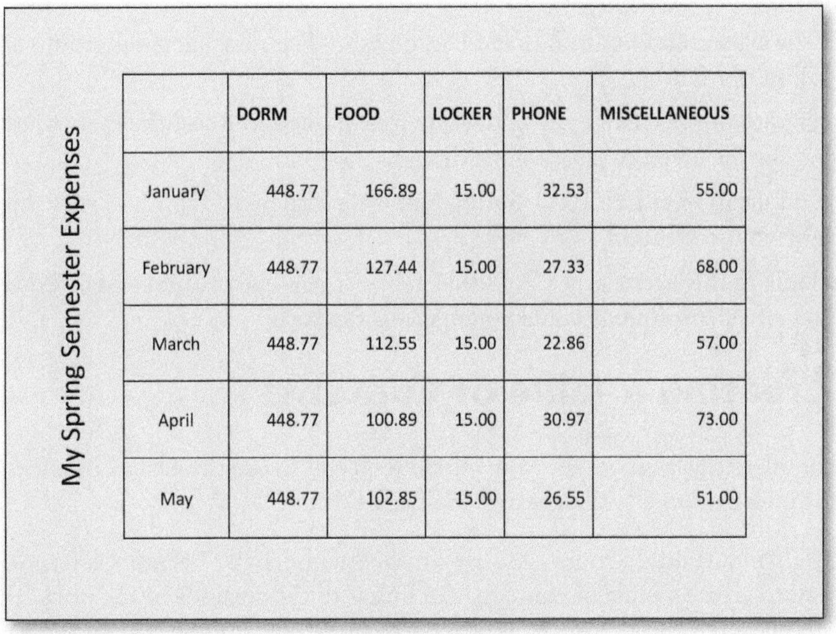

	DORM	FOOD	LOCKER	PHONE	MISCELLANEOUS
January	448.77	166.89	15.00	32.53	55.00
February	448.77	127.44	15.00	27.33	68.00
March	448.77	112.55	15.00	22.86	57.00
April	448.77	100.89	15.00	30.97	73.00
May	448.77	102.85	15.00	26.55	51.00

My Spring Semester Expenses

Figure 10–91

Perform the following tasks:

1. Run Publisher and open a blank 11 × 8.5" publication in landscape orientation.
2. Set the font scheme to Office 1 and the color scheme to Office.
3. To create a heading with a vertical text direction:
   a. Create a text box on the left side of the publication, approximately 1-inch wide, which runs from the top to the bottom of the publication.
   b. Set the font size to 28 and change the text direction to vertical text.
   c. Select the text box and display the Home tab.
   d. Click the Rotate Objects button (Home tab | Arrange group) and then click Flip Vertical in the Rotate Objects gallery to rotate the text box.
   e. In the text box, type **My Spring Semester Expenses** to create the heading and then deselect the text box.

Continued >

In the Labs *continued*

4. To create the table:

a. Display the Insert tab.

b. Click the 'Add a Table' button (Insert tab | Tables group) and create a 6 × 6 table that fills the rest of the page.

c. Enter the text from Table 10–4.

d. Select the first column of the table and then display the Table Tools Layout tab.

e. Click the Align Center button (Table Tools Layout tab | Alignment group) to center the cells.

f. Select all of the cells with dollar amounts and right-justify them.

g. Select the table. Click the Cell Margins button (Table Tools Layout tab | Alignment group) and then click Wide in the Cell Margins gallery to change the cell margins.

5. To add a tint to the page background:

a. Display the Page Design tab.

b. Click the Background button (Page Design tab | Page Background group) and then click '10% Tint of Main'.

6. If instructed to do so, change the budget figures in one month of the table to estimates of what you spend for the given categories in a month.

7. Save the publication as Lab 10–1 Spring Semester Expenses Table and then submit the file as directed by your instructor.

8. ✳ The table in this exercise is a Publisher table. If you had created an embedded Excel table, what kinds of enhancements could you make to the table?

Lab 2: **Creating a Table of Contents**

Note: To complete this assignment, you will be required to use the Data Files. Please contact your instructor for information about accessing the Data Files.

Problem: Highland Middle School is nearly finished with its 2017 yearbook template. The staff would like you to create a table of contents and link it to the sections in the book. In addition to selling print copies, Highland posts its yearbook as a PDF file online. You decide to use Publisher bookmarks to design a table of contents, as shown in Figure 10–92.

Perform the following tasks:

1. Run Publisher and open the file named Lab 10–2 Student Yearbook from the Data Files.

2. Press CTRL+F to open the Find and Replace task pane.

3. Search for the first occurrence of the word, Students.

4. Display the Insert tab and then use the Bookmark button (Insert tab | Links group) to create a bookmark named Students. Drag the bookmark to the top of the page.

5. Repeat Steps 2 through 4 to search for the words, Sports, Drama & Music, Class Officers, and Teachers. At the first occurrence of each term, create a bookmark on that page with the appropriate name.

6. Use the 'Go to Page' command to return to the third page of the publication. Using Figure 10–92 as a guide, fill in the table of contents with the following information: Students on page 1; Sports on page 5; Drama & Music on page 8; Class Officers on page 11; and Teachers on page 12.

7. One at a time, select the text in the first column. Press CTRL+K to display the Insert Hyperlink dialog box. Click the 'Place in This Document' button (Insert Hyperlink dialog box) and then select the appropriate bookmark.

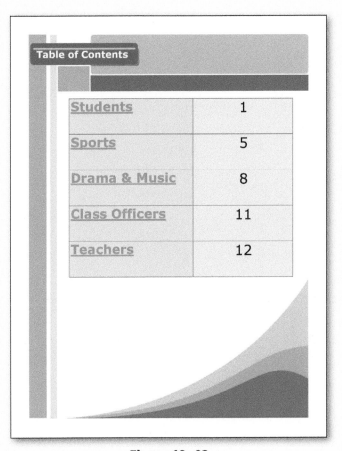

Figure 10–92

8. If instructed to do so, insert your picture on the Students page.

9. Save the publication with the file name, Lab 10–2 Student Yearbook Complete.

10. CTRL+click each of the links to make sure they work.

11. Save the file in the PDF format and test the links.

12. Submit this assignment as directed by your instructor.

13. ✸ Describe the process of merging this kind of document with a database of pictures. How would that be easier than inserting all of the pictures?

Lab 3: **Consider This: Your Turn**

Creating a Research Paper Template

Problem: Because you often write research papers for your courses, you decide it would be convenient to have a template in which you can type or import text.

Perform the following tasks:

Part 1: Run publisher and open a blank 8.5 × 11" publication. Set the font scheme to Office 1 and the color scheme to Black & White. Create a large text box that fills the page. Set the margin of the text box to 0.5 inches. Duplicate the page several times to create a total of seven pages. Go to page 2 and create a section. Link the text box to the one on page 3 and then link subsequent pages. Insert page numbering on every page except the title page. Submit the assignment in the format specified by your instructor.

Part 2: ✸ Microsoft Word contains templates for research papers and includes citation tools. Make a list of three publications that are easier to create in Word and three publications that are easier to create in Publisher. How does familiarity with the software affect your list?

11 Advanced Features in Publisher

Objectives

You will have mastered the material in this project when you can:

- Download online templates
- Convert a graphic to a Microsoft drawing object
- Fill with a custom RGB color
- Install a new font
- Change the size of a webpage
- Customize ruler guides
- Insert a web masthead and navigation bar
- Insert an animated graphic and alternative text

- Publish and test a website
- Insert form controls
- Use return data labels
- Edit form control and form properties
- Set webpage options
- Use VBA to create a message box
- Set the security level in Publisher

Introduction

Publisher has some advanced features that you may not use every day; however, these features are important for a full understanding of the app. These include online templates, font installation, website editing tools, macros, and Visual Basic for Applications.

Online templates, other than those installed with Publisher, offer new and different templates so your publications look fresh. You also can download new fonts to give your publications more variety.

Publisher 2016 no longer includes any web templates in the template gallery, but you can edit a blank webpage file or edit existing web publications that were created with Publisher. If you open an existing web publication, the Web tab will appear on the ribbon to provide you with web publication tools. Programs, such as Visual Studio and Dreamweaver, provide more tools specifically for advanced website development; however, Publisher's web capabilities allow for the creation of basic websites and interactive feedback.

When you click a web form control or any command or button, Publisher follows a prewritten, step-by-step set of instructions to accomplish the task. For example, when you click the Save button on the Quick Access Toolbar, Publisher follows a precise set of steps to save your publication. In Publisher, this series of instructions is called a **procedure**. A procedure also is referred to as a **program** or **code**.

The process of writing a procedure is called **computer programming**. Each Publisher command or button has a corresponding procedure that executes when you click the command or button. **Execute** means that the computer carries out the step-by-step instructions. In a Windows environment, an event causes the instructions associated with a task to be executed. An **event** is an action, such as clicking a button, clicking a command, dragging a scroll box, or right-clicking selected text.

Although Publisher has many buttons and commands, it does not include a command or button for every possible task. Thus, Microsoft has included with Publisher a powerful programming language called Visual Basic for Applications. The **Visual Basic for Applications (VBA)** programming language allows you to customize and extend the capabilities of Publisher to suit your own needs.

Project — Creating an Interactive Website

To illustrate some of the advanced features of Microsoft Publisher, this module presents a series of steps to create an interactive website about ladybugs. You will create a graphic from an online template to use on the home page. You will install and use a new web font. Then, you will create a form for the website that sends data to its owner, as well as other web objects, including a navigation bar, animated graphics, a background audio, and form controls.

You do not need extensive knowledge of HTML. Recall that HTML (Hypertext Markup Language) is a formatting language that programmers use to format documents for display on the web. Publisher provides user-friendly tools and controls to make it easy for even beginners to design interactive and highly-effective websites.

Figure 11–1a shows the home page for the website, and Figure 11–1b shows a web form created for the website. This project also demonstrates the use of a VBA-generated message box to remind the designer to upload the most recent copy of the publication to the web (Figure 11–1c).

The following roadmap identifies general activities you will perform as you progress through this module:

1. USE ONLINE TEMPLATES.
2. INSTALL FONTS.
3. INSERT a web MASTHEAD and NAVIGATION BAR.
4. ADD WEB GRAPHICS and alternative text.
5. PUBLISH and TEST a website.
6. CREATE FORM CONTROLS and set properties.
7. SET webpage OPTIONS and add audio.
8. USE VBA CODE to create a macro.
9. SET SECURITY LEVELS.

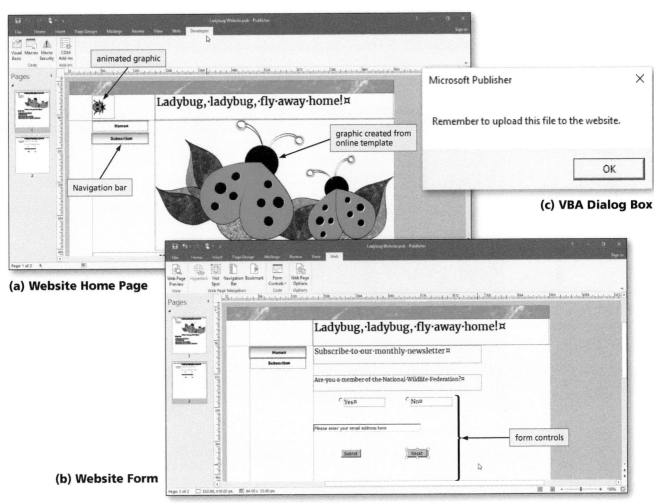

(a) Website Home Page

(b) Website Form

(c) VBA Dialog Box

Figure 11–1

Using Online Templates

In addition to the templates and blank publications in the BUILT-IN gallery, Publisher users have access to thousands of online templates in various categories. Some featured online templates appear when you run Publisher or when you click the New tab in the Backstage view. Other online templates can be located by entering search terms in the 'Search for online templates' box. You can enter terms, such as business, industry, holiday, or illustrations, among others. In addition, you can enter the type of publication you are looking for, such as invoice, newsletter, brochure, and so forth.

To Search for an Online Template

The following steps run Publisher and search for a template related to coloring pages. *Why? Many teachers use Publisher to create activities for their students. In this case, one of the coloring page templates contains an appropriate graphic for a website created later in the module.* You must be connected to the Internet in order to search for online templates.

1

- Run Publisher and display the template gallery.

- Type **coloring** in the 'Search for online templates' box to enter the search term (Figure 11–2).

 Experiment

- Scroll through the featured online templates.

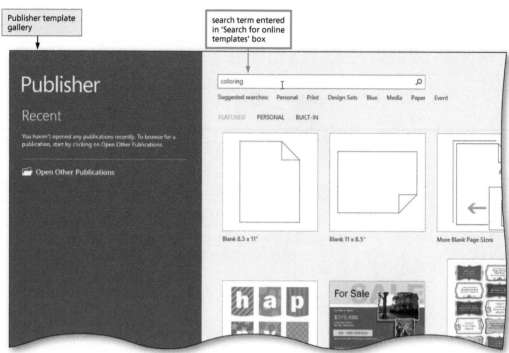

Figure 11–2

2

- Press the ENTER key to display online templates related to the search term in the New gallery (Figure 11–3).

 Experiment

- Scroll through the online templates.

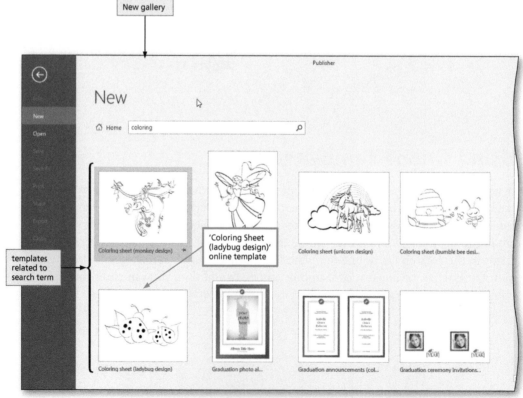

Figure 11–3

3
- Click the 'Coloring Sheet (ladybug design)' online template to select it and display a dialog box (Figure 11–4).

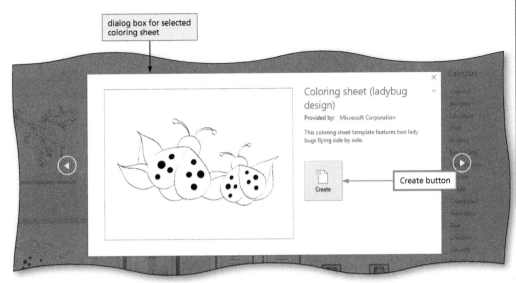

dialog box for selected coloring sheet

Coloring sheet (ladybug design)

Provided by: Microsoft Corporation

This coloring sheet template features two lady bugs flying side by side.

Create

Create button

Figure 11–4

4
- Click the Create button to download the template and to display it in the Publisher window (Figure 11–5).

template downloaded

Figure 11–5

To Choose a Color Scheme and Save

The following steps choose a color scheme and save the publication.

1 Display the Page Design tab.

2 Click the More button (Page Design Tab | Schemes group) and then click the Parrot color scheme.

3 Click the Save button on the Quick Access Toolbar. Navigate to your storage location and then save the file with the file name, Ladybug Coloring Page.

4 If you wish to print the publication for someone to color, ready the printer, press CTRL+P to display the Print gallery, and then click the Print button in the Print gallery.

Picture Formats

Pictures or graphic files are created and stored using many different file types and extensions. The type of file sometimes is determined by the hardware or software used to create the file. Other times, the user has a choice in applying a file type and makes the decision based on the file size, the intended purpose of the graphic file — such as whether the file is to be used on the web — or the desired color mode.

A few common graphic file types are listed in Table 11–1.

Table 11–1 Graphic File Types		
File Extension	**File Type**	**Description**
BMP	Bitmap	BMP is a standard Windows image format used with Windows-compatible computers. BMP format supports many different color modes.
EMF	Enhanced Metafile	EMF is an improved version of the standard Windows-based graphic format that provides for scaling, built-in descriptions, and device independence.
EPS	Encapsulated PostScript	EPS files can contain both bitmap and vector graphics. Almost all graphics, illustration, and page-layout programs support the EPS format, which can be used to transfer PostScript artwork between applications.
GIF	Graphics Interchange Format	GIF commonly is used to display graphics and images on webpages. It is a compressed format designed to minimize file size and electronic transfer time.
JPG or JPEG	Joint Photographic Experts Group	JPG files commonly are used to display photographs on webpages. JPG format supports many different color modes and retains all color information in an RGB image, unlike GIF format. Most digital cameras produce JPG files.
PDF	Portable Document Format	PDF is a flexible file format based on the PostScript imaging model that is cross platform and cross application. PDF files accurately display and preserve fonts, page layouts, and graphics. PDF files can contain electronic document search and navigation features, such as hyperlinks.
PNG	Portable Network Graphics	PNG is a format that does not lose data when compressed or zipped. This format can display millions of colors and supports transparency.
PSD	Photoshop Document	PSD format is the default file format in Photoshop and is the only format that supports all Photoshop features. Other Adobe applications can import PSD files directly and preserve many Photoshop features due to the tight integration among Adobe products.
RAW	Photoshop Raw	RAW format is a flexible file format used for transferring images among applications and computer platforms. This format has no pixel or file size restrictions. Documents saved in the Photoshop Raw format cannot contain layers.
TIF or TIFF	Tagged Image File Format	TIF is a flexible bitmap image format supported by almost all paint, image-editing, and page-layout applications. This format often is used for files that are to be exchanged among applications or computer platforms. Most desktop scanners can produce TIF images.
WMF	Windows Metafile Format	WMF is a format portable across Office applications, composed of drawn graphics and shapes.

Publisher can import, save, and perform minor editing on most of the picture file types in the preceding table, except the PDF, PSD, and RAW formats.

To Convert a Picture and Ungroup

1 USE ONLINE TEMPLATES | 2 INSTALL FONTS | 3 INSERT MASTHEAD & NAVIGATION BAR | 4 ADD WEB GRAPHICS
5 PUBLISH & TEST | 6 CREATE FORM CONTROLS | 7 SET OPTIONS | 8 USE VBA CODE | 9 SET SECURITY LEVELS

You have grouped and ungrouped objects in previous modules; however, the ladybug graphic is a WMF picture, not a grouped object. You must convert the picture to a Microsoft drawing object in order to ungroup it in the following steps. *Why? You have limited capabilities to edit individual parts of a WMF picture. After converting and ungrouping, you will have access to each part of the picture and can use tools on the Drawing Tools Format tab.*

1

- Select the picture (in this case, the ladybug picture).

- If necessary, display the Picture Tools Format tab.

- Click the Ungroup button (Picture Tools Format tab | Arrange group) to ungroup, which will display a Microsoft Publisher dialog box (Figure 11–6).

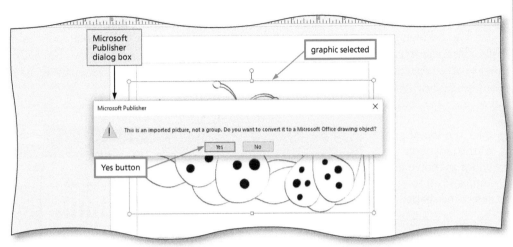

Figure 11–6

Q&A Can I convert every picture this way?

No. Conversion is limited to a few file types, such as the Windows Metafile Format (.wmf) format and some gif, png, and bmp files.

2

- Click the Yes button (Microsoft Office dialog box) to convert the picture to a grouped drawing object (Figure 11–7).

Q&A What do all of the dots mean?

The dots represent the corners of each shape within the grouped shape.

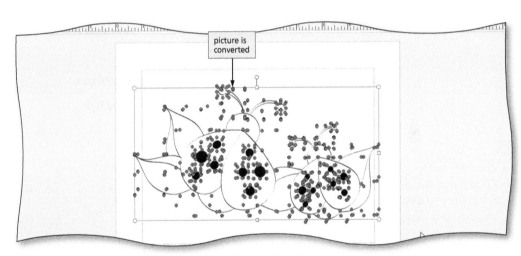

Figure 11–7

3

- Click the Ungroup button (Drawing Tools Format tab | Arrange group) to ungroup the drawing object (Figure 11–8).

4

- Click outside of the picture to deselect.

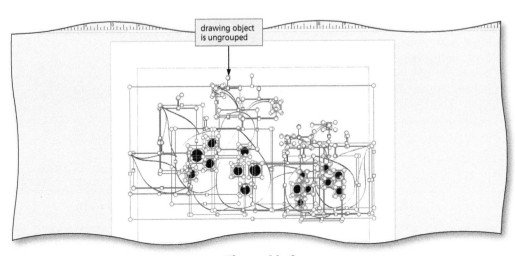

Figure 11–8

To Fill with a Custom RGB Color

The following steps fill portions of the image with a unique color created by using RGB settings. *Why?* *None of the color schemes includes an exact red/orange color; and, because this image eventually will appear on the web, using an RGB color is appropriate.* Recall that RGB stands for red, green, blue and is the color mode used on monitors and projectors.

1

- Click the top of one of the ladybug's wings as shown in Figure 11–9 to select the shape.

- Display the Drawing Tools Format tab.

- Click the Shape Fill arrow (Drawing Tools Format tab | Shape Styles group) to display the Shape Fill gallery (Figure 11–9).

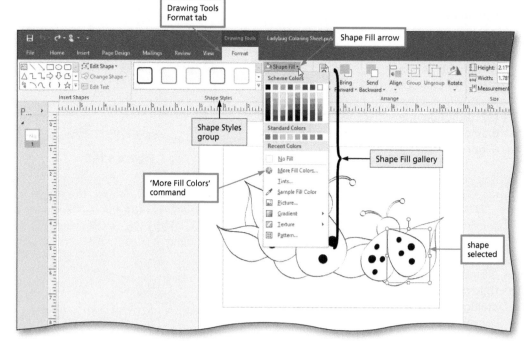

Figure 11–9

2

- Click 'More Fill Colors' in the Shape Fill gallery to display the Colors dialog box.

- Click the Custom tab to display the commands related to creating a custom color.

- If necessary, type **255** in the Red box, type **51** in the Green box, and type **0** in the Blue box (Figure 11–10).

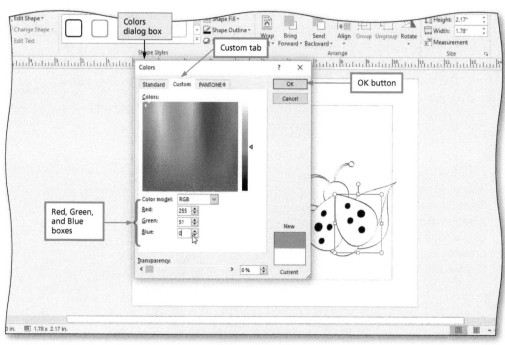

Figure 11–10

3

- Click the OK button (Colors dialog box) to apply the color and fill the shape (Figure 11–11).

Q&A Why does my color look different?
Subtle color differences occur when colors are printed on paper in the CMYK mode versus the color you may see on your screen in RGB mode.

Figure 11–11

To Copy the Formatting

The following steps copy the red/orange fill color to other parts of the picture using the format painter.

1 With the shape still selected, display the Home tab.

2 Double-click the Format Painter button (Home tab | Clipboard group).

3 One at a time, click each of the other large, wing portions of the lady bugs. As you click, stay inside the shape, but close to the border of the shape to avoid selecting anything else. If you make a mistake, press CTRL+Z and then click again.

4 Click the Format Painter button again to deselect it.

5 Click the scratch area to deselect any shape (Figure 11–12).

BTW

Color Modes
A color mode describes the way in which colors combine to create other colors. The most commonly used color modes are RGB (used with screens and projectors), CMYK (used in color printing), and LAB (used in photographic retouching and color correction).

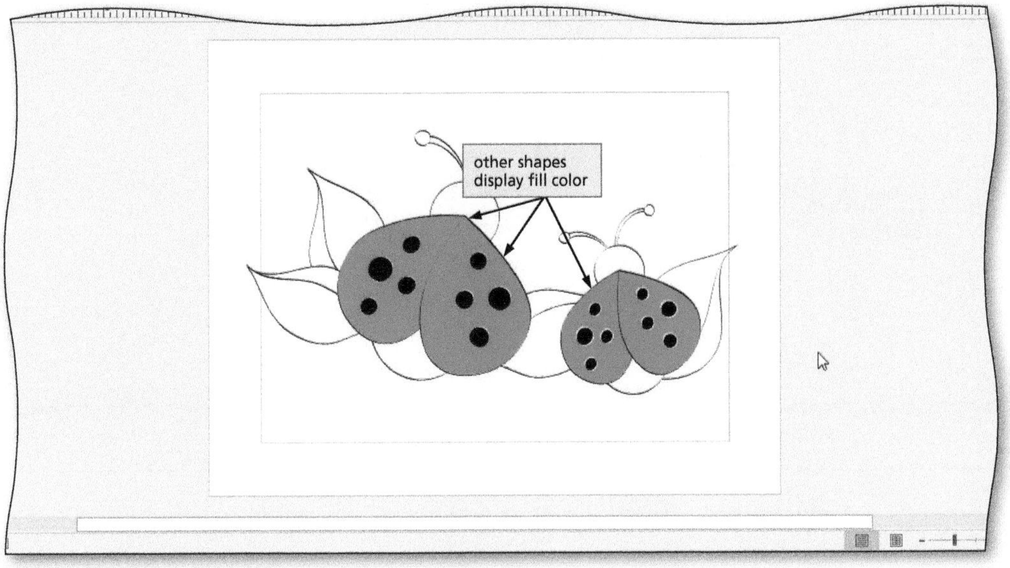

Figure 11–12

To Fill Other Shapes

The following steps fill other parts of the picture.

1 Click the head of the ladybug and fill it with black. Repeat for the head of the other ladybug.

2 Click the tail of the ladybug. Click the Shape Fill arrow (Drawing Tools Format tab | Shape Styles group), point to Texture, and then click Granite. Repeat for the tail of the other ladybug.

3 To simulate leaves, select the larger leaf-like shape to the left of the left ladybug. Click the Shape Fill arrow (Drawing Tools Format tab | Shape Styles group), point to Texture, and then click Green marble.

4 Use the format painter to copy the texture to the other three large, leaf-like shapes.

5 Select one of the smaller leaf-like structures. Click the Shape Fill arrow (Drawing Tools Format tab | Shape Styles group), point to Texture on the Shape Fill menu, and then click More Textures in the Texture gallery.

6 In the Format Shape dialog box, click the Texture arrow and then click Green marble. Drag the Transparency slider to 50%. Click the OK button (Format Shape dialog box).

7 Use the format painter to copy the texture to the other smaller, leaf-like structures.

8 Click the small circle at the end of one of the antennae. Click the Shape Effects button (Drawing Tools Format tab | Shape Styles group), point to Glow in the Shape Effects gallery, and then, in the Glow Variations area, click 'Accent 1, 11 point glow'. Repeat the process for the other antennae (Figure 11–13).

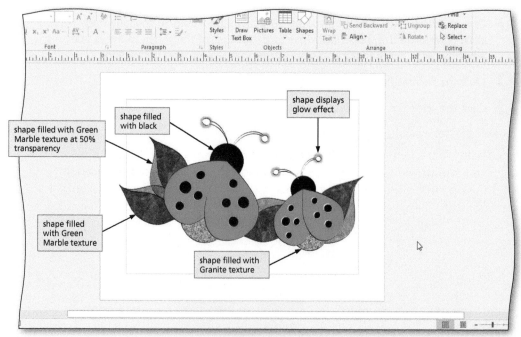

Figure 11–13

To Regroup and Save as a Picture

The following steps regroup the picture and save it as a picture file. Then, because you saved the coloring page separately, you can close the Publisher file without saving it.

1 Drag around all of the objects on the page to select them.

2 Press CTRL+SHIFT+G to regroup the image.

3 Right-click the grouped object and then click 'Save as Picture' on the shortcut menu.

4 When Publisher displays the Save As dialog box, type **Ladybugs Graphic** in the File Name box and then navigate to your storage location.

5 Click the Save button (Save As dialog box) to save the picture.

6 Exit Publisher. If Publisher asks you to save the Publisher file again, click the No button to keep the coloring page intact.

TO CHANGE THE PICTURE RESOLUTION WHILE SAVING

If you were going to print the picture, you might want to increase the picture's resolution. If you want to change the resolution while saving, you would perform the following steps:

1. Right-click the picture and then click 'Save as Picture' on the shortcut menu.
2. When Publisher displays the Save As dialog box, click the Change button and choose the appropriate resolution.
3. Enter a name in the File name box and then navigate to your storage location.
4. Click the Save button (Save As dialog box) to save the picture.

BTW
PNG
The PNG file format is a good option for logos and line art and is used when you need transparency in an image.

Break Point: If you wish to take a break, this is a good place to do so. To resume at a later time, continue following the steps from this location forward.

Installing Fonts

While many fonts are installed when you install Microsoft Office 2016, sometimes you need a specialized font to provide a certain look and feel for your publication, or a font that looks good on the web. Other times, businesses may have developed a personalized font. In any of those cases, you may need to download and install that font on your computer. Installing fonts is a function of the operating system and provides access to that font across publications and across apps.

BTW
Storing Font Files
Most installed fonts are stored in a folder named C:\Windows\Fonts on your hard drive.

To Install a New Font

1 USE ONLINE TEMPLATES | 2 INSTALL FONTS | **3 INSERT MASTHEAD & NAVIGATION BAR** | 4 ADD WEB GRAPHICS
5 PUBLISH & TEST | 6 CREATE FORM CONTROLS | 7 SET OPTIONS | 8 USE VBA CODE | 9 SET SECURITY LEVELS

The following steps install a new font on your computer. If you are in a lab environment, check with your instructor before performing these steps. *Why? Some lab settings are restricted to running apps and are unable to make changes to the installation.* To complete these steps, you will be required to use the Data Files. Please contact your instructor for information about accessing the Data Files.

- Click the File Explorer button on the Windows taskbar to open a File Explorer window.

- Navigate to the location of your font file, in this case the Data Files.

- Right-click the file named Merriweather-Regular (Figure 11–14).

Q&A How would I install a downloaded font?
Most downloaded fonts are stored in a compressed file. You must extract the files, read and agree to the license agreement, if any, and then use these steps to install the font.

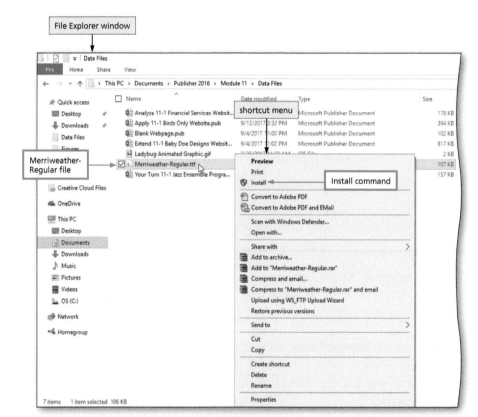

Figure 11–14

②

- Click Install on the shortcut menu.

Q&A How do I know if it installed correctly?
You can look in the font list in any of the Office apps.

Where are fonts stored?
Fonts are stored in the registry of your computer, but they can be viewed and manipulated via the Control Panel.

BTW
Web Labels
Some Publisher form controls do not include text to prompt the web user for specific kinds of data entry. In these cases, it is appropriate to use a text box, placed close to the form control, as a label. A **label** is an instructive word or words directing the user to enter suitable data. Because the web form will collect three pieces of individual information entered by the user into text boxes, each one needs a label to instruct and assist the user in filling out the form.

Webpages and Websites

Over the last few versions of Publisher, Microsoft has deprecated many of the web commands and the Web tab. Microsoft recommends using other programs, such as Microsoft Visual Studio, to create websites; however, you still have some choices for creating web content in Microsoft Publisher, including the following:

- Save a print publication as a single file webpage in the MHTML format.
- Save a print publication as an HTML file, with supporting files, such as images and sounds, included in a folder of supporting files.
- Open a blank web publication template and use the limited tools on the Web tab.
- Edit a previously saved Publisher web publication.

In this module, you will create a simple, two-page website in order to learn the web tools.

Should you use Publisher for web publications?

Use Publisher when you want to create, publish, and manage simple, static websites that match your business brand and that require revisions of only text and graphics. Publisher can be used to create a simple data collection site, such as a visitor list. Publisher is not intended for blogs or shopping carts; it cannot validate data, such as credit cards. Do not use Publisher if you expect to alter the raw HTML code at a later time.

While other programs, scripting languages, and web content management systems provide more efficient ways to create advanced websites, Publisher may be suitable for people who do not want to program in HTML or do not wish to learn another app.

To Open a Web Publication

The following steps open a blank web publication. To complete these steps, you will be required to use the Data Files. Please contact your instructor for information about accessing the Data Files.

1 Run Publisher.

2 Click the Open Other Publications tab in the Backstage view and then click Browse in the Publisher Open gallery.

3 Navigate to the Data Files and double-click Blank Webpage to open the selected file and to display the opened publication in the Publisher window.

4 Change the color scheme to Parrot.

To Change the Size of the Webpage

1 USE ONLINE TEMPLATES | 2 INSTALL FONTS | 3 INSERT MASTHEAD & NAVIGATION BAR | **4 ADD WEB GRAPHICS**
5 PUBLISH & TEST | **6 CREATE FORM CONTROLS** | **7 SET OPTIONS** | **8 USE VBA CODE** | **9 SET SECURITY LEVELS**

Because monitor resolutions lately have increased, new webpages can be much wider than those in the past; however, some users still may have older monitors, so it is a good practice to use a standard 960 pixels wide webpage. *Why? Visitors who use a mouse to navigate websites do not like to scroll from left to right. A setting of 960 pixels will display fully on most monitors.* The length of the webpage is not as defined. Research shows that interested visitors — those with and without a mouse — will scroll down to read more on the page.

The following steps set the page width to 960 pixels and the page length to 1022 pixels.

1

• Click the 'Choose Page Size' button (Page Design tab | Page Setup group) to display its menu (Figure 11–15).

Q&A What unit is shown on the ruler?
Because webpages are measured in pixels, the ruler displays pixel measurements.

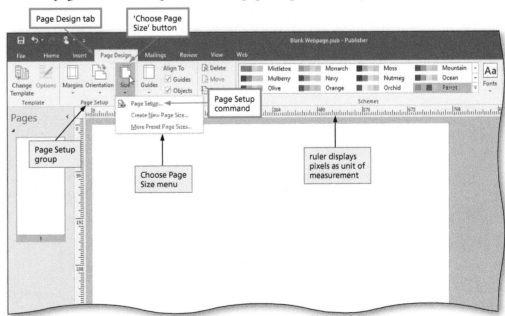

Figure 11–15

- Click Page Setup on the Choose Page Size menu to display the Page Setup dialog box.

- Type **960px** in the Width box and **1022px** in the Height box to set the dimensions of the webpage (Figure 11–16).

- Click the OK button (Page Setup dialog box) to apply the settings.

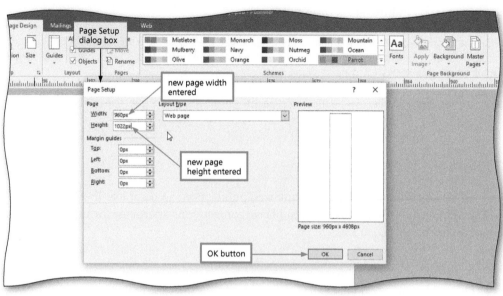

Figure 11–16

To Apply a Background

You have inserted backgrounds before. Recall that a stark white background is less effective in web publications than it is in print publications. For this website, you will use a light blue background. You also will change the display to page width.

① Click the Background button (Page Design tab | Page Background group) to display the Background gallery.

② In the Solid Background area, click '10% tint of Accent 2' to apply the background.

③ Display the View tab and then click the Page Width button (View tab | Zoom group) to view the page as wide as possible (Figure 11–17).

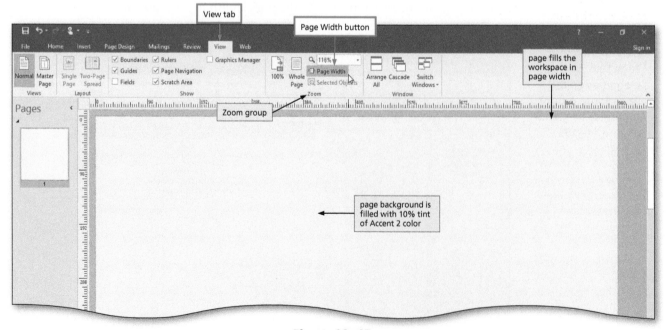

Figure 11–17

To Create Custom Ruler Guides

Recall that you used built-in ruler guides for publication pages to help you align objects and create sections on the page. In this web publication, you will create custom ruler guides. *Why? With custom ruler guides, you can align objects at unique places on the page.* The following steps create vertical and horizontal ruler guides.

1

- Display the Page Design tab.

- Click the Guides button (Page Design tab | Layout group) to display the Guides menu (Figure 11–18).

Q&A What is the purpose of the Add commands?
They create a horizontal or vertical line in the middle of the page, which you then can move to any location.

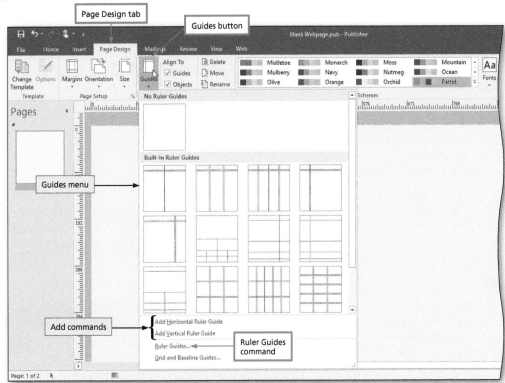

Figure 11–18

2

- Click Ruler Guides on the Guides menu to display the Ruler Guides dialog box. If necessary, click the Horizontal tab.

- In the Ruler Guide position box, type **112** to enter a horizontal ruler guide (Figure 11–19).

Q&A Could I drag from the ruler to create ruler guides?
Yes, but often it is difficult to drag the ruler guides to an exact pixel location.

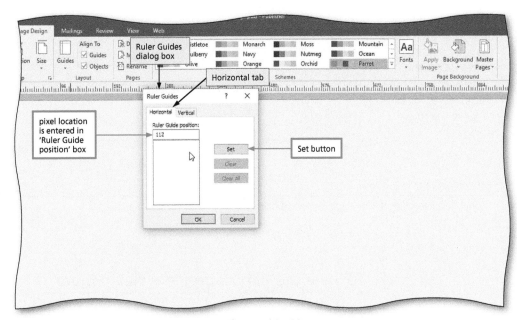

Figure 11–19

- Click the Set button (Ruler Guide dialog box).
- Click the Vertical tab.
- Type 68 in the Ruler Guide position box and then click the Set button.
- Type 255 in the Ruler Guide position box and then click the Set button (Figure 11–20).

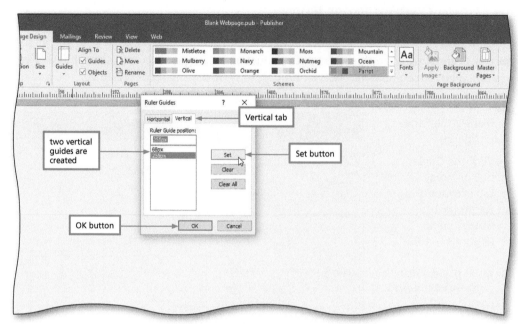

Figure 11–20

4

- Click the OK button (Ruler Guide dialog box) to create the ruler guides (Figure 11–21).

🔎 **Experiment**

- Point to a ruler guide. When the pointer changes to a double-headed arrow, drag the ruler guide to move it. Click the Undo button on the Quick Access Toolbar to move the ruler guide back.

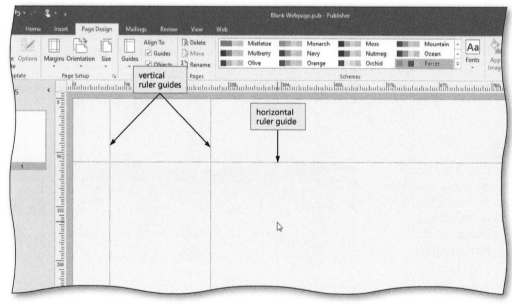

Figure 11–21

Other Ways

1. Drag from horizontal or vertical ruler to desired ruler guide position

To Save the Publication in a New Folder

The following steps create a new folder as you save the publication as a Publisher file. Later in the module, you will publish it as an HTML file. If you plan on creating multiple websites on your storage location, it is a good idea to keep them in separate folders so that HTML files with similar file names do not overwrite one another.

1 Click File on the ribbon to open the Backstage view.

2 Click Save As in the Backstage view and then browse to your storage location.

3 Click the New Folder button on the Save As dialog box toolbar. Type `Module 11 Project` as the name of the folder and then press the ENTER key.

4 Double-click the new folder to open it.

5 In the File name text box (Save As dialog box), select the text and then type `Ladybug Website` to name the Publisher file.

6 Click the Save button (Save As dialog box) to save the publication in the new folder.

Web Mastheads and Navigation Bars

In print publications, mastheads appear on the first page of a newsletter or newspaper and include information about the title, the edition, the date, and perhaps other information, such as the owner, name of the company, department, motto, or logo. A **web masthead** includes many of the same pieces of information, but usually appears on all pages of a website and may include links and navigation.

A **navigation bar** is a set of buttons or hyperlinks that allows visitors to move to any page within the website. You can place navigation bars on a page vertically, horizontally, along the top, along the bottom, or down the side. Additionally, navigation bars can be duplicated in multiple places on the page for easy access while scrolling through the page. Publisher navigation bars are grouped objects and are synchronized across pages. In fact, when you add a page to your website, Publisher automatically adds a new button to the navigation bar on each page.

You can insert navigation bars from the Web tab on the ribbon. Figure 11–22 displays the various groups and buttons on the Web tab.

BTW
Navigation Bar Properties
If you right-click the navigation bar and then click 'Navigation Bar Properties', Publisher will display the Navigation Bar Properties dialog box, which allows you to change the page title of each page and reorder the hyperlinks.

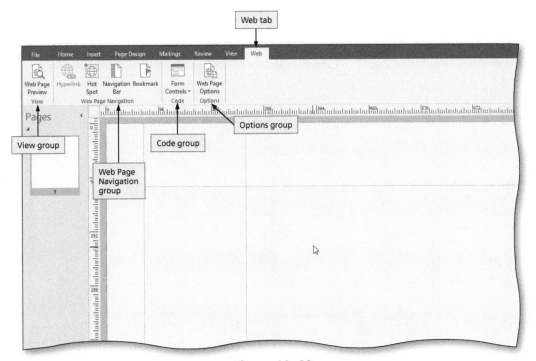

Figure 11–22

CONSIDER THIS

How do you decide on navigation?
The most important feature of a website is its navigation capabilities. Visitors need to be able to find information easily. They expect a navigation bar with links to other pages on your website. Use a logical order to present the pages and to create a navigation bar that virtually is identical on all pages. Publisher has navigation bars in its Building Block Library. Make sure you edit the bars appropriately, and make sure you use terms that are common to most websites, such as Home, Locations, Contact Us, or About.

To Create a Web Masthead

1 USE ONLINE TEMPLATES | 2 INSTALL FONTS | 3 INSERT MASTHEAD & NAVIGATION BAR | **4 ADD WEB GRAPHICS**
5 PUBLISH & TEST | 6 CREATE FORM CONTROLS | 7 SET OPTIONS | 8 USE VBA CODE | 9 SET SECURITY LEVELS

The following steps create a masthead for the website. *Why? A masthead identifies the website to visitors.* Sample mastheads are located in the Building Block Library in the Page Parts folder.

1

- Display the Insert tab.
- Click the Show Building Block Library Dialog Box Launcher (Insert tab | Building Blocks group) to display the Building Block Library dialog box (Figure 11–23).

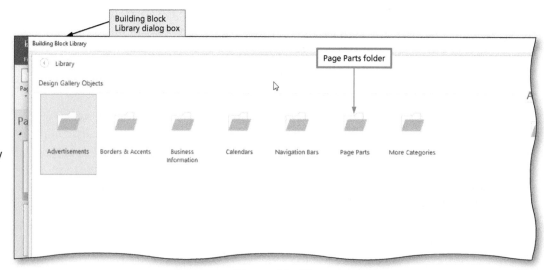

Figure 11–23

2

- Click the Page Parts folder to open it and then, if necessary, scroll to the Mastheads area.
- Click the All Mastheads folder.
- Scroll to and then click the Marble thumbnail to select it (Figure 11–24).

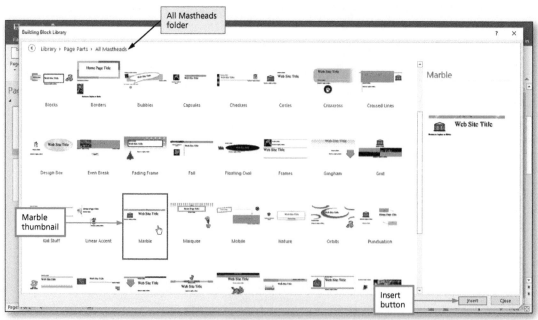

Figure 11–24

③
- Click the Insert button (Building Block Library dialog box) to insert the masthead in the publication.
- Drag the masthead to the top of the page and resize it horizontally to fit the page, as shown in Figure 11–25.
- Zoom to 100% if necessary.

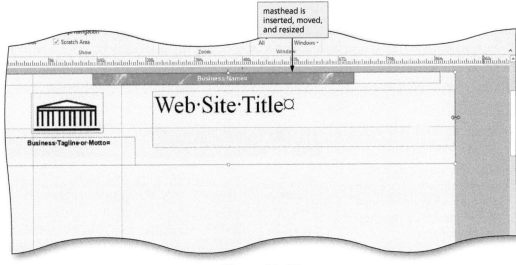

Figure 11–25

To Reformat the Masthead

The following steps ungroup the masthead. You also will delete, resize, and move objects.

① With the masthead still selected, click the Ungroup button (Picture Tools Format tab | Arrange group) to ungroup the masthead.

② Delete the text in the Business Name text box. Also delete the Business Tagline or Motto text box and the graphic.

③ Resize the gradient shape to fill the area between the margins and the area above the Web Site Title text box.

④ Move the Web Site Title text box to align with the ruler guide as shown in Figure 11–26. Resize the text box to fill the area between the ruler guide and the margin.

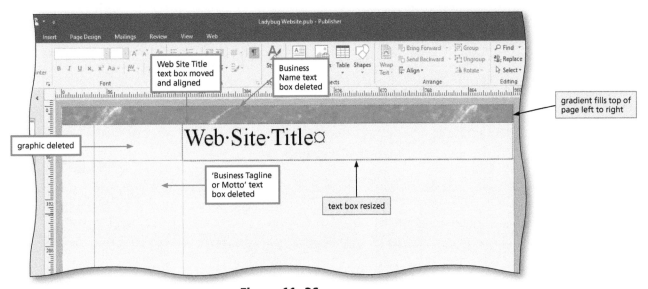

Figure 11–26

To Use the Installed Font

The following step uses the newly installed font in the title for the webpage. You will type in the name of the newly downloaded web font name. *Why? The font list in Publisher web publications presents a limited number of fonts.*

- Select the text in the Web Site Title text box.

- Click the current font name in the Font box (Home tab | Font group) and then type **Merriweather** to enter the new font name.

- Click the Font Size arrow (Home tab | Font group) and then click 24 in the Font Size list.

- Click the Bold button (Home tab | Font group) to bold the text.

- Type **Ladybug, ladybug, fly away home!** to replace the text (Figure 11–27).

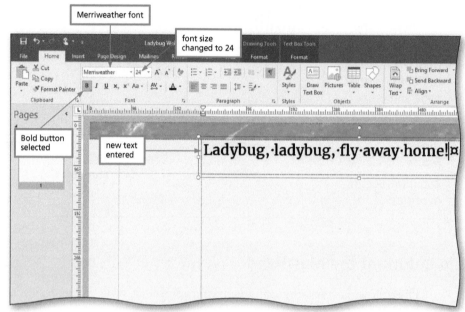

Figure 11–27

To Insert a Navigation Bar

The following steps insert a navigation bar. *Why? Websites should have an easy-to-use mechanism to move from page to page.*

- Display the Web tab.

- If necessary, click the scratch area to deselect any selected object.

- Click the Navigation Bar button (Web tab | Web Page Navigation group) to display the Building Block Library dialog box.

- Scroll to and then click the Top Drawer thumbnail to select it (Figure 11–28).

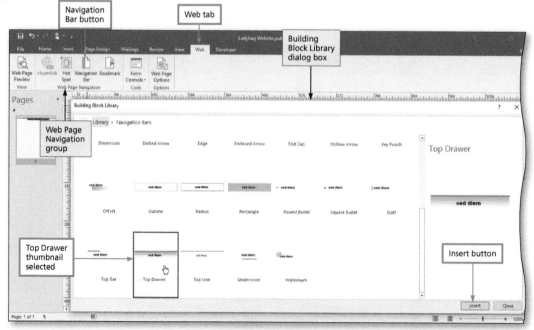

Figure 11–28

2
- Click the Insert button (Building Block Library dialog box) to insert the navigation bar in the publication.
- Drag the navigation bar inside the first vertical ruler guide and below the horizontal ruler guide as shown Figure 11–29.

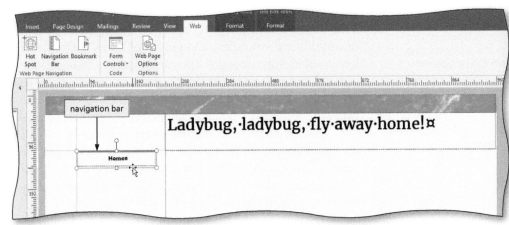

navigation bar

Ladybug, ladybug, fly away home!¤

Home¤

Figure 11–29

Q&A
Why does only one button appear in the navigation bar?
You have only one page in the website so far. As you add other pages, the navigation bar will expand to include more buttons.

Other Ways

1. Click Building Block Library Dialog Box Launcher (Insert tab | Building Blocks group), click Navigation Bars folder (Building Block Library dialog box), select navigation bar, click Insert button

To Add a Secondary Page to a Website

A **home page** is the opening page or main document that is displayed when you visit a website. Typically, the home page welcomes you and introduces the purpose of the website and the sponsoring business. The home page is the first page that website visitors will see, so it should explain the website's purpose, content, and layout. Home pages commonly provide links to the **secondary pages** or lower-level pages in the website. Secondary pages provide additional information, such as contact pages, detail pages, website maps, forms, or other accompanying materials.

The following steps duplicate the home page to create a secondary page.

1 Right-click the Page 1 thumbnail in the Page Navigation pane to display the shortcut menu.

2 Click 'Insert Duplicate Page' on the shortcut menu to create a duplicate page (Figure 11–30).

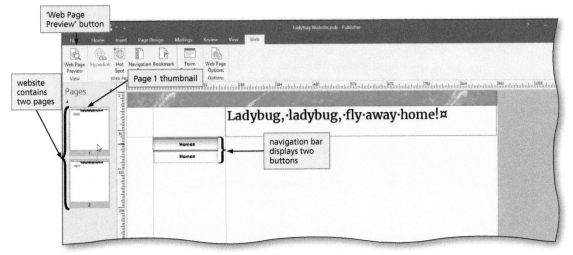

Figure 11–30

BTW
Picture Resolution on the Web
The resolution at which you save a picture file does not affect how it appears on the web; it is dependent only on the size. Picture size is determined by the pixel dimensions of the image and the display resolution of your screen.

Web Graphics

When using graphics on webpages, you must take into consideration visual appeal, download time, resolution, and purpose. Unless the home page is a picture gallery, just a few graphics are sufficient to create visual appeal and catch the visitor's eye. Keep in mind that each image added to a webpage increases the amount of time it takes to download the page. In addition, some people browse the web with images turned off in order to speed up the process; others turn off graphics to make the page more accessible.

Even though the computer screen is lower in resolution than most printed pages, web graphics easily can rival the quality of color images printed on paper. **Resolution** refers to the number of horizontal and vertical pixels in a display device or the sharpness and clarity of an image. A high-resolution graphic makes a webpage more visually appealing but increases the download time.

Purpose may be the most important consideration in using web graphics; they should help convey the website's message, not clutter the layout. The graphics should add interest or color, brand a company, draw attention, show relationships, or simplify complex information.

The number and type of graphics you use on your page will be a compromise between what is appealing visually and what makes the best sense for your target audience.

An **animated graphic** is a picture that displays animation when viewed in a browser. When Publisher is installed, Microsoft provides a folder of pictures, animations, and sounds on the local computer, located at C:\Program Files\Microsoft Office\ CLIPART\PUB60COR\ or sometimes installed at C:\Program Files\Microsoft Office\ root\CLIPART\PUB60COR. Because the Online Pictures command no longer provides a way to search for only video or audio, inserting animated graphics from a file is the easiest method to add an animated graphic to your webpage. A **static graphic** is one that does not display any animation.

BTW
GIF File Format
The GIF file format is used with animated effects and is a good option for clip art, flat graphics, and images that use minimal colors and precise lines, such as logos or blocks of colors.

To Insert an Animated Graphic

1 USE ONLINE TEMPLATES | 2 INSTALL FONTS | 3 INSERT MASTHEAD & NAVIGATION BAR | 4 ADD WEB GRAPHICS
5 PUBLISH & TEST | 6 CREATE FORM CONTROLS | 7 SET OPTIONS | 8 USE VBA CODE | 9 SET SECURITY LEVELS

The following step inserts an animated graphic on page 1 of the website. *Why? While too much animation may distract users, a simple animated graphic can convey the website owner's message or style. When you publish the website, Publisher will place a copy of the animated graphic in the folder that accompanies your website.* To complete this step, you will be required to use the Data Files. Please contact your instructor for information about accessing the Data Files.

- Navigate to page 1.
- Click the Pictures button (Insert tab | Illustrations group) to display the Insert Picture dialog box.
- Navigate to the Data Files and double-click the file named Ladybug Animated Graphic to insert it in the publication. Move it to the position shown in Figure 11–31.

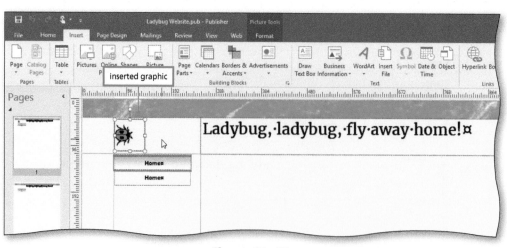

Figure 11–31

Q&A | My folder list displays the file names only. How can I see the graphic itself?
Click the 'More options arrow' on the Insert Picture dialog box toolbar and then click 'Extra large icons' in the list.

To Preview an Animated Graphic

The following steps preview the animated graphic. *Why? It always is a good idea to see what a graphic is going to look like and how it is going to perform in a browser.*

1

- Display the Web tab.

- Click the 'Web Page Preview' button (Web tab | View group) shown in Figure 11–30 to preview the webpage in a browser.

- If necessary, double-click the browser title bar to maximize the window (Figure 11–32).

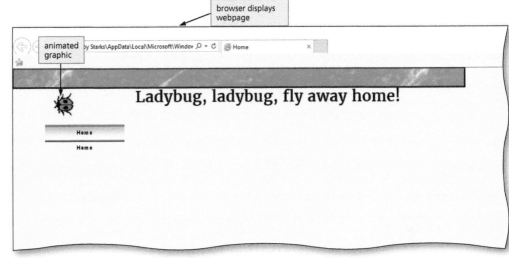

Figure 11–32

Where can I find other animated graphics?
While the web may have a variety of animated graphics, some come with a standard Publisher installation. Try looking in the following location: C:\Program Files\Microsoft Office\CLIPART\PUB60COR\ for files with the extension, .gif. Some installations store the clip art files at C:\Program Files\Microsoft Office\root\CLIPART\PUB60COR.

2

- Click the Close button on the browser title bar to close the browser window and return to Publisher.

Other Ways

1. Press CTRL+SHIFT+B

Alternative Text

A special consideration when using graphics on the web is accessibility. Screen readers that read webpages for people with disabilities can provide feedback about pictures, but only if the picture has alternative text. **Alternative text** is descriptive text that appears as an alternative to a graphic image on webpages. Graphics without alternative text are not usable by screen readers. Browsers may display alternative text while graphics are loading or when graphics are missing. Screen readers read the alternative text out loud.

To Add Alternative Text

The following steps insert alternative text for the animated graphic on the home page. *Why? You want the webpage to be accessible by everyone, including those with screen readers.*

1

- Right-click the ladybug animated graphic and then click Format Picture on the shortcut menu. When Publisher displays the Format Picture dialog box, click the Alt Text tab.

- Type **An animated graphic displays a clip art image of a flying ladybug.** in the Alternative text text box (Figure 11–33).

Q&A How can I test the alternative text? When you view the website in most browsers, a ScreenTip displays the alternative (or alternate) text when you point to the picture. If you have a screen reader, you would hear a voice speak those words.

- Click the OK button (Format Picture dialog box) to apply the alternative text.

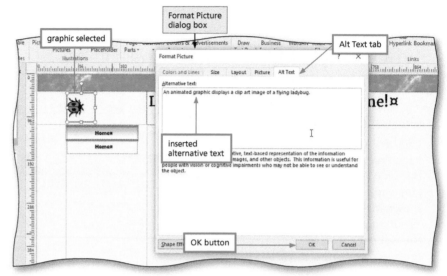

Figure 11–33

To Insert Another Graphic

The following steps add a static graphic you created earlier in the module and alternative text to page 1 of the website.

1 If necessary, navigate to page 1.

2 Click the Pictures button (Insert tab | Illustrations group) to display the Insert Picture dialog box.

3 Browse to your storage location and then insert the picture named Ladybugs Graphic.

4 Move and resize the picture to fit below the horizontal ruler guide and to the right of the second vertical ruler guide, as shown in Figure 11–34.

5 Right-click the graphic, and then click Format Picture on the shortcut menu.

6 If necessary, click the Alt Text tab (Format Picture dialog box). Type **A coloring page image of two ladybugs** in the Alternative text text box (Figure 11–34).

7 Click the OK button (Format Picture dialog box) to assign the alternative text to the image.

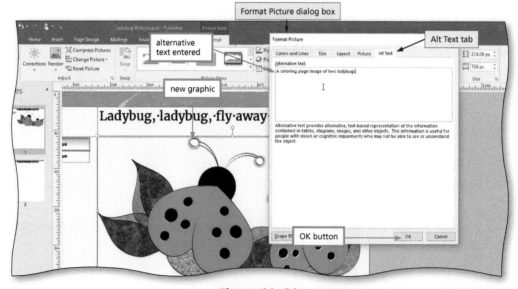

Figure 11–34

To Complete Page 1

To finish page 1, the following steps create a text box and insert hyperlinks. Table 11–2 displays the text and hyperlinks. You also will save the publication again.

Table 11–2 Text and Hyperlinks for Page 1

Text	Hyperlink
Welcome to our page about ladybugs.	none
Helpful links:	none
National Geographic Website	http://animals.nationalgeographic.com/animals/bugs/ladybug/
LadybugLady.com	http://www.ladybuglady.com/
Scholastic First Discovery Video	https://www.youtube.com/watch?v=JiTH7SvasJ8
Nursery Rhyme Lyrics from Poetry Foundation	http://www.poetryfoundation.org/poem/176337

1 Create a text box that fills the area below the large graphic to include the area between the first vertical ruler guide and the right margin.

2 Set the font to Merriweather and the font size to 20.

3 Enter the text from Table 11–2. Center the first line.

4 Create the hyperlinks as listed.

5 Click the Save button on the Quick Access Toolbar to overwrite the previously saved file (Figure 11–35).

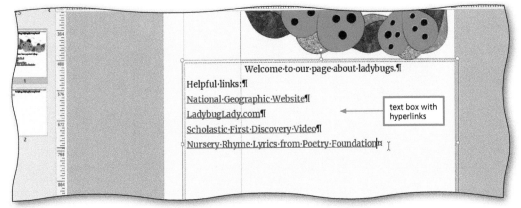

Figure 11–35

Break Point: If you wish to take a break, this is a good place to do so. Exit Publisher. To resume at a later time, run Publisher, open the file named Ladybug Website, and then continue following the steps from this location forward.

Publishing the Website

Even before you finish all of the webpages in your website, it is a good idea to publish the file in the HTML format. The act of publishing the HTML creates the file and folder structure, which you can use to add additional components and files that are external to Publisher. Recall that in an earlier module, you created a single file webpage in the MHTML format. For a website with multiple pages, you should use the standard HTML format. Typically, websites use the file name index.htm or index.html for the home page. The secondary pages and all other objects, such as pictures and audio files, are stored in a folder named index_files. Publisher creates this structure for you when you publish a webpage.

BTW

Hyperlinks vs. Hot Spots
No functional difference exists between a hyperlink and a hot spot. Hot spots, however, can be created anywhere on the page; hyperlinks must be a graphic or text. In addition, hot spots do not change the text font as hyperlinks do.

BTW

Audio Files
Make sure you have legal access to any audio file you plan to include on your webpage. The audio files that come with a licensed installation of Publisher are legal to use in your webpages.

Publishing is different from saving. You need to do both. Saving the publication saves the .pub file and its inclusive pages. You edit that file using Publisher. Publishing the website converts all of the components and interactivity to HTML code so that it can viewed with a browser.

To Publish a Website

The following steps publish the website to your storage location. *Why? Publishing creates the file structure you need to store upcoming files.* You can publish it to a web server, but until your website is complete, it is a good idea to publish it to a storage location.

- Click File on the ribbon to open the Backstage view.
- Click the Export tab to display the Export gallery.
- Click Publish HTML in the left pane to display the Publish HTML area in the right pane.
- Click the Publish HTML button to display the Publish to the Web dialog box.
- If necessary, navigate to your storage location and the Module 11 Project folder you created earlier in the module (Figure 11–36).

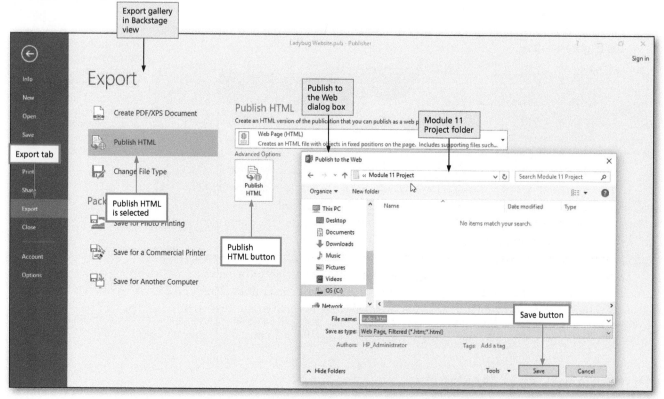

Figure 11–36

- Click the Save button (Publish to the Web dialog box) to publish the website.

Q&A What did Publisher save?
In the current folder, Publisher created an HTML file named index and a folder named index_files.

Form Controls

Form controls are the individual boxes and buttons used by website visitors to enter data. Each form control has editable properties and values that change its appearance and functionality. The data from a form control is transmitted from the visitor to the website's owner via a Submit button. Publisher supports six types of form controls.

How should you design your form?

Functionality is key. Ask only for information you need. Make sure your form controls are the correct type for each piece of data. Design a well-thought-out draft of the form, and be sure to include all essential form elements. Sketch the form on paper first to view the overall affect and placement of the objects before creating the elements on the computer screen. Essential elements include the form's title, text, and graphics; data entry fields; and data entry instructions. A form control or data entry field is a placeholder for data that a user enters in the form. If the data entered in the form will be analyzed by a program other than Publisher, create the data entry fields so that the entries are stored in separate fields that can be shared with other programs and, therefore, filtered, sorted, and exported easily. Determine the properties for each control, such as its return data type, and then make a list of possible values that it can contain. Arrange data entry fields in logical groups on the form and in an order that users would expect. Data entry instructions should be succinct and easy to understand. Ensure that users can change and enter data only in designated areas of the form.

CONSIDER THIS

A **check box** is a square box that presents a yes/no choice. It displays a check mark or x when selected. Several check boxes may function as a group of related but independent choices. An **option button**, or **radio button**, is a round button that presents one choice. When selected, an option button circle is filled in. When grouped, option buttons function like multiple-choice questions — they are mutually exclusive. The difference between an option button and a check box is that users can select only one option button within a group, but any number of check boxes. In Publisher, checkbox form controls and option button form controls both display a label you can edit. Furthermore, you can choose to display either of the form controls as selected or not selected at start up.

A **list box** presents a group of items in a list. Visitors can scroll to select from one or any number of choices in the list box. You determine the available choices and the number that may be selected when you set list box properties.

If you want web visitors to type information in a text box, you insert a **textbox form control.** Sensitive information, such as credit card information or passwords, can be displayed as asterisks or bullets. Textbox form controls are different from regular text box controls that display text entered during the design process. Textbox form controls appear as white boxes, with an insertion point for data entry by the web user.

A **text area**, or multiline text box, provides a means of entering information by making available to the visitor a larger text box with multiple blank lines. Most websites include regular text boxes as instruction labels next to textbox and text area form controls to assist visitors in entering the correct information.

You must include a **submit button** on every form. This button allows visitors to send you their form data. You can create a **reset button** by using a second submit button form control with different properties. Reset buttons are optional, but they provide a simple way to clear form data and allow the web visitor to start over. A submit button can display any words in its visible label, such as Send or Clear. In a production environment, in order for the submit button to work properly, the server to which you upload the HTML files must have **FrontPage Server Extensions**, a software technology that allows Microsoft products to communicate easily with the server and provides additional functionality intended for websites.

Each form control has a set of **properties** or attributes, such as a return data label, text, width, or other settings. These properties change the appearance and functionality of the form control. To edit the properties of a form control, you double-click the control. One of those properties is a logical **return data label**, also called an **internal data label**.

BTW

Checkbox Form Control
A checkbox form control allows users to submit yes and no responses without having to type the words in a text box. Like option button form controls, checkbox form controls come with their own labels.

BTW

Checkbox Form Control Properties
When editing the checkbox form control properties, you must double-click the box portion of the control rather than its text label to display the Checkbox Properties dialog box. The assigned check box value accompanies the return data label when the form is submitted.

This return data label references and identifies the visitor-supplied information when it is submitted to the website owner. For instance, a return data label with the word, Course#, could accompany a user-supplied course number in an email submission. Without a return data label, a random number in the email might be difficult to decipher.

To Create Text Boxes

Before creating any form controls, the following steps create regular text boxes on page 2 to help the user identify the purpose of the webpage.

1 Navigate to page 2.

2 Draw a text box approximately 500 pixels wide and 50 pixels tall. Move the text box to the corner of the right vertical ruler guide and below the horizontal ruler guide.

3 Change the font to Merriweather and the font size to 16.

4 Type `Subscribe to our monthly newsletter` to complete the text and then click outside the text box to deselect it.

5 Create another text box approximately the same size and approximately 25 pixels below the previous one.

6 Change the font to Merriweather and the font size to 12. Type `Are you a member of the National Wildlife Federation?` to complete the text (Figure 11–37).

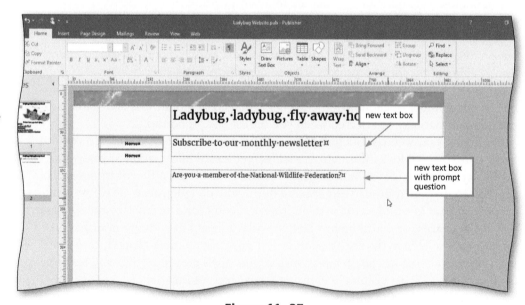

Figure 11–37

To Change a Navigation Button

1 USE ONLINE TEMPLATES | 2 INSTALL FONTS | 3 INSERT MASTHEAD & NAVIGATION BAR | 4 ADD WEB GRAPHICS
5 PUBLISH & TEST | 6 CREATE FORM CONTROLS | **7 SET OPTIONS** | 8 USE VBA CODE | 9 SET SECURITY LEVELS

The following step changes the label on the Navigation button. *Why? Currently both buttons are set to Home. You will need to change the second one to Subscribe.*

• Double-click the text in the second Home navigation button.

• Type `Subscribe` to change the text on the button (Figure 11–38).

Q&A

Should I change the button's text on page 1, as well?
No. The navigation bar is synchronized and will change automatically.

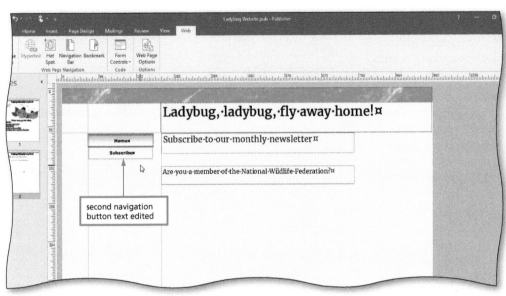

Figure 11–38

To Insert Option Button Form Controls

1 USE ONLINE TEMPLATES | 2 INSTALL FONTS | 3 INSERT MASTHEAD & NAVIGATION BAR | 4 ADD WEB GRAPHICS
5 PUBLISH & TEST | 6 CREATE FORM CONTROLS | **7 SET OPTIONS** | 8 USE VBA CODE | 9 SET SECURITY LEVELS

Publisher provides option button form controls to allow users to make one choice from a group of options. Option button form controls provide their own labels. When selected, the option button form control displays a filled-in circle or bullet.

Publisher groups multiple option button form controls automatically so that users can select only one. The following steps create two option buttons. **Why?** *The options will indicate the website visitor's answer regarding membership in the National Wildlife Federation.*

1

- Deselect any selected object and then display the Web tab.

- Click the Form Controls button (Web tab | Code group) to display the Form Controls menu (Figure 11–39).

🔍 **Experiment**

- Click Checkbox on the Form Controls menu to create a checkbox form control. Double-click the control to view the Checkbox Properties dialog box. Click the Cancel button and then delete the control from your webpage. Click the Form Controls button again.

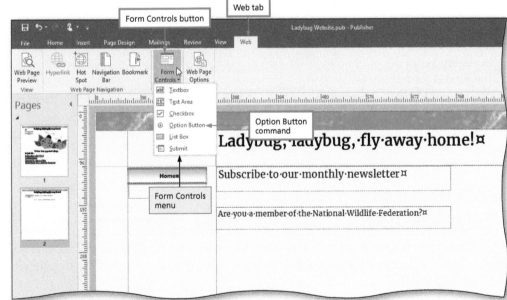

Figure 11–39

2

- Click Option Button on the Form Controls menu.

- When the Option Button form control is inserted in the publication, drag it to a location below the previous text box, as shown in Figure 11–40.

- Resize the form control as necessary to display all of the text (Figure 11–40).

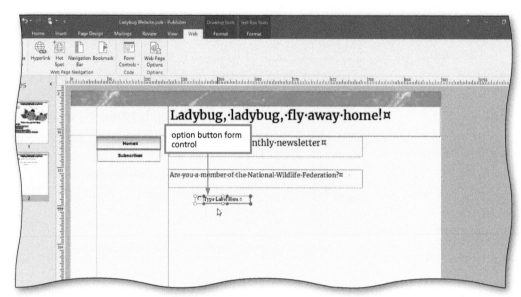

Figure 11–40

3

- Click the label to select its text. Set the font to Merriweather and the font size to 12. Type **Yes** to replace the text.

- CTRL+drag the first option button to create another option button form control to the right of the first one. Type **No** as the text. If necessary, resize the format control and format the text (Figure 11–41).

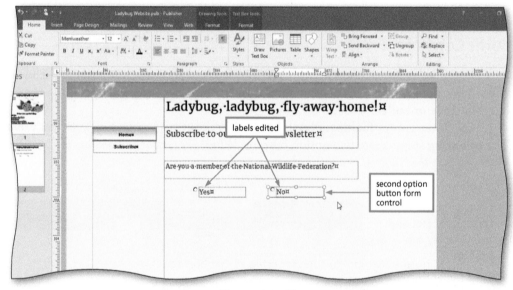

Figure 11–41

To Edit Option Button Form Control Properties

1 USE ONLINE TEMPLATES | 2 INSTALL FONTS | 3 INSERT MASTHEAD & NAVIGATION BAR | 4 ADD WEB GRAPHICS
5 PUBLISH & TEST | 6 CREATE FORM CONTROLS | **7 SET OPTIONS** | 8 USE VBA CODE | 9 SET SECURITY LEVELS

Each form control has a set of properties or attributes that change the appearance and functionality of the form control, including default text, the number of characters, the capability to hide sensitive information with asterisks, and a return data label.

Option button form control properties include the capability to display the option button as selected or not selected, a return data label to name the option button group, and an option button value to name the individual button.

A special consideration with option button form controls is their logical grouping. At times, you may want to use multiple groups of option buttons. For example, a website that sells T-shirts might need option button groupings for size, for color, and for neckline. Because option buttons are mutually exclusive, selecting a color could turn off a previously selected size, unless you specify the logical grouping. To group the buttons logically, Publisher requires that you use the same return data label for each member within a group. *Why? The return data label value identifies the group and accompanies the option button value when the form is submitted.* Typically, the option button value is a word that describes the selected option button.

The following steps edit the option button form control properties.

- Select the first option button form control. Double-click the circular part of the option button (to the left of the text label) to display the Option Button Properties dialog box.

- Select the text in the 'Return data with this label' box and then type **Member** to replace the text and indicate the grouping.

- Select the text in the 'Option button value' text box, and then type **Member_Yes** to replace the text (Figure 11–42).

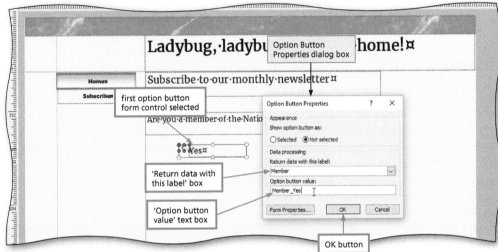

Figure 11–42

Q&A
Why does the 'Return data with this label' box display an arrow?
You might have multiple groups of option buttons, each group with a different name. The arrow allows you to choose in which group the button should belong.

Do I need to use an underscore between words?
If the data from the web form updates a database, the return data label must match the database field name exactly for the data to be stored correctly. The underscore enhances readability while following the rule that database field names may not contain a space.

- Click the OK button (Option Button Properties dialog box) to set the properties.

- Select the second option button form control. Double-click the circular part of the option button to display the Option Button Properties dialog box.

- Click the 'Return data with this label' arrow and then click Member in the list.

- Select the text in the 'Option button value' text box and then type **Member_No** to replace the text (Figure 11–43).

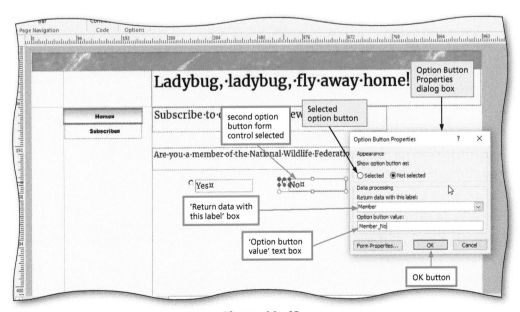

Figure 11–43

Q&A

When will the Option button value box be used?
Text in the Option button value box will appear in submitted data. For example, the website owner would see the return data label, Member, followed by the word, Member_Yes, and thus know how to use the data.

When would it be appropriate to choose Selected?
The Selected option button (shown in Figure 11–43) is used to display a bullet in the option button when website visitors first view the form. You might want to display a selected option button to encourage visitors to inquire about specific options or if it is the owner's practice to include information by default.

3

● Click the OK button (Option Button Properties dialog box) to set the properties.

To Insert Textbox Form Controls

1 USE ONLINE TEMPLATES | 2 INSTALL FONTS | 3 INSERT MASTHEAD & NAVIGATION BAR | 4 ADD WEB GRAPHICS
5 PUBLISH & TEST | 6 CREATE FORM CONTROLS | 7 SET OPTIONS | 8 USE VBA CODE | 9 SET SECURITY LEVELS

The web form contains a textbox form control to collect an email address from visitors. As a website designer, you should provide instruction to users as to what they should enter in a textbox form control; either provide a separate text box label or enter text in the textbox form control itself in order to assist users. *Why? By providing instructions and by changing the size or width of the controls to approximate the amount of data expected from the user, you can help the user to enter information correctly.* Later, you will set properties to provide additional help for users. The following step inserts a textbox form control.

1

● Click the Form Controls button (Web tab | Code group) to display the list of form controls and then click Textbox to place a textbox form control in the publication.

● Move the text box form control below the options buttons aligned with the right ruler guide, and resize it so that it is wider, as shown in Figure 11–44.

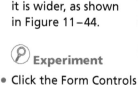
Experiment

● Click the Form Controls button (Web tab | Code group) and then click Text Area on the Form Controls menu to create a text area form control. Double-click the control to view the Text Area Properties dialog box. Click the Cancel button and then delete the control from your webpage.

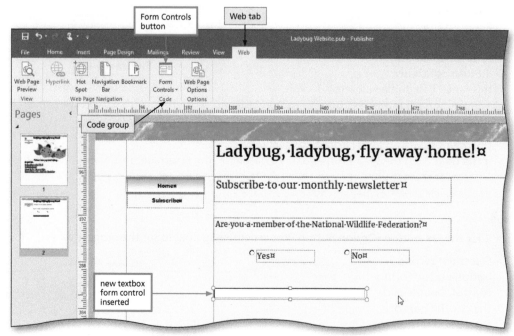

Figure 11–44

To Edit Textbox Form Control Properties

1 USE ONLINE TEMPLATES | 2 INSTALL FONTS | 3 INSERT MASTHEAD & NAVIGATION BAR | 4 ADD WEB GRAPHICS
5 PUBLISH & TEST | 6 CREATE FORM CONTROLS | 7 SET OPTIONS | 8 USE VBA CODE | 9 SET SECURITY LEVELS

With a textbox form control, the return data label is an important property. *Why? If the data is submitted to a database, the return data label must match the database field name exactly for the data to be stored correctly.* If the data is submitted to the website owner via email or some other tool, a return data label helps differentiate among the various data fields.

The width of a textbox form control keeps the user from entering too much information. For example, the width of a ZIP code should be 10 characters, so that the user can enter a dash and the 4-digit ZIP code extension. Limiting the user to 10 characters will help ensure that he or she is entering the correct data in the correct box. Unless it is set otherwise, a textbox form control allows the user to enter a maximum of 255 characters, no matter how wide the visible box is on the form.

The following steps edit the properties of the textbox form controls by assigning return data labels and setting field widths.

- Double-click the textbox form control to display the Text Box Properties dialog box.

- In the Default text text box, type **Please enter your email address here** to complete the prompt.

- Select the text in the 'Return data with this label' text box and then type **Email_Address** to replace the text.

- Do not change the value for the number of allowable characters (Figure 11–45).

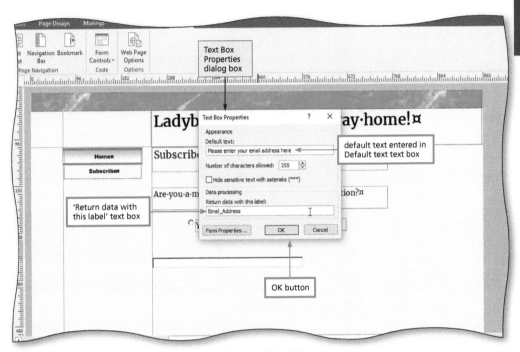

Figure 11–45

- Click the OK button (Text Box Properties dialog box) to set the properties.

Other Ways
1. Right-click form control, click 'Format Form Properties' on shortcut menu, enter properties, click OK button (Text Box Properties dialog box)

To Insert Submit Form Controls

1 USE ONLINE TEMPLATES | 2 INSTALL FONTS | 3 INSERT MASTHEAD & NAVIGATION BAR | 4 ADD WEB GRAPHICS
5 PUBLISH & TEST | 6 CREATE FORM CONTROLS | **7 SET OPTIONS** | **8 USE VBA CODE** | **9 SET SECURITY LEVELS**

A submit form control creates a Submit button, which the user clicks to submit data from all controls on the form. Three kinds of submission are available: saving the data in a file on the web server, sending the data via email, and using a program provided by an Internet service provider (ISP).

The owner of the Ladybug website wants the data from the web form sent via email and wants a second button labeled Reset. *Why? A Reset button allows users to clear previous entries.* The submit button form control is a special kind of command button used to issue commands in a graphical user interface. You can tailor the button by changing its caption and its type or purpose. The two available types of command buttons in Publisher are submit and reset. The following steps create these two buttons.

- Click the Form Controls button (Web tab | Code group) and then click Submit to display the Command Button Properties dialog box.

- If necessary, click the Submit option button to select it (Figure 11–46).

Q&A Can I add a picture to the button?

Yes. If you click the Image check box (Command Button Properties dialog box), you can browse to select a picture file that becomes a clickable button when the webpage is displayed in a browser. You cannot combine words and pictures on a button unless the picture file already contains the words. Pictures

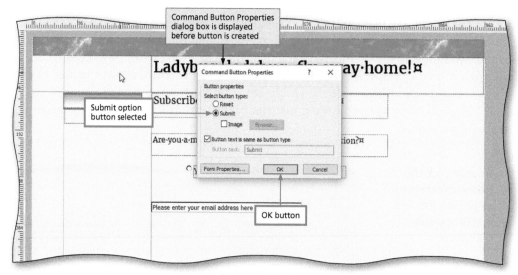

Figure 11–46

or graphics with plain backgrounds and distinctive shapes work best. You may need to resize the graphic once it is inserted into the publication.

2

• Click the OK button (Command Button Properties dialog box) to place the control on the page.

• Drag to reposition the Submit button to a location below the textbox form control as shown in Figure 11–47.

Q&A Can I change the words on the button?

Yes. If you remove the check mark in

Figure 11–47

the 'Button text is same as button type' check box (Command Button Properties dialog box), you can type new text in the Button text text box.

3

• Click the Form Controls button (Web tab | Code group) and then click Submit to display the Command Button Properties dialog box.

• Click the Reset option button to select it (Figure 11–48).

Figure 11–48

4

- Click the OK button (Command Button Properties dialog box) to place the control on the page.

- Drag to reposition the Reset button to the right of the Submit button, as shown in Figure 11–49.

Experiment

- Click the Form Controls button (Web tab | Code group) and then click the List Box

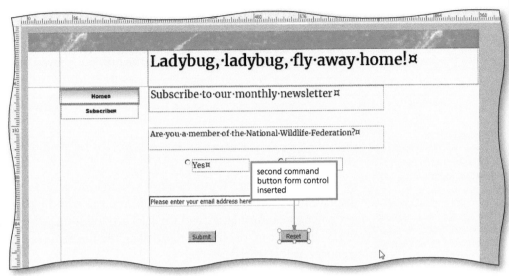

Figure 11–49

command to create a List Box form control. Double-click the control to view the List Box Properties dialog box. Click the Cancel button and then delete the control from your webpage.

To Edit Form Properties

1 USE ONLINE TEMPLATES | 2 INSTALL FONTS | 3 INSERT MASTHEAD & NAVIGATION BAR | 4 ADD WEB GRAPHICS
5 PUBLISH & TEST | 6 CREATE FORM CONTROLS | **7 SET OPTIONS** | **8 USE VBA CODE** | **9 SET SECURITY LEVELS**

The following steps edit form properties. *Why? Setting the form properties allows you to specify the data retrieval method and enter data retrieval information.*

1

- Double-click the Submit button form control to display the Command Button Properties dialog box.

- Click the Form Properties button (Command Button Properties dialog box) to display the Form Properties dialog box.

- Select the 'Send data to me in e-mail' option button (Form Properties dialog box) to display the settings.

- Select the text in the 'Send data to this e-mail address' box and then type **info@ ladybugwebsite .biz** to replace the text (Figure 11–50).

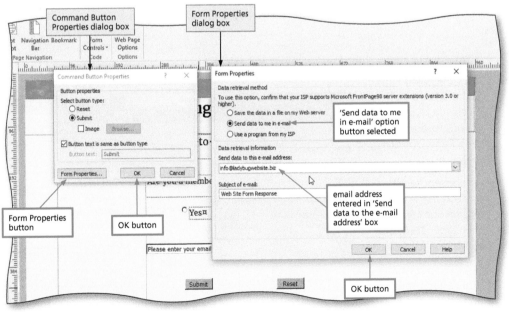

Figure 11–50

Experiment

- Click each of the option buttons to view what type of data is needed for each of the retrieval methods.

- Click the OK button (Form Properties dialog box) to set the form properties.

- Click the OK button (Command Button Properties dialog box) to return to the publication.

- Click the Save button on the Quick Access Toolbar to overwrite the previously saved file.

Other Ways

1. In any properties dialog box, click Form Properties button, choose data retrieval method (Form Properties Dialog box), enter settings, click OK button

BTW
Relative References
A **relative location** is a reference to a file in the same folder or a subfolder of the current folder. Relative locations are typed in, rather than browsed to, and always begin with the symbols ..\ preceding the file name.

Web Page Options

Publisher's **Web Page Options** allow you to customize the way the webpage is displayed and how it works on the web. You can edit the page title, the file name, search engine information, and the background sound. While the page title is the text that will appear on the browser's title bar, the file name is the name of the individual webpage as it is stored on a server.

The search engine information, such as description and keywords, create **meta tags** in web publications; these tags are HTML specification tags that tell search engines what data to use. The **description** is a sentence or phrase that you create to describe a website. The description appears in most search engine results pages. The description should encourage people to click the link to a website. The **keywords** are a list of words or phrases that some search engines may use to locate a webpage. While keywords are used less frequently than they once were, you still should insert them and make sure they accurately reflect the content of the webpage for effective searching. The **page title** is displayed on the browser title bar or tab and can be the same or different for each page. Page titles also appear in the Insert Hyperlink dialog box, making it easy to follow links from page to page.

To Edit Webpage Options

1 USE ONLINE TEMPLATES | 2 INSTALL FONTS | 3 INSERT MASTHEAD & NAVIGATION BAR | 4 ADD WEB GRAPHICS
5 PUBLISH & TEST | 6 CREATE FORM CONTROLS | **7 SET OPTIONS** | **8 USE VBA CODE** | 9 SET SECURITY LEVELS

The following steps enter webpage options for page 1 of the website. *Why?* *Entering a page title, description, and keywords helps users find the website when they use a search engine.*

- Navigate to page 1. If necessary, display the Web tab.

- Click the 'Web Page Options' button (Web tab | Options group) to display the Web Page Options dialog box.

- If necessary, select any text in the Page title text box and then type **Ladybug Website** to replace the text.

- If necessary, select any text in the File name text box and then type **index** to replace the text (Figure 11–51).

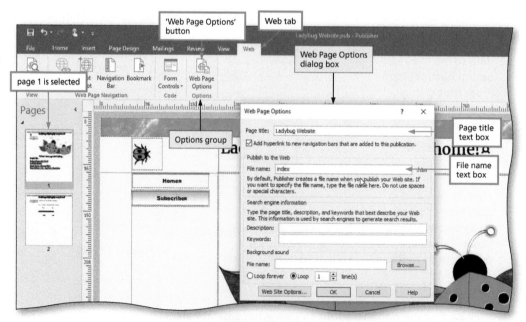

Figure 11–51

Q&A Why is the home page named index?
It is standard practice to assign the name, index, to the main page of any website or directory. Web servers recognize index as the main page and, thus, do not require visitors to type the file name at the end of the web address when navigating to the webpage.

2

- In the Description text box, type a **site all about ladybugs** to describe the website.

- In the Keywords text box, type **ladybug, lady beetle, ladybird beetle** to create the keywords list.

- Do not close the dialog box (Figure 11–52).

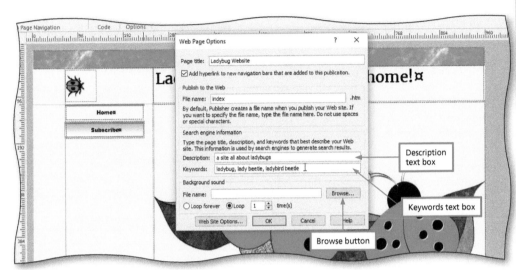

Figure 11–52

Experiment

- Click the Web Site Options button (Web Page Options dialog box) to view additional settings. Click the Cancel button (Web Options dialog box) to return to the Web Page Options dialog box.

Audio

Many websites include audio, sounds, or music. In Publisher, you can add audio to your publication in various ways. You can insert links to audio clips that play when a user clicks the link, you can use the Insert Object command to insert an audio file, or you can include an automatic **background sound** that plays when the page first is displayed. Adding sound generates interest, attracts attention, and can add a certain style to your website. Disadvantages of adding sound include additional download time and visitors who navigate away from the website because they may not want to listen. You should use sound only to enhance the website and do so only in appropriate amounts.

Some websites use MIDI files for their sound and music. **MIDI** stands for **Musical Instrument Digital Interface**, which is a standard music file protocol used by a variety of electronic musical instruments, computers, and other related devices to connect and communicate with one another.

If you use music on your website, make sure you have the legal permission to do so. Most music is copyrighted; for example, you may have purchased a song on iTunes, but that does not give you the legal right to post it on a website. If you want to link to other music on the web, make sure you link to legal sites. In this project, you will be inserting only audio that is part of the Publisher installation.

BTW
Audio Hot Spots
If you want a hot spot to play music, copy the audio file to the index_files folder. Then, use the Insert Hyperlink dialog box and the 'Existing File or Web Page' button to select the relative location of an audio file, such as ..\index_files\MYSONG.MID.

To Insert an Audio File

1 USE ONLINE TEMPLATES | 2 INSTALL FONTS | 3 INSERT MASTHEAD & NAVIGATION BAR | 4 ADD WEB GRAPHICS
5 PUBLISH & TEST | 6 CREATE FORM CONTROLS | 7 SET OPTIONS | 8 USE VBA CODE | 9 SET SECURITY LEVELS

The following steps insert an audio file. *Why? The owner of the website would like music to play when visitors come to the website.*

1

- Click the Browse button (Web Page Options dialog box) (shown in Figure 11–52) to display the Background Sound dialog box.

- Scroll as necessary and then click MUSIC_01.MID to select the file (Figure 11–53).

 Q&A Can I hear what the music sounds like now?
Yes. You can right-click the file and then click Play on the shortcut menu. Depending on your default music app, you may have to install Windows Media Player or a compatible app.

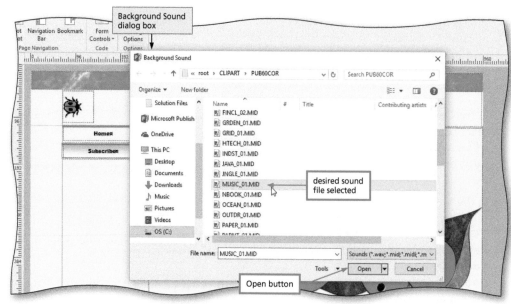

Figure 11–53

2

- Click the Open button (Background Sound dialog box) to select the sound.
- Click the OK button (Web Page Options dialog box) to return to the publication.

To Edit Webpage Options on Page 2

The following steps edit the webpage options on the second page of the website to create a page title.

① Navigate to page 2. If necessary, display the Web tab.

② Click the 'Web Page Options' button (Web tab | Options group) to display the Web Page Options dialog box.

③ If necessary, select any text in the Page title text box and then type **Ladybug Web Form** to replace the text (Figure 11–54).

④ Click the OK button to close the Web Page Options dialog box.

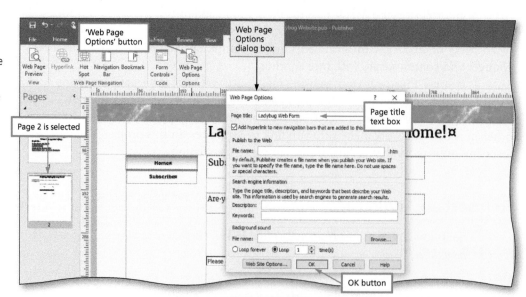

Figure 11–54

To Republish to the Web

The following steps save the Publisher file and republish the HTML files to the web.

1 Click the Save button on the Quick Access Toolbar to overwrite the previously saved file.

2 Click File on the ribbon and then click the Export tab in the backstage view to display the Export gallery.

3 Click Publish HTML in the left pane to display the Publish HTML gallery in the right pane.

4 Click the Publish HTML button to display the Publish to the Web dialog box.

5 Navigate to your storage location and the Module 11 Project folder you created earlier in the module.

6 Click the Save button to publish the website. If Publisher displays a Confirm Save As dialog box, click the Yes button.

Testing a Website

When you test a website, typically you will check the animation, listen to any sounds if your system has speakers, test the navigation bar, view all the pages, and test all hyperlinks and hot spots. You also should enter data in the web form and test the Submit and Reset buttons.

BTW

Hot Spots
To facilitate user interaction, webpages also may contain hot spots. Recall that a hot spot is a location other than text that contains a hyperlink, typically a graphic, picture, or other identifiable area.

How should you test the form?
Be sure that the form works as you intended. Fill in the form as if you were a user. Have others fill in the form to be sure it is organized in a logical manner and is easy to understand and complete. Correct any errors or weaknesses in the form, and test the form again. Finally, publish the form on the web.

CONSIDER THIS

To Test a Website

1 USE ONLINE TEMPLATES | 2 INSTALL FONTS | 3 INSERT MASTHEAD & NAVIGATION BAR | 4 ADD WEB GRAPHICS
5 PUBLISH & TEST | 6 CREATE FORM CONTROLS | 7 SET OPTIONS | **8 USE VBA CODE** | **9 SET SECURITY LEVELS**

In the following steps, you will preview and test the website. *Why? Testing will reveal any errors in navigation or hyperlinks.*

1
- Click the Page 1 thumbnail in the Page Navigation pane and then display the Web tab.
- Click the 'Web Page Preview' button (Web tab | View group).
- When Publisher runs the browser, if necessary, maximize the browser window (Figure 11–55).

 Experiment
- One at a time, click each link to display each page. Click the browser's back button to return to the ladybug website.

My music did not play. What should I do?

Your computer may not have an installed media player. If your screen displays a dialog box at the bottom of the screen, click the Open button and then install the suggested media player. See your instructor for other ways to listen to the music.

Figure 11–55

2

- Click the Subscribe button on the navigation bar.

- Select an option button.

- Select the text in the email address textbox form control and then enter your email address (Figure 11–56).

Will the Submit button work?

It is possible to enter text, make choices, and click the Reset button in the webpage preview; however, the Submit button will not work until the webpage is uploaded to an appropriate server that has FrontPage Extensions, a software technology for servers. See your instructor for ways to upload the files.

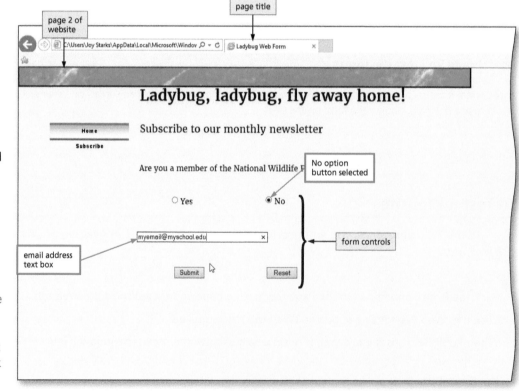

Figure 11–56

③

• Click the Reset button to verify that it works and resets all of the form controls.

• Click the Close button on the browser title bar to close the window and return to the publication.

Break Point: If you wish to take a break, this is a good place to do so. Exit Publisher. To resume at a later time, run Publisher, open the file named Ladybug Website, and continue following the steps from this location forward.

Visual Basic for Applications

Visual Basic for Applications (VBA) is a powerful tool used to program how Publisher and other applications perform while creating documents. In Publisher, VBA provides you with the ability to run macros, write procedures, and create new menus and buttons.

Should you customize applications with macros and events?
Many casual Microsoft Office users do not know that customization is available. Creating special tabs and buttons on the ribbon can help a user to be much more productive. Creating a macro for repeating tasks also saves time and reduces errors. If you understand how to do so, customization is an excellent productivity tool.

CONSIDER THIS

A **macro** is a set of instructions, keystrokes, or commands saved with a unique name that acts a shortcut to execute those instructions at a later time. In some applications, you can create new macros by recording keystrokes of common tasks that you wish to automate. In Publisher, you can run macros recorded elsewhere or program the macros yourself.

Publisher has seven prenamed macros, called **document events**, which execute automatically when a certain event occurs. Table 11–3 lists the name and function of these document events.

Table 11–3 Document Events	
Macro Name	**Runs**
BeforeClose	Immediately before any open publication closes
ShapesAdded	When one or more new shapes are added to a publication; this event occurs whether shapes are added manually or via program code
Undo	When a user undoes the last action performed
Redo	When reversing the last action that was undone
Open	When you open a publication containing the macro
ShapesRemoved	When a shape is deleted from a publication
WizardAfterChange	After the user chooses an option in the wizard pane that changes any of the following settings in the publication: page layout (page size, fold type, orientation, label product), print setup (paper size or print tiling), adding or deleting objects, adding or deleting pages, or object or page formatting (size, position, fill, border, background, default text, text formatting)

The name you use for an automatic macro depends on when you want certain actions to occur. In this project, when a Publisher user exits the Ladybug Website, you want a message box to appear, reminding the user to upload the appropriate files to the web. Thus, you will see how to create a BeforeClose macro using the Visual Basic Editor.

To Display the Developer Tab

1 USE ONLINE TEMPLATES | 2 INSTALL FONTS | 3 INSERT MASTHEAD & NAVIGATION BAR | 4 ADD WEB GRAPHICS

5 PUBLISH & TEST | 6 CREATE FORM CONTROLS | 7 SET OPTIONS | 8 USE VBA CODE | **9 SET SECURITY LEVELS**

The following steps edit the ribbon settings to display the Developer tab on the ribbon. *Why? You need the Developer tab to write VBA code and macros.*

- Right-click an empty area on the ribbon to display the shortcut menu (Figure 11–57).

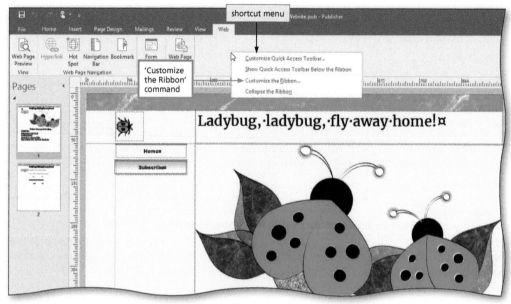

Figure 11–57

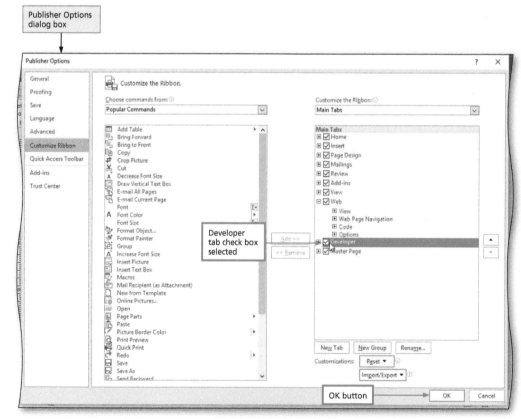

2

- Click 'Customize the Ribbon' on the shortcut menu to display the Publisher Options dialog box.

- In the Main Tabs list, click to display a check mark in the Developer check box (Figure 11–58).

Figure 11–58

3

- Click the OK button (Publisher Options dialog box) to accept the setting change.

- Click Developer on the ribbon to display the Developer tab (Figure 11–59).

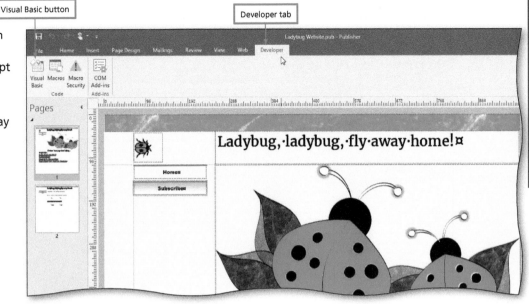

Figure 11–59

Using the Visual Basic Editor

The **Visual Basic Editor** is a full-screen editor that allows you to enter a procedure by typing lines of VBA code as if you were using word processing software. VBA displays a **code window** in which you may choose document events and type code.

Because the code window is similar to a text box or word processor window, at the end of a line, you press the ENTER key or use the DOWN ARROW key to move to the next line. If you make a mistake in a code statement, you can use the arrow keys and the DELETE or BACKSPACE keys to correct it. You also can move the insertion point to lines requiring corrections.

To Open the VBA Code Window

1 USE ONLINE TEMPLATES | 2 INSTALL FONTS | 3 INSERT MASTHEAD & NAVIGATION BAR | 4 ADD WEB GRAPHICS
5 PUBLISH & TEST | 6 CREATE FORM CONTROLS | 7 SET OPTIONS | **8 USE VBA CODE** | **9 SET SECURITY LEVELS**

The following step opens the VBA coding window. The document event will apply only to the current publication. *Why? VBA procedures and macros are unique; other publications will not have access to the code created in this publication.*

1

- Click the Visual Basic button (Developer tab | Code group) (shown in Figure 11–59) to open the Microsoft Visual Basic for Applications window.

- If necessary, double-click the Microsoft Visual Basic for Applications title bar to maximize the window.

- If the Project window does not appear, click View on the menu bar and then click Project Explorer. If the Properties panel appears below the Project window, click its Close button.

- In the Project window, if a plus sign appears next to Project (Ladybug Website.pub), click the plus sign.

- If a plus sign appears next to Microsoft Publisher Objects, click the plus sign.

- Double-click ThisDocument to open the code window. If necessary, double-click the code window title bar to maximize the window (Figure 11–60).

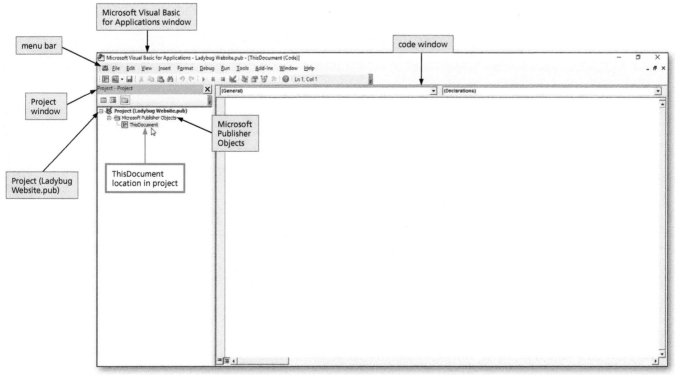

Figure 11–60

Other Ways

1. Press ALT+F11

Entering Code Statements and Comments

The BeforeClose event in the Ladybug Website includes a code statement that calls, or executes, a function. A **function** is a keyword, already programmed in VBA, that activates a procedure. You will code the **MsgBox function,** which displays a message in a dialog box and then waits for the user to click a button. In its simplest forms, the code statement includes the function keyword, MsgBox, and the text that will appear in the message box enclosed in quotation marks. VBA programmers use a message box to display copyright information about a publication, remind users to save publications in a certain location, or let web users know their submission was successful.

Adding comments before and within a procedure helps you remember the purpose of the macro and its code statements later. **Comments** begin with the keyword, Rem, or an apostrophe (') and are displayed in green in the code window. Comments have no effect on the execution of a procedure; they simply provide information about the procedure, such as its name and description.

To Program a BeforeClose Event

1 USE ONLINE TEMPLATES | 2 INSTALL FONTS | 3 INSERT MASTHEAD & NAVIGATION BAR | 4 ADD WEB GRAPHICS
5 PUBLISH & TEST | 6 CREATE FORM CONTROLS | 7 SET OPTIONS | **8 USE VBA CODE** | **9 SET SECURITY LEVELS**

The following steps insert a comment and code statement in the BeforeClose event. VBA provides beginning and ending code statements for document event procedures. It is common practice to indent comments and code within these statements. *Why? Indenting code enhances readability.*

1

- In the code window, click the Object arrow and then click Document in the list to choose the object.
- Click the Procedure arrow, and then click BeforeClose in the list to choose the procedure to code (Figure 11–61).

Q&A Why did Publisher create two procedures?
The beginning and ending code statements for the BeforeClose and Open procedures appear in the code window. Publisher automatically displays the Open procedure by default, but it will have no effect on this publication.

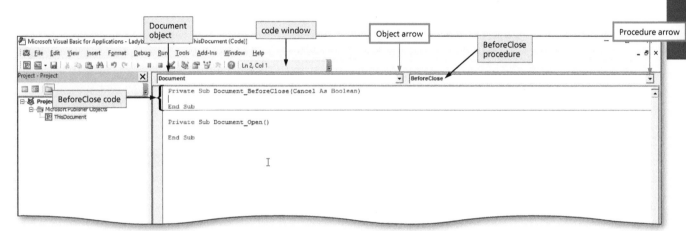

Figure 11–61

2

- Press the TAB key. Type `'When the publication closes, a reminder message box will be displayed.` and then press the ENTER key to enter the comment line.
- Type `MsgBox "remember to upload this file to the website."` to complete the code (Figure 11–62).

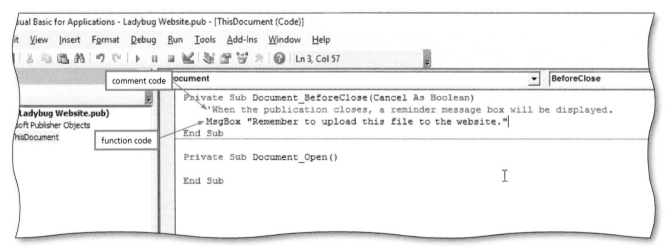

Figure 11–62

Q&A Why did I press the TAB key?
Pressing the TAB key indents the lines of code. The TAB key has no effect on how the code executes; it merely aids in readability.

3

- Click the Close button on the Microsoft Visual Basic for Applications title bar to close the VBA code window.

Security Levels

A **computer virus** is a potentially damaging computer program designed to affect, or infect, your computer negatively by altering the way it works without your knowledge or permission. Currently, more than one million known computer viruses exist, and new viruses are discovered each day. The increased use of networks, the Internet, and email has accelerated the spread of computer viruses.

To combat this problem, most computer users run antivirus programs that search for viruses and destroy them before they ever have a chance to infect the computer. Macros are a known carrier of viruses because of the ease with which a person can write code for a macro. For this reason, you can reduce the chance your computer will be infected with a macro virus by setting a **security level** in Publisher. Security levels allow you to enable or disable macros. An **enabled macro** is a macro that Publisher will execute, and a **disabled macro** is a macro that is unavailable to Publisher.

Table 11–4 summarizes the four available security levels in Publisher.

Table 11–4 Publisher Security Levels	
Security Level	**Condition**
Very High	Publisher will execute only macros installed in trusted locations. All other signed and unsigned macros are disabled when the publication is opened.
High	Publisher will execute only macros that are digitally signed. All other macros are disabled when the publication is opened.
Medium	Upon opening a publication that contains macros from an unknown source, Publisher displays a dialog box asking if you wish to enable the macros.
Low	Publisher turns off macro virus protection. The publication is opened with all macros enabled, including those from unknown sources.

If Publisher security is set to very high or high and you attach a macro to a publication, Publisher will disable the macro when you open the publication. If the security is set to medium, each time you open the Publisher publication or any other document that contains a macro from an unknown source, Publisher displays a dialog box warning that a macro is attached and allows you to enable or disable the macros. If you are confident of the source (author) of the publication and macros, you should click the Enable button in the dialog box. If you are uncertain about the reliability of the source of the publication and macros, you should click the Disable button.

To Set a Security Level in Publisher

1 USE ONLINE TEMPLATES | 2 INSTALL FONTS | 3 INSERT MASTHEAD & NAVIGATION BAR | 4 ADD WEB GRAPHICS
5 PUBLISH & TEST | 6 CREATE FORM CONTROLS | 7 SET OPTIONS | 8 USE VBA CODE | **9 SET SECURITY LEVELS**

The following steps set Publisher's security level. *Why? Because you created a macro with VBA code in this project, you should ensure that your security level is set to medium.*

- Click the Macro Security button (Developer tab | Code group) to display the Trust Center dialog box.
- If necessary, click Macro Settings in the left pane to display the macro options.
- If necessary, click the 'Disable all macros with notification' option button to select it (Figure 11–63).

- Click the OK button (Trust Center dialog box) to apply the settings.

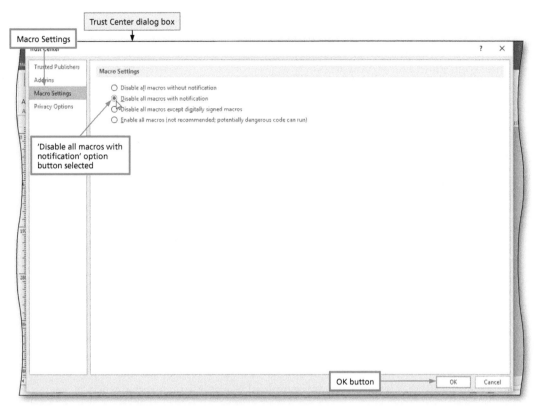

Figure 11–63

Completing the Website

To complete the website, the final tasks are to check for spelling and design errors, save the publication as both a Publisher publication and as a web file, and then test the macro.

To Check the Publication

Recall that Publisher's Design Checker scans the publication for overlapping errors and large graphics that may prevent the page from loading quickly on the web. The following steps check for spelling errors and run the Design Checker.

1. Click the Spelling button (Review tab | Proofing group). If Publisher flags any words that are misspelled, fix them.

2. When Publisher asks to check the entire publication, click the Yes button.

3. Fix any other errors.

4. Open the Backstage view and then click the 'Run Design Checker' button. If the Design Checker identifies any errors, fix them. You can ignore references to low resolution images.

5. Close the Design Checker task pane.

To Save and Republish

Now that the form is complete, it is a good time to save the publication again and republish the files to the web.

1 Click the Save button on the Quick Access Toolbar to overwrite the previously saved file.

2 Click File on the ribbon and then click the Export tab to display the Export gallery.

3 Click Publish HTML in the left pane to display the Publish HTML gallery in the right pane.

4 Click the Publish HTML button to display the Publish to the Web dialog box.

5 If necessary, navigate to your storage location and the Module 11 Project folder you created earlier in the module.

6 Click the Save button (Publish to the Web dialog box) to publish the website. If Publisher displays a Confirm Save As dialog box, click the Yes button.

Testing the Website

After you have published it to a web server, you should test your electronic form to make sure it functions as you intended and returns the form data to you. To receive results, change the email address to your own in the Form Properties dialog box (Figure 11–50). See your instructor to upload your files to an appropriate server.

To Check Form Controls for Accuracy

If you wanted to check the form for accuracy, you would perform the following steps.

1. See your instructor for ways to upload your web files to a server.
2. Use a browser to locate your website on the web.
3. Enter information into several of the text boxes, and click one of the option buttons.
4. Click the Reset button.
5. Complete the electronic form. As you use the form, make sure the controls work as you intended.
6. Click the Submit button.
7. Verify that you received the data you entered. If you did not, contact your Internet service provider and ask about its ability to support Microsoft FrontPage server extensions, version 3.0 or above.
8. Check the data to make sure you understand the format in which the responses were returned to you.

To Hide the Developer Tab

The following steps hide the Developer tab so that it no longer appears on the ribbon.

1 Display the Backstage view and then click the Options tab to display the Publisher Options dialog box.

2 Click Customize Ribbon in the left pane. In the Main Tabs list, click to remove the check mark in the Developer check box.

3 Click the OK button (Publisher Options dialog box) to accept the setting change.

To Test the Macro

The following steps show the reminder message box that appears when the user exits Publisher. *Why? To test the automatic macro, you activate the event that causes the macro to execute.* For example, the BeforeClose macro runs whenever you close the Publisher publication.

- Click the Close button on the Publisher title bar to display the message box created by the macro (Figure 11–64).

- Click the OK button (Microsoft Publisher dialog box) to close the message box. If Publisher asks you to save the publication again, click the Save button.

Figure 11–64

Summary

In this module, you were introduced to some advanced Publisher features. You downloaded an online template, installed a new font, converted a picture to a Microsoft drawing object, and created a custom RGB color to create a web graphic. You opened a blank web publication and added ruler guides, a masthead, a navigation bar, an animated graphic, hyperlinks, and alternative text. You then created additional pages and set webpage options. You inserted, edited, and set properties for form controls, including an audio to play when the website first is displayed. You created a web form and learned that each form control should have a unique name and a return value for submission purposes. Finally, you used Visual Basic for Applications to program a message box in the publication itself and changed the security level.

STUDENT ASSIGNMENTS

CONSIDER THIS: PLAN AHEAD

What decisions will you need to make when creating your next website?
Use these guidelines as you complete the assignments in this module and create your own publications outside of this class.

1. Download any online templates you might need.

2. Install any specific fonts.

3. Determine the size, layout, and number of pages in the website.

    a) Select a page size.

    b) Create repeatable objects, background, and guides that you wish to appear on every page.

    c) Duplicate pages.

4. Insert objects.

    a) Insert graphics and alternative text.

    b) Insert animation.

    c) Insert text.

5. Publish the website on your local storage location.

6. Choose audio carefully.

    a) Copy audio files to index_files folder.

    b) Create relative links to audio clips as hot spots.

7. Create necessary form controls.

    a) Insert controls and set appropriate properties.

    b) Set form properties.

    c) Align all objects.

8. Set webpage options.

9. Set navigation bar properties.

10. Test the website both in preview and by using the index.html file.

11. Use VBA to customize a publication with macros.

12. Set security levels to run macros.

Apply Your Knowledge

Reinforce the skills and apply the concepts you learned in this module.

Working with Form Controls

Note: To complete these steps, you will be required to use the Data Files. Please contact your instructor for information about accessing the Data Files.

Instructions: You have been hired as an intern for an online store that sells custom birdhouses. As it builds its website, it would like you to complete the webpage order form. You are to add a new page, update it, and then insert form controls to create an electronic form. You decide to investigate Building Block Library forms. The resulting form is shown in Figure 11–65.

Perform the following tasks:

1. Run Publisher and open the file named Apply 11–1 Birds Only Website from the Data Files. Click the Page Width button (View tab | Zoom group).

2. Navigate to page 5. Right-click the Page 5 thumbnail in the Page Navigation pane and then click 'Insert Duplicate Page' on the shortcut menu.

3. On the new page 6, change the page title, Service, to Order Form. Change the navigation bar text on the last button to Order Form.

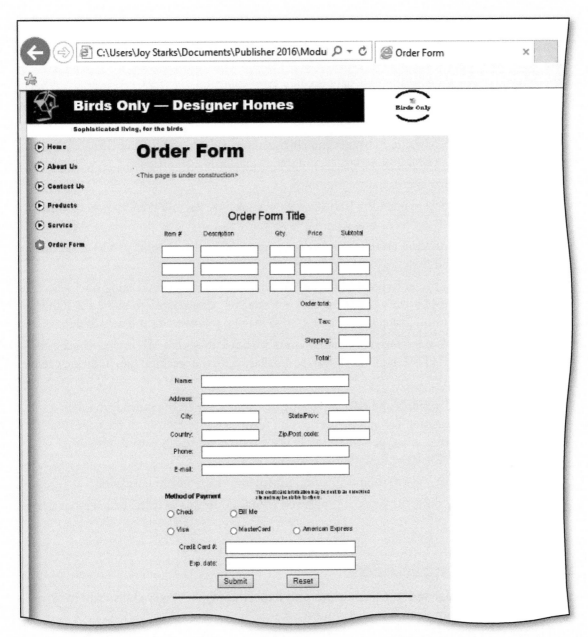

Figure 11–65

4. Right-click the navigation bar and then click 'Navigation Bar Properties' on the shortcut menu. Click Order Form in the Links text box (Navigation Bar Properties dialog box) and then click the Modify Link button. Click the Change Title button (Modify Link dialog box). Type **Order Form** in the Page Title text box (Enter Text dialog box). Click the OK button three times to close each of the dialog boxes.

5. At the bottom of page 6, edit the synchronized navigation text box by placing the insertion point after the word, Service, and inserting a space. Then, type **| Order Form** as the new text. Select the new text and then click the 'Add a Hyperlink' button (Web tab | Web Page Navigation group). Link the new text to the Order Form page.

6. Show the whole page. Click the Show Building Block Library Dialog Box Launcher (Insert tab | Building Blocks group) and then click the Page Parts folder (Building Blocks Library dialog box). Scroll to display the Reply Forms section. Insert the Order Form building block, and move it as necessary to fill the middle of page 6.

Continued >

Apply Your Knowledge *continued*

7. Zoom in on the credit card area. Double-click the Credit Card # textbox form control. When the Text Box Properties dialog box is displayed, click the 'Hide sensitive text with asterisks (***)' check box. Do the same for the Exp. date textbox form control.

8. Double-click the Submit button and then click the Form Properties button. If instructed to do so, have the data sent to your email address and use an appropriate message for the subject line.

9. If instructed to do so, navigate to page 1 and change the email address to your own.

10. Run the Design Checker and check the spelling. Fix any errors other than objects partially off the page or objects that encroach the printable area.

11. Click File on the ribbon to open the Backstage view, click Save As, and then browse to your storage location.

12. Click the New folder button on the Save As dialog box toolbar. Type **Apply 11-1** as the name of the folder and then press the ENTER key.

13. Double-click the new folder to open it. In the File name text box (Save As dialog box), select the text and then type **Apply 11-1 Birds Only Website Complete** to name the Publisher file. Click the Save button (Save As dialog box) to save the publication in the new folder.

14. Open the Backstage view and then click the Export tab. Click Publish HTML in the left pane and then click the Publish HTML button in the Export gallery. Save the resulting files in the new folder.

15. Exit Publisher.

16. Open a File Explorer window and navigate to the new folder. Open the index.htm file in a browser. Test the navigation bar and the navigation text box at the bottom of the page. Navigate to the Order Form page, and type something in the Credit Card text box to test that the numbers are hidden. Click the Reset button.

17. See your instructor for ways to submit this assignment and/or publish the website.

18. ✷ Make a list of five different kinds of things you could add to this website. List reasons why you would do so.

Extend Your Knowledge

Extend the skills you learned in this module and experiment with new skills. You may need to use Help to complete the assignment.

Editing Graphics

Note: To complete these steps, you will be required to use the Data Files. Please contact your instructor for information about accessing the Data Files.

Instructions: Run Publisher. Open the publication, Extend 11–1 Baby Doe Designs Website, from the Data Files. The file contains a home page photo gallery with six additional pages containing full-size images.

You will edit the website shown in Figure 11–66 so that it displays compressed, thumbnail pictures for each photo. The first thumbnail is displayed in Figure 11–66.

Perform the following tasks:

1. Use Help to learn more about thumbnail images and reducing download times.

2. Browse through the pages in the publication to become familiar with the page names, layout, and photographs.

Courtesy of Amanda Mansheim

Figure 11–66

3. For each photo:
   a. Navigate to the page and copy the photo. Paste the photo into the scratch area.
   b. Navigate back to page 1. Resize the photo to create a thumbnail image that fits in the area below its caption.
   c. Compress the photo for the web. *Hint:* Right-click the image, click Format Picture on the shortcut menu, and then use the Compress button in the Format Picture dialog box.
   d. Create a hyperlink or hot spot to link the thumbnail to the appropriate webpage in the website.

4. Navigate to page 2. Click the Picture Placeholder button (Insert tab | Illustrations group) and then drag the empty picture placeholder to the left of the photo. Search for a clip art image of a back button and insert it into the empty picture placeholder.

5. Press CTRL+K to create a hyperlink back to Page 1.

Continued >

STUDENT ASSIGNMENTS

Extend Your Knowledge *continued*

6. Below the back button, create a label that says, Back to the Photo Gallery.

7. Select both the back button and the label. Copy and paste them on pages 3 through 7.

8. Navigate to page 1. Below the photo gallery, create a welcome message label that says `Welcome to my website! Please fill out the form below to receive my newsletter.`

9. Below the welcome message label, create a web form to collect the visitor's name and email address. Include a submit button.

10. Edit the textbox form control properties to name the two text boxes. One should be named, name, and the other should be named, email_address. Change the Form Properties to send the data via email.

11. If requested by your instructor, use your email address.

12. On your storage location, create a folder named Extend 11–1. Save the publication in the new folder with the file name, Extend 11–1 Baby Doe Designs Website Complete.

13. Test the webpage by previewing it and clicking each photo. Fix any errors.

14. Export the publication and publish the HTML. Store the resulting files in the new folder.

15. See your instructor for ways to submit this assignment.

16. ✷ What modifications could you make to this website to upload the pictures from a database? How would that facilitate website maintenance?

Expand Your World

Create a solution that uses cloud or web technologies by learning and investing on your own from general guidance.

Using an Online Service for Website Creation

Instructions: You decide to investigate other ways to generate a website quickly and easily, without having to learn advanced HTML or a framework, such as Dreamweaver.

Perform the following tasks:

1. Run a browser and navigate to www.weebly.com (Figure 11–67). As directed by your instructor, enter your name, email address, and create a password. Alternately, sign in with your Facebook account.

2. In the first screen, choose to create a website or click the Site button. Choose a theme.

3. In the second screen, select the 'Use a Subdomain of Weebly.com' option button and type your name in the text box. Click the Continue button.

4. In the third screen, click the 'Build My Site' button.

5. When the design page opens, scroll to the lower part of the page. Drag objects from the toolbox on the left into the design. Click the Edit button, and follow the directions to edit the inserted object. If necessary, click the Save button.

6. Investigate the tabs across the top of the toolbox. Try adding an audio clip. Try adding a button.

7. If instructed to do so, insert a text box with your name.

8. Investigate the tabs across the top of the design screen. Make appropriate changes.

9. When you are finished, click the PUBLISH button and follow the steps. The address of your new website will be http://yourname.weebly.com. Send the link to your instructor.

10. ✷ Was weebly.com easier to use than Publisher? What are the advantages and disadvantages that you noticed?

Figure 11–67

In the Labs

Design, create, or modify, and/or use a publication using the guidelines, concepts, and skills presented in this module. Labs 1 and 2, which increase in difficulty, require you to create a solution based on what you learned in the module; Lab 3 requires you to apply your creative thinking and problem-solving skills to design and implement a solution.

Lab 1: **Using Online Templates**

Note: To complete these steps, you will be required to use the Data Files. Please contact your instructor for information about accessing the Data Files.

Problem: Only Cakes is a local bakery with a website in place; however, they have decided to start taking orders over the web. They would like a web order form for customers to order cakes online, as shown in Figure 11–68. Data should be collected about the name and address of the customer, and the size, flavor, and icing of the desired cake. Also, include a check box for return customers and option buttons for delivery or pick-up. Finally create a text area where customers can list additional instructions.

Perform the following tasks:
1. Run Publisher and then open the file, Blank Webpage, from the Data Files.
2. Choose the Parrot color scheme and the Casual font scheme.
3. Click the Background button (Page Design tab | Page Background group) and then click More Backgrounds in the gallery. Click the 'Picture or texture fill' option button (Format Background dialog box) and then click the Texture button. Choose the 'Blue tissue paper' texture. Click the OK button to close the Format Background dialog box.
4. Create a horizontal guide at 139 pixels. Create a vertical guide at 148 pixels.

Continued >

In the Labs *continued*

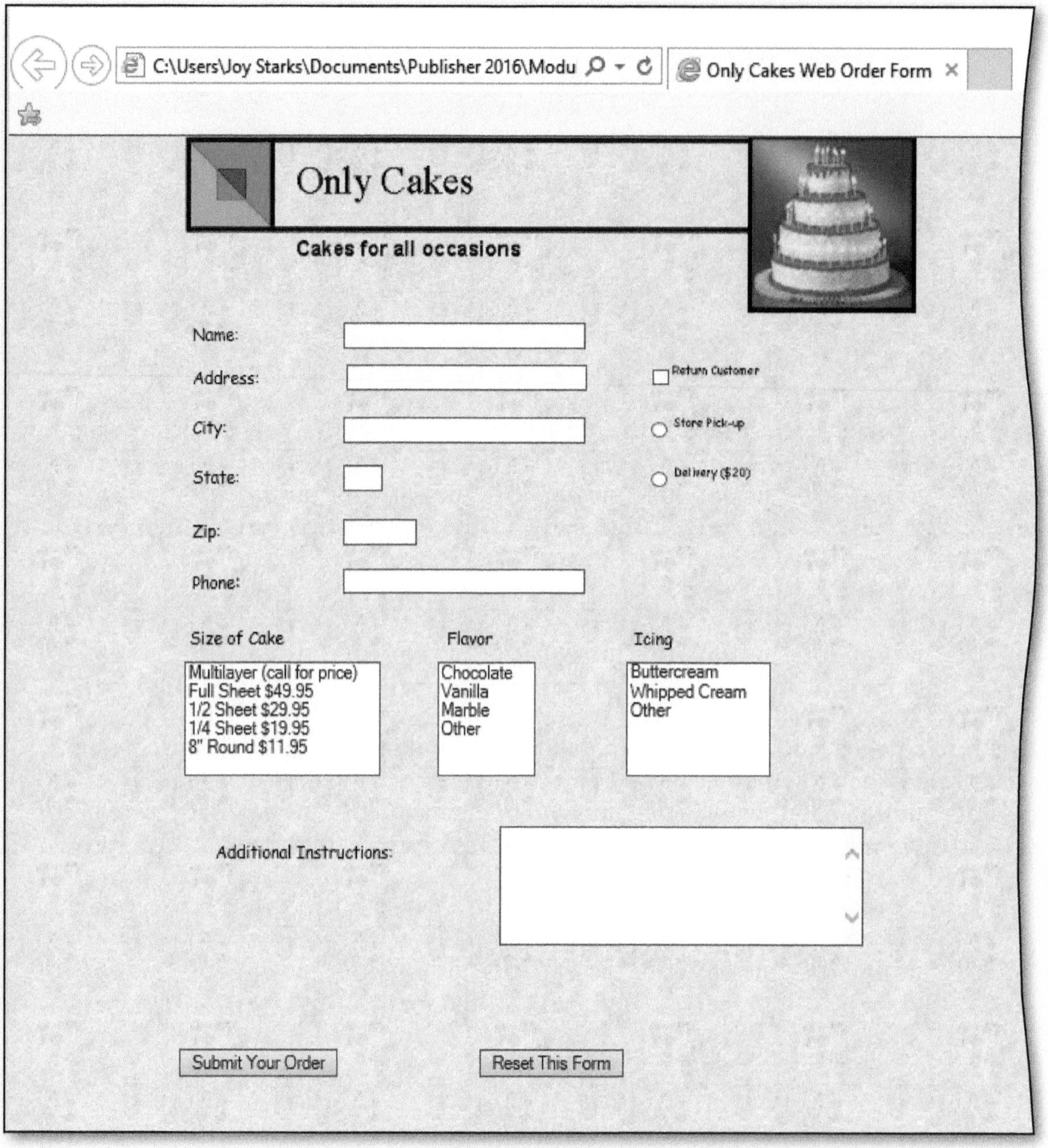

Figure 11–68

5. Use the Building Block Library and the Page Parts folder to choose the Accent Box masthead. Align it with the top of the page and on the right side of the vertical guide.

6. In the masthead, click the text in the Home Page Title text box and then type **Only Cakes** to replace the text.

7. Select the text in the Business Name text box and then type **Cakes for all occasions** as the new tag line. Right-click the text box and then click Best Fit on the shortcut menu.

8. With the masthead selected, click the Ungroup button (Drawing Tools Format tab | Arrange group) to ungroup the masthead. Click outside of the masthead objects to deselect them.

9. Right-click the picture and then click Delete Object on the shortcut menu. Right-click the 'Business Tagline or Motto' text box and then click Delete Object on the shortcut menu.

10. Search for a clip art image using the search term, cake. Choose a graphic similar to the one shown in Figure 11–67. Move it to the upper-right corner of the page, and resize it to fit the area between the top margin and horizontal guide.

11. Below the masthead and right of the vertical guide, create text box labels for Name, Address, City, State, Zip, and Phone. Position them as shown in Figure 11–67. Create a textbox form control to accompany each of the labels. Resize the form controls and place them appropriately. Double-click each form control, and set the return data label to be the same as the accompanying label. Align and distribute the controls as necessary.

12. To the right of the form controls and labels, create a checkbox form control. Use the label, Return Customer. Set the return data label to Return_Customer.

13. Create two option button form controls. Change the label text on the first option button to read Store Pick-up. Change the label text on the second option button to Delivery ($20). For each Option Button form control, set the return data label to the word, Service. Set each Option button value to be the same as the accompanying label. Align and distribute the controls as necessary.

14. Below the previously inserted form controls, create three labels: Size of Cake, Flavor, and Icing. Create a list box form control for each label. Use the items shown in Table 11–5.

Table 11–5 Data for List Box Form Controls

Return Data Label	Size	Flavor	Icing
Data Items	Multilayer (call for price) Full Sheet ($49.95) 1/2 Sheet ($29.95) 1/4 Sheet ($19.95) 8" Round ($11.95)	Chocolate Vanilla Marble Other	Buttercream Whipped Cream Other
Selection	Nothing selected	Nothing selected	Nothing selected

15. Below the previously inserted form controls, create a label containing the following text: Additional Instructions. Create a text area form control beside the label. Use the return data label, Additional_Instructions.

16. Finally, create a Submit button with the label, Submit Your Order, which sends data to an email address.

17. If instructed to do so, use your email address in the Submit button properties.

18. Create a Reset button with the label, Reset This Form.

19. Click the 'Web Page Options' button (Web tab | Options group). Insert an appropriate page title, file name, description, keywords, and background sound.

20. Check the publication for spelling and design errors. Preview the publication using the 'Web Page Preview' button (Web tab | View group).

21. Click File on the ribbon to open the Backstage view, click Save As, and then browse to your storage location.

22. Click the New folder button on the Save As dialog box toolbar. Type **Lab 11-1** as the name of the folder and then press the ENTER key.

23. Double-click the new folder to open it. Name the file Lab 11–1 Only Cakes Web Order Form.

24. Open the Backstage view and then click the Export tab. Click the Publish HTML tab in the Export gallery and then click the Publish HTML button. Save the resulting files in the new folder.

Continued >

In the Labs *continued*

25. Open a File Explorer window and navigate to the new folder. Open the index.htm file in a browser. Test the boxes and buttons.

26. See your instructor for ways to submit this assignment and/or publish the website.

27. ✺ How would you merge this file with the company's current website? What changes might you need to make?

Lab 2: **Adding VBA Procedures to a Publication**

Problem: The owner of the Ladybug Website wants a change to the website you created in this module. The owner now has asked you to insert a copyright message box each time the publication is opened, as shown in Figure 11–69a. The message box should display the information icon that is represented in VBA by the code, vbInformation. The title bar of the message should contain the name of the business. Table 11–6 lists the code and its purpose to create a copyright message box.

The owner also wants to warn any employees who edit the publication of accidental deletions (Figure 11–69b). Table 11–7 lists the code and its purpose to create a warning message box that will be displayed when an object in the publication is deleted.

Table 11–6 VBA Code for a Copyright Message Box	
VBA Code	**Purpose**
'When the publication opens, a copyright message box will be displayed.	Comment
MsgBox "This publication is copyrighted by the Ladybug Website.", vbInformation, "Ladybug Website"	Function to display message box prompt, icon, title bar caption

Table 11–7 VBA Code for a Warning Message Box	
VBA Code	**Purpose**
'When a user deletes an object in the publication, a confirmation message box will be displayed.	Comment
Dim intResponse As Integer	Declares a storage location for the user's response
intResponse = MsgBox("Do you really want to delete this object?", vbYesNo)	Function to display message box prompt and two command buttons
If intResponse = vbNo Then Publisher.ActiveDocument.Undo	Tests to see if the user clicked the No button and then calls the Undo button procedure

Perform the following tasks:

1. Run Publisher and open the Ladybug Website file, created earlier in this module, or contact your instructor for information about accessing the required files.

2. Click the Enable Macros button (Microsoft Publisher Security Notice dialog box).

3. Press ALT+F11 to open the Visual Basic Editor window. If necessary, click the plus sign next to 'Project (Ladybug Website.pub)' and then click the plus sign next to 'Microsoft Publisher Objects'. Double-click ThisDocument.

4. Click the Object arrow and then click Document in the list. Click the Procedure arrow and then click Open. Press the TAB key and then enter the VBA code from Table 11–6.

5. Click the Procedure box arrow and then click ShapesRemoved. Press the TAB key and then enter the VBA code from Table 11–7.

6. If instructed to do so, add a comment line in the code with your name and course number.

7. Close the Microsoft Visual Basic for Applications window.

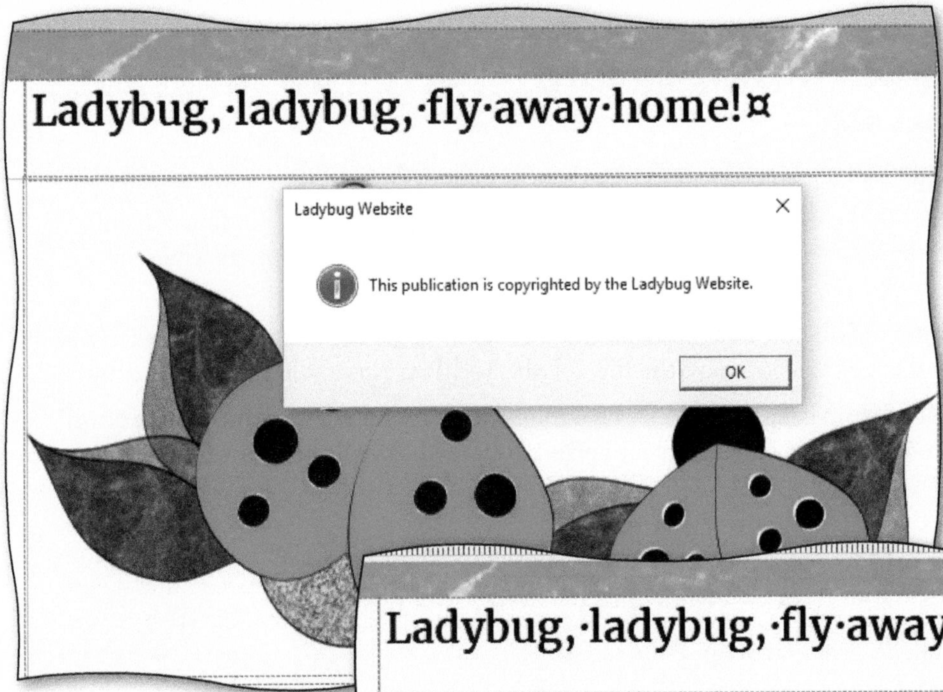

(a) Copyright Message Box

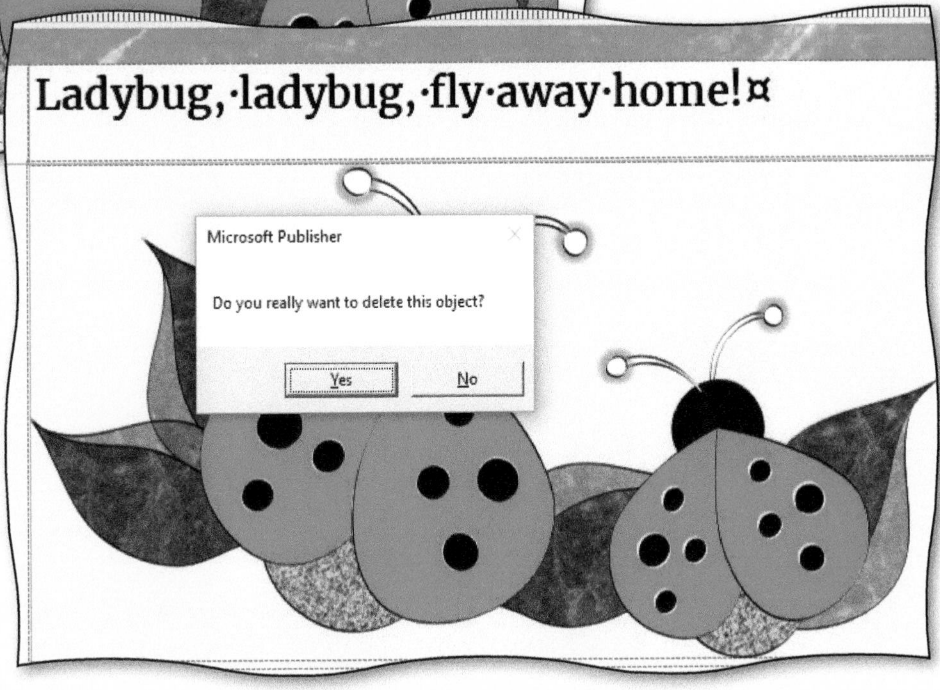

(b) Warning Message Box

Figure 11–69

8. Display the Developer tab. Click the Macro Security button (Developer tab | Code group) to display the Trust Center dialog box. If necessary, click Macro Settings in the left pane to display the macro options. If necessary, select the 'Disable all macros with notification' option button. Click the OK button (Trust Center dialog box) to apply the settings.
9. Save the publication and then test the two macro events by exiting Publisher and reopening the publication.
10. When the Microsoft Office Publisher dialog box appears warning you of possible macro viruses, click the Enable Macros button. When Publisher displays the information dialog box, click the OK button.
11. Delete an object in the publication. When Publisher displays the message box, click the No button. Hide the Developer tab when you are finished.
12. Write down a specific instance of when you might use each of the events listed in Table 11–3, other than those listed and used in the module. How did you decide on those specific instances?

Continued >

In the Labs *continued*

Lab 3: **Consider This: Your Turn**

Creating a Message Box

Problem: Several student workers are editing the Department of Music's latest musical program publication. The chair of the department would like you to write VBA code reminding students to upload the latest copy of the program to the server. A message box should appear when the publication closes.

Part 1:   Open the file named Lab 11–3 Jazz Ensemble Program from the Data Files and then add the VBA code to create the message box. Save the file as Lab 11–3 Jazz Ensemble Program Complete.

Part 2:   ✹ Think of other messages that designers might want to include in print publications. Make a list of when the message should appear and what it needs to tell the user of the publication.

Index

Note: Bold page numbers refer to pages where key terms are defined.

3-D Rotation shape effect, PUB 280–283
10-month calendar, creating, PUB 305–307
20-lb. bond paper, **PUB 93**

A

active tab, **OFF 17**
add-in, **PA 10**
adding. *See also* inserting
 alternative text, PUB 587–588
additions to publications, PUB 34
address bar, folder windows, **OFF 29**
address lists, **PUB 345**
adjustment handle, PUB 13
advertisements, **PUB 196**
 check publication for errors, PUB 199–200
 closing publication without exiting publisher, PUB 200
 editing and formatting coupon, PUB 198
 entering other texts, PUB 199
 inserting coupon, PUB 197
 resizing, moving, duplicating coupon, PUB 198
align, **PUB 30**
aligning
 objects, Catalog Tools Format tab, PUB 419–420
 other cells, PUB 300
 text, PUB 32
 text and format, PUB 186–187
alternative text, **PUB 587**
 adding, PUB 587–588
 hyperlinks and text, PUB 589
 inserting another graphic, PUB 588
animated graphics, **PUB 586**
 inserting, PUB 586
 previewing, PUB 587
animation emphasis effects, **PA 8**
annotating webpages, PA 15
applications. *See* apps
apps, **OFF 3**
 exiting Office, with one document open, OFF 42

Microsoft Office Web Apps, OFF 8–9
 running from File Explorer, OFF 52
 running from start menu, OFF 10–12
 running using Search box, OFF 46–47
 switching from one to another, OFF 31–32
arrange thumbnails, **PUB 82**
ASCII, **PUB 464**
attachment, **PUB 483**
 best practices, PUB 484
 sending postcard as, PUB 486
audio, PUB 601
 editing webpage options, PUB 602
 inserting, PUB 601–602
 republishing to web, PUB 603
AutoCorrect Options button, PUB 54–55
autofit, **PUB 25**
autofit headings, PUB 69
AutoFit text, PUB 25–26
autoflow, **PUB 118**
automatic hyphenation, **PUB 145**
Award certificates, **PUB 255**
 creating, PUB 255–256
 editing, PUB 255–256

B

B2B (business-to-business), **PUB 389**
background sound, **PUB 601**
backgrounds, using pictures as, PUB 63–64
Backstage view
 closing file using, OFF 49–50
 creating new publication from, OFF 48
 opening recent file using, OFF 50
black-and-white printing, **PUB 94**
blade-coated paper, **PUB 93**
blank page, customized, PUB 200–201
blank publication, OFF 10–12, **PUB 163**
 selecting, PUB 276, PUB 502–503

body copy, **PUB 503**
bold, **PUB 23**
bold text, PUB 23
bookmark, **PUB 549**
 creating, PUB 549–550
 hyphenation rules, PUB 552
 navigating in PDF file, PUB 553–554
 saving in PDF format, PUB 553
 spelling and design errors, PUB 552–553
 testing hyperlinks, PUB 552
 using to create hyperlinks, PUB 550–551
border, **PUB 293**
 changing color and weight, PUB 66–67
 formatting inside, PUB 297–298
BorderArt
 adding, PUB 309–311
 definition, **PUB 309**
 inserting building block, PUB 311–312
 inserting Clip Art, PUB 313
boundary, **PUB 11**
brightness, PUB 182, **PUB 363**
 editing, PUB 365–367
brochure paper, **PUB 95**
brochures, **PUB 49**
 creating trifold, PUB 52–55
 editing inside panels of, PUB 73–77
 medium, PUB 51
 options, PUB 52
 page size, PUB 52
 selecting template, PUB 52–53
Building Block Library, **PUB 180**
 adding objects, PUB 283
 deleting content from, PUB 203
building blocks, **PUB 180**
 inserting, PUB 202, PUB 315–316
 inserting in BorderArt, PUB 311–312
 saving, PUB 180–181
 snapping object to margin guide, PUB 181–182
built-in templates, **PUB 4**
bulleted list, **PUB 194**
 creating custom, PUB 194–195
 entering text, PUB 196
business cards, **PUB 256**

creating, PUB 256–257
printing, PUB 258–259
setting publication properties,
    PUB 260
business information field
data for, PUB 277
inserting, PUB 230–231
business information sets,
    PUB 218
changing existing publications,
    PUB 230
creating, 277–278, PUB 227–230
data for, PUB 227
deleting, PUB 264–265
inserting business information
    field, PUB 230–231
business-to-business (B2B),
    PUB 389
buttons
AutoCorrect Options, PUB 54–55
mouse, OFF 4
Paste Options, PUB 58

C

calendar
creating, PUB 305–307
definition, **PUB 304**
description, PUB 304–305
editing, PUB 135
editing other pages, PUB 313
printing, PUB 314
saving pages as images, PUB 314
Caption gallery, PUB 86–88
captions, **PUB 83**
editing, PUB 84
ungrouping, PUB 85
card, **PA 6**
catalog, **PUB 391**
planning layout of, PUB 392
reopening, PUB 433
catalog merge area, **PUB 410**
catalog pages, **PUB 410**
deleting two-page spread,
    PUB 412–413
formatting, PUB 411–412
inserting, PUB 411
selecting data sources,
    PUB 413–414
Catalog Tools Format tab,
    PUB 414–415
aligning objects, PUB 419–420
excluding entries, PUB 422
finding entries, PUB 421

inserting other text fields,
    PUB 418–419
inserting picture field,
    PUB 415–416
inserting text fields, PUB 417–418
moving and resizing picture field,
    PUB 417
previewing merge, PUB 422–423
turning off boundaries, PUB 422
viewing boundaries, PUB 416
cell, **PUB 284**
editing alignment, PUB 299
merging, PUB 290–291
splitting, PUB 292
cell and text box margins
changing cell margins,
    PUB 518–519
changing text box margins,
    PUB 520
collapsing front matter section,
    PUB 520
creating table of contents,
    PUB 517–518
cell diagonal, **PUB 292**
creating, PUB 292–293
removing, PUB 293
certificates, **PUB 255**
changing
publication properties,
    OFF 23–24
publications, PUB 33–36
character spacing, **PUB 335**
kern character pairs, PUB 336
tools, measurement task pane,
    PUB 335
tracking charatcers, PUB 337
Character Spacing dialog box,
    PUB 338
creating text box, PUB 338–339
check box, **PUB 591**
click mouse operations, OFF 4
Clip Art, inserting, PUB 313
Clipboard task pane
pasting from, PUB 531
using, PUB 530–531
clipping, **PUB 223**
clips, **PUB 27**
capturing video, PA 11
described, **PA 11**
closing
Graphics Manager task pane,
    PUB 426
Mail Merge task pane, PUB 357
publication, email newsletter, 483

code, **PUB 566**
code window, **PUB 607**
collapsing
front matter section, PUB 520
Page Navigation pane, PUB 12
ribbon, OFF 18–19
sections, PUB 514–515
color-matching library, **PUB 94**
color printing, PUB 94
colors
borders, changing, PUB 66–67
font, changing, PUB 67–68
color scheme, **PUB 6**, PUB 52
color stop, **PUB 187**
column
deleting, PUB 287–288
inserting, PUB 290
commands, **OFF 10**
and shortcut menus, OFF 19–20
Comments, **PUB 608**
common knowledge, **PUB 115**
compress, **PUB 363**
picture settings, PUB 363
compress pictures, PUB 368
computer programming, **PUB 566**
computer virus, **PUB 610**
content, PUB 529
changing text wrapping options,
    PUB 534–535
Clipboard task pane,
    PUB 530–531
copying and pasting sidebar, PUB
    532–533
copying wrapping style,
    PUB 536
editing WordArt, PUB 532
importing text, PUB 529–530
inserting picture, PUB 533–534
content pages, **PUB 503**
continued notices, **PUB 122**
formatting with, PUB 122–124
contrast, PUB 182, **PUB 363**
editing, PUB 365–367
converting, picture to drawing
    object, PUB 179–180
copy fit, **PUB 25**
copying, **PUB 56**
data source files, PUB 410
embedded table, PUB 319
folder to OneDrive, OFF 42–44
linked table, PUB 319
and pasting, PUB 56–57
section heading, page breaks,
    PUB 547

sidebar, PUB 532–533
text, methods (table), PUB 56
wrapping style, PUB 536
Cortana, **PA 14**
creating
  Award certificates, PUB 255–256
  background on Master Page,
    PUB 394
  blank publication from File
    Explorer, OFF 51
  bookmarks, PUB 549–550
  business cards, PUB 256–257
  cell diagonal in tables,
    PUB 292–293
  cited reference, Research task
    pane, PUB 469–470
  custom bulleted list,
    PUB 194–195
  custom page size, PUB 164–166
  custom ruler guides,
    PUB 579–580
  data source, PUB 344–348
  drop cap, PUB 140–141
  embedded table, PUB 317–319
  envelopes, PUB 252–253
  folders, OFF 27–29
  folder within a folder, OFF 30
  header, PUB 395–396
  hot spot, PUB 474–475
  letterhead, PUB 218–220,
    PUB 315
  logo, PUB 221–222
  mirrored header, PUB 396
  new color scheme,
    PUB 167–168
  new font scheme, PUB 170–172
  new publication from Backstage
    view, OFF 48
  new style, PUB 234–236
  numbered lists, PUB 246–248
  OneNote notebook, PA 2
  page border, pagination,
    PUB 516
  portable files, PUB 260–262
  publication, email templates,
    PUB 450
  reflection, front cover,
    PUB 407–408
  section heading, page breaks,
    PUB 546–547
  sections, designing layout,
    PUB 505–506
  Sway presentation, PA 6–7
  table of contents, PUB 517–518

templates, PUB 148–151
text box, Character Spacing dialog
  box, PUB 338–339
text box, form control, PUB 592
text box, users, PUB 239
text breaks, PUB 544–546
title graphic, front cover,
  PUB 409
title, pagination, PUB 512–513
trifold brochure, PUB 52–55
two-page spread, PUB 392–394
web masthead, PUB 582–583
Creative Commons license,
  PA 7
cropping, **PUB 221**
cropping pictures, PUB 221–222
crop to shape, **PUB 223**
CTRL key, keyboard shortcuts
  and, OFF 5
custom bulleted list,
  PUB 194–195
custom color scheme, **PUB 166**
  applying, PUB 201–202
  choosing color not in gallery,
    PUB 169
  creating new color scheme,
    PUB 167–168
  deleting, PUB 204
custom font scheme, **PUB 170**
  applying, PUB 201–202
  creating new font scheme,
    PUB 170–172
  deleting, PUB 205
customize, **PUB 126**
customized blank page,
  PUB 200–201
customizing
  data source fields, PUB 347–348
  drop cap, PUB 141–142
  letterhead for interactivity,
    PUB 238–240
  Quick Access Toolbar,
    OFF 20–21
  ribbon, OFF 14, PUB 126–128
  template, greeting card,
    PUB 487–489
  templates, PUB 6–10
  workshop, email templates,
    PUB 450
custom letterhead template,
  PUB 245–248
  creating numbered lists,
    PUB 246–248
  increasing indent, PUB 248

open publication from recent list,
  PUB 245
typing beginning of letter,
  PUB 245–246
custom page size
  creating, PUB 164–166
  deleting, PUB 205–206
custom-sized publications,
  PUB 163
  creating custom page size,
    PUB 164–166
  selecting blank publication,
    PUB 163
cutting, **PUB 56**

D

data
  deleting, table, PUB 303–304
  entering, table, PUB 301–303
  filtering, PUB 374–375
database, **PUB 344**
data-driven publication, **PUB 389**
data field, **PUB 345**
data file, **PUB 329**
data formats, PUB 344
data record, **PUB 344**
data source, **PUB 329**
  connecting with, PUB 358–359
  copying files, PUB 362,
    PUB 410
  creating, PUB 344–348
  customizing fields, PUB 347–348
  editing, PUB 360–362
  entering data, PUB 348–349
  saving, PUB 350
  selecting, catalog pages,
    PUB 413–414
  using Mail Merge Wizard,
    PUB 345–346
default text, **PUB 17**
  replacing, PUB 17–18
deleting. *See also* removing
  business information set,
    PUB 264–265
  columns, table, PUB 287–288
  content from Building Block
    Library, PUB 203
  custom color scheme, PUB 204
  custom color scheme, greeting
    card, PUB 491
  custom font scheme, PUB 205
  custom page size, PUB 205–206
  data, table, PUB 303–304

deleting *(continued)*
files, OFF 55
objects, PUB 19–20
objects, on pages, PUB 125–126
pages from newsletters, PUB 113
rows, table, PUB 288
two-page spread, PUB 412–413
deletions from publications,
PUB 34
description, **PUB 600**
deselecting objects, PUB 18
Design Checker, **PUB 88,**
PUB 144
running, PUB 90
Design Checker dialog box,
PUB 477–478
designing layout
creating sections, PUB 505–506
inserting pages, PUB 504–505
merge sections, PUB 506
design issues
Design Checker dialog box,
PUB 477–478
editing color schemes, PUB 476
email, PUB 475
publication checking errors,
PUB 478
spelling errors, PUB 479
troubleshooting, PUB 479
desktop publishing (DTP),
PUB 105
destination, **PUB 249, PUB 315**
Developer tab
displaying, PUB 606–607
hiding, PUB 612
diagonal border, PUB 299
dialog boxes, navigating in,
OFF 35
Dialog Box Launcher, **OFF 16**
digital printing, **PUB 94**
dimension, **PUB 284**
directory, **PUB 391**
planning layout of, PUB 392
disabled macro, **PUB 610**
displaying. *See also* viewing
Developer tab, VBA,
PUB 606–607
formatting marks, PUB 60
KeyTips, OFF 17
measurement task pane,
PUB 232–233
Docs.com, **PA 8**
document events, **PUB 605**
document properties, OFF 24

double-tap gesture, OFF 3
drag-and-drop editing,
PUB 143–144
drag gesture, OFF 3
dragging
to move or resize windows,
OFF 56–57
selecting multiple objects by,
PUB 81–82
drag mouse operations, OFF 4
drawing
rectangle, PUB 184
text box, PUB 186
drawing canvas, **PA 3**
drawling line, PUB 370
drop cap, **PUB 140**
creating, PUB 140–141
customizing, PUB 141–142
duplicating
coupon, advertisements,
PUB 198
Master Page, PUB 396–397
pages, PUB 523
two-page spread, PUB 524–527

E

edit, **PUB 15**
editing
Award certificates, PUB 255–256
calendar, PUB 135
captions, PUB 84
cell alignment, PUB 299
color schemes, PUB 476
comment text box, PUB 459
coupon, advertisements,
PUB 198
data source, PUB 360–362
form properties, PUB 599–600
forms, PUB 76–77
heading, PUB 455
heading text in left panel, PUB 59
headlines for continued story,
PUB 124
inside panels of brouchers,
PUB 73–77
Lead Story Headline, PUB 116
left and middle panels,
PUB 74–76
masthead, in styles, PUB 238
merged publications,
PUB 358–362
objects, PUB 131
objects in middle panel, PUB 55

objects in right panel, PUB 53–54
option button, PUB 594–595
other text boxes, PUB 455–456
pages, PUB 124
postcard, PUB 485
pull quotes, PUB 134–135
Secondary Story Headline,
PUB 118
sidebars, PUB 132–133
stories in Word, PUB 128–131
text boxes, form control,
PUB 596–597
text, greeting card, PUB 490–491
ticket stub, PUB 371–372
webpage options, PUB 600–601
webpage options, audio,
PUB 602
WordArt, PUB 532
WordArt alignment, PUB 279
email, **PUB 445**
design issues, PUB 475
HTML-enabled, PUB 446
email merge, **PUB 446**
email newsletters
listserv, PUB 480
modifying paper size and margins,
PUB 482–483
previewing, PUB 480–481
sending print publications,
PUB 482–483
sending, using Publisher,
PUB 481–482
email templates, PUB 448
changing newsletter page size,
PUB 450–451
creating publication, PUB 450
customizing workshop, PUB 450
selecting of, PUB 449
setting background using patterns,
PUB 452–454
types of, PUB 449
embed, **PUB 263**
fonts, PUB 263–264
embedded table, **PUB 314,**
PUB 317–321
copying, PUB 319
creating, PUB 317–319
creating from scratch, PUB 318
formatting, PUB 319–320
moving, PUB 321
pasting, PUB 319
positioning, PUB 321
summing, PUB 320–321
embedding, type of, PUB 263

enabled macro, **PUB 610**
end matter, **PUB 503**
envelopes, **PUB 252**
  addressing, PUB 254
  creating, PUB 252–253
  printing, PUB 254–255
  setting options, PUB 254–255
e-postcards, **PUB 483**
errors, eliminating in brochures,
    PUB 88
event, **PUB 566**
Excel-enhanced table, **PUB 314**
execute, **PUB 566**
exiting
  Office apps, OFF 53
  Office apps with one document
    open, OFF 42
  Publisher, PUB 150–151
  Word, PUB 130
expanding
  Page Navigation pane, PUB 12
  ribbon, OFF 18–19

F

featured templates, **PUB 4**
field, **PUB 227**
field code, **PUB 351**
  grouped, PUB 351
  individual, PUB 354–355
  inserting, PUB 351–355
field name, **PUB 345**
File Explorer
  creating blank publication from,
    OFF 51
  running apps from, OFF 52
file name, **OFF 24**
  invalid naming characters,
    OFF 34
files, **OFF 8**
  closing using Backstage view,
    OFF 49–50
  deleting, OFF 55
  moving, OFF 54–55
  naming, OFF 34
  opening existing, OFF 47
  opening using Backstage view,
    OFF 50
  PostScript, PUB 95
  renaming, OFF 54
  saving in folder, OFF 49
  saving in folders, OFF 32–35
fill, **PUB 185**
  changing, PUB 298

filling shape, PUB 223
  grouping objects, PUB 225
  with pictures, PUB 223–225
  saving as pictures, PUB 226
filtering data, PUB 374–375
Find and Replace commands,
    PUB 536–540
  finding whole words only,
    PUB 539
  using Find command,
    PUB 537–538
  using Replace command,
    PUB 539–540
  wildcard and format searching,
    PUB 537
Find command, PUB 537–538
fine-tuning, shape effects,
    PUB 282–283
First-Line Indent marker,
    PUB 339
fitting
  another pictures, PUB 463–464
  pictures, PUB 462–463
flags, **PUB 20**
flip, **PUB 176**
flipping objects, PUB 176–177
flyers
  creating, PUB 2–10
  described, **PUB 1**
folders, **OFF 10**
  creating, OFF 27–29
  creating within folders, OFF 30
  expanding, scrolling through,
    collapsing, OFF 30–31
  saving file in, OFF 49
  saving files in, OFF 32–35
folder windows, **OFF 29**
font colors, changing, PUB 67–68,
    PUB 298
fonts, **PUB 6**
  installing new, PUB 575–576
font scheme, **PUB 6**, PUB 8
font size
  adjusting, PUB 86
  described, **PUB 23**
  increasing, PUB 26
footers, **PUB 395**
  alternating, inserting,
    PUB 400–401
format, **PUB 22**
  applying, table, PUB 285–286
  borders, PUB 293
  diagonal border, PUB 299
format painter, **PUB 249**

saving letter, PUB 250–251
  using, PUB 249
Format Painter button, PUB 249
formatting
  catalog pages, PUB 411–412
  with continued notices,
    PUB 122–124
  coupon, advertisements,
    PUB 198
  embedded table, PUB 319–320
  shapes, PUB 73–74
  single *vs.* multiple characters and
    words, PUB 23–24
  with stylistic sets, PUB 78–79
  text, PUB 22–26
  while editing in Word, PUB 130
formatting marks, **PUB 59**
  displaying, PUB 60
form control, PUB 591–592
  changing Navigation button,
    PUB 592–593
  checking for accuracy, PUB 612
  creating text boxes, PUB 592
  editing form properties,
    PUB 599–600
  editing option button,
    PUB 594–595
  editing text boxes, PUB 596–597
  inserting option button,
    PUB 593–594
  inserting submit button,
    PUB 597–599
  inserting text boxes, PUB 596
  text box, PUB 591
form letters, **PUB 329**
  previewing, PUB 356–357
form options, **PUB 52**
forms, editing, PUB 76–77
free-response quiz, **PA 12**
front cover
  creating reflection,
    PUB 407–408
  creating title graphic, PUB 409
  cropping to shape,
    PUB 405–406
  formatting border,
    PUB 406–407
  inserting pictures, PUB 405
front matter, **PUB 503**
FrontPage Server Extensions,
    PUB 591
Full Screen Mode, **OFF 17**
function, **PUB 608**
function key, zoom using, OFF 21

G

galleries, touch, PUB 56
gallery, **OFF 15, PUB 166**
gestures
  described, **OFF 3**
  for touch screen (table), OFF 3
glossy paper, **PUB 93**
glyph, **PUB 77**
gradient, **PUB 187**
graphics, **PUB 27**
  bringing forward button,
    PUB 178
  changing proportion, PUB 174
  converting picture to drawing
    object, PUB 179–180
  editing, PUB 172
  flipping objects, PUB 176–177
  grouping objects, PUB 178–179
  inserting, PUB 139, PUB 364
  inserting pictures,
    PUB 172–173
  moving, PUB 31
  opening file, PUB 364
  replacing, PUB 136–138
  resizing, PUB 178
  resizing castle graphic,
    PUB 173
  rotating, PUB 173–174
  saving as picture, PUB 181
  setting transparent color,
    PUB 175–176
  ungrouping objects, PUB 179
  using in newsletters,
    PUB 136–139
Graphics Manager
  closing, PUB 426
  redisplaying pictures, PUB 426
  working with, PUB 423–426
green computing, **PUB 33**
greeting card, **PUB 487**
  customizing template,
    PUB 487–489
  deleting custom color scheme,
    PUB 491
  editing text, PUB 490–491
  inserting design accent,
    PUB 489–490
  printing folded publication,
    PUB 491
group, **OFF 14, PUB 178**
grouped field code, **PUB 351**
  inserting, PUB 351–353
grouped object, **PUB 76**

grouping
  graphics, PUB 178–179
  objects, filling shape, PUB 225
  and ungrouping objects,
    PUB 178–179

H

handles, **PUB 13**
hard copy, **PUB 33**
hard return, **PUB 59**
header, **PUB 395**
  creating, PUB 395–396
header record, **PUB 344**
header row, **PUB 344**
headings, editing text in left panel,
    PUB 59
headlines, **PUB 115**
  editing for continued story,
    PUB 124
health, minimizing wrist injuries,
    OFF 5
Help
  Office Help, OFF 57
  Publisher, PUB 115
  using Search text box, OFF 58
  working in Office apps, OFF 59
home page, **PUB 585**
HOME tab, OFF 18
HTML-enabled email,
    PUB 446
Hub, **PA 14**
hyperlinks, **PUB 35**
  alternative text, PUB 589
  creating hot spot, PUB 474–475
  creating, using bookmarks,
    PUB 550–551
  inserting, PUB 35, PUB 471–472
  inserting mailto, PUB 472–474
  mailto, PUB 472–474
  testing, bookmarks, PUB 552
Hypertext Markup Language
    (HTML), **PUB 37**
hyphenation, **PUB 145**
hyphenation rules, PUB 552

I

image setter, **PUB 94**
importing, **PUB 115, PUB 344**
  text files, PUB 116–117
importing style, PUB 237–238
Increase Font Size button, PUB 69
indentation, **PUB 239**

individual field code, PUB 354–355
inked handwriting, **PA 3**
Inking, **PA 15**
Ink to Text, **PA 3**
inserting
  alternating footers, PUB 400–401
  animated graphics, PUB 586
  audio file, PUB 601–602
  author information, pagination,
    PUB 516–517
  automatic date, text wrapping,
    PUB 242–243
  building block, BorderArt,
    PUB 311–312
  building blocks, PUB 202,
    PUB 315–316
  business information field,
    PUB 230–231
  catalog pages, PUB 411
  Clip Art, PUB 313
  coupon, advertisements, PUB 197
  design accent, greeting card,
    PUB 489–490
  empty table, PUB 284–285
  field code, PUB 351–355
  graphic, alternative text, PUB 588
  graphic in table cells, PUB 303
  graphics, PUB 139, PUB 364
  graphics, pagination, PUB 513
  grouped field codes,
    PUB 351–353
  hyperlinks, PUB 35,
    PUB 471–472
  individual field code,
    PUB 354–355
  linked table, PUB 318–319
  merge field codes, PUB 376–378
  multiple pictures from storage
    devices, PUB 61–62
  option button, PUB 593–594
  other text fields, Catalog Tools
    Format tab, PUB 418–419
  page numbers, pagination,
    PUB 507–508
  pages to newsletters, PUB 113
  picture field, Catalog Tools
    Format tab, PUB 415–416
  pictures, PUB 29, PUB 172–173,
    PUB 461
  pictures, front cover, PUB 405
  pictures in content, PUB 533–534
  quizzes, live Webpages and apps,
    PA 12
  rows, table, PUB 289

shapes, PUB 70, PUB 73–74
special characters from Symbol
  Dialog Box, PUB 466–467
submit button, PUB 597–599
symbol from Symbol Dialog Box,
  PUB 464–466
text boxes, form control,
  PUB 596
text fields, Catalog Tools Format
  tab, PUB 417–418
text in ticket, PUB 369
texture, Master Page,
  PUB 398–400
WordArt object, PUB 190–191
installing, new fonts,
  PUB 575–576
internal data label, **PUB 591**
italic, **PUB 24**
italicizing text, PUB 24

J

jump lines, **PUB 122**

K

kerning, **PUB 335**
keyboards, copying, cutting,
  pasting, deleting text (table),
  PUB 56
keyboard shortcuts, **OFF 5**
KeyTips, **OFF 17**
keywords, **PUB 600**

L

landscape, **PUB 62**
landscape orientation, **PUB 276**
large-scale publication, PUB 543
  using Go to Page command,
  PUB 543–544
layering, **PUB 72**
layout guides, **PUB 30**
Lead Story Headline, PUB 116
left-handed mouse functions,
  OFF 4
letter
  saving, format painter,
  PUB 250–251
  typing, PUB 316
letterhead, **PUB 218**
  creating, PUB 218–220,
  PUB 315

customizing for interactivity,
  PUB 238–240
custom template, PUB 245–248
opening template, PUB 220
Paragraph dialog box,
  PUB 239–240
setting publisher display settings,
  PUB 221
libraries, **PUB 94**
line, drawling, PUB 370
linen paper, **PUB 93**
line spacing
  changing, PUB 193
  described, **PUB 193**
lining style, PUB 402
  proportional, PUB 402
linked table, **PUB 314**
  copying and pasting, PUB 319
  inserting, PUB 318–319
linked text boxes, **PUB 115**
  breaking links, PUB 120–121
linking text boxes, using menu,
  PUB 527–529
links, breaking text box,
  PUB 120–121
list box, **PUB 591**
listserv, **PUB 480**
live preview, **OFF 15**, **PUB 166**
lock screen, **OFF 5**
logging in to user accounts, OFF 5
logo, **PUB 221**
  creating, PUB 221–222
  cropping pictures, PUB 221–222

M

macro, **PUB 605**
  disabled, PUB 610
  enabled, PUB 610
  testing, PUB 613
Mailers, **PUB 161**
Mail Merge task pane, PUB 357
Mail Merge Wizard, PUB 345–346
mailto hyperlink, **PUB 472**
manual hyphenation, **PUB 145**
manual line break, **PUB 133**
marginal elements, PUB 132–139
margin guides, **PUB 11**
margin marker, **PUB 339**
marquee, **PUB 320**
master page
  alternating footers, PUB 400–401
  applying, PUB 402–404
  closing, PUB 312

creating background on, PUB 394
definition, **PUB 307**
duplicating, PUB 396–397
footers, PUB 395
header, PUB 395–396
inserting texture, PUB 398–400
removing colored background
  shapes, PUB 397–398
renaming, PUB 397
viewing, PUB 307–308, **PUB 394**
Masthead, **PUB 113**
  editing, PUB 113–114
maximize, **OFF 12**
  Page Navigation pane, PUB 53
measurement task pane, **PUB 231**
  character spacing tools,
  PUB 335
  displaying, PUB 232–233
  positioning objects using,
  PUB 233
  settings, PUB 232
menu, **OFF 10**
merge area, **PUB 391**
merged pages, printing, PUB 357
merged publications
  editing, PUB 358–362
  Mail Merge task pane, PUB 357
  options, PUB 356
  previewing form letters,
  PUB 356–357
  printing merged pages, PUB 357
merge field codes, inserting,
  PUB 376–378
merge sections, PUB 506
merging, **PUB 344**
merging catalogs
  exiting Publisher, PUB 433
  merging printer, PUB 430–433
merging cells, PUB 290–291
merging printer, PUB 430–433
merging with Excel
  adding text to shape,
  PUB 375–376
  checking publications, PUB 378
  copying shape to ticket stub,
  PUB 378
  exiting Publisher, PUB 381
  filtering data, PUB 374–375
  inserting merge field codes,
  PUB 376–378
  printing page of tickets,
  PUB 378–380
  saving files, PUB 381
  selecting recipients, PUB 372–373

meta tags, **PUB 600**
Microsoft Access 2016, **OFF 9**
Microsoft Account Area, OFF 17
Microsoft accounts, signing out of,
   OFF 38–39
Microsoft Edge
   browsing with, PA 14
   locating information with
      Cortana, PA 14–15
Microsoft Excel 2016, **OFF 9**
Microsoft Office 365, **OFF 9**
Microsoft Office Online, **OFF 9**
Microsoft OneNote 2016, **OFF 9**
Microsoft OneNote Mobile app,
   PA 2
Microsoft Outlook 2016, **OFF 9**
Microsoft PowerPoint 2016,
   OFF 9
Microsoft Publisher 2016, **OFF 9**
Microsoft Word 2016, **OFF 8**
MIDI (Musical Instrument Digital
   Interface), **PUB 601**
Mime Hypertext Markup
   Language (MHTML), **PUB 37**
minimized window, **OFF 36**
minimizing and restoring windows,
   OFF 36
mini toolbar
   described, **OFF 16**
   turning off, OFF 16
mirrored header, creating,
   PUB 396
misspelled words, PUB 21
modifications to publications,
   PUB 34
monospacing, **PUB 335**
mouse
   operations (table), OFF 4
   using, OFF 3–4
move, **PUB 30**
moving
   coupon, advertisements, PUB 198
   embedded table, PUB 321
   files, OFF 54–55
   graphics, PUB 31
   picture field, Catalog Tools
      Format tab, PUB 417
   text, PUB 142–144
   text box, PUB 31
   windows, OFF 56
MsgBox function, **PUB 608**
Multiple Sheets Grid, PUB 92
Musical Instrument Digital
   Interface (MIDI), **PUB 601**

N

naming. *See also* renaming
   files, OFF 34
navigating, **OFF 35**
   in dialog boxes, OFF 35
navigation bar, **PUB 581**
navigation pane, folder windows,
   OFF 29
newsletters, PUB **105**
   benefits, advantages of,
      PUB 107–108
   choosing template, options,
      PUB 108–109
   design choices, PUB 108–112
   editing Masthead, PUB 113–114
   marginal elements,
      PUB 132–139
   printing, PUB 147–148
   revising, PUB 140–148
   text, PUB 114–126,
      PUB 115–126
   using graphics in, PUB 136–139
nonbreaking hyphens, **PUB 145**
nonprinting character, **PUB 59**
Normal style, **PUB 234**
Normal view, **PUB 394**
numbered lists
   creating, PUB 246–248
   definition, **PUB 246**

O

Object Position button, **PUB 11**
objects, **PUB 10**
   aligning, Catalog Tools Format
      tab, PUB 419–420
   converting picture to drawing,
      PUB 179–180
   deleting, PUB 19–20
   deselecting, PUB 18
   editing, PUB 131
   editing in middle panel, PUB 55
   editing in right panel,
      PUB 53–54
   flipping, PUB 176–177
   grouping, PUB 178–179
   inserting WordArt, PUB 190–191
   positioning, measurement task
      pane, PUB 233
   resizing, PUB 30
   selecting multiple, by dragging,
      PUB 81–82
   snapping to margin guide,
      PUB 181–182
   ungrouping, PUB 179
   WordArt, PUB 190–191
Object Size button, **PUB 11**
Office apps
   exiting, OFF 53
   Office Help, OFF 56–57,
      OFF 59
   opening Help windows in,
      OFF 56
   Publisher window, ribbon and
      elements common to,
      OFF 13–22
Office Clipboard, **PUB 56**
Office Help, OFF 56–57
Office Mix
   adding to PowerPoint, PA 10
   capturing video clips, PA 11
   inserting quizzes, live Webpages
      and apps, PA 12
   sharing, PA 12
offset, **PUB 398**
offset printing, PUB 94
OneDrive, **OFF 9**
   account, unlinking, OFF 44–45
   copying folder to, OFF 42–44
   saving files on, OFF 37–38
OneNote notebook
   converting handwriting to text,
      PA 3–4
   creating, PA 2
   recording lecture, PA 4
   syncing, PA 2–3
   taking notes, PA 3
one-page spread, **PUB 108**
online pictures, **PUB 79**
   searching for, PUB 79–81
online templates
   chossing color scheme,
      PUB 569
   picture formats, PUB 570–575
   searching for, PUB 568–569
opening
   file using Backstage view, OFF 50
   Help windows in Office apps,
      OFF 56
   Page Navigation pane, PUB 53
   publications, PUB 34
OpenType fonts, **PUB 83**
operating system
   described, **OFF 2**
   Windows 10, OFF 2–8
operations, mouse (table), OFF 4
option button, **PUB 591**
   editing, PUB 594–595

inserting, PUB 593–594
  selecting paste, PUB 58
order form, **PUB 52**
ordering, **PUB 72**
organizing, files and folders,
    OFF 26–29
orphan, **PUB 544**
outline, **PUB 185**
outsource, **PUB 92**
overflow, **PUB 120**

P

Pack and Go Wizard, **PUB 95,**
    PUB 95–97
page breaks, PUB 544
  copying and pasting section
      heading, PUB 547
  creating section heading,
      PUB 546–547
  creating text breaks,
      PUB 544–546
  inserting other breaks, PUB 546
page layout, **PUB 10**
Page Navigation pane
  collapsing, expanding, PUB 12
  hiding, PUB 12
  opening and maximizing, PUB 53
Page Number button, **PUB 11**
page orientation, PUB 276–277
pages
  changing in newsletters, PUB 113
  continuing stories across, PUB
      118–119, PUB 121–122
  deleting objects on,
      PUB 125–126
  editing, PUB 124
  following stories across,
      PUB 119–120
  formatting with continued notices,
      PUB 122–124
  setting options, PUB 110–112
  switching between, PUB 73
pages for content
  duplicating pages, PUB 523
  duplicating two-page spread,
      PUB 524–527
  linking text boxes using menu,
      PUB 527–529
  rearranging pages, PUB 523–524
  viewing two-page spread,
      PUB 524
page size, **PUB 52, PUB 164**
page title, **PUB 600**

pagination, **PUB 507**
  applying background, PUB 512
  collapsing sections, PUB 514–515
  creating page border, PUB 516
  creating title, PUB 512–513
  entering subtitles, PUB 514
  inserting author information,
      PUB 516–517
  inserting graphics, PUB 513
  inserting page numbers,
      PUB 507–508
  removing page numbering,
      PUB 511
  specifying starting page number,
      page navigation pane, PUB 510
  specifying starting page number,
      ribbon, PUB 508–509
paper considerations for printing,
    PUB 93–94
Paragraph dialog box,
    PUB 239–240
Paragraph group, PUB 192
paragraphs, typing text, PUB 59
password, **OFF 5**
Password text box, OFF 7
Paste Options, **PUB 58**
pasting, **PUB 56**
  from Clipboard task pane,
      PUB 531
  embedded table, PUB 319
  linked table, PUB 319
  section heading, page breaks,
      PUB 547
  sidebar, PUB 532–533
  text, methods (table), PUB 56
path, **OFF 26, PUB 409**
PDF (Portable Document Format),
    PUB 260
picture, PUB 460–461
  changing border colors and
      weight, PUB 66–67
  compress, PUB 368
  compress settings, PUB 363
  converting to drawing object,
      PUB 179–180
  cropping in logo, PUB 221–222
  drawing rectangle, PUB 184
  editing brightness and contrast,
      PUB 365–367
  filling shape saving in,
      PUB 226
  filling shape with, PUB 223–225
  fitting, PUB 462–463
  fitting another, PUB 463–464

inserting, PUB 172–173,
    PUB 461
inserting, content, PUB 533–534
moving logo onto page, PUB 184
placing other graphics, PUB 367
recoloring, PUB 364–365
resetting, PUB 64–65
resizing, PUB 65
saving graphics as, PUB 181
selecting corrections, PUB 183
swapping, placing and resetting,
    PUB 83
using as backgrounds,
    PUB 63–64
picture formats
  converting pictures,
      PUB 570–571
  copying format, PUB 573
  filling other shapes, PUB 574
  filling with custom RGB color,
      PUB 572–573
  regrouping, PUB 575
  saving as pictures, PUB 575
  ungrouping, PUB 570–571
picture placeholders, **PUB 27**
picture styles, **PUB 64,**
    PUB 65–66
pinch gesture, OFF 3
placeholder text, **PUB 15**
  replacing, PUB 15–17, PUB
      115–126
placing, pictures, PUB 83
point, **PUB 23**
point mouse operation, OFF 4
Portable Document Format (PDF),
    PUB 260
portable files
  creating, PUB 260–262
  publishing in portable format,
      PUB 261–262
portrait, **PUB 62**
portrait orientation, **PUB 276**
positioning, embedded table, PUB
    321
postcard, **PUB 483**
  editing, PUB 485
  opening template, PUB 484
  sending as attachment, PUB 486
PowerPoint, adding Office Mix to,
    PA 10
press and hold gesture, OFF 3
press mouse wheel, OFF 4
press thumb button on mouse,
    OFF 4

previewing
  animated graphics, PUB 587
  Catalog Tools Format tab,
    PUB 422–423
  email newsletters, PUB 480–481
  form letters, PUB 356–357
  and printing, PUB 91–92
  web publications in browsers,
    PUB 38–39
Previous Locations arrow, folder
  windows, **OFF 29**
printer memory, PUB 93
printing
  business cards, PUB 258–259
  calendar, PUB 314
  choosing options, PUB 109
  color, PUB 94
  conserving ink, toner, PUB 33,
    PUB 94
  considerations, PUB 92–93
  envelopes, PUB 254–255
  folded publication, greeting card,
    PUB 491
  merged pages, PUB 357
  newsletters, PUB 147–148
  Pack and Go Wizard,
    PUB 95–97
  page of tickets, PUB 378–380
  PostScript files, using, PUB 95
  previewing and, PUB 91–92
  publications, OFF 24–26,
    PUB 33
  on special paper, PUB 95
printout, **PUB 33**
procedure, **PUB 566**
process-color printing, **PUB 94**
product list, **PUB 409**
program, **PUB 566**
projects
  brochures, PUB 49–51
  flyer, PUB 1
  newsletter, PUB 105–106
promotional piece, **PUB 305**
proofreading, **PUB 140**
properties, **PUB 591**
  described, **PUB 15**
proportional lining style,
  PUB 402
propotional spacing, **PUB 335**
publication
  business cards, PUB 260
  business information sets,
    PUB 230–231
  changing, PUB 33–36

checking design errors,
  PUB 478
checking for errors,
  PUB 199–200
checking spelling, PUB 89
closing without exiting publisher,
  PUB 200
creating, email templates,
  PUB 450
creating new blank from File
  Explorer, OFF 51
custom letterhead template,
  PUB 245
custom-sized, PUB 163–166
Design Checker, PUB 88,
  PUB 144
entering text in, OFF 22, OFF 49,
  OFF 52
hyphenation, checking,
  PUB 145–147
merging data into, PUB 343–357
merging with Excel, PUB 378
opening, PUB 34
options, choosing, PUB 7–10
printing, OFF 24–26, PUB 33
properties, OFF 23–24
saving and closing, email
  newsletter, 483
spell checking, PUB 20–22,
  PUB 144
translating text, PUB 430
publication set, **PUB 108**
Publisher
  display settings, PUB 109
  email newsletters using,
    PUB 481–482
  exiting, PUB 150–151
  Help, PUB 94, PUB 115
  merging catalogs, PUB 433
  running, PUB 331
  security level, PUB 610
  setting security level,
    PUB 610–611
Publisher window, OFF 13–22,
  PUB 10–12
publishing
  portable format, PUB 261–262
  Sway, PA 8
  to web, **PUB 37**
  websites, PUB 589–590
Publishing HTML, **PUB 37**
pullouts, **PUB 132**
pull quotes, **PUB 132**
  editing, PUB 134–135

Q

Quick access area, folder windows,
  OFF 29
Quick Access Toolbar, **OFF 17**
  customizing, OFF 20–21
  relocating using shortcut menu,
    OFF 19–20

R

radio button, **PUB 591**
reading online, PUB 454
  completing lead story,
    PUB 456–457
  completing second story,
    PUB 457–458
  completing sidebar, PUB 460
  completing third story,
    PUB 458–459
  editing comment text box,
    PUB 459
  editing heading, PUB 455
Reading view, **PA 14**
Recent list, **PUB 34**
recipient lists, **PUB 345**
recolor, **PUB 363**
  picture, PUB 364–365
  shapes, PUB 71–72
record, **PUB 344**
recto page, **PUB 108**
Recycle Bin, **OFF 8**
reflection, **PUB 407**
  creating, PUB 407–408
  settings, PUB 407
Refresh button, folder windows,
  OFF 29
relocating Quick Access Toolbar,
  OFF 19–20
removing, ribbon customization,
  PUB 150–151
renaming. *See also* naming
  files, OFF 54
  Master Page, PUB 397
reopening catalogs, PUB 433
repeatable area, **PUB 410**
Replace command, PUB 539–540
replacing
  default text, PUB 17–18
  graphics, PUB 136–138
  placeholder text, PUB 15–17,
    PUB 115–126
replication, **PUB 320**
republishing websites, PUB 612

Research task pane, PUB 467
 creating cited reference,
  PUB 469–470
 options, PUB 470
 using, PUB 468–469
reset button, **PUB 591**
Reset command, **PUB 64**
resetting, **PUB 363**
 pictures, PUB 64–65, PUB 83
resize, **PUB 30**
resizing
 castle graphic, PUB 173
 coupon, advertisements, PUB 198
 graphics, PUB 178
 objects, PUB 30
 picture field, Catalog Tools
  Format tab, PUB 417
 pictures, PUB 65
 table, PUB 290
 windows, OFF 57
resolution, **PUB 586**
response form, **PUB 52**
responsive design, **PA 6**
Restart command, OFF 6
restoring minimized windows,
  OFF 36
return data label, **PUB 591**
reusable parts, PUB 274
RGB, **PUB 94**
ribbon, **OFF 14**
 collapsing, expanding,
  OFF 18–19
 copying, cutting, pasting, deleting
  text (table), PUB 56
 customizing, OFF 14,
  PUB 126–128
 displaying different tab on,
  OFF 17–18
 folder windows, **OFF 29**
 office app, OFF 13–22
 removing customization,
  PUB 150–151
 screen resolution and, PUB 64,
  PUB 115
Ribbon Display Options, OFF 17
right-handed mouse functions,
  OFF 4
roadmaps to chapters, OFF 2
rotate mouse wheel, OFF 4
rotation handle, **PUB 13**
rows
 changing, PUB 297
 deleting, PUB 288
 inserting, PUB 289

selection of, PUB 297
ruler, **PUB 10, PUB 339**
 tools, PUB 340
ruler guides, PUB 520
 creating custom, PUB 579–580
 selecting, PUB 521–522
running
 apps from File Explorer, OFF 52
 apps using Search box,
  OFF 46–47
 apps using start menu, OFF 10–12
 Design Checker, PUB 90
 Publisher, PUB 4

S

sample, **PUB 234**
 font color, PUB 234–235
sandbox, **PA 15**
sans serif, **PUB 78**
saving
 bookmark, PDF format, PUB 553
 building blocks, PUB 180–181
 data source, PUB 350
 existing Office file with same or
  different file name, OFF 52–53
 file in folder, OFF 49
 files in folders, OFF 32–35
 files in merging with Excel,
  PUB 381
 files on OneDrive, OFF 37–38
 graphics as picture, PUB 181
 letter, format painter,
  PUB 250–251
 pages as images, calendar,
  PUB 314
 publication, email newsletter, 483
 publications as web publications,
  PUB 37–38
 websites, PUB 612
scaling, **PUB 335**
scratch area, **PUB 61**
screen recording, **PA 11**
screen resolution, **OFF 39**
 changing, OFF 40–41
 ribbon and, PUB 64, PUB 115
ScreenTips, **OFF 15**
scroll arrows, **OFF 4**
scroll bar, **OFF 4, OFF 13**
scroll box, **OFF 4**
scrolling, OFF 4
Search box
 folder windows, **OFF 29**
 running apps using, OFF 46–47

windows, OFF 59–60
Search text box, Help using,
  OFF 58
secondary page, **PUB 585**
Secondary Story Headline,
  PUB 118
section heading
 copying and pasting, PUB 547
 creating, PUB 546–547
sections, **PUB 505**
 creating, PUB 505–506
security level, **PUB 610**
 settings for Publisher, PUB
  610–611
select, **PUB 12**
selecting
 brochure template, PUB 52–53
 built-in template, PUB 5–6
 objects, PUB 12–14
 text, PUB 15–19
selection rectangle, **PUB 12**
separated, **PUB 94**
serif, **PUB 77**
set up, **PUB 93**
shape effects, **PUB 280**
 applying, PUB 280–281
 fine-tuning, PUB 282–283
shapes
 filling, PUB 223
 inserting, PUB 70
 inserting and formatting,
  PUB 73–74
 recoloring, PUB 71–72
 sending backwards, PUB 72
sharing
 Office Mix presentation, PA 12
 Sway, PA 8
shortcut menus, **OFF 19**
 copying, cutting, pasting, deleting
  text (table), PUB 56
 delete using, PUB 36
 relocating Quick Access Toolbar
  using, OFF 19–20
 replacing graphics using,
  PUB 136–138
Shut down command, OFF 6
sidebars, **PUB 132**
 editing, PUB 132–133
signing in, to user account, OFF 5,
  OFF 6–7
sign-in screen, **OFF 5**
sign-up form, **PUB 52**
Sleep command, OFF 6
slide gesture, OFF 3

Slide Notes, **PA 11**
slide recording, **PA 11**
snapping, PUB 181–182
soft return, **PUB 133,**
    PUB 133–134, **PUB 246**
source, **PUB 249, PUB 315**
spacing
  character, PUB 335
  line, PUB 193
  proportional, PUB 335
special characters, **PUB 464**
  inserting from Symbol Dialog
    Box, PUB 466–467
spelling
  checking, PUB 20–22, PUB 89,
    PUB 144
  errors, PUB 552–553
splitting cells, PUB 292
spot color, **PUB 94**
spot-color printing, **PUB 94**
spread, **PUB 392**
Start button, **OFF 10**
Start menu, **OFF 10**
  running apps from, OFF 10–12
status bar, **OFF 13,** PUB 11
storage devices, inserting pictures
    from, PUB 61–62
story, **PUB 115**
  adding content to build, PA 7
  continuing across pages,
    PUB 118–119, PUB 121–122
  editing in Word, PUB 128–131
  following across pages,
    PUB 119–120
Storyline, **PA 6**
stretch gesture, OFF 3
style, **PUB 234**
  applying, PUB 237–238
  creating new, PUB 234–236
  editing masthead, PUB 238
  importing, PUB 237–238
  sampling font color,
    PUB 234–235
stylistic alternate, **PUB 78**
stylistic sets, **PUB 77**
  formatting with, PUB 78–79
submit button, **PUB 591**
  inserting, PUB 597–599
subset, **PUB 263**
suites, Microsoft Office 2013,
    OFF 9
summing, embedded table,
    PUB 320–321
swap icon, **PUB 61**

swapping, pictures, PUB 61–64,
    PUB 83
swashes, PUB 78
Sway
  designing, PA 8
  Publishing, PA 8
  sharing, PA 8
Sway presentation, creating,
    PA 6–7
Sway site, **PA 6**
swipe gesture, OFF 3
switching
  from one app and another,
    OFF 31–32
  between pages, PUB 73
symbol, **PUB 464**
  inserting from Symbol Dialog
    Box, PUB 464–466
Symbol Dialog Box
  inserting special characters,
    PUB 466–467
  inserting symbols,
    PUB 464–466
syncing, **PA 2**
  OneNote notebook, PA 2–3
synonym, **PUB 541**

T

tab, **PUB 339**
  Catalog Tools Format tab (*See*
    Catalog Tools Format tab)
  displaying different, on ribbon,
    OFF 17–18
  entering tabbed text,
    PUB 342–343
  setting, PUB 340–343
  types of alignments, PUB 341
table, **PUB 284**
  applying format, PUB 285–286
  changing column width, PUB 297
  changing rows, PUB 297
  content selection, PUB 287
  copying embedded, PUB 319
  creating cell diagonal, PUB
    292–293
  creating embedded, PUB 317–319
  deleting column, PUB 287–288
  deleting data, PUB 303–304
  deleting rows, PUB 288
  embedded, PUB 314,
    PUB 317–321
  entering data, PUB 301–303
  Excel-enhanced, PUB 314

finishing, PUB 304
  formatting embedded,
    PUB 319–320
  inserting column, PUB 290
  inserting empty, PUB 284–285
  inserting graphic in cells,
    PUB 303
  inserting rows, PUB 289
  linked, PUB 314
  merging cells, PUB 290–291
  moving embedded, PUB 321
  pasting embedded, PUB 319
  positioning embedded, PUB 321
  resizing, PUB 290
  splitting cells, PUB 292
  summing embedded,
    PUB 320–321
table borders
  adding borders, PUB 295–296
  changing border color, PUB 295
  changing line weight, PUB 294
  formatting and creating borders,
    PUB 293
  selection of table, PUB 293
table of contents, **PUB 132**
  updating, PUB 548
tabloid, **PUB 147**
tab selector, **PUB 339**
tab stop, **PUB 339**
  setting, PUB 341–342
tab stop marker, **PUB 339**
tabular style, PUB 402
tags, PUB 148
tap gesture, OFF 3
task pane, **OFF 16**
tear-offs
  described, **PUB 18**
  entering, PUB 18–19
template information pane,
    PUB 5
templates, **PUB 2**
  choosing newsletter,
    PUB 108–109
  creating, PUB 148–151
  creating flyers, PUB 2–10
  customizing, PUB 6–10
  saving, setting file properties,
    PUB 149–151
  selecting brochure, PUB 52–53
testing
  macro, PUB 613
  websites, PUB 603–605
text
  aligning, PUB 32

autofitting, PUB 25–26
bold, PUB 23
converting handwriting to, PA 3–4
copying, cutting, pasting,
    PUB 56–58
editing heading in left panel,
    PUB 59
entering in publications, OFF 49,
    OFF 52
italicizing, PUB 24
moving, PUB 142–144
in overflow, PUB 114
selecting and entering,
    PUB 15–19
underlining, PUB 24
text area, **PUB 591**
text boxes, OFF 7, **PUB 15**
  deleting, PUB 20
  linked, PUB 115
  linking, PUB 120–121
  moving, PUB 31
text box form control, **PUB 591**
text effects
  aligning text and format,
    PUB 186–187
  applying gradient to text,
    PUB 187–189
  drawing text box, PUB 186
  fill, PUB 185
  outline, PUB 185
text files, importing, PUB 116–117
text scaling, **PUB 335**
text wrapping
  changing options, PUB 534–535
  description, PUB 240
  inserting automatic date,
    PUB 242–243
  options, PUB 241
  setting, PUB 241–242
  setting read-only attribute,
    PUB 243–244
thesaurus, **PUB 541**
  using, PUB 541–542
ticket, **PUB 362**
  changing text direction,
    PUB 370–371
  editing ticket stub, PUB 371–372
  inserting text, PUB 369
  printing page of, PUB 378–380
tiling option, **PUB 398**
tilt mouse wheel, OFF 4
tool tabs, **OFF 14**
touch keyboard, OFF 13
Touch Mode, OFF 16

touch screen
  gestures (table), OFF 3
  touch galleries, PUB 56
  using, OFF 3–4
tracking, **PUB 335**
track kerning, **PUB 335**
translating text, PUB 426–430
  entering text, PUB 427
  ignoring flagged words,
    PUB 430
  inserting text, PUB 428–429
troubleshooting, design errors,
    PUB 479
two-page spread, **PUB 108,
    PUB 392**
  creating, PUB 392–394
  deleting, PUB 412–413
  viewing, PUB 524
type ornamentation, **PUB 170**
typing
  checking spelling while,
    PUB 20–22
  letter, PUB 316
  paragraphs of text, PUB 59
typography, **PUB 78**

U

underlined, **PUB 24**
underlining text, PUB 24
undo, **PUB 15**
ungroup, **PUB 178**
ungrouping
  captions, PUB 85
  objects, PUB 179
Unicode, **PUB 464**
uniform resource locator (URL),
    PUB 471
unlocking screens, OFF 5
unsubscribe, **PUB 445**
up cap, **PUB 141**
URL (uniform resource locator),
    PUB 471
user account
  described, **OFF 5**
  signing in, OFF 5, OFF 6–7
user icon, **OFF 5**
user name, **OFF 5**, OFF 7

V

VBA (Visual Basic for
    Applications), **PUB 566**
verso page, **PUB 108**

viewing. *See also* displaying
  boundaries, Catalog Tools Format
    tab, PUB 416
  built-in templates, PUB 4
  Master Page, PUB 394
  master pages, PUB 307–308
  single pages, PUB 394
  two-page spread, PUB 524
  whole pages, PUB 32
virus, computer, PUB 610
Visual Basic Editor, **PUB 607**
Visual Basic for Applications
    (VBA), **PUB 566**
  displaying Developer tab,
    PUB 606–607
  document events, PUB 605
  opening VBA code window,
    PUB 607–608
  programming BeforeClose event,
    PUB 608–609

W

watermarks, **PUB 332**
  changing transparency of graphics,
    PUB 333–334
  inserting and placing, PUB 332
web masthead, **PUB 581**
  creating, PUB 582–583
  inserting navigation bar,
    PUB 584–585
  reformatting, PUB 583
  using installed font, PUB 584
Web Note, **PA 15**
webpage, PUB 576
  applying background, PUB 578
  changing size of, PUB 577–578
  creating custom ruler guides,
    PUB 579–580
  opening web publication,
    PUB 577
  saving in new folder,
    PUB 580–581
webpage options, **PUB 600**
  editing, PUB 600–601
web publication, **PUB 37**
  previewing in browsers,
    PUB 38–39
  saving a publication as,
    PUB 37–38
websites
  adding secondary page, PUB 585
  checking publication, PUB 611
  publishing, PUB 589–590

websites *(continued)*
  saving and republishing, PUB 612
  testing, PUB 603–605
widow, **PUB 544**
windows
  maximizing, OFF 12
  minimizing, restoring, OFF 36
  moving, resizing, OFF 56–57
Windows 10, **OFF 2**
  introduction, OFF 2–8
  running apps using Search box,
    OFF 46–47
  running apps using Start menu,
    OFF 10–12
  starting, OFF 5–7
  using touch screen and mouse,
    OFF 3–4

Windows 10 desktop, OFF 8
Windows Clipboard, **PUB 56**
Windows Metafile Format (.wmf),
    PUB 179
Windows search box, OFF 59–60
wizard, **PUB 345**
Word
  editing stories in, PUB 128–131
  exiting, PUB 130
WordArt, PUB 189
  changing shape, PUB 191–192
  editing, PUB 532
  editing alignment, PUB 279
  formatting object, PUB 278–279
  inserting object, PUB 190–191,
    PUB 278–279
wordwrap, **PUB 59**

  as you type, PUB 60
  workspace, **PUB 10**
  wrapping, **PUB 240**
  wrapping points, **PUB 240**

X

XML Paper Specification (XPS),
    PUB 260
XPS (XML Paper Specification),
    PUB 260

Z

zoom, **PUB 13**
  using function key, OFF 21
  zoom methods (table), PUB 14